The Regulation of Financial Planning in Australia

This book investigates the legitimacy of the current Australian Financial Services Licensee-Authorised Representative (AFSL-AR) licensing model, as specified in the Commonwealth Corporations Act 2001.

The book rectifies the deficiency in scholarly attention to this matter by developing a new conceptualised framework for the financial planning discipline. It takes into account theories in agency, legislation, legitimacy and the *independent* individual regulatory regimes in other professions; thereafter integrating this framework with financial planning theory to examine the legitimacy, or what was found to be the illegitimacy, of licensing advisers via multiple third party conflicted commercially oriented licensees.

This book makes a very useful reference to understanding financial planning licensing in Australia.

Angelique Nadia Sweetman McInnes is an unorthodox wife, mother, entrepreneur, author, academic, publication reviewer and presenter. Her research interests include international finance, financial services, financial planning, financial technology and digital finance.

Banking, Money and International Finance

Expert Systems in Finance
Smart Financial Applications in Big Data Environments
Edited by Noura Metawa, Mohamed Elhoseny, Aboul Ella Hassanien, M. Kabir Hassan

Equity Home Bias in International Finance
A Place-Attachment Perspective
Kavous Ardalan

Frontier Capital Markets and Investment Banking
Principles and Practice from Nigeria
Temitope W. Oshikoya and Kehinde Durosinmi-Etti

French Banking and Entrepreneurialism in China and Hong Kong
From the 1850s to 1980s
Hubert Bonin

Banking, Lending and Real Estate
Claudio Scardovi and Alessia Bezzecchi

The Regulation of Financial Planning in Australia
Current Practice, Issues and Empirical Analysis
Angelique Nadia Sweetman McInnes

Financial Risk Management in Banking
Evidence from Asia Pacific
Shahsuzan Zakaria; Sardar M. N. Islam

The Economics of Financial Cooperatives
Income Distribution, Political Economy and Regulation
Amr Khafagy

For more information about this the series, please visit www.routledge.com/series/BMIF

The Regulation of Financial Planning in Australia

Current Practice, Issues and Empirical Analysis

Angelique Nadia Sweetman McInnes

Routledge
Taylor & Francis Group
LONDON AND NEW YORK

First published 2020
by Routledge
2 Park Square, Milton Park, Abingdon, Oxon OX14 4RN

and by Routledge
52 Vanderbilt Avenue, New York, NY 10017

Routledge is an imprint of the Taylor & Francis Group, an informa business

British Library Cataloguing-in-Publication Data
A catalogue record for this book is available from the British Library

Library of Congress Cataloging-in-Publication Data
Names: McInnes, Angelique Nadia Sweetman, 1967– author.
Title: The regulation of financial planning in Australia : current practice, issues and empirical analysis / by Angelique Nadia Sweetman McInnes.
Description: First Edition. | New York : Routledge, 2020. | Series: Routledge advances in management and business studies | Based on author's thesis (doctoral – RMIT University, 2018) issued under title: Licensee-authorised representative licensing model : theory and Australian empirical evidence.
Identifiers: LCCN 2019015085 | ISBN 9780367149970 (hardback) | ISBN 9780429054372 (ebook)
Subjects: LCSH: Financial services industry—Law and legislation—Australia. | Financial planners—Legal status, laws, etc.—Australia.
Classification: LCC KU885 .M375 2020 | DDC 346.9409—dc23
LC record available at https://lccn.loc.gov/2019015085

ISBN: 978-0-367-14997-0 (hbk)
ISBN: 978-0-429-05437-2 (ebk)

Typeset in Galliard
by Apex CoVantage, LLC

DEDICATION/TOEWYDING

Aan my oorlede liefste liefdevolle ouers, Alettha, Elizabetha Sweetman (nee Horn) (7 Desember 1945–10 Oktober 2009) en Aidan Albert Fredrick Sweetman (2 Februarie 1945–9 September 2014) Ek dra hierdie werk aan u toe. Met u jare lange aanmoediging en geloof het ek uiteindelik 'n Doktor in die Filosofie behaal, net soos u verwag het. Alhoewel u nie meer saam met my is om in hierdie prestasie te deel nie, Ek weet u is altyd met my in die gees. Ek dank u vir u toegewyde offers en liefde wat my tot hierdie oomblik toe gelei het. Met rose liefdevolle liefde, u dogter.

Contents

Figures

Graphs

Tables

Acknowledgements

Now this work is completed, I acknowledge foremost, my Saviour. Next, I am grateful to the people unknowingly involved in this journey. Most important, my earnest gratitude goes to Hugh, a husband like no other, as well as our loving children, Kaitlin, Calum and Tegan. While you watched me sit behind my laptop in the living room for several years, together we experienced a rollercoaster ride of setbacks and breakthroughs. Your love, sacrifices, understanding and support were the main contributors to the success of this research. Sorry for the high emotional, mental, social and even physical toll we all paid during this difficult PhD journey. Apologies for my neglect of my obligations as wife and mother to you all during this ride. Forgive me for not being present when you needed me most. Recognition extends to my extended family, friends and acquaintances for keeping in touch with the hermit I have become.

I acknowledge the supervision of Associate Professor Abdullahi D. Ahmed [Ahmed]. Doctors Maryam Safari and Daniel Richards, your encouragement, together with the support from the academic and professional staff at RMIT's School of Accounting, Flinders University's Business School and Central Queensland University's School of Business and Law, has not gone unnoticed. A special mention goes to Professor Pi-Shen Seet. Unknown to him, he played a vital role in the success of this research. To you, I am grateful for your suggestion to read the literature on legitimacy and institutional theory during a question-and-answer session at one of my presentations on the topic. Doing so led to the formulation of a key part of the theoretical framework for this study.

Next, I thank Simon Hoyle for giving this research media attention. I am grateful to Tom Reddacliff, Russell Galt, Troy Penney, Sonnie Bailey, Aleks Vickovich and the many unnamed financial planners for their constructive critical commentaries via survey, social media, email, face-to-face and telephone. Thank you to the attendees at the Annual Personal Finance and Investment Symposiums of 2014, 2015, 2016 and 2017 for providing valuable critical feedback on several conference papers relating to this research. My gratitude extends to the *Financial Planning Research Journal* team for publishing a paper on this controversial matter.

To Gill Lilley and my sister Antoinette Sweetman, thank you for your contributions during proofreading of this work. Finally, to the authors in the reference list, thank you for your dedication to publish your respected works for me to critique.

Abbreviations

AARP	American Association of Retired Persons
aBIC	Sample size-adjusted Bayesian information criterion
ACL	Australian Credit Licence
ACT	Australian Capital Territory
the Act	Commonwealth Corporations Act 2001 or Corporations Act 2001
ADF	Asymptotically distribution free
AFA	Association of Financial Advisers
AFS	Australian Financial Services
AFSL	Australian Financial Services Licence
AFSL-AR	Australian Financial Services Licensee-Authorised Representative
AGFI	Adjusted goodness of fit
AIC	Akaike information criterion
ANOVA	One-way analysis of variance
ANZ	Australia and New Zealand Banking Group Limited
APES 230	Accounting Professional Ethical Standards 230
APESB	Accounting Professionals and Ethics Standards Board
APL	Approved product list
AQF	Australian Qualifications Framework
AR	Authorised representative
ASIC	Australian Securities and Investments Commission
ASV	Average shared variance
AVE	Average variance extracted
BCHEAN	Business College Human Ethics Advisory Network
BD	Broker-dealer's institution
BDM	Business Development Manager
BIC	Bayesian information criterion
BOLR	Buyer of last resort
CA ANZ	Chartered Accountants Australia and New Zealand
CAIC	Consistent Akaike information criterion
CAR	Corporate authorised representative
CBA	Commonwealth Bank of Australia Limited
CFA	Confirmatory factor analysis
CFI	Comparative fit index

CFP	Certified Financial Planner
CI	Confidence interval
CIO	Credit and Investments Ombudsman
CLERP	Corporate Law Economic Reform Program
CLF	Common latent factor
CMIN	Chi-square value
CN	Critical sample size
COB	Conduct of business
CPAA	Certified Practising Accountants Australia
CR	Composite reliability
CRCMM	Composite reliability for congeneric measures model
DF/df	Degrees of freedom
DOL	United States Department of Labor
E/CFA	Exploratory factor analysis within the confirmatory factor analysis framework
ECVI	Expected cross-validation index
EFA	Exploratory factor analysis
EM	Explanatory Memoranda/Statements
EM	Expectation-maximization
$F [df_1, df_2]$	Variance ratio for Levene's test with degrees of $freedom_1$ and df_2
FAI	Financial advisory institution
FAMR	Financial Advice Market Review
FASEA	Financial Adviser Standards and Ethics Authority
FCA	Financial Conduct Authority
FINRA	Financial Industry Regulatory Authority
FINTECH	Financial technology
FOFA	Future of Financial Advice
FOS	Financial Ombudsman Scheme
FPA	Financial Planning Association
FSA	Financial Services Authority
FSR	Financial Services Reform
FSRA	Commonwealth Financial Services Reform Act 2001
FUM	Funds under management
GFC	Global financial crisis
GFI	Goodness of fit index
GOF	Goodness of fit
IAPD	Investment Adviser Public Disclosure
IAR	*Independent* Advice Representatives
IARD	Investment Advisers Registration Depository
IFA	*Independent* Financial Adviser
IFAAA	*Independent* Financial Advisers Association of Australia
IFP	Institute of Financial Planning
IPFPSB	*Independent* Professional Financial Planning Standards Board
KPI	Key performance indicator
LIC	Life insurance corporation or life insurance company

M	Mean
MAR	Missing at random
MAX	Maximum
MGCFA	Multigroup confirmatory factor analysis
MI	Modification indices
MIN	Minimum
MLE	Maximum likelihood estimation
MSV	Maximum shared variance
NAPFA	National Association of Personal Financial Advice
NASAA	North American Securities Administrators Association
NFI	Normed fit index
NNFI	Non-normed fit index
N.S.	Not significant or insignificant
NSW	New South Wales
OCIE	Office of Compliance Inspections and Examinations
PCLOSE	Closeness of fit
PI	Professional indemnity
PJC	Parliamentary Joint Committee
PS	Policy Statements
PSA	Professional Standards Authority
PSC	Professional Standards Councils
QCF	Qualifications and Credit Framework
RAR	'Restricted' advisers or appointed representatives
RDR	Retail Distribution Review
RG	Regulatory Guides
RIA	Registered investment advisers
RIAR	Registered *independent* advice representative
RMSEA	Root mean square error of approximation
RO	Ruler-option
RR	Broker-dealer registered representative
SB	Satorra & Bentler
SD	Standard deviation
SE	Standard errors
SEC	Securities and Exchange Commission
SEM	Structural equation modelling
SMSF	Self-managed superannuation funds
SOA	Statement of Advice
SPS	Statement of Professional Standing
SRC	Standardised residual covariance
SRO	Self-regulatory organisation
STD	Standard
TFI	Tucker-Lewis fit index
UK	United Kingdom
US	United States of America
VIF	Variable inflation factor

%	percent
c.r.	critical ratios
n	sample size
p	statistical significance level
r^2	squared multiple correlation
S. or sig.	significance or significant
β	beta, correlations
λ	Lambda standardised or unstandardised regression weights
χ^2	chi-square
z	z-score

Glossary

Agent Financial adviser or authorised representative.

Conflict of interest by or from association Conflict advisers face by being directly or indirectly associated with, owned by or affiliated to licensees distributing, issuing and/or manufacturing in-house financial products.

Dual-agency role Licensee–adviser–client role.

Independent **or independence** Refers to the definition of s923A of the Act.

Licensing Includes appointing, authorising and regulating individual financial advisers.

Principal Client or Licensee.

True professional Professionals formally recognised and accredited under the Professional Standards legislation and schemes.

cum With.

ditto The same thing again.

etc. Et cetera.

ex Without.

inter alia Among other things.

vice versa In the opposite direction from the way it was previously stated.

vis-à-vis In relation to or about.

viz Videlicet, namely.

Dual [a_1] Advisers are dual agents.

Simult [a_2] Simultaneously serving licensee and client.

BestRev [a_3] Generating revenue for licensees and serving clients' best interests.

CoIASS[a_4] Conflict of interest from association

AlignAct [a_5] Aligning adviser–client interests is difficult.

CoIAct [a_6] Unavoidable conflicts of interest present.

FiducAct [a_7] Greater risk of breaching best interest duty.

CompAct [a_8] Advisers limited from competing fairly.

Regulative [a_9] Regulative illegitimacy – Risk of unintentional Act compliance breaches.

Consequential [a_{10}] Consequential illegitimacy – Licensee commercial interests compromising adviser best interest duty.

Procedural [a_{11}] Procedural illegitimacy – Sales policies, procedures and practices window dressed to appear to comply with the Act.

Structural [a_4] Structural illegitimacy – conflicts of interest from association.

Personal [a_{13}] Personal illegitimacy – individual leaders of aligned licensees aim to protect their product distribution channels when lobbying government.

Cognitive [a_{14}] Cultural-cognitive illegitimacy – public cannot clearly distinguish s923A *independent* advisers from those advisers who are not.

Trust [a_{16}] Individual adviser licensing will improve public trust and confidence in advisers.

Independence [a_{17}] Individual adviser licensing will promote independence from product-biased licensees.

Professions [a_{18}] Individual licence should be in line with other professions, such as accounting, legal and medical.

IPFPSB [a_{19}] Advisers prefer individual licence through a single *independent* registration, competency, education, conduct, standards and disciplinary board.

EliminateCoI [a_{21}] Individual licensing through a single *independent* professional standards board will eliminate conflict of interest from association.

Old Structural (deleted) [a_{12}] When advisers leave their licensee, unless they sign up with another licensee, they lose their ability to work.

Defend (deleted) [a_{15}] Media exposure of scandals has resulted in financial advisers defending their relationship/association/affiliation with their licensee to clients.

Takeover (deleted) [a_{20}] Accountants are taking over strategic *independent* advice by redefining and repositioning financial planning within their self-regulatory model.

Appendices

Publications, papers and media interest

Publication

McInnes, A & Ahmed, AD 2016, 'Examining the legitimacy of the current "authorised representative" licensing model', *Financial Planning Research Journal*, vol. 2, no. 2, pp. 64–90.

Symposium papers and media interest

McInnes, A & Ahmed, AD 2017, 'Australian Financial Services licensee-authorised representative licensing model: Current practice, issues and empirical analysis', paper presented to the 6th Annual Personal Finance and Investment Symposium, University of Tasmania, Hobart, Tasmania.

McInnes, A & Ahmed, AD 2016, 'Is the term "*independent*" misunderstood and are financial advisers in Australia truly *independent*? A preliminary analysis', paper presented to the 5th Annual Personal Finance and Investment Symposium, Western Sydney University, Parramatta, Melbourne.

McInnes, A & Ahmed, AD 2015, 'Examining the legitimacy of the current "authorised representative" licensing model', paper presented to the 4th Annual Personal Finance and Investment Symposium, Ship Inn Conference Centre, Griffith University, Southbank, Brisbane.

McInnes, A, Ahmed, AD & Delpachitra, S 2014, 'An overview of the legitimacy of the current licensing of financial advisers', paper presented to the 3rd Annual Personal Finance and Investment Symposium, Flinders University, Victoria Square Campus, 182 Victoria Square, Adelaide, South Australia.

Nine media articles on the topic were published because of this research.

1 Introduction

Introduction

This research investigates the legitimacy of the current Australian Financial Services licensee-authorised representative licensing model [financial adviser or adviser licensing], as specified in the Commonwealth Corporations Act 2001. A long-standing debate in the media and practice initiated examining the legitimacy of appointing, authorising and regulating [licensing] individual financial advisers through third-party, institutional product-conflicted commercially oriented licensees. Unsupported damaging statements, personal assertions seem evident in most commentaries. A sticking point was the lack of a theoretical framework within financial planning theory to define, model and measure legitimacy. Therefore, this study rectifies the deficiency in scholarly attention to this matter by developing a new framework for the financial planning discipline. It does so by considering theories in agency, legislation, legitimacy and the *independent* individual regulatory regimes in other professions. Then it applies these theories to financial planning theory to examine the legitimacy of current financial adviser licensing.

Understanding the underlying problem of licensing authorised representatives [ARs] via third-party licensees in this chapter starts with a brief historical background discussion on the legislative framework of AFSL-AR licensing. A simple description of the licensee–adviser licensing structure continues the discussion. Then the trends in licensing advisers in the United States and United Kingdom compared with Australia is deliberated. Against this brief backdrop, this chapter develops the argument to clarify the nature of the problem further. Afterwards, to narrow the scope of this study, the objectives shadow the conversation. At that point, this introductory chapter outlines the methodology used to conduct the investigation. Subsequently, the chapter highlights the importance of examining the legitimacy of existing licensee–adviser licensing. In the closing statements of this introductory chapter, the author presents the plan of the study.

Background to the study

Legislative background to AFSL-AR licensing

The start of the licensing debate, in and outside of the Australian Parliament, has roots dating back to 1996. The Wallis Financial Systems Inquiry recommendations published in 1997 and the implementation of the subsequent Corporate Law Economic Reform Program [CLERP] (Corbett 1999; Overland 2007) led to the implementation of the Commonwealth Financial Services Reform Act 2001 [FSRA] (Hutson & Vonnessen 2003; Parliamentary Joint Committee on Corporations and Financial Services 2014). FSRA repealed the old licensing system of multiple licences regulating the activities of insurance agencies, brokers, securities dealers, accountants and solicitors (Pearson 2006b). Chapter 7 in the new Commonwealth Corporations Act 2001 replaced the old corporation's legislation. From early 2002 (Australian Securities and Investments Commission 2016j), a single licensing system existed (Banister *et al.* 2013). The AFSL, enforced by the regulator ASIC, authorised financial licensees and their ARs to offer financial products and services to the public (Hutson & Vonnessen 2003; Pearson 2006b).

Then the 2008 GFC happened. This was followed by subsequent corporate scandal exposures of licensees' and their advisers' unethical behaviour. These scandals damaged public trust and confidence in the financial advice industry (Ap 2011; Taylor, Juchau & Houterman 2013). To deal with the unethical behaviour triggered by conflicts of interest (Alexander 2011) from product sales (Burke & Hung 2015), the government responded with the Parliamentary Joint Committee on Corporations and Financial Services (2009a) [Ripoll Inquiry] (Parliamentary Joint Committee on Corporations and Financial Services 2009a; Australian Government The Treasury 2014). This inquiry led to the enactment of the Future of Financial Advice [FOFA] legislation (Australian Government The Treasury 2014). One of FOFA's intentions included improving public trust and confidence in advisers (Ap 2011). Thus began a measured legal process of professionalising the financial advice sector away from a sales-driven distribution network (Burke & Hung 2015). Although Ripoll (Parliamentary Joint Committee on Corporations and Financial Services 2009a) recommended individual licensing and an *independent* industry standards board, the government decided to start with the enactment of the National Consumer Credit Protection Regulations 2010 (Holley Nethercoate Commercial & Financial Services Lawyers 2014a) from mid-2010 to enforce an Australian Credit Licence [ACL]. Subsequently, additional regulation moved FOFA away from single licensing back to multiple overlapping ACLs, AFSLs and limited AFSLs (Banister *et al.* 2013).

More financial corporate scandals ensued, specifically the well-known Trio Capital and Storm Financial debacles (Commonwealth of Australia 2016c). Further confirming critics' misgivings of FOFA, *vis-à-vis:* FOFA proposals did not prevent licensees' and their advisers' unethical behaviour (West 2009; Hartnett 2010). Subsequently, three tranches of FOFA legislation were implemented to amend specifics clauses of the Act (Kell 2013). Operative mid-2012, with mandatory compliance commencing mid-2013 (Burke & Hung 2015), the Corporations Amendment (Future of Financial Advice) Act 2012 [first tranche] and Corporations Amendment (Further Future of Financial Advice Measures) 2012 [second tranche] were enacted as separate yet related FOFA regulations (North 2015). Initially, ASIC took a facilitative approach to compliance. Thereafter, all AFSL licensees had to comply (Australian Securities and Investments

Commission 2016g). The Corporations Amendment (Streamlining of Future of Financial Advice) Act 2014 [third tranche] was mooted on 19 November 2014 (Australian Securities and Investments Commission 2016g). The Corporations Amendment (Revising Future of Financial Advice) Regulation 2014 and the Corporations Amendment (Financial Advice) Regulation 2014 reinstated a few provisions in the disallowed legislation.[1] These three tranches and successive regulations unambiguously covered increasing ASIC's powers, clients' best interest duty, annual fee disclosure statements and renewal notices where clients would opt in every two years to continue ongoing fee payments, as well as banning conflicted remuneration (Burke & Hung 2015; Corones & Irving 2016). In addition to the regulatory changes, amendments were made to the previous accountants' FSRA AFSL licensing exemptions clauses (Banister *et al.* 2013). Until mid-2016, accountants' Regulation 7.1.29A exemption (Halsey & Halsey 2014) applied, allowing accountants to advise on certain financial products and services, *inter alia* self-managed superannuation funds [SMSFs] without an AFSL (Adams 2002). Since then, the government has repealed this exemption.[2] Now accountants must hold a full, limited AFSL or become ARs under another licensee's AFSL when making any recommendation relating to financial products and services, including SMSFs (Global Accounting Alliance, Chartered Accountants Worldwide & charteredaccountantsanz.com 2016).

With FOFA reforms taking hold, opponents asserted the reforms were reactive (Valentine 2013). It reduced advice availability to the public by increasing advice costs (Mennen 2014). Accordingly, towards the end of 2013, the government announced a Financial System Inquiry [Murray Inquiry] reviewing the financial services industry's overall strength (Commonwealth of Australia 2014a). Together with recommendations to simplify the system's overall complexity, provide certainty, reduce compliance costs and lower administrative burdens (North 2015), Murray endorsed lifting professional, ethical and education standards among advisers (Parliamentary Joint Committee on Corporations and Financial Services 2014). Thus, the implementation of the Corporations Amendment (Professional Standards of Financial Advisers) Act 2017 began influencing the future licensing of advisers.[3] Notably, during the Murray review's consultation phase, a brief dialogue in the Australian Senate explored a single individual financial licence for each financial adviser, rather than advisers being licensed via multiple institutional licensees (Commonwealth of Australia 2014e). The final Murray report made no recommendations regarding individual licensing (Commonwealth of Australia 2014a). Instead, his report concluded the existing regulatory framework of product design, product distribution, disclosure and financial advice was insufficient to deliver reasonable adviser conduct to clients (Commonwealth of Australia 2014a). However, "*coercive measures*" (Ariely, Amir & Lobel 2008, p. 2098) followed this "*policy nudge*" (Ariely, Amir & Lobel 2008, p. 2098) from the government to advance the process of professionalising advisers with the establishment of an *independent* standard-setting body,[4] the Financial Adviser Standards and Ethics Authority (O'Dwyer 2017). At the time of finalising this book, the government has accepted the recommendations in the Royal

Commission into Misconduct in the Banking, Superannuation and Financial Services Industry established on 14 December 2017 to include a single statutory disciplinary body in the list of bodies responsible for overseeing the behaviour of financial advisers.[5,6] Accordingly, this research explores advisers' views of an *independent* body.

Existing Australian licensee–adviser licensing

The Act plays a key role in licensing financial institutions and their ARs (Jones 2012; Banister *et al.* 2013). With a few exceptions, the Corporations legislation permits three licensing options[7]: (1) limited license, (2) full license (Teale 2008) or (3) AR of an AFSL licensee. Under a limited AFSL, licensees may allow their ARs to advise on SMSFs, superannuation products, securities, simple managed investment schemes, insurances plus basic deposit products. Alternatively, licensees can obtain a full licence offering comprehensive 'holistic' personal advice (Parliamentary Joint Committee on Corporations and Financial Services 2009a, p. 23).[8]

Insufficiently addressed in scholarly literature, s923A of the Act distinguishes between two categories, identities, roles and/or definitions of licensees, advisers and/or advice. Namely, licensees and their advisers are either truly "*independent*" ["*non-aligned*," "*non-institutionally owned*," "*independently owned*," "*unbiased*" and "*impartial*"], otherwise they are product or remuneration conflicted (Australian Securities and Investments Commission 2017b). In addition to the categories of licensees and advisers, North (2015) confirmed the licensing regulations permitted the development of a range of business models among licensees and advisers covering a broad range of different structures and sizes.

ASIC enforces a legal process to appoint, authorise and regulate individual advisers through third-party licensees (Beal & McKeown 2009) prescribed in the Act.[9] Fundamentally, licensees comply with the selection process (Bender 2011) and compliance system of authorising advisers as prescribed in the legislation (Bennett 2000). From 31 March 2015, ARs must register with the publicly accessible ASIC Financial Adviser Register. Consequently, apparent in practice, yet deficient in scholarly works (Holley Nethercoate Commercial & Financial Services Lawyers 2014a; Power 2015; Global Accounting Alliance, Chartered Accountants Worldwide & charteredaccountantsanz.com 2016), outwardly ARs can practise their craft only when they are either (1) self-employed and *independent* with their own AFSL, (2) self-employed by becoming contracted/franchised via institutional licensees and using the licensees support services or (3) employees of institutional licensees with AFSLs. A more in-depth discussion on licensing regimes in Australia, the United Kingdom [UK] and the United States [US] follows in Chapter 2.

International trends of professional adviser licensing

Numerous writers (see, e.g. conversations by Brean, Kryzanowski & Roberts 2011; Adamson 2012; Inderst & Ottaviani 2012e; Walker 2012; McMeel 2013;

Bateman & Kingston 2014; Deloitte & Financial Services Council 2014) documented international interest in regulating individual advisers operating in the retail financial services sector. Like in Australia, policymakers in the US (Stolz 2009a; Trone 2009; Laby 2010; Kaissar 2016) and the UK (Reichman 2013) focus much of their regulations on lowering the risk to the public when dealing with financial services providers (Valentine 2008; Hartnett 2010; Bruce 2012; Kwon 2013).

Apparent in these three specific countries, principal institutions or third-party affiliates appoint advisers to work as their agents to deliver financial and/or product sales recommendations on their behalf (Zabel 2010; Bateman & Kingston 2014; Burke & Hung 2015; Financial Conduct Authority 2015). These third-party affiliates and their advisers must register with their respective regulator (Zabel 2010; Bateman & Kingston 2014; Burke & Hung 2015; Financial Conduct Authority 2015).

Arman and Shackman (2012) discussed the ability of the Australian public to distinguish between the different designations in the medical, legal and accounting professions. Yet they found the public could not distinguish between the different designations of advisers, *vis-à-vis* differentiate between *independent* and conflicted advisers. Bhargava (2009) and Finke, Huston and Waller (2009b) concurred, the US public faces a similar situation. In contrast to the approach by the US and Australia, the UK has dropped the idea of a clear distinction between sales and advice, settling instead for *independent* advice and restricted advice (McMeel 2013). In Australia, whether institutions are product aligned or *independent*, they all have statutory fiduciary duty obligations as well as legal obligations to disclose all conflicts of interest (Bateman & Kingston 2012) and, since Hayne's recommendations, their independence status (Commonwealth of Australia 2019; Deloitte 2019). All US advisers, whether affiliated to product advisory institutions or truly *independent* institutions, are fiduciaries required to comply with statutory best interest duties and conflicts of interest requirements (United States Department of Labour 2017). Although the UK Government has disregarded a specific fiduciary duty requirement for UK advisers, it has imposed a duty of care of a comparable standard to the Australian statutory fiduciary duty (Deloitte & Financial Services Council 2014).

Documented by McDermott (2016), the UK Retail Distribution Review [RDR] aims to promote adviser personal accountability. Yet it is questionable how advisers in any of these nations achieve personal accountability under their current licensing regimes. Especially if advisers are licensed, regulated and authorised at the institutional level, rather than being accountable at the individual level like other true accredited professionals.

Notably, true professionals have independence (Carnegie & O'Connell 2012) and autonomy within their job role (Rubin 2015). As argued by many (Bamber & Iyer 2002; Horsley & Thomas 2003; Breakey 2017; Breakey & Sampford 2017), this independence and autonomy puts them in a stronger position to avoid conflicts of interest. Although the literature survey showed some scholarly writings from the UK and the US reflecting on the issue of '*independent* advisers' and '*independent* advice' (Gough 2005; Zabel 2010; Bender 2011; Chaston 2013; Bateman & Kingston 2014; Burke & Hung 2015), in drawing a comparison, a void was observed in the existing Australian literature on these issues. Furthermore, unlike the UK and Australia,[10] the US has not yet established minimum professional standards, education and ethics for advisers to improve the quality of advice (Valentine 2013; Burke & Hung 2015). Most important, compelling evidence is absent in financial planning theory, confirming the current approach of regulating advisers via multiple third parties is desired, suitable and a fitting approach to protect the public while encouraging professionalism.

Conceptualised framework of licensing advisers

Against this setting, the development of the prototype model to explain, model and measure the legitimacy of current AFSL-AR licensing by abstracting the reality occurred. Simply, emerging from the literature review, licensing individual advisers via third-party commercial product-aligned licensees, as specified in the Act, creates a dual-agency role. This licensee–adviser–client role leads to conflicts of interest, specifically from association, because advisers serve licensees' commercial and clients' best interests simultaneously. Consequently, licensing advisers via third-party licensees is inconsistent with four identified objectives of the Act. Therefore, current licensee–adviser licensing is delegitimised on the basis of the criteria of Suchman's legitimacy theoretical framework applied to financial planning theory. Accordingly, any threats to AFSL-AR licensing legitimacy strengthens arguments for an individual professional licensing model, like other professions.

Dual-agency role of financial advisers

Licensees as the principal appoints, registers and regulates ARs to act on their behalf (McKeown, Kerry & Olynyk 2014). This model forms the licensee–adviser [principal–agent] contractual legislated agency (Gor 2005) relationship (Eisenhardt 1989; Smith & Walter 2001). Prominent in academic financial planning literature (McKeown, Kerry & Olynyk 2014; Taylor & Juchau 2017), yet inadequately defined in the Act, the second principal–agent contractual relationship between the client [the principal] and the financial adviser [the agent] (Corones & Galloway 2013) completes the dual-agency role of advisers.

Clearly, under the current legislation, advisers serve two principals, the licensee and the client, simultaneously (Kingston & Weng 2014). Kingston and Weng (2014) noted when an agent tries to serve two principals simultaneously, it creates a conflict of interest. This research specifically focuses on the financial planning academic neglect of this conflict of interest from association, because Valentine (2008) emphasised the need to place conflict of interest from association at the head of further research. Especially in the presence of allegations, the majority of advisers are licensed via product-conflicted third-party licensees to act as their product distribution pipeline (Starke 2013a). From the perspective of Corones and Galloway (2013), conflict of interest from association challenges advisers' best interest duty obligation. Notably, while licensees direct their agents to act in the best interests of clients, simultaneously the profit motive drives them (Lewis 2013). The literature remarks on the tension between the commercial interests of the licensee and the best interests of the clients (Perkins & Monahan 2011) – an issue yet not critically evaluated. Hiller, Mahlendorf and Weber (2014) emphasised, institutional-professional conflict is evident when individuals, lacking independence, confront the issues of loyalty to their institution and loyalty to their profession. From a structural, operational, ethical (Arnold & McCartney 2008) and legal point of view, advisers under the current licensing regime are hindered to act as true professionals, who characteristically should be *independent* (Murphy & Watts 2009; Smith, Clarke & Rogers 2017) and free of conflicts. Consequently, making it problematic for them to achieve the objectives of the Act.

Four objectives of the Commonwealth Corporations Act 2001

The Australian Government, and ASIC, aims to protect retail financial consumers by a complex set of rules (Corones & Irving 2016), including regulating ARs through third-party AFS licensees via the Act.[11] Four identified objectives of the Act underlie this main social aim (Simes, Harper & Green 2008) when it comes to regulating advisers: (1) encouraging alignment of advisers' interests with their clients' best interest; (2) managing, controlling or avoiding conflicts of interest; (3) ensuring compliance with the statutory fiduciary duty; and (4) promoting competitive behaviour between financial service providers (Bora & Lewis 1997; Corbett 1999; Mutton 2001; Collier 2003; Serpell 2008; Jones 2009; Alexander 2011; Ap 2011; Ireland & Gray 2011; Kell 2012). They are vital to this study, because until now, a critical evaluation of their role in the legitimacy of current AFSL-AR licensing has not occurred. Therefore, the study highlights how licensing advisers via multiple third-party licensees with a product bias is inconsistent with the intent and purpose of four of the objectives of the Act. Licensing advisers via third parties potentially threatens the legitimacy of their licensing, because Bender (2011) determined legitimacy is threatened by conflicts of interest, while Kury (2007) noted, complementary to agency theory.

Integrating Suchman's theoretic legitimacy framework to AFSL-AR licensing

Despite international work in legitimacy theory (Gualini 2004; Díez-Martín, Prado-Roman & Blanco-González 2013) covering various sectors (Low 2010; Sonpar, Pazzaglia & Kornijenko 2010; Pellegrino & Lodhia 2012) and professions, namely accounting (Fisher, Swanson & Schmidt 2007; Andon, Free & Sivabalan 2014) and law (Rogers, Smith & Chellew 2017), deficiencies applying legitimacy theories in financial planning literature exist. This gap is addressed by specifically applying all the criteria in Suchman's (1995) complete legitimacy framework to current licensing. This approach differs from common legitimacy research practice, noted by Doh *et al.* (2010) of examining only one or two legitimacy criteria at a time.

In this regard, Suchman (1995, p. 574) defined legitimacy as a "*generalized perception or assumption that the actions of an entity are desirable, proper, or appropriate within some socially constructed system of norms, values, beliefs, and definitions.*" Understanding the legitimacy of AFSL-AR licensing is dependent on examining Suchman's (1995) three broad, yet specific, types of legitimacy: (1) pragmatic [regulative], (2) normative [moral], and (3) cultural-cognitive [cognitive]. Importantly, Scott (2014) noted, entities exhibiting pragmatic, normative and cultural-cognitive legitimacy increase their survival rates.

Starting with **pragmatic legitimacy**, Suchman (1995) outlined this legitimacy; as the perception of the social support for an entity's activities operating within some socially acceptable system. On the basis of existing literature, **regulative legitimacy**, derived from pragmatic legitimacy (see Rao 2004; Chen & Roberts 2010), occurred when regulatory entities use laws to create perceptions of trust and confidence in society (Kostova & Zaheer 1999) by regulating behaviour (Scott 2013, p. 59; see also Scott 2014). Legitimacy studies (e.g. Bitektine 2011; Chelli, Durocher & Richard 2014) indicated entities gain and maintain regulative legitimacy in the presence of the perception of compliance with the legislation. On these grounds, determining licensing's regulative legitimacy involves examining the presence of perceptions licensing advisers through third-party aligned licensees risks them unintentionally breaching regulatory compliance of the Act, because of their affiliations to product issuers.

With **normative [moral] legitimacy**, attention shifts to specific morals, values or ethics (Chen & Roberts 2010; Chua & Rahman 2011) of an entity's outcomes, goals, activities and/or structures, within a socially accepted (Johnson & Holub 2003) constructed value system (Bitektine 2011). Consequently, understanding the licensing model's normative [moral] legitimacy requires assessing Suchman's (1995) (1) consequential, (2) procedural, (3) structural and (4) personal legitimacies.

Consequential moral legitimacy considers an entity's socially valued outcomes from an ethical perspective (Suchman 1995, p. 579). In the literature, specifically aligned licensees allegedly perform as "*commercial businesses using advisers as a sales force*" (Parliamentary Joint Committee on Corporations and Financial Services 2014, p. 24) to support shareholder theory (Griffiths 2007, p. 231; Lindorff & Peck 2010; Kofman & Murawski 2015).[12] This focus on shareholder wealth maximisation is contrary to developing social capital (Lindorff & Peck 2010) by supporting stakeholders' interests instead of shareholders' interests.[13] However, ASIC expects licensees and their ARs, when managing conflicts of interest, to always put their clients' best interests first, even when not in the licensees' or the licensees' shareholders' best interests (Australian Securities and Investments Commission 2016i). Conflicts of interest should be managed through disclosures (Serpell 2008). However, Bruhn and Miller (2014) concluded, disclosures were ineffective in managing conflicts. Confirmed by Smith's (2009) mixed methods study, employee advisers face conflicts between their professional obligations to provide quality advice to clients and their commercial obligations of business profit. Maclean and Behnam (2010) claimed, critical to ensure legitimacy, institutions should resolve their struggle to manage their regulatory compliance, especially when the legal requirements compromise their commercial activities. Therefore, whether licensing advisers through third-party aligned licensees creates tension between the licensees' commercial interests and their clients' best interest should determine the existence of consequential moral legitimacy.

Procedural moral legitimacy considers the moral perspective of an entity's socially acceptable practices, standards and procedures (Suchman 1995, p. 579). In legitimacy theory, decoupling (Cole & Salimath 2013) occurs where formal policies, processes and rules for legislative compliance differ from actual practice (Carruthers 1995) and behaviour (Scott 2014). Licensees implement legislated practices, standards and procedures reinforcing the advisers' product distribution role (Ferguson, Masters & Christodoulou 2014; Parliamentary Joint Committee on Corporations and Financial Services 2014, p. 24; Commonwealth of Australia 2019). In this way, Sampson (2010) noted, sometimes done without detection, they decouple legislative compliance from practice. Newnham (2012) agreed adding licensees are adept at keeping in place distribution channels masquerading as sources of advice. A deficiency exists in Australian inquiry verifying their claims. Therefore, to address this deficiency by examining licensing's procedural moral legitimacy requires testing the existence of perceptions licensing advisers through licensees results in deceptive sales procedures, standards and practices to reinforce product distribution, while giving the appearance [window dressing] of satisfying regulatory requirements. If not, then licensee–adviser licensing demonstrates procedural legitimacy.

Suchman (1995) defined **structural moral legitimacy** as the moral evaluation of adopting formal structures acceptable to society. Presently under the existing licensing regime, licensees, particularly with strong product affiliations whether by ownership, affiliation or association, appoints, authorises and regulates multiple representatives (Australian Government The Treasury 2014). Licensees control advisers as quasi-employees (Pokrajac 2014). Consequently, this "*cohabitation*" (Money Management 2014) when product distributors and advisers toil together as co-workers servicing clients' needs leads to conflict of interest from association. The available evidence seems to suggest even highly qualified advisers lack professional autonomy (Smith, Armstrong & Francis 2009) to practise their craft like other professionals under the present licensing regime. In principle, the Australian financial advisory industry is buying into a formal structure of conflict of interest from association to conflicted licensees without critical assessment or evaluation. Evaluating licensing structural moral legitimacy requires investigating whether licensing advisers through third-party licensees leads to conflict of interest from association. On these grounds, if it does not, then licensing advisers in this way shows structural legitimacy.

To achieve **personal moral legitimacy** requires the moral and social evaluations of charismatic individual's roles (Carnegie & O'Connell 2012; Goretzki,

Strauss & Weber 2013) exerting their personal influence to dismantle or create new entities (Suchman 1995). Young and Thyil (2014) and the recommendations in the Hayne Royal Commission (Commonwealth of Australia 2019) suggested financial institutional leaders have a duty and moral obligation to all stakeholders, not only shareholders, to be doing the right thing to obtain their implicit or explicit consent to operate. Therefore, if individual leaders of aligned licensees' contributions to the debate surrounding the licensing of advisers do not have the objective of protecting their product distribution channels, then licensing displays personal legitimacy.

Additionally, **cultural-cognitive legitimacy** occurs in the presence of a perception of shared understanding, activities, norms and beliefs (Santana 2012), with the aim to perpetuate an institutional order (Kury 2007) based on cognition or awareness (Meyer 2007). With legislation, clients and their advisers should have a shared understanding as to (1) who advisers are [identity] (Zimmerman & Zeitz 2002, p. 420), (2) what is expected of them [role] (Zimmerman & Zeitz 2002, p. 420) and (3) how effective they are [performance] (Scott 2014). For the same reason, clients and their advisers should have a shared understanding of the adviser's identity and role, so the objectives of the Act can be achieved [performance]. Considering this previous dialogue, cultural-cognitive legitimacy of licensing exists if the Australian public can clearly distinguish between *independent* financial advice [s923A *independent* advisers] and conflicted financial advice [aligned advisers], which subsequently should lead to achieving the objectives of the Act.

To the contrary, if all the criteria are unfulfilled, then licensing lacks legitimacy. Illegitimacy strengthens arguments for a move from the rhetoric of an alternative solution [individual licensing] (Parliamentary Joint Committee on Corporations and Financial Services 2009a, 2014; Vickovich 2014c; Vickovich & Garber 2014; Hoyle 2017a, 2017c, 2017d, 2017b, 2017e; Professional Planner 2017b; Reddacliff 2017) to implementation.

Individual licensing as an alternative solution

Balasubramnian, Brisker and Gradisher (2014) found, trust counts as a major determining factor to influence a member of the public to seek financial advice. Widely publicised, there exists a climate of instability and lack of confidence in financial planning (Hely 2012; Australian Securities and Investments Commission 2013a; Taylor, Juchau & Houterman 2013; Commonwealth of Australia 2019). Therefore, this research assesses whether advisers think individual licensing, rather than licensee–adviser licensing, will improve public trust and confidence.

Sanders and Roberts (2015, p. 18) highlighted in a white paper, the business models within the financial advisory sector, together with the licensing model, favours the **institutional commercial licensee** over the **individual professional adviser**. They acknowledged, despite the "*legitimate legislative basis for this*" (Sanders & Roberts 2015, p. 18), it is contrary to the approach of accredited professions. Although arguably advisers can self-license, corporation (Australian Government Corporations and Markets Advisory Committee 2012) and 'natural persons' [such as self-licensing advisers] are subject to the same licensing regime. Questionable is whether corporate institutions and professional 'natural persons' should be grouped together under the same corporate regulations. Unknown is whether the Act, to achieve its intent and purpose, is a suitable legislative vehicle to license advisers through multiple third-party licensees.

Many authors (see, e.g. North 2015; Australian Securities and Investments Commission 2017b; Smith, Clarke & Rogers 2017; Vickovich 2017a) agreed professional independence is a key, yet controversial, issue facing the advisory sector. Great Southern Limited, Storm Financial, TimberCorp Group and CBA are four illustrative cases where the focus included narrow sales recommendations and culturally endorsed unethical adviser behaviour (Australian Government Corporations and Markets Advisory Committee 2012; North 2015). Arguably, licensing advisers through third parties in this way is a direct threat to **independence** and creates conflicts. North (2015) confirmed this threat results in unethical behaviour.

Recent developments in behavioural theory (Dolan *et al.* 2012) pointed out that making even subtle changes to contexts, environment or choice architecture can affect behaviour powerfully. As advised by Steen, McGrath and Wong (2016), removing the connection between product issuers and individual advisers may lead to a culture shift in the financial advisory sector to consequently reduce risks to the public of more financial scandals. This research considers the extent to which advisers want disconnection from AFSL institutions. If so, then should **individual licensing via a single body replace** the current licensing model? Legal scholars O'Brien and Gilligan (2014) supported this idea. They expect professional obligations should be framed by considering the proof around the failure of the prevalent codes of conduct, together with the risks associated with the existing institutional licensing regime. Especially when principally this system of institutional licensing is absent in other true professions. Also Hayne has made recommendations of a statutory single *independent* disciplinary body (Commonwealth of Australia 2018, 2019) to further this ideal.

The Australian financial planning emerging **profession** is likened to other professions in the literature (Ap 2011; Bruce 2012; Knutsen & Cameron 2012; Australian Securities and Investments Commission 2014f; Burke *et al.* 2015). Yet upon closer inspection, the way the Act, as ASIC enforces, structurally licenses individual advisers makes these proclamations of similarity misleading. Doctors may prescribe certain pharmaceutical products they favour (Everingham 2014). Although they are beholden to corporations (Breakey & Sampford 2017, p. 262), they are not licensed to practise their craft through these third parties. Lawyers, doctors and accountants work for large corporate commercial institutions, but they retain autonomy and control within their job roles (Rubin 2015; Breakey & Sampford 2017). When these professionals leave their workplace, they retain their professional status (Evetts 2011), their licence to practise and ability to work without needing to transfer to other corporate institutions.

Among many others, Bearden (2002) and Cheetham and Chivers (2005) set out numerous characteristics of traditional professions believed to provide professions legitimacy. Fundamentally, through their ***independent*** bodies, Tom (1995) noted, all new entrants into these professions must meet their specific entrance and ongoing membership requirements, including standards of ethics, education and performance, on a continual basis (Breakey & Sampford 2017). In contrast to the attributes of other true professionals, advisers are not self-regulatory, collegial, ***independent***, structured, hierarchical and only client focussed (Riaz, Buchanan & Bapuji 2011). Nor do they operate within a recognised professional body with status (Evetts 2011) within society (Riaz, Buchanan & Bapuji 2011). Nor do they control their specialised knowledge and skills observed in other professionals (Schuchardt *et al.* 2007). Evetts (2011) found professionals employed in public services organisations [hospitals and universities] were closed to being controlled through managerial interventions and institutional controls. He claimed these professional groups have autonomy over their work practices, are accompanied by high status, while holding power and authority. In comparison, even highly qualified professional advisers do not have professional autonomy (Smith, Armstrong & Francis 2009), power and authority. Reinforced by the literature (see, e.g. Rogers 2004; Watts & Murphy 2009; Frumento & Korenman 2013; Rogers, Smith & Chellew 2017), contemporary professions are constantly developing to address new challenges. This development is around professional ethics (Breakey 2017) autonomy, power and authority from corporatisation of professions and professionals (Evetts 2011; Breakey & Sampford 2017; Rogers, Smith & Chellew 2017). Like other professions, seemingly advisers face a struggle for autonomy, power and authority around professional ethics (Smith, Armstrong & Francis 2009). However, arguably it is for completely different reasons from other professions. This research considers one of the reasons for advisers' struggle to achieve autonomy, power and authority, namely licensing via multiple third-party licensees. Consequently, Steen, McGrath and Wong (2016) and Hayne (Commonwealth of Australia 2018, 2019) are correct when they contend the emerging financial planning profession has some way to go before it can be considered a true profession.

Since the Ripoll Inquiry in 2009 (Parliamentary Joint Committee on Corporations and Financial Services 2009a), government support for professionalising financial planning via **industry self-regulatory approaches** is obvious. However, no commitment from them, until the passing of the Corporations Amendment (Professional Standards of Financial Advisers) Bill 2017, the setting up of FASEA (Newnham 2017) followed by Hayne recommending a single regulatory disciplinary oversight body where advisers are mandated to register with (Commonwealth of Australia 2019; Deloitte 2019) has occurred. Although the regulator ASIC has not been in favour of a self-regulatory model (Australian Securities and Investments Commission 2012a), they do acknowledge the potential benefit of such an approach, namely making employee advisers more visible to everyone (Vickovich 2014c). Omarova (2010) argued, like professional self-regulation evident in law and medicine, industry self-regulation is critical to the proper functioning of the financial services industry. Mainly, he reasoned, because private profit-seeking institutions are not trustworthy enough to regulate their own activities in the best interests of the public. Self-regulation in the advice sector is supported by the Professional Standards Authority (Professional Standards Councils 2014; Sanders & Roberts 2015).

Tuch (2005) maintained complying by managing the conflict, not necessarily avoiding or eliminating it, may leave an institution and its advisers in breach of their fiduciary duty. In rebuttal, Angel and McCabe (2013) asserted, society tolerates conflicts of interest as inescapable. However, Hayne would disagree given his preference for the **elimination of conflicts** (Commonwealth of Australia 2019; Deloitte 2019). With this lack of consensus on conflicts of interest, this study considers the extent to which licensing advisers with an individual licence via a single *independent* professional body eliminates this conflict.

Research objectives and contribution

Guided by the theories in agency, legislation, legitimacy and professions, integrated into financial planning theory, the primary research objective of this work is to examine the extent to which current financial adviser licensing is legitimate. The first key point for investigation is the extent to which licensing advisers through third-party licensees creates a dual-agency role, leading to a conflict of interest from association. The second key issue scrutinised is the degree a conflict of interest from association, by licensing advisers through multiple third-party licensees, is inconsistent with the objectives of the Act. The third key issue examined involves a critical evaluation of the level current licensee–adviser licensing is legitimate based on Suchman's (1995) legitimacy framework. This study finishes with the fourth key issue, namely an enquiry into the degree individual licensing through an *independent* professional standards board, like other professions, is a worthy alternative to consider.

Statement of importance

An intensive search of textbooks, journals and reports, including mainstream and professional media reports, government documents and white papers, occurred. This literature exploration included the lists and abstracts of Australian theses using the National Library of Australia's Trove service, as well as the library theses search engines at Central Queensland, Flinders and RMIT University. This secondary data search showed the topic to be under-researched and under-reported in Australia and further afield. Further searches and review of the literature over the duration of this research project revealed its distinctiveness and importance. Hence, the need for deeper scholarly attention was evident. The findings of this investigation will highlight some of the important issues surrounding licensing, while providing policymakers, domestically and internationally, with initial data and preliminary evidence of some of the problems and possible solutions to licensing individual advisers. Thus, this information could potentially influence the role of the regulators, the professional associations, licensees and advisers. Well documented, the focus continues to be the inherent conflicted remuneration of financial services (Australian Securities and Investments Commission 2013b; Batten & Pearson 2013; Bird & Gilligan 2015a; Commonwealth of Australia 2019; Deloitte 2019)[14]; they too have concentrated on professional, education and ethical standards,[15] to address advisers' wrongdoings. Merely concentrating on these issues to improve the conduct of advisers is misguided. Many recognised conflicts between advisers and their clients also arose from ownership, affiliations or association structures between particularly conflicted licensees and their ARs distributing product (Valentine 2008; Parliamentary Joint Committee on Corporations and Financial Services 2009a; Kennedy 2012; Banister *et al.* 2013, p. 1436; Johnston 2014; Pokrajac 2014; Vickovich & Garber 2014; Hoyle 2017a).

Illustrated in Tables 1.1 and 1.2, commonly found are most advisers have affiliations to product producers. Particularly, from Table 1.1 less than 1% (33/4,351) of licensees regulate 50.6% of all ASIC registered advisers (Professional Planner 2017a). Prominent in Table 1.2, it appears none of these 33 licensee groups employing more than 250 ARs listed in Table 1.1 meets the s923A independence definition as specified in the Act. This data confirm the findings during the literature review (Parliamentary Joint Committee on Corporations and Financial Services 2009a; Smith, Armstrong & Francis 2009; Sandlant 2011; Accounting Professional & Ethical Standards Board Limited 2012; Australian Government The Treasury 2014; North 2015; Spits 2015); explicitly, most advisers are associated with product issuers with a legal shareholder wealth maximisation obligation. Although Power (2017) reported a total of 85 well-known, truly ***independent*** advisers affiliated to 45 licensees exist, it is unclear how many advisers in Australia satisfy s923A independence definition of the Act.[16] A clear imbalance between the number of product-biased and ***independent*** advisers, notwithstanding a shortage in ***independent*** advisers, is apparent. Together with the review of the existing literature, under-representation of ***independent*** advisers is undesirable, because

Table 1.1 Total number of licensees and advisers registered on the ASIC Adviser Register on 5 April 2017.

Category	*Licensee*		*Adviser*	
	Frequency	*Percent*	*Frequency*	*Percent*
250+ ARs	33	.8	12,312	50.6
50–249 ARs	56	1.3	5,114	21.0
20–49 ARs	75	1.7	2,204	9.1
5–19 ARs	3,133	72.0	2,617	10.8
2–4 ARs	608	14.0	1,642	6.7
1 AR	446	10.3	446	1.8
Total	4,351	100	24,335	100

Source: *(Professional Planner 2017a, citing Adviser Ratings and ASIC)*

Table 1.2 Frequency of the top licensee groups and their advisers registered on the ASIC Adviser Register on 5 April 2017.

Licensees with more than 250 advisers	*Advisers*	
	Frequency	*Percent*
AMP Limited	2,870	11.8
Commonwealth Bank Limited	1,719	7.1
National Australia Bank Limited	1,667	6.9
Australia and New Zealand Banking Group Limited	1,151	4.7
Westpac Banking Corporation Limited	1,136	4.7
IOOF Holdings Limited	860	3.5
SMSF Advisers Network Pty Ltd	715	2.9
Morgans Financial Limited	468	1.9
Centrepoint Wealth Pty Ltd	380	1.6
Synchronised Business Services Pty Ltd	424	1.7
Dover Financial Advisers Pty Ltd	366	1.5
Bell Potter Securities Limited	280	1.2
GPS Wealth Limited	276	1.1
Total	12,312	50.6

Source: *(Professional Planner 2017a, citing Adviser Ratings and ASIC)*

the Australian public claimed they trust ***independent*** over conflicted advice more (Egan 2008; Australian Securities and Investments Commission 2010b). Adding to this independence debate, the public should be able to clearly differentiate advisers providing ***independent*** from conflicted advice (Parliamentary Joint Committee on Corporations and Financial Services 2009a; Boutique Financial Planners 2014). Arman and Shackman (2012) pointed out this is not the case, which was further supported by a Roy Morgan survey (Morris 2013). Thus, making the issue of independence an important consideration here.

To add to the discussion, the accounting profession incorporated ethical standards for accountants providing financial services into their APES 230 standards (Accounting Professional & Ethical Standards Board Limited 2013). Accountants repositioning financial planning within their profession, according to Brown (2008), sets the expectations of the accounting profession and the public, as well as what advisers should be doing for their clients in the future. In turn, Lambert (2013) suggested this redefinition should significantly influence the future of financial planning, specifically when it comes to the issue of professionalising financial planning.

Scholars contended the FOFA legislation and current licensing was unsuccessful in bringing tangible benefits to the public (Pearson 2006b; Kingsford Smith 2011; Mennen 2014; Bird & Gilligan 2015a; Commonwealth of Australia 2015; Coorey & Eyers 2015; North 2015; Commonwealth of Australia 2016d, 2016b; Ferguson 2016; Henderson & Conifer 2016; Australian Securities and Investments Commission 2017c). Investigating the legitimacy of AFSL-AR licensing is imperative politically, given Burke and Hung (2015) documented evidence of scant research on the impacts of FOFA and the Hayne Inquiry during the research.

During the study, *ASIC Report 515: Financial advice: Review of how large institutions oversee their advisers* released in March 2017 (Australian Securities and Investments Commission 2017e) indicated the top five licensees in Table 1.1 were failing on many levels when overseeing their ARs. This is further supported by research conducted by Bird *et al.* (2016) on the number of enforceable undertakings accepted by ASIC for reasons of misconduct by advisers and licensees. Specifically, they identified three common issues of misconduct: (1) promotion, marketing, advertising and sales of financial products and services infringements; (2) contraventions around specific financial product advice provided; and (3) governance of financial advisory or product and services businesses by supervision, training and monitoring of ARs for compliance. Thus, current licensing could be a potential source of the lack in public confidence and trust (Taylor, Juchau & Houterman 2013), notwithstanding possible class action (Corones & Irving 2016) under various regulations (Bird & Gilligan 2015a). By this argument, inquiry in this area will highlight the extent to which current licensing is responsible for and adds to the contraventions by advisers licensed via licensees with product bias and commercial interests leading to lack of public trust and confidence.

The feasibility of implementing individual licensing was only briefly considered during the Ripoll (Parliamentary Joint Committee on Corporations and Financial Services 2009a) and Murray Inquiries (Commonwealth of Australia 2014a; O'Brien & Gilligan 2014; Vickovich & Garber 2014), although it was never implemented, because many conflicting submissions were presented about the matter, especially during the Murray Inquiry (see, e.g. Financial Rights Legal Centre, Choice & Consumer Action Law Centre 2016; Koh 2016). Although uncommitted to individual licensing, the government demonstrated continued interest in individual licensing (Commonwealth of Australia 2014a). Keeping it on the negotiating table (Commonwealth of Australia 2014e) opened up opportunities for Hayne to make recommendations (Commonwealth of Australia 2019; Deloitte 2019) that could ultimately lead to professionalising financial planning via individual licensing, making this research important for the future of licensing advisers in Australia.

Furthermore, this study will contribute to other projects such as the work undertaken by the Professional Standards Councils in partnership with the University of New South Wales about professions, professional obligations and regulation in the 21st century (Breakey 2017; Greenleaf 2017; Morgan & Hanrahan 2017; Rogers, Smith & Chellew 2017; Smith, Clarke & Rogers 2017; Deloitte 2019). Its focus is on financial planning as a profession, professional obligations of advisers and their regulation during this century. Moreover, it adds to the work undertaken by the Centre for International Finance and Regulation in partnership with the University of Melbourne concerning enforceable undertakings and penalties (Bird & Gilligan 2015b; Gilligan *et al.* 2015a; Gilligan *et al.* 2015b; Bird *et al.* 2016; Gilligan *et al.* 2017).

The lack of enough peer-reviewed financial planning literature supported by sound definitions, principles, models, norms and decision rubrics (Paulo 2003) to define, model, measure, test and challenge the legitimacy of licensing is due to the conceptual construct being difficult to define and quantify. However, research in the Australian financial planning discipline has no sanctioned methodological or concrete research frameworks (Wiseman & Anderson 2013) adequately developed for such a challenge. Thus, the development of a framework to examine the legitimacy of current financial adviser licensing is important. The proposed rectification of this deficiency is embedding agency theory further into financial planning theory, while integrating legitimacy theory into financial planning theory within the context of legislation governing licensing of advisers as true professionals. This research advances financial planning theory, while raising questions for further investigation.

If the agenda for policymakers is professionalisation of advisers to operate with the same standards and ethics as other professions, then this research informs policymakers of better solutions to protect the public, while restoring public trust and confidence in advisers.

Outline of the book

This book comprises seven chapters. Chapter 1 here provides the standard introduction. Then a secondary study in Chapter 2 serves to discuss the background to licensing advisers in Australia, the US and the UK. On the basis of an extensive literature review, Chapter 3 develops the theoretical framework for examining the legitimacy of current AFSL-AR licensing. Chapter 4 presents the questions and hypotheses, the decision behind using a post-positivist research paradigm, mixed methods methodology and the research strategy. Chapter 5 explains the results of the study. In Chapter 6, the discussion focuses on the main findings. The study closes with concluding remarks in Chapter 7. This final chapter includes a summary, implications, practical application and recommendations for further research, major contributions and limitations of the study.

Notes

1 Corporations (Statements of Advice) Repeal Regulation Select Legislative Instrument No. 210, 2014, <www.legislation.gov.au/Details/F2014L01704>.
2 Corporations Amendment Regulation 2013 (No 3) F2013L00905, <www.comlaw.gov.au/Details/F2013L00905>.
3 Corporations Amendment (Professional Standards of Financial Advisers) Act 2017, <www.legislation. gov.au/Details/C2017A00007/Download>.
4 Corporations Amendment (Professional Standards of Financial Advisers) Act 2017, <www.legislation. gov.au/Details/C2017A00007/Download>.
5 Details of this Royal Commission, known as the Hayne Inquiry, https://financialservices.royalcommission.gov.au/Pages/default.aspx.
6 Licensee [mandatory], Professional Associations [voluntary], FASEA code monitory body [mandatory] and ASIC [mandatory] (Deloitte 2019).
7 Commonwealth Corporations Act 2001, <www.legislation.gov.au/Details/C2017C00328/Html/Volume_1#primary-nav>.

8 Regulatory Guide 244: Giving information, general advice and scaled advice.
9 Commonwealth Corporations Act 2001, <www.legislation.gov.au/Details/C2017C00328/Html/Volume_1#primary-nav>.
10 Corporations Amendment (Professional Standards of Financial Advisers) Act 2017, <www.legislation.gov.au/Details/C2017A00007/Download>.
11 Commonwealth Corporations Act 2001, <www.legislation.gov.au/Details/C2017C00328/Html/Volume_1#primary-nav>.
12 Shareholder wealth maximisation and/or profit maximisation.
13 Goodwill, reputation and/or sustainability.
14 Regulatory Guide 246: Conflicted remuneration.
15 Corporations Amendment (Professional Standards of Financial Advisers) Act 2017, <www.legislation.gov.au/Details/C2017A00007/Download>.
16 Commonwealth Corporations Act 2001, <www.legislation.gov.au/Details/C2017C00328/Html/Volume_1#primary-nav>.

2 International trends in regulation

Introduction

This chapter sets the stage by providing a detailed contextual background account of the licensing topic. The conversation begins here with a detailed discussion of the historical background on licensing advisers within the Australian regulatory framework. The current Australia licensee–adviser licensing structure is explained by building on the introduction chapter. The evolution of the US adviser model follows. Then a similar discussion of the implementation of the UK's Retail Distribution Reform commences. In closing, the Australian licensing of advisers is discussed in conjunction with the regulatory trends and challenges taking place in the US and UK.

Australia

Legislative background to Australian adviser regulation

Illustrated in Figure 2.1, the beginnings of current AFSL-AR licensing began with the Wallis Inquiry in 1996 and the Corporate Law Economic Reform Program (Corbett 1999; Cooper 2006; Haigh 2006; Overland 2007). The government appointed Wallis to conduct a Financial Systems Inquiry into the efficiency, competitiveness, consumer interests and regulatory framework of the financial system (Bora & Lewis 1997; Edwards & Valentine 1998; Australian Banking & Finance 1999). Although present at the time was little evidence of financial problems within the Australian setting requiring regulatory changes, the old regime was considered an obstructive constraint (Bakir 2003). CLERP 6, the sixth policy reform, formed part of an improvement suite modifying the old Corporations Law of Australia (Den-Toll 2001). Subsequently, the Wallis Inquiry and CLERP led to the implementation of the Commonwealth FSR Act 2001 on 11 March 2001 (Hutson & Vonnessen 2003).[1] The main aim of this specific legislation was to protect consumers whenever they dealt with financial institutions and their agents (Harvey 2002; Overland 2007; Serpell 2008; Sinodinos 2013d; Australian Securities and Investments Commission 2014a). Here, the government imposed higher standards on financial services providers by implementing more

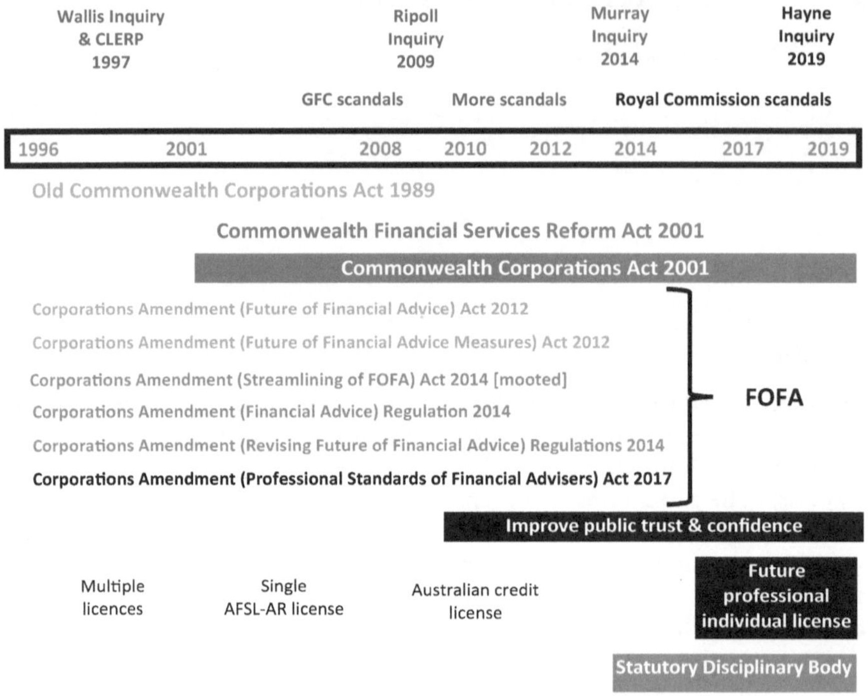

Figure 2.1 Background to adviser licensing.

consistent uniform regulations for all financial instruments at the institutional level (Knutsen & Cameron 2012).

Prior to FSRA, the Australian Financial System comprised several market participants, operating within numerous overlapping financial institutions and markets, with licences issued by various entities and regulators (Bora & Lewis 1997). Bennett (2000) informed, one of the features of the CLERP regulatory framework was considerations around the most appropriate mechanism for licensing financial institutions and their advisers. Consequently, one of Wallis's recommendations published in 1997 included changing the licensing regime for financial sales, advice and dealing (Hanratty 1997). Depending on the classes of financial products and services offered, the old licensing system of multiple licences for providers as specified in Chapter 7 and 8 of the old Commonwealth Corporations Act 1989 was repealed and was then replaced by a new Chapter 7 of the new act (Harding 2001; Pearson 2006b).[2,3] This came into force on 15 July 2001 (Harding 2001). All the old existing range of approvals regulating the activities of insurance agencies, brokers and licensed securities dealers, accountants and all solicitors disappeared (Cotter & Von Nessen 2001). From 11 March 2002, the focus was on a single licensing system (Clayton Utz Financial Services Reform

Group 2002; Australian Securities and Investments Commission 2009; Banister *et al.* 2013; Australian Securities and Investments Commission 2014b) in the form of an AFS Licence (Pearson 2006b) for licensees and their advisers. Henceforth, licences issued provided one or more specific classes of financial products or services under the Act (Davis 2002; Hutson & Vonnessen 2003; Pearson 2006b). The new legislation unified a disjointed legislated environment (Clayton Utz Financial Services Reform Group 2002) by consolidating many different laws into one key piece of legislation for the financial services industry(Parliament of Australia 2001; Haigh 2006; Overland 2007).[4] In this way, FSRA systematically changed the financial services regulatory environment of Australia for licensees and their advisers (Adams 2002; Clayton Utz Financial Services Reform Group 2002; Overland 2007; Bruce 2012).

Then, in 2008, the GFC, and significant financial losses suffered by clients associated with the high-profile corporate scandals (Ellis 2010) by Opes Prime (Julian 2009; Ap 2011; Lewis 2013), Westpoint Corporation (Valentine 2008; Beal & McKeown 2009; Fitzpatrick 2011) and FinCorp (Valentine 2008; Australian Securities and Investments Commission 2013a), caused a climate of instability and lack of confidence in the financial services sector (Taylor, Juchau & Houterman 2013). Most of the headlines pointed to unethical behaviour as one of the leading reasons for this loss in public trust and confidence in financial advice (Ap 2011; Taylor, Juchau & Houterman 2013). The government responded with the Parliamentary Joint Committee on Corporations and Financial Services (2009a) *Inquiry into financial products and services in Australia*, well known in Australia as the Ripoll Inquiry (Australian Government The Treasury 2014). Ripoll's recommendations (Parliamentary Joint Committee on Corporations and Financial Services 2009a) resulted in FOFA reforms (Australian Government The Treasury 2014) to deal with conflicts of interest (Alexander 2011) from remuneration and product sales (Burke & Hung 2015). Furthermore, the government suggested the need for better quality of advice and greater access to advice for Australian retail clients (Corones & Galloway 2013) in the financial advisory sector. Public discussions emerged around professionalising the financial advice sector away from a sales-driven distribution network (Taylor, Juchau & Houterman 2013; Burke & Hung 2015) to improve the lost public trust and confidence (Ap 2011). Ripoll contemplated the effectiveness of licensees overseeing and taking responsibility for the conduct of their ARs (Parliamentary Joint Committee on Corporations and Financial Services 2009a). As part of this contemplation, individual licensing and an industry-based professional standards entity was considered a possible solution to overcome inadequate oversight of advisers by their licensees (Parliamentary Joint Committee on Corporations and Financial Services 2009a). However, the government put aside the matter of individual licensing and a professional standards body during the FOFA legislative reforms.

Instead, FOFA reforms started with consumer credit legislation.[5] Under this legislation, effective 1 January 2010 (Ap 2011), the government regulated conflicts of interest relating to loan products (Banister *et al.* 2013). ASIC enforced from 1 July 2010 an Australian Credit Licence (ACL) on licensees and their credit representatives (Holley Nethercoate Commercial & Financial Services Lawyers 2014a), who were, in many instances, also ARs (Banister *et al.* 2013). This additional regulation moved FOFA away from a single licence back to multiple licences. Banister *et al.* (2013) maintained the overlap between the ACLs, full AFSLs and the limited AFSLs initially confused everyone.

After implementation of the first phase of FOFA reforms, critics contended its proposals would not prevent unethical behaviour (West 2009; Hartnett 2010). Their concerns were confirmed when more financial corporate collapses ensued, specifically Trio Capital (Taylor 2012; Commonwealth of Australia 2016a) and Storm Financial (Kingsford Smith 2009; Ap 2011; Lewis 2013; Commonwealth of Australia 2016a, 2016c). Subsequently, three tranches of FOFA legislation were implemented to amend specific clauses of the Act (Kell 2013). Operative 1 July 2012, with mandatory compliance commencing 1 July 2013 (Burke & Hung 2015), the first and second tranches were implemented as separate yet related FOFA regulations (North 2015),[6,7] covering clients' best interests duty, annual fee disclosure statements and renewal notices where clients would opt in every two years to continue ongoing fees. It banned conflicted commission and volume payments (Burke & Hung 2015). Implementation of a voluntary transition period and grandfathering arrangements to provide time for licensees and advisers to adjust their business models to comply with FOFA ensued. Initially, ASIC took a facilitative approach to compliance; afterwards, all AFSL licensees had to comply (Australian Securities and Investments Commission 2016g). The third tranche covering commissions, best interests duty, opt-in requirements and fee disclosure statements was mooted on 19 November 2014 (Australian Securities and Investments Commission 2016g).[8] In addition, the Corporations (Statements of Advice) Repeal Regulation 2014 revoked the Corporations Amendment (Statements of Advice) Regulation 2014. The Australian Senate reversed some of the laws back to the initial regulations before their implementation (Australian Securities and Investments Commission 2016g). Subsequently, the government worked on foundations of the disallowed regulation. Two regulations, implemented on 16 December 2014 and 1 July 2015, reinstated a few provisions in the disallowed legislation.[9,10]

In addition to the foregoing changes, amendments were made to the previous qualified accountants' FSRA AFSL licensing exemptions (Banister *et al.* 2013) commencing 1 July 2013.[11] Until 30 June 2016, accountants' Regulation 7.1.29A exemption (Halsey & Halsey 2014) applied, allowing them, for example, to set up SMSF or advise on the tax implications of financial products, or provide 'incidental advice' (Adams 2002). Operative 1 July 2016, this exemption was repealed.[12] Now recognised accountants must hold a full or limited AFSL or become ARs under another licensee's AFSL should they advise on certain financial products and services, such as SMSFs (Global Accounting Alliance, Chartered Accountants Worldwide & charteredaccountantsanz.com 2016), tax implications of financial products and 'incidental advice' on securities, insurance products, basic deposit products, superannuation, managed investment schemes, *etc.* To assist accountants to adjust their business models, they had until 30 June 2019 under a streamlined application process to apply for a full or limited licence as specified in Regulation 7.6.01BA. However, after 1 July 2019, this regulation was removed and any future licence applications from accountants must comply with the full obligation of s912 (1e) of the Act, like other licensees.

With FOFA reforms taking hold, some maintained the reforms were reactive (Valentine 2013) while reducing advice availability to the public by increasing advice costs (Mennen 2014). Accordingly, on 20 November 2013, the government announced a Financial System Inquiry [Murray Inquiry] reviewing the financial services industry's overall strength (Commonwealth of Australia 2014a). To encourage advice cost flow-on-effects to clients, the review's purpose was to simplify the system's overall complexity, provide certainty, reduce compliance costs and lower administrative burdens by decreasing red tape (North 2015). On that account, the review pointed to the claim professional, ethical and education standards among advisers should be lifted (Parliamentary Joint Committee on Corporations and Financial Services 2014). At this stage, acceptable standards for admission into the emerging financial planning profession in Australia, notwithstanding internationally, had been lacking. For instance, by educational standards, all Australian advisers had to comply with *ASIC Regulatory Guide 146 Licensing: Training of financial product advisers* by undergoing some initial minimum competency tests, continuing with ongoing and specialised training and education with accredited training providers.[13] Although previously recognised as sufficient to address the regulators' minimum licensing requirements, inconsistent standards of financial planning qualifications were evident at the Graduate Diploma and/or Advanced Diploma level offered at various vocational education institutions of variable standards as part of competency-based programs (Bruce 2012). This indicated advisers needed only a diploma in financial planning and/or specialist accreditations in the areas of SMSF, gearing and derivatives (Deloitte & Financial Services Council 2014). The PJC's consideration from March 2015, based on Murray's recommendations in 2014, to raise advisers' educational standards by expecting all new advisers to complete a minimum degree qualification, obligatory ongoing professional development, as well as a structured professional year as a prerequisite for registration as a financial adviser (Parliamentary Joint Committee on Corporations and Financial Services 2015), started moving advisers away from a product sales focus to a professional advisory focus.

Aside from the professional standards issue during the Murray Review's consultation phase, a brief, yet separate, dialogue in the Australian Senate took place with regard to a single financial licence for each individual financial adviser, rather than one licence for an institutional licensee contractually engaging a number of advisers (Commonwealth of Australia 2014e). Recall from ponderings, this was not the first time a government inquiry contemplated individual licensing. The Ripoll Inquiry considered individual licensing and a professional standards body "*to share responsibility with ASIC for establishing, monitoring and enforcing competency and conduct standards for financial advisers*" (Parliamentary Joint Committee on Corporations and Financial Services 2009a, p. 136). Despite a second inquiry contemplating individual licensing, surprisingly, the Murray Report made no recommendations regarding the matter (Commonwealth of Australia 2014a). Instead, his report concluded the existing regulatory framework of product design, product distribution, disclosure and financial advice is insufficient to deliver reasonable treatment to clients (Commonwealth of Australia 2014a). However, as was mentioned earlier, with more financial scandals emerging, notably CBA (Mennen 2014), the government had no choice but to implement a "*policy nudge*" (Ariely, Amir & Lobel 2008, p. 2098) in the form of new legislation passed on 9 February 2017 to further spearhead the process of professionalising advisers away from financial product sales.[14] This prod was followed by "*coercive measures*" (Ariely, Amir & Lobel 2008, p. 2098) of including an *independent* professional standards setting body,[15] FASEA (O'Dwyer 2017). This body develops and sets educational standards and examinations for all new advisers, professional year requirements and continuing professional development requirements and develops a code of ethics for advisers. In the new legislation, existing advisers are given a transition period to complete an appropriate degree equivalent, transition through a recognised pathway and pass an exam. Legislating a code of ethics for all advisers is an indication Hayne (Commonwealth of Australia 2019) and the government realises, as anticipated by Heath (2009), merely urging more ethical behaviour upon advisers does not present a solution to prevent the unethical behaviour of rogue advisers. Consequently, at the time of writing, individual advisers were now being regulated by two main regulators, namely ASIC via third-party licensees and FASEA directly. Equivocally, although still in early stages, FASEA and ASIC share overlapping licensing powers to prevent or cancel the authorisation of individual advisers from practising their craft, albeit for different reasons. Thus, these latest regulatory requirements around professionalism are yet to take hold to protect the Australian public when receiving financial advice. Additionally, Hayne's recommendations of professional discipline of advisers focuses on reforms to continue evolving financial advice into a profession providing current business models and structures time to adjust or exit the industry (Commonwealth of Australia 2019; Deloitte 2019).

Current adviser licensing regime in Australia

Part 7 Division 5 are key parts in the Commonwealth Corporations Act 2001, licensing financial institutions and authorising their agents. In addition to Chapter 7 of the Act, Teale (2008) highlighted, the regulations are continually updated to be legally enforceable with a separate process from the government involving Corporations Regulations 2001,[16] plus Schedule 2 and 3 in the Corporations Amendment Regulations 2013 (No 3) as additional support (Beal & McKeown 2009; Global Accounting Alliance, Chartered Accountants Worldwide & charteredaccountantsanz.com 2016).[17] ASIC introduced Regulatory Guides [RG],[18] previously known as Policy Statements, as guidance to 'regulated entities' within the financial planning industry when considering the interpretation and compliance of the law (Beal & McKeown 2009). Although not legally enforceable, they assist in the understanding, interpretation and regulation of the licensing of licensees and adviser (Bennett 2000; Tomlinson 2001; Clayton Utz Financial Services Reform Group 2002; Pearson 2006b; Australian Securities and Investments Commission 2014a). Illustrated as part of the process of keeping participants in the advice industry informed or to clarify any confusion, ASIC continues to amend existing regulatory guidance over the course of the changes to reflect the FOFA reforms where necessary (Australian Securities and Investments Commission 2014d). Furthermore, Explanatory Memoranda and Statements issued by the Commonwealth Government accompanies every new bill (O'Neill 2006).[19] Although they are not legally enforceable, they form part of the additional guidance notes to the Act and the Regulations to offer insights into the intention behind any rules and how the Commonwealth Government intends for it to operate in practice. This legislation is backed up by other important protections in common law (Sinodinos 2014; Boyle 2015). The law of contract and duty of care exercised by advisers are of specific relevance in common law (Adams 2002). Thus, principles of common law built up through successive court decisions complements the Act.

The Act and supporting documents require institutions providing financial services and products (Beal & McKeown 2009) to hold an AFS Licence with a few exceptions (Beal & McKeown 2009; Jones 2012; Banister *et al.* 2013). AFS licensees are individuals, partnerships or companies, but not trusts, unless held in their capacity as trustees, but not in the name of the trustees, as qualified in the Act (Australian Securities and Investments Commission 2016d). The AFSL regime is available to financial institutions, accountants, credit licensees, trustees of superannuation funds, fund managers and individuals who qualify. Notably, licensees once licensed are registered on the Professional Register (Australian Securities and Investments Commission 2016f). An AFSL imposes a range of ongoing obligations (Adams 2002) and minimum standards of conduct provisions on the licensees at institutional level and on their advisers at the individual level (Harvey 2002; Teale 2008; Australian Securities and Investments Commission 2016d). To illustrate further, these obligations include: general or personal advice; audit requirements; uniform product disclosures obligations; and AR competency standards (Holley Nethercoate Commercial & Financial Services Lawyers 2014b; Australian Securities and Investments Commission 2016d). All licensing, conduct and disclosure requirements apply to all providers in relation to financial services offered to wholesale and retail client (Banister *et al.* 2013). Banister *et al.* (2013) and Rantall (2014) mentioned, the policies, processes and procedures licensees have in place to ensure their compliance with the law serve as critical proof to ASIC of their, and their ARs', competency to deliver financial services in an efficient, honest and fair manner.

Since implementation of FSR, ASIC has introduced three licensing options to provide financial product and financial advice services with some common legal responsibilities as shown in Table 2.1: a full AFS licence (Teale 2008) or a limited AFSL licence option (Serpell 2008; Halsey & Halsey 2014) or where the AR is licensed via AFSL licensees. Obtaining full AFSL enables the licensee and their

Table 2.1 Summary of licensing options available to advisers with some legal obligations.

Licensing obligations[26]	*Limited license*[27]	*Full license*[28]	*AR of an AFSL licensee*[29]
Definitions	Describes licensees authorised to provide only one or more of a limited range of financial services for SMSFs, superannuation products, securities, simple managed investment schemes, general insurance products, life risk insurance products and basic deposit products.	Describes licensees authorised to provide a full range of financial services and products.	Describes individuals, bodies corporate, partnerships, of CARs appointed by AFSL licensees to provide specific financial services and products on its behalf.
Provide all financial services covered under the AFS Licence efficiently, honestly and fairly.	Licensees and ARs must comply.	Licensees and ARs must comply.	Licensees and ARs must comply.
Adequate arrangements to manage conflicts of interest.	Licensees and ARs must comply.	Licensees and ARs must comply.	Licensees and ARs must comply.
Comply with licensing terms and conditions.	Licensees and ARs must comply.	Licensees and ARs must comply.	Licensees and ARs must comply.
Ensure AFSL licensees and ARs comply with financial services laws, such as they are competent and trained.	Informal action plans developed by the licensees must be in place.	Formalised action plans developed by the licensees must be in place.	AFSL licensees' obligation.
Must have adequate resources and compensation arrangements in place.	Licensees require limited resources, as they do less research and have lower compensation obligations.	Licensees require sufficient resources to implement their research plans and have greater compensation obligations.	AFSL licensees' obligation.
Comply with other statutory laws.	Licensees and ARs must comply.	Licensees and ARs must comply.	Licensees and ARs must comply.

Table 2.1 Summary of licensing options and the legal obligations available to advisers, cont.

Licensing obligations[30]	*Limited license*[31]	*Full license*[32]	*AR of an AFSL licensee*[33]
Financial product research capacity.	Not necessary.	Need to provide proof to ASIC.	AFSL licensees' obligation.
Dispute resolution and risk-management systems in place.	Member Financial Ombudsman Scheme (FOS) or Credit & Investments Ombudsman (CIO)	Member Financial Ombudsman Scheme (FOS) or Credit & Investments Ombudsman (CIO)	AFSL licensees' obligation.
Notify ASIC of compliance breaches and any significant changes, like the appointment and cessation of ARs.	AFSL licensees' obligation.	AFSL licensees' obligation.	AFSL licensees' obligation.
Lodge annual returns.	Unaudited annual returns.	Audited annual returns.	AFSL licensees' obligation.
Ensure licensees and ARs have adequate PI.	AFSL licensees' obligation.	AFSL licensees' obligation.	AFSL licensees' obligation.
Privacy and Anti-Money Laundering and Counter-Terrorism Financing policy in place.	Licensees and ARs must comply.	Licensees and ARs must comply.	Licensees and ARs must comply.
Keep registers: business document, service providers, authorised representatives and advertising and promotions.	AFSL licensees' obligation.	AFSL licensees' obligation.	AFSL licensees' obligation.
Engage an employee, director and/or third party contractor of 'good fame and character' to be directly involved in overseeing the provision of financial services, referred to as a responsible manager.	Appoint at least one person per license with business references, police clearances and bankruptcy checks, meet education and relevant experience requirements.	Appoint at least one person per license with business references, police clearances and bankruptcy checks, meet education and relevant experience requirements.	The AFSL licensee must appoint at least one person per license with business references, police clearances and bankruptcy checks, meet education and relevant experience requirements.

adviser to offer comprehensive personal financial product and services advice, including recommendations in a broad range of areas (Halsey & Halsey 2014).[20] Obtaining a full licence requires the employment of experienced and qualified responsible manager(s) for the licensees too (Holley Nethercoate Commercial & Financial Services Lawyers 2014a; Australian Securities and Investments Commission 2016k). A limited advice licence is available to a range of institutions and individuals, such as industry superannuation trustees, advisers and potential accountants to offer clients 'one-off advice' or 'scaled advice' (Australian Securities and Investments Commission 2012b; Sinodinos 2013b).[21] Consumers receive 'scaled advice' to meet a restricted or limited quantity of their financial planning needs, such as insurance advice only, SMSF advice only, or advice on superannuation products, securities, simple managed investment schemes, general and life insurance and basic deposit products. Thus, licensees engineer their business models around the expertise of their advisers by the following classifications: expert, generalist, holistic advisers and/or product specialists (Chene, Gold & Gramlich 2010; Banister *et al.* 2013).

Along similar lines, prominent in the legislation,[22] media and in practice (Fox 2014; Pokrajac 2014; Spits 2014a; Jacobson 2016; Lester 2016; Power 2016b), yet insufficiently addressed in scholarly literature, is the identification and definitions of the categories of licensees and their ARs. Well-documented (Senate Economics References Committee 2014; Ferguson 2015; Commonwealth of Australia 2016b; Steen, McGrath & Wong 2016) is the government concern about the detriment of misconduct within financial services. Thus, in October 2014, ASIC established the Wealth Management Project (Australian Securities and Investments Commission 2016a). The objective was to lift conduct and standards of the largest financial advice institutions [NAB, Westpac, CBA, ANZ, AMP and Macquarie] (Australian Securities and Investments Commission 2016a). As part of this project, on 2 March 2016, ASIC announced they will increase their surveillance, seek out, publicly name and shame financial services licensees or their advisers who illegally refer to their financial services as "***independent***" (Australian Securities and Investments Commission 2016e; Jacobson 2016).

Reading the Act carefully, s923A states financial services providers must operate without any conflicts of interest from remuneration, affiliation, association and ownership links to product issuers(Jacobson 2016).[23] It prohibits advisers, any related body corporates or their associates receiving remuneration in the form of commissions, some asset-based fees, volume-based payments, bonuses, gifts and/or other benefits (Elliott 2006; Jacobson 2016).[24] Asset-based fees are remuneration in the form of a percentage incentive payment for FUM (Brown 2011). If turning off commissions is impractical, the Act instructs the rebate of these commissions back to the client.[25] Moreover, this law disallows restricting recommendations of financial products by a narrow APL (Elliott 2006; Jacobson 2016).

Currently, s923A permits receiving or charging asset-based fees for FUM (Power 2016b) but bans asset-based fees on investments limited to borrowed

FUM [s964D and s964E] (Australian Securities and Investments Commission 2013b) (Australian Securities and Investments Commission 2013b) (Australian Securities and Investments Commission 2013b) (Australian Securities and Investments Commission 2013b).[34] Permitting asset-based fees is a controversial issue. For Industry Super Australia (2014), and others, like the Accounting Professional and Ethical Standards Board (Brown 2011), receiving asset-based fees via a specific platform is technically a commission from platforms [product sales]. To the contrary, the Financial Planning Association (2014) claimed asset-based fees are advice fees, not commissions. These fees are charged through the product under the direction of the client for ongoing services to obtain regular information on each investment in the client's portfolio from respective platforms and product issuers. Like Australia, the UK Financial Conduct Authority [previously Financial Standards Authority] permits asset-based fees with the condition it fairly represents services provided to the client (International Financial Law Review 2009).

Section 923A of the Act creates two categories of advisers licensed via licensee, namely advisers who are either not *independent* or *independent*. These categories were based on ownership and remuneration, with limited reference to s923A. Colloquially, they were known as "*independent*" (Power 2016b), "*aligned*" and "*non-aligned*" (Lester 2016). Seemingly, these terms were inconclusively debated in non-scholarly literature, in practice (Tucker 2009; Starke 2013b; May 2014; Spits 2014a; Vickovich 2014a) and in online blogs (Lester 2016). Licensees and their advisers considering themselves aligned to product issuers providing aligned advice seem clear, they cannot legally use the terms "*independent*," "*impartial*" or "*unbiased*", because they do not meet the requirements in s923A [e.g. AMP-owned and the bank licensees and advisers]. Characteristically, salaried employee or self-employed advisers licensed to licensees affiliated to product issuers provide aligned advice (Perri 2014; Spits 2014b). Aligned institutions tend to control and restrict the products and platforms on their approved product lists [APLs] (Smith 2009; North 2015; Certified Practising Accountant 2016). A fundamental challenge for aligned advisers, Sandlant (2011) and Power (2016b) claimed, is their role as distribution channels for product providers for revenue benefits. Furthermore, the media reported (*Independent* Financial Adviser News 2016c) these licensees restrict adviser ownership of the client by, for example offering BOLR terms.[35] In the agreements, self-employed advisers retire or transfer to another licensee, they sell the clients to the abandoned licensee or sell these clients to an AR approved by the abandoned licensee. Some formula specified in the BOLR agreement calculates the selling price.

ASIC estimated around 80 to 85% of the unconfirmed numbers of 15,000, 18,000 or 22,500 advisers in Australia were associated with product issuers (Smith, Armstrong & Francis 2009; Accounting Professional & Ethical Standards Board Limited 2012; Australian Government The Treasury 2014; North 2015). Spits (2015) reported the snapshot findings of the annual Money Management Top 100 Financial Planning Group Survey. In 2015, they found the total aligned ownership of advisers was 72% of advisers in the Top 100 advice groups. Between these, AMP and the big four banks, licensed 57.2% of the Top 100 advice groups.

There were allegations (see, e.g. Munro 2011; Sandlant 2011; Australian Securities and Investments Commission 2013b, 2013c; Vickovich 2015) claiming mid-sized licensees and their ARs advertised themselves as '*independent.*'[36] While under the misconception of following the *independent* advice principles, they were selling their own 'white label' or 'private label' products recommended from single platforms and/or allowing commissions or asset-based fees (Parliamentary Joint Committee on Corporations and Financial Services 2009a; Smith, Armstrong & Francis 2009; Sandlant 2011; North 2015; Spits 2015).[37,38] To the contrary, ASIC's (2014f) interpretation of s923A is different (Santacruz 2016a). They asserted licensees are not necessarily "*independent*" just because no affiliation to a product issuer exists. Subsequently, ASIC sought legal advice around the terms "*independently-owned*" (Santacruz 2016a), "*non-institutionally owned*" and "*non-aligned.*" This was after they penalised two licensees, because they used these terms when they did not meet the requirements of s923A (*Independent* Financial Adviser News 2016a). The argument proposed by one of these licensees for using the term "*independently-owned*" was to inform the public, the financial institutions do not own them (Santacruz 2016c). Despite this, advisers failing the requirements of s923A independence definition were referring to themselves with related terms to independence, such as "*independently owned,*" "*non-institutionally owned*" and "*non-aligned,*" without using the terms "*independent,*" "*impartial*" and "*unbiased.*" Arguably, if they can make this claim, then on these grounds, any self-employed adviser authorised via an aligned licensee could make the same argument. Namely, they can argue they are *independently* owned, because their licensee does not own them, just authorises them and restricts their activities or actions. Some viewed this play on words as potentially misinterpreting and misapplying the requirements in s923A of the Act. Thus, potentially misleading the public to think they were dealing with an *independent* adviser. On legal advice, the Australian Securities and Investments Commission (2017a) clarified the terms "*independently owned,*" "*non-institutionally owned*" and "*non-aligned*" or related terms could be used only if advisers complied with the requirements of s923A. Consequently, they have updated *Regulatory Guide 175 Licensing: Financial product advisers – conduct and disclosure* explaining how to interpret s923A of the Act.

Although ASIC has clarified two categories of licensee and advice under s923A, at the time of finalising the editing of this book, this section of the Act remains contentious, with lobby groups wanting it amended or repealed (Johnston & Walker 2017; Vickovich 2017b, 2017c). Notably, Elliott (2006) defended it, saying s923A was difficult for advisers and licensees to implement. She explained, in practice, a fee-for-service business sometimes finds it almost impossible to rebate commissions back to clients when these commissions cannot be turned off. Another financial planning practitioner confirmed, advisers find it difficult to structure their business to meet the independence requirements, because "*the industry is not set up to support this kind of ethics – it actually drives against it*" (Beaman 2010c, p. 9). However, it is argued any potential misapplication or misrepresentation of s923A of the Act places licensees and advisers at risk of ASIC taking action (Pearson 2008; Australian Securities and Investments Commission 2016b), as well as legal liability consequences subject to various other regulations (Bird & Gilligan 2015a).

Licensees and advisers who are truly *independent* providing *independent* advice are legally able to use the terms "*independent,*" "*impartial,*" "*unbiased,*" "*independently owned,*" "*non-institutionally owned,*" "*non-aligned*" and/or related terms, as specified in s923A of the Act, for several reasons. They meet either (1) the *Independent* Financial Advisers Association of Australian's gold standard and strict independence conditions, with no direct or indirect ownership, affiliation or association links to product issuers, and charge no commissions or asset-based fees [e.g. licensees Roskow *Independent* Advisory and Brocktons *Independent* Advisory]; or (2) all the requirements in s923A of the Act, with no direct or indirect affiliation links to product issuers, and charge no commissions but charge asset-based fees [e.g. licensees Pitcher Partners Wealth Management and Aspire Financial Consultants]. These licensees do not restrict the ownership of the client with, for example, BOLR terms (Perri 2014; Spits 2014b, 2014a). Unlike in many aligned cases, clients are transferred with their advisers to another licensee without any encumbrance (Perri 2014; Spits 2014b, 2014a). Allegedly, they are not vertically integrated. They enjoy broad APLs not commonly controlled by their licensees (Pokrajac 2014). The clients of the non-aligned advice sector allegedly receive a greater degree of *independent* advice (Starke 2013b), because allegedly product bias in the recommendations is obscured (Pokrajac 2014).

Licensees obtain an AFSL by lodging an application with ASIC once it meets regulatory standards as prescribed in the Act and several ASIC regulatory guides(Deloitte & Financial Services Council 2014).[39] Only once licensed are licensees permitted to appoint ARs, who are their agents comprising either 'natural persons,' body corporates or partnerships [s916A of the Act] providing advice on financial products and services to the public (Beal & McKeown 2009; Deloitte & Financial Services Council 2014). Accordingly, among their numerous regulatory responsibilities, ASIC enforces a demanding legal process (Jones 2012; Banister *et al.* 2013) prescribed in s916A, s916B, s916C, s916D, s916E and s916F of the Act to appoint, authorise and regulate individual advisers through third-party licensees (Beal & McKeown 2009). The licensees' role involves providing internal and external legitimacy for the actions of their advisers.

Outwardly, this is demonstrated by a rigorous selection process (Bender 2011) using a monitoring, supervising and training compliance system (Bennett 2000) aimed to meet the requirements of the legislation. For instance, some of the statutory duties imposed on licensees and advisers are providing appropriate advice, offering adequate warnings of the risks, managing controlling and/or avoiding conflicts of interest through disclosure,[40] utilising some form of documented risk-management system and always placing the clients' best interest with 'safe harbour' requirements ahead of their own interests (Deloitte & Financial Services Council 2014). Section 916B of the Act states, where advisers are body corporates, its employees and directors must be appointed as ARs of the licensees (Bearden 2006). Notably, individual ARs do not require a licence as specified in s911A, unless they deliver financial advice without supervision via an AFSL licensee (Parliamentary Joint Committee on Corporations and Financial Services 2009a, p. 23). From 31 March 2015, ARs of licensees must be registered on the ASIC Financial Adviser Register available to the public online (Bateman & Kingston 2014).

Apparent in practice (Holley Nethercoate Commercial & Financial Services Lawyers 2014a; Power 2015; Global Accounting Alliance, Chartered Accountants Worldwide & charteredaccountantsanz.com 2016), but subtly defined in scholarly works, ARs can practise their craft only if licensed in one of three ways: (1) licensed as ***independent*** individual self-employed advisers with their own licence [self-licensing], (2) contracted to licensees like a franchise arrangement using the licensees' support services (Parliamentary Joint Committee on Corporations and Financial Services 2009a), or (3) becoming employees of licensees (Bennett 2000; Holley Nethercoate Commercial & Financial Services Lawyers 2014a). First, ***independent*** advisers, complying with s923A of the Act, can take out an AFSL and be themselves legally accountable (Teale 2008). This involves following a process as prescribed by the law and ASIC to set up a practice on their own after meeting ASIC's education, experience and licensee licensing requirements (Bennett 2000). In Australia, the s923A ***independent*** self-licensed adviser has the freedom to recommend from a choice of products for their clients, because they operate open product lists of all the products in the marketplace (Pokrajac 2014). Second, the contracted or franchised advisers wanting to be self-employed without taking on the legal and financial responsibility of an AFSL may enter a contract or franchise arrangement with licensee groups. The licensee groups remain legally responsible for the education, training supervision and conduct of the franchised advisers, while the advisers operate their own business with comparative autonomy. In exchange for a fee, these licensee groups offer ARs subsidised support services (Parliamentary Joint Committee on Corporations and Financial Services 2009a; Professional Planner 2017b), such as education, compliance, marketing and software (Bennett 2000). Third, ARs can become employees of licensees and be paid, generally, a base salary with additional performance-based remuneration (Bennett 2000). Notably, employees of AFSLs can provide financial product advice on behalf of their AFSL employer without requiring to become an AR or holding an AFSL as long as their employer has an AFSL (Simes, Harper & Green 2008).

From the foregoing, it is apparent the financial services regulator, ASIC, is responsible for licensing and monitoring the activities of the AFSL holders and their agents. This involves taking the necessary action for any violations identified; imposing or changing licence conditions; reviewing sales, marketing material and investment schemes of licensees; and reviewing selected documents, such as product disclosure statements and financial statements lodged with them (Jones 2012; Banister *et al.* 2013). ASIC takes action against advisers offering financial services beyond the scope of their licence conditions (Pearson 2006b) by suspending or cancelling a licence or banning a 'natural person' from acting as an adviser (Simes, Harper & Green 2008; Serpell 2012). If problems with the information disclosed occurs or if the offer documents require additional or corrective disclosure, then ASIC is expected to enforce appropriate disclosures (Jones 2012). The enforcement involves an administrative remedy in addition to any civil or criminal remedies (Jones 2012), including enforceable undertakings and related penalties (Bird & Gilligan 2015b; Gilligan *et al.* 2015a; Gilligan *et al.* 2015b; Bird *et al.* 2016; Gilligan *et al.* 2017).

Australian reform consequences and challenges

Implementation of the Act, plus its subsequent amendments by Financial Services (see Tomlinson 2001; Bulling 2003; Moutsopoulos 2005; Haigh 2006; Jackling & Sullivan 2007) and FOFA Reforms (see, e.g. Serpell 2008; Bowen 2010; Alexander 2011; Australian Securities and Investments Commission 2014e) have not been without its critics. Pearson (2006b) claimed the FOFA rules are so wide in scope, complex and confusing, it continually requires further explanation. Illustrated earlier was such a situation, namely the recent review by ASIC of the legal interpretation of s923A of the Act (Australian Securities and Investments Commission 2017a; Tran 2017; Vickovich 2017b; Waterson & Vickovich 2017). Valentine (2008, p. 283) critically argued, some parts of the financial services industry is heavily regulated, while others lightly regulated. He noted, not all advisers operate on a level playing field, nor carry uniform regulatory burdens under the existing licensing model. For example, S765A of the Act disregards physical assets such as direct real estate [property], wine, art, stamp collections and credit facilities as financial products. Therefore, insurance brokers, mortgage brokers, real estate agents, art dealers, coin and stamp dealers, jewellers and sellers of sporting memorabilia do not require an AFSL or are only partially covered by the AFSL. Furthermore, Smith, Armstrong and Francis (2009) noted, the Act excludes estate planning or non-product strategic advice.

Although FSR was supposed to result in efficiencies and cost savings for financial services providers, Pearson (2006b) felt it has been an expensive endeavour for the industry by compliance costs and financial adviser turnovers within licensees, as well as from the exit of advisers from the advisory sector.

Although unverified in scholarly literature, advisers transferring between licensees place licensees, the clients and advisers at risk, legally and financially. For example, clients are adversely affected concerning PI insurance and when BOLR agreements are in place, especially when individual advisers change licensees. In 2010, Guardian and Synchron licensees had a disagreement over a clause in an adviser transfer agreement. Unless Guardian agreed to the transfer conditions, Synchron would not be covered by PI insurance if a transferring client was unhappy with the advice given to them while at Guardian, and before moving over to Synchron (Levy 2010).

Where clients are 'owned' by the licensees, particularly when BOLR agreements are in place, the client is expected to wait for the licensee to allocate a new adviser to the client, often not of their choosing. Although ARs can leave their licensees at any time, they lose their authority to continue working until they sign up with another licensee, or obtain their own licence (Clayton Utz Financial Services Reform Group 2002). This potentially leaves clients, who have invested considerable time building a relationship of trust with a particular adviser (Banister 2016), without a designated adviser during the transition time of the transfer to another licensee. This void for clients could gravely impact any existing trust relationships between adviser and client (Banister 2016), notwithstanding future trust associations.

Haigh (2006) observed, despite FSR legislation introducing a legal and ethical framework governing advisers and licensees, commensurate levels of accountability are missing when shared between licensee and adviser. Under FOFA legislation, accountability is not at the individual level, but at the institutional level, especially where the majority of advisers are affiliated to product producers (Parliamentary Joint Committee on Corporations and Financial Services 2009a). Prior to statutory best interest duty obligation, Gor (2005) noted, the accountability burden rested entirely on licensees to authorise representatives to offer financial services. Thereafter, he argued, accountability rested with the licensees and their ARs, in indistinguishable proportions. In this regard, Haigh (2006) and Pearson (2006b) may be correct when they decided the legislation produced no tangible benefits to the Australian public.

North (2015) contended the licensing regulations disseminated a range of business models covering different sizes. Debatably, this led to inconsistent standards between licensees (Vickovich 2014d) for compliance audits, education, training, supervision, licensee licensing requirements and conduct (Bennett 2000). Highly questionable, the Act validates commercial product-aligned licensees to acquire advisers to be their financial product distributors (Parliamentary Joint Committee on Corporations and Financial Services 2014, p. 24) and hence, arguably, condones conflict of interest from association, which threatens independence and professionalism.

Furthermore, agency theory, according to Scott (2013, p. 61), highlighted the cost and difficulty of monitoring the regulation through third parties who may not necessarily be neutral. Another problem with the legislation is the potential for licensees to take advantage of detailed technical licensing rules of the Act to develop formal compliance programs on paper to give the appearance of satisfying the regulatory requirements [window dressing], while allowing for sales-based culture (Parliamentary Joint Committee on Corporations and Financial Services 2009a; Smith 2009; Newnham 2012; Parliamentary Joint Committee on Corporations and Financial Services 2014; North 2015).

Subject to deficits in academic works, yet apparent in media commentaries (Vickovich & Micallef 2013), were discussions on the advantages and disadvantages of licensing advisers through third-party licensees. Some advantages are third-party licensees allowing advisers to focus their attention on the client while leaving back office, compliance burdens to the licensees. Licensees affiliated to large institutions are in a better position to pay compensation to clients for losses suffered if legal compliance violations or unethical behaviour occurred (Pokrajac 2014). Disadvantages include, *inter alia*, advisers unable to market themselves as *independent* to clients who consider independence important, as well as being restricted by the licensees' APL when providing advice to clients (Santhebennur 2014).

Valentine (2013) proposed the legislation did not deal with the fragmentation of financial advice, limited licences, tax agents, grandfathering and horizontal and vertical integration adequately. The underlying argument by Valentine (2013) was against reforms being reactive, such as when the use of the descriptions 'financial planner' or 'financial adviser' by licensed individuals were added to the Act at the eleventh hour.

Burke and Hung (2015) documented the scant evidential research in Australia studying the impacts of FOFA. For example, Australian Government The Treasury (2014) released a FOFA Regulation Impact Statement titled *Future of Financial Advice Amendments – Details-stage regulation Impact Statement* in March 2014, noting the decline in the number of advisers since implementation of FOFA. They conceded two contributory factors to this decline in adviser numbers, namely FOFA reforms and the ailing economy. It is unclear, Burke and Hung (2015), suggested, what contributed more to the decline given these two impacts were connected. They could not deduce from their findings whether increased industry concentration and compliance costs, together with increased costs of advice, reduced access to financial advice for retail clients.

Another bit of research reported in the *Review of the financial advice industry's implementation of the FOFA reforms (Report 407)* reviewing the industry's implementation of FOFA was conducted by ASIC with their findings released in September 2014 (Australian Securities and Investments Commission 2014f). They found although most licensees increased scaled advice and strategic advice, they did no change advice services they offered post-FOFA implementation. ASIC found the statutory fiduciary duty obligations did not have any impact on most institutions' APLs, except for a few amendments such as a reduction in the number or types of products on the list. However, they did find the presence of an estimated reduction in commissions paid by product issuers, a reduction in fees based on volume of assets under advice and an increase in fixed fees paid by clients. Yet they stated that after implementation of FOFA, the [unweighted] average income source for these licensees changed little. Burke and Hung (2015) determined in post-FOFA some institutions were continuing to receive most revenues from commissions, because of grandfathering arrangements existing before July 2013, or because of excluding banning insurance commissions. Seemingly, FSR and FOFA has been a long, difficult road, with many sections in the Act appearing to have been omitted (Roberts 2012), unresolved or continuing as a work-in-progress for Australian policymakers. Interestingly, Australia is not alone in finding a suitable model to regulate the financial advice sector. Thus, the focus shifts internationally, to the US and the UK, because other countries face similar challenges.

United States

Legislative background to United States adviser regulation

Prior to 2010, US providers of financial services operated in a relatively unregulated environment (Baily, Klein & Schardin 2017). They would distinguish themselves, for example, by registering with private self-regulatory organisations, such as the Certified Financial Planner Board of Standards Incorporated (Finke & Langdon 2012). Historically, documented by Inderst and Ottaviani (2012e), advice provided by US investment advisers was rarely in the best interests of the public. For instance, Finke, Huston and Waller (2009b) explained that US retail consumers struggled to clearly distinguish between investment advisers and brokers designations, because of the similarity in their job titles. On top of this, the GFC in 2008 nearly destroyed the US financial system and led to financial hardships for many Americans (Kelleher, Hall & Medina 2016).

This all changed with the enactment of the Dodd-Frank Wall Street Reform and Consumer Protection Act 2010 [Dodd-Frank Act] in response by the US Government to the calamities of the GFC (Himstreet 2012; Kennedy, McCoy & Bernstein 2012; Burke & Hung 2015; Kelleher, Hall & Medina 2016). A major component of this legislation focussed on the regulation of two distinct categories of financial services providers. Namely, to regulate product- and remuneration-conflicted broker-dealer institutions and *independent* investment adviser institutions separately by a different regulator with a different set of rules to make them more distinguishable (Carosa 2012; Rubin 2015). Specifically, the primary regulator, the Securities and Exchange Commission [SEC] regulates the financial advisory institutions [FAIs], together with their registered investment advisers [RIAs] or registered *independent* advice representatives [RIARs] (Zabel 2010; Himstreet 2012), while broker-dealer institutions [BDs], with their broker-dealer registered representatives [RRs] (Bateman & Kingston 2014; Burke & Hung 2015) are now regulated by Financial Industry Regulatory Authority [FINRA] under the supervision of the SEC.

The primary regulator, SEC, is authorised to write and enforce the legislative rules, as well as conducting examinations (Inderst & Ottaviani 2012e). Together with the Consumer Financial Protection Bureau, they track consumer complaints (Inderst & Ottaviani 2012b). SEC, for example, deals with matters of competence, standards and disclosures of any unavoidable conflicts of interest in the financial sector (Balasubramnian, Brisker & Gradisher 2014; fi360 FiduciaryPath 2015, p. 26). Burke and Hung (2015) claimed, SEC has, on an ongoing basis, been expected to evaluate the effectiveness of the existing regulatory provisions, while identifying any gaps, duplication or shortcomings in the regulations protecting retail clients (U.S. Securities and Exchange Commission 2011).[41] Interestingly, Balasubramnian, Brisker and Gradisher (2014) recommended in their paper, s913 of the Dodd-Frank Act obligates the SEC to consider changes in how different financial professional designations apply their fiduciary responsibilities to their clients. SEC, with the US Department of Labor [DOL], was in the process of considering some rule changes in this regard. Specifically, on 8 April 2016, DOL announced a 'fiduciary rule' to define US advisers as fiduciary (United States Department of Labour 2017). This is expected to affect all advisers in the US. However, the controversial rule with final compliance initially scheduled to be phased in from 10 April 2017 to 1 January 2018 was delayed until 9 June 2017. Illustrating the difficulty of the issue, a further delay until 1 July 2019

[18 months] was granted on 28 August after DOL lodged a legal document to the US District Court for Minnesota in this regard (Waddell 2017).

Interestingly, Baily, Klein and Schardin (2017) concluded, Dodd-Frank legislation has made the financial sector much safer and more stable without loss of efficiency and economic growth. They concluded further, the legislation is addressing the "*too-big-to-fail*" (Baily, Klein & Schardin 2017, p. 43) problem, with clear procedures for dealing with institutions in trouble. In their view, by removing misleading financial products, the legislation ensures the public is protected. Yet they acknowledged improvement in agency supervision has some way to go, with the need to continue tweaking Dodd-Frank to improve its performance. Accordingly, in the next section, an explanation is presented considering how the Dodd-Frank reform legislation resulted in US policymakers' incorporating a financial advisory structure (Demina 2014) to impact the relationship between product providers, advisers and clients of financial services with consumer protection as a main objective (Inderst & Ottaviani 2009).

Adviser licensing regime in the United States

To permit financial institutions and their agents to provide *independent* financial advice, SEC enforces the definitions and specifications of the US Investment Advisers Act 1940 [54 Stat. 847] (Laby 2010) on FAIs. FAIs are not 'natural persons', but legal entities comprising investment advisory institutions obligated to register with the SEC (Rubin 2015). Notably, FAIs can be registered with state agencies, depending on the size of funds under their management (Balasubramnian, Brisker & Gradisher 2014). To register with the SEC, the FAIs must meet a FUM threshold (fi360 FiduciaryPath 2015). Accordingly, institutions with less than $100 million in FUM, instead of registering with SEC, are required to register with the states when they have clients (fi360 FiduciaryPath 2015). Additionally, Bateman and Kingston (2014) mentioned, an extensive list of exclusions from this legislation of FAIs who do not have to register with the SEC is available.

FAIs must comply with the regulations promulgated by the SEC when engaging the services of RIAs (Burke & Hung 2015; Rubin 2015). Zabel (2010) penned, *independent* advice representatives [IARs] are either *independent* [self-employed, while affiliated to an FIA or having their own FAI] or they can join existing FAI as supervised employees. *Independent* advice representatives may include CFPs and/or others with similar designations (Balasubramnian, Brisker & Gradisher 2014). IARs, according to the writings of Rubin (2015), provide ongoing financial advice for compensation in the form of a fee-for-service, regardless of whether the client purchases or sells a particular financial product. Consequently, earning a transaction-based commission incentivises them to distribute any financial products (Demina 2014; Burke & Hung 2015; Egan, Matvos & Seru 2016). Noteworthy, the majority, Burke and Hung (2015) established, earned FUM-based percentage fees. This confirmed the US had not placed a widespread ban on commissions for these agents. However, IARs must disclose their qualifications and background (United States Securities and Exchange Commission 2017). Fee-for-service disclosures are required as well (United States Securities and Exchange Commission 2017). FAI licensees must provide a written internal compliance program of policies and procedures (United States Securities and Exchange Commission 2017).

Whether the FAIs are either state registered or SEC registered, these institutions and their IARs are required to comply with a statutory fiduciary duty of care, as defined by the Investment Advisors Act (Himstreet 2012; Tittsworth 2013; Burke & Hung 2015). To reflect their fiduciary duty, SEC enforces SEC rule204A-1, where the FAIs adopt and enforce a code of ethics as part of the code of conduct standards for all their IARs (Balasubramnian, Brisker & Gradisher 2014). Finke, Huston and Waller (2009b) mentioned, CFPs agree to uphold a fiduciary standard higher than required by the Investment Advisers Act. Apparently, inconsistency in the application of the best interests duty occurred, because Rubin (2015) argued, for the state-registered FIAs, the application of fiduciary duty to advisers varies from state to state. Consequently, many financial clients did not realise, unlike CFPs or SEC-registered IARs, some state-registered IARs are not required to owe a high level of fiduciary responsibilities to their retail clients (Rubin 2015).

Unlike in Australia and the UK, to become an IAR requires limited competency assessment with no formal educational requirements (United States Securities and Exchange Commission 2017). The only exception is where an IAR wants to advise on mutual funds. Then, depending on where they operate, they have to pass a securities examination (United States Securities and Exchange Commission 2017). At the minimum, advisers need to pass the Uniform Investment Adviser Law Examination with a grade of 72% (Kaissar 2016). This is simply a three-hour exam, covering different legal investment-related subjects for a token fee (Kaissar 2016). The US has yet to raise the educational standards. Kaissar (2016) recommended, in a non-scholarly article, for example, new entrant advisers should complete a rigorous admissions process. In his article, he proposed, like in Australia, after completing a minimum amount of undergraduate or graduate-level coursework in finance, accounting, or economics, entrants should also pass examinations in law, regulation, economics, financial statement analysis and portfolio management similar in difficulty to the CPA, bar or medical board examinations. He argued an effective deterrent to misconduct and non-compliance is ensuring advisers invest a substantial amount of resources into joining the profession. His underlying argument suggests making it difficult for an individual to obtain a licence through a demanding admissions standard process to encourage high ethical standards. Although Kaissar (2016) admitted, it may be unjustly impractical to impose new licensing requirements on existing advisers, it does not give advisers any reason to neglect continuing professional development.

Arguably, Frumento and Korenman (2013) informed not all advisers in the US may lack the necessary educational standards, because the CFP Board of Standards Incorporated has developed a complete program to certify US fee-only advisers with specific curricula and examinations criteria. According to a paper published by the Financial Planning Coalition (2014), the CFP Board has had limited success in encouraging increased CFP certification, setting and enforcing competency and ethical standards plus identifying qualified advisers to fill some of the gaps in the regulation. Of note, Frumento and Korenman (2013) mentioned, the National Association of Personal Financial Advice [NAPFA], the professional body for fee-only US advisers, accepts only CFP-designated advisers for membership. The NAPFA National Board increasingly was supporting the emerging financial planning profession with a singular professional designation they want the public to trust in the same way Certified Practising Accountants, medical doctors or lawyers do by meeting education, training and ethics requirements (Frumento & Korenman 2013).

Balasubramnian, Brisker and Gradisher (2014) claimed to provide retail clients a degree of assurance about any financial adviser's registration, licensing, conduct, reliability, educational and professional experience competence – they have access to some of this information and education from the SEC. With the assistance of Investment Adviser Public Disclosure [IAPD], SEC provide consumers with background checks of RIA and their affiliated institutions (Demina 2014). In a joint venture with North American Securities Administrators Association [NASAA], SEC maintain the [IARD] (Balasubramnian, Brisker & Gradisher 2014). Moreover, various institutions, such as the CFP Board, various individual state agencies and American Association of Retired Persons [AARP] provides information to retired retail clients regarding how to conduct background checks on advisers and what should be considered when dealing with advisers. Through its Office of Compliance Inspections and Examinations [OCIE], the SEC monitors the activities and conduct of IARs to identify higher-risk advisers of any misconduct the SEC's Division of Enforcement should pursue (Demina 2014). All advisers who have been disciplined are listed on a public record for misconduct (Egan, Matvos & Seru 2016). However, despite the US Government's intent to protect retail consumers with legislation, the onus continues to lie ultimately with the retail clients to take responsibility for selecting their financial adviser and negotiating arrangements with them on the basis of the disclosures they receive (United States Department of The Treasury 2009).

In contrast to FAIs, broker-dealers are subject to the provisions of the Securities Exchange Act of 1934 [Exchange Act] [48 Stat. 881] (Laby 2010; Demina 2014; Burke & Hung 2015). They must become members of the *independent* non-profit self-regulatory organisation (Inderst & Ottaviani 2009; fi360 FiduciaryPath 2015) FINRA (Balasubramnian, Brisker & Gradisher 2014; Egan, Matvos & Seru 2016), registered with the SEC (Rubin 2015). Interestingly, Powell (2008) found, US advisers would prefer regulation by a professional regulatory organisation such as the CFP Board than self-regulation by SRO boards administered by FINRA.

Like IFAs, the BDs are not 'natural persons'. They are business entities performing brokerage activities, such as purchasing and disposing of financial instruments (United States Department of The Treasury 2009) for profit (fi360 FiduciaryPath 2015). In addition to earning transaction-based commissions

(Burke & Hung 2015), these institutions are referred to as dealers when they purchase or dispose of financial instruments not only for third parties, but also for their own account (United States Department of The Treasury 2009). The employees of BDs are registered representatives [RRs] who are 'natural persons' (fi360 FiduciaryPath 2015). BD entities do not have their own licensing requirements. However, their RRs are generally subject to the licensing requirements of FINRA, which include Series 6, 7 licences, which come with educational requirements. Affiliated individuals of BDs have no qualification requirements, unless they also provide advice in securities transactions (Burke & Hung 2015).

Unlike IARs, RRs are incentivised to sell products to receive remuneration in the form of commission payments (Demina 2014). So as not to mislead retail consumers, Rubin (2015) clearly stated, these institutions are obligated to be transparent in their advertising, informing consumers RRs are arms-length sales people. FINRA, authorised by Congress, Rubin (2015) enlightened further, promulgates and enforces the Exchange Act provisions, as well as FINRA rules (fi360 FiduciaryPath 2015). For example, they enforce the requirement that BDs disclose to FINRA all customer complaints and arbitrations, regulatory actions, employment terminations, bankruptcy and criminal or judicial proceedings (Egan, Matvos & Seru 2016). They implement educational standards (Egan, Matvos & Seru 2016), as well as rules governing the activities and conduct of brokers-dealers and market transparency (Balasubramnian, Brisker & Gradisher 2014). FINRA is responsible for educating retail consumers (Balasubramnian, Brisker & Gradisher 2014) while monitoring the outcomes of risk assessment audits of the broker-dealer institutions for compliance (Demina 2014). Noteworthy, despite all these requirements, the onus remains with the retail consumer to access and select a suitable broker-dealer using FINRA Broker-Check10 of background information on brokers (Balasubramnian, Brisker & Gradisher 2014).

Instead of a higher fiduciary standard of care (Balasubramnian, Brisker & Gradisher 2014), RRs' fiduciary duty is much broader (Deloitte & Financial Services Council 2014). However, it is a legal requirement under current US securities regulations for BDs to make financial recommendations 'suitable' to the portfolio, financial situation, needs (Balasubramnian, Brisker & Gradisher 2014; Burke & Hung 2015; Rubin 2015) and risk profile of their clients (United States Department of The Treasury 2009). They have disclosure requirements to provide to clients in plain English a narrative brochure containing all information as specified in Part 2 of Form ADV (Deloitte & Financial Services Council 2014).[42] To do so, it is mandatory for commission BDs to make a reasonable attempt to obtain personal financial information of their non-institutional client. Failing this, they face FINRA's disciplinary procedures and regulatory sanctions, such as the loss of their licence and/or possible litigation (Inderst & Ottaviani 2009). Thus limiting their self-interests to some extent (fi360 FiduciaryPath 2015). Although Demina (2014) warned, retail clients run the risk of being placed into sub-optimal investments under the 'suitability rule.' Arguably, it is a subordinate standard to fiduciary duty, because it is not a requirement to avoid conflicts of interest. The requirement is to disclose them for specific financial products (fi360

FiduciaryPath 2015, p. 26). Consequently, the riskier products yielding higher returns and product commissions tied to their riskiness misaligns BDs', RRs' and their clients' interests (Demina 2014). Hence, conflicts of interest from remuneration may potentially bias the product sales.

Balasubramnian, Brisker and Gradisher (2014) wrote consumers have the means to determine if any advisers have been involved in professional misconduct by going to the Misconduct Register. Despite US advisers being named and shamed on a public misconduct register, according to Egan, Matvos and Seru (2016), the resultant loss of reputation and increased competition from good advisers has not deterred many rogue advisers. Remarkably, Egan, Matvos and Seru (2016) found in their study, US advisers who were punished for misconduct are able to continue providing financial advice after being dismissed from their institution for their bad behaviour as a means of discipline. They claimed their results indicated evidence of misconduct matching of institutions and advisers. Here, whereby advisers with a history of misconduct transfer to institutions with a history of misconduct. This, they argued, weakens to some extent the disciplining mechanism of the US regulator as well as decreasing the punishment for the misconduct. By implication, a systemic problem for the whole industry.

United States reform consequences and challenges

Apparently, the reforms legally regulate BDs' and FAIs' relationships with their clients (Demina 2014) differently (Bhargava 2009) by definitions, registration, duties, compensations, legal requirements, legal obligations and standards of care (Bhargava 2009; Baris & Cohn 2012; Demina 2014; Burke & Hung 2015; Egan, Matvos & Seru 2016). However, Frumento and Korenman (2013) observed, despite these reforms, retail consumers continue to find it difficult to separate the advice and services they offer. Bhargava (2009) and Finke, Huston and Waller (2009b) concurred, the US public cannot clearly distinguish between conflicted broker-dealers licensed to sell securities or insurance products and *independent* registered investment-advisers regulated to deliver investment advice, because they are perceived to offer similar services. Especially when investment advisers and broker-dealers are perceived by clients to offer similar financial advice services (Demina 2014). This perception, Demina (2014) pointed out, put clients at risk of harm, because it may result in divergence between adviser–client interests.

Interestingly, FINRA and SEC regulate some advisers. Thus, they receive commissions for product transactions as well as fee-for-service for offering advice (Deloitte & Financial Services Council 2014). This was confirmed in a study by Burke and Hung (2015) when they found a hybrid business model is evident in practice where SEC-registered FAIs are either registered as BDs or they have affiliations with BDs. They found in their study, some IARs are also registered representatives of BDs, or RRs are registered as FAIs. A later study by Egan, Matvos and Seru (2016) supported their findings by confirming, those registered as brokers and investment advisers account for about 50% of all US active advisers.

While the US financial planning market is developing (Treasury 2015), SEC has been continually working on changes, innovation and setting new rules to help retail clients distinguish between the different FAI designations with a fiduciary duty from RRs without (Balasubramnian, Brisker & Gradisher 2014). Furthermore, penalties for misconduct include fines, probation and restitution, such as a prison sentence for fraudulent misconduct (Egan, Matvos & Seru 2016).

Although US regulators continue to consider adding to the oversight legislation for advisers (Stolz 2009b), Varriale (2012) claimed, the US regulators are struggling to decide how to regulate advisers (Baris & Cohn 2012). For example, Frumento and Korenman (2013) reported, two pieces of legislation, Investment Advisory Oversight Act of 2012, known as the 'Bacchus Bill,' and Investment Adviser Examination Improvement Act of 2012, were introduced by the US Government with the purpose to increase what was perceived as not enough regulation regulating professionalism and investment advisers. The Investment Adviser Oversight Act of 2012 was introduced. Yet it was never enacted to mandate many SEC and state-RIA to become a member in an SRO (Tittsworth 2013).

They reported evidence of uncertainty as to who should supervise advisers. However, despite support for this legislation by several private bodies, namely FINRA (Tittsworth 2013), Securities Industry and Financial Markets Association, National Association of Insurance and Financial Advisers and Financial Services Institute (Frumento & Korenman 2013), the Investment Advisers Association opposed it (Frumento & Korenman 2013). They opposed it for a number of reasons highlighted in a paper by Tittsworth (2013), such as unnecessary costs and lack of transparency or accountability. Both legislations were mooted after reaching the House of Financial Services Committee. Although the legislation was unpassed, it reopened the debate to professionalism of the financial advice industry and who should regulate advisers in the US (Frumento & Korenman 2013).

Schulaka (2009) observed just under a decade ago the move by US advisers to an independence advisory model. In his critique, he concluded, independence is unsuitable for some advisers. Furthermore, reports indicate mainly the affluent clients seek out *independent* holistic advisory services (Journal of Financial Planning 2009). Yet Zabel (2010) noted the US independence institutional business models are growing faster than broker-dealer institutional models, because of higher revenue increases, more control over client accounts, improved brand-building ability as well as the opportunity to maximise value for their businesses.

Difficulties with the independence channel in the US, Aschkenasy (2009) pointed out, include the duplication of support services, such as marketing plans, compliance and regulatory matters, in addition to the power wielded by a large wire house, bank or insurance-owned broker-dealer when negotiating fees or deals on behalf of their representatives. If a US representative should depart from his or her principal licensed institution, then the adviser immediately becomes a non-affiliate third-party and, from this point, the institution [FAIs or BDs] retains the client (Hansen 2008). Questionable is whether this is in the best interest of the clients.

Evident from the literature writings by Bateman and Kingston (2014) and Burke and Hung (2015), apparently the US is looking towards the developments in the UK since the implementation of RDR in 2012. However, Salka (2015) indicates US reforms will be delayed or limited, should the US attempt to imitate the UK model. This they base on the power of broker-dealers, multiple collage of regulations and a litigious US society. Therefore, further developments involving licensing, regulating and authorising advisers in the US is yet unrealised.

United Kingdom

Legislative background to United Kingdom adviser regulation

From 2005 to 2008, data were collected and reported in three separate thematic reports, involving mystery shopping expeditions proving the presence of inherent and widespread weaknesses in the manner UK institutions and their representatives sold products across much of the UK financial services industry (Pain 2013). This scrutiny of consumer protection, financial service integrity and competition initiatives by the UK Government (Walker 2012) resulted in the launch of RDR in 2006. Important for this study are the RDR reforms and legislation effective from 1 January 2013 (Clare *et al.* 2013) to address the scandals in the UK retail advice sector (Ring 2015). Its purpose was to regain the lost UK consumer trust and confidence in the retail market for financial products and services (United Kingdom House of Commons Treasury Committee 2011; Financial Services Authority 2012b; Atkin *et al.* 2013) by identifying and eliminating the root causes of poor advice (Burke & Hung 2015).

Until the enactment of Financial Services Act 2012 (Inderst & Ottaviani 2012b), the initial RDR UK supervisory responsibilities of FAIs and their representatives was vested in the Financial Services Authority [FSA]. Subsequently, the FSA, a single regulatory body for the entire UK financial services markets (Kwon 2013), was replaced with a new Financial Conduct Authority [FCA] (McMeel 2013) by the Financial Services Act 2012. The FCA was empowered to regulate the institutions and individuals who advise on, sell or distribute financial products and services (Inderst & Ottaviani 2012e). The Financial Services and Markets Act 2000 defines their purpose and responsibilities in FCA as a single non-government *independent* body, accountable to the UK Treasury, who, in turn, is accountable to the UK Parliament (Inderst & Ottaviani 2012e).[43] The record of FCA legal rules and guidance are set out in the FCA Handbook.[44] The statutory duties, such as best interest,[45] disclosure[46] and suitability rule[47] imposed in them are set out in the Conduct of Business Source Book [COBS] (Financial Conduct Authority 2017a).

Specifically, FCA's attention to supervise individual advisers via third parties (Financial Services Authority 2010; Adamson 2012; Bateman & Kingston 2014) to ensure "*appropriate, affordable, and fair advice and intermediary services*" (Salka 2015, p. 87). For example, one of the broader objectives of RDR in Policy Statement PS13/1, issued by the Financial Conduct Authority (2013a), is to restrict the undesirable influence on consumer outcomes product providers have on distribution and adviser remuneration. Furthermore, the legislation has the objectives of aligning advisers' interests with their clients' as well as promoting effective competitive behaviour between the product providers (Financial Conduct Authority 2014a) by removing product provider influence over the distribution of products (Financial Conduct Authority 2013a). McDermott (2016) determined the FCA was, in the first instance, tasked with continuing arrangements for supervising authorised persons for compliance, and second to manage the risk of non-compliance by financial institutions [of course their representatives] of managing conflicts of interest between their clients and themselves.

If UK firms want to offer financial services, including financial advice, then they must apply for permission from the FCA by lodging a Part IV Permission (Deloitte & Financial Services Council 2014) application as specified in the Financial Services and Markets Act 2000 (Financial Conduct Authority 2016b). Furthermore, FCA must approve a person wanting to deliver advice. Similar to ASIC, FCA assesses an institution against strict criteria 'fit and proper' (Deloitte & Financial Services Council 2014) to provide *independent* advice (Financial Services Authority 2012b; Financial Conduct Authority 2014c; Burke & Hung 2015).

Furthermore, individual advisers must meet a minimum standard of education, including a minimum of 35 hours of continual professional development hours annually. They must be issued with a statement of professional standing by a recognised professional body (Deloitte & Financial Services Council 2014). The UK policymakers from 31 December 2012 imposed additional requirements. Like Australia, new pre-sale disclosure requirements and point-of-sale disclosure requirements were imposed (Deloitte & Financial Services Council 2014; Financial Conduct Authority 2017a).[48],[49] Commissions were banned after 31 December 2012 (Deloitte & Financial Services Council 2014). Notably, financial services institutions and their representatives were obligated to describe or self-label their financial services to fall in one of two regulated activities, namely as either 'restricted' or '*independent*' advice (Bateman & Kingston 2014; Burke & Hung 2015).

Adviser licensing regime in the United Kingdom

The first category of UK advisers, namely *independent* financial advisers [IFAs], Burke and Hung (2015) defined as advisers legally obliged to consider all types of retail investment products distributed across the whole financial services market by all financial institutions, in addition to making unbiased and unrestricted recommendations. IFAs, whether individuals or institutions, according to Thorpe (2012) and supported by information from the Financial Conduct Authority (2016c), must show they have adequate structures and processes in place to ensure compliance. Specifically, concerning the twin tests of "*comprehensive and fair analysis*" (Financial Services Authority 2012b, p. 6; Thorpe 2012) and "*unbiased and unrestricted*" (Financial Services Authority 2012b, p. 6) criteria for independence. To demonstrate achievement of the twin tests, Thorpe (2012) concluded may involve the use of software, third-party research providers, review panels of selected products and/or product providers to show how the market and selected products are aligned with a client's risk tolerance and suitability. What needs clear articulation to retail clients, he further recommended, is the nature of the service and restrictions, the types of products, size of product range and access to different product providers, together with specialisations offered to differentiate *independent* from 'restricted' advice. Unlike restricted advisers, the UK *independent* advisers are authorised and regulated by FSA [now FCA] to work in the best interest of clients by not representing any financial institutions such as insurance companies, banks or other product providers when providing recommendations to clients (Fernandez-Aviles & Davila 2012).

The second category, 'restricted' advisers or appointed representatives [RAR], Burke and Hung (2015) explained can only recommend certain products, product providers or both. Fernandez-Aviles and Davila (2012) documented, RAR are like the traditional 'aligned' or 'tied' UK advisers. Therefore, performing 'regulated activities' effectively means 'appointed representatives' act as agents either for authorised restricted institutions, such as product distributors, banks or insurance companies or authorised *independent* institutions (Financial Services Authority 2012a).[50] As far as licensing is concerned, 'restricted' institutions, like their *independent* counterparts, must recruit, appoint and supervise one or more 'appointed representatives,' complying with the FCA's 'fit and proper' test to deliver tied advice restricted by products or providers (Financial Services Authority 2012b; Financial Conduct Authority 2014c; Burke & Hung 2015). Like their counterparts, restricted 'appointed representatives' can be either institutions or 'natural persons' performing regulated activities as agents for the FCA authorised principals (Financial Conduct Authority 2015).

Independent financial 'appointed representatives' and restricted 'appointed representatives' must register with the FCA (Burke & Hung 2015), paying them a levy (Financial Conduct Authority 2014c). This includes a written contract between the principals and the 'appointed representatives' documenting the arrangements. The principals of IFA and RAR take full responsibility for ensuring the 'appointed representatives' complies with FCA rules.[51] For example, the 'appointed representatives' must comply with the Statements of Principle and Code of Practice (Financial Conduct Authority 2014c). These principles explains the behaviour FCA expected of 'appointed representatives' and together with a further requirement for advisers, the Statement of Professional Standing [SPS] (Financial Conduct Authority 2014c). 'Appointed representatives' are expected to comply with the regulatory requirements of their affiliated institutions (whether *independent* or 'restricted' (Financial Conduct Authority 2015). If they conduct any 'regulated activities' outside this scope, they are expected to become authorised in their own right (Financial Conduct Authority 2015). If affiliated 'appointed representatives' wish to transfer and become 'authorised,' they have to give notice to their principals as well as coming to some agreement with their principals as to how they can have direct access to ex-client files if the client complained (Financial Conduct Authority 2015). Once 'appointed representatives' leave their authorised institutions, their agreement with their principals will determine whether they can continue dealing with existing clients. All FCA-authorised institutions or individuals are responsible for having systems in place to deal with, *inter alia*, PI insurance, compliance and related business liabilities (Financial Conduct Authority 2015).[52] The directly authorised institutions are responsible for ensuring their ARs, while carrying out 'regulated activities' [controlled functions] and meeting the relevant selling standards, such as the *independent* advice rules (Financial Services Authority 2012b; Financial Conduct Authority 2014c). The principals have access to all employees, their premises and records to carry out regular audits to ensure they are financially stable and competent (Financial Conduct Authority 2015). They are obligated to report anything affecting the ongoing suitability of 'appointed representatives' to FCA and the authorised institutions (Financial Conduct Authority 2014c).

United Kingdom reform consequences and challenges

Reported in popular media, some institutions, such as Sanlam, created a hybrid advisory model, where their advisers offer Sanlam-only ['restricted'] or whole of market investment recommendations [*independent*] (Trudeau 2012). Trudeau (2012) put forward the claim; this practice is permitted if representatives of hybrid models call themselves 'financial planners' and not *independent* advisers. Although Brittain (2013), in their paper, presented the difference between advisers and financial planners by stating the former performs product transactions with a sales focus and the latter tends to charge separately for advice and so is not reliant on securing a sale, this distinction is confusing.

Unlike the US, the UK has placed a widespread ban on commissions, except for commissions on life insurance products and percentage assets-based fees set by the advisers to mirror the clients' service (Boynton & Mathieson 2009, p. 15; Bateman & Kingston 2014).[53] Along similar lines, depending on the product provider or the product type, it is alleged the fees charged should neither "*vary inappropriately*" (Boynton & Mathieson 2009, p. 15) nor be prejudiced by facilities offered by product providers to, for example, recuperate the financial product charges. Furthermore, in addition to the conditions on remuneration practices, RDR rules have included disclosure of remuneration and services (Financial Conduct Authority 2014a). Other benefits of RDR include the unlikelihood larger clients would subsidise smaller clients, because technology helps meet the needs of smaller clients (Financial Conduct Authority 2014d; Burke & Hung 2015). At the time of this study, and confirmed in a paper written by Bateman and Kingston (2014), although an ongoing debate about the matter of best interests of the retail client in the UK is ever present, they have not imposed a statutory fiduciary duty on advisers.

Traditionally, most IFAs carried out basic financial advisory services with the minimum of educational competencies. Whereas others sat the Certificate of Financial Planning with the Chartered Insurance Institute or the CFP exam with the Institute of Financial Planning [IFP], affiliated to the US CFP Standards Board (Brittain 2013). Cole and Salimath (2013) contended, CFP-qualified advisers are generally more highly qualified, with backgrounds in accountancy or the law. Starting 1 January 2013, to become 'appointed representatives' in the UK requires meeting minimum specified professional education requirements and experience (Financial Services Authority 2012a). In the works of Burke and Hung (2015), clearly all existing and new 'appointed representatives' entrants have to meet the same qualification requirements and educational standards. This, they mentioned, included the prerequisite to hold an approved Qualifications and Credit Framework [QCF] Level 4 qualification, namely Diplomas in Financial Planning, Investment Planning, Banking, Investment Advice, or Financial Advice, which is equivalent to one year of university study.

Benefits of better qualified UK advisers and advisers working for *independent* institutions free from product or provider bias (Reichman 2013) should increase their professionalism. By implication, their clients should then receive more appropriate, affordable and fair advisory services (Reichman 2013). However, although RDR seemingly has initiated moves towards increased professionalism among advisers (Financial Conduct Authority 2014c), it is not without its critics. For instance, not everyone thinks all retail clients need *independent* professional advice (Harvey 2011). Ferran (2012) is unsure whether retail clients of financial advice approve of RDR. Reichman (2013) questioned whether the reforms introduced following RDR de-risked the advice process. They offered compelling reasons, arguing RDR may have created an advice gap where lower asset clients are unable to obtain advice, cost of advice has not necessarily decreased and, unless specifically identified, rogue advisers were able to put retail clients at risk of loss. Coghill (2013) found professional bodies, such as the Law Society, Solicitors' Regulation Authority and Institute of Chartered Accountants had opposing views on whether particularly 'restricted' institutions and their 'appointed representatives' are truly competent.

Since RDR implementation, before intervening, UK policymakers and their regulator require significant evidence-based data on any financial services issue (Pain 2013). From 2013 to 2017, Europe Economics, an *independent* external European consultant, was commissioned to undertake a three-stage thematic review looking at how financial institutions and their advisers were managing with the RDR requirements and to determine the extent to which RDR has delivered on its original objectives (Financial Conduct Authority 2014a, 2014b, 2014c; Burke *et al.* 2015). Burke and Hung (2015) summarised Europe Economics' latest research findings, considering the impacts of UK's RDR since its implementation. The first stage review completed in July 2013 indicated, it was unclear whether *independent* and 'restricted' institutions were acting within their scope of independence or restrictions, respectively. Further, problems were identified with regard to remuneration disclosures and transparency issues with ongoing services propositions (Financial Conduct Authority 2013b; Burke *et al.* 2015). In addition, despite the distinction between 'restricted' and '*independent*' advisers, findings by Europe Economics indicated, confusion and uncertainty reigned amongst UK retail clients about these designations (Financial Conduct Authority 2014b).

Although one of the initial impacts of RDR was adviser numbers declined, Europe Economics claimed they found these numbers were on the rise again as advisers became more confident about their futures (Financial Conduct Authority 2014c). To the contrary, Clare *et al.* (2013) argued the increase in the minimum education standards for advisers under RDR, the increased regulatory and compliance costs, downward pressure on revenues, challenges of adjusting business models, declining business value and the decline in cross-subsidisation from larger to smaller clients did not bode well for the future numbers of advisers. Clare *et al.* (2013) claimed RDR led to some major UK banks withdrawing from providing wealth management advice to small investors, which affected the number of appointed representatives to supply financial advisory services. Clare *et al.* (2013) wrote RDR has taken the past role of advisers from product distributors to a new role of financial planner or a combination of fund selector and financial planner. They claim computer literacy will lead the mass market of consumers in the future to do their own financial planning using technology.

Thus, like in Australia, technology (Morgan Stanley 2018) is forcing UK financial advice business models to evolve. The second review concluded in March 2014 found, although not compelling enough to be certain, institutions were describing themselves as *independent*, when perhaps it was questionable whether they were operating an *independent* practice (Financial Conduct Authority 2014e; Burke & Hung 2015). In this review, they found a significant number of institutions were not disclosing the cost of advice, or how they were charging for the advice, types of services offered and the nature of any ongoing services within a reasonable time frame (Financial Conduct Authority 2014f; Burke & Hung 2015). However, the third and final review found the institutions became better at disclosing costs, scope and nature of services and were providing ongoing services to clients. However, inadequate ongoing service fee disclosures (Financial Conduct Authority 2014d; Burke & Hung 2015), including transparency of concealed fees of underlying products (Salka 2015, still happens. Furthermore, their research indicated business models have adapted. A decline in sales of high commission-paying products and increases in sales of low commission or no commission pre-RDR financial products (Salka 2015) now exists. However, Salka (2015) claimed the data appeared to prove evidence of an issue surrounding adviser reputations.

Increasingly, advances in technology, particularly the increasing availability of online services, mobile app services and blockchain (Morgan Stanley 2018), are leading changes in how people seek advice for their financial planning needs (Financial Conduct Authority 2014a). Therefore, FCA is keen to remove unnecessary regulatory obstacles to affordability and accessibility standing in the way of innovations in advice models (Financial Conduct Authority 2014a). Jointly with Her Majesty's Treasury, the FCA launched the FAMR in August 2015 (Treasury 2015). Their final report found despite post-RDR, trust, affordability and accessibility remains relatively low (Financial Conduct Authority 2016a). Thus, they make recommendations in their report to improve these. From the report, it is clear the UK has moved away from deciding how to regulate advisers to looking at ways to protect consumers and improve access, affordability and quality of advice under the existing regulatory model (Financial Conduct Authority 2017b). While the next review by Europe Economics was planned for 2017, in July 2017, FCA decided to delay its review until 2019 to overlap with the review on the impact of Financial Advice Market Review [FAMR] Reforms.[54] Although several scholars, namely Walker (2012), Bateman and Kingston (2014) and Salka (2015) feel RDR may be a blueprint for policy reform discussions and regulatory implementations of licensing advisers in other nations, this research considers a different blueprint for Australian advisers.

Comparisons between the three nations

Australian regulators argued, the best protection for consumers is compliance by the financial services industry with a fair and transparent principles-based regulatory system (Pearson 2006b). Likewise, the US has been moving from a rules-based approach with lower standards of care to a principles-based framework, which requires advisers to provide a higher standard of care to clients (Trone 2009). Whereas the UK is wondering whether the principle-based approach is working for them and are apparently moving back to a rules-based approach. Kwon (2013) commented, it does not matter whether supervision and regulation of financial service is rule based or principle based, what matters is lowering the risk to the public dealing with financial services providers.

According to Deloitte and Financial Services Council (2014), Australia has higher standards of regulation encompassing narrow requirements than the US and the UK. Reading articles presented at a symposium titled *Revolution in the regulation of financial advice: The U.S., the U.K. and Australia* (Facciolo 2013), evidently regulating advisers in the US, the UK and Australia continues to be a controversial matter, polarising many with an interest in the financial advisory industry. Plainly, similarities and differences between these three countries in the way they license regulate and authorise their advisers. UK and Australian models are closer in similarity than the US model (Deloitte & Financial Services Council 2014) exists. Licensing is at the institutional level for all three nations. All these nations have disclosure requirements of information found in the Australian FSGs. However, UK and Australia are more prescriptive by disclosures (Deloitte & Financial Services Council 2014). The Australian SOA is more comprehensive compared with suitability letters in the UK (Deloitte & Financial Services Council 2014). With a few exceptions, Australia and the UK are the only countries having banned conflicted remuneration.

Similar to Australia (Valentine 2008; Hartnett 2010; Bruce 2012), the UK (Bateman & Kingston 2014) and the US (Laby 2010; Kaissar 2016) having significant impact on individual advisers' financial services are regulatory reforms to protect retail clients. The underlying objectives of all these nations' regulations is to promote managing, controlling, avoiding or eliminating conflicts of interest, ensuring statutory fiduciary duty [US and Australia only] and aligning the institutions [principals] and their representatives' interests with the clients' interest, as well as encouraging competition between financial service providers.

In Australia, the UK or the US, all advisory or financial institutions and their appointed agents must register with their respective regulator.[55,56,57] Evident in all these countries, their advisers are agents of institutions or third-party affiliates when they provide financial advice and/or product sales. State regulators via third-party affiliates or principals effectively regulate them. Yet there is insufficient compelling evidence to validate this as the most effective approach to achieve the objective of protecting the public. What has been overlooked in the scholarly literature, in contrast to other professions, such as accounting, law and medicine, is that once any of these agents [IARs, RRs, IFAs, 'appointed representatives' and 'authorised representatives'] departs from or terminates their contractual arrangements with any of these principals [FAIs, BDs, 'restricted' advice institutions, *independent* advice institutions and Australian licensees], they immediately are no longer legally allowed to offer advice. Generally, the representative's possession or use of any client information obtained, while at the principal, is prohibited without prior agreement to the contrary. In effect, these authorised financial institutions principals [FAIs, BDs, 'restricted' advice institutions, *independent* advice institutions and Australian licensees] generally owns the client, depending on the terms of the contract between principal and agent, irrespective of any relationship established between client and 'natural person' adviser. Neglected in the literature is the potential consequences of severing this relationship between adviser and client, because of the departure of the adviser.

Observations by Bateman and Kingston (2014) and Burke and Hung (2015) indicated US and UK policymakers have put legal provisions in place to distinguish between two categories of FAIs and advisers. For them, a prominent feature of their regulations was the separation of '*independent*' advice from advice not *independent*, in terminology and categories. Australian legal and accounting professionals concurred, legislating and disclosing the difference between financial product sales and *independent* financial advice should resolve the best interest duty and APLs disputes (Certified Practising Accountants 2014; Hewison 2014; Mitchell 2014). Trends in the UK (Brittain 2013), the US (Frumento & Korenman 2013) and Australia (Arman & Shackman 2012) indicate the public struggle to clearly distinguish between two categories of advisers, namely conflicted [product advisory institutions] and non-conflicted advisers [*independent* advisory institutions]. The US and Australia have tried to distinguish between sales and advice. In contrast to the US and Australia, the UK has dropped this idea by settling instead for *independent* advice and restricted advice (McMeel 2013). Further, the impact of Brexit is yet unrealised as the UK negotiates with the European Union its exit (Deloitte 2016). Advisers in Australia have been restricted in practice and restricted in the use of occupational title of '*independent* financial adviser.' Interestingly, the Australian definition of independence is attached to product and remuneration independence, and dissimilar to the UK, cannot be overcome through an expansive product list (Anonymous 2011). The definition of independence in Australia is more rigorous. It is more difficult to achieve than the UK definition (Anonymous 2011).

In the US, the product advisory institutions are not legally obligated to follow a fiduciary standard or disclose any conflicts of interest to their clients (Balasubramnian, Brisker & Gradisher 2014). Whereas their *independent* advisory institutions owe a statutory fiduciary duty and conflicts of interest are as specified in the Investment Advisors Act 1940 (United States Department of The Treasury 2009). Although, at the time of writing, clearly no uniformity in their fiduciary standards for IAs and their RRs is obvious, SEC is considering exercising its rulemaking authority to implement a uniform fiduciary standard of conduct for all of them (Burke & Hung 2015). In Australia, whether institutions are product aligned or *independent*, they all have a statutory fiduciary duty obligation, as well as a legal obligation to disclose all conflicts of interest. Although under debate at the time of writing this book, the UK Government has disregarded a fiduciary duty requirement for UK advisers.

Unlike Australia and the UK, the US allows commissions or regulated remuneration practices. Although the ban on commission in Australia is far more widespread than the position evident in the UK, on the grounds of ongoing scandals in Australia, such as the Commonwealth Bank (North 2015), banning commissions has not prevented clients suffering at the hands of advisers of large banking institutions. With conflicts of interest dealt with by the regulators, perhaps conflict of interest from association to product-aligned licensees need further scrutiny.

Currently, s923A of the Act permits receiving or charging asset-based fees for FUM(Power 2016b).[58] However, specified in s964D and s964E of the Act, the ban on asset-based fees on investments are limited to borrowed FUM.[59] The available non-scholarly literature supposes permitting asset-based fees is a contentious matter. For Industry Super Australia (2014), and others, like the Accounting Professional and Ethical Standards Board (Brown 2011), receiving remuneration in the form of a percentage incentive payment for FUM (asset-based fees) through a specific platform is technically a commission from product sales. Whereas contrary views by the Financial Planning Association (2014) claimed asset-based fees are advice fees, not commissions, charged through the product under the direction of the client for ongoing services to obtain regular information on each investment in the client's portfolio from respective product issuers.

Notably, platforms are not considered financial products under the present legislation.[60] Interestingly, the UK FCA permits asset-based fees with the condition it fairly represents services provided to the client (International Financial Law Review 2009). Curiously, during this research, a journalist reported ASIC was seeking *independent* legal guidance to establish whether advisers claiming independence, while charging asset-based fees, are conflicted (Santacruz 2016b).

Disparate from the UK and Australia, the US has not yet established minimum standards for advisers to improve the quality of advice (Valentine 2013) to retail clients by raising the professional and educational standards of advisers (Burke &

Hung 2015). Debates in the US about professional standards, education and ethics are happening. Whereas the UK has implemented professional standards and educational requirements for their advisers. Australia has just legislated and set up a body to implement standards, education and ethics.

Shortcomings in licensing advisers' post-regulatory reforms for all these nations are evident. So seemingly the policymakers in these nations are looking at developments in each other's respective countries (McMeel 2013) to overcome these shortcomings. For example, the Financial System Inquiry panel has sought feedback on the push to more clearly distinguish between *independent* and restricted financial advice, looking to the UK model as a potential blueprint (*Independent* Financial Adviser News 2014b). Fernandez-Aviles and Davila (2012) claimed in their paper, referring to the UK market, although the *independent* financial adviser is rarely evident in financial institutions, and hence misconstrued by clients, they are increasingly becoming relevant.

Evident in the literature, the UK's RDR (Anonymous 2011; *Independent* Financial Adviser News 2014b; Burke & Hung 2015) and Australia's FOFA (Burke & Hung 2015) developments are being watched by other nations as a possible blueprint. Compared with the UK and the US, Australia is in a better position to take reforms further. Australia does not face a society as litigious as the US (Salka 2015), nor do they face the constraints imposed by Markets in Financial Instruments Directive (MiFID) to harmonise regulation in the financial markets across the European Union (Burke & Hung 2015) or arguably the ramifications of Brexit once implemented (Deloitte & Financial Services Council 2014).[61] However, professional media mentioned, although RDR may go further than the Act, FOFA goes much further than RDR (Anonymous 2011). Just as the US regulators are considering SROs should regulate investment advisers in the retail market without any clues as to how to do so (Varriale 2012), so too does Australia and the UK need to consider where to next with their reforms.

In closing, if personal accountability is what RDR is promoting (McDermott 2016), and if lessons should be learnt from the UK by the US and Australia (Bateman & Kingston 2014; Salka 2015), then it is questionable how this personal accountability is achieved if advisers are licensed, regulated and authorised at the institutional level where accountabilities are indistinguishable, rather than at the individual level as true professionals.

Conclusion

Licensing advisers is problematic for Australian policymakers. *Ditto* for the UK and the US policymakers too. The overriding collective goal financial services regulation pursues is the protection of the public from rogue advisers. Licensing plays a vital role in regulating and authorising commercially driven financial institutions. From the readings surrounding licensing of advisers in the US, the UK and Australia, similarities and significant differences as to how advisers are regulated, authorised and supervised occur. Clearly, the legislative focus for all countries appears to remain on the macro-level rather than at the micro-level, at the institutional level rather than the individual level, particularly to solve the conflict of interest from association problem. Yet their approach of licensing via multiple third parties is questionable, because the client does not receive financial recommendations from the institutional entities. Instead, retail clients trust 'natural persons' to provide them with recommendations in their best interests.

Undoubtedly, policymakers have been legislating the attributes of a professional financial adviser, such as meeting the fit and proper test, best interest duty, independence, professional standards and educational and training standards, as well as ethical standards, when reviewing licensing, regulating and authorising individual advisers, neglecting to consider conflict of interest from association by licensing advisers through commercially driven third-party licensees. Neglected is conflict of interest from association, where the focus has been on conflict of interest from remuneration. The main argument advanced here is the licensing of individual advisers via institutions prevents a clear separation between the institution and the individual provider of financial advice, leading to potential of conflict of interest from association.

Totally ignored as a potential risk for all the Financial Services stakeholders is licensing individual advisers through conflicted third parties [IAs, BDs, 'restricted' advice institutions, *independent* advice institutions and Australian licensees]. Arguably, current licensing may be inconsistent with the objectives of any legislation aiming to protect the retail consumer of financial products and services.

Despite licensing's wide acceptance to protect the public from being sold unsuitable financial products, this project considers whether it has limited application to regulate and authorise individual professional advisers through numerous third-party institutions, rather than a single professionals board like other true professions. In the last few years, a growing interest in individual licensing of advisers in Australia by an *independent* industry professional body has emerged. Without finding current licensing for Australian advisers illegitimate, there is no basis to consider an *independent* industry professional body by Australian policymakers. Therefore, to provide a more evidence-based approach for policymakers considering changes to licensing, regulating and authorising individual advisers, specifically in Australia, the next chapter develops the framework to test with research the extent of the legitimacy of current AFSL-AR licensing. This chapter serves as a basis for Chapter 3 where the researchers develop the model of the research for the inquiry.

Notes

1 For more information on the Commonwealth Financial Services Reform Act 2001 please go to <www.legislation.gov.au/Details/C2004A00891>; Note FSRA was subsequently superseded by the Commonwealth Financial Services Reform Amendment Act 2003 <www.legislation.gov.au/Details/C2004A01226> as well as amended by Financial Services Reform (Consequential Provisions) Act 2001 and Financial Services Reform (Consequential Provisions) Act 2002.

2 For more information on the Commonwealth Corporations Act 1989, which is no longer in force, please go to <www.legislation.gov.au/Series/C2004A03857>;

Note FSRA was subsequently superseded by the Commonwealth Financial Services Reform Amendment Act 2003 <www.legislation.gov.au/Details/C2004A01226> as well as amended by Financial Services Reform (Consequential Provisions) Act 2001 and Financial Services Reform (Consequential Provisions) Act 2002.

3 For more information on the Commonwealth Corporations Act 2001, see <www.legislation.gov.au/Details/C2017C00328>.

4 Financial Services Reform Act 2001.

5 Australian Credit Licence was specified in the National Consumer Credit Protection Regulations 2010, <www.legislation.gov.au/Details/F2014C00815>.

6 Corporations Amendment (Future of Financial Advice) Act 2012 (Tranche 1), <www.legislation.gov.au/Details/C2012A00067>.

7 Corporations Amendment (Further Future of Financial Advice Measures) 2012 (Tranche 2), <www.legislation.gov.au/Details/C2013C00529>.

8 Mooted Corporations Amendment (Streamlining of Future of Financial Advice) Act 2014 (Tranche 3), <www.legislation.gov.au/Details/C2014B00043>.

9 Corporations Amendment (Revising Future of Financial Advice) Regulation 2014, <www.legislation.gov.au/Details/F2014L01707>.

10 Corporations Amendment (Financial Advice) Regulation 2015, <www.legisla tion.gov.au/Details/F2015L00969>.

11 Corporations Amendment Regulation 2013 (No 3), <www.legislation.gov.au/Details/F2013L00905>.

12 Corporations Amendment Regulation 2013 (No 3) F2013L00905, <www.comlaw.gov.au/Details/F2013L00905>.

13 Details <http://asic.gov.au/regulatory-resources/find-a-document/regulatory-guides/rg-146-licensing-training-of-financial-product-advisers/>.

14 Corporations Amendment (Professional Standards of Financial Advisers) Act 2017, <www.legislation. gov.au/Details/C2017A00007>.

15 Corporations Amendment (Professional Standards of Financial Advisers) Act 2017, <www.legislation. gov.au/Details/C2017A00007/Download>.

16 Access to Corporations Regulations 2001, <www.legislation.gov.au/Series/F2001B00274>

17 Corporations Amendment Regulations 2013 (No 3), <www.legislation.gov.au/Details/F2013L00905>.

18 List of ASIC's regulatory guides, <http://asic.gov.au/regulatory-resources/find-a-document/regulatory-guides/>.

19 IndexofEM,<www.aph.gov.au/About_Parliament/Parliamentary_Departments/Parliamentary_Library/Browse_by_Topic/law/explanmem>.

20 Regulatory Guide 244: Giving information, general advice and scaled advice.

21 Regulatory Guide 244: Giving information, general advice and scaled advice.

22 Commonwealth Corporations Act 2001, <www.legislation.gov.au/Details/C2017C00328/Html/Volume_1#primary-nav>.

23 Commonwealth Corporations Act 2001, <www.legislation.gov.au/Details/C2017C00328/Html/Volume_1#primary-nav>.

24 Commonwealth Corporations Act 2001, <www.legislation.gov.au/Details/C2017C00328/Html/Volume_1#primary-nav>.

25 See page 222 of the Commonwealth Corporations Act 2001, <www.legislation.gov.au/Details/C2017C00328/Html/Volume_1#primary-nav>

26 Refer to S.912A of the Commonwealth Corporations Act 2001 for the licensing obligations of the AFSL holders.

27 See regulations 7.8.12A (4) and 7.8.14B (3) of the Corporations Regulations referred to at <https://asic.gov.au/for-finance-professionals/afs-licensees/apply ing-for-and-managing-an-afs-licence/limited-financial-services/>.

28 See details at <https://asic.gov.au/for-finance-professionals/afs-licensees/do-you-need-an-afs-licence/>.
29 See s916A, 916B and 916F of the Corporations Act and regulation 7.6.08(1) and (3) of the Corporations Regulations 2001 referred to at <https://asic.gov.au/for-finance-professionals/afs-licensees/appointing-and-ceasing-an-afs-authorised-representative/who-can-be-an-authorised-representative-of-an-afs-licensee/>.
30 Refer to S.912A of the Commonwealth Corporations Act 2001 for the licensing obligations of the AFSL holders.
31 See regulations 7.8.12A (4) and 7.8.14B (3) of the Corporations Regulations referred to at <https://asic.gov.au/for-finance-professionals/afs-licensees/applying-for-and-managing-an-afs-licence/limited-financial-services/>.
32 See details at <https://asic.gov.au/for-finance-professionals/afs-licensees/do-you-need-an-afs-licence/>.
33 See s916A, 916B and 916F of the Corporations Act and reguation 7.6.08(1) and (3) of the Corporations Regulations 2001 referred to at <https://asic.gov.au/for-finance-professionals/afs-licensees/appointing-and-ceasing-an-afs-authorised-representative/who-can-be-an-authorised-representative-of-an-afs-licensee/>.
34 Regulatory Guide 246: Conflicted remuneration.
35 Buyer of last resort agreement is a contract between a licensee, who usually distributes financial products, and their AR, allowing the licensee to purchase the client base from the adviser when they retire or exit the licensee. The capital purchase value is calculated on the basis of formula applied to the funds under management [FUM] or revenue the adviser had generated. Generally, a higher percentage is paid if the FUM is with the licensee. Thus, encouraging advisers to increase the capital value of the business by recommending mainly the licensee's in-house financial products (Francis 2006).
36 Regulatory Guide 246: Conflicted remuneration.
37 Australian Securities and Investments Commission (2013b, p. 24) defined a platform 'white label' arrangement as a contractual agreement between a platform owner and licensee to rebrand the platform to give the appearance it is the licensees' own platform.
38 'Private label' agreements occur when the licensee is the platform owner and characteristically contracts out the administration of the platform to another platform operator (Australian Securities and Investments Commission 2013b, p. 27).
39 Regulatory Guide 104. Licensing: Meeting the general obligations. Issued 1 July 2015.

Regulatory Guide 105 Licensing: Organisational competence. Issued 15 December 2016.

Regulatory Guide 126 Compensation and insurance arrangements for AFS licensees. Issued 20 December 2010.

Regulatory Guide 146. Licensing: Training of financial product advisers. July 2012.

Regulatory Guide 165. Licensing: Internal and external dispute resolution. Issued July 2015.

Regulatory Guide 166. Licensing: Financial requirements. Issued December 2009.

Regulatory Guide 175. Licensing – Financial product advisers – conduct and disclosure. Issued April 2011.

Regulatory Guide 181. Licensing: Managing conflicts of interest. Issued 30 August 2004.

Regulatory Guide 182. Dollar disclosure. Issued 19 June 2008.

40 Disclosure is in the form of a Financial Services Guide, Statement of Advice, which includes a Fee Disclosure Statement and Product Disclosure Statements.

41 Prescribed in s913 of Title IX of the Dodd-Frank Wall Street Reform and Consumer Protection Act of 2010.
42 For more information, go to <www.sec.gov/about/forms/formadv-part2.pdf>.
43 Financial Services and Markets Act 2000, <www.legislation.gov.uk/ukpga/2000/8/contents>.
44 FCA Handbook is accessible at this link, <www.handbook.fca.org.uk/handbook>.
45 COB 2.1.1 "A firm must act honestly, fairly and professionally in accordance with the best interests of its client (the client's best interests rule)."
46 COBS 2.2.1 "A firm must provide appropriate information in a comprehensible form to a client."
47 COBS 9.2.1 "A firm must take reasonable steps to ensure that a personal recommendation, or a decision to trade, is suitable for its client."
48 COBS 6.3 Services and Costs Disclosures or Combined Initial Disclosure Document at <www. handbook.fca.org.uk/handbook/COBS/6/3.html?date=2016–07–03>.
49 COBS 9 Suitability (including basic advice) at <www.handbook.fca.org.uk/handbook/COBS/9.pdf>.
50 For more information, see <www.the-fca.org.uk/appointed-representatives-and-principals>.
51 See more at <www.the-fca.org.uk/appointed-representatives-and-principals?field_fcasf_sector= unset&field_fcasf_page_category=unset#sthash.VmHl0PBx.dpuf>.
52 See more at <www.the-fca.org.uk/appointed-representatives/move-being-ar-being-authorised?field_fcasf_sector=unset&field_fcasf_page_category=unset#sthash.nmfTxEu7.dpuf>.
53 COBS 6.1.A Adviser charging and remuneration <www.handbook.fca.org.uk/handbook/COBS/6/ 1A.html>.

COBS 6.1B.5 Retail investment product provider, operator of an electronic system in relation to lending, and platform service provider requirements relating to adviser charging and remuneration <www.handbook. fca.org.uk/handbook/COBS/6/1B.html>.

54 Details can be found here <www.out-law.com/en/articles/2017/july/financial-conduct-authority-to-merge-rdr-review-with-assessment-of-famr/>.
55 US financial advisory institutions, US broker-dealer institutions, 'UK restricted' advice institutions, UK *independent* advice institutions and Australian Financial Services licensees.
56 US *independent* registered investment advisers, US broker-dealer registered representatives, UK *independent* appointed representatives, UK 'restricted' appointed representatives and Australian s923A *independent* authorised representatives and Australian authorised representatives.
57 US Securities and Exchange Commission, US Financial Industry Regulatory Authority, UK Financial Conduct Authority and Australian Securities and Investments Commission.
58 Commonwealth Corporations Act 2001, <www.legislation.gov.au/Details/C2017C00328/Html/Volume_1#primary-nav>.
59 Regulatory Guide 246: Conflicted remuneration.
60 Commonwealth Corporations Act 2001, <www.legislation.gov.au/Details/C2017C00328/Html/Volume_1#primary-nav>.
61 For more information, see <www.the-fca.org.uk/focus-areas/mifid-ii?field_fcasf_page_category=426 &field_fcasf_sector=unset>.

3 Legitimacy of licensee–adviser licensing

Introduction

Against the backdrop of the previous chapter on licensing advisers in Australia, the US and the UK, the stage is set to develop the theoretical framework evaluating the legitimacy of AFS licensee–adviser licensing. This requires relying on integrating principal–agent theory, the objectives of the Act, legitimacy theory and theory of *independent* regulatory regimes of other professions into financial planning theory.

Starting with the central argument [Figure 3.1], licensing advisers via third-party commercial product-aligned licensees, as specified in the Act, creates a dual-agency [licensee–adviser–client] role. A dual-agency role involves advisers serving the licensees' commercial interests and their clients' best interests simultaneously (Beal & McKeown 2009; Evetts 2011; Banister *et al.* 2013; Taylor, Juchau & Houterman 2013; Kingston & Weng 2014). This licensee–adviser–client role leads to conflicts of interest, specifically a conflict of interest from association, ownership or affiliation. Consequently, this licensing approach is inconsistent with four of the objectives of the Act. It threatens the legitimacy of current licensee–adviser licensing, when assessed against the criteria of Suchman's (1995) legitimacy theoretical framework extended and applied to financial planning theory. If the AFSL-AR licensing is proven illegitimate, then arguments for *independent* individual professional licensing (Parliamentary Joint Committee on Corporations and Financial Services 2009a; Sanders & Roberts 2015), like other professions, are strengthened.

Dual agency role of advisers

To understand the principles underlying the dual-agency role of individual advisers, the first part of the model in Figure 3.1 considers agency theory, particularly principal agent theory.

Agency theory integrated into financial planning theory

Early literature (Eisenhardt 1989; Leslie 2008) commonly identified an agency relationship exists whenever principals engage agents to create value for them.

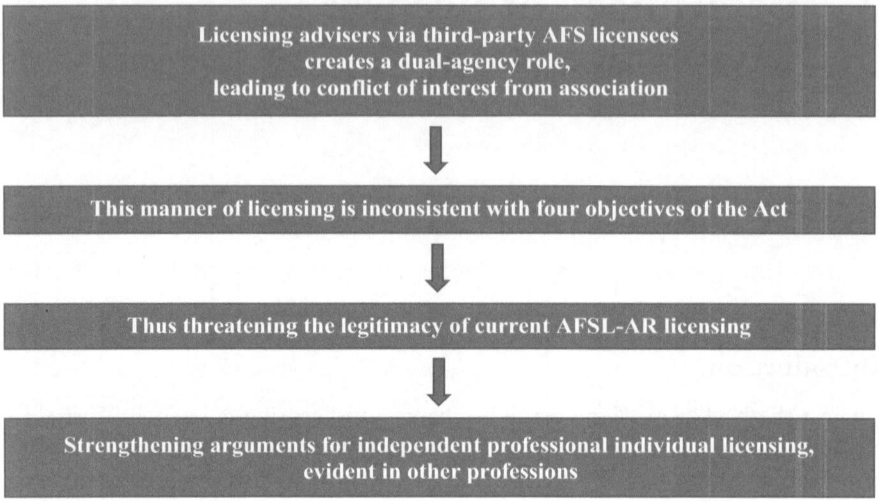

Figure 3.1 Conceptualised model to examine licensee–adviser licensing legitimacy.

Dawson, Watson and Boudreau (2010) pointed out agents and their principals assumedly hold symmetric knowledge. This encourages them to engage each other in formalised relationships of trust in the form of written contractual agreements. They proposed the difficulties of this assumption were the complications created by the reality of information asymmetry and moral hazard. Eisenhardt (1989) and Haigh (2006), drawing on a substantial body of literature, observed these problems were because of the assumption: agents and principals put their personal interests first without regard for others. The pre-contractual information asymmetry problem (Bergen, Dutta & Walker Jr 1992), or problems of adverse selection, operate *ex ante* where agents hide information about the true reality (Haigh 2006). For instance, Steen, McGrath and Wong (2016) explained licensees issuing products have product knowledge superior to their agents' [advisers] knowledge, who, in turn, know more about the products than their clients. According to them, this information asymmetry is evident between product licensees–advisers–clients in all financial services markets, causing inefficiency in financial products or services by prices and quantities. Consequently, they felt this meant clients end up with unsuitable financial products.

Likewise, post-contractual problems (Bergen, Dutta & Walker Jr 1992) of moral hazard operate in a similar way to adverse selection, but *ex post* (Haigh 2006). Agents conceal their action while failing to deliver what they are supposed to deliver (Aras & Crowther 2011). As illustration, advisers may be tempted to overrate the merits of the financial services or products they sell on behalf of their licensees (Sandlant 2011). They do so to secure business from clients to achieve key performance indicators or gain positive recognition from their licensees for earning them revenues (Sandlant 2011). Clients of advisers, Schwarcz (2014) wrote, have limited cognitive resources, background knowledge and time to devote to understanding complex yet ever-changing financial products. Therefore, principals spend time continually trying to discover the true intentions of their agents, albeit with varying success (Bolton, Freixas & Shapiro 2007; Bhattacharya *et al.* 2012; Carlin & Gervais 2012).

When products are sold through institutions' distribution channels – as in many retail banks, financial product issuers, superannuation funds and/or platforms – or whether sales or advice is reliant on third parties – as is often with insurance institutions – a trilateral agency problem arises between the client, the agent and the product providers (Inderst 2009). Two key agency problems come into play, because the interests, goals, values or expectations of the principal–agent are incongruent (Eisenhardt 1989). Arthurs and Busenitz (2003) were of the view that agency theory is inapplicable when no agency problem exists. Consequently, the greater the gap between agents' and principals' interest, the greater the agency problem, and hence the agency costs (Wasserman 2006; Leslie 2008; Balasubramnian, Brisker & Gradisher 2014), such as monitoring costs, bonding and residual losses (Balasubramnian, Brisker & Gradisher 2014).

Licensee–adviser–client dual-agency relationship

Rees (1985) contended most principal–agent models assumed a single principal and a single agent. Yet, acknowledged by financial planning scholars (Beal & McKeown 2009; Banister *et al.* 2013; Taylor, Juchau & Houterman 2013), advisers serve two principals, namely the licensee and client. This essentially leads to challenges of reconciling the various conflicts of interest among these principals. For instance, empirically confirmed licensees are earning various permutations of technical questionable types of revenue. Licensing advisers via third-party commercially driven licensees leads to a **conflict of interest** from association. Conflict of interest from association is defined here as the conflicts arising when a licensee is either directly or indirectly affiliated to financial product issuers, retail superannuation or aligned platforms. These include but are not limited to:

- financial product issuers [e.g. Commonwealth Bank of Australia, National Australian Bank, Westpac and AMP aligned groups].
- retail superannuation [e.g. Westpac's BT Super (Westpac), National Australian Bank's MLC, Commonwealth Bank's Colonial First State and ANZ Bank's OnePath].
- aligned platforms [e.g. Westpac's BT Wrap, Macquarie Wrap, Commonwealth Bank's Colonial First State FirstChoice Wrap and AMP's North Wrap].

Agency theory, models and propositions produced in personal financial planning courses and their textbooks in Australia (Beal & McKeown 2009; Banister *et al.* 2013; Taylor, Juchau & Houterman 2013) revealed the emphasis is the client–adviser relationship. The financial planning theory (Beal & McKeown 2009; Hartnett 2009; Banister *et al.* 2013; Taylor, Juchau & Houterman 2013) described the purpose of advisers is to follow a six-step financial planning process (Boone 2000) to provide strategic advice to ensure their clients achieve their financial and lifestyle goals. Product does not feature in the definitions presented in scholarly financial planning literature. Thus, it is reasoned from the definition in the literature (Beal & McKeown 2009; Hartnett 2010; Arman & Shackman 2012; Taylor, Juchau & Houterman 2013), the adviser should be client focussed when providing advice rather than product focussed.

Yet with some level of uncertainty when reflecting on the licensee–adviser–client agency role, advisers sanctioned their agency relationship is an adviser–client (Corones & Galloway 2013) agency relationship (Moutsopoulos 2005; Finke, Huston & Waller 2009a) and a licensee–adviser relationship. While the financial planning literature emphasises the adviser–client agency relationship, it neglects the licensee–adviser and seemingly the licensee–client relationship.

It is specified in the Act, advisers' purpose is to recommend financial products and services to their clients on behalf of licensees. Section 761G defines the client as the person receiving the financial product advice. Thus, the legislation focuses on product advice definitions of the financial adviser role. Leading from the foregoing statements, the Act embeds the second competing agency relationship, namely the licensee–adviser agency relationship (Moran 2014), while neglecting the adviser–client relationship. Expressed in s911B of the legislation

> a person [the provider] must only provide a financial service in this jurisdiction on behalf of another person (the principal) who carries on a financial services business if . . . the principal holds an Australian financial services licence covering the provisions of the service.1

Evident from the legislation, advisers' occupational contractual duty to their licensees as authorised representatives, which is specified in s916A and s916B, is "*to provide a specified financial service or financial services on behalf of the licensee*" (Tuch 2005; Australian Securities and Investments Commission 2012a).[2] Found in the writings of Beal and McKeown (2009) the purpose of licensees is to provide financial products, comply with the Act and, as specified in s912, screen, appoint, monitor, train and supervise ARs for ASIC. However, in practice, under the current licensing regime, advisers see the adviser–licensee relationship as merely an unimportant legal arrangement of compliance, which they must accept.

Contrary to the terms in s916A and s916B, Australian advisers may no longer perceive themselves as operating on behalf of AFS licensees. Interestingly, there is no suggestion evident in the relevant sections of the Act the adviser works on behalf of the client. However, Sitkoff (2014) asserted the fiduciary obligation implies the adviser operates as an agent for the client. Since the implementation of statutory best interest duty, the legislated adviser–licensee relationship of agent (Den-Toll 2001) and principal providing services to the public seems to be changing.[3],[4] Therefore, a division exists between how financial planning theory and practice seem to define their and their licensees' role in practice, compared with how the Corporations Act defines these roles.

Facciolo (2011) and others (Smith & Walter 2001; Gor 2005; Hackethal, Haliassos & Jappelli 2012) found advisers play a dual role as distributors of financial products for product providers. They are advisers to the ultimate purchasers of these products. From agency theory perspectives, advisers serve at least two principals, the licensee and the client, simultaneously (Kingston & Weng 2014, p. 294) when complying with the Act. Kingston and Weng (2014, p. 294) argued, "*An agent should not try to serve two principals simultaneously – they create the possibility of a conflict of interest between adviser and client.*"

Inderst and Ottaviani (2009) claimed the risk of mis-selling is complicated when an adviser faces a dual-agency role of canvassing for clients while providing advice to clients to commit to a product. In a later paper, Inderst and Ottaviani (2012b) demonstrated mathematically a conflict arises when, instead of a single role of getting to know and providing recommendations to clients, an adviser is faced with searching for clients, learning new products and then finally providing product recommendations on behalf of the product providers. There may be several reasons why serving both parties simultaneously is difficult, which this study explores further.

For instance, during the Hayne Inquiry (Commonwealth of Australia 2018, 2019) how licensees were earning revenues came under scrutiny. Seemingly, the benefit of having complex product distribution networks services via advisers complements licensees' revenues. Licensees' remuneration models [fee for no service, flat fee, percentage of revenue, licensee split of fees charge for advice, platform fees, product fees or fees they charge advisers to use their services and/or any volume rebates for specific products], including product sold, looks to be a key conflict. From the findings during the Royal Commission consultation there was discomfort from licensee leaders, while Hayne, the public and media were aghast when it came to light how licensees earned their revenues. Charging clients who have passed away and fee for no service serves as some of the allegedly "greedy" practices occurring (Commonwealth of Australia 2018, 2019).

Legitimacy integrated into financial planning theory

According to Kury (2007), legitimacy is complementary to agency theory. Thus, having given attention to agency, legitimacy of the entity as suggested by Clegg (2010) should come next. Because, if licensing advisers via third-party licensees creates a dual-agency role leading to conflict of interest from association for advisers, then this conflict is inconsistent with the four objectives of the Act. Therefore, the legitimacy of the current licensee–adviser model is threatened when considered within the context of four relevant objectives of the Act and using criteria from the legitimacy framework of Suchman (1995) integrated into financial planning theory.

Overview of legitimacy theory

Researchers Díez-Martín, Prado-Roman and Blanco-González (2013), substantiated in their paper, secondary sources provide extensive studies in legitimacy theory since the mid-1990s. Empirical work in legitimacy theory internationally focussed on organisational theory (Ellis 2006; Golant & Sillince 2007; Díez-Martín, Prado-Roman & Blanco-González 2013), management theory (Bitektine 2011), economic theory and political science (Gualini 2004; Ellis 2006). Some studies in legitimacy centred on specific industry fields, such as mining (Pellegrino & Lodhia 2012), telecommunications (Low 2010) and healthcare (Sonpar, Pazzaglia & Kornijenko 2010). Others focussed research attention on specific professions, for example the accounting profession (Greenwood, Suddaby & Hinings 2002; Tilling 2004b; Fisher, Swanson & Schmidt 2007; Kury 2007; Andon, Free & Sivabalan 2014). Yet researchers in business schools in Australia and internationally have neglected the topic of legitimacy within the context of financial planning theory.

As with any developing theory, Tilling (2004b) acknowledged, defining, understanding and suitably applying legitimacy is challenging. Accordingly, the most cited definition of legitimacy given by Suchman (1995, p. 574) stated:

> ***Legitimacy*** *is a generalized perception or assumption that the actions of an entity are desirable, proper, or appropriate within some socially constructed system of norms, values, beliefs, and definitions.*

Suchman's (1995) theoretical definition of legitimacy was understood by Bitektine (2011) and Pellegrino and Lodhia (2012) as the perceptions, beliefs, values and judgements by various actors about the social acceptability of the goals, which entities pursue. However, according to Tilling (2004b), although legitimacy has concrete outcomes, it is an abstract concept based on the biased perceptions of the actors. As Suchman (1995, p. 583) stated, "*Legitimacy is possessed objectively, yet created subjectively.*" Santana (2012) reaffirmed this statement in a later paper. Furthermore, a "*socially constructed system*" (Suchman 1995, p. 574), found within the definition, refers to the institutional frameworks, which consists of, for example, legal, moral or cognitive elements (Scott 2013). For purposes of this investigation, it is inferred the Act is the "*socially constructed system*" (Suchman 1995, p. 574), which arguably qualifies current AFSL-AR licensing, while simultaneously endorsing conflict of interest from association.

Hence, the rules and the requirements of the Act influences the perceptions, beliefs and considerations of the institutional constituents, including the public, government, the regulators, professional associations, media, licensees and the advisers. Thus, according to Zimmerman and Zeitz (2002) and de Queiroz, de Vasconcelos and Goldszmidt (2007), legitimacy is a valuable resource for an institution. To the contrary, Scott (2013, p. 72) reasoned "*it is not a specific resource, but a fundamental condition of social existence.*" Whether legitimacy is a "*resource*" (Scott 2013, p. 72) or "*condition of social existence*" (Scott 2013,

p. 72), this study drew on Kury's (2007) conviction. Namely, perception is the element which determines through judgement the entity's standing, survival and activities. Therefore, the legitimacy of current licensing is an intangible (Bender 2011), dynamic, general societal perception (Santana 2012) or "*assumption, that the actions of*" (Suchman 1995, p. 574) licensing advisers through third-party, often commercially oriented product-conflicted licensees, as specified presently in the Act "*are desirable, proper, or appropriate*" (Suchman 1995, p. 574). This perception should rise above the adverse financial scandals (Kury 2007).

Noteworthy is that legitimacy affects how the actors understand and behave towards (de Queiroz, de Vasconcelos & Goldszmidt 2007) licensee–adviser licensing. Perceptions reflect the expectations of congruence (Zimmerman & Zeitz 2002) between the behaviours and beliefs (Santana 2012) of the licensee, adviser and the shared, or assumedly shared, interests of their clients, with the purpose to create social order, according to Chen and Roberts (2010). Although Ellis (2006) argued, the legitimacy judged from outside audiences matters, it is contended by other scholars (see, e.g. Bitektine 2011; Rocha & Granerud 2011; Cole & Salimath 2013), so are judgements by inside audiences.

Legitimacy theory, including the broad societal-level definition of legitimacy itself, does not provide the means as to how legitimacy achieves social expectations, social support or congruency. However, it hints at certain actions and events which either increase or decrease legitimacy (Chua & Rahman 2011). As illustration, the scandals creating distrust among clients, licensees and advisers facing conflicts of interest, the challenge of fiduciary duty obligations and misaligned interests between licensee–adviser and client either intensify or diminish the legitimacy of AFSL-AR licensing.

Legitimation is the process by which an institution builds, maintains or retains legitimacy (Díez-Martín, Prado-Roman & Blanco-González 2013) by continuously testing and redefining the entity operating within its surroundings (Kostova & Zaheer 1999). Significantly, Suchman (1995) reasoned, legitimation is purposeful, calculating and often oppositional. Regulation, as viewed by Yeung (2009) and Santana (2012), is an attempt at legitimation to achieve the status of legitimacy. Therefore, the study surmises, the "*tool of legitimation*" as defined by Chen and Roberts (2010, p. 654), is the Act enforcing current AFSL-AR licensing.

Following the approach by Riaz, Buchanan and Bapuji (2011), this investigation framed the discussion further, into institutional fields. Greenwood, Suddaby and Hinings (2002) defined an institutional field as the social structure comprising collections of collective related institutions, organising to form a part of institutional life. Here, the emerging financial planning profession's institutional field is defined as the financial advisory sector operating within the financial services sector.

Central to the field are the sources of legitimacy (Díez-Martín, Prado-Roman & Blanco-González 2013). They include all the internal and external social actors (Chalmers & Godfrey 2004) judging licensee–adviser licensing and conferring legitimacy if observed valuable (Suchman 1995). Thus, the sources of legitimacy comprise policymakers, regulators, professional associations, licensees, advisers, clients [or the public] and the media. Institutional logics are the symbolic constructions used by these social actors to evaluate legitimacy (Bitektine 2011) within the institutional field (Soin & Huber 2013).

The literature on legitimacy theory is indeed fragmented (Sonpar, Pazzaglia & Kornijenko 2010). Hence, legitimacy experts (Suchman 1995; Kury 2007; Chen & Roberts 2010) felt the division of legitimacy into institutional [social] legitimacy and organisational [strategic] legitimacy was necessary, because then researchers have a means of examining legitimacy. Chelli, Durocher and Richard (2014) claimed, when doing research in legitimacy, researchers should clearly determine whether these legitimacies are of relevance in their research. Therefore, this book considers both divisions to understand the legitimacy of current licensing, because on the basis of observations of Kostova and Zaheer (1999), legitimacy affects an entity [like licensing] externally and internally. At the macro-level, **institutional [social] legitimacy** asserts, external institutional pressures will be sufficient to achieve (Soin & Huber 2013) or to maintain legitimacy (Chelli, Durocher & Richard 2014). Considering the roles of ASIC, licensees and their advisers, the Act, although enforced by ASIC, is present externally. In other words, it influences the internal advisers from externally. In their paper, Wenzel and Jobling (2006) argued legitimacy is gained or lost depending on the level and consistency of the power used by the enforcers. Therefore, to achieve or maintain legitimacy requires licensees and their advisers to consistently conform to the legislation and ASIC's compliance rules. A key legitimation strategy is to keep the entity and legal surroundings closely aligned (Suchman 1995, p. 595; Chelli, Durocher & Richard 2014). Sonpar, Pazzaglia and Kornijenko (2010) alleged, the institutional approach, although generally appealing, has been criticised in various studies. For instance, they mentioned a shortcoming, namely it downplays how different institutional powers may put pressure on entities to prioritise different sets of values. To further exemplify this criticism by Sonpar, Pazzaglia and Kornijenko (2010) within the context of this investigation, the following issue is apparent: who should license individual advisers? Should it be ASIC, licensees, an *independent* industry professional standards board or advisers themselves? How should advisers be licensed? Should it be current licensee–adviser licensing or new alternative licensing? Finally, why should individual advisers be licensed in this manner? Is it to achieve the objectives of the Act? Furthermore, they reiterate, this view of legitimacy neglects the fact, legitimacy is temporary and dynamic in nature.

Thus, institutional legitimacy investigates what institutional structures [e.g. for purposes of this study aligned or *independent* licensee business models], activities [stakeholder maximisation, shareholder wealth maximisation, aligning the interests of clients and advisers, managing conflicts of interest, competitive behaviour and fiduciary duty obligations] and procedures [licensing compliance sales procedures] are legitimate. Utilise these as the variables to evaluate legitimacy (Chen & Roberts 2010). At the macro-level, institutional [social] illegitimacy (Chen & Roberts 2010) of current licensing may be present.

The external institutional forces (Soin & Huber 2013), in the form of the legal requirement to achieve the objectives of the Act as unsuccessfully enforced by ASIC (Commonwealth of Australia 2018, 2019) via AFSL licensees, are contributing to the potential illegitimacy (Chelli, Durocher & Richard 2014) of AFSL-AR licensing. Licensing advisers via third parties makes **it hard to align adviser–client's interests, eliminate conflicts of interest, comply with the statutory best interest duty and maintain fair competition**.

In contrast, Suchman's (1995) **strategic [organisational]** perspective placed legitimacy under the control of the internal actors of the institution. Instead of operating at the 'macro-level' as Tilling (2004b) expressed for institutional legitimacy, strategic legitimacy is an examination at the 'micro-level'. Thus, legitimacy is malleable, like an operational resource or tool to meet the desires of the internal actors according to Suchman (1995, p. 576) to give them credibility (Kury 2007) and to gather societal support (Durocher, Fortin & Côté 2007). Consequently, institutions develop strategies affecting the external surroundings to achieve legitimacy. For instance, licensees may develop specific internal policies, procedures and practices to meet the compliance requirements of the legislation, while concurrently achieving their business goals. Legitimacy thus becomes an internal instrument or resource (Tilling 2004b) of self-construction (Santana 2012) for licensees to give integrity to their actions and their advisers. In contrast to the institutional view of legitimacy, strategic legitimacy acknowledged, legitimacy is temporary and dynamic (Sonpar, Pazzaglia & Kornijenko 2010). Thus, it requires renegotiation periodically. According to Chelli, Durocher and Richard (2014), the institutional and strategic legitimation cannot happen together. However, these two views of legitimacy assist with understanding how congruency is reached, the legitimacy gap closed (Pellegrino & Lodhia 2012) or how it is justified (Chen & Roberts 2010).

Evaluating AFSL-AR licensing

Several legitimacy scholars have proposed various legitimacy typologies to evaluate legitimacy (Bitektine 2011). Although legitimacy is difficult to measure, by using proxy variables, quantitative analysis is achievable (Zimmerman & Zeitz 2002). On these grounds, this study applied to financial planning theory Suchman's (1995) complete framework. Furthermore, Suchman's framework covers institutional and strategic legitimacy issues. Consequently, underlying institutional legitimacy issues are four important objectives of the Act pertinent to this study. They include as follows: (1) managing, controlling or avoiding conflicts of interest; (2) ensuring statutory fiduciary duty is implemented; 3) aligning the adviser's interests with the client's best interest, as well as; (4) encouraging competitive behavior between financial service providers (Bora & Lewis 1997; Corbett 1999; Mutton 2001; Collier 2003; Serpell 2008; Jones 2009; Alexander 2011; Ap 2011; Ireland & Gray 2011; Kell 2012). Furthermore, the strategic legitimacy criteria include Suchman's (1995) broad, yet specific legitimacy criteria, namely regulative, normative (moral) and cultural-cognitive legitimacy.

Conceptually, it is argued here the legitimacy of the AFSL-AR licensing model needs to be evaluated in terms of these legislative four objectives, and Suchman's (1995) legitimacy criteria to safeguard the integrity of professionalising the emerging financial planning profession while ensuring the effective protection of retail financial consumers.

Contraventions of the objectives of the Corporations Act 2001

Carlin and Gervais (2012) claimed two forces are at work between institutions [principals] and their agents [advisers], namely the contracts agreed between them, together with the legal environment imposed by the government. According to Hackethal, Haliassos and Jappelli (2012), the financial regulation policy debate and theoretical work centring on harmful adviser behaviours and conflicts of interest damages public trust. Underlying the main aim by the government to protect retail financial consumers and to improve public trust and confidence in advisers (Australian Government The Treasury 2016) are four important objectives of the Act: (1) managing, controlling or avoiding conflicts of interest; (2) ensuring statutory fiduciary duty is implemented; (3) aligning the adviser's interests with the client's best interest; (4) encouraging competitive behaviour between financial service providers (Bora & Lewis 1997; Corbett 1999; Mutton 2001; Collier 2003; Serpell 2008; Jones 2009; Alexander 2011; Ap 2011; Ireland & Gray 2011; Kell 2012). The argument suggests the legitimacy of AFSL-AR licensing needs evaluation by these four objectives to safeguard the integrity of professionalising the emerging financial planning profession, while ensuring the effective protection of retail financial consumers.

CONFLICTS OF INTEREST CONTRAVENTIONS

Researchers have studied conflicts of interest extensively for decades with published articles prolific in the literature (see *inter alia* Vessenes 1997; Bearden 2002; Tuch 2005; Bolton, Freixas & Shapiro 2007; Palazzo & Rethel 2008; Felsenthal & Guttenberg 2009; Bird 2011; Loewenstein, Cain & Sah 2011; Inderst & Ottaviani 2012b; Angel & McCabe 2013; Burke *et al.* 2015; Calcagno & Monticone 2015). With regard to the first objective, managing, controlling or avoiding conflicts of interest is a difficulty for advisers and for other professionals in medicine, accounting and law (Bruce 2012; Burke *et al.* 2015). Subsection 912A[1][a] [aa] of the Act states "*adequate arrangements*" should be put in place to manage, control or avoid any conflicts of interest "*in relation to activities undertaken by the licensees or their representatives when providing financial advice*" (Zammit 2004, p. 20; Tuch 2005). Licensees and their representatives are obligated to manage (Tuch 2005) actual, apparent or potential (Pearson 2006b) conflicts of interest where the interests of clients diverge from the interests of the licensee or its representatives.

The government of the Commonwealth of Australia (2014a) conceded, although conflicts of interest are morally wrong, they are legally permitted as long as they are disclosed and clients consent to them. However, in accordance with ASIC's Regulatory Guide 181,[5] it is insufficient to just disclose conflicts and obtain consent. Johnston (2014) claimed since 2005, post-FSR, it was no longer necessary for advisers from mostly vertically integrated institutionally aligned/ owned licensees (Australian Securities and Investments Commission 2016i) to disclose on all marketing material their licensee's institutional logos. They argued, with no reference to the licensees of the many advisers, consumers were unable to recognise with whom they were engaging. Consequently, clients were ending up with 'in-house-products' without realising it (Morris 2013; Johnston 2014; Australian Securities and Investments Commission 2017c). Advisers reported in the study, the disclosures have not been as transparent as they intended in the legislation. Thus, these different interpretations of disclosure rules are confusing. Journalist Vickovich (2014a) recommended additional amendments to the legislation should include full disclosure of licensee ownership on all marketing material as evident pre-FSR. In addition, government commentators have conceded, significant room is inevitable for improvement concerning inadequate disclosures to retail clients (Australian Securities and Investments Commission 2013a, 2014c; Sinodinos 2014; Australian Securities and Investments Commission 2016i).

Apparent during the literature review among the many other types of conflicts was the primary focus (see, e.g. Bailey 2000; Palazzo & Rethel 2008; Beal & McKeown 2009; Inderst & Ottaviani 2012d; Walton 2012; Banister *et al.* 2013; Kingston & Weng 2014) specifically on conflict of interest from remuneration. Legislators in the US, the UK and Australia too have given remuneration much attention (Australian Securities and Investments Commission 2003; Collier 2003; Australian Securities and Investments Commission 2012c; Inderst & Ottaviani 2012c, 2012e; Commonwealth of Australia 2018). Burke *et al.* (2015) confirmed, after reviewing and summarising their research, prevalent conflicts affected the behaviour of advisers when remuneration schemes existed. Undoubtedly, to date conflicted remuneration remains the main reason cited for the loss of confidence by the public in advisers (Batten & Pearson 2013; Steen, McGrath & Wong 2016; Commonwealth of Australia 2018).

Support for the banning of commissions [s961J of the Act] to eliminate this conflict of interest (Julian 2009) led to some of the FOFA legislative reforms discussed in Chapter 2. However, Inderst (2009), as well as Bateman and Kingston (2014), highlighted the unintended consequences of banning commissions. They concluded banning commissions has made the financial service uneconomic for people of humble means seeking advice. It lowered social efficiency. Even government commentators (Sinodinos 2013c) have acknowledged, eliminating commissions was proven problematic in the UK. Specifically, advice has become unaffordable for many in the UK, making advice accessible to mainly high-income investors (Financial Conduct Authority 2016a). On the plus side, *independent* research undertaken by Europe Economics (Financial Conduct Authority 2014b, 2014c) found in the UK, post-RDR implementation, after banning commissions, a decline in high commission-paying product sales and product prices occurred. UK policymakers are presently in the process of working on solutions to address affordability, accessibility and quality of advice (Financial Conduct Authority 2017b).

Importantly, the Australian Parliamentary Joint Committee on Corporations and Financial Services (2009a) found the conflicts between advisers and their clients arose from commission remuneration practices, and from ownership, affiliations or association structures between particularly conflicted licensees and their ARs distributing product. Conflict of interest from association has received some comment in the media (Brown 2007; Beaman 2010a; Vickovich & Stewart 2014), from advisers in favour of independence (Brammall 2012) and from government commentators (Parliamentary Joint Committee on Corporations and Financial Services 2009a; Sinodinos 2013a, 2013c, 2014) and in trade publications (Kennedy, McCoy & Bernstein 2012; Pokrajac 2014). Evidence during this literature review, among them presented by Valentine (2008), demonstrated scholars and legislators have tended to ignore this issue of conflicts from association, resulting in a deficiency in scholarly research and literature about this matter. This is surprising, given estimates of 80% to 85% (Bearden 2002; Parliamentary Joint Committee on Corporations and Financial Services 2009a; Kingston & Weng 2011, 2014; Steen, McGrath & Wong 2016) of advisers are sponsored by product issuers to allegedly act as their product distribution pipeline (Starke 2013a). Thus, this research addresses Valentine's (2008) view, namely corporate scandals within the financial planning sector emphasised the need to place conflict of interest from association at the forefront of further research. If Perkins and Monahan (2011) are correct when they claim a primary responsibility of a professional adviser is to avoid conflicts with that of the client, then it is imperative changing current licensing is supported theoretically.

BEST INTEREST DUTY VIOLATIONS

Since FOFA reforms were designed to tackle conflicts of interest (Alexander 2011), they included amending the Act to introduce an explicit statutory fiduciary duty obligation (Ireland & Gray 2011). Arguable from the government and ASIC's perspective, FOFA addressed conflicts of interest by introducing the principle of putting the priorities of clients first (Australian Securities and Investments Commission 2013a, 2014c; Sinodinos 2014). This fiduciary duty, defined in s961A, is a key obligation of Australian licensees and their representatives (Banister *et al.* 2013). The Australian regulator makes it clear in their *Future of Financial Advice: Best interests duty and related obligations: Regulation Impact Statement* (Australian Securities and Investments Commission 2012a) as to who, when and how a fiduciary owes another a best interest duty. A critical aspect of financial advice is the professional obligations and duties of the Australian financial adviser to put the interest of their clients first or above their own [and/or the licensee's] interest when providing financial advice or services. This duty includes 'safe harbour' requirements set out in s961B[2] (Australian Securities and Investments Commission 2013a).

For Tuch (2005), evident is an inconsistency between the regulations of managing, controlling or avoiding conflicts of interest and the statutory obligations.

In this regard, considering his views, despite statutory fiduciary duty obligations, retail clients may receive personal advice persuading them to purchase unsuitable products of unacceptable quality, because of conflicts of interest. Moreover, fiduciary duty is influenced by advisers' occupational contractual duty to their licensees as authorised representatives [s916A or 916B of the legislation] (Tuch 2005; Australian Securities and Investments Commission 2012a), while simultaneously they are legally obligated to serve the best interests of their clients. Conceivably, fiduciary duty is of relevance, because advisers' statutory fiduciary duty to their Australian clients influences conflicted association, and *vice versa*.

Most of the international and national literature emphasises the various legal interpretations of fiduciary duty by case law formulated through the courts, common law of agency and from a corporate perspective under corporation legislation, such as the Act (Tuch 2005; Australian Securities and Investments Commission 2016h).[6] Although Tuch (2005) claimed the courts, which was reaffirmed by Hayne (Commonwealth of Australia 2019), commercial banks owe a fiduciary duty to their customers when providing product advice, he claimed this best interest duty is unnecessary in cases where banks provide general financial advice on a sales transaction or where the retail clients did not rely on the bank's advice to transact, or expect the transaction, may not be in their best interest. A legal case during this project highlighted the interpretation and application of the fiduciary duty in this way may be problematic. On 22 December 2016, ASIC commenced civil penalty proceedings against Westpac Securities Administration Limited and BT Funds Management Limited in the Australian Federal Court for failing to comply with the best interest duty (Australian Securities and Investments Commission 2016c). Westpac allegedly claimed to deliver general advice [telephonically]. ASIC disagreed, arguing it was personal advice (Australian Securities and Investments Commission 2016c). At the time of writing, the matter remained unsettled in court.

Furthermore, Batten and Pearson (2013) argued, the best interest duty standard as defined in the Act does not refer to the outcome of the advice. Rather, it refers to a process of automatic compliance. They claimed, with outcomes likely to fail a common law test of financial adviser duty of care, the definition of conflicts of interest in the legislation is non-existent. Moreover, the examples provided in the Explanatory Memorandum are insufficient to comply with the common law best interest duty. They further explained the licensee seemingly has the requirement to manage conflicts of interest. Whereas the individual financial advice provider has the requirement to act in the client's best interests. In addition, advisers comply only with the best interest requirement if they are aware of any conflicts.

It is important to note, currently almost two-thirds of investors do not believe advice providers act in their best interests (Australian Securities and Investments Commission 2013a). Degeling and Hudson (2014) suggested limiting advisers' recommendations to the authorisations of their AFSLs leads to unintentional violations of the best interest duty. This enquiry validates claims by secondary non-academic sources, Australian aligned licensees limited their ARs to recommendations of mainly products they select and assess for the APL (Australian Government The Treasury 2014; Sheehan 2016). Becoming evident during the Royal Commission (Commonwealth of Australia 2018, 2019), it is difficult for bank advisers facing limited APLs to align their interests with the best interests of the client. Advisers agree it is difficult to manage conflicts if financial products on APLs are linked to PI insurance (Stewart 2013) to reduce the licensees' risk. Seemingly, the practice to link PI to products on the APLs is questionable, because it limits APLs. Limiting APLs to PI-approved products, arguably, serves to 'encourage' advisers to recommend only these products. Debatably, this practice increases the risk of advisers breaching the best interest duty. Although secondary evidence suggests PI's purpose is to reduce the licensees' risk, no mention is made of the potential risks clients of advisers face by the practice of linking PI to APLs. Although best interest duty should override conflicts in theory, from the discussion so far, it is impractical to implement in practice, because in the presence of conflict of interest from association, complying with the best interest duty is tricky.

Licensees and their advisers are unsuccessful in achieving the best interest duty, because in practice, the presence of a poor product sales culture within aligned licensee, validated and verified, confirmed secondary research findings (Smith 2009; Steen, McGrath & Wong 2016) and by Hayne (Commonwealth of Australia 2018, 2019). It is argued here, this culture is facilitated by the ownership structures between licensees and advisers (Goedecke 2001). Closely associated with a poor product sales culture, Smith (2009, p. 316) confirmed, licensees' compliance, business development and area and/or distribution managers 'encourage' them to sell the licensees' in-house financial products. Thus, this control of licensees over advisers can make them powerless in avoiding contraventions of the best interest duty.

LICENSEE–ADVISER–CLIENT INTEREST MIS-ALIGNMENT

Attempts of Chapter 7 of the Act to reduce information asymmetry between product-aligned licensees, advisers and their clients is thwarted by licensing advisers via multiple third-party profit motivated licensees. Until this research, scholarly literature discussed alignment of institution-adviser interests (Bewley *et al.* 2008; Aschkenasy 2009) with client interests (Black 2005; Nyberg *et al.* 2010; Finke & Langdon 2012; Inderst & Ottaviani 2012d; Knutsen & Cameron 2012; Mazzola 2013; Starke 2013b) to a limited extent. The *Review on Retail Life Insurance Advice Report* (Trowbridge 2015) indicated a problem of misaligned interests, especially by remuneration models between licensees and insurers, and licensees and advisers. This misalignment is allegedly impacting the quality of advice negatively and contributing to the underinsurance in Australia (Trowbridge 2015).

Goedecke (2001) claimed Australian banks and financial planning practices acknowledge investment and risk insurance products are often non-aligned to the client's best interests. Despite licensees' obligations by law to monitor their agent's work in accordance with ASIC's (2007) enforcement requirements to prevent moral hazard, together with questionable licensee practices, it seems licensees demand alternative adviser behaviour. This burden to sell products leads to the misalignment of adviser–client interests. Thus, advisers could face ethical dilemmas they are unable to control if licensees dictate the terms or have influence over the adviser.

Many articles (see, e.g. Black 2005; Bowen 2010; Johnsen 2010; Australian Securities and Investments Commission 2012a; Inderst & Ottaviani 2012d; Kell 2012; Kingsford Smith 2012; Commonwealth of Australia 2019) focussed on remuneration practices and incentives or lack of educational and ethical standards as reasons why mis-selling has led to adviser-clients' interests to be non-aligned. The Parliamentary Joint Committee on Corporations and Financial Services (2009a) acknowledged, remuneration practices and ownership structures serve as the reasons for the incongruence of interests between adviser–client. Although remuneration practices is a focus for government, theorists have neglected the impact institutional financial advisory ownership structures may have had on aligning advisers' interests with the client. This is surprising, because aligning the interests of advisers to their clients more closely [specified in Schedule 1, item 13, division 2, and s961K of the Act] is one of the broader FOFA objectives. Notably, the Australian Financial Systems Inquiry (Commonwealth of Australia 2014a) singled out aligning financial institutions, presumably licensees and consumers' interests, rather than individual advisers' and their clients' interests. Perhaps it is so because the legislation about licensing, regulating and authorising individual advisers is at the corporate commercial institutional licensee level, rather than at the individual professional adviser level. If no misaligned interests are present, then no agency costs are present (Balasubramnian, Brisker & Gradisher 2014). However, the broader the gap between the interests of agents and principals, the more the agency costs (Wasserman 2006; Leslie 2008; Balasubramnian, Brisker & Gradisher 2014). Furthermore, with an additional agency relationship between licensees and advisers, an actual and/or potential incongruence between the interests of the advisers and their licensees may exist. This potentially leads to incongruence between the interests of advisers and their clients. Starke (2013b) asserted, congruency between the interests of clients and individual professional advisers is essential to any profession. Thus, he claimed alignment of licensee–adviser–client interests should be an important part of any regulatory reforms.

COMPETITIVE FINANCIAL ADVISORY ENVIRONMENT VIOLATIONS

The initial philosophy of FSR regulation was "*free and competitive markets can produce an efficient allocation of resources and provide a strong foundation for economic growth and development*" (Pearson 2006b, p. 103). Viable competition between financial services providers, according to Inderst and Ottaviani (2009), generally ensures protection for all consumers of financial products. They maintained further when faced with intense competition for retail customers, financial services sales force [advisers], while complying with specified standards, required more incentives from their institutions. Using mathematics, they argued these additional incentives make the regulation so costly for their institutions and advisers, making the opportunity to mis-sell financial products increasingly attractive.

Product-aligned licensees and dealer groups enter vertically integrated (Commonwealth of Australia 2018) or franchise-type business models to improve their product distribution channels (Christie 2015). Common among the aligned advisers was the practice of third line forcing. This occurs when loan applications are approved only if the client obtains insurance from the same provider. Furthermore, advisers alleged banks subsidise their advice delivery from vertical integration in practice by defraying the costs and support services of running the licence onto other parts of the business. Starke (2013b) argued vertical integration was resulting in anti-competitive consequences between various financial services providers within the financial planning sector. Anti-competitive behaviour was confirmed during the Murray (Commonwealth of Australia 2014a) and ASIC (Australian Securities and Investments Commission 2016i) review when they considered the increasingly high concentration of vertical integration in financial services. Financial services in Australia are considered by Steen, McGrath and Wong (2016) as less competitive than the US markets because of the highly concentrated and vertically integrated financial services sector. Findings reported in the interim report of the Hayne Royal Commission (Commonwealth of Australia 2018) suggested competition in the banking sector to be lacking, but the final recommendation did not make any suggestions that would affect vertical integration.

Suchman's legitimacy theoretical framework extended and applied

Chua and Rahman (2011) pointed out; the basis of legitimacy is the concept of 'social contract.' 'Social contract' is derived from political economic theory (Pellegrino & Lodhia 2012). It is central to legitimacy theory (Chelli, Durocher & Richard 2014), because it exemplifies the unspoken and obvious perceptions or expectations of society regarding how an entity is expected to be (Pellegrino & Lodhia 2012). Whether current licensing is "*desirable, proper, or appropriate*" as Suchman (1995, p. 574) viewed it depends upon the perceptions of the relevant social audience of actors shown in Table 3.1 of a breach of the social contract, in addition to how they influence three forms of legitimacy.

Legitimacy is threatened if violations of the 'social contract' occur (Pellegrino & Lodhia 2012) by some of the actors intervening (Suchman 1995) and possibly rescinding on their contract stated Johnson and Holub (2003). Seemingly, the appropriation of scandals in financial services signalled severe contraventions by the emerging financial planning profession of their 'social contract.'

In the book *Institutions and Organizations: Ideas, Interests, and Identities* (Scott 2013), it is apparent rules, norms and meanings can be accessed by inspecting events, beliefs [perceptions] and behaviours. Consequently, to understand the legitimacy of AFSL-AR licensing depends on the examination of Suchman's (1995) three broad, yet specific, types of legitimacy: pragmatic, normative and

Table 3.1 Institutional actors within financial planning adapted from the taxonomy of Kury (2007).

Pragmatic [Regulative] legitimacy	*Normative [Moral] legitimacy*	*Cultural-cognitive legitimacy*
Institutional actors regulating the licensing of advisers	**Institutional actors offering normative or a professional platform for advisers**	**Institutional actors having a shared understanding of current licensing**
• ASIC • FASEA	• Financial planning associations such as the FPA and AFA, *etc.* • AFS licensees	• Individual financial advisers • Clients of financial advisers • Public • Media

cognitive. Importantly, Scott (2014) highlighted, entities exhibiting these three typologies of legitimacy increase their survival rates. On the basis of a study by Carnegie, Edwards and West (2003), these three forms of legitimacy – consisting of elements of rules, norms and meanings (Scott 2013), respectively – are interrelated, yet can be mutually exclusive. Figure 3.2 illustrates the criteria used to investigate the legitimacy of AFSL-AR licensing.

PRAGMATIC [REGULATIVE] LEGITIMACY

Suchman (1995) defined pragmatic legitimacy as the perception of the social support for an entity's intentions, objectives and activities operating within some socially acceptable system. Johnson and Holub (2003) claimed this social support depends on the expected benefit to the conferring body. Therefore, it is a form of self-interest-based (Scott 2013) and audience-based legitimacy (Bitektine 2011), because it captures the degree to which an entity represents its audiences' self-interests (Díez-Martín, Prado-Roman & Blanco-González 2013).

Regulative legitimacy, derived from pragmatic legitimacy (Baum & Oliver 1991; Deephouse 1996; Zimmerman & Zeitz 2002; Rao 2004; Chen & Roberts 2010), occurs when regulatory entities use rules and laws to create trust, confidence, stability and order in society (Kostova & Zaheer 1999) by regulating and constraining certain types of behaviour (Scott 2013, p. 59). Yeung (2009) felt, regulative legitimacy is a form of political legitimacy, where researchers have tried to understand why or when actors comply with a country's authorities. Carruthers (1995) made the point, traditional approaches of legislating assume the rules and compliance requirements are present to influence the choices actors make in response to or in compliance with their institutional surroundings. Thus, the legislation embodies a form of social control (Yeung 2009; Santana 2012). Translating this for the purposes of this enquiry, it means ASIC under the authority of the Act authorised licensees to grant or withhold legitimacy (Bitektine

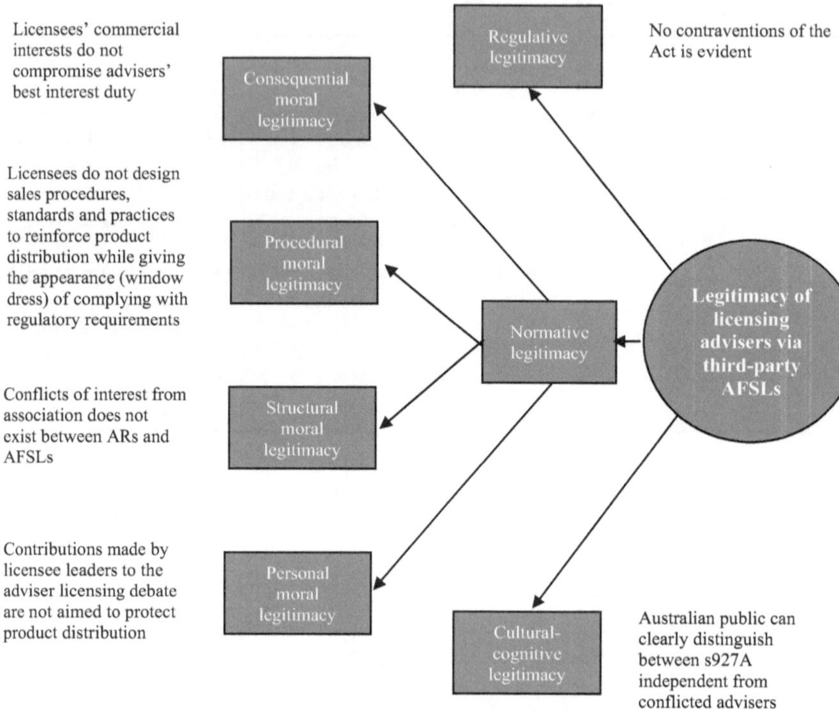

Figure 3.2 Legitimacy of current AFSL-AR licensing.

2011) by appointing or removing ARs from practising. From Table 3.1, the immediate influential regulative actors regulating the licensing of advisers with an institutional power base is the government assisted by the regulators ASIC and FASEA. The Act guides how conducting the licensing of advisers occurs and in theory support regulative legitimacy.

Thus, licensees do not have the "*right to exist*" (Bitektine 2011, p. 153) without an AFSL and advisers do not have the "*right to exist*" (Bitektine 2011, p. 153) without an authorisation from a licensee with an AFSL. Therefore, the current regulatory licensing system as authorised by the Act forms the basis of individual financial adviser's regulative legitimacy or "*right to exist*" (Bitektine 2011, p. 153). Serpell (2008) asserted the sources and legal form of legitimacy influence the trust actors have for any financial system. Regulative legitimacy serves as a defence for the "*right to exist*" (Bitektine 2011, p. 153), which arguably is being tested by the loss in public confidence and trust (Kell 2013) and the Royal Commission into Misconduct in the Banking, Superannuation and Financial Services Industry. Thus, to qualify as legitimate, the licensing model's "*right to exist*" (Chen & Roberts 2010, p. 654; Bitektine 2011, p. 153; Pellegrino &

Lodhia 2012, p. 70) is achieved by obtaining approval or avoiding sanction from the public (Tilling 2004b) or other relevant stakeholders listed in Table 3.1.

Licensees are responsible for the actions of their representatives. Specifically, s917B and s917D of this Act regulate licensees' responsibility for compliance contraventions by their advisers,[7] even if their advisers operate outside the scope of their licensees' rules (Chen 2009). If a client is dealing with an AR, the law protects them as though they are dealing with the licensee (Harvey 2002; Overland 2007; Serpell 2008; Sinodinos 2013d; Australian Securities and Investments Commission 2014a). From a legislator's and licensees' perspective, this is entirely appropriate; licensees must ensure compliance with ASIC rules and regulations to retain their licence by monitoring, supervising and training their advisers. The rest is up to the adviser. However, Smith (2009, p. 326) found a focus group of advisers she interviewed was frustrated, because they were of the opinion their AFS licensees are unable and do not have the desire to implement consistent behaviour or adviser conduct standards across their financial advisory groups. Furthermore, although compliance has become a liability, its repetitive mantra (Pearson 2006b), according to results from studies by Smith (2009), is that compliance officers of licensees were hindered in their ability to prevent compliance failure, especially by disciplining rogue advisers for misconduct or related performance issues.

According to Bruce (2012), the government's regulation has a significant influence on the activities of advisers. ASIC considered the legal requirements in the Act to be sufficient to achieve legitimacy (Australian Securities and Investments Commission 2013d). They have available various strategies as incentive to enforce compliance with the rules and principles. Legal coercion, repercussions of litigation, penalties, sanctions, the courts and police (Wenzel & Jobling 2006) provide additional compliance incentives (Chalmers & Godfrey 2004) for licensees and their ARs. Yet it is argued by Wenzel and Jobling (2006), these forms of deterrence mechanisms are not necessarily the most efficient means to regulate, because of the agency cost of the need to constantly and unsuccessfully monitor. Kingsford Smith (2011) commented on financial regulations as well as criticising ASIC in his paper as ineffective in their ability to investigate, enforce and prosecute, because they are not properly equipped with the necessary power, resources and a culture of regulatory relationships required in responsive financial regulation. Research by Melbourne Law School researchers (Bird & Gilligan 2015b; Gilligan *et al.* 2015a; Gilligan *et al.* 2015b; Bird *et al.* 2016; Bird, Gilligan & Ramsay 2016) considered the influence with which ASIC must sanction and discipline the Financial Services sector. Gilligan *et al.* (2015a) suggested, financial penalties are viewed by large corporates as an operational risk rather than a deterrence to prevent compliance offenses. Gilligan *et al.* (2017) advocated and supported the Hayne Royal Commission findings (Commonwealth of Australia 2019), namely ASIC's enforcement powers and practices are inadequate, inconsistent and ineffective. Arguably, ASIC is inadequately resourced from a personnel and surveillance perspective to regulate a large number and wide range of bodies to prevent misconduct. Gilligan *et al.* (2017) found, when ASIC does impose corporate finance law, it is often too late. Black (2012) warned if inconsistencies were evident in the performance of any regulation, then this would lead to its failure and its unintentional consequences by behaviour, risks or objectives. After all, Slattery and Nellis (2005) acknowledged, while regulators face political pressures and media attention when regulating financial services, their flexibility and certainty is limited when using legal rulemaking. Thus, recommendations by Hayne focuses on better enforcement by the regulators (Commonwealth of Australia 2019).

Legitimacy studies (e.g. Bitektine 2011; Chelli, Durocher & Richard 2014) revealed, to gain desired legitimacy, a perception of compliance with the legislation imposed by the external surroundings must exist (Carruthers 1995). Therefore, to determine licensing's regulative legitimacy involved examining the presence of the perception licensing advisers through third-party aligned licensees risks their advisers unintentionally breaching regulatory compliance duty (Degeling & Hudson 2014), because of their licensees' affiliations to product issuers. If, indeed, the advisers of licensees comply with the Act, then arguably current licensing is legitimate [Figure 3.2]. Important to note, Bender (2011) made the claim compliance with the law does not necessarily mean legitimacy. Highlighted in the literature review as important (Considnine & Ali Afzal 2011; Carlin & Gervais 2012) was the issue as to who [advisers, or the licensees or both] is ultimately accountable and in what proportions after a compliance breach.

Verifying regulative legitimacy is imperative, because Australian regulators argued the best protection for consumers is compliance by the financial services industry with a fair and transparent principles-based regulatory system (Pearson 2006b). Any infringements may result in ASIC or even public class action (Pearson 2008; Australian Securities and Investments Commission 2016b), as well as legal liability consequences for licensees and/or their advisers under various regulations (Degeling & Hudson 2014; Bird & Gilligan 2015a). In addition, licensees and advisers will lose their reputations if or when breaches in compliance are discovered and make headline news. Furthermore, the financial losses suffered by clients results in the public choosing to avoid seeking financial advice when the ensuing distrust sets in (Carlin & Gervais 2012).

NORMATIVE [MORAL] LEGITIMACY

Normative [moral] legitimacy is considered by theorists as a feature-based (Suchman 1995) and a judgement-based (Scott 2013) typology. This definition of legitimacy focuses on the perceptions of specific morals, values or ethics (Chen & Roberts 2010; Chua & Rahman 2011) of an entity's outcomes, goals, activities and/or structure (Bitektine 2011), within some socially accepted (Johnson & Holub 2003) or socially constructed value system (Bitektine 2011).

Normative legitimacy provides the moral justification to support regulative legitimacy through social norms. Whereas regulative legitimacy shapes the legal surroundings with formal rules to influence the structure, operation and responsibility of institutions (Thynne 2011). Moreover, normative legitimacy shapes the moral or professional foundation through institutions (Scott 2013) [policymakers, regulators ASIC and FASEA, professional associations and AFS licensees as illustrated in Figure 3.1] applying the law. These normative actors interpret the regulative rules, implement the rules and perpetuate the institutional order (Carnegie & O'Connell 2012).

Thus, this legitimacy's purpose is to provide a moral foundation, a basis to aid as a tool to foster positive images of the emerging profession amongst the public. It is about what is perceived and judged as the "*right thing to do*" (Yeung 2009, p. 286) morally to promote societal welfare. For instance, the Australian financial regulations aim to clean up the financial services sector (Hii & Su-King 2009). Owen (2003) noted, regulations drove the way financial institutions developed the manner in which they structured and distributed their financial products. Suchman (1995) categorised normative legitimacy into consequential, procedural, structural and personal moral legitimacy. Understanding and assessing moral legitimacy of current licensing requires further scrutiny of these four variables.

CONSEQUENTIAL MORAL LEGITIMACY

Consequential moral legitimacy contemplates the moral assessment of an entity's socially [incorporating a political element] acceptable and socially valued deeds, outputs and outcomes (Suchman 1995, p. 579). Lindorff and Peck (2010) wrote legitimacy requires institutions to manage their businesses for the benefit of all stakeholders, not just shareholders and employees.

Observed during the literature review, legislating stakeholder wealth maximisation is challenging, because numerous effects are in play. Yun (2012, p. 66) wrote, within the US context: "*Corporate executives have a fiduciary duty to act in the best interests of the corporation and its shareholders.*" Likewise, Australian Corporate Law [s180–s184] applies this principle to corporate executives of Australian corporations (Jones & Welsh 2012, p. 373). According to the writings of Jones and Welsh (2012, p. 373), this fiduciary duty included avoiding conflicts of interest between shareholders and management. They maintained further, in addition to their fiduciary duties, Australian directors, other officers and their employees, such as employee ARs, are legally expected not to work for self-interest or cause any detriment to the corporation [s182[1] and s183[1]] (Jones & Welsh 2012, p. 373) without disclosure to, and consent from, the corporation (Hargovan 2011).

Agency theory works under the assumption that the principal's main interest is profit maximisation and agents acting on behalf of their principals should advance the principal's goals (Moran 2014). By implication, then, the adviser must advance the licensees' goals who, in turn, according to Australian Corporate Law [s180–s184], must advance the interests of the shareholders, including complying with the fiduciary duty to shareholders. Unsurprisingly, the Act expects licensees and their ARs, when managing conflicts of interest, to put the client's best interests first [s961B], even if not in the licensees' or the licensees' shareholders' interests (Australian Securities and Investments Commission 2016i). Having to put the clients' and their shareholders' best interest first puts licensees in a Catch-22 situation. AFS licensees must always be able to prove they have given priority to the interests of clients over other interests (Australian Securities and Investments Commission 2016i). Yet evidence collected in the UK exposed financial institutions, such as banks, focus on profitability rather than what is in the best interests of clients or treating them fairly (Pain 2013). Seemingly, the same holds true for the US, when Finke, Huston and Waller (2009b) reported commission-based investments sold through brokers sacrificed best interests in favour of profitability. Recently, the Australian Hayne Inquiry (Commonwealth of Australia 2019) confirmed Bennett's (2000) argument, namely it is indisputable licensees are in the business to make money. Even though the client's best interest duty should legally trump shareholders' interests in practice, the Royal Commission findings (Commonwealth of Australia 2019) suggest otherwise. According to Rubin (2015), institutions' financial interests makes clients' interests secondary in practice to that of the institutions.

Smith (2009) found a shift away by institutions from merely profit making [shareholders' wealth maximisation] to ethics and social responsibility [stakeholders' wealth maximisation]. Yet she concluded in her study when behaving ethically is perceived as financially loss-making, then the question of what firms should do as opposed to what they actually do may, in fact, be two different things (Smith 2009, p. 62). Her quantitative findings confirmed employee advisers face conflicts between their professional obligations to deliver appropriate advice to clients and commercial obligations of business profit within their current advisory models. Fund managers or product issuers paid for licensees' main source of revenue according to data gathered during two ASIC reviews in 2011 and 2014 and the FS Royal Commission findings (Commonwealth of Australia 2019).[8,9] In the literature, specifically aligned licensees are seen as "*commercial businesses using advisers as a sales force*" (Parliamentary Joint Committee on Corporations and Financial Services 2014, p. 24) to support shareholder theory (Griffiths 2007, p. 231; Lindorff & Peck 2010; Kofman & Murawski 2015) instead of stakeholders' interests to develop social capital (Lindorff & Peck 2010).[10,11] Furthermore, in the *Review of Retail Insurance Advice Report*, it was recommended insurers remove misaligned financial incentives in their distribution channels being offered to advisers and licensees (Trowbridge 2015).

Maclean and Behnam (2010) maintained financial institutions struggle to manage their regulatory compliance when the legal requirements appear to conflict with or compromise commercial activities. They maintained resolving this tension is critical to ensure legitimacy. According to several studies assessed by Carnegie and O'Connell (2012), consequential legitimacy appeared challenging to measure. They found especially testing perceptions objectively to obtain reliable evidence. Despite these potential problems, this study assesses whether licensing advisers through third-party aligned licensees creates tension between the licensees' commercial interests and their clients' best interests to determine the existence of consequential moral legitimacy. The premise is if aligned licensees' commercial interests are consistent with the clients' best interests, perceived or otherwise, then licensing advisers through third-party aligned licensees is more difficult to challenge and existing licensing retains consequential moral legitimacy [Figure 3.2].

Establishing this legitimacy is important, Smith (2009) maintained further, because financial services firms owe economic, social, legal and ethical responsibilities to all stakeholders. Moreover, clarified by Griffiths (2007), focussing on immediate shareholder profits results in undesirable social costs to retail clients. Furthermore, Bearden (2002) pointed out financial interests can compromise advisers' professional judgement, hence damaging the adviser–client professional relationship of trust notwithstanding the quality in the advisers' work. Compromise is required for any incompatibility between the institutions' values and the adviser's professional values; otherwise, this will manifest into institutional-professional conflicts (Bamber & Iyer 2002). Consequential illegitimacy makes professionalisation of advisers illusive.

PROCEDURAL MORAL LEGITIMACY

Procedural moral legitimacy studies the moral assessment of the entity's socially acceptable and desired economic and non-economic (Meyer 2007) practices, techniques, systems, standards and procedures (Suchman 1995, p. 579; Carnegie & O'Connell 2012). According to Carruthers (1995) and Bender (2011), institutions emulate, reproduce and implement these to achieve legitimacy. Documented by Banister *et al.* (2013), professional financial planning associations support their member licensees and advisers to put in place socially desired best practices, standards, procedures, rules and structures such as codes of conduct, educational standards and programs. This is followed by a strict compliance system of monitoring involving audits, supervision and training (Bennett 2000).

Yet some legitimacy theorists argued decoupling (Rocha & Granerud 2011; Cole & Salimath 2013) occurs when these formal codes of conduct, policies, processes and rules for legislative compliance differ from actual practice (Carruthers 1995) and behaviour (Scott 2014). Decoupling seems present in financial services, based on several pieces of available evidence. For instance, scholarly evidence was produced by Smith (2009, p. 319) when she demonstrated licensee compliance officers failed to follow internal procedures and policies, such as keeping appropriate records of advice and ensuring the integrity of records kept. In addition, in a review, the Australian Securities and Investments Commission (2017e) found that the largest banking and financial institutions' licensees were ineffective in overseeing their advisers.[12] They reported the audit process of a sample of 160 client files audited by the licensees' compliance manager were found ineffective in 25%, partially effective in 57% and effective only in 18% of the cases (Australian Securities and Investments Commission 2017e; Graham 2017). Smith (2009, p. 316) identified, irrespective of whether it was in the clients' best interest, practices supporting financial product sales and recommendations associated with their AFS licensee were evident among financial planners. Also the FS

Royal Commission exposed policies, procedures and practices of charging clients fees for no services (Commonwealth of Australia 2019).

Apparent in practice, licensees were found to employ business practice managers and compliance managers to monitor and supervise advisers to ensure they comply with the law (Australian Securities and Investments Commission 2007). Yet the available evidence verified compliance officers of licensees were hindered in their ability to discipline advisers when their performance or conduct was inadequate or to prevent compliance failure from occurring (Smith 2009). In addition, Sampson (2010) expressed, the product distribution role is performed without detection. Additionally, Carruthers (1995) theorised in his accounting research paper institutions decouple by developing relatively elaborate administrative systems so institutional rules appear technical in nature. Newnham (2012) and Valentine (2013) argued, licensees are adept at keeping in place actual distribution networks masquerading as sources of advice. For instance, product sales targets are set (Jones 2009; Smith 2009; Mennen 2014; Burke & Hung 2015) to 'encourage' their aligned financial planning practices and employees to achieve revenue benchmarks (Industry Super Australia 2014; Morris 2014), which results in their distribution networks promoting in-house products (Valentine 2013). Notably, Smith (2009), Starke (2013b) and Mennen (2014) confirmed the financial planning business of CBA, a bank financial product distributor controlled advice channels, set product sales targets for their salaried representatives and threatened them with dismissal to ignite a sales-driven culture of 'cross selling' and 'up selling.'

Equally important, practices involving setting sales targets to reinforce product distribution are evident internationally too (United Kingdom House of Commons Treasury Committee 2011; Inderst & Ottaviani 2012b; Brannan 2017). For instance, Inderst and Ottaviani (2012b) explored how product providers can distort advice by promoting employees achieving specific sales targets. Inderst (2009) argued, if combining the sale of financial products with the provision of financial advice, then opportunities of mis-selling and unsuitable advice opens. Evidence from the high volume of Financial Ombudsman Services complaints, mystery shopping findings and sales file reviews in the UK between 2005 and 2011 demonstrated consumers were at high risk of suffering losses from widespread flaws in sales practices [mis-selling of products] across much of the UK financial services industry (Ferran 2012; Pain 2013). Inderst and Ottaviani (2009) proved when the agents face greater competition for clients, compliance with a regulatory standard becomes costly for the institution, increasing the risk of potential mis-selling.

Secondary non-academic sources claimed Australian aligned licensees limited their ARs to recommendations of mainly products they select and assess for the APL (Australian Government The Treasury 2014; Sheehan 2016). The existence of APLs are justified by licensees as important for risk-management purposes (Stewart 2013). Furthermore, Hutson and Vonnessen (2003) indicated, designing systems for risk management, dispute resolution, client compensation and general compliance may be beyond even proficient financial service providers. Achieving an acceptable standard of risk management is challenging. For instance, to lower their risks, PI insurers require licensees to make provisions for APLs to prevent advisers from selling just any product on the market (Stewart 2013). Thus, investment committees will assess products for the APL for all their advisers to use to ensure product is covered by the licensee's PI insurance (Stewart 2013). Although *Regulatory Guide 175* (Australian Securities and Investments Commission 2017d) explicitly states advisers may need to go outside their licensee's APL to serve their clients' best interests, West (2009) and Stewart (2013) expected no reason why aligned licensees would want their representatives to retain, recommend or include a competitor's financial products in their recommendations. This practice is confirmed in the literature (Collier 2003; Parliamentary Joint Committee on Corporations and Financial Services 2009a) whereby most product-aligned ARs are expected to recommend the product of the parent institutions. In practice, ASIC shadow shopping (Australian Securities and Investments Commission 2003, 2006, 2010a, 2012c) and reviews (Australian Securities and Investments Commission 2016i) identified aligned ARs tend to favour recommending strategies linked to the specific branded products of their licensee.

Yet advisers have the opportunity to apply for one-off approvals, where an investment committee of the licensee will evaluate products not on the APL to either reject or approve for use by that adviser only (Stewart 2013; Australian Securities and Investments Commission 2017d). Despite one-off approvals, Batten and Pearson (2013) claimed advisers are inclined to recommend only a few key products from APLs including if linked to platforms of different investment choices.[13] ASIC found in a review the statutory fiduciary duty obligations failed to impact most institutions' APLs, except for a few amendments such as a reduction in the number or types of products on the list (Australian Securities and Investments Commission 2014f).[14]

According to Maclean and Behnam (2010), these forms of decoupling produce formal compliance programs symbolising gestures of myth, ceremony and window dressing. In the meantime, it is "*business as usual*" (Maclean and Behnam (2010), effectively manipulating backstage to maintain appearances (Kury 2007). To achieve a better outcome, institutions use their time and resources to create processes and rules for compliance purposes, instead of following them (Carruthers 1995). For example, ASIC found some evidence licensees adopted policies designed to meet compliance without adequate implementation into their business culture, systems and processes (Australian Securities and Investments Commission 2016i). Additionally, Smith (2009, pp. 316–317) discovered, when she considered the ethical decision making of AFS licensee compliance managers, not only was deceptive behaviour linked to a failure of the compliance systems and procedures of AFSL licensees to specifically prevent the unethical behaviour surrounding product recommendations, but also an ineffective ethical climate and culture. Valentine and Hollingworth (2015) supported the hypothesis, employees make decisions around an institution's ethical values on the basis of the verbal and non-verbal messages conveyed to them within a context, situation and around an issue. A more recent international case study (Brannan 2017) concurred with these findings. Namely, the culture plays a significant role in influencing the conduct of financial services operators.

Achieving procedural legitimacy is not as straightforward as following rules and codes (Considnine and Ali Afzal 2011) or having best practice procedures and processes (Maclean & Behnam 2010) in place as a defence against accusation of bias, imprudence or violations of the Act. Except for the inductive qualitative case study analysis by Maclean and Behnam (2010) of a US financial services organisation where widespread deceptive sales practices occurred, while a deficiency in Australian research with regard to this matter of undetected sales compliance deception is apparent. An Australian study discovered an ethical culture promoting ethical behaviour within AFSL licensees is dependent on the presence of formal and informal systems and procedures (Smith 2009), yet unassessed for their legitimacy.

Thus, to verify procedural moral legitimacy requires examining declarations licensing advisers via third-party product-aligned licensees has resulted in deceptive sales procedures, standards and practices designed to give the appearance [window dressing] of satisfying regulatory requirements, while reinforcing product distribution. If this is not the case, then there is no question mark placed on its procedural legitimacy. This information is significant, because Maclean and Behnam (2010) demonstrated decoupling the compliance program from practice results in the loss of external legitimacy, because internal legitimacy of the formal compliance program is damaged, which then culminates in unethical practices becoming institutionalised. Furthermore, it is well documented (Senate Economics References Committee 2014; Ferguson 2015; Commonwealth of Australia 2016b; Steen, McGrath & Wong 2016) the government is concerned about the detriment of misconduct within financial services. Regulators internationally consider at the root of many conduct risks is the exploitation of conflicts of interest built into financial sector structures, processes and management over time (Australian Securities and Investments Commission 2016i). Moreover, Smith (2009) maintained, AFS licensees do not have the breadth of systems and procedures in place necessary to ensure an effective ethical climate and culture.

STRUCTURAL MORAL LEGITIMACY

Structural moral legitimacy is defined by Suchman (1995) as the moral evaluation of the adoption of formal structures acceptable to society to make it the appropriate structure for the job. Thus, this research considers whether the licensing system is "*worthy of support because its structural characteristics locate it within a morally favoured taxonomic category*" (Suchman 1995, p. 581). Applying this definition to financial planning theory within the context of the current licensing regime was challenging at first, because Suchman (1995) noticed similarity between procedural and structural *legitimacy*. However, he distinguished between them as follows: (1) procedural depends on "*discrete routines viewed in isolation*" (Suchman 1995, p. 581), namely do the product-aligned licensees control their affiliated advisers to distribute their in-house products? (2) structural depends on whether "*entire systems of activities recur consistently over time*" (Suchman 1995, p. 581) namely do advisers structurally licensed via licensees confront conflict of interest from association?

Extending the foregoing within the context of the current licensing regime, the Parliamentary Joint Committee on Corporations and Financial Services (2009a) confirmed conflicts between advisers and their clients arise from licensee ownership structures. Conflict of interest from association with the associated agency problems is a long-standing issue, because Davis (1995) claimed a conflict of interest from association is at odds with aligning financial advisers' interest to that of the client's interests. Additionally, Smith (2009, p. 317) wrote, AFS ownership structures of institutions, together with the management of the conflicts of interest linked with these ownership structures, contributed to advisers' unethical behaviour. ASIC agreed, when a legal relationship between product issuers and advisers were shared, this results in conflicts of interest (Money Management 2014). Valentine (2013) identified, more specifically, the conflict of interest where product providers, for example, banks and insurance institutions, owned financial advisory services businesses.

Controversial debate in the media has revolved around advisers being viewed as quasi-employees controlled by their licensees (Pokrajac 2014). This situation creates institutional-professional conflicts (Bamber & Iyer 2002). This conflict may be a problem, because Smith, Armstrong and Francis (2009) determined in their research licensees lack the breadth within their systems and procedures to ensure an effective ethical climate and culture for professional advisers. Smith (2009, p. 66) questioned whether advisers can balance their professional agency obligations to their clients with their agency responsibilities to their licensees. Especially in the presence of a moral hazard when advisers face weighing the importance of their agency relationship with third parties against their professional obligations to clients.

A willingness on the part of advisers to observe professional obligations by avoiding competing with their clients or profiting at their expense is apparent, but this seems more challenging when affiliations to conflicted licensees arises (Collier 2003; Banister *et al.* 2013). The reason for this is the Act is encouraging licensees to exert legal control and discipline over their advisers (Carruthers 1995), while at the same time expecting them to serve the best interests of their clients. Smith (2009, p. 324) found, advisers felt tension between their obligations around profit, together with the pressure to sell financial products, which have led to unresolved conflicts of interest.

Many large licensees have adopted vertically integrated business sales models with platforms for competitive advantage (Valentine 2013) to develop financial products for distribution via their own financial planning advice channels through cross-selling (Mennen 2016; Steen, McGrath & Wong 2016). Furthermore, Sampson (2010) asserted, concentrated among a handful of large licensees is the ownership of financial planning practices. The purpose is to ensure an efficient structure and business environment for distribution, albeit structurally corrupt.

Steen, McGrath and Wong (2016, p. 3) argued the structural issue of the vertically integrated model contributes to the undesirable effects of information asymmetry, adverse selection and moral hazard consequences.

For instance, Suciu (2011) wrote moral hazard refers to agents' willingness to take excessive risks, because they can be bailed out during an adverse event. For instance, Pokrajac (2014) claimed advisers are aware their institutionally owned licensee is large enough and has the means to pay for remedies, such as client compensation, out-of-court settlements, and other legal remedies imposed by the regulators should they fail in complying with the Act. Notably, Egan, Matvos and Seru (2016) found in the US, misconduct is often more evident in some of the largest financial institutions, and lower in established older institutions managed by ethical executives with clean records of misconduct. On the basis of the actions taken against CBA and Westpac (Nehme 2010; Corones & Irving 2016) and the 50% of 414 enforceable undertakings accepted by ASIC over 17.5 years [1 July 1998 until 31 December 2015] concerning financial services misconduct for financial planning and wealth management advice (Bird *et al.* 2016), the Royal Commission on misconduct came to the same conclusions (Commonwealth of Australia 2019).

Interestingly, Young and Thyil (2014) found during their qualitative study some financial institutions' leaders hold the view individuals' behaviour cannot be regulated – only structures can be put in place for individuals to buy into. The premise here is the Australian financial advisory industry is buying into a formal structure without critical assessment or evaluation. Hence, to evaluate licensing's structural moral legitimacy means examining the claim, licensing advisers through product-aligned licensees results in conflict of interest from association. Valentine (2008) claimed the underlying structural issue of ownership of advice by product issuers is the crux of the problems in the financial advisory sector. Conflicts of interest are undesirable, because as we saw in the literature review (Goedecke 2001; Parliamentary Joint Committee on Corporations and Financial Services 2009a; Commonwealth of Australia 2014a), it misaligns adviser–client interests. Smith (2009, p. 317) suggested the management of conflicts of interest linked with licensee ownership structures contributed to advisers' unethical behaviour. The statements by the Parliamentary Joint Committee on Corporations and Financial Services (2009a) and Valentine (2013) with regard to the cohabitation of licensee–advisers being conflicted by ownership and their own products was tested and found to be true. Interestingly, the recommendations by Hayne on misconduct focussed on regulators and failure of legal enforcement and compliance to give the public greater powers, rather than the legal structural problems within the industry (Commonwealth of Australia 2019). In line with the views of Bearden (2002), the harmful consequences of the current structure include financial interests can compromise advisers' professional judgement and damage the adviser–client professional long-term relationship of trust, notwithstanding the quality in the advisers' work. Licensees seemingly control advisers like quasi-employees (Pokrajac 2014). Advisers generally do not have autonomy like other true professionals (Smith, Armstrong & Francis 2009). Furthermore, in support of the works of Scott (2013, p. 61), the cost and difficulty of monitoring the regulation through third parties, not necessarily neutral, is a significant problem.

This conflict is an important issue, because policymakers are trying to professionalise financial planning with legislation (Parliamentary Joint Committee on Corporations and Financial Services 2015) within an existing system plagued by conflict of interest from financial product association, ownership or affiliation. This trilateral agency structure qualified by the Act places the licensee in control, rather than the client. This puts the client at risk of conflict of interest from association.

According to Pearson (2006b), risks to the financial product retail consumer with regard to the regulation of financial services have not been sufficiently articulated. Specifically, the legal scholar Walton (2012) claimed, what is often neglected in regulation is a discussion on the real risks to individual members of the public when third parties are involved in a relationship. Along similar lines, professionalisation of advisers will likely be illusive so long as clients' interests are secondary in practice to that of the institutions (Rubin 2015). Pertinent is that conflicts of interest are exacerbated if the licensees offered monetary or other soft dollar benefits (Australian Securities and Investments Commission 2004; Pearson 2006b; Professional Planner 2017b).[15] Peretz and Schroedel (2009) mentioned, rather than product innovations, conflicting incentives for participants are the underlying problem. ASIC acknowledged,

> At the employee level, a conflict of interest could also arise when similar incentives or an inappropriate remuneration structure encourages the employee to promote group-manufactured products or platform products in priority to a third party's products, which may not be in the best interests of the client.
>
> (Australian Securities and Investments Commission 2016i, p. 14)

BOLR agreements, depending on their terms and conditions, advisers claimed, are an inducement for advisers to prefer recommending in-house products (Australian Securities and Investments Commission 2004; Pearson 2006b; Industry Super Network 2011; Australian Securities and Investments Commission 2016i).[16] These arrangements can be considered, according to Beal and McKeown (2009), as motivation to trap advisers to work with only one financial institution for most of their career. BOLR agreements sever adviser–client relationships when an adviser leaves a licensee for another licensee. Severed adviser–client associations are a problem, because NMG Consulting (2014) found in the UK once client–adviser relationships are established, clients are often loath to switch advisers, even for the opportunity of making small financial gains, because trusted associations underpin ongoing service arrangements (Financial Conduct Authority 2014c). Therefore, BOLR is not in the best interest of the client, because no continuity for the client is present (Kendell 2017). Moran (2014) and Kennedy (2012) concluded the current licensing legislation encourages advisers towards larger conflicted licensees to protect business value, save cost and obtain subsidisation of support services, while managing their uncertainty. Arguably, an *independent* adviser is at a competitive disadvantage by comparison.

In addition, qualified competent advisers lose their accreditation to provide financial advice when they leave a licensee. Although they may be highly qualified, competent and ethical, unlike other professionals, they cannot practise their craft unless another licensee institution employs them or they become self-licensed. Furthermore, advisers licensed through a third-party commercial conflicted rather than a professional *independent* institution may act as a disincentive for potential new entrants to pursue a career in financial planning. Further contributing to the shortage of advisers is baby boomers starting to retire.

PERSONAL MORAL LEGITIMACY

The fourth and largely uncommon form of moral legitimacy identified in the article "*Legitimacy: strategic and institutional approaches*" (Suchman 1995) is personal moral legitimacy. According to the few collected works, personal moral legitimacy is achieved through the moral and social evaluations of the roles of charismatic individuals (Carnegie & O'Connell 2012; Goretzki, Strauss & Weber 2013) exerting their personal influence to dismantle or create new entities depending on their vested interests (Suchman 1995). Mainly the role changes of influential individuals and their impact on legitimacy is discussed in the literature (Goretzki, Strauss & Weber 2013).

Non-scholarly literature makes allegations about certain key people as members of seniority of multiple diversified licensees (Vickovich 2014d) and financial planning professional bodies (Vickovich 2014c) with varying stakes (Commonwealth of Australia 2014d) presenting as committee members on panels to respond as lobby groups at roundtables (Vickovich 2014d) and private and public hearings making submissions (Australian Bankers' Association Inc 2014) to persuade or dissuade the government to increase or decrease the amount of legislation. Sampson (2010) claimed some financial services industry participants lobby government to water down elements of the reforms to protect the relationship between advisers and companies offering financial products. Campo (2014) confirmed this when she posted a blog explaining the FOFA reforms are being stymied by financial institutions who control around 80% of all advisers through their lobby efforts. For example, mentioned in popular media reports, Senator David Fawcett [Chair of the PJC of Corporations and Financial Services from 9 December 2013 to 9 May 2016], initially focussed on the issue of alternative licensing models for advisers during the Murray Inquiry (Vickovich 2014c; Vickovich & Garber 2014). However, seemingly, submissions and direct lobbying shifted the focus to other issues (Commonwealth of Australia 2014c, 2014b; Perri 2014; North 2015).

Earlier findings during ASIC investigations into the National Australia Bank Limited and Australia and New Zealand Banking Group Limited over their sales practices on separate occasions (Bailey 2000) confirmed a culture of product sales focus. Although unfounded, each contribute different, sometimes opposing, recommendations to the debate surrounding regulating individual advisers while simultaneously implementing competing training, accreditation and professional recognition programs (Reese 2011). In addition, the FPA allows their members to be affiliated to product providers. This affiliation makes it very difficult for Australians to identify advisers not torn between their client's interests and that of their licensees' (Moisand 2008b). Yet no research searching secondary scholarly literature has considered the influence of these influential men [and women] in this emerging profession, particularly pertaining to the licensing of advisers. Therefore, examining personal moral legitimacy may be substantiated by considering whether the contributions made by individual leaders of product-aligned licensees to the debate surrounding the licensing of advisers is mainly protection of their product distribution channels. If it is found not to be the case, then licensing displays personal legitimacy.

CULTURAL-COGNITIVE LEGITIMACY

Cultural-cognitive legitimacy is about an entity pursuing goals incorporating shared understanding, shared norms, common beliefs and common knowledge systems (Santana 2012) to perpetuate an institutional order (Kury 2007) based on cognition or awareness (Meyer 2007). Cognitive legitimacy considers the "*taken-for-granted*" (Kury 2007, p. 373) identity, roles, rules and performance of taking certain actions (Scott 2013). In other words, cognitive legitimacy is about "*this is how we do things*" (Kury 2007, p. 373) where elements of inevitability, necessity and replication or "*mimicking*" (Kury 2007, p. 378) of the status quo within such a belief system is present (Suchman 1995, p. 582; Durocher, Fortin & Côté 2007; Kury 2007; Carnegie & O'Connell 2012). Unlike the self-interest-based and judgement-based regulative and normative legitimacy, the source of this form of legitimacy is communal based (Kury 2007).

The cultural-cognitive actors [Table 3.1] include the media [external actors], the clients of advisers [external actors] and the individual advisers [internal actors]. The media stories and general rhetoric exposed, manipulated and/or shifted logics by which legitimacy is assessed (Suddaby & Greenwood 2005). Rhetoric, per Suddaby and Greenwood (2005, p. 39), is a critical ingredient to intentionally influence cognitive legitimacy. The media serves to expose the lack, or existence, of cultural-cognitive legitimacy. The reaction of the external actors, namely the public, by having trust and confidence in advisers further reinforces this lack of cognitive legitimacy. Notably, although the media, media professionals and their audiences (Pellegrino & Lodhia 2012) are considered as unfairly hostile (Harvey & Schaefer 2001), Bird (2011) is of the opinion, the role of the media in increasing accountability of the regulators, licensees and advisers should be recognised. Therefore, the news media coverage (Hoyle 2016; Vickovich 2017a) informs the public of aspects of deeds within the financial advice industry previously unknown or requiring some attention. The media thus creates legitimacy gaps or crisis, which run against the values and beliefs (Chelli,

Durocher & Richard 2014) of the public. Noteworthy is that many of the gaps identified come from media reports, although much of the news was damaging.

For instance, with regard to the shared understanding of the identity, role and performance of advisers, a press release about the main research findings of a Roy Morgan study (Morris 2013) reported, the public were generally unsure whether advisers were product aligned or s923A *independent*. They reported the majority incorrectly perceived and claimed, for example, Financial Wisdom [owned by CBA] or Godfrey Pembroke [National Australian Bank/MLC Australia] or RetireInvest [ANZ Bank] provide *independent* financial advice (Morris 2013; Vickovich 2013). What is questionable, Sampson (2009) maintained in earlier years, is the common practice for the licensee to own or have an interest in the financial planning group, to rebrand its aligned advisers so that the link is not immediately apparent to clients seeking *independent* advice. He maintained, and noted earlier when discussing conflicts of interest, further disclosure is often inconspicuous. Notably, this problem is not limited to the Australian financial advisory sector. Interestingly, Inderst and Ottaviani (2012e) mentioned a survey undertaken in Europe among 6,000 purchasers of retail investment products, where findings in this report (Chater, Huck & Inderst 2010) indicated, participants were ill-informed on conflicts of interest, believing aligned advisers provided completely *independent* advice.

Although elements of this cognitive concept have been researched, Scott (2013) and Yeung (2009) claimed this form of legitimacy is problematic to determine, because all the other forms of legitimacy have an influence on it. Despite their views, an attempt is made to determine cognitive legitimacy, by starting with the concept cognitive legitimacy is judged by placing an entity into a category or classification using identifiable variables, such as the observable structural properties and technical and procedural features of the entity (Bitektine 2011). Therefore, if the legitimacy to financial planning theory is extended and applied, then clients and their advisers should have, as Scott (2013) notably theorised, a shared understanding as to 'who advisers are' [identity] (Zimmerman & Zeitz 2002, p. 420), 'what is expected of advisers' [role] (Zimmerman & Zeitz 2002, p. 420) and 'how effective advisers are' [performance] (Zimmerman & Zeitz 2002, p. 420). In this regard, the perceptions of the internal actors, namely advisers, are the main concern, because operationally they enact the rules, while sharing, or assumedly sharing, common beliefs with their clients and the media (Kury 2007).

Although Faherty (2010) and my discussion in Chapter 2 pointed out two categories of advisers, namely advisers providing advice and selling product, Moisand (2008b) wrote, the line between sales and advice is blurred. The Australian legal and accounting professionals concurred that legislating and disclosing the difference between financial product sales and *independent* financial advice should resolve the best interest duty, APL disputes (Certified Practising Accountants 2014; Hewison 2014; Mitchell 2014) and misunderstandings by the public. One of the Hayne Royal Commission recommendations was disclosure of the lack of independence to address public confusion. Whether this disclosure will deal with the confusion when Bruhn and Miller (2014) demonstrated, disclosure does not work, remains unclear.

To assess cultural-cognitive legitimacy depends on establishing whether licensing advisers through third-party aligned licensees provides clients with a clear distinction between independence [identity] and conflicted association to product-aligned licensees [identity], hence *independent* advice [role] and conflicted advice [role], to achieve the objectives of the Act [performance]. If the distinction between *independent* financial advice and conflicted product advice is clear, then the author concludes here licensing advisers via licensees displays cognitive legitimacy. Clearly defining and differentiating advisers providing s923A *independent* advice from conflicted advice (Parliamentary Joint Committee on Corporations and Financial Services 2009a; Boutique Financial Planners 2014) is important to avoid clients being misled.[17] As was mentioned earlier, a Roy Morgan study (Morris 2013) provided some evidence licensees failed to display their affiliated institutional brand. Thus, placing clients under the misconception they are dealing with an *independent* financial adviser, when they were not (Vickovich 2013). Arguably, misleading clients in this way contravenes the Act, potentially leading to civil and criminal legal action and/or penalties against licensees and their advisers (Bird & Gilligan 2015a). Therefore, visibly defining and differentiating advisers complying with s923A from those who do not (Parliamentary Joint Committee on Corporations and Financial Services 2009a; Boutique Financial Planners 2014) is important to avoid clients being misled. Furthermore, an article in *Money Management* (2012) stated financial planning is unable to be recognised as a true profession until the public understands the clear division between financial planning and product distribution. North (2015) claimed for Australians to receive high-quality reasonably priced financial advice, the advice industry needs more advisers who are *independent*.

Individual professional licensing like other professions

A crisis, exposed by the media, according to Riaz, Buchanan and Bapuji (2011), forces actors to recognise the end and inevitability of change in practice. In agreement with the reasoning of Scott (2013), if the existing set of rules, norms and beliefs are under siege, hence undergoing delegitimisation, then it inevitably should be superseded by new rules, norms and scripts. Various researchers (see Suchman 1995; Zimmerman & Zeitz 2002; Chelli, Durocher & Richard 2014) have proposed various legitimation strategies in the company of a legitimacy crisis. Low (2010) theorised, once one makes a branding of 'illegitimacy', it is difficult to defend or repair the legitimacy. While a myriad of alternative adviser licensing solutions is available, the focus here is individual licensing to professionalise advisers, like other professionals. Hayne recognised in his recommendations the financial advice industry needs to evolve into a profession. Therefore, individual licensing is a consideration, with the underlying reasons expressed in the next section covering topics such as public trust and confidence, *independent* professional individual over conflicted institution, other professions licensing regimes, a single [*independent* professional financial planning standards board] rather than multiple licensing entity/ies [AFS licensees] and elimination of conflict of interest from association. In line with Hayne's recommendation (Deloitte 2019), an environment more conducive to professional ethics and individual accountability to improve protection of the public is evolving financial advice into a profession.

Client trust and confidence

FOFA reforms' purpose was to build trust and confidence in advisers (Ap 2011; Gray & Ireland 2011; Kell 2012; Moran 2014). Balasubramnian, Brisker and Gradisher (2014) found, trust is one of two most important determining factors to influence whether a person seeks financial advice. The other is cost. The legal fraternity refers to trust and confidence relationships as fiduciary relationships (Himstreet 2012; Lazaro 2013; Campbell 2014; Corones & Irving 2016).

The public is confused or unsure when confronted by advisers of various competing financial planning institutions (Beaman 2010b). Hely (2012) mentioned an ANZ Bank financial literacy survey (The Social Research Centre 2011) found approximately 42% of Australians distrust what advisers recommended. Nearly 67% of investors, according to findings by Australian Securities and Investments Commission (2013a) distrust advisers to take their fiduciary best interest duty seriously. In the annual Roy Morgan Image of Professions survey of 2015, only 24% [down by 4% since the previous year] of Australians over the age of 14 rated advisers very high or high for 'ethics and honesty' (Morgan & Levine 2015). A year later, the annual Roy Morgan Image of Professions survey found only 27% [up by 3% since the previous year] rated advisers very high or high for the same variables (*Independent* Financial Adviser News 2016b). Accountants were up by 6% from the previous year, rating 51% (*Independent* Financial Adviser News 2016b). These statistics are important to consider, because underlying elements of trust and confidence is ethical behaviour (Chua & Rahman 2011). Another underlying element of trust and confidence is best interest duty (Himstreet 2012; Lazaro 2013; Campbell 2014; Corones & Irving 2016). Trust and confidence issues are a difficulty for advisers and many other professionals in medicine, accounting and law (Bruce 2012; Burke *et al.* 2015). Given the continuing low level of financial literacy (The Social Research Centre 2015) among the public means clients need to trust professional advisers' intentions (Worthington 2006; Evetts 2011). US legal scholars agree, trust and confidence favour a long-term personal relationship considering one's personal circumstances (Black 2005; Kay 2012; Frumento & Korenman 2013). It is not, or should not be, simply a short-term, arms-length financial product sales transaction between strangers (Black 2005; Kay 2012; Frumento & Korenman 2013). Therefore, trust and confidence between principal and agent is imperative in professionalism (Evetts 2011, 2014).

Thus, the use of legal rules to create legal trust relationships (Haigh 2006), such as current licensing, is a potential source of distrust among the public. Kay (2012) believed an ethos of trust and confidence generated from long-term personal relationships and low-volume personal sales should address information asymmetry and misalignment of incentives. Additionally, Calcagno and Monticone (2015) showed non-*independent* advisers cannot solve the low financial literacy problem. According to the disclosures by most advisers, the lack of trust and confidence can be rectified with the implementation of an individual professional licensing regime. This finding further supports the discoveries of the Professional Standards Councils (2014), namely licensees confirm improvement in trust and confidence would be one of the many benefits of professionalism.

Independent professional versus conflicted institutional licensing

Although the numbers are unconfirmed, probable from the discussion so far, only a few advisers work for s923A *independent* AFS licensees. Most advisers are associated with various product issuers with numerous financial services business models, including financial advisory services (Steen, McGrath & Wong 2016) offering differing roles for them (Sanders & Roberts 2015). Even advisers representing themselves as IFAs follow the institutional model, whereby conflicted recommendations involve indirect investments and platform options, ignoring direct investments and 'off platform' options for clients (Vickovich 2017a). When product issuers and advisers are co-workers, this leads to conflicts of interest as a consequence of this cohabitation (Money Management 2014).

Sanders and Roberts (2015, p. 18) highlighted in a white paper, licensee–adviser licensing within the financial advisory sector together with the Act favours the institutional commercial licensee over the individual professional adviser. They acknowledged despite the "*legitimate legislative basis for this*" (Sanders & Roberts 2015, p. 18), it is contrary to the approach of professions where the individual professional advisers' obligations override licensees. Consistent with this view, research by Hackethal, Haliassos and Jappelli (2012) indicated, both multitasking and effective monitoring agency costs lead to institutions with employed agents, such as bank financial advisers, choosing lower standards of product recommendations to both unsophisticated and inattentive experienced sophisticated clients, than the more entrepreneurial *independent* financial advisers. Thus, private profit-seeking institutions are untrustworthy to regulate their own activities in the best interests of the public (Omarova 2010). Nearly 20 years ago (Bakir 2003), institutional regulation in financial services was suggested as becoming obsolete where institutional, sectoral and product boundaries were being eroded by technological and technical innovations in finance.

Additionally, Haigh (2006) interpreted, the introduction of the legislation through FSR has produced incommensurate levels of accountability in financial services nor tangible benefits to the public. Rogue advisers (Valentine 2008; Beal & McKeown 2009; Cull 2009; Chua & Rahman 2011; Fitzpatrick 2011; Kingsford Smith 2011; Taylor 2011; Walton 2012), for example Don Nguyen and Anthony Awkar of Commonwealth Bank Financial Planning (Staff Reporter 2011; *Independent* Financial Adviser News 2014a; Mennen 2014) could easily hide within large institutions. According to Starke (2013a), large institutions make supervising individual advisers for compliance contraventions problematic.

Prior to statutory fiduciary duty obligation, Gor (2005) claimed the burden of accountability rested entirely on the licensee to authorise the representative to offer financial services. However, post-statutory best interest duty has made individuals personally accountable to some extent, yet current licensing makes the licensee responsible for the actions of their agents (Smith, Clarke & Rogers 2017). Carlin and Gervais (2012) argued, when a retail client is financially hurt, in theory two parties are liable, namely the product provider [licensee] and their agent [adviser]. Yet evidently, in practice, despite licensees auditing their advisers to ensure they comply with the requirements of the licence, large licensees are ineffective in making individual advisers accountable when things go wrong (Australian Securities and Investments Commission 2017e).

Carlin and Gervais (2012) proposed the legislation must take into consideration compliance by the product provider regarding product quality, transparency and cost effectiveness. Important to note is compliance concerning the behaviour of the advisers in placing clients into financial instruments and the contractual agreements between these parties. Yet current licensing does not reinforce their best interest duty to clients, because evidence (Australian Securities and Investments Commission 2017e) demonstrates it makes identifying the rogue advisers within large institutions challenging.

For Considnine and Ali Afzal (2011), effective accountability necessitates the ability to determine the contributions of each actor, before apportioning responsibility to the true actors. Furthermore, important is the extent to which these writers view how the accountability is shared in indistinguishable proportions between two actors with overlapping vertical and horizontal domains and responsibilities. Vertical [e.g. managing conflict of interest from *association*] and horizontal [e.g. putting the interest of the client first] (Valentine 2013) domains and responsibilities between Australian licensees and their representatives under the current licensing regime occurs. No scholarly research measuring the extent to which advisers and licensees share accountability for breaches is evident. The reason may be because Considnine and Ali Afzal (2011) contended, identifying each one's contribution to the violation, as well as identifying individuals responsible for infringements within entities, is difficult.

Transgressions in Australia were at the institutional level, where licensees encouraged their agents to deliver narrow sales-focussed recommendations to their clients (Australian Government Corporations and Markets Advisory Committee 2012; Australian Securities and Investments Commission 2017e). Thus, identifying whether licensee, adviser or both are responsible for violations under the current licensing regime is difficult. This difficulty is confirmed by Dr George Gilligan during his submission to the Murray Review (O'Brien & Gilligan 2014, p. 7). He claimed,

> There is a certain imbalance between the privileged position that participation in the financial sector allows through the mechanism of the licence – which is a gift of the state – and what might be termed the civic duties and obligations that potential carries with it. We think the balance has shifted

> too far towards an almost automatic expectation of assuming a licence. This has been compounded because of the organisational context – many of the financial planners and advisers in Australia are employed by large organisations, so there is a diminution of accountability and transparency in relation to the activities of individuals who are selling products or recommending products to consumers.

With this issue being problematic, individual accountability affords strong incentive for agents to align their actions with the principals' preferences (Considnine & Ali Afzal 2011), namely the client as opposed to institutional-individual [licensee–adviser] accountability. Thus, questionable under the current licensing regime is how individual advisers can be accountable to their clients under statutory fiduciary duty, when they are not ***independent***ly licensed from institutional licensees.

Well-documented in academic works, independence is considered one of the attributes of a professional (Riaz, Buchanan & Bapuji 2011). ***Independent*** financial advice and how it is applied is recognised in practice by the leaders of financial planning professional associations (Slattery 2014) and the Professional Standards Authority (Power 2016a) as a critical ingredient in ensuring the professionalism of the financial advisory industry. Corporation [institutional licensees] (Australian Government Corporations and Markets Advisory Committee 2012) and natural persons [individual advisers, including self-licensed advisers] are subject to the same licensing regime when clients do not receive financial recommendations from the institutional entities. Instead, retail clients develop a supposedly long-term relationship (Knie-Andersen 2002; Johnsen 2010; Siddiqui & Sharma 2010; Bruce 2012, p. 86) of trust with 'natural persons' offering recommendations in their best interests. Moreover, Considnine and Ali Afzal (2011) cautioned individual accountability is determined retrospectively when an assessment of the agent's actions by principals is made after the fact.

Providing an alternative licensing solution is important, because although current licensing may have made some inroads to protect clients, it has neglected to adequately define and categorise the different services advisers offer in a manner to assist the public to clearly differentiate (Australian Government 2016) between s923A ***independent*** and conflicted advisers. Furthermore, the structure of the current licensing system needed a review of this nature, as this is one of the determining factors of how licensees and their advisers define and develop their business models. From observations made by Sanders and Roberts (2015, p. 11), as financial planning professionalises, one of the challenges the financial advisory sector faces is identifying and defining the professional and seemingly non-professional roles.

Furthermore, Evetts (2011) discovered, when investigating professionals [specifically, doctors and academics] employed in public services organisations [hospitals and universities], he found professionals are closed to being controlled through managerial interventions and institutional controls. His research established, accompanied by high status, these professional groups have autonomy over their work practices, providing them with power and authority. Furthermore, for him it is difficult to measure and standardise these professionals' outputs or their work. In other words, they cannot be controlled using institutions or the market. His findings showed the state-employee medical practitioners use their cultural authority and legitimacy to maintain dominance to retain occupational control of work processes and relations with their patients. According to him, what is detrimental to professionalism are institutional audits, targets and key performance indicators, because they lead to distorting work processes, procedures and priorities, while causing 'unintended' consequences for the doctors and their patients. Arguably, professionalising advisers will lead to similar detriments, albeit absent under the current institutional licensing model. Evetts (2011) recommended, a practitioner's identity, work culture and opportunity to engage with peers all contribute to improving professionalism benefiting practitioner and patient.

A matter of contention is whether institutions and 'natural persons' should be subject to the same regulations. Many authors agreed (see, e.g. North 2015; Australian Securities and Investments Commission 2017b; Smith, Clarke & Rogers 2017; Vickovich 2017a), professional independence is a key controversial issue facing the advisory sector. From the discussion so far, the focus of previous studies, but with scant attention, has been on corporate licensing of advisers. Serpell (2008) supports the view of individual advisers having a separate standalone licensing or registration system, separate from financial product and service institutions. Financial planning is a multidisciplinary profession, which can support a standalone regulatory system (Macey 2002b). Especially as the financial planning discipline increasingly specialises, the need to develop standards for comprehensive advice separate from specialities along similar lines to medical boards responsible for reviewing medical specialities is inevitable (Macey 2002a). Thus, it is time to consider individual licensing of 'natural persons,' like other professions. Especially when principally this system of institutional licensing is absent in other true professions.

Advisers' affiliation to product issuers threatens **independence**. Under-representation of *independent* advisers is undesirable, because Australians trust *independent* over conflicted advice more (Egan 2008; Australian Securities and Investments Commission 2010b). Advisers seek independence from licensees, because it would remove advisers from being bonded to an employer and/or licensee. Independence will provide the power and autonomy required to manage better any undue force from licensees to sell products. Seemingly, the system the adviser is forced to operate within is a contributing factor to contraventions of the Act.

Licensing, regulating and authorising individual advisers at the corporate commercial institutional licensee level, rather than at the **individual** professional adviser level (Sanders & Roberts 2015, p. 18), is preventing alignment of adviser–client interests. Largely problematic is subjecting the corporation [institutional licensees] (Australian Government Corporations and Markets Advisory Committee 2012) and 'natural persons' [individual advisers, including self-licensed advisers] to the same licensing regime when clients do not receive personal financial advice recommendations from the institutional entities. Instead, retail clients develop a supposedly long-term relationship (Knie-Andersen 2002; Johnsen 2010; Siddiqui & Sharma 2010; Bruce 2012, p. 86) of trust with 'natural persons' to provide recommendations supposedly in their best interests. Removing the connection between product institutions and individual advisers may lead to a culture shift the financial adviser sector needs to minimise the ongoing scandals (Steen, McGrath & Wong 2016).

Individual licensing in line with other Australian professions

Troubling in practice and the media (see Macey 2002b; Horsley & Thomas 2003; Moisand 2008a; Valentine 2008; Australian Government Treasury 2009; Parliamentary Joint Committee on Corporations and Financial Services 2009a; Smith 2009; Financial Services Authority 2010; Laby 2010; Ap 2011; Bruce 2012, p. 303; Inderst & Ottaviani 2012a; Knutsen & Cameron 2012; Frumento & Korenman 2013; Australian Securities and Investments Commission 2014f; Campo 2014; Financial Planning Coalition 2014; McInnes, Ahmed & Delpachitra 2014; Burke *et al.* 2015; fi360 FiduciaryPath 2015; North 2015; Rubin 2015), the Australian financial planning emerging profession is often compared to being similar in professionalism to other professions. Advisers have been likened to other professionals (Ap 2011; Bruce 2012; Knutsen & Cameron 2012; Australian Securities and Investments Commission 2014f; Burke *et al.* 2015). For example, just as doctors manage their patients' health needs following a logical process, so advisers do the same for their clients' regarding their future financial needs following a financial planning process.

Yet upon closer inspection, these proclamations of similarity are misleading. Medical practitoners may work for corporations (Breakey & Sampford 2017, p. 262) and/or prescribe pharmaceutical products from preferred suppliers (Everingham 2014), but they are not licensed by these third parties. Similarly, lawyers and accountants may work for large corporate commercial institutions, yet they hold professional autonomy and control within their employment roles (Rubin 2015; Breakey & Sampford 2017). Once accountants (Bamber & Iyer 2002; Institute of Chartered Accountants of Australia 2012), lawyers (Arteta 2016; Australian Bar Association 2016) and doctors (Medical Board of Australia 2012) leave their workplace, they may retain their professional status (Evetts 2011), plus their licence to practise and are permitted to continue working without needing to transfer to any licensee.

Therefore, upon closer examination, the way individual advisers are licensed makes this claim of similarity deceptive for several reasons. Despite this comparative likeness, Cull (2009) reported in her paper, some accountants do not see financial planning as meeting all the requirements of a profession in light of their historical and current embedded sales culture. What is missing in the FOFA legislation is the question of whether advisers are indeed able to become a true profession, in substance, like doctors, accountants and lawyers when not licensed in a similar manner as these professionals (Sanders 2015). Thus, Hayne recommended reforms to evolve financial planning into a profession (Deloitte 2019).

A substantial body of literature (see, e.g. Watts & Murphy 2009; Frumento & Korenman 2013) supports this perspective. Key attributes to being a profession include it being self-regulatory, collegial and client focussed (Bearden 2002). Bearden (2002) stated all of this adds up to a profession with status within a society operating within a recognised professional body. These characteristics give the profession its legitimacy (Cheetham & Chivers 2005). Initially, it was the legal profession adopting a self-regulatory model where its ethical standards are managed through legal professional associations, within law firms and by barristers using the rules of the court (Parker 2004). Accountants drew on the experience of lawyers in their efforts to professionalise according to Cooper and Robson (2006) by working together on an independence model (Carnegie & O'Connell 2012).

Surprisingly, Cull (2009) observed on the basis of her research results no amount of legislation has led the emerging financial planning profession to pursue self-regulation in their efforts to professionalise. This is surprising, given the advice sector can draw on the history, experiences and model of these other professions to develop their own professional licensing model. Bruce (2012, p. 344) observed, historically, advisers have not formally belonged to a profession or were formally classified as professionals.

Notably, a wide variety of academic research define these professions as altruistic in nature whereby they are oriented towards service rather than profit operating with autonomy within their job role (Rubin 2015). This has not been the case with advisers facing conflict of interest from their ties with product issuers. Distinct from the financial advice profession, the medical, legal and accounting professions are *independent*, structured and hierarchical (Riaz, Buchanan & Bapuji 2011). Noted by several authors (Riaz, Buchanan & Bapuji, 2011), in contrast to other professions, Australian advisers were not self-regulatory, collegial, *independent*, structured, hierarchical and client focussed. Nor do even highly qualified and professional advisers have professional autonomy (Smith, Armstrong & Francis 2009). Nor do they operate within a recognised single *independent* professional body with status within a society, as observed in other professionals (Riaz, Buchanan & Bapuji 2011). Unlike advisers, other true professionals are personally and individually licensed or registered with a national licence and/or with a state-based licence to practise; their profession in Australia via a professional standards board typically use a single enforcement body. Through their *independent* bodies such as the Medical Board of Australia, Law Societies of each state, Australian Bar Association, Institute of Chartered Accountants Australian Board and the CPA Board, Tom (1995) noted, all new entrants into the profession must meet their specific requirements, including specific entrance and ongoing membership requirements and standards of ethics, education and performance, on a continual basis (Breakey & Sampford 2017). Similar to doctors (Medical Board of Australia 2012) and lawyers (Arteta 2016; Australian Bar Association 2016), when accountants leave public practice, they can retain their registration with their professional association (Bamber & Iyer 2002; Institute of Chartered Accountants of Australia 2012; Certified Practising Accountant 2016). Therefore, once medical, accounting and legal professionals acquire a license or become registered, they never lose their licence to practise their profession unless barred by their *independent* professional bodies. This contrasts with what happens to Australian advisers. According to Clayton Utz Financial Services Reform Group (2002), advisers lose their ability to earn a living once they leave a licensee. They either must join another licensee or apply for their own licence. Although unconfirmed, this could act as a disincentive for potential new entrants to pursue a career as a financial adviser, notwithstanding the loss individuals highly skilled in financial advice who do not wish to be authorised via an institutional AFSL model. Despite competent advisers investing in degree qualifications, unless affiliated to a licensee, they are no longer legally or technically 'authorised' to provide financial advice. This contributes to the shortages of professional advisers, and more so the *independents*. The professional associations of other professions, such as the CPA Australia, Institute of Chartered Accountants Australia and Law Society of NSW are formally recognised as professions under the Professional Standards legislation and schemes (Sanders & Roberts 2015). The entrants are required to meet entry prerequisites, formalised education, ongoing training and work experience.

Doctors, lawyers and accountants possess independence, knowledge and skills based on theoretical knowledge gained at a university or tertiary educational institution or a training provider where entry is on a selective basis in contrast to occupations of a more manual nature such as the trades and sales. They meet the five key elements of 40 separate units of a profession and professionalism (Sanders & Roberts 2015). Within this framework, they can work in different sectors of their profession with different competencies and specialisations. Unsurprisingly, advisers also work with varying competencies and specialisations, *inter alia*, estate planning, SMSF, age-care and retirement planning, as well as in different sectors of the financial services industry. Unlike other professionals, Schuchardt *et al.* (2007) confirmed advisers do not control their specialised knowledge and skills. Nor do they have any autonomy when operating under the licence conditions and engagement contractual arrangements of their AFSL licensees.

Reinforced by a substantial body of literature (see, e.g. Rogers 2004; Watts & Murphy 2009; Frumento & Korenman 2013; Rogers, Smith & Chellew 2017), contemporary professions are constantly evolving to address new challenges. Especially around professional ethics (Breakey 2017) autonomy, power and authority from corporatisation of professions and professionals (Evetts 2011; Breakey & Sampford 2017; Rogers, Smith & Chellew 2017), notwithstanding technological consequences (Greenleaf 2017). This includes problems created by large corporate professional services institutions employing them [corporatisation of professions and professionals] (Breakey & Sampford 2017) and of course, technology (Rogers, Smith & Chellew 2017; Smith, Clarke & Rogers 2017), specifically FINTECH disruptions (Morgan Stanley 2018). Like other professions, seemingly advisers face a struggle for autonomy, power and authority around professional ethics too (Smith, Armstrong & Francis 2009).

Importantly, Arman and Shackman (2012) argued, the Australian general public can distinguish between the different designations in the medical, legal and accounting professions by their title, qualification and competencies [specialisations]. However, allegedly with no compelling proof in Australia, they cannot readily identify the different designations for advisers (Australian Government Treasury 2009; Parliamentary Joint Committee on Corporations and Financial Services 2009a; Ap 2011). Financial adviser regulation covers various titles and are subject to different, and arguably inconsistent (Laby 2010), educational, regulatory and ethical standards. North (2015) was of the view lawyers, doctors and accountants of a range of skills and experience charging varying fees operate via regional and non-regional large and small practices across Australia with services provided to a broad spectrum of people. Along these lines, what sets true professions apart from the emerging financial advice profession is all professionals observe a code of practice and ethics. They also have the characteristic of being non-commercial. Qualified professionals are subject to discipline should they infringe upon the profession's code of practice or ethics (see, e.g. Australian Medical Association [AMA] 2009; Accounting Professional and Ethical Standards Board Ltd 2011; Law Council of Australia [LCA] 2011).

To promote financial planning to be more in line with the other professions, and following the footsteps of the UK's RDR, new legislation – the Corporations Amendment (Professional Standards of Advisers) Bill 2017 – aimed to raise the existing professional, educational and ethical standards of Australian advisers wanting to enter the emerging profession. To operate within the emerging profession, it is legislated by this law that all new entrants will require an undergraduate degree, completion of a professional year and passing of an exam, in addition to complying with a code of ethics and ongoing professional training.

Particularly important is the view of Rubin (2015) about confusion around titles and designations undermining the trust society requires to justify granting individuals professional autonomy. Bearden (2006) was adamant, uncompromised professional judgement without conflicts of interest is the most valuable service financial advisers can give to their clients. Unlike other professions, Schuchardt *et al.* (2007) confirmed advisers do not monopolise their expert knowledge and skills to practise their craft. North (2015) claimed if the financial advice industry is to be competitive and innovative while transitioning into profession, then similar features to other professions will be important. If advisers want to be trusted professionals, then Kaissar (2016) recommended they must first become a profession. As professionals, they are then answerable to their clients and their regulator, where they have the freedom to set their own standards of registration, education, practice, ethical conduct and discipline like other professions as proposed in the literature by Frumento and Korenman (2013).

Single independent monopoly self-regulatory adviser licensing body

While much has been done by the policymakers, according to Steen, McGrath and Wong (2016), financial planning has some way to go before it will be considered a true profession. However, it is argued here this maybe is not so, because government support was present during the Ripoll Inquiry (Parliamentary Joint Committee on Corporations and Financial Services 2009a), Murray Review (Commonwealth of Australia 2014a; Vickovich & Garber 2014) and the Professional Standards Authority (Sanders & Roberts 2015) for encouraging financial planning to professionalise by, for instance, considering self-regulatory approaches. Yet to date, no clear decisive commitment by the government to self-regulation has been evident, except perhaps setting up FASEA. Yet professional associations such as the SMSF Professionals' Association of Australia has called for a new licensing system to encourage a proliferation of *independent* advisers, akin to the Registered *Independent* Advisor regime in the US (Vickovich 2014b). Efforts by the FPA of Australia are focussing on encouraging Commonwealth policy to accept a so-called SRO (Taylor 2014). Therefore, self-regulation in the form of a single *independent* professional financial planning self-regulatory body to license or accredit individual advisers as true professionals is a possibility.

From the literature review, evidently the debate surrounding self-regulation is nothing new in Australia (Carroll & McGregor-Lowndes 2001), or abroad (Omarova 2010). Numerous government inquiries and public comment have spanned many years into the nature of self-regulation in Financial Services in Australia (Bell 1975; Carroll & McGregor-Lowndes 2001; Pearson 2006a) and the US (Gillis 1986; ICFP 1999; On Wall Street 2003; Powell 2008). Various speeches by regulators wondering about self-regulatory approaches (Pearson 2006b) complemented these inquiries and commentaries. Professional media in Australia has made anecdotal reference to self-regulation (Vickovich & Stewart 2014).

Omarova (2010) observed neither the US reform legislation nor the Australian FOFA considered the role of self-regulation. The researcher in this enquiry concurs with them. Any long-term regulatory reform in the financial services sector must consider the potential role of self-regulation (Omarova 2010). Notably, an *independent* professional standards board was mooted in the UK when feedback to FSA surmised this would potentially incur duplicative operating costs, roles and responsibility, as well as potentially lead to contradictory decision making between a professional standards board and the FSA (Complinet – Thomson Reuters – Governance Risk & Compliance 2010; Financial Services Authority 2010). FSA [now FCA] decided to focus on supervising the competence and ethical conduct of advisers within the regulated financial institutions as well as development of standards for advisers (Complinet – Thomson Reuters – Governance Risk & Compliance 2010; Financial Services Authority 2010). Yet US financial planner groups supported a single SRO as a means to restrict anyone else from offering financial planning services unless registered with the SRO and maintaining fiduciary standards (Thompson 2001). The merits of an SRO were considered by the SEC in the US, because SEC examiners are spread too thin trying to perform their regulatory duties overseeing advisers (Schapiro 2009). Specifically, FINRA believed, self-regulation is the most effective and efficient solution (Bhargava 2009) to ensure consumer protection and market integrity for an efficient and effective securities market (Balasubramnian, Brisker & Gradisher 2014).

Yet some authors disagreed (Hansen 2008; Powell 2008) on the basis that any regulation by the SRO would be too excessive. Powell (2008) found from an FPA survey, US advisers prefer regulation by a professional regulatory organisation such as the CFP Board, rather than self-regulation as investment advisers under an SRO board administered by the FINRA. For this main reason, advisers viewed the CFP Board better understands the difference between advisers and RIAs or registered representatives than FINRA or SEC. Unlike the SEC and FINRA, ASIC believes self-regulation and self-licensing at the individual level or a professional standards board is not an appropriate solution, rather opting for retention of co-regulation with licensee institutions (Tyson-Chan 2006; Australian Securities and Investments Commission 2012a). ASIC argued, self-licensing of individuals is difficult to achieve, given presently, financial advice providers of varying competencies work in different sectors of financial services (Australian Securities and Investments Commission 2012a). Whereas FPA called for self-regulation through professional association membership (Spits 2013). The same arguments prevailed in the US since 1999 (ICFP 1999), when the Institute of CFP and life insurers (Thompson 2001) opposed efforts by the US government to establish an SRO. The prevailing argument centred on the financial service community to be considered too diverse for this type of regulatory structure, as well as adding another layer of supervision.

Corbett (1999) contended self-regulation is an indirect form of deregulation. To the contrary, Omarova (2010) proposed it is not identical to deregulation at all, but a far more complex and flexible system combining direct government regulation with participation by private industry participants. For purposes of this study, Omarova (2010, p. 700) defined "*self-regulation as a regime of collective rule-making, a regulatory process whereby an industry-level [as opposed to a governmental or firm-level] organization sets rules and standards.*" In this way, they oversee, monitor and enforce compliance of the rules, while governing the behaviour of the members of that industry. Omarova (2010) theorised, self-regulation is a move away from policing the conduct of financial institutions to a more comprehensive idea.

The literature review revealed numerous advantages and disadvantages of industry self-regulation. For example, compared with regulators regulating financial service sector-wide conduct, industry self-regulation supplements the law with more effective governance setting, customer service or technical standards in the presence of the potential for commercial interests to undermine standards (Commonwealth of Australia 2014a). Ojo (2011) construed, contribution to the advantages of self-regulation included proximity, flexibility, compliance and resources. Supported by the writings of Omarova (2010), Ojo (2011) claimed, in contrast to government regulators, self-regulatory institutions can identify, assess and resolve problems and obtain information quicker, because of their closer access to the industry. However, he warned, proximity to the industry can be a disadvantage of self-regulation, especially when conflicts of interest are present. For the reason, political limitations and processes faced by regulators, especially during times of unpopular or difficult decisions, make self-regulation much more flexible. In addition to articulating the theoretical basis for a self-regulatory body, Overton (2008) believed this body is more likely to commit to greater compliance. However, he does caution, this will depend on adequate disciplining of serious perpetrators breaching the rules. Pearson (2006b) claimed self-regulation might reduce the costs for government and business, if targeted and needs specific. From a funding point of view, Overton (2008) felt it is easier to procure resources through a self-regulatory private institution as opposed to through the government. Yet not everyone agrees costs will decrease, because for some stakeholders in Australia (Sanders & Roberts 2015) and in the US (Tittsworth 2013), it is likely to send many businesses into insolvency. Notwithstanding the increase to advice costs for financial planning clients from regulatory reforms and changing the licensing model (Mennen 2014). Although accountants of Chartered Accountants Australia and New Zealand and CPA Australia supported individual licensing for advisers, they felt the individual compliance costs may act as a disincentive for individual licensees (Parliamentary Joint Committee on Corporations and Financial Services 2014). Yet, on the basis of a qualitative study to establish some of the challenges the public, government and industry face, together with the drivers and barriers with regard to professionalism (Sanders & Roberts 2015), some financial services stakeholders interviewed felt the costs of compliance and regulation should reduce by 38% by professionalising (Sanders & Roberts 2015).

Despite the barriers identified, importantly the interviewees claimed professionalisation should outweigh the costs (Sanders & Roberts 2015). Furthermore, Pearson (2006b) cautioned, to achieve the regulatory objectives, self-regulation depends on not only the cost, but also how responsive to rule-making the body is, and the extent to which the regulatees engage in the process. Especially if Omarova (2010) is correct in trusting the ability of private industry participants to better regulate themselves within a dynamic global context than government regulators would be able to. Furthermore, Omarova (2010) argued, self-regulation, similar to professional self-regulation evident in law and medicine, is critical to the proper functioning of the financial services industry. Although papers written on self-regulation for professions such as for legal (Parker 1999, 2004) and accounting (Cooper & Robson 2006; Raar 2008) are around, this has been more the case in the US, with less research evident in Australian financial planning literature. This is surprising, because a white paper (Sanders & Roberts 2015) and several legal journal articles (Tuch 2005; Tuffin 2009; Sanders 2014) consider self-regulation as a viable option for the emerging financial planning profession.

It is well-documented there is the need to put in place appropriate, properly working systems to maintain the integrity (Thynne 2011), acceptability, credibility, approval and support (Considnine & Ali Afzal 2011) among all the participants within the emerging financial planning profession of self-regulation. If the government is serious about professionalising financial planning, then *independent* financial planning professional education, registration, competence, conduct and disciplinary standards board is the proposed model for individual licensing of advisers to ensure financial planning moves towards a recognised profession operating in a similar manner to other professions. By linking into the government regulatory purpose, this professional body would then enforce their own conditions of membership, formulate their own rules, carry out their own discipline and impose their own conditions of dismissal (Black 1996). For instance, according to the white paper by Sanders and Roberts (2015), for a profession to exist requires a self-regulatory entity, regulated by the Professional Standards Board as qualified by the professional standards regulation. On behalf of the Australian public, this entity oversees and administers professional entry, professional standards of educational and ethics, a professional year requirement as well as registration examination requirements, notwithstanding the compliance expectations (Sanders & Roberts 2015). Included in its list of requirements, the professional must be a member of a professional body operating under a Professional Standards Scheme approved by the Professional Standards Councils. If advisers were to become true professionals, they would need to observe the regulations governing professions, namely the state-based Professional Standards Act(Power 2016a).[18] Applied to individual licensing of advisers effectively means regulating advisers at the individual financial planning professional level, not regulator ASIC or institutional licensee level.

Thus, a single *independent* professional financial planning body to set the rules and standards to govern the entry, behaviour and exit of the members of the emerging profession, while monitoring and enforcing compliance rules specific to advisers, should be a consideration by policymakers. ASIC lacks confidence one industry body can effectively be disciplined enough to enforce a self-regulatory code across the different industry sectors (Australian Securities and Investments Commission 2012a). Yet Sanders and Roberts (2015, p. 20) agreed, if the rules and "*regulations are specified, administered and enforced by a combination of the state and the regulated organisations,*" it will lead to a principle-based, rather than rules-based approach. In other words, the government identifies and legislates the principles and the profession regulates the detail to regulation (Sanders & Roberts 2015).

Recently, the government has made a concerted move towards a single professional body to set rules and standards to govern behaviour of advisers with the passing of the Corporations Amendment (Professional Standards of Financial Advisers) Bill 2017 and setting up of the FASEA (Newnham 2017). FASEA will be responsible for governing the conduct of financial advice professionals whereby all advisers will complete mandatory educational and training requirements and an industry exam, and will adhere to a Code of Ethics commencing 1 January 2019 (O'Dwyer 2017). Kohler (2017) is raising some important points in popular media to make everyone aware so they start thinking about this new body. Specifically, he claimed it is unclear how FASEA and the licensing powers of the Australian Securities and Investments Commission will work together. For instance, he noted advisers must now comply with ASIC and FASEA requirements. ASIC can cancel advisers' authority to practise their craft for specific infringements of the Act and FASEA for breaching educational and ethical standards. Thus, he wonders if this an opportunity for FASEA to eventually be fully responsible for the licensing of individual advisers or not. In addition, FASEA's current funding model of being funded by AFSL licensees opens it up to conflicts of interest from association too.

Additionally, one of Hayne's recommendations is that a single statutory ***independent*** disciplinary body (Commonwealth of Australia 2019) could eventually lead to individual licensing via a single self-regulatory body.

Importantly, previous legitimacy literature warned, according to Suddaby and Greenwood (2005), any proposed and implemented new institution must attain legitimacy too. If a change to a legitimate new system occurs, then a significant difference between the old and the new system is required (Rao, Morrill & Zald 2000).

Where there are no existing solutions, innovators and researchers will identify the gaps to come up with FINTECH solutions (Morgan Stanley 2018). Interestingly, in the debate, there are some rumblings of using FINTECH to make compliance and providing advisory services more inexpensive, efficient and cost effective (Morgan Stanley 2018). Thus, discussions with Simon Hoyle, Tom Reddacliff and Troy Penney, who have respected track records within the financial advisory sector, indicated solutions to address these concerns are available (Hoyle 2017f; Reddacliff 2017).

Eliminate conflict of interest from association

Walker (2006) and West (2009), claimed the public in reality seeks advice free of all conflicts of interest. In light of Australian policymakers' push for professional standards advice to ensure higher standards of protection for the public (Parliamentary Joint Committee on Corporations and Financial Services 2015), conflict of interest from association should be eliminated. Applying behavioural research to the licensee–adviser relationship, evidently advisers face institutional-professional conflict within institutional licensing. To illustrate how advisers face institutional-professional conflict, this study briefly draws on social identity theory, whereby Bamber and Iyer (2002) proposed, individuals put themselves into either compatible or competing categories, social groups or identities, such as occupation and institution. Applying this to the current project, licensing individual advisers through product-aligned licensees allegedly has resulted in advisers having to choose between serving their clients as a 'professional,' where conflicts of interest should matter (Bearden 2002), while simultaneously being regulated by conflicted licensee institutions distributing product. This identification impacts their decision making and behaviour (Smith 2009). For instance, employee advisers face conflicts between their professional obligations to deliver appropriate advice to clients and commercial obligations of business profit and time pressures within their current advisory models (Smith 2009).

Abernethy and Wai Fong (1996) made the claim; institutions tend to mimic the behavioural expectations or rules of institutions within or outside their fields similar in complexity. Therefore, whatever the norm, irrespective of whether explicitly stated or implicitly observed, it will be imitated (Dolan *et al.* 2012). The manner in which advisers communicate, reason or understand information has meant they have been faced with choosing between internalising the norms and values of either the occupation, institutions (Bamber & Iyer 2002) or both.

Smith (2009, p. 324) found unethical behaviour because of remuneration sources is unrelated to the cognitive ethical reasoning of a decision maker. Instead, her findings provided evidence of the contextual factors, such as the financial services institutions' ethical climate and culture influenced unethical patterns of conduct associated with remuneration structures. By implication, the licensees' ethical climate and culture should, therefore, influence the ethical behaviour of their representatives. Thus, the corporate personality of the licensee may possibly interfere with the operation of the professional obligation of the adviser employed by the licensee. When institutions' values are incompatible with individuals' professional values, it manifests into institutional-professional conflicts (Bamber & Iyer 2002). Bamber and Iyer (2002) noted when studying auditors, a conflict exists between the institutions' wish for control, expectations of institutional loyalty, compliance with rules and regulations and professional employees' [agents'] wish for professional autonomy to maintain high standards when serving their clients. Within the current licensing regime, a similar incompatibility occurs between licensees and their representatives. Arguably, licensees subject to their licensing conditions and commercial interests dictate advisers' use of knowledge and skills to provide unbiased professional financial advice to clients. Accordingly, he surmised, this conflict between meeting institutional demands, while acting in accordance with professional values and judgements, needs some form of compromise. He added further, the greater the compromise, the greater the institutional-professional tension and hence the greater the incompatibility between institutional and professional demands. English (2008) indicated professionals working in institutions sharing the same values and goals as the profession are less likely to experience the tension between their commitment and loyalty to their institution and their occupation.

Although conflicts of interest can be managed, controlled and avoided through disclosures according to Bruhn and Miller (2014), they have their limitations. Disclosure to minimise bias in advice (Inderst 2009) is rarely the best way to protect clients (Commonwealth of Australia 2014a; Demina 2014). For instance, more than a handful of international scholars (see, e.g. papers by Inderst & Ottaviani 2009; Loewenstein, Cain & Sah 2011; Inderst & Ottaviani 2012a) held the view mandatory disclosure could be publicly harmful. Inderst and Ottaviani (2012a) found previous experimental studies predicted disclosed commissions might prevent clients overloaded with facts from effectively digesting all the relevant information. More recently, Egan, Matvos and Seru's (2016) research on US retail clients showed unsophisticated clients are often unaware disclosures exists and do not know where to source the disclosures or how to interpret them adequately. In addition, Inderst and Ottaviani (2012a) and others (e.g. Loewenstein, Cain & Sah 2011; Walton 2012) found previous experimental studies predicted any disclosures may lead advisers to be incentivised or morally justified to deviate from observing their professional standards. Specifically, Rubin (2015) generalised, disclosure and client consent could be used as reasons for advisers to dismiss their statutory fiduciary duty. Schwarcz (2014) provided an interesting discussion on the limitations and ineffectiveness of disclosure surrounding financial products, especially by their design and implementation. Rubin (2015) reasoned clients trust their advisers so much, they will agree to disclosures in error or out of ignorance, unaware of the full extent of any unintended future consequences.

Considerable evidence is available in behavioural finance theory, demonstrating the risk-averse public are irrational in making investment choices (Valentine 2013). Especially when irrelevant attributes of the financial products they invest in distract them from fully appreciating the risk of potential losses (Valentine 2013). Evidence reported by the Commonwealth of Australia (2014a) highlighted financial institutions and their representatives should consider their clients' behavioural prejudices and information asymmetry. Arguably, disclosure to minimise bias in advice (Inderst 2009) is rarely the best way to protect clients (Commonwealth of Australia 2014a; Demina 2014).

Although Angel and McCabe (2013) asserted, society tolerates conflicts of interest as inescapable, Tuch (2005) maintained complying by managing the conflict, and not necessarily avoiding or eliminating it, may leave institutions in breach of their fiduciary duty. This fact implies that not only are advisers and licensees at risk of unintended non-compliance of their fiduciary duty, but also their licensees. Schwarcz (2009) says this is an example of unintended, adverse consequences created by the regulation. Especially, if government commentators (Sinodinos 2013c, 2013a) claimed at various conferences in 2013, the political agenda is about eliminating conflicts of interest within financial planning. Hayne has a preference for eliminating conflicts (Deloitte 2019). Therefore, with this lack of consensus on some of the issues around conflicts of interest, this study considers the extent to which licensing advisers with an individual licence via a single *independent* professional body eliminates this. This is important because Bearden (2002) noted a defining characteristic of a profession is conflicts of interest matter. He stated further, professional bodies expect avoidance of conflicts of interest, because they theoretically damage not only the professional relationship of trust between adviser and client, but also the quality of work provided by the adviser.

Conclusion

Whether the appointment, authorisation and regulation of advisers through third-party licensees as specified in the Commonwealth Corporations Act 2001 is a significant problem is unclear. Therefore, questioned in this inquiry is the support for the legitimacy of the current licensee–adviser licensing model for individual financial advisers. Mainly because predominantly negative mixed messages from various stakeholders confront this matter without any compelling scientific-based evidence of what is appropriate for this emerging profession. Until empirical research based on a conceptualised theoretic construct is undertaken, a vacuum in financial planning scholarly theory and empirical research literature, as well as the myths and unsubstantiated arguments surrounding licensing advisers through third-party licensees, will remain.

From the previous discussion, the lack of academic attention to define, model and measure legitimacy of the licensing model was seemingly due to the difficulty to define and quantify the conceptual construct. In addition, financial planning literature on this topic is inconclusive and under-researched. Thus, this document addresses the deficiencies in financial planning theory on the matter of licensing with a conceptual model built on various established theories. Therefore, the proposed rectification of these deficiencies to obtain a balanced view is applying agency theory, legislation, Suchman's theoretical legitimacy framework and theory of the professions and/or professionals integrated with financial planning theory. This serves as a theoretical foundation to obtain conclusive evidence to validate the extent of the legitimacy of the current AFSL-AR licensing model.

By applying these theories, licensing advisers via third-party licensees as specified in the Commonwealth Corporations Act 2001 creates a dual-agency role. Advisers serving the commercial interests of licensees and the best interests of clients simultaneously leads to conflict of interest from association.

Debatably, this conflict is inconsistent with four objectives of the Act, namely aligning adviser–client interests, avoiding conflicts of interest, promoting best interest duty and encouraging competitive behaviour.

Consequently, threatening the legitimacy of the current licensing model based on criteria in Suchman's legitimacy framework extended and applied to financial planning theory. Therefore, arguably here if by ASIC outsourcing the licensing to product-aligned licensees leads to regulative, consequential normative, procedural normative, structural normative, personal normative and/or cultural-cognitive legitimacy, then the current AFSL-AR licensing model is legitimate. Apparent from journal articles and related secondary sources, financial advisers will enjoy regulative legitimacy by following the formal legal rules of the Act as enforced by ASIC. Normative or moral legitimacy is evident when the licensing model is perceived to display socially acceptable outcomes [commercial interests do not compromise best interests], procedures [not window dressed for compliance purposes], structure [no conflict of interest from product affiliations] and/or values [product-aligned leaders do not lobby legislators to protect their product distribution channels]. The licensing model faces cultural-cognitive legitimacy if, as framed by the media and accepted by the public, the Australian public can clearly distinguish between s923A *independent* financial advice and conflicted financial advice. Thus, contraventions of any of these criteria mean the current licensing model has lost its legitimacy.

Fundamentally, if the claim, the current licensing model is illegitimate, then proposals for an individual professional licensing model like other professions over the institutional licensee licensing model is strengthened. This thesis considers whether financial advisers should operate at the same level of professionalism with the same status, *independent* self-regulatory standards, governance and structures as lawyers, accountants, doctors or other professionals. In the last few years, interest in individual licensing of financial advisers in Australia by an *independent* professional body has emerged.

This epistemologically conceptual framework will serve as an important theoretical contribution to empirically evaluate and verify the legitimacy of the current licensing model for individual financial advisers. This enquiry will not only advance financial planning theory but also raise questions and provide a scholarly platform for further investigation. Furthermore, empirical data collected using this framework will provide policymakers concrete evidence to make decisions around licensing individual advisers without having to rely on unconfirmed claims. In closing, evaluating the legitimacy of the current licensing model is important in achieving the FOFA aim of protecting the clients of advisers and creating trust and confidence in the advisory sector by professionalising financial advisers into a recognised and accredited profession.

Notes

1. Commonwealth Corporations Act 2001, page 186, <www.legislation.gov.au/Details/C2017C00312>.
2. Commonwealth Corporations Act 2001, page 206, <www.legislation.gov.au/Details/C2017C00312>.
3. Section 761A and Section 916A of the act.
4. Section 761G of the act.
5. Regulatory Guide 181. Licensing: Managing conflicts of interest. Chapter 7 – Financial services and markets outlines the ASIC's approach to how conflicts should be controlled, avoided and disclosed.
6. Regulatory Guide 181. Licensing: Managing conflicts of interest. Chapter 7 – Financial services and markets.
7. Commonwealth Corporations Act 2001, <www.legislation.gov.au/Details/C2017C00328/Html/Volume_1#primary-nav>.
8. Report 251: Review of Financial Advice Industry Practice Report.
9. Report 407: Review of the financial advice industry's implementation of the FOFA reforms.
10. Shareholder wealth maximisation and/or profit maximisation.
11. Goodwill, reputation and/or sustainability.
12. Report 515: Financial advice: Review of how large institutions oversee their advisers.
13. Notably, platforms are not considered financial products under the present legislation.
14. Report 407: Review of the financial advice industry's implementation of the FOFA reforms.
15. For example, licensees offer financial support, invitations to overseas conferences or holidays, subsidised office equipment, shares in financial services companies, fee rebates, subsidised dealer fees, subsidised professional indemnity insurance, paraplanning support, training and continuous professional development, marketing allowances, transition payments and access to cheap capital and enhanced buyback agreements.
16. BOLR agreements are prevalent among one-third of AFS licensees (Australian Securities and Investments Commission 2011) who offers their advisers a guaranteed minimum sale value for their client base, usually when they retire or leave the licensee, and if they cannot find a buyer on the open market (Australian Securities

and Investments Commission 2004). The sale value is based on a multiple of revenue, with a higher multiple offered for the licensees' in-house products (Australian Securities and Investments Commission 2004).

17 Commonwealth Corporations Act 2001, <www.legislation.gov.au/Details/C2017C00328/Html/Volume_1#primary-nav>.

18 This legislation specifies for Australian professions rules around being a professional, with independence requirements being prominent. To gain access to the legislation that governs the Professional Standards Scheme covering every Australian jurisdiction, please go to <www.psc.gov.au/legislation>.

4 Research paradigm, methodology, SEM

Introduction

Previous chapters indicated unsubstantiated controversial debate about licensing advisers. Recommended by Black (2012), eventually any debate should move to peer-reviewed academic works. To achieve this, this chapter builds on the previous theoretical discussion with the development of the hypothetical model to test the legitimacy of current AFSL-AR licensing.

The plan of the chapter begins with stating the main research question, investigative questions and hypotheses. Following this is a brief discussion on the researcher's selected paradigm or research philosophy. Then the mixed methods methodology of choice for the research is recognised. Towards the end of the chapter, a discussion follows on the research design, together with aspects of the sampling procedure and research analysis techniques.

Research question with hypothesis

To evaluate the legitimacy of current AFSL-AR licensing, the research started with the primary research question. Put simply, to what extent do advisers agree the current AFSL-AR licensing is legitimate?

Accordingly, to find answers to this main research question, this chapter provides four proposed secondary investigative questions and hypotheses in Figure 4.1. Figure 4.2 highlights the formulated investigative research questions and hypotheses.

The first key point under investigation framed hypothesis H1 [Figure 4.1], namely the advisers' dual-agency role devised by financial planning scholars (Banister *et al.* 2013; Taylor *et al.* 2013; Beal & McKeown 2009) as the adviser–client and the legislated licensee–adviser agency relationships (Finke, Huston & Waller 2009; Kingston & Weng 2014). Thus, with hypothesis H1 [a] [Figure 4.2] it is investigated how advisers see, and hence, portray, their dual-agency role in practice. Recall Kingston and Weng (2014, p. 294) asserted advisers serving the licensees' and the clients' interest simultaneously leads to conflicts of interest in the adviser–client relationship. Therefore, hypothesis H1 [b] may provide valuable

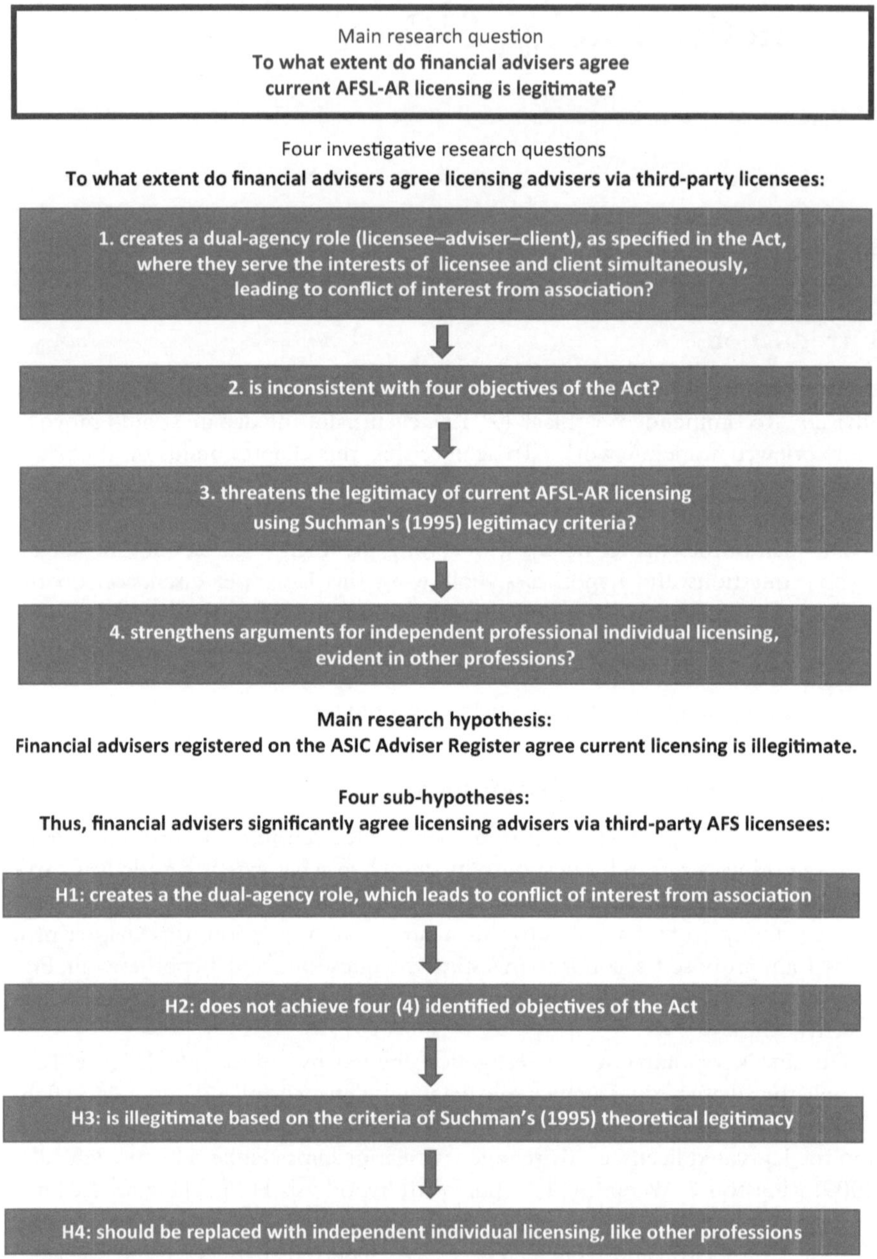

Figure 4.1 Main research question, investigative questions and their hypotheses.

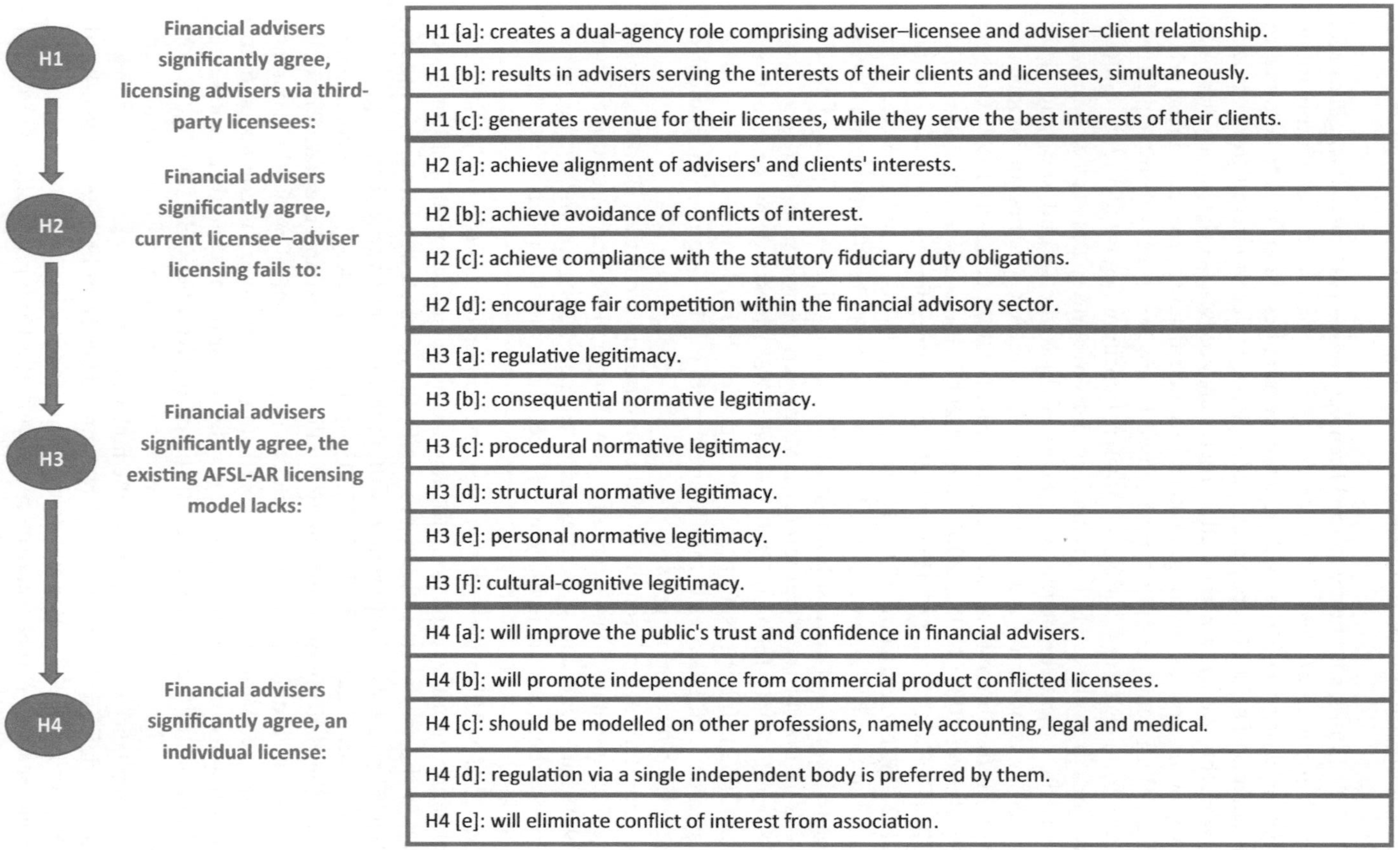

Figure 4.2 Sub-hypotheses to test the four investigative hypotheses of the respecified model.

insights into how advisers understand their roles under the current licensing regime.

In the literature, specifically aligned licensees are seen as "*commercial businesses using advisers as a sales force*" (Parliamentary Joint Committee on Corporations and Financial Services 2014, p. 24), while meeting best interest duty compliance requirements. The study, specifically, addresses conflict of interest from association, whereby advisers are generally structurally licensed via third-party licensees to earn revenue by distributing financial products from approved financial product lists. With remuneration from licensee to adviser dealt with by legislators, revenues from client to licensees via advisers remains a neglected and unresolved topic. Thus, hypothesis H1 [c] tentatively aims to address this neglected matter.

Next, the objectives of the Act [Figure 4.1] is the second key issue [H2] examined by considering four sub-hypotheses. The Act specifies the importance of aligning the interests of advisers with clients (Bora & Lewis 1997; Corbett 1999; Mutton 2001; Collier 2003; Serpell 2008; Jones 2009; Alexander 2011; Ap 2011; Ireland & Gray 2011; Kell 2012), so does financial planning theory (Black 2005; Nyberg *et al.* 2010; Finke & Langdon 2012; Inderst & Ottaviani 2012d; Knutsen & Cameron 2012; Mazzola 2013; Starke 2013b). Davis (1995) postulated conflict of interest from association was at odds with aligning financial adviser's interest to the client interests. Moreover, many articles (see, e.g. Black 2005; Bowen 2010; Johnsen 2010; Australian Securities and Investments Commission 2012a; Inderst & Ottaviani 2012d; Kell 2012; Kingsford Smith 2012) indicated cultural practices within financial planning leading to misalignment of adviser–client interest happens.

An important unexplored licensing issue pursued here is the acknowledgment of the Parliamentary Joint Committee on Corporations and Financial Services (2009a) that ownership structures serve as the reasons for the incongruence of interests between adviser–client. Hence, the reasons for hypothesis H2 [a] [Figure 4.2].

Persuaded by Valentine's (2008) belief the corporate scandals within the financial planning industry emphasised the need to place conflict of interest from association at the forefront of further research, the research considered hypothesis H2 [b] [Figure 4.2] of importance within the context of adviser licensing.

Recall from Chapter 3, Tuch (2005) concluded, clearly an inconsistency between the regulations of managing conflict of interest and the statutory obligation occurs, requiring the institutions to manage, control or avoid the conflict of interest. He maintained, merely complying by managing the conflict, and not necessarily avoiding or eliminating it, may leave institutions and their representatives in breach of their fiduciary duty. Therefore, hypothesis H2 [c] [Figure 4.2] serves to highlight the potential danger of current licensing threatening unintentional compliance contraventions of the fiduciary duty.

Except brief discussions in papers by Simes, Harper and Green (2008), Bhati (2009), Milne (2007), Parliamentary Joint Committee on Corporations and Financial Services (2009a) and more recently the Commonwealth of Australia (2014a) report on *Future of Financial Advice Amendments – Details-stage regulation Impact Statement*, the secondary study revealed a deficiency in data addressing competitive behaviour between financial services providers within the context of current adviser licensing. However, Steen, McGrath and Wong (2016) claimed the high concentration and vertically integration makes financial services in Australia less competitive than the US markets. Therefore, hypothesis H2 [d] [Figure 4.2] will test the validity of these claims from the advisers' perspective.

The third key issue in Figure 4.1 is assessing the legitimacy of licensee–adviser licensing by considering Suchman's (1995) legitimacy criteria [H3] formulated into six sub-hypotheses. Addressing the lack of models to define, measure and assess the legitimacy of the current AFSL-AR licensing was the rationale for interpreting, extending and applying Suchman's (1995) criteria of legitimacy to financial planning theory. Legitimacy studies (e.g. Bitektine 2011; Chelli *et al.* 2014) indicated entities maintain regulative legitimacy if a perception of compliance with the legislation occurs. Consequently, the licensing will not enjoy regulative legitimacy as specified in hypothesis H3 [a] [Figure 4.2] should advisers agree licensing advisers via third parties can lead to unintentional compliance contraventions of the Act (Degeling & Hudson 2014).

The literature pointed out, the Act qualifies commercially driven conflicted licensees to exert legal control over their representatives (Carruthers 1995) with the objective to achieve profitability,[1] while simultaneously (Kingston & Weng 2014) expecting their agents to serve the best interests of their clients. Although Smith (2009) found in her study a shift away from merely profit making [shareholders' wealth maximisation] to ethics and social responsibility [stakeholders' wealth maximisation]. She concluded only when behaving ethically is perceived as profitable does stakeholder wealth maximisation come into play (Smith 2009, p. 62). Her quantitative findings confirmed employee advisers face conflicts between their professional obligations to deliver appropriate advice to clients and commercial obligations of business profit within their current advisory models. Maclean and Behnam (2010) maintained financial institutions struggle to manage their regulatory compliance, when the legal requirements appear to conflict with or compromise commercial activities. Moreover, they maintained resolving this tension is critical to ensure legitimacy. Hence, H3 [b] [Figure 4.2] validates consequential moral legitimacy will be deficient with regard to AFSL-AR licensing if a perception licensees' commercial interests compromise the clients' best interest is found.

It has been alleged licensees implemented legislated deceptive practices, standards and procedures to reinforce the product distribution role of advisers (Collier 2003; Lee 2007; West 2009), and sometimes without detection (Sampson 2010). Newnham (2012) and Valentine (2013) reasoned, licensees are adept at keeping in place distribution channels masquerading as sources of advice. Therefore, it is surmised with hypothesis H3 [c] [Figure 4.2], if current licensing is prone to encourage deceptive sales procedures, standards and practices designed to give the appearance [window dressing] of satisfying regulatory requirements, then it fails the procedural moral legitimacy criteria.

Parliamentary Joint Committee on Corporations and Financial Services (2009a) and ASIC (Money Management 2014) reported, conflicts between advisers and their clients arise from ownership structures, namely a sharing of a legal relationship between product distributors and advisers. Additionally, Smith (2009, p. 317) established in her study, a contributory factor to advisers' unethical behaviour was AFS ownership structures of institutions, together with the management of conflicts of interest linked with these ownership structures. Valentine (2013) identified, more specifically, the conflict of interest is where product providers [e.g. banks and insurance institutions] own financial advisory services businesses. Thus, hypothesis H3 [d] [Figure 4.2] considers, if a perception exists suggesting actors do not support the structure (Suchman 1995, p. 581) of licensing advisers via third-party licensees, then on ethical grounds, the literature suggests this model is questionable (Davis 1995; Smith 2009; Valentine 2013). Then AFSL-AR licensing displays a shortfall in structural moral legitimacy.

To assess personal moral legitimacy the theory implies requires the moral assessment of the influence of key people of seniority (Carnegie & O'Connell 2012; Goretzki, Strauss & Weber 2013) of multiple diversified licensees (Vickovich 2014d) and financial planning professional bodies (Vickovich 2014c) with their own vested interests (Suchman 1995; Commonwealth of Australia 2014d). They present as committee members on panels or make submissions (Australian Bankers' Association Inc 2014) to respond as lobby groups to persuade or dissuade the government to increase or decrease the amount of legislation affecting advisers. Each contributes different, sometimes opposing, recommendations to the licensing regulation debate, while simultaneously implementing competing training, accreditation and professional recognition programs (Reese 2011). In this regard, hypothesis H3 [e] [Figure 4.2] tested, if advisers perceive the contributions by specifically individual leaders of product-aligned licensees to the licensing regulation have the regard only of protecting their product distribution channels, then it can be argued licensing will not have personal moral legitimacy.

With cultural-cognitive legitimacy, clients and their advisers should have a shared understanding as to "*who they are*" (Zimmerman & Zeitz 2002, p. 420) [advisers' identity], "*what is expected of them*" (Zimmerman & Zeitz 2002, p. 420) [advisers' role] and "*how effective they are*" [advisers' performance] (Scott 2013). Therefore, hypothesis H3 [f] [Figure 4.2] verifies if the public can clearly distinguish between *independent* and conflicted advisers [identity], thus between *independent* financial advice and conflicted financial advice [role] to achieve the identified four (4) objectives of the Act [performance], then cultural-cognitive illegitimacy is apparent.

Finally, the framework finishes with the fourth key issue and hypothesis [Figure 4.1], namely whether a single *independent* individual professional licence should replace the existing conflicted multiple AFS licence. This question required consideration of five sub-hypotheses. Balasubramnian, Brisker and Gradisher (2014) found, trust is one of two most important determining factors influencing whether a person seeks financial advice. The use of legal rules to create legal trust relationships (Haigh 2006), namely the Act, to licensing individual advisers through third-party, often conflicted licensees, may have over the past few years contributed to the levels of distrust among the public (Hely 2012; Australian

Securities and Investments Commission 2013a). The same can be said for using legal licensee compliance deterrence mechanisms (Tucker 2009). Therefore, by implication, hypothesis H4 [a] [Figure 4.2] wonders whether advisers think individual licensing would improve trust and confidence in advisers.

It is clear from statements by the leaders of financial planning professional associations (Slattery 2014) and the Professional Standards Authority (Power 2016a), *independent* financial advice and how it is applied is a critical ingredient in ensuring the professionalism of the financial advisory industry. Hence, the justifying hypothesis H4 [b] [Figure 4.2].

Advisers have been likened to other professionals, including doctors, lawyers and accountants, within a prolific number of papers (Macey 2002b; Horsley & Thomas 2003; Moisand 2008a; Valentine 2008; Parliamentary Joint Committee on Corporations and Financial Services 2009b, 2009a; Smith 2009; Financial Services Authority 2010; Laby 2010; Ap 2011; Bruce 2012, p. 303; Inderst & Ottaviani 2012a; Knutsen & Cameron 2012; Frumento & Korenman 2013; Australian Securities and Investments Commission 2014f; Campo 2014; Financial Planning Coalition 2014; McInnes, Ahmed & Delpachitra 2014; Burke *et al.* 2015; fi360 FiduciaryPath 2015; North 2015; Rubin 2015). Yet these are misleading statements, because advisers are not accredited to practise their craft like other professionals. What is missing in the FOFA legislation is the question whether advisers are indeed able to, or should become, a true profession, in substance, like doctors, accountants and lawyers, when they are not licensed in a similar manner as these professionals (Sanders 2015). Leading from the foregoing, this research, therefore, tried to establish with hypothesis H4 [c] [Figure 4.2] the extent of adviser support for individual licensing like other professions.

Initially, a professional industry standards board was recommended by Parliamentary Joint Committee on Corporations and Financial Services (2009a), but mooted after consultations with the financial services industry, without evidenced-backed research. Nearly two decades later, in a bid to raise professional, educational, training and ethical standards of advisers (Parliamentary Joint Committee on Corporations and Financial Services 2015), legislation passed in 2017 included an *independent* financial planning standard setting body, namely FASEA (Newnham 2017).[2] This body is presently tasked only with setting professional standards, education and ethics. In light of the views expressed by Kingsford Smith (2014), namely a single monopoly body is the most effective way to regulate professionals, an important question with regard to individual licensing is advisers' attitudes regarding whether a single body should also be tasked with registration, conduct and disciplinary standards like other professions' standards boards. The co-regulatory or self-regulatory bodies tend to compete is the main reason she claimed. This competition, according to Kingsford Smith (2014, p. 19), tends to lead to "*a race to the bottom*" by conduct standards and enforcement. Therefore, licensing advisers via a single entity with monopoly powers will be a distinguishing feature of this profession. Leslie (2008) wrote further in his paper, most agency theory literature stated, the agency problem and related costs were undesirable and should be minimised, because it may lead to inefficiency in professional relationships. On the basis of the writings of Evetts (2011), if advisers become true professionals employed in financial institutions, they will be less open to being controlled through managerial interventions and institutional controls. Expressly, it capitalises on the advantages of monopolies, while overcoming some of the shortcomings of co-regulation or self-regulation via multiple entities. For instance, if observations by Toms Reddacliff (2017), a consultant to the financial services sector, are true, then ASIC and licensees are spending valuable resources to complete their duties when regulating advisers, often involving large volumes of complex data processed and collected from licensees on a daily basis using manual, ineffective and inefficient systems. Moreover, a single body may be more suited to deal with some of the new problems that profession and professional corporatisation through employment causes (Breakey & Sampford 2017; Rogers, Smith & Chellew 2017). Therefore, hypothesis H4 [d] [Figure 4.2] considers adviser support for a single *independent* body.

Although regulator ASIC is against a self-regulatory model (Australian Securities and Investments Commission 2012a), they acknowledged the potential benefit of individual licensing making employee advisers more visible to everyone (see Vickovich 2014c). Unsurprisingly, the Professional Standards Authority supports self-regulation designed for the advice sector (Professional Standards Councils 2014; 2015 Sanders & Roberts 2015). However, they can approve a professional standards scheme only if the financial planning body can demonstrate a high level of self-regulation by complying with the professional standards legislation controlling other professionals (Professional Standards Councils 2015). Also, Hayne has made recommendations for a single *independent* regulatory discipline body for individual advisers, which could replace FASEA (Commonwealth of Australia 2019; Deloitte 2019) or merge with FASEA as financial planning evolves into a true profession. Omarova (2010) argued self-regulation is critical to ensure the proper functioning of financial services. He reasoned private profit-seeking institutions are unreliable to regulate their own activities in the public's best interests. This reasoning is supported by evidence produced in report number 515 by Australian Securities and Investments Commission (2017e). Furthermore, Tuch (2005, p. 515) maintained, complying by only managing conflicts using disclosures may still leave parties in breach of their fiduciary duty. In rebuttal, Angel and McCabe (2013) asserted, society endures conflicts of interest, because it is unavoidable. With consensus absent on issues around conflict of interest from association, hypothesis H4 [e] considers the extent to which licensing advisers with an individual licence via a single *independent* professional body will eliminate conflicted association.

Research paradigm

To find answers to the research questions, the researcher measured and tested 18 sub-hypotheses [Figure 4.2] by engaging in the scientific research process illustrated in Figure 4.3. Before going on to look at a specific methodology, the researcher felt it important to consider the various research paradigms to start the

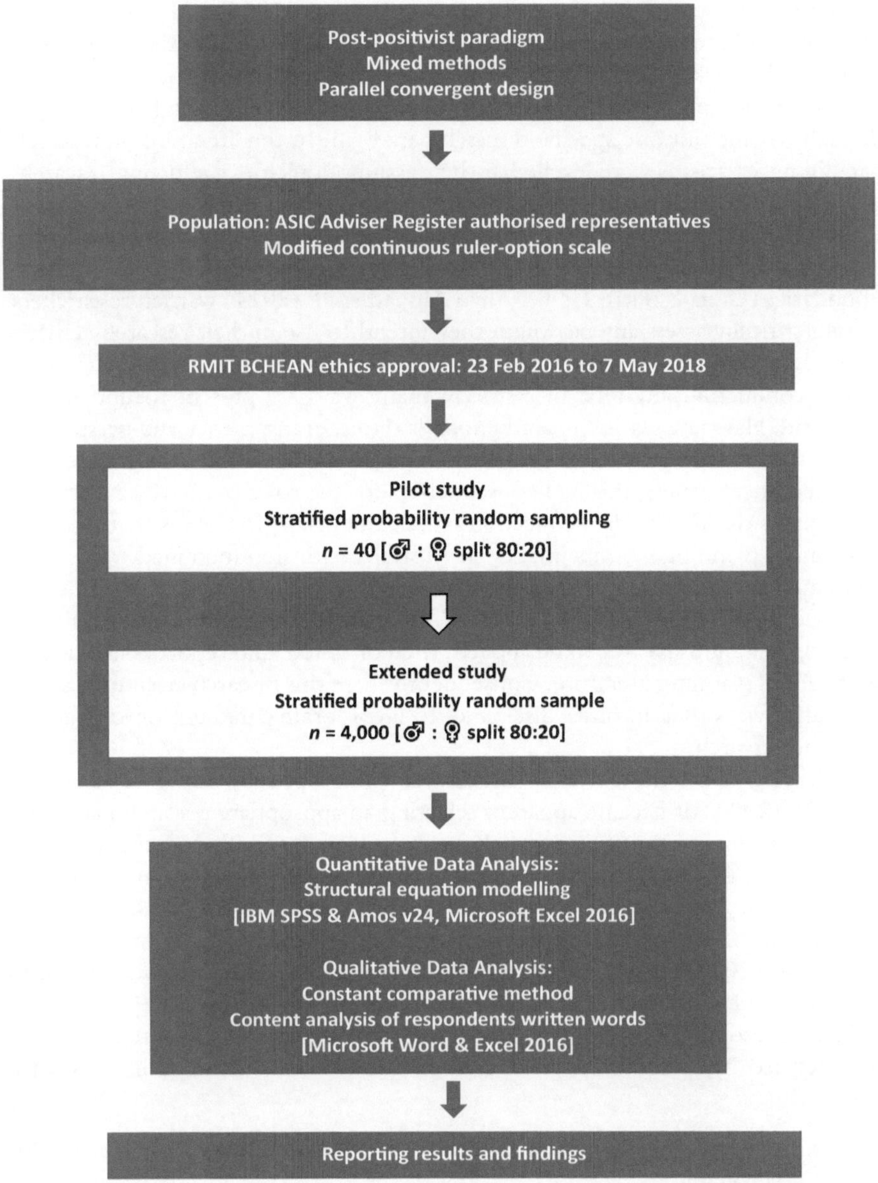

Figure 4.3 Research process for this study.

research journey. From the proliferation of the number of [scientific] research paradigms in the applied, social and behavioural science literature (Gioia & Pitre 1990; Willmott 1993; Creswell 2003; Mertens 2005; Kakkuri-Knuuttila, Lukka & Kuorikoski 2008; Caginalp & Desantis 2011; Taneja, Taneja & Gupta

2011; Venable 2013; Aliyu Ahmad *et al.* 2014), it was evident, the theory of the various research paradigms was still evolving (Willmott 1993) and changing over time (Taneja, Taneja & Gupta 2011; Venable 2013). Hence, the researcher concurred with Mackenzie and Knipe (2006) who claimed, this proliferation of new research paradigms is confusing to a first time or early career researcher, making it difficult to pinpoint one specific research paradigm. In the literature on research paradigms, criticisms were levelled at their assumptions for conducting research. For example, assumptions of mutual exclusivity (Willmott 1993; Kakkuri-Knuuttila, Lukka & Kuorikoski 2008) clarified in some research comprised overlapping multi-paradigms (Onwuegbuzie, Johnson & Collins 2009) with blurred boundaries (Gioia & Pitre 1990). Aliyu Ahmad *et al.* (2014) warned researchers should critically assess any paradigm they intend to use in their research activity. While Laughlin (2004) recommended, it was necessary to choose a paradigm, before conducting any type of research, many ways are present to understand the world. Having a research paradigm adds rigour, transparency and perspective to the research project. He explained further, once one made the ontological and theoretical choice, this had consequences for the roles of the researcher and participants during the data collection phase. Important to note is that research in financial planning is in its infancy in Australia with no sanctioned framework (Wiseman & Anderson 2013) adequately developed. Therefore, to ensure sufficient acceptable standards for research (Willmott 1993), the multitude of available research paradigms has yet to be applied, tried or tested, and reported in Australian financial planning literature. Consequently, here this research attempted some alternative ways used in other disciplines to incorporate paradigms into financial planning research.

Reflecting upon the writings of research philosophy by Lowe (2004) and Laughlin (2004), it became apparent selecting an appropriate research paradigm meant focussing on the main research question from a specific paradigmatic perspective. Even though other appropriate paradigmatic viewpoints are available. Therefore, in light of these recommendations, to determine a suitable research paradigm for this research, a framework classifying research paradigms developed by Venable (2013), as shown in in Table 4.1, was used. This framework was combined with the writings of Onwuegbuzie, Johnson and Collins (2009).

The philosophical view of the post-positivist paradigm was adopted, because the specified hypothesised *a priori* framework was built with the intention to

Table 4.1 Applied classification framework of Venable (2013) – post-positivist paradigm.

Dimension	*Value-naïve*	*Value-aware*	*Value-critical*	*Dimension*
Empirical	**Realism/Post-Positivist Paradigm**			**Descriptive**
Non-Empirical				**Evaluative or Normative Descriptive**

test hypotheses about associations through deductive reasoning (Arghode 2012). Moreover, these hypotheses were based on a framework originally developed inductively from extant theories from numerous disciplines [namely legislative, agency, financial planning, legitimacy theories and theories of true professionals] to investigate the licensing of individual Australian advisers. Consequently, a post-positivist [realism] paradigm was determined an appropriate approach. Thus, the study represented multiple and differing attributes, composing one [1] main research hypothesis, four [4] investigative hypotheses and eighteen [18] measurement sub-hypotheses about a single ***independent*** reality [the legitimacy of current licensing], which can differ from the reality (Krauss 2005). Therefore, in an attempt to find out the truth of the legitimacy of licensing, it was appropriate to test these multiple relationships in a linear scientific manner (Onwuegbuzie, Johnson & Collins 2009). However, on the grounds of the sensitive and controversial nature of the topic, it was clearly not completely a positivist study. Necessary was some qualitative interpretation of the quantitative data, resulting in entering the realms of post-positivist research.

To illustrate, by referring to Table 4.1, Venable's (2013) framework positioned post-positivist within three dimensions, where according to the literature it is empirical, rather than non-empirical [coloured light grey in column one of Table 4.1]. As far as the second dimension [last column in dark grey in Table 4.1] was concerned, this study involved descriptive knowledge to predict the way the world works without the researcher being completely value ladened. Philosophically, this research appeared descriptive and evaluative, because the literature review explained and predicted a qualitatively determined framework for assessing the legitimacy of current conflicted licensing, with some value judgements and interpretations of the literature.

Furthermore, it was important researcher bias was acknowledged throughout the research process (Wiseman & Anderson 2013). Therefore, the third dimension in Venable's (2013) framework included value-naïve versus value-aware versus value-critical dimensions [first row in Table 4.1]. Here, the researcher considered the different value perspectives she may carry during the research. Therefore, illustrated in Table 4.1, this project is post-positivist, because a theory needed revising by theoretical reasoning as well as some experimentation. This makes this paradigm value aware (Krauss 2005). After reading the works of Kline (2010), Krauss (2005) and Borsboom, Mellenbergh and Van Heerden (2003), it was evident for this research, one did not need to rely solely on the research objectives and the quantitative data collected, but also on knowledge about the choice of variables to analyse during data analysis. The researcher relied on the interpretation of the theory, specifically the theoretical framework. Thus, the researcher's experience, beliefs and intuition influenced the development of the framework. Therefore, it was expected this model would need adjustment if in anticipation it misfit the initial raw data. It was important for the data to fit the model, because then there is a valid model to interpret the theory and results. In other words, on the basis of the findings of the research, the model may need revision by controlling the variables to better predict the reality (Krauss 2005), because it is acknowledged, the model of Chapter 3 is not infallible. Thus, these examples of potential researcher bias in the way they may objectively perceive the real world is another reason why post-positivism [realism] and positivist paradigm views differ (Onwuegbuzie, Johnson & Collins 2009). Although it was not ascertained and critically examined [axiology] (Venable 2013), and hence not value critical, the researcher was conscious her values may have formed part of the research (Venable 2013). Every effort was made to minimise this.

In summary, this study is not purely quantitative, because the researcher and participants may bias the interpretations of the research observations. In other words, this research is not completely positivist, but post-positivist. Furthermore, this project is value naïve, because values are completely ignored during quantitative analysis in the research (Venable 2013). Thus, to encourage reliability (Carr 1994), objectivity (Carroll & McGregor-Lowndes 2001) and control (Arghode 2012) to this enquiry, the researcher wanted to be isolated from the randomly selected participants during data collection (Arghode 2012) and during data analysis, to avoid biasing the data.

Research methodology

Mackenzie and Knipe (2006) asserted, the research paradigm is the theoretical approach, whereas quantitative and qualitative data determines the data collection methods, analysis and reporting modes. Thus, during the literature review, previous research revealed, many scholars claimed measuring legitimacy challenging (Suchman 1995; Zimmerman & Zeitz 2002; Carnegie, Edwards & West 2003; Kline 2010). Most research evaluated legitimacy qualitatively (Low 2010; Maclean & Behnam 2010; Sonpar, Pazzaglia & Kornijenko 2010; Pellegrino & Lodhia 2012; Díez-Martín, Prado-Roman & Blanco-González 2013; Andon, Free & Sivabalan 2014) using mainly the case study approach. Tilling (2004a) warned research in legitimacy is a subjective activity potentially partial to the researcher's biases. On the other hand, Wimmel (2009) maintained, it is possible to measure legitimacy using structured survey questionnaires to measure perceptions of whether societal support for a particular system occurs. There is little evidence available relating to quantitative research measuring legitimacy, and particularly in financial planning theory. Van der Stede, Young and Chen (2005) clearly explained acceptable evidence is not dependent on the method, but on how well the method is used.

Caginalp and Desantis (2011) claimed if no quantitative procedure for determining whether a hypothesised effect has statistical validity is attainable, then the theory remains a philosophy, rather than becoming a science. The same applies for qualitative procedures. Although all methods (Clark & Creswell 2008) are suitable to research this project's reality (Krauss 2005). The decision to pursue mixed methods was based on the strengths and weaknesses (Carr 1994; Al-Dossary 2008) as well as the similarities and differences (Jean Lee 1992; Arghode 2012) between quantitative, qualitative and mixed methods (Clark & Creswell 2008). Furthermore, a mixed methods approach is valid under any of the research paradigms (Clark & Creswell 2008). The mixed methods design the researcher applied was the convergent parallel design (Creswell & Plano Clark 2011), whereby the quantitative and qualitative data collection occurred simultaneously in a single phase from the same participants using one source of collection [a single survey]. Integrating data forms into the overall interpretation of the results (Baran & Jones 2016) resulted in the numerical and non-numerical data complementing each other to provide a more comprehensive analysis than if done on their own (Classen *et al.* 2007). I chose mixed methods methodology (Creswell & Plano Clark 2011; Baran & Jones 2016), because this research integrated several theories for the first time.

SEM research design

To obtain a comprehensive quantitative picture regarding the legitimacy of adviser licensing, the investigator measured, collected and analysed the data following the research process of Figure 4.3.

Structural equation modelling (SEM) was my statistical technique of choice. SEM is a useful tool for the post-positivist researcher, because it comprises mixed components. Qualitative contextual information can be used within a post-positivist paradigm (Mertens 2005). SEM is arguably a procedure conducive to mixed analysis procedures, because it is a tool to describe, control, estimate, explain and interpret data while allowing for recommendations, particularly around relationships (Arghode 2012). Furthermore, before this study, SEM had been used in different disciplines (Kirby & Bollen 2009), such as accounting (Herda 2013), psychology (Anderson & Gerbing 1988; MacCallum & Austin 2000; McDonald 2011), behavioural studies (Hox & Bechger 1998), operations management, management information systems (Shah & Goldstein 2006), educational, medical and marketing (McNally & Griffin 2005) (Siddiqui & Sharma 2010; Al-Shirawi, El-Hajjar & Charles 2014), organisational research (Shah & Goldstein 2006), psychometric, biostatistics and education (Rovine & Molenaar 2001), other social sciences (Chiu 2014) and so the list goes on. Al-Shirawi, El-Hajjar and Charles (2014) used SEM in a study of the financial services sector in Bahrain (Al Qeisi & Al Zagheer 2015) to investigate determinants of knowledge sharing behaviour among Jordanian banking staff. Although attitudes (Jackson, Gillaspy & Purc-Stephenson 2009) or perceptions (Chiandotto & Masserini 2011) of subjects were evaluated using SEM, only a few studies used it in previous financial planning theory studies in Australia, but not to study perceptions of advisers relating to licensing. Consequently, on the basis of others' research (Bacon 1997; Chin 1998; Akhtar 2011), the team identified SEM appropriate.

By specifying *a priori* hypotheses about relations between variables as already discussed, methodologically hypotheses testing meant an element of objectivity is required. Priority was given to the quantitative data [Figures 4.1 and 4.2] and analysis (Onwuegbuzie, Johnson & Collins 2009). In this way, researcher's biases found evident in purely qualitative research are minimised for non-experimental (MacCallum & Austin 2000) as well as experimental observation and measurement (Lee 2011) when measuring abstract concepts. Tabachnick and Fidell (2007) and Hair *et al.* (2010), explained SEM can be used to simultaneously measure subjective abstract concepts as specified by the four investigative questions with concrete consequences. This methodology represents a series of hypotheses about how the variables in the analysis are generated and related (Hu & Bentler 1999).

Given the researcher was new to SEM, the traditional SEM methodology for non-experimental research requires several equations (Blunch 2008). This focus involved multiple regression analyses of factors of many interrelated dependence associations (Herda 2013) of complex hypotheses with a network of paths (Grace 2008) estimated simultaneously while taking into account the measurement error (McFadyen, Maclaren & Webster 2007). Maximum likelihood estimation [MLE] was the method of estimation, because according to Hu and Bentler (1999), it is the most widely used estimation technique for large sample sizes. In SEM, large sample sizes are samples greater than 250 (Hu & Bentler 1999). Measurement error is a special feature of SEM. Whereas for multiple regression, the predictor latent factors are estimated without any errors (McCoach, Black & O'Connell 2007; Kline 2010), SEM corrects for measurement errors (Kim, Pratt & Wallace 2014). Thus, this technique is useful in separating 'true variance' [variance common among indicators of a single construct] from 'error variance' or 'disturbance' [variance from other factors, including error in measurement] (McCoach, Black & O'Connell 2007).

Techniques such as analysis of variance and multiple regression analyse only measures means of observed variables, and certainly not simultaneously for all variables (Kline 2010). Thus, they were considered inappropriate. Shortcomings of SEM as a data analytic technique according to McCoach, Black and O'Connell (2007) include that it cannot solve problems in theory, or researcher errors of inference. They warned, any misconceptions and misinterpretations during statistical hypothesis testing, model equivalence, model modification, model fit versus model prediction and causality is important to note. Insight and judgement were critical to applying SEM involving covariance structure analysis and latent variable analysis (Hair *et al.* 2010; Nebojsa 2014) correctly (Shook *et al.* 2004).

Interpreting the quantitative data and results to make sense of it, Marsh, Hau and Wen (2004) theorised, was a subjective activity. Therefore, it was critical the researcher collected qualitative data to further appreciate the results of the associations between the variables, while obtaining a richer understanding of the quantitative results (Onwuegbuzie, Johnson & Collins 2009) from the participants' point of view. It served to describe and validate the quantitative estimates where qualitative views overlapped while collecting additional contradictory information (Feldon & Kafai 2008; Creswell & Plano Clark 2011). Especially, when Marsh, Hau and Wen (2004) felt despite the quantitative statistical results, two or more researchers may come to different factor solutions where the researcher served as research instrument as well. Post-positivist researchers should acknowledge and try to eliminate the possibility of this happening (Onwuegbuzie, Johnson & Collins 2009). According to Lichterman (2015), incorporating interpretative explanation is an acknowledgement the quantitative data collected is incomplete and needs interpretation of qualitative data to show what the participants meant in their responses. Consequently, the researchers integrated both data alongside each other at the interpretation and discussion stage (Creswell & Plano Clark 2011; Baran & Jones 2016).

Preliminary a priori *confirmatory factor analysis measurement model*

Using symbols from the McArdle-McDonald reticular action model (Kline 2010, p. 95), the model and hypothesis were graphically visualised (Herda 2013) in an *a priori* model with the assistance of the IBM SPSS & Amos graphic version 24 software [Figure 4.3]. An important aspect of this *a priori* model is that the initial model highlighted in Chapter 3 and illustrated in Figure 3.1 was based on well-grounded substantive theory (Blunch 2008). Accordingly, the structural equation model incorporated a set of observed variables and unobserved variables (McCoach, Black & O'Connell 2007). The abstract constructs in Figure 3.1 were all difficult to measure directly, thus some working definitions of the latent factors were designed. Illustrated in the form of ellipses in Figure 4.4, they were defined as:

- dual-agency role [b_1]: representing the extent to which licensing advisers via third parties creates a dual agency, whereby advisers serve the interests of the licensees and clients simultaneously, leading to conflict of interest from association.
- objectives of the Act [b_2]: representing the extent to which licensing advisers via third-party licensees achieves four identified objectives of the Act.
- legitimacy of the current AFSL-AR licensing of individual financial advisers [b_3]: representing the extent to which licensing advisers via third parties meets the criteria of Suchman's (1995) legitimacy theoretical framework.
- individual licensing as an alternative option [b_4]: representing individual licensing via a single ***independent*** professional self-regulatory body as an alternative licensing option for individual advisers.

No known measures to understand the latent constructs were available. Therefore, the preliminary endogenous, observed parameters; manifest, indicator variables; or factor loadings captured, estimated or observed the different aspects of the factors. They represented as squares in Figure 4.4 as follows:

- a_1 to a_4 [four endogenous indicators]: representing functions of financial adviser's dual-agency role [b_1].
- a_5 to a_8 [four endogenous indicators]: representing functions of objectives of the Act [b_2].
- a_9 to a_{15} [seven endogenous indicators]: representing functions of legitimacy of current AFSL-AR licensing [b_3].

- a_{16} to a_{21} [six endogenous variables]: representing functions of the individual licensing option for individual professional advisers [b_4].

The causal paths or hypothesised directional effects or direct linear effects (Kline 2010) of the model in Figure 4.4 are represented by one-headed arrows running from the exogenous predictor unobserved latent construct or factors to

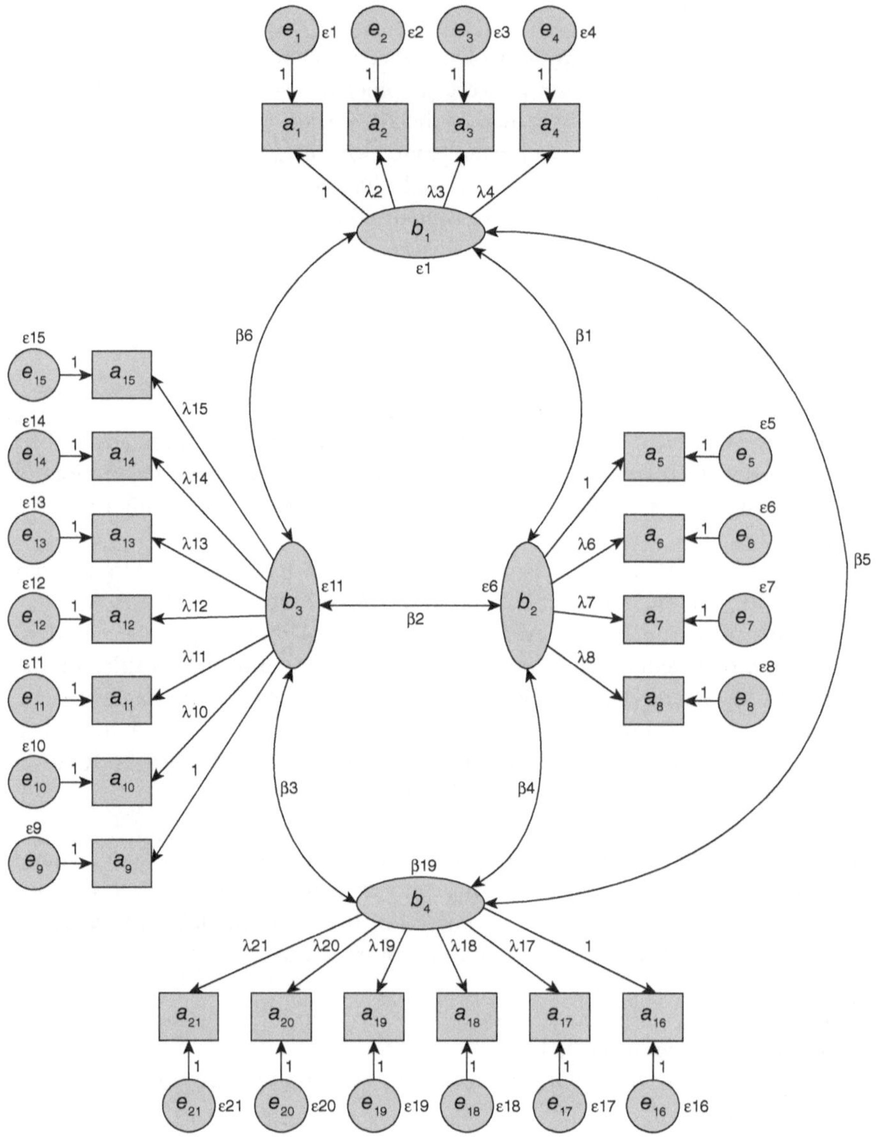

Figure 4.4 Preliminary *a priori* recursive acyclic confirmatory factor analysis model.

the endogenous measured observed outcome variables in the form of squares (Ullman & Bentler 2012). Mathematically, these associations are represented as λ [lambda]. They represent regression coefficients [path, factor loadings or pattern coefficients] in the unstandardised or the standardised model between exogenous factors and endogenous variables (Kline 2010).

Evident in the literature, when considering the relationship between observed measures and unobserved latent constructs, it is important to specify the direction of the regression weights (Edwards & Bagozzi 2000). They are either formative or reflective (Bagozzi 2007; Howell, Breivik & Wilcox 2007; Nebojsa 2014). However, when reading the articles published in academic journals on the matter, disagreement in some of the social science writings (Bagozzi 2007; Howell, Breivik & Wilcox 2007; Nebojsa 2014) about whether a social science study should be reflective or formative was present. In other words, whether a construct causes, or is caused by, its observed measures (Edwards & Bagozzi 2000). An underlying assumption for my SEM analysis is the items or indicators used to measure a factor are reflective (Shah & Goldstein 2006). This means the observed variables depend on the latent variables or are the reflections of the construct (Schmitt 2011).

Interestingly, Diamantopoulos and Siguaw (2006) cautioned Type I errors are more likely when a model is erroneously reflective. Therefore, decision rules for assessing whether the SEM should be reflective rather than formative (Chin 1998; Edwards & Bagozzi 2000; Howell, Breivik & Wilcox 2007; Bollen & Bauldry 2011) were established using a process developed by Coltman *et al.* (2008). Their process is helpful in clarifying the similarities and differences between reflective and formative features (Bollen & Bauldry 2011). Furthermore, recommendations made by Borsboom, Mellenbergh and Van Heerden (2003) made it clear to us the importance of defining the latent constructs (Rossiter 2002) in the preliminary *a priori* model in this enquiry. They must be *independent* of the observations. Simply, a reflective model shows any variation in the construct causes variation in the observed measures. Whereas it is expected observed measures do not cause variation to the latent construct (Bollen & Lennox 1991; Rossiter 2002; Coltman *et al.* 2008). To explain, if current licensing is changed, then effectively this should change the measurement of the indicators. For instance, the indicators: licensee–adviser–client relationship [a_1] and serving two principals simultaneously [a_2] are caused by the dual-agency role of advisers [latent variable b_1]. Another example, aligning adviser–client interests [a_5], conflict of interest [a_6], best interest duty [a_7], and competition [a_8] are surmised to be instigated by objectives of the Act [latent variable b_2]. Regulative [a_9], normative [$a_{10,11,12,13}$] and cultural-cognitive [a_{14}] legitimacies are triggered by the legitimacy [latent variable b_3] of licensing advisers via third-party licensees. Similarly, individual licensing [latent variable b_4] influences elimination of conflict of interest [indicator variable a_{21}] or promotion of public trust and confidence [indicator variable a_{16}]. Thus, this study is unconcerned with indicators a_1 to a_{21} predicting the latent variables b_1 to b_4. Instead, it is concerned the direction of causality runs from the latent construct to the measured items.

Furthermore, the interchangeable endogenous variables share a common theme, *vis-à-vis*, and the legitimacy of licensing (Rossiter 2002; Coltman *et al.* 2008). Thus, by adding or dropping any indicators does not change the constructs' theory (Rossiter 2002; Coltman *et al.* 2008). For this *a priori* confirmatory factor analysis model, theoretically a choice of a reflective measurement over a formative model is appropriate. The variable error 'ε' [epsilon], represented as a circle [e] in Figure 4.4, is the unexplained variance or unmeasured causes of the corresponding endogenous variables and latent constructs.

They are initially set to a scaling constant or unstandardised residual path coefficient of one, to give the latent factor an interpretable value, before the software can estimate it and not yield an undetermined result too (Kline 2010, p. 105).

This study is mainly concerned with the regression coefficients (Hox & Bechger 1998) between the endogenous [a_1 to a_{21}] and exogenous variables [b_1, b_2, b_3 and b_4]. Thus, in this way, the study estimates the unstructured population covariance matrix compared with the observed sample covariance matrix [the data set] (Schreiber *et al.* 2006; Ullman 2006). In other words, covariance tests the relationships among a set of variables to determine the existence of a match between hypothesised model and the sample data. Thus, this SEM research tested the extent to which four exogenous factors explained the 21 endogenous indicators under the assumption the SEM model was true. It tested the extent to which the latent factors co-vary. According to Kline (2010, p. 252), any SEM study detects a false model, rather than claim the retained model is true and correct.

Important to note from Figure 4.4, the researchers fixed one of the path coefficients of each of the covariates to one, while allowing the rest to run freely during the analysis phase. Effectively, this fixing ensured the factor variance is the same as the measured variance and assigns a scale to the factor (Ullman & Bentler 2012).

Thus creating what Chiu (2014) refers to as an anchor variable. An anchor or reference variable enables statistically testing of the differences in the path coefficient estimates (Ullman & Bentler 2012; Chiu 2014). Otherwise, without an anchor variable, the software cannot estimate the model (Kline 2010, p. 105). These parameters are either unknown (Chiu 2014) and estimated free [unconstrained] (Al-Dossary 2008) or are fixed [constrained] to a known specific value of zero or one (Al-Dossary 2008). To choose an anchor variable for Figure 4.4, Chiu (2014) endorsed to find the observed variable of each latent variable with the highest coefficient of determination or squared multiple correlation [r^2] on the covariate. Thus, for the first estimation, the initial reference variable with unit loading identification constraint were allocated to a_1, a_5, a_9 and a_{16} endogenous variables to assign a scale to latent factors b_1, b_2, b_3 and b_4 respectively, until an indicator with a more reliable score was identified.

Quantitative SEM is a technique evaluating models of linear relationships whereby the sample data are assumed to follow a multivariate normal distribution and the means and covariance matrix contain all the information (Shah & Goldstein 2006). Therefore, in the foregoing, the preliminary indicators and predictors, together with the preliminary inter-relationships between the constructs (Nebojsa 2014), are translated into a series of mathematical covariance matrices and regression Equations 4.1, 4.2, 4.3 and 4.4. These equations and matrices were adaptations of the basic model common in most statistical textbooks, *vis-à-vis* data equals model plus error (Hox & Bechger 1998, p. 361; Field 2014), including equations and matrix models of Dr Charles Hofacker (2007) and Wei *et al.* (2010).

Equation 4.1

$$a_p = \lambda_{p,q} b_1 + \lambda_{p,q} b_2 + \lambda_{p,q} b_3 + \lambda_{p,q} b_4 + \varepsilon_p$$

Equation 4.2

$$a_p = \lambda_{p,q} b_q + \lambda_{p,q} b_q + \lambda_{,pq} b_q + \lambda_{p,q} b_q + \varepsilon_p$$

Equation 4.3

$$a_p = \beta_{p,q} a_p + \lambda_{p,q} b_q + \varepsilon_p$$

Equation 4.4

$$a = \beta a + \lambda b + \varepsilon$$

The key latent constructs and endogenous indicators of the covariance structure assuming the mean is equal to zero is mathematically represented in Equation 4.4 and illustrated in Figure 4.4.

The initial reflective model in matrix terms:

$$\begin{pmatrix} a_1 \\ a_2 \\ \cdots \\ a_{21} \end{pmatrix} = \begin{pmatrix} 0_{1,1} & 0_{1,2} \cdots & 0_{1,21} \\ \beta_{2,1} & 0_{2.2} \cdots & 0_{2,21} \\ \cdots & \cdots & \cdots \\ \beta_{21,1} & \beta_{21,2} & 0_{p,p} \end{pmatrix} \begin{pmatrix} a_1 \\ a_2 \\ \cdots \\ a_{21} \end{pmatrix} + \begin{pmatrix} \lambda_{1,1} & \lambda_{1,2} & \lambda_{1,3} & \lambda_{1,4} \\ \lambda_{2,1} & \lambda_{2,2} & \lambda_{2,3} & \lambda_{2,4} \\ \cdots & \cdots & \cdots & \cdots \\ \lambda_{21,1} & \lambda_{21,2} & \lambda_{21,3} & \lambda_{p,q} \end{pmatrix} \begin{pmatrix} b_1 \\ b_2 \\ \cdots \\ b_4 \end{pmatrix} + \begin{pmatrix} \varepsilon_1 \\ \varepsilon_2 \\ \cdots \\ \varepsilon_{21} \end{pmatrix}$$

The previous matrix and Equations 4.1, 4.2, 4.3 and 4.4 illustrate initially *p* equals 21 simultaneous equations were set. The column vector *A*, contains *p* endogenous observed measured variables and the column vector *E*, contains *q* exogenous unobserved factors. Therefore, the observations are found in the rows [*p*] and the latent variables in the columns [*q*]. The measured variables serve as response variables (Chiu 2014). The regression coefficients λ [lambda] denote the amount of effect the latent variables have on the observed variables (Chiu 2014). The standardised or unstandardised regression coefficients λ is found in column vector *D* and variance ε [epsilon] is found in column vector *F*. The 21 endogenous variables [*a*] are demonstrated as a function of the four exogenous covariates [*b*]. Noteworthy, the sum of λ plus the error variance for each variable is equal to one (Streiner 2006). In column vector *B*, β [beta] the unknown element represents the regression slopes estimated using maximum likelihood estimates, which according to Kline (2010, p. 154) is the method used to derive the estimates. Beta [β] represents the non-directional hypothesised correlation relationships between the constructs and illustrated by double-headed arrows in Figure 4.4. In column vector *F*, ε [epsilon] are the errors-in-variables or measurement errors for endogenous variables or disturbances. They account for the uncommon variance unique to each *a* endogenous variable (Bacon 1997; Hofacker 2007) under a few assumptions (Chiu 2014).

The factor loadings between the measured variables are assumed random and uncorrelated with each other and the latent variables (Cole, Ciesla & Steiger 2007a; Chiu 2014). Namely they are initially assumed identical and constrained to expected values equal to zero (Chiu 2014) and so no arrows between parameters (Hox & Bechger 1998). Commonality between the endogenous variables is measured by their variance (Bacon 1997; Hofacker 2007). In the β matrix [column vector *B*], the *p* by *p* contains the coefficients of the regressions of covariates *a* on other covariates of *a* with zeroes on the diagonal, because a variable cannot cause itself. All factors in the CFA model are assumed to covary and are unanalysed (Kline 2010). In these regression equations, the latent variable serve as a covariate (Chiu 2014). The *p* by *q* λ contains the regression coefficients of the *a*s on the *b*s in column vector *D*. The error vector or unique factors, ε [epsilon], are *p* by one in column vector *F*. These errors are not factor analysis errors, but errors-in-equations or specification errors. Hence, all the measurement errors are assumed *independent* of each other (Chiu 2014) and the factors.

Considering the linear equation $a_p = \beta_{pq}\, a_p + \lambda_{pq}\, b_q + \varepsilon_p$ [Equation 4.4], it represents the perceived dependent endogenous value *a*, for case *p*, is the sum of the exogenous variable *a*, for case *p*, multiplied by the coefficient β, for *pq*, the exogenous variable *b*, for case *q*, multiplied by coefficient λ, for *pq*, plus an estimated error term or variance ε_p [epsilon] for the endogenous observed variables *a* for case *p*. This model allows for the endogenous variable *a* to estimate other endogenous variables (Ullman & Bentler 2012).

The first subscript *p* in the equation refers to the equation and the second subscript *q* refers to the cause. The error term is the difference between the observed and predicted values for each *pqs*. Thus, this model includes more than one linear equation to describe how the variables depend on each other with path coefficients describing how the exogenous variables *b* affects the endogenous variables of *a* covariates. Precisely, the matrix algebra is explained further as follows:

Equation 4.5

$$a_p = \beta_{pq}\, a_p + \lambda_{pq}\, dual\, agency\, role_q + \varepsilon_p$$

Equation 4.6

$$a_p = \beta_{pq}\, a_p + \lambda_{pq}\, objectives\, of\, the\, Act_q + \varepsilon_p$$

Equation 4.7

$$a_p = \beta_{pq}\, a_p + \lambda_{pq}\, legitimacy\, of\, the\, current\, licensing_q + \varepsilon_p$$

Equation 4.8

$$a_p = \beta_{pq}\, a_p + \lambda_{pq}\, individual\, licensing_q + \varepsilon_p$$

To assess the model, the expected *a* and *b* are assumed equal to zero. The goal is to estimate how much variation or loadings, represented as λ in Equations 4.1 to 4.4 and Figure 4.4, namely the observed endogenous covariates [a_1 to a_{21}] can be attributed to the latent unobserved exogenous constructs [b_1, b_2, b_3 and b_4]. Although the four exogenous constructs will be correlated with each other, all the measured indicator variables are consigned to only one construct each and endogenous. The latent constructs were assumed measurable with a test of positively correlated items. The error terms shown in Figure 4.4 were initially unrelated to any other measured variable, making the initial measurement model co-generic. This was further confirmed by the measurement model's initial degrees of freedom [df] using Jöreskog congeneric model (Rigdon 1994). In SEM, the initial df are calculated on the basis of the size of the covariance matrix, not on the sample size (Yusoff & Mohd Janor 2014). Degrees of freedom is the difference between the number of endogenous observed manifest variables [*m*], and the exogenous latent constructs [ϱ] (Blunch 2008). This value should be greater or equal to zero for amenable analyses (Byrne 2013). This CFA's df based on Equation 4.9 where *m* is 21 and ϱ is four equates to 21 (21 + 1) / 2–2 (21) – 4 (4–1) / 2 = 183 degrees of freedom.

Equation 4.9

$$Degree\ of\ freedom\ formula = m(m+1)/2 - 2m - \delta(\delta - 1)/2$$

Another important attribute of the measurement model is making sure a unique set of parameters consistent with the sample data, commonly known as model identification, is present (Al-Dossary 2008; Bollen & Noble 2011). Model identification determines whether the model fits the data (Al-Dossary 2008; Bollen & Noble 2011). Identification problems, especially under-identification issues, lead to admissible or spurious solutions and a waste of research resources (Kline 2010). The issue is whether the parameters estimated are unique. Software such as IBM Amos version 24 is able to detect and notify across a range of identifications and provide recommended remedies (Arbuckle 2014), such as using more constraints (Bacon 1997). Although only once data has been collected and estimated could the investigator determine if a problem with the data about under-identification is happening. Thus, the researcher followed additional recommendations of Blunch (2008) during model development. For instance, he proposed starting with four manifest variables per latent factor when developing an *a priori* measurement model. However, later literature indicated the standard measurement model is identified, because each factor has more than two [2] indicators per factor, meeting the two and three indicator rule (Kline 2010, p. 138). Both writers advanced this should ensure the model is initially identified before any data collection and analysis, because Brito and Pearl (2002) reasoned, models tend to change during research analysis while impacting the identification status of the model. Thus, for this study, the measurement portion of the model in Figure 4.4 was identified, because each factor had more than three indicators. The complexity of the model affects the identification. Complexity is determined by the number of parameters, hence number of observations or data points [v] the researcher estimates (Kline 2010). To estimate the model in different ways, the initial measurement model in Figure 4.5 was designed to be over-identified with 2,352 data points [v] to 48 parameters [r] [21 regression coefficients λ, six covariance β and 21 variance [ε] as calculated by Equation 4.10.

Equation 4.10

$$\textit{Number of data points formula } (v) = r(r+1)/2$$

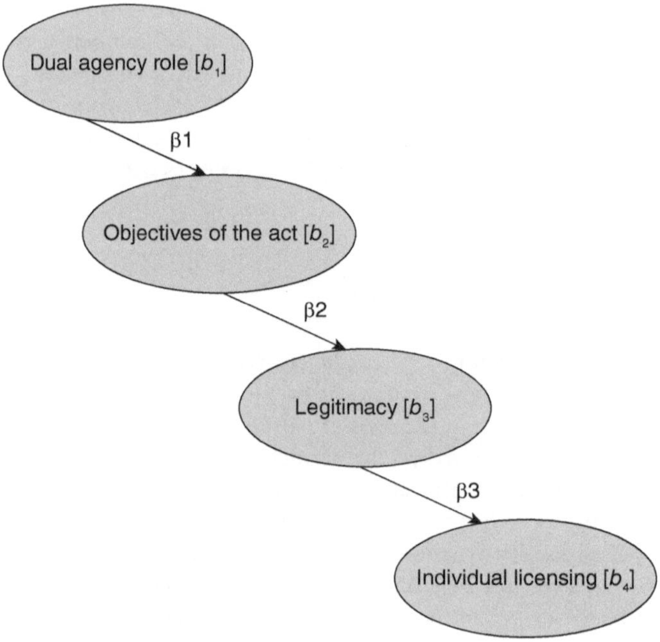

Figure 4.5 The *a priori* structural model.

Having more data points than parameters is necessary to test the hypotheses using a statistical test such as the chi-square statistic and fit indices (Ullman & Bentler 2012). Thus, this initial SEM model was designed with df of 183. Additionally, this preliminary *a priori* model is a recursive model, because its equations are acyclic, where the variance errors and error covariance are uncorrelated (Brito & Pearl 2002; Shah & Goldstein 2006; Blunch 2008). It is unidimensional, because each manifest variable is predicted only by its respective factor (Brito & Pearl 2002; Shah & Goldstein 2006; Blunch 2008).

In closing, in the four-factor *a priori* measurement model [Figure 4.4] started with six paths among the constructs with non-directional covariance. Therefore, they represent all possible unanalysed associations. In contrast, the investigator took one step further and designed the *a priori* structural path between the factors, illustrated in Figure 4.5, to have three paths among the factors to indicate the direct effects of the measured relationships in the normative model as specified in Figure 3.1 and discussed in Chapter 3. On the basis of the CFA correlation [β] results, the researcher confirmed the structural model depicted in Figure 4.5 by making assumptions about the covariance. Thus, the researcher used β results of the hypothesised respecified model depicting the relationships between dual-agency role, legitimacy of the licensing model to achieve the objectives of the Act and individual licensing to determine if the posited model structure and their hypotheses [relationship between latent variables and manifest variables and among latent variables] was reasonable (Chiu 2014).

Population and sample

Defining the population and sample was critical, because Van der Stede, Young and Chen (2005) claimed it is a key determining factor when making valid inferences. Given it is the first time this topic has been addressed by scholars, the main concern was the views of advisers. Especially given the issues about licensing influenced advisers directly as already noted in previous chapters. Thus, the population was drawn from the list of ARs registered on the ASIC Adviser Register.

Prior to sourcing contact details of potential participants to collect the data, the principal researcher emailed the Information Services Team of ASIC on 20 March 2016 requesting them to complete a customised search of the ASIC Adviser Register to produce a full list of ARs' names and email addresses for use. ASIC responded by email with a link to this register, explaining they do not hold email addresses of ARs.[3] Subsequently, a population of 15,623 authorised representatives listed in the ASIC Adviser Register was downloaded on 21 March 2016 as indicated in the timeline of Figure 4.8. Since publications claimed the Adviser Register comprised a population of 23,309 financial planners/advisers registered on the ASIC Adviser Register (Financial Service Council & UBS Asset Management 2016), this number of only 15,623 was surprising. Therefore, a second file was downloaded in case an irregularity occurred in the download. However, the researcher met with the same result. Evident from an initial examination and analysis of this adviser register, the gender distribution based on an examination of first names was approximately 81% males and 19% females. However, note during this analysis of the population, unisex names were allocated to males, because according to media reports (Chaplin 2015) significantly fewer female advisers than males work in the financial advisory industry, with a ratio comprising 80% male and 20% female reported. By implication, if a different gender split ratio was selected for this study, then collecting a suitable representative number of female respondents may be problematic. Therefore, a gender split of 80% males and 20% females was considered appropriate for this project. Accordingly, the downloaded database was split into male and female genders, based on the first names, with unisex names allocated to the list of males.

Then the investigator selected a probability random sample (Cooper & Schindler 2003; Garner 2005; Black *et al.* 2010; Swift & Piff 2010; Argyrous 2011; Yusoff & Mohd Janor 2014) of 4,040 [80% male and 20% females] using the <RAND> function in Microsoft Excel. The sample of 4,000 was allocated to the extended main study. For the main study, the sample comprised 3,200 males and 800 females. Four thousand was considered cost effective and sufficient to ensure MLE procedures were possible. This sample size was also selected to avoid sampling error (Kline 2010).

As already noted, the list of prospective participants' email addresses was unavailable on the ASIC Adviser Register. Therefore, prior to commencing the study's data collection, the investigator performed a search via Google search engine for valid email addresses of this selected sample from 2 April 2016 to 29 May 2016.

Although a more difficult approach to source prospective participants in this way, according to literature (Niemierko & Goitein 1990; Cooper & Schindler 2003; Garner 2005; Black *et al.* 2010; Swift & Piff 2010; Argyrous 2011; Yusoff & Mohd Janor 2014), a probability simple random sampling method was considered far more scientific. Particularly when this method allows for the calculation of sampling error (Niemierko & Goitein 1990; Cooper & Schindler 2003; Garner 2005; Black *et al.* 2010; Swift & Piff 2010; Argyrous 2011; Yusoff & Mohd Janor 2014). Thus, keeping sampling bias to a minimum more effectively than other approaches (Field 2014). Moreover, McCoach, Black and O'Connell (2007) claimed applications of SEM using non-probability samples in numerous studies places generalisability of research results in doubt. Although Niemierko and Goitein (1990) found random sampling significantly reduces estimation errors, they do concede it does have a few disadvantages, such as the possibility of low response rates.

Therefore, in the uncertain event of a too low response rate for the SEM technique, the investigators made the decision to revert to convenience sampling to increase the number in the collection sample. To do so required the plan to approach the professional associations for help to recruit more respondents from their membership lists. Fortunately, the data collection sample size was sufficient, and this plan B did not eventuate. Therefore, recruiting from the membership lists of professional associations was unnecessary, because a major drawback would have been the compromised independence of this sensitive and controversial research. Note, instead of providing participants a financial or other incentive for participation, the investigators offered a summary of the results if they sent their email addresses to the researcher once the research findings were concluded.

Research instrument, measurement items and measurement scale

Data collection occurred electronically in a single snapshot, cross-sectional, newly developed self-administered, web-based semi-structured survey questionnaire. Some researchers (Al-Debei, Akroush & Ashouri 2015; Al Qeisi & Al Zagheer 2015) claimed this is a common approach in many other social studies involving SEM. According to Yanamandram and White (2010), previous research showed, online surveys produce quicker responses and were more cost effective to reach the target group located in different geographical states of Australia, while producing the same accuracy and completeness as mail surveys. Furthermore, the survey was easily accessible by mobile smartphones, tablets and computers. However, Akbulut (2015) highlighted some of the limitations of online questionnaires. Typically, email invitations can be perceived as junk mail, unclear instructions may reduce the quality of responses, the lack of human contact may limit the ability of the researcher to obtain in-depth details and privacy and security concerns of respondents' needs proper consideration.

The questionnaire was designed to connect the structural equation model [Figures 4.4 and 4.5] developed from the underlying theory [Figure 3.1] to the data collected to test the hypotheses [Figures 4.1 and 4.2] from which the researcher deduced the inferences (Nebojsa 2014). The questionnaire was designed to take about 35 minutes to complete. Furthermore, given the *a priori* model was solely constructed on the basis of theoretical principles and no evidence of similar studies available, the C-OAR-SE [Construct definition, Object classification, Attribute classification, Rater identification, Scale formation, and Enumeration] theory offered useful guidelines to develop the measurement variables (Rigdon *et al.* 2011). Additionally, each endogenous variable was estimated using one question for reasons as specified in C-OAR-SE theory (Rossiter 2002; Dolnicar, Grün & Leisch 2011). The questionnaire consisted of closed questions, to collect quantitative data, and open-ended questions, to collect qualitative data. This research was mainly concerned with measuring levels of perceptions commonly found in other social science research (e.g. Yanamandram & White 2010; Bendixen & Yurova 2011). The questionnaire was divided into two parts. The first part of the survey asked respondents to reflect on their current perceptions as the operational procedure and indicated their approximate percentage level of agreement to 21 statements.

For this enquiry, the continuous numerical scale developed by Yusoff and Mohd Janor (2014) for measuring perceptions, namely the ruler-option [RO] scale, was modified. According to Yusoff and Mohd Janor (2012), RO is consistent with operational measurement theory. The Qualtrics Survey Software technical support specifically customise their existing scale option and create the Yusoff and Mohd Janor (2014) RO scale to collect the data measuring attitudes, feelings or opinions. Mainly, because it was unavailable in their options of scales. Operational measurement theory contended intangible qualitative attributes such as perceptions are quantifiable for measurement if there is the understanding a concept can be understood only once a method to estimate it is found. This makes the RO measurement scale appropriate for this research. Furthermore, there is agreement here with the views of Yusoff and Mohd Janor (2014), namely human thinking and feeling are continuous concepts by definition with little evidence it can be broken down into minute discrete amounts of thinking and feeling. When Yusoff and Mohd Janor (2014) tested their newly developed scale, they found for respondents it was easy to use and for researchers easy to administer. Confirmed in a later study by Akbulut (2015), RO scale compared with the Likert scale resulted in a stronger relationship between indicator and its associated construct. Furthermore, they all found the RO scale compared with the Likert scale in the measurement model data produced higher internal reliability and produced greater internal consistency of the observations, percentage of variance explained by the observations and ratio of df to number of parameters. The former providing more mathematical information to estimate model parameters. By validity of the regression coefficients, they confirmed the measurement model for data using RO scale had higher convergent validity. However, they confirmed both models attained almost the same level of discriminant and construct validity. Thus, this scale is ideally suited to SEM, because compared with conventional ordinal Likert scale (Beal & Dawson 2007; Yanamandram & White 2010), it is less likely to distort or miss information. This could lead to adversely impacting the measurement errors (Beal & Dawson 2007) and interpretation (Rossiter 2002). Although Likert scale response categories have a rank order, the intervals between the categories are unequal (Jamieson 2004).

Given that a scale measuring perceptions should have a number of characteristics (Yusoff & Mohd Janor 2014), modified RO scale of this study reflects these characteristics. For example, it is continuous and metric, *vis-à-vis* scaled from zero to 100% level of agreement. Thus, with its measurement unit of a percentage provided options to respondents to avoid ambiguity of the status of respondents who rate the middle point. This scale included a zero point for no agreement, with a clearly defined operational procedure as the basis for measurement. Additionally, a clear description of the operations involved was included.

In Figure 4.6, example 1 shows the proposed scale developed by Yusoff and Mohd Janor (2014). Here, the RO scale consisted of a continuous straight line with 100 points and three options illustrated in example 2. The second part of the survey asked respondents for their unidentifiable demographic information.

Method of data collection

To ensure the data on adviser licensing are collected systematically, data collection happened in two phases: a pre-test pilot study and then the extended main study. The timeline of the data collection is illustrated in Figure 4.7.

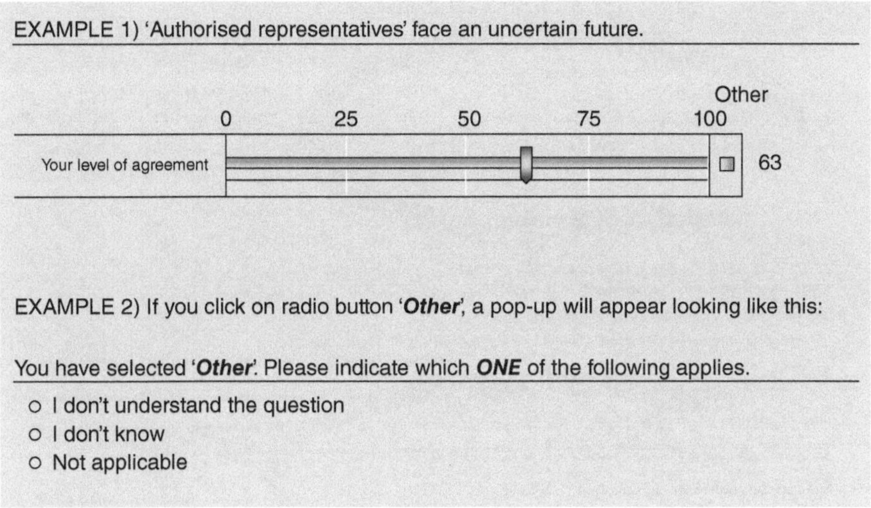

Figure 4.6 Ruler-option scale for the extended main study.

Ethics approval

Flinders University's Social and Behavioural Sciences Ethics Committee's Low Risk Sub-Committee granted conditional ethics approval on 4 July 2014 [Project number 6459]. Submission of a full ethics application to the Business College Human Ethics Advisory Network [BCHEAN] transpired from 25 August 2015. Subsequently, the final approval was granted through ethics approval number 19784 where the main window for data collection was run from 23 February 2016 to 7 May 2018. Please refer to the data analysis flowchart in Figure 4.8 summarising the data analysis process of the study.

Pre-test pilot study

To increase the main study's probability of success according to van Teijlingen and Hundley (2002), a pre-test pilot study was conducted (Leon, Davis & Kraemer 2011). It identified problems with the quantitative research design, particularly biases in the questions (van Teijlingen & Hundley 2002; Van der Stede, Young & Chen 2005; Fain 2010) and weaknesses in the sampling techniques (Fain 2010), as well as issues in the preliminary data collection and analysis. Janghorban, Roudsari and Taghipour (2014) claimed pre-test pilot studies improve a novice researcher's data collection, analytical skills, research competence and knowledge. Thus, the pilot study helped improve the data collection process,

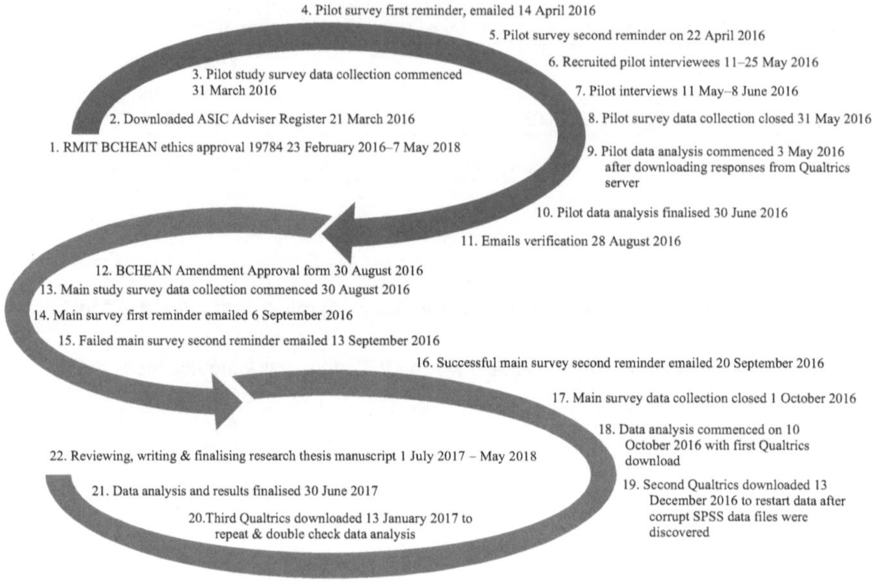

Figure 4.7 Timeline of the data collection and analysis phase.

data entry by respondents and coding of the items for analysis (Dolnicar, Grün & Leisch 2011; Dolnicar 2013).

The construction, ease of use, access, language, wording, comprehension, adequacy and appropriateness of the questions and content (Dolnicar, Grün & Leisch 2011; Dolnicar 2013) of the survey questionnaire, including its content and scale, was tested for suitability of purpose, reliability and validity, specifically content validity (Rossiter 2008). This face and content validity of the study design was especially important, because current financial adviser licensing is a relatively unexplored area in financial planning research. Thus, in this way, minimal misleading results is assured, notwithstanding decreasing the risk of incorrect theories or hypotheses (Rossiter 2008). This is particularly important, because the survey questionnaire was newly designed. Its content was based on the theory discussed in Chapter 3.

Extended main study

After the pre-test pilot study was finalised, the extended main study phase commenced. This stage included preparation, data collection, data analysis and the write-up of the findings as scheduled in the timeline in Figure 4.7. Given Van der Stede, Young and Chen (2005) claimed obtaining valid inferences using the SEM technique depended on the sample size of useable data, the investigator began with considering the minimum sample size and response rate needed for this study. Teo (2010) and Schmitt (2011) noted when determining the sample size for any SEM study, one should consider model size by indicators per factor, estimation procedures and the possibility of model misspecification, as well as departures from a normal distribution with regard to degree of multivariate normality. Shah and Goldstein (2006) contended, sample size has a major impact on reliability of estimates, model fit and statistical power. According to them, the larger the size of the model when using MLE procedures, together with the likelihood of misspecification or departures from normality, the larger the sample sizes required. Thus, determining an appropriate sample size for a SEM study can be challenging. The size of the sample for the main study and performing power analysis for SEM is important to obtain enough data so where relationships exist they can be estimated (Bacon 1997). Past literature mistakenly recommend rules of thumb, which could lead to incorrect conclusions about the defensibility of a model (Jackson, Voth & Frey 2013). Overestimations are a waste of research resources (Jackson, Voth & Frey 2013). Therefore, instead of using rules of thumb, a more acceptable scientific approach was used, *vis-à-vis*, an online sample size and power (MacCallum & Hong 1997; Chin 1998; Shah & Goldstein 2006) analysis software calculator developed by Soper (2016) based on the works of Cohen (1988) and Westland (2010). This mathematical approach is documented in a manuscript by Schumacker and Lomax (2010). Consequently, given an initial *a priori* model of 21 observed and four latent constructs [Figure 4.4] in the model, with a desired probability of .05 and statistical power level of .8, Soper's (2016) online calculator calculated a recommended minimum sample of 137 participants for anticipated effect sizes above the acceptable minimum for this study of .300. When increasing the effect size to .700, the sample size required decreased to 116.

Note, a factor loading of .300 according to Harrington (2009) is interpretable. Van der Stede, Young and Chen (2005) regarded a response rate of 80 to 90% increased the representativeness and generalisability of the survey results. Thus, it makes for better inferences about the population. However, a paper by Aguinis and Edwards (2014) predicted it is a mistake to think increasing response rates or findings from a large sample were always generalisable. Furthermore, the Akaike information criterion and Bayesian information criterion are measures of fit for models in SEM. They adjust with sample size and number of parameters to evaluate generalisability (Pitt & Myung 2002; Lubke & Muthen 2005). To clarify, generalisability is the ability of Figure 4.4 "*to fit all data samples, not just the observed sample*" (Pitt & Myung 2002, p. 422). Although, ideally a high response rate is desirable in any study (Van der Stede, Young & Chen 2005), a response rate of at least 3.5% [137 participants] of the *n* of 4,000 would be sufficient to perform estimation procedures in this enquiry. Consequently, with some idea of the minimum required for a SEM study, the data collection phase proceeded.

An invitation letter of introduction was emailed to 4,000 potential respondents. The email invitation provided the research background and objectives. The letter of introduction invited the selected participants to click on an embedded URL link to Qualtrics securely hosting the survey instrument for the main study. Once they accessed the survey form, they could download the participant information sheet as well as provide their electronic consent. Unsurprisingly, the response rate was initially below the required 137 respondents. Therefore, implementation of follow-up procedures included a reminder emailed. To provide potential participants with a third opportunity to participate in the survey, as illustrated on the timeline in Figure 4.7, a second reminder invitation was successfully emailed to the unresponsive invitees, in case they deleted, missed or forgot about the survey. The survey closed on 1 October 2016.

Data transfer, preliminary analysis and storage

After collection, importation of the data occurred electronically into password-protected CSV files. Conversion of these files into spreadsheets ready for data screening as per the timeline in Figure 4.7 for study occurred. Three downloads were made for the extended study, so the data could be cross-checked and cross-validated to ensure it had not been corrupted at any stage during the analysis. All files relating to the data analysis for this study were secured with password protection throughout the analysis.

The statistical software of choice for the analysis was IBM SPSS version 24, IBM SPSS Amos version 24, Microsoft Excel [Microsoft Office 365 ProPlus suite] and G*Power 3.1.9.2 software. These are relatively simple software to use for a beginner SEM researcher compared with other SEM software (Al-Shirawi, El-Hajjar & Charles 2014). The researchers selected IBM SPSS Amos version 24, because it was available as an additional module within IBM SPSS Statistics for Windows version 24. For the study, data were reported in non-identifiable format in associated publications. For instance, pseudonyms by referring to participants as respondent, participant or informant A, B, C, *etc.*, were used in place of actual names for the respondents' qualitative commentary. Once the project was finalised, apart from any personal identifiable information, all data collected, data analysis and supporting files were securely stored for the required period of five years on the RMIT server. After five years, RMIT will obliterate the data. All other copies of data on the Qualtrics Server and supplementary hardware used by the student researcher was removed once the results became public. The final research paper/s will remain online indefinitely.

Quantitative methods of data analysis

The analyses were initially pre-planned prior to data collection with the purpose of making amendments as required as the data analyses, interpretation and reporting stage progressed. The timeline of the data analysis depicted in Figure 4.7, indicated downloading the pilot data from Qualtrics occurred once and three times for the main study.

Extended main study phase

As recommended by Leon, Davis and Kraemer (2011), to avoid any corruption of data during the main study, none of the data from the pilot study or any of the pilot participants were included in the main study. New data were collected from a new randomly selected list of potential participants (Leon, Davis & Kraemer 2011). The data analysis process illustrated in Figure 4.8 started with data screening. Before going on to testing the model for goodness of fit, the cases were examined for electronic consent, invalid responses, unengaged responses, any data needing recoding into appropriate format for analysis and missing data for cases and outliers on the continuous data. It was impossible to follow Cooper and Schindler's (2014) recommendations to contact the respondents to obtain the missing information, because both surveys were completed anonymously. Dropping any outliers was not an option either, because it will affect the generalisability of the findings (Harrington 2009). With regard to missing data for each variable, Harrington (2009) wrote it can cause problems in SEM. For example, it can result in insufficient data points to run the analyses and compute the estimates, or it might reflect bias common to the respondents. The pattern of missing data was examined, because Harrington (2009) claimed this was more important than the amount of missing data. If reviewers or examiners questioned the methods used, several approaches offered by Lynch (2003) were considered to deal with the missing data. The variables were screened for skewness and kurtosis. Multivariate normality is more restrictive than univariate normality (Tomarken & Waller 2005). In addition, the 'Other' option in RO scale was addressed using an imputation method (Lynch 2006; Tabachnick & Fidell 2007).

"*Nonlinearity occurs when the change in the dependent variable associated with a one-unit change in the independent variable depends on the value of the independent variable*" (Menard 2002, p. 72). "*Non-additivity occurs when the change in the dependent variable associated with a one-unit change in the independent variable depends on the value of one of the other independent variables*" (Menard 2002, p. 72). To ensure the outcome [*independent*] variable is linearly related to the predictor [dependent] variable and the data do not violate this assumption (Field 2014), the ANOVA test in SPSS was applied (Field 2014, p. 43; Gaskin 2016c). To determine the extent of the non-linearity, an ordinal least square regression and curve-linear regression ['curve estimation'] was performed to see if the relationship is more linear than non-linear (Gaskin 2016c). Violations of additivity and linearity means the model will be invalid, therefore, the researcher used robust methods, specifically bootstrapping (Field 2014).

Homoscedasticity tests were completed, because it tests whether the residual [error] values of the variables are consistent across different levels of the variable (Hair *et al.* 2010). With heteroscedasticity, standard errors are overstated, making statistical significance inaccurate (Menard 2002). Thus, high SE is a symptom of non-additivity or non-linearity (Hair *et al.* 2010). Heteroscedasticity can lead to serious distortion of findings while weakening the analysis, thus increasing the possibility of a Type I error (Tabachnick & Fidell 2007). So to determine the homogeneity [small standard deviations] and heteroscedasticity [large standard deviations] of the variances, the ratio of the range to standard deviations was calculated. The range of the variables fell between a minimum value of 0% and a 100% maximum level of agreement. Notably, although the debate on heteroscedasticity is still inconclusive (Gaskin 2016d), in case a reviewer wants this tested for, it was conducted.

Well-documented, multicollinearity, where the variance of the *independent* variable to explain the variance in the dependent variable overlap each other (Gaskin 2016d), is undesirable. In this case, the dependent variable's variance is thus common (Gaskin 2016d). In addition, the *independent* variables are highly correlated with each other. Multicollinearity of the ith *independent* variable with the other *independent* variables in the model is checked using the variable inflation factor [VIF] and tolerance value for each *independent* variable after running a multivariate regression (O'Brien 2007; Gaskin 2016d). "*The VIF [hence tolerance] is based on the proportion of variance the ith independent variable shares with the other independent variables in the model*" (O'Brien 2007, p. 684). Perfect multicollinearity is indicated by the coefficient of multiple determination for multiple regression [r^2] equals one for each of the *independent* variables (Menard 2002). Using SPSS regression collinearity was checked where the tolerance statistic is $1-r^2$ [*independent* variable], where r^2 [*independent* variable] is the variance in each *independent* variable explained by all of the other *independent* variables (Menard 2002). Menard (2002) claimed a tolerance of less than .20 is a concern, but a tolerance of less than .10 is more concerning, because it indicates serious collinearity issues. Whereas O'Brien (2007) claimed greater than four to ten shows potential problems. Prominently, this study is disinterested in the effect of multicollinearity on the ith regression coefficient, but instead whether the regression coefficient is statistically significant despite the limitation of multicollinearity issues (O'Brien 2007). Consequently, no attempt was made to delete any variables and risk changing the theory. Instead, bootstrapping was applied, because it is a common approach to correct SE for multivariate non-normality in MLE (Hancock & Nevitt 1999). Bootstrapping is a method estimating the parameters of a model with SE from the sample, without reference to a theoretical sampling distribution (Aguinis, Gottfredson & Joo 2013). This technique is particularly useful, especially if the sample is large (Menard 2002). Large sample sizes are defined as *n*s greater than or equal to 250 (Hu & Bentler 1999). The results of the central limit theorem in large *n*s are considered inconsequential given the distribution of the regression coefficients in repeated sampling for large enough samples will approach a normal distribution with known mean [equal to the population mean] and variance (Menard 2002). However, it is argued in the literature the normally distributed error assumption is ignored by bootstrapping the confidence intervals (Field 2014). Notably, a limitation of bootstrapping is some cost to power (Nevitt & Hancock 2001). For bootstrapping the 95%, CI for percentile and bias-corrected CI was applied. On the basis of the recommendations by Kline (2010), no questions were phrased in the opposite direction or in reverse order to the other questions. Kline (2010) viewed reverse coded items as an unnecessary additional problem for researchers. Therefore, no reverse coding was necessary prior to handling the data for analysis.

Once the data were screened to establish the sample of useable cases, descriptive data analysis proceeded as planned. This included analysing the response rate, nomenclature and biographical details of the respondents.

Exploratory/confirmatory factor analysis tests

Although the preliminary indicator-factor relationships modelled in Figure 4.5 was specified on the basis of the normative theory discussed in Chapter 3, Menard (2002) wrote the most important assumption in linear regression analysis is the model is correctly specified. This he explained was vital to ensure unbiased regression coefficients are not systematically overestimated or underestimated. Although, the initial plan at the beginning of this project was to move straight into a CFA framework, to do so was premature. Kline (2010) recommended when one is developing a theory for the first time using a new data set, an exploratory factor analysis [EFA] should be done first. Besides, most studies are to some extent exploratory and confirmatory (Joreskog 1978). The *a priori* model, shown in Figure 4.4, was based on an untested model developed by combining numerous disciplines for the first time. The measures were newly developed with no evidence of any existing measures (Harrington 2009) available to test legitimacy of licensee–adviser licensing. Thus, EFA made sense because the associations, as conceptualised within the model, were unknown. The model in Figure 4.4 seasoned SEM researchers, such as Bentler (2006), would likely consider incomplete, rather than biased, because only a normative sense of the number of common factors and the hypothesised pattern of item-factor relationships, based on investigative theory-driven development, was evident (Brown 2006). Consequently, validation of the appropriateness of the observed variables and factors for the population took place before making inferences from the data.

EFA was used to explore the possible underlying factor structure to test for construct validity of the priori model within the CFA framework to obtain preliminary valid model fit. Before examining the associations among variables within the model, the appropriate number of common factors and pattern of indicator-factor relationships to minimise any gross misspecifications was established (Brown 2006). Thus, the scope during data analysis was extended to include EFA incorporated within the CFA framework [E/CFA] (Brown 2006) prior to the main CFA analysis (Mulaik & Millsap 2000; Maslowsky, Jager & Hemken 2015) as illustrated in Figure 4.8. Starting with EFA dimension reduction in IBM SPSS, the investigator considered the differential magnitude of the factor loadings to produce a refined model. The researcher used pattern matrices and Cronbach's alpha estimates to indicate removal of the appropriate measurement variables from further analysis where they did not meet EFA's statistical criteria or to determine if substitution made more sense (Brown 2006; Yanamandram & White 2010; Al-Shirawi, El-Hajjar & Charles 2014). EFA was implemented only to determine the appropriate number of common factors, and appropriate pattern of indicator-factor relationships, by the differential magnitude of the factor loadings, to minimise gross misspecifications (Brown 2006). Poorly behaved items were identified and gross misspecifications were respecified before the model was re-estimated (Anderson & Gerbing 1988). This led to revisions of the model to create a realistic confirmatory solution (Brown 2006). During EFA, the scientist did preliminary tests, GOF, convergent validity, discriminant validity and scale reliability.

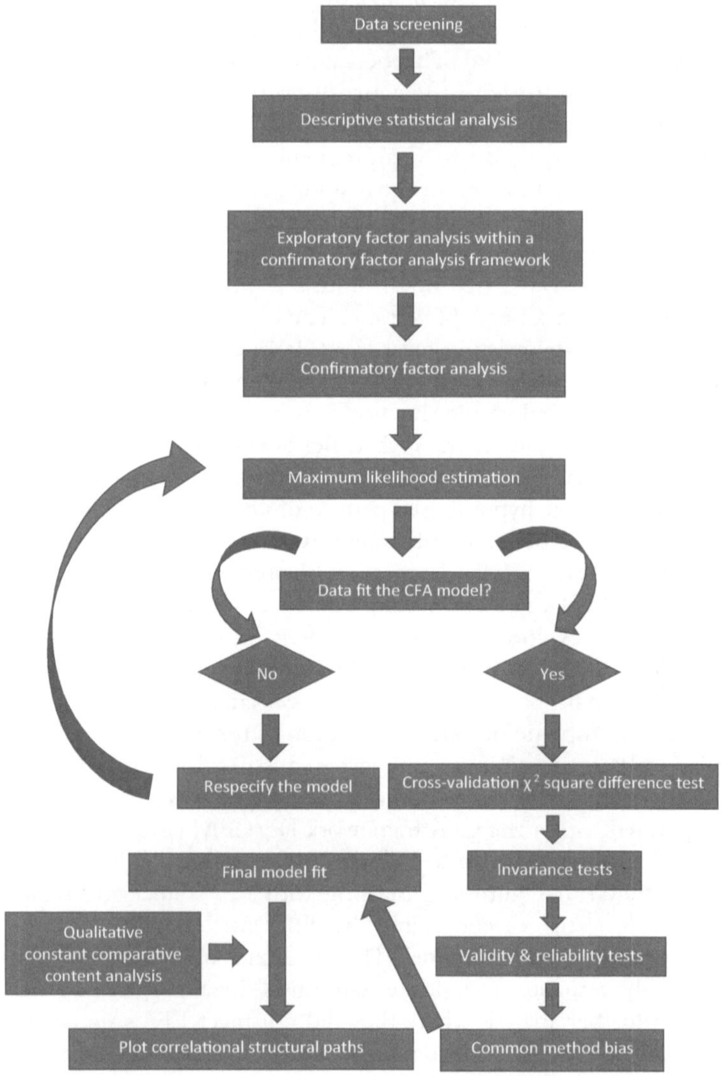

Figure 4.8 Flowchart of the data analysis phase.

Confirmatory factor analysis maximum likelihood estimation

After E/CFA, simple CFA technique (Kline 2010), which is common in many SEM studies (Anderson & Gerbing 1988; Yanamandram & White 2010; Chiandotto & Masserini 2011; Awasthi & Sangle 2013; Al-Shirawi, El-Hajjar & Charles 2014), was applied. During this phase, the associations were evaluated using MLE to determine if they were consistent and supported the theoretical expectations. Hence, ensuring the measurement model was valid (Al-Shirawi, El-Hajjar & Charles 2014). The aim was to have a model producing an estimated population covariance matrix fitting as closely as possible the sample [observed] covariance matrix. Then the parameters, including path coefficient, variance and covariance of the model, were used to assess the population covariance matrix (Ullman & Bentler 2012). To address violation of the assumptions (Aguinis, Gottfredson & Joo 2013), bootstrapping MLE at the 95% bias-corrected CI was the most feasible choice (Brown 2006; Kline 2010; Byrne 2013; Brown & Moore 2016). Kline (2010) and Byrne (2013) recommended using bootstrapping as a nonparametric distribution free technique where no normality assumption is present. However, Byrne (2013) warned it assumes the sample and the population distributions have the same shape. To check the correctness of the model, the estimated parameters using Bollen-Stine bootstrapping (Byrne 2013) was calculated. Other methods proposed by Byrne (2013) were considered, but found impractical. For instance, asymptotically distribution free [ADF] could not be used, because it requires a minimum sample (Byrne 2013) of at least 480. Another solution was to correct the test statistic rather than change the mode of estimation (Chou, Bentler & Satorra 1991; Hu, Bentler & Kano 1992). Byrne (2013) indicated the Satorra-Bentler χ^2-square is such a test. However, this correction procedure for non-normal samples is unavailable in Amos. Furthermore, Amos bootstrapping and the Satorra-Bentler scaled χ^2-square tests produce the same *p*-value for large *n*s. Simulation results (see Fouliadi 1998; Nevitt & Hancock 1998) found bootstrapping may be better than the Satorra-Bentler scaled χ^2-square. Bootstrapping was used, because χ^2-square is sensitive to linearity, additivity, multicollinearity and normality (Joreskog 1978).

Face validity, model fit and specification searches

After every application of MLE, the GOF statistics were checked first, followed by checking the data for non-convergence (Chen *et al.* 2001), Heywood cases (Byrne 2013), any missing constraint errors and indications the estimation was unable to reach its iteration limit (Gaskin 2016e). Evidence of inadmissible solutions, such as non-positive factor variance estimates and/or non-positive-definite sample or model-implied and covariance matrices [correlations smaller than one or larger than negative one], was checked (Raykov 2004). This included evidence values greater than one for factor correlations, or evidence of negative factor loadings [regression weights] (Blunch 2008), any identification issues (Harrington 2009) and model misspecification errors (Brown 2006). Factor loadings were scrutinised to determine if they were greater than .30, because these values are interpretable if sample size is ignored (Tabachnick & Fidell 2007; Harrington 2009). Then the SE of the estimates or how closely the model's estimates approximate the true population parameters (Brown 2006) was checked. Next, the investigator examined the squared multiple correlations, which provides the proportion of explained variance in the indictors. The information about whether the measures are meaningfully related to their purported latent dimension (Brown 2006) were examined. Squared multiple correlations is an indicator's reliability (Brown 2006). The variance-covariance matrix and the model-implied variance-covariance matrix was checked to ensure eigenvalues greater than zero (Brown 2006). Then the GOF indices of MLE of the raw data, which represented the average discrepancy between the sample observed and hypothesised correlation matrices (Byrne 2013), were scrutinised.

Well-documented (Anderson & Gerbing 1988; Hox & Bechger 1998; Herda 2013), an initial model never fits the data well when solving a set of structural or regression equations. Good fit was vital before the researcher proceeded with interpreting the results (Tabachnick & Fidell 2007; Jackson, Gillaspy & Purc-Stephenson 2009; Hair *et al.* 2010; Yanamandram & White 2010; Hair, Ringle & Sarstedt 2013). Therefore, model fit was addressed to increase the chance of replication of the findings by following some of the best practice recommendations of Aguinis, Gottfredson and Joo (2013). Thus, resulting in more accurate interpretation and conclusions. Given all the regression lines between latent and observed variables were already in place [Figure 4.4], they were unfeasible to correct model fit (Hermida 2015, p. 6).

Instead, data-driven MI (Raykov 2004) provide specific information for how the fit of the model can be improved (Hermida 2015). When measurement errors or estimates of the "*other unique sources of variance*" (Hermida 2015, p. 6), or referred to in the literature as "*a true score unique variance*" (Hermida 2015, p. 6) and "*unsystematic error variance*" (Hermida 2015, p. 6), are present, then correlation or regression analysis might lead to biased estimates (Yuan & Bentler 2004). Although Hermida (2015) cautioned against specification searches using MI, based on current practice, MI with cut-off threshold greater than 4.0 (Raykov 2004; Brown 2006) were used to sequentially modify the model post hoc until adequate fit was achieved (Maccallum & Necowitz 1992). Furthermore, no clear guidelines as to the appropriate error correlation practices were found in the literature. If you recall, initially in the hypothesised model [Figure 4.4], the covariances among measurement errors were fixed to zero, because measurement errors were considered unique to each indicator (Hermida 2015, p. 6). By correlating the unique variance, the observed relationship between any two indicators loading on the same factor is the shared influence of the latent variable and other external factors (Brown & Moore 2016). Correlated errors demonstrate the indicators are related, because of something other than the shared influence of the latent factor. Correlated errors could result from method effects, such as using a common measurement method. Alternatively, similar wording of items and positive or negative phrasing can cause correlated errors. MI can indicate systematic error based on respondent characteristics such as the nay-saying respondents who may have been stressed answering the questions in ways considered socially desirable (Byrne 2013). Given the sensitive nature of the topic, as well as the overlapping central theme of the questions (Byrne 2013), MI greater than four were expected during this study's data analysis. Hermida (2015) claimed other authors have demonstrated if indicator variables share components, then it is appropriate to covary the error terms. Furthermore, Cole, Ciesla and Steiger (2007b) claimed leaving out MI-driven correlated residuals can result in not detecting model misspecifications. This they claimed resulted in latent variables misrepresenting the constructs being examined. Therefore, the researcher continued to retest and respecify the measurement model [Figure 4.4] using MI several times until achieving adequate model fit.

Note though, model respecification is a controversial issue in the literature (Shook *et al.* 2004; McCoach, Black & O'Connell 2007). For instance, Maccallum (1986) warned, the process of modifying must be conducted very judiciously, with the outcome viewed with great caution. Thus, respecification was pursued only if they were justified on empirical and conceptual grounds (Maccallum & Necowitz 1992). They were significant at $p < .05$ level (Harrington 2009). It is dangerous to correlate measurement errors after post-hoc specification searches without theoretical justification, Hermida (2015) cautioned, as it results in model fit improvement from capitalisation of chance. Theoretical specification searches, namely revising the model solely based on large statistical standardised residuals or MI, could result in further model misspecification overfitting. Overfitting occurs when estimates are superfluous or because of chance associations in the sample data (Hermida 2015). Therefore, no paths were added to improve fit, because this would compromise the theory and reduce replication of the estimates, notwithstanding theoretically unjustifiable (Hermida 2015). Thus, the modifications were made only to represent the true model producing the data (Raykov 2004).

The standardised residual covariance [SRC], much like MI, pointed out where the discrepancies between the proposed and estimated models were evident. Thus, these values were inspected to determine whether the developed model is a good model with small residuals on average with thresholds no greater than 1.96 [for $p < .05$] or 2.58 [for $p < .01$] (Bentler 2006). The SRCs greater than 2.5 (Matsunaga 2010) to 4.0 with one degree of freedom at alpha level of .05 (Brown 2006) were investigated. The investigator looked for positive standardised residuals to determine if the model's parameters underestimated the relationship. Negative standardised residuals indicate the model's parameters overestimated the relationship. If the fit statistics indicated the data fit the model adequately, the SRC estimates were merely noted, rather than used to produce better-fit statistics by deleting violators of the SRC thresholds. Mainly, for the reason, deleting variables would threaten the integrity of the data to solve the statistical problems of explaining the factors (Clark & Watson 1995; Osborne & Costello 2005). Therefore, specification searches were performed using MI only, because it provided recommendations to correct discrepancies or differences between the proposed and estimated model (Hermida 2015, p. 6). Respecifying the model did not rely entirely on the modification statistics. Therefore, using the relevant theory and research findings as recommended in SEM literature justified the respecification (Brown & Moore 2016).

Acknowledged, SEM goodness of fit [GOF] is a contentious issue (see Ke-Hai 2005; Bentler 2006; Hayduk *et al.* 2006; Barrett 2007). For instance, Byrne (2013) claimed the plausibility of a model cannot be determined merely by chi-square fit indices, namely CMIN, CMIN *p*-value and relative or normed CMIN [CMIN/DF], which measures discrepancy between the population's true covariance structure and the target model (Ke-Hai 2005; Bentler 2006; Hayduk *et al.* 2006; Barrett 2007; Byrne 2013). CMIN is criticised for generally being unreliable for large *ns* greater than 250 (Matsunaga 2010). Consequently, as recommended by many SEM researchers (Marsh, Kit-Tai & Zhonglin 2004; Markland 2007; Byrne 2013), other fit statistics, shown in Table 4.2, were considered important for this enquiry to overcome the limitations of each one (Kline 2010).

Specifically, the root mean square error of approximation [RMSEA] measures the extent to which the population matrix is the same as the sample matrix within the

Table 4.2 Goodness of fit statistics and their thresholds.

Measure	*Meaning*	*Thresholds for good fit*
CMIN	Sample matrix and estimated matrix are the same	Compare obtained $\chi 2$-square value with tabled chi-square value for given degrees of freedom [DF]
DF		
P		$p > .05$ or $p > .01$
CMIN/DF		< 3
GFI		> .95; > .90 permissible; 0 [no fit] to 1 [perfect fit]
AGFI		> .95 to > .80 [adjusted for DF); 0 [no fit] to 1 [perfect fit]
CFI	Over-identification condition is met	> .95 good; > .90 permissible; 0 [no fit] to 1 [perfect fit]
TLI/NNFI	Over-identification condition is met	value close to .95 reflects good fit; 0 [no fit] to 1 [perfect fit]
NFI		value close to .95 reflects good fit; 0 [no fit] to 1 [perfect fit]
PCFI	Estimated parameter is robust against other samples (Mulaik 1998)	Compare alternative models; 0 [no fit] to 1 [perfect fit]
AIC	A value as low as possible	Compare alternative models and should be smaller than the saturated and independence model, the smaller the better
BIC	A value as low as possible	Should be smaller than the saturated or independence model for the model to be more generalisable, the smaller the better (Myung, Tang & Pitt 2009)
SRMR	Average error in the model is minimal	< .09; 1 [poor fit] to 0 [perfect fit]
RMSEA	Population matrix and estimated matrix are the same.	< .05; .05–.10 moderate; > .10 poor
PCLOSE		> .05

Source: Adapted from various sources: Hu & Bentler 1999; Hair *et al.* 2010; Kline 2010; Byrne 2013; Pittayachawan 2013.

bounds of a 90% CI (Byrne 2013). If PCLOSE [closeness of fit] is less than .05, then RMSEA fails the test of minimal discrepancy between the observed and predicted covariance matrix. The GFI [goodness of fit index] measures the relative amount of variance and covariance in the sample matrices jointly explained by the population matrices (Byrne 2013). Whereas AGFI is the adjusted GFI for the df value (Byrne 2013). GFI, AGFI, normed fit index [NFI] and Tucker-Lewis fit index [TFI] or non-normed fit index [NNFI] compares the hypothesised model with null [no] model (Byrne 2013). TFI is usually lower than the GFI (Hu & Bentler 1999).

Comparative fit index [CFI] is an incremental fit index comparing the hypothesised model against some standard baseline [independence and null] model (Byrne 2013). In *independent* models, the variables are uncorrelated. Thus, the value of the index is the amount the target model improves the fit relative to the null or independence models (Byrne 2013). Of interest were models approaching the value of one to indicate they are better than the independence models. Now the information theory indices are the Akaike information criterion [AIC] and consistent Akaike information criterion [CAIC], Bayesian information criterion [BIC] and sample size-adjusted BIC [aBIC] (Byrne 2013). They explain the extent to which the observed covariance matrices differ from the predicted covariance matrices by comparing the target model to the saturated and independence models (Byrne 2013). Therefore, smaller or lower values for AIC and CAIC, BIC and aBIC (Lubke & Muthen 2005) are preferred. Their values should be less than either the independence or saturated models (Byrne 2013). Byrne (2013) recommended current practice incorporates GOF thresholds, but cautions these thresholds are an unnecessary and insufficient basis to establish validity of a model. Especially given GOF is inversely related to sample size (Byrne 2013). They recommended the researcher's judgement around interpretability of estimates, model complexity and *a priori* theory should be considered when looking at the fit indices. The various GOF indices guidelines [see Table 4.2] proposed by various scholars were used to help evaluate the extent to which the model is supported by the data (Blunch 2008).

Cross-validation test

Once respecification of the model led to acceptable GOF results of MLE (Kline 2010) in Amos, the respecified model's estimates could be interpreted to confirm the improved model fit was not from capitalisation of chance. Thus, the results were generalisable (Hermida 2015). The next step was cross-validation [Figure 4.8 Flowchart of the data analysis stage] using another sample drawn from the same population. Therefore, to cross-validate the model, multigroup confirmatory factor analysis [MGCFA] was used, because it is the most widely used methodology (Cheung & Rensvold 2009; Steinmetz *et al.* 2009) involving constrained models nested within less constrained models (Harrington 2009). The multiple group gender [male and female] formed the new sample from the same population to estimate freely measurement parameters and compared these results to constrained measurement estimates (Anderson & Gerbing 1988). The χ^2 difference test was used to cross-validate the data of these two samples. Seemingly, it is the difference in χ^2 values rather than the absolute χ^2 values themselves determining whether the model is realistic, because chi-square is sensitive to linearity, additivity, multicollinearity and normality (Joreskog 1978). Recommended by Byrne (2013), the χ^2 difference test can be used to determine whether adding constraints significantly worsens the fit of the model. In other words, the χ^2 statistic and associated df of the constrained models were subtracted from the base unconstrained model (Byrne 2013). Evidence of cross-validation was claimed if χ^2 difference was statistically non-significant (Byrne 2013). In other words, a non-significant χ^2 difference value indicated the unconstrained model fits the data better than the constrained model. If the χ^2 difference value was significant, then the improvement in chi-square was significantly larger. Hence, the constrained model fails the cross-validation test (Byrne 2013). Put another way, if the null hypothesis of equal distributions could not be rejected, namely the results were non-significant, the chi-square increase was insignificant compared with its df and the groups had equivalent covariance structures (Byrne 2013) and have been cross-validated.

Invariance tests

Invariance tests [Figure 4.8] followed cross-validation. Raykov (2004) claimed a scale could be accepted only if it assessed the same, latent variable in different populations as well as the scale's factorial structure is invariant in all groups [configural invariance] "*and the baseline-level performance on each of its components is on average equal in the groups*" (Raykov 2004, p. 308). Like cross-validation, to test for invariance MGCFA was used (Cheung & Rensvold 2009; Steinmetz *et al.* 2009) involving constrained models nested within less constrained models (Harrington 2009). Seven models were tested comprising configural, metric, latent factor mean differences test for scalar and equality of uniqueness [residual variance] associated with observed variables invariance to determine measurement invariance. For structural invariance, the researcher tested for equivalence of factor means, equivalence of factor covariance and variance (Brown 2006, pp. 269–270; Schmitt & Kuljanin 2008). In the MGCFA framework, invariance of parameter matrices was tested by constraining cross-group equality of these matrices. Then the models were compared statistically using the difference in the χ^2 statistics and df (Steinmetz *et al.* 2009). Evidence of invariance was claimed if χ^2 difference was statistically non-significant (Byrne 2013). In other words, a non-significant χ^2 difference value indicated the unconstrained model fits the data better than the constrained model. If the χ^2 difference value was significant, then the improvement in chi-square was significantly larger and hence the constrained model failed the invariance test (Byrne 2013). Put another way, if the null hypothesis of equal distributions could be accepted, namely the results were non-significant, the chi-square increase was insignificant compared to its df, the groups had equivalent covariance structures and were invariant (Byrne 2013). Consequently, if the CMIN for each model was much larger than the df, the baseline model adequately explained the observed data on statistical grounds [$p > .10$, .05 or 01] (Reise, Widaman & Pugh 1993). Another practical approach to test for invariances was to report the difference in CFI [CFI difference tests] (Byrne 2013), rather than χ^2 difference values only (Cheung & Rensvold 2002; Steinmetz *et al.* 2009; Locander *et al.* 2015). Cheung and Rensvold (2002) proposed evidence of invariance was based on difference in CFI values exhibiting probability greater than .01 cut-off. Although Locander *et al.* (2015) made use of this approach in their research, Byrne (2013) claimed the change in CFI was still unsanctioned. Hence, both methods were thus implemented. Notably, where the two disagreed the χ^2 statistic value decision in the first instance was followed, because this method permit testing for invariance easily by setting cross-group constraints and comparing more restricted with less restricted models. The χ^2 statistic difference test argues for non-invariance if significant and the CFI indifference tests argues for invariance if changes in CFI is less than .01 and significant (Byrne 2013).

The first step in invariance assessment involved establishing configural invariance by computing covariance among the observed variables for each group without any constraints. There are three conditions for factorial structure invariance to be met, namely each population measured the same number of factors, the same predictors load onto the same factors and factor loadings were identical in each group (Raykov 2004). Here, no constraints were present, meaning the same pattern of fixed and non-fixed parameters and thus the model is the same across groups (Steinmetz *et al.* 2009). Measuring configural invariance data was split along gender [male and female] lines to determine whether the factor structure achieves reasonable fit when two groups are tested together and freely, namely no cross-group path constraints were evident. Although Schmitt and Kuljanin (2008) confirmed in the literature, if configural invariance is established, then there is no further need to carry on with additional tests. However, to see how restricting the model further affects the results, additional tests of invariance were applied too.

Measurement invariance was added to the well-established criteria of reliability, homogeneity and validity (Byrne 2013). Measurement invariance determines whether the questionnaire assesses identical or different latent variables in more than one group or the indicator loadings and manifest variable intercepts are equal across groups (Raykov 2004). Testing measurement invariance assumes the numerical values under consideration are on the same measurement scale. Thus, they are assumed comparable across groups for the purpose to uncover population heterogeneity (Steinmetz *et al.* 2009). It is an important aspect of scale development, as this determines whether the testing instrument was appropriate for use in various groups. In multigroup application, invariance of a single measurement instrument (Byrne 2013) across gender was tested, because it determined whether the questionnaire assessed identical or different latent variables in more than one group (Raykov 2004). Thus, it determined whether the indicator loadings and manifest variable intercepts are equal across groups (Raykov 2004). Thus, measurement invariance examines the similarities and differences in covariance patterns of item-factor relations (Reise, Widaman & Pugh 1993) and variance-covariance matrices across gender. Thus, predictors must be adequately equivalent and measure the identical underlying latent construct of the two groups (Schmitt & Kuljanin 2008). By validating whether the factor structure and loadings were equivalent across groups ensured, the composite variables measured the same underlying latent constructs for different groups within the same sample. Therefore, it validates the generalisability of the model across population (Vandenberg & Lance 2000). The construct scales should demonstrate full invariance to prevent biased and potentially misleading indicators of individual and group difference of a common set of factor loadings used to estimate factor scores within each group (Reise, Widaman & Pugh 1993). Only then can the researcher make meaningful comparisons across populations or measurement cases (Raykov 2004). Metric invariance is a stronger form of measurement invariance, whereby values of factor loadings of each variable on each factor are fixed to be the same across groups (Schmitt & Kuljanin 2008). The loadings for factors are constrained to equality for each of the groups compared (Byrne 2013). Thus, the factor structure and loadings are equivalent across groups. The composite variables measure the same underlying latent constructs for different groups within the sample, and hence are generalisable across population (Vandenberg & Lance 2000).

Structural covariance invariance tests for factor covariance equivalence (Byrne 2013) or the factor covariance are equivalent across groups and hence displays invariance (Byrne, Shavelson & Muthen 1989). Strict invariance tests the equality of indicator residual variances by computing the equality of reliability of an assessment scale across groups (Byrne 2013). Thus, the equality of uniqueness associated with each observed variable is tested when the residuals of the regression equations are equivalent across groups (Schmitt & Kuljanin 2008). Notably, testing the equality of indicator residual variances is optional, because it rarely holds in real data and is highly restrictive according to Brown (2006). If the restricted, nested model results in a non-significant increase in chi-square compared with the less restricted model, then the hypothesis of full measurement invariance is tenable (Brown 2006).

Structural invariance is divided into three tests of equality, namely latent means, factor variances and tests of equality of covariance. Structural invariance tests for population heterogeneity (Brown 2006). To assess population heterogeneity, the invariance of the measurement and structural part of the MGCFA across two gender groups was tested. Differences between measurement errors, factor loadings and latent means among gender groups given measurement invariance is expected. Equivalence of factor means [scalar invariance] differences test for scalar invariance is done when the intercepts of regression equations of observed variables on latent factors are equivalent across groups (Schmitt & Kuljanin 2008). In other words, it tests the equality of indicator intercepts (Byrne 2013). Equally constraining vector with item intercepts results in the same systematic response bias in the groups prerequisite for latent mean comparison. Scalar invariance refers to invariance of the item intercepts in the regression equations linking the indicators' item intercepts to interpret systematic biases in the responses of a group to an item. As a result, the manifest mean can be systematically higher or lower [upward or downward biased] than one would expect. Scalar invariance is present if the degree of upward or downward bias of the manifest variable is equal across groups. To test for scalar invariance, one constrains the tau-vectors to be equal across groups ($\tau A = \tau B = \ldots = \tau G$). This check involves equally constraining vector with latent means invariance of the latent means if equal intercepts with the same latent means in the groups (Brown 2006). Equivalence of factor covariance test evaluates a further constraint, namely the equality of the factor covariance (Schmitt & Kuljanin 2008). This examination determines whether equivalence of factor covariance occurs and whether all items are related in the same way across groups (Schmitt & Kuljanin 2008). Equivalence of factor variance test of invariance of the error variances is less important in SEM, because relationships between latent variables are corrected for measurement error (Steinmetz *et al.* 2009). In this case, one mean is set to zero and the significance of the other model parameters represents a test of differences of latent means (Byrne 2013). Therefore, equivalence of factor variance across groups is present.

Validity and reliability tests

Next, the convergent, discriminant and scale reliability were evaluated using the appropriate tests such as Cronbach's alpha, composite reliability [CR], average variance extracted [AVE], average shared variance [ASV], factor correlations, tau- and parallel equivalent tests (Brown 2006; Harrington 2009). Although CFA does assess convergent and discriminant validity (Curran, West & Finch 1996), EFA is the better technique to assess validity, especially discriminant validity (Farrell & Rudd 2009). So both methods were used to test for validity.

Convergent validity evaluated whether the variables in the model correlate well with their latent factor (Hair *et al.* 2010). To reliably interpret the estimates (Campbell & Fiske 1959), acceptable estimates of a given indicator loaded onto an underlying latent variable had to be above threshold of .35 based on an n greater than 250 (Gaskin 2016b). Although Harrington (2009) claimed a threshold of .30 is interpretable. A model achieves convergent validity if for all items in the measurement model, AVE is greater than .5 for all the factors (Harrington 2009). Furthermore, if MLE estimates in Amos are statistically significant $p < .001$ or $p < .05$, then the indicator has a large degree of true score common variance (Harrington 2009).

Discriminant validity is the degree to which concepts were not interrelated (Campbell & Fiske 1959; Gaskin 2016b). This is important to avoid the possibility of a Type II error, namely accepting a poor model, because this error could result in the incorrect interpretations and conclusions of the factor analysis (Farrell & Rudd 2009). A Type II error occurs when it is believed there is no effect in the population, when there is (Field 2014). Gaskin (2016b) proposed numerous methods to determine discriminant validity during an EFA. The first method was to examine the EFA pattern matrix (Table 5.4 Pattern matrix[a] after E/CFA.) and check for cross-loadings where indicator variables load on multiple factors (Gaskin 2016b). No cross-loadings should occur, and they must not differ by less than .2, or else shared variance occurs (Gaskin 2016b). The second method is to examine the factor correlation matrix (Gaskin 2016b). In the factor EFA correlation matrix, correlations between factors should be less than .7 to ensure discriminant validity (Gaskin 2016b). A third method proposed in the literature (Fornell & Larcker 1981; Hair *et al.* 2010) is to use CFA by calculating AVE. The ASV, representing the amount of variance in measured variables relating to another construct explained by a latent construct, was examined. Finally, to determine discriminant validity the maximum shared variance [MSV] values were calculated and assessed. Each structural equation model represents only one possible fit to the data; therefore, the AVE of each construct is compared with the ASV between constructs. If the AVE for each construct is greater than its ASV with any other construct, discriminant validity is supported (de Almeida *et al.* 2014). A fourth method proposed by Harrington (2009) to establish discriminant validity is to assess whether the CFA correlations between latent factors is less than .85. In other words, the indicators of the theoretical distinct constructs are not highly intercorrelated (Harrington 2009).

Before the results of the respecified model can be trusted, reliability tests are critical to any research, because the presence of errors in the scores and inconsistency in the measurement or proportion of true individual differences of the observed variables can lead to incorrect conclusions (Harrington 2009). Consequently, three methods were used. Cronbach's alpha (Field 2014) was the first test. Field (2014) confirmed when dealing with psychological constructs values, Cronbach's alpha of .8 is appropriate. In the early stages of research, values as low as .5 will suffice and values greater than .7 is usually expected. Interestingly, Raykov (2004) showed Cronbach's alpha underestimates reliability in a multi-component measuring instrument like a multiple item questionnaire. Therefore, interpreting Cronbach's alpha should be done with caution (Field 2014), Consequently, the CRCMM (Raykov 1997, 2004) was a useful online statistics tool (Colwell 2016) based on the works of Raykov (1997) to test reliability further. CR was considered an appropriate test for this investigation, because it is more reliable for large samples (Raykov 1997). To pass the reliability test, CR should be greater than .7 (Hair *et al.* 2010; Malhotra & Dash 2011). Further tests for reliability included congeneric, tau equivalent and parallel equivalent (Kline 2010). Tau-equivalent tests have equal true score variances [$\acute{\varepsilon}_1 = \acute{\varepsilon}_2$, *etc.*], but possibly different error variances [$\varepsilon_1 \neq \varepsilon_1$] (Brown & Moore 2016). It assumes the components of an instrument [scale] are measures of the same latent constructs in the same units of measurements with different precision [tau-equivalent] (Raykov 1997, 2004). Indicators have equivalent relationships with the underlying factor they measure. Thus, a one-unit change in the latent variable is associated with a one-unit change in each indicator loading on that factor. In other words, indicators measure the same units of measurement (Harrington 2009). More restrictive is parallel where observed measures have equal factor loadings [$\acute{\varepsilon}_1 = \acute{\varepsilon}_2$, *etc.*] and equal error variances [$\varepsilon_1 = \varepsilon_1$, *etc.*]. They measure the latent construct with the same level of precision (Harrington 2009), namely equivalent error variances. It is assumed to measure the latent construct with the same level of precision [equivalent error variance ε] this study used the χ^2-square difference test to evaluate nested model comparisons for tau and parallel equivalents (Yuan & Bentler 2004).

Common methods bias tests

On the recommendation of Gaskin (2013), the researcher then tested the responses for common method bias. Common method bias refers to a bias in the data set when something external to the question or measure may have resulted in influencing the responses given (Podsakoff, MacKenzie & Podsakoff 2012).

Method effects creates a correlation between two measures which cannot easily be identified – as either the result of a true relationship or the result of shared methods. Thus, different methods, wording or response options available may result in a lower-than-expected correlation between constructs or may result in two or more constructs when there is only one (Harrington 2009). This is a problem, because it affects hypothesis tests, can lead to Type I or Type II errors, result in incorrect conclusions about how much variance is accounted for by a latent construct and provide incorrect discriminant validity findings (Podsakoff, MacKenzie & Podsakoff 2012).

Three tests (Gaskin 2013) were identified as most suitable for this study: the Harman test (Nebojsa 2014; Choi, Ullah & Kwak 2015), common latent factor [CLF] test (Podsakoff *et al.* 2003; Podsakoff, MacKenzie & Podsakoff 2012) and CLF marker test (Podsakoff, MacKenzie & Podsakoff 2012; Williams & O'Boyle 2015). When measuring perceptions, Podsakoff, MacKenzie and Podsakoff (2012) recommended researchers should make sure a subset of all the measures do not measure a single latent factor. This is the Harman's single factor test. Although this test has been shown to display inconsistent reliability, it is still used in current research (Nebojsa 2014; Choi, Ullah & Kwak 2015), while, allegedly, many reviewers still publish it (Nebojsa 2014; Kang & Jindal 2015). To see if most of the variance can be explained by a single factor, and hence the model has significant common method bias (Gaskin 2016a), all the variables in the study were loaded into EFA (Gaskin 2013). The number of factors extracted in the model in SPSS were constrained to equal one in an unrotated solution, rather than extracting via eigenvalues (Gaskin 2013).

Another method used by various researchers (Groza, Locander & Howlett 2016; Kuzucu 2016) to assess the common method bias in the measurement and structural model the investigator implemented is the CLF method (Podsakoff *et al.* 2003; Podsakoff, MacKenzie & Podsakoff 2012). When the specific source of the common method bias cannot be identified, the CLF serves as a solution. In this method, a CLF to capture the common variance among all observed variables in the model was used. To do this, a single latent factor was added to the respecified CFA model, and then connected to all observed items in the model. Then the standardised regression weights from this model was compared with the standardised regression weights of a model without the CLF. If the results of the latent methods model are consistent with the structural model, then this indicates the relationships are unaffected by common method bias (Groza, Locander & Howlett 2016). If large differences [like greater than .200] occur, then the CLF must be retained after the regression weights were estimated (Podsakoff *et al.* 2003).

Another widely used technique is the CLF marker technique, zero constraint test or the CFA marker technique (Podsakoff, MacKenzie & Podsakoff 2012; Williams & O'Boyle 2015). Here, one includes a marker variable, such as a CLF as the previous method. The difference this time is all the factor loadings loading onto the CLF are first unconstrained and then constrained to zero (Podsakoff, MacKenzie & Podsakoff 2012). This approach controls for the portion of the variance attributable to gathering all the measures with the same method (Podsakoff, MacKenzie & Podsakoff 2012). Then after performing MLE for the constrained and unconstrained models, a chi-square difference test between the unconstrained model and the zero constraint model is undertaken (Podsakoff, MacKenzie & Podsakoff 2012; Williams & O'Boyle 2015). This approach tests whether the amount of shared variance across all variables was significantly different from zero based on chi-square difference test (Podsakoff, MacKenzie & Podsakoff 2012; Williams & O'Boyle 2015). If the chi-square is significant, then it was concluded method bias does exist in my measures. Strengths of this approach were that it modelled the effects of method biases at the indicator level, rather than at the construct level, and it provided a statistical test of method bias based on model comparisons. Furthermore, it is a test determining whether method biases affect all measures equally or differently (Podsakoff, MacKenzie & Podsakoff 2012; Williams & O'Boyle 2015).

Common method bias was solved by retaining the CLF, namely the unmeasured common latent method factor to estimate the model parameters (Podsakoff *et al.* 2003). Mainly, for the reason, it was the most common solution to control all systematic sources of bias during hypotheses testing of relationships between constructs (Podsakoff, MacKenzie & Podsakoff 2012). Other statistical remedies were considered, such as correlation-based and/or regression-based marker variable technique. However, they were considered inappropriate, because a suitable marker variable completely unrelated to the indicators could not be identified, notwithstanding they came with several other limitations (Podsakoff, MacKenzie & Podsakoff 2012). The instrumental variable technique was inappropriate, because the researcher could not identify the possible sources of method bias potentially affecting the variables.

The common factor analysis marker technique is too complex. It was overlooked, because it has the shortcoming of providing incorrect SE and GOF statistics. Notably, the findings by Meade, Watson and Kroustalis (2007) claimed, common method bias may be in many cases inconsequential. They claimed common method bias does not necessarily threaten the validity of study conclusions in every project. Consequently, to confirm or deny this claim, this book reported results in Chapter 5 by retaining and excluding the CLF.

Structural path model

CFA was the main component of this SEM analysis. To close the data analysis for interpretation of the results, the structural model was finalised using the correlation results to confirm the relationship and hypotheses β_1 to β_6 between the factors b_1, b_2, b_3 and b_4. Qualitative analysis proceeded after the hypotheses were tested.

Qualitative phase of data analysis

Given that quantitative data was given priority, analysis of the qualitative data was kept simple. Therefore, for the qualitative data, a constant comparative technique (Glaser 1965; Maykut & Morehouse 1994; Kolb 2012) with a focus on content analysis (Smith 2009; Steen, McGrath & Wong 2016) of specific respondents' written words only was applied. To generate common concepts, dimensions and categories, as well as emerging patterns and themes, frequency and meanings, together with relationships of words, the survey informants' quotes were inspected, sorted and analysed (Webb, Sweet & Pretty 2002; Sonpar, Pazzaglia & Kornijenko 2010). These commonalities were integrated into the overall interpretation of the quantitative results using insight and judgement by following some of the approaches used by Maykut and Morehouse (1994). Following the guidelines offered by Baran and Jones (2016), the collected data were organised. Thoughtfully, the transcript of each case was read in isolation of the quantitative data several times to obtain a general sense of the qualitative responses. This led to the emergence of themes or categories for each quantitative survey question. Then the data were coded into a list of themes for each question using the words emerging from the data. Coding took place manually to sort, organise, code and create the categories. Thus, the rate of recurrence, connotations and associations of the words (Webb, Sweet & Pretty 2002) respondents used to express themselves were analysed. This analysis was followed by categorising several overall themes supported by the repetitive words and themes of each question. According to Baran and Jones (2016), themes create categories and summarise the findings for sense making. Next, each quantitative result in conjunction with the qualitative findings considered interesting, yet important, phrases or categories were analysed. Furthermore, other meanings, ideas or interpretations associated with the data were considered. Thus, the constant comparative method was purposely used with the main aim to understand the phenomenon under investigation with minimum of interpretation (Maykut & Morehouse 1994). Consequently, respondents' actual words quoted were used, which included how they felt about an issue to validate the themes emerging from their responses. This form of content analysis has the main purpose to find specific words, concepts or categories within the text, which allowed us to make interpretations with regard to the quantitative results (Webb, Sweet & Pretty 2002).

Conclusion

The project was approached from a post-positivist [realism] paradigm using a quantitative research methodology. SEM was the quantitative methodology used, because this project was about validating a theoretical perspective by EFA within a CFA framework. This analysis was followed by CFA to calculate structural relationships simultaneously between the four constructs. A sample of 4,000, with an 80/20 split between male and females, was drawn from the ASIC Adviser Register using probability random sampling. The study used a Qualtrics, web-based, cross-sectional designed, semi-structured survey questionnaire during the study using a continuous data Ruler-Option scale.

Notes

1 Regulatory Guide 181. Licensing: Managing conflicts of interest. Chapter 7 – Financial services and markets.
2 The Corporations Amendment (Professional Standards of Financial Advisers) Bill 2017.
3 <https://data.gov.au/dataset/asic-afs-authorised-representative>.

5 Contextualising current licensing of advisers

Preliminary analysis using confirmatory factor analysis

Introduction

After the development of an empirical model in Chapter 4 based on the theoretical construct of the legitimacy of current AFSL-AR licensing in Chapter 3, this chapter reports the main study results. Starting with a dialogue on screening the data collected, while performing EFA applied within a CFA framework. Subsequently, the results are offered before and during CFA. Then after respecification, the model is tested for contraventions of any statistical assumptions leading to greater accuracy in data interpretations.

Main study result analysis

Response rate and screening the data

Of the respondents satisfying the eligibility criterion of being registered on the ASIC Adviser Register, 608/4,000 [15.2%] authorised representatives responded. Long-standing, it is typical for survey response rates to be generally low (Sekaran 2000). Next, these cases were screened to determine the useable data suitable for SEM technique. Only 17.94% [47/262] in 98 instances out of 5,502 data points (1.78%) [Table 1 in Appendix 5.1] claimed the questions in the survey were irrelevant to them or they misunderstood the question.

The missing data in the survey questionnaire were negligible [Figure 5.1]. Section A of the survey produced evidence of five [1.90%] cases out of 262 cases with about half [47.62%] of the variables with missing data. Only .2% [11] missing values in the entire sample as illustrated in Figure 5.1. When data were examined by the pattern of missing data in the Table 2 in Appendix 5.2, case 171 had missing data of less than 5%. To avoid losing efficiency, the method Lynch (2003) proposed to just listwise delete the missing observations if less than 5% missing, was not implemented. Furthermore, Harrington (2009) claimed any listwise deletion can result in a loss of power by reducing the sample size, leading to inefficiency in estimating SE of a parameter. Cases 165 and 108 in Table 2 in Appendix 5.2 had missing values greater than 5%, but less than 10%. A method recommended for these cases is a regression-based imputation method whereby

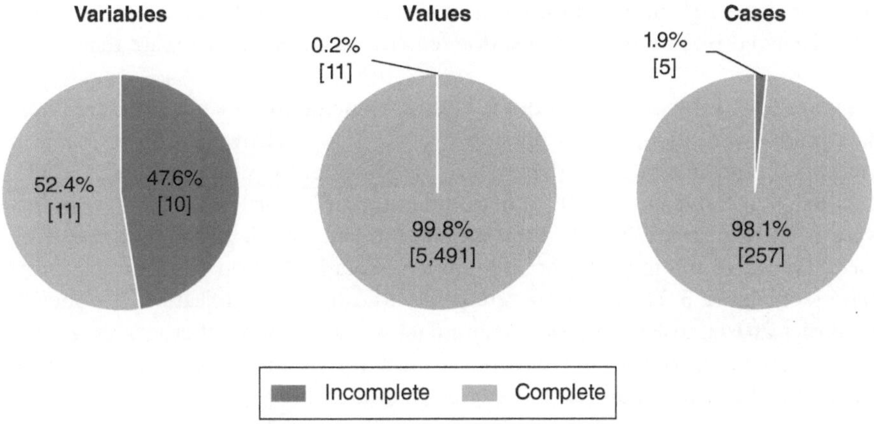

Figure 5.1 Overall summary of missing values for Section A of the questionnaire.

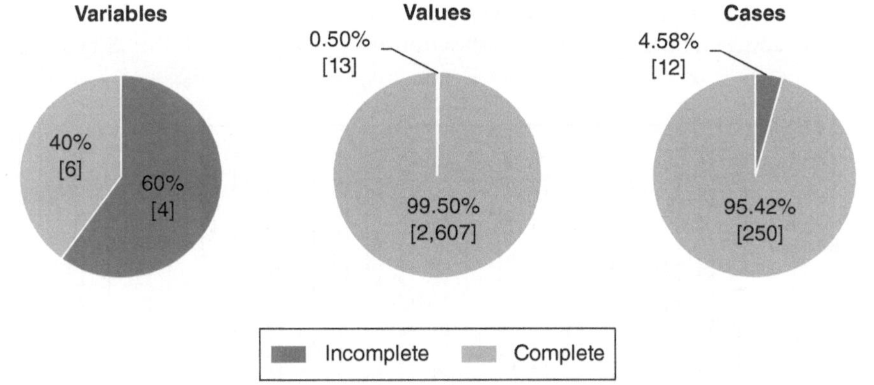

Figure 5.2 Overall summary of missing values for Section B of the questionnaire.

the missing data are replaced with regression means for missing values between 5% and 10% (Lynch 2003). This remedy was rejected, because Lynch (2003) claimed a limitation of this approach found during their simulation is that it produces mean imputation or correction biases. Cases 198 and 261 had missing data greater than 10%, but less than 20%. Thus, Lynch (2003) endorsed using a selection model or sophisticated technique for handling the missing data for data clearly not missing at random [MAR]. If MAR, then one can then either listwise delete or use some method of imputation, for example, multiple, hot decking and expectation-maximization.

Although all these proposed solutions seem reasonable, the dummy variable adjustment method was used, whereby the missing values on a variable are replaced with the neutral value of 50%, signifying undecided or unsure [neither agree or disagree], non-committal, inapplicable or misunderstanding the question. To avoid biasing the findings, this remedy was more appropriate than other methods.

Figure 5.1 [Table 2 in Appendix 5.2] shows a negligible 11 out of 5,502 [.2%] data points were identified as missing overall. The dummy variable imputation method should not bias the parameters, or importantly, the SE (Lynch 2003). As Tabachnick and Fidell (2007) recommended, if 5% or less of the data points were MAR for large samples, then any method to handle missing data can be used. The small number of ignorable missing data in Section B of the questionnaire [see Figure 5.2], were only reported without any modification (Cooper & Schindler 2014). Tolerating the missing data was appropriate, because they form a small percentage of the total data points, did not exist in critical areas and were not worth the cost to correct (Cooper & Schindler 2014, p. 378).

When the data for outliers were inspected, 21 or .382% [21/5,502] univariate outliers for model fit (Aguinis, Gottfredson & Joo 2013) were detected in the boxplots in Graph 5.1. These boxplots generated in SPSS indicated just a small number of responses were heavily weighted towards the upper half of the RO away from the mean. Three variables, namely Dual [nine outliers], BestRev [six outliers] and Personal [six outliers] show outliers [Graph 5.1] in SPSS analysis.

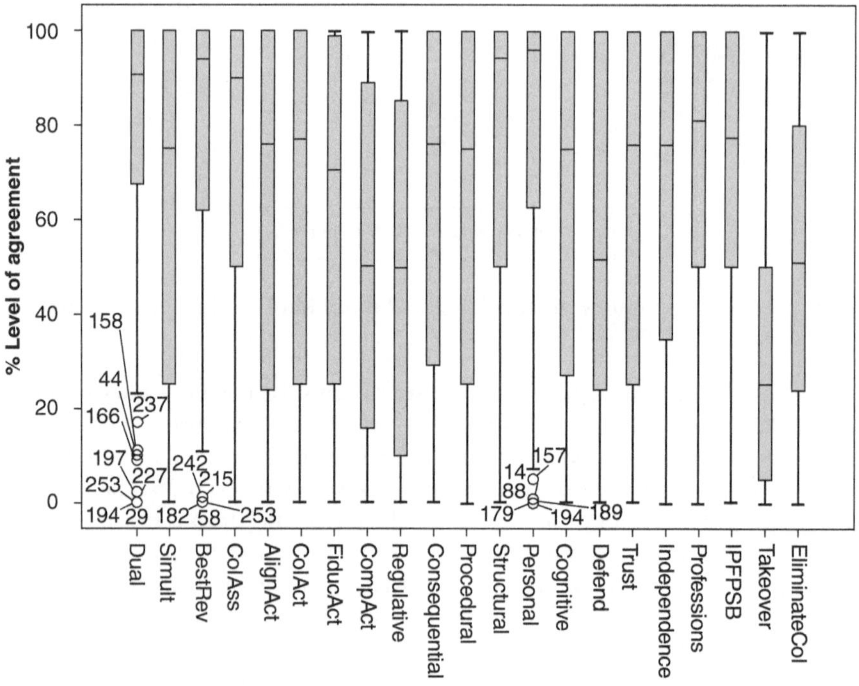

Graph 5.1 Box plots of univariate normality and outliers.

The responses collected did not fall into a normal distribution. Violations of univariate normality is confirmed by the SPSS-generated histograms and PP-plots which were clearly indicated by s-shape skewness, resulting in the distributions being significantly different from a normal distribution.

To detect model fit outliers in the space of the predictors standing distinctly apart from all the other, Mahalanobis d-squared (Stevens 1984; Gaskin 2011; Byrne 2013) was used. A review of Table 3 in Appendix 5.3 shows in p1 column and p2 column the correlations between the variables for these responses are abnormal or significantly different to the rest of the data set for this model (Byrne 2013).[1,2] However, there was no justification to remove these records.

Furthermore, the multivariate kurtosis value of 87.028 in Table 5.1 referred to the Mardia's coefficient (Byrne 2013) confirmed non-normality of the data. In this table, negative skewness statistics for all variables, except for Regulative [a_9], was evident. Evidence of highly skewed distributions [values less than –1 or greater than +1] occurred for variables Dual [a_1], BestIRevenue [a_3], ColAssociation [a_4] and Personal [a_{13}]. Evidence of distributions moderately symmetrical [skewness values between –1 to –.5 and +1.5 to +1]. Likewise, negative kurtosis scores seem evident for most variables. The fairly flat and light-tailed distribution kurtosis values were within the acceptable range of –2 and +2 (Sposito, Hand & Skarpness 1983). Although no clear consensus exists in the literature as to how large the values should be, only variables with skew index absolute values greater than three (Kline 2010) and kurtosis index absolute values greater than seven (Byrne 2013) or ten were considered troublesome (Kline 2010). Therefore,

Table 5.1 Assessment of normality [Group number 1].

Variable	*Min*	*Max*	*Skewness*	*c.r.*	*Kurtosis*	*c.r.*
a_1	0	100	-1.381	-9.126	.728	2.405
a_2	0	100	-.453	-2.996	-1.237	-4.086
a_3	0	100	-1.329	-8.779	.808	2.669
a_4	0	100	-1.130	-7.467	-.093	-.307
a_5	0	100	-.413	-2.728	-1.421	-4.696
a_6	0	100	-.673	-4.450	-1.100	-3.634
a_7	0	100	-.406	-2.680	-1.312	-4.334
a_8	0	100	-.062	-.406	-1.465	-4.841
a_9	0	100	.091	.600	-1.485	-4.905
a_{10}	0	100	-.635	-4.193	-1.081	-3.573
a_{11}	0	100	-.508	-3.357	-1.278	-4.224
a_{13}	0	100	-1.294	-8.550	.641	2.118
a_{14}	0	100	-.567	-3.749	-1.140	-3.768
a_{16}	0	100	-.587	-3.882	-1.203	-3.976
a_{17}	0	100	-.687	-4.538	-.975	-3.221
a_{18}	0	100	-.818	-5.404	-.812	-2.683
a_{19}	0	100	-.779	-5.145	-.815	-2.692
a_{21}	0	100	-.118	-.778	-1.318	-4.354
Multivariate					**87.028**	**26.249**

visibly none of the reported skewness and kurtosis indicated problematic levels of concern.

Additionally to guard against overall Type I errors, whereby an effect in the population is statistically mistakenly identified, when none was present (Field 2014), Cook's distance [D] (Stevens 1984) was plotted on a scatter plot (Gaskin 2012) to identify the outliers. From Cook's D, clearly the outliers were neither errors nor influential. Instead, they were considered interesting outliers (Aguinis, Gottfredson & Joo 2013), because each individual outlier case appeared engaged on the basis of the amount of time spent on the survey. They attempted to complete the optional comments box. These comments are shown in Tables 4a, b and c in Appendix 5.4.

Furthermore, Cook's D for each case were less than the highest value of .26143 as illustrated in the scatterplot in Graph 5.2. Hence, the entire Cook's D were less than the threshold of one. Thus, not influencing the regression of the variable (Stevens 1984; Gaskin 2012).

From advisers' comments, the main reasons behind the outliers were how they understood or interpreted the survey questions about their role within the licensee–adviser–client relationship, as well as their perceptions of leaders' influence when lobbying government during consultation phases of proposed legislative changes. According to Aguinis, Gottfredson and Joo (2013),

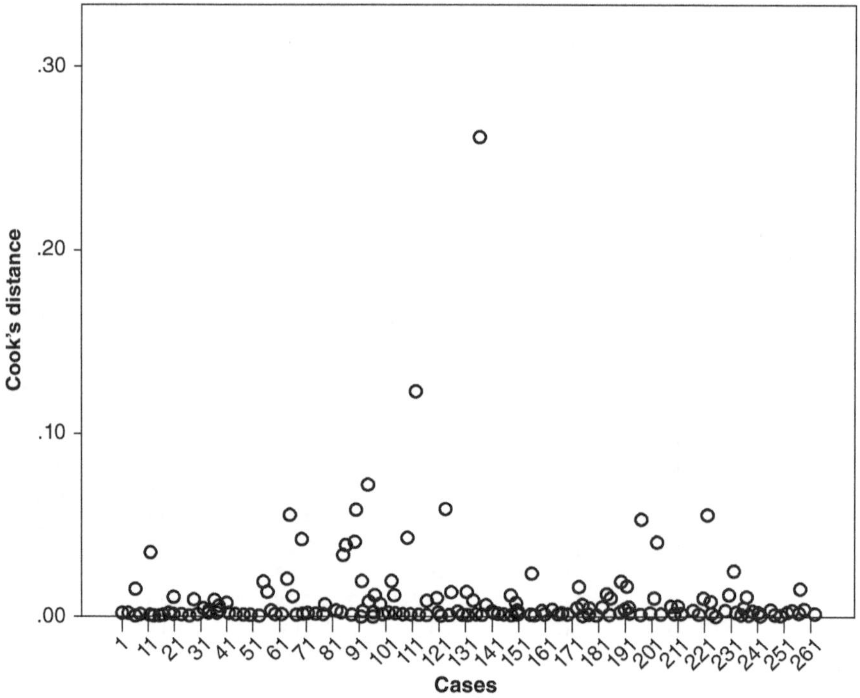

Graph 5.2 Scatterplot of highest Cook's difference on variable a_{11}.

interpretations of survey questions will change the model fit [the substantive estimates]. Despite this, there was no need to remove these global prediction outliers (Stevens 1984), because they formed part of the population of interest (Chan & Bishop 2013). This is further supported in a paper by Aguinis, Gottfredson and Joo (2013) arguing to exercise caution before deleting outliers, because in doing so ends up potentially supporting the hypothesis being tested. According to them, when researchers define, identify and handle outliers impacting the parameter relationships, effect sizes, directions and existence, this has significant implications and conclusions for a project.

On the basis of the multivariate kurtosis value [87.028] in Table 5.1 and their critical value [referred to as the "*normalised estimate of multivariate kurtosis*" (Byrne 2013, p. 123)] of 26.249, which was greater than five, the data in the sample were clearly non-normally distributed (Byrne 2013). Evidence of multivariate non-normality was found, because critical ratio [c.r.] value of 23.763 is greater than the z statistic threshold of 1.96 (Byrne 2013). Using the criteria provided by some authors (Harrington 2009), skewness and kurtosis do not appear problematic.

Especially when Wang and Wang (2012) explained maximum likelihood estimates are less likely to be biased in the presence of non-normality. However, they cautioned to be aware, SE of maximum likelihood estimates and model fit indices were underestimated when non-normality was evident. They claimed non-normality inflates the model χ^2 statistics. They endorsed as solutions adjusting the normal theory ML χ^2 and SE using rescaling methods or to use the bootstrap method. A technique they claimed provided robust SE and mean-adjusted χ^2 test statistic equivalent to Satorra & Bentler [SB] χ^2. During this analysis, the bootstrap method was applied, because of its accessibility in Amos.

With regard to linearity, the values in the ANOVA Table 5.2 were significant only for Structural * FiducAct [$p = .002$] and for Professions * IPFPSB [$p = .029$], which indicated these relationships deviated from linearity (Gaskin 2016c).

The assumption of homogeneity of variance, which is the opposite of heteroscedasticity, was not violated, because estimates of the data range divided by their SDs all fell between acceptable thresholds two and six (Field 2014), with all estimates less than 3.496. See Table 5 in Appendix 5.5 for the estimates for all the variables in the model. If these values were greater than six, then heterogeneity issues would have been present. Therefore, there was no need to reduce this particular bias using the robust method of bootstrapping (Field 2014). This outcome was confirmed by a second test to assess homogeneity.

Using SPSS regression linear graph scatterplot function [see an example of variable Structural variable a_4 in Graph 5.3] for each relationship, the researcher plotted the variables' regression standardised error residual value on the y-axis against the regression standardised *independent* or predictor variables on the x-axis and added a fit line (Gaskin 2015). In all the variables' cases, there is homoscedasticity, because the fit line appeared relatively flat and the data were roughly consistent around the fit line (Gaskin 2015). Given the sample size was large, the Levene's test to determine whether the variance is potentially heteroscedastic or there is homogeneity, was considered inappropriate (Field 2014).

Table 5.2 ANOVA table to test deviation from linearity.

			Sum of Squares	*df*	*Mean Square*	*F*	*Sig.*
Structural * FiducAct	Between Groups	[Combined]	184119.9	56	3287.856	6.629	0
		Linearity	136020.5	1	136020.5	274.226	0
		Deviation from Linearity	48099.41	55	874.535	1.763	.002
	Within Groups		101683.5	205	496.017		
	Total		285803.4	261			
Professions * IPFPSB	Between Groups	[Combined]	203755.9	52	3918.383	5.821	0
		Linearity	152887.2	1	152887.2	227.114	0
		Deviation from Linearity	50868.74	51	997.426	1.482	.029
	Within Groups		140693.2	209	673.173		
	Total		344449.1	261			

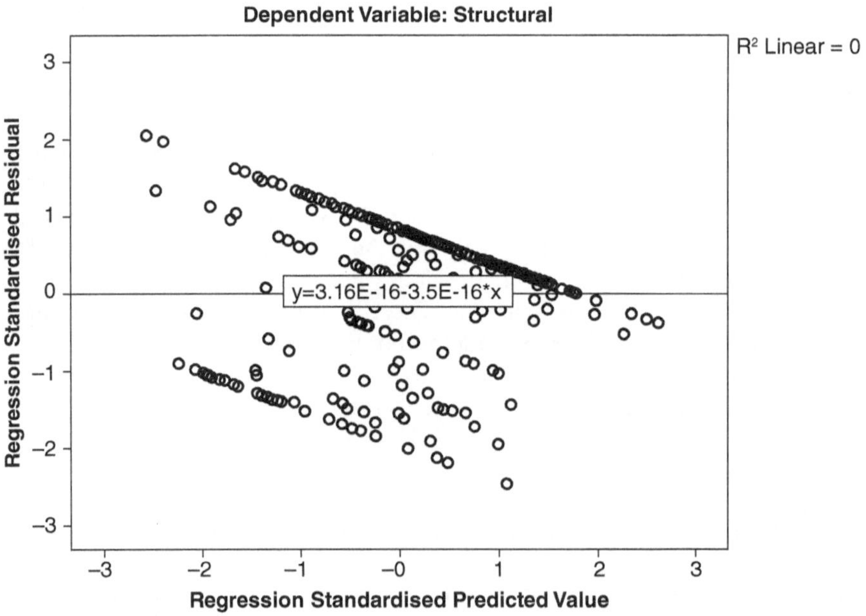

Graph 5.3 Scatterplot to test homogeneity of variable Structural [a_4].

Next, a multicollinearity errors test was performed by running a multivariate regression. Here, it was found all variables' tolerance statistic of $1-r^2$, where r^2 is the variance in each *independent* variable explained by all of the other *independent* variables, were greater than the threshold of .1 and .2 (Menard 2002) in Table 6 in Appendix 5.6. Additionally, from evidence in Table 6 in Appendix 5.6, no serious multicollinearity problems occurred (Gaskin 2016d), because for most of the *independent* variables the VIF is below three, with only a handful of variables with VIFs greater than 5.206. Thus the statistics verifies VIFs were not violated to a great extent, but were tolerable, and hence, should not invalidate the CIs and significance tests (Field 2014). It was concluded the variables did not correlate too highly and there were non-zero variances, thus the CIs where the population values of estimates are likely to fall are reliable and valid. Thus, the model can be generalised to the population and the significance tests accepted as valid (Field 2014).

Despite the limitation of multicollinearity issues, this research is interested not in the effect of multicollinearity on the ith regression coefficient, but instead in whether the regression coefficient is statistically significant (O'Brien 2007). Therefore, there was no specific need to solve for multicollinearity and *independent* errors. Furthermore, the literature on this issue authenticated it safe to focus on the combined effects of all of the variables in the model (Menard 2002). In addition, for large samples, the lack of normality of distributed errors [not predictors] will not invalidate CIs and significance tests, because of the central limit theorem (Field 2014).

In closing, to address additivity and linearity violation by ColAss * FiducAct [p = .002] and for Professions * IPFPSB [p = .029] evident in Table 5.2, and multivariate non-normality, as proposed in the literature (Aguinis, Gottfredson & Joo 2013), the analysis utilised bootstrapping in Amos at a 95% CI for bias-corrected CI, rather than some of the numerous approaches evident in research practice (Byrne 2013).

In summary, overall, the quantitative screening statistical results of this investigation were positive, with the bias of data and any assumption violations defensible and hence manageable. Consequently, the main study research methodology of using SEM was proven feasible.

Descriptive statistical analysis results

After data screening, only 6.55% [262/4,000 respondents] of the responses on the legitimacy of current licensing contained useful data for analysis, as illustrated in Table 5.3. This level of participation was disappointing, because it was evident, from discussions held with professional media, academics, senior members of the emerging financial planning profession, some financial planning practitioners, attendees at three Personal Finance and Investment Symposiums in November of 2014, 2015, and 2016 and a representative of the Professional Standards Authority, this controversial matter of current adviser licensing is [or should] be important to all financial planning stakeholders. Evident during these discussions,

Table 5.3 Types of responses.

Types of Responses	*Frequency*	*Percent*
Qualtrics email failed to send	1	.03
Opt out [Unsubscribed]	272	6.80
Consents declined	4	.10
Non-responses	3,391	84.77
Incomplete responses	70	1.75
Complete responses (Data analysis useable responses)	262	6.55
Total probability random sample selected	4,000	100

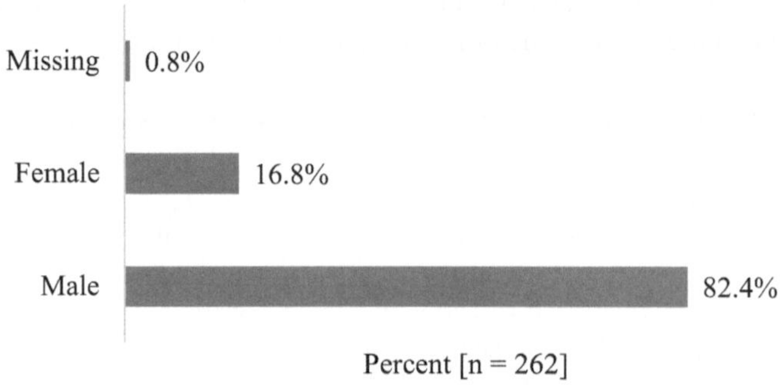

Graph 5.4 Frequency of gender split of respondents.

as well as during the survey itself, the study was timely given the government's attempt at driving for professionalising financial planning. Despite the low useable data response rate, recruiting more participants was sidestepped. Recruiting more, would have potentially caused additional sampling bias. It was unnecessary, because there were more than enough data to perform MLE in Amos.[3]

Graph 5.4 and Table 7 in Appendix 5.7 indicate the gender split. Two respondents failed to offer details of their gender.

The bar chart in Graph 5.5 and Table 8 in Appendix 5.8 indicate most survey respondents were unsurprisingly Baby Boomers [approximately 55.7%] born between 1946 and 1964 followed by Gen X, then Gen Y or Millennials and Traditionalists. Only one respondent evaded providing details of his or her age.

From Table 9 in Appendix 5.9 and Figure 5.3, it is apparent the recruits covered the whole of Australia, with the majority [nearly one-third] from New South Wales, followed by Queensland, Victoria, South Australia, Western Australia, Tasmania, Australian Capital Territory and then Northern Territory. Everyone offered their locations of work.

From the histogram in Graph 5.6 [Table 10 in Appendix 5.10], it was evident the frequency of the number of years' respondents have been ARs followed a normal distribution reasonably closely. Only four [1.5%] respondents failed to provide details of the length they have been ARs.

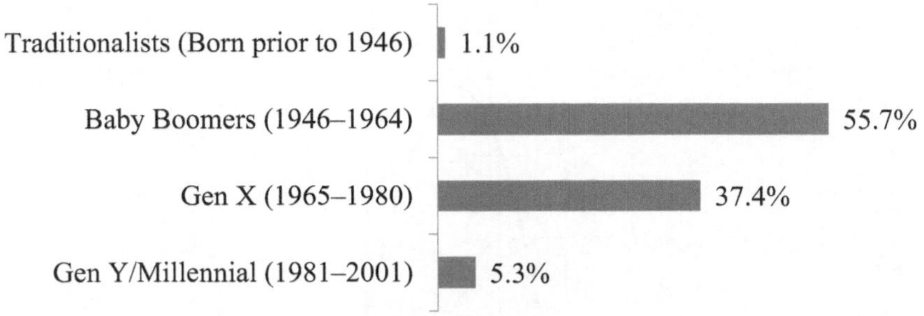

Graph 5.5 Frequency of age of survey respondents.

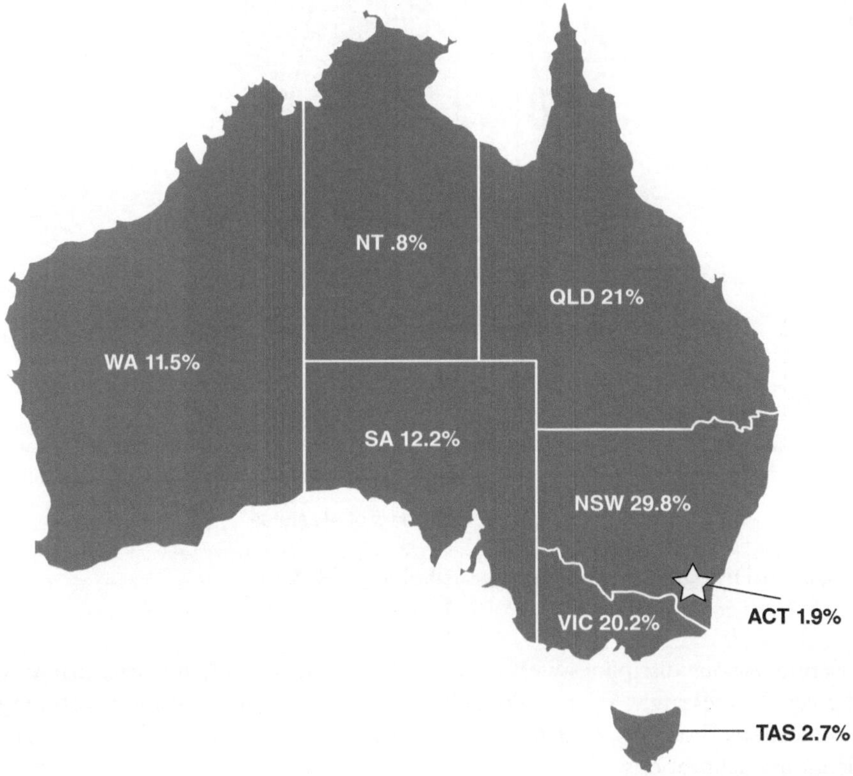

Figure 5.3 Frequency of the location of respondents.

It was evident there were no doctorates [Graph 5.7; Table 11 in Appendix 5.11] among the recruits. In addition, 27.1% [70] had a financial planning degree and postgraduate financial planning qualifications, with 69.7% [180] claiming they held other forms of financial planning qualifications. Most [63.7%] had degrees

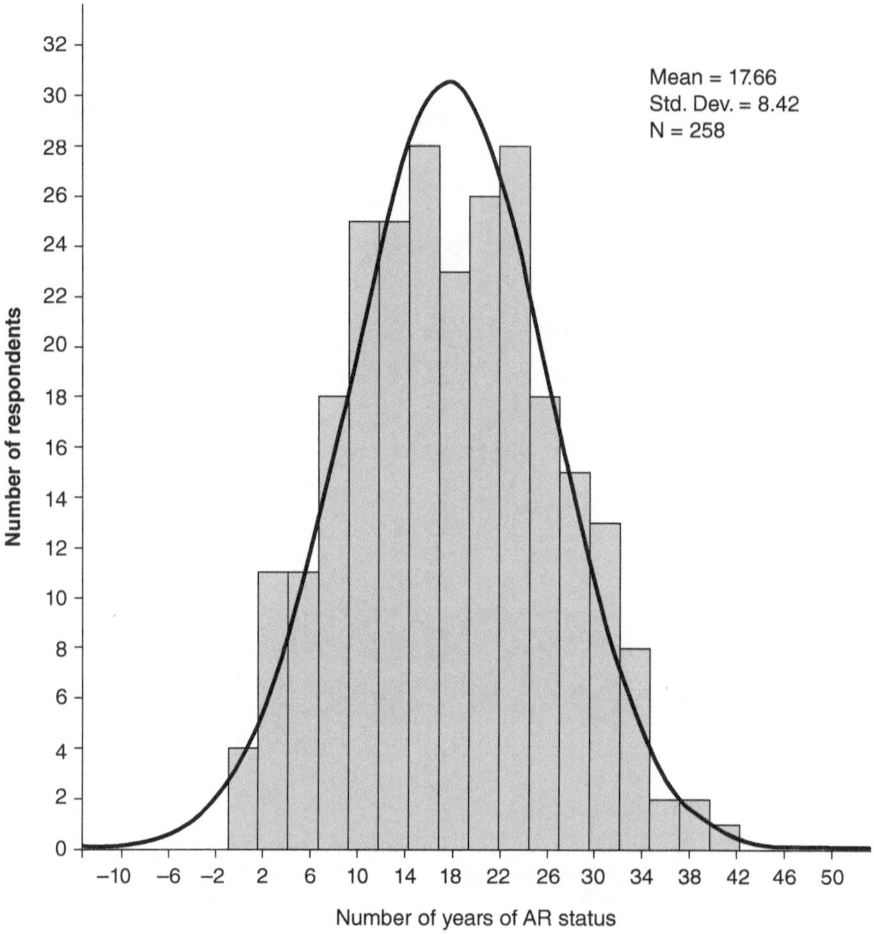

Graph 5.6 Histogram of number of years holding AR status.

covering various disciplines with only 26.7% with specifically financial planning degrees. Interestingly, six recruits held no AQF recognised financial planning qualifications. Four respondents evaded providing any details of their financial planning qualifications.

When advisers were asked about their professional association membership, evident from Table 12 in Appendix 5.12, survey respondents claimed membership of a diverse range of professional associations. Unsurprisingly, the majority were members of the FPA, followed by the Self-Managed Super Fund Association and Association of Financial Advisers. Interestingly, 8.8% represented non-membership of any association. One participant indicated he or she was a member of six associations, with five claiming membership of three professional

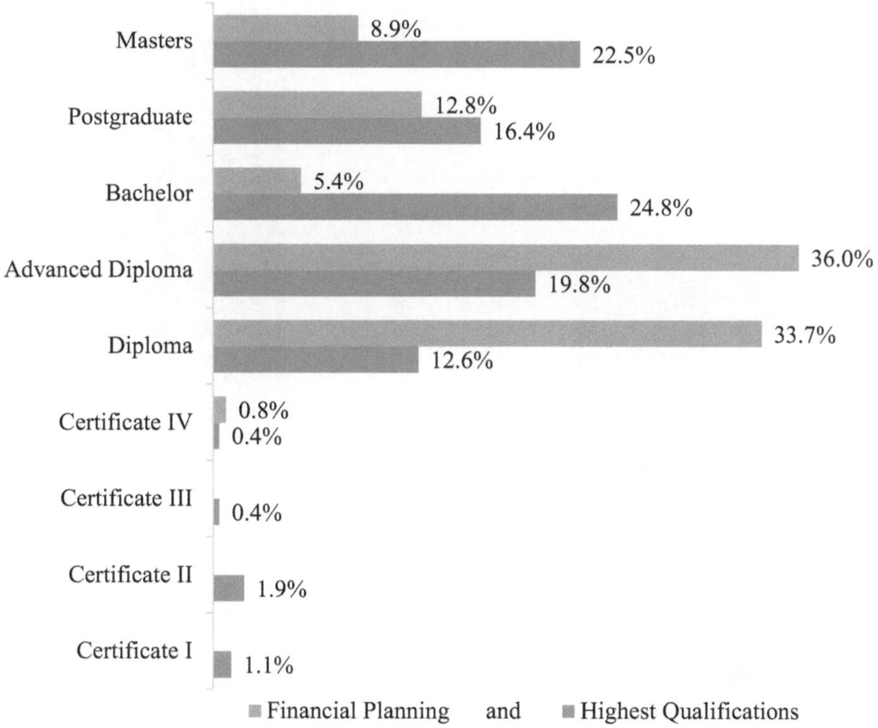

Graph 5.7 Frequency of the highest and financial planning AQF qualifications [$n = 262$].

associations and 50 claiming membership of two associations listed in Table 12 in Appendix 5.12. Although 53.8% of survey respondents claimed to hold a CFP qualification, 25.6% of the recruits held no professional qualifications [see Table 13 in Appendix 5.13]. Of the 67 who held no formal professional qualifications, four claimed they were studying towards a CFP. One AFA adviser claimed he or she was completing the FChFP professional qualifications. About 15.3% indicated they were certified practicing accountants.

Most respondents were self-employed ARs [Graph 5.8] and Table 14 in Appendix 5.14. No missing responses in this part of the survey after data screening was found.

Table 15 in Appendix 5.15 and Graph 5.9 illustrated, 47.7% of cases perceived themselves to be aligned. Most striking was that a smaller proportion, 14.9%, considered themselves affiliated to s923A *independent* licensees. The non-aligned nearly made up 37% of respondents, yet were not s923A *independent*, because at this stage, the use of the term "non-aligned" was not limited to s923A *independent* licensees and advisers.

The biographic details indicate the survey covered a broad range of advisers of various ages, from a diverse range of backgrounds, operating across Australia and

Graph 5.8 Frequency of AR status [*n* = 262].

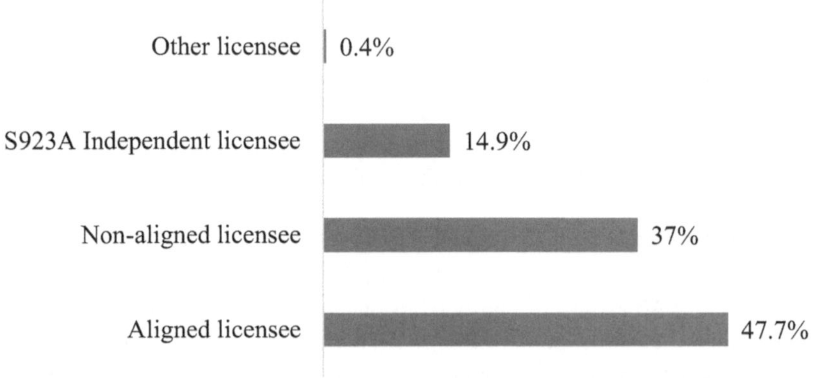

Graph 5.9 Frequency of licensee status [*n* = 262].

included s923A *independents*. On these grounds, this research is important to advisers on the basis of their willingness to participate in a lengthy survey regarding licensing advisers.

Structural equation modelling results

Exploratory/confirmatory factor analysis results

Evident from the initial results of MLE, the researcher realised there may have been a theoretical basis for the *a priori* model illustrated in Figure 4.4 in Chapter 4, but initially not an empirical one. Furthermore, from the GOF results in column 1 of Table 5.6, noticeably this *a priori* model is misspecified. It is well-documented, any initial specified measurement models almost invariably fail to deliver acceptable fit (Anderson & Gerbing 1988). Acceptable fit meaning the most variance is accounted for by the best fit (Myung, Tang & Pitt 2009). Consequently, a data-driven EFA approach within a CFA MLE method (Brown & Moore 2016) disclosed the first initial source of misspecification was too many factors, because the inter-item correlations were greater than .85 (Clark & Watson 1995). This over-factoring confirmed further evidence of multicollinearity (Byrne 2013). The higher the correlations between two factors, the greater the discrepancy between the pattern loadings and the structure loadings on some variables (Matsunaga 2010). Consequently, factors b_2 and b_3 were collapsed into one factor [b_3]. Thus, indicators AlignAct [a_5], CoIAct [a_6], CompAct [a_8] and FiducAct [a_7], were merged into the Legitimacy factor [b_3]. This merge was confirmed appropriate per the initial pattern matrix during E/CFA analysis in SPSS [see Table 16, Appendix 5.16]. Coefficients of the pattern matrix are the unique loads of the given factor into variables, namely regression coefficients (Gaskin 2016b). To simplify and clarify the data and confirm the conclusions so far, Promax rotation, an oblique rotation, using SPSS's default kappa four, was performed, because it allowed the factors to correlate (Osborne & Costello 2005). It produced a more accurate reproducible solution with more information compared with other methods (Osborne & Costello 2005). Employing an oblique-rotation approach assists with conceptual consistency across the EFA and CFA analysis (Matsunaga 2010). EFA using oblique rotation helps identify unrelated factors and irrelevant indicators (Matsunaga 2010). The higher the kappa, the higher the correlations (Matsunaga 2010). Therefore, it was decided to use the default low kappa value of four.

The EFA structure matrix was used to determine which variables to drop. Matsunaga (2010) claimed this was a better method to use than pattern matrix. Although the initial structure matrix analysis [see Table 17, Appendix 5.17] indicated most items on each question adequately represented their constructs, three variables were identified problematic. First, EFA structure matrix in Table 17 in Appendix 5.17 indicated CoIAss [a_4] loaded significantly better onto construct legitimacy [b_3] compared with latent factor dual [b_1]. After re-evaluation of its theoretical explanation and content, it was concluded substantively the definition of Structural legitimacy [a_{12}] was better explained by the variable CoIAss [a_4]. Instead of conflict of interest from association being explained by the agent–principal relationship, it arguably made more sense to apply it as a structural issue within current licensing regime, because by being licensed via third-party licensees is structurally debase if it leads to conflict of interest from association. Subsequently, based on EFA pattern matrix, the financial planning theory for structural legitimacy was normatively and empirically re-evaluated and replaced with a more appropriate theoretical underpinning, sourced from the secondary theory, concurrent with an appropriate measure. Thus, the measure CoIAss [a_4] loading initially onto the factor dual [b_1] in the *a priori* model [a_4], was renamed Structural [a_4] and replaced Structural [a_{12}]. This new measure for structural legitimacy was better explained by the latent factor legitimacy [b_3]. Furthermore, comments made by some respondents for the Structural variable a_{12} indicated their interpretation and understanding of the question was not as it was intended in the survey. For example, one respondent, who reflected others' views, claimed for the statement meant this excluded self-licensed advisers, "*Surely the option is there to apply for your own licence?*"; "*They can get their own license.*" The intention of this statement was to include self-licensed advisers. The objective of this account was to find out whether it was structurally legitimate for advisers to lose their right to work when they have been no longer an authorised representative. Thus, the analysis confirmed the view of Brown and Moore (2016), EFA was useful in improving flaws in the theory too. Especially concerning how the various theories from other disciplines were applied and integrated with financial planning theory.

Additionally, based on the EFA pattern matrix, Structural [a_{12}], Defend [a_{15}] and Takeover [a_{20}] were eliminated from latent factors b_3 and $b_{4,}$ respectively. They had factor loadings less than .30 and their cross-loadings differed by less than .2. With regard to the Takeover [a_{20}] statement 'Strategic *independent* advice is being taken over by the accounting profession, as accountants redefine and re-position financial planning within their self-regulatory model,' was not interpreted by the intent of the statement and context of the topic. This view was reflected in comments such as "*That's laughable*" and "*This is rubbish I've got a lot of my clients from accountants as they would not give advice.*"; "*In my experience accountants do not have the knowledge to provide appropriate advice regarding areas such as Centrelink and aged care.*"; "*No. Accountants do not have the necessary expertise in the eyes of the clients.*" Therefore, on quantitative [very low loadings] and on qualitative statistical grounds [comments], this measure was deleted.

Variable Defend [a_{15}] ['Since the media has exposed the financial planning scandals, advisers have had to defend their relationship/association/affiliation with their licensee to clients'], indicated some statistical issues, with unacceptable low factor scores. Once again, advisers were answering the statement from their practice's experience, emotional or from a desirability point of view, rather than as the question tried to elicit, namely advisers in general. For example, "*The answer to this question is both yes and no. There have been some scandals however the majority of financial advisers and their clients have not been involved and/or impacted. Not all advisers are bad. I have a large business [when compared to the market], I have never had to defend a relationship.*" Some found the question offensive, others responded defensively. For example, "*Again, I am offended by the tone of these questions. This appears to be a witch hunt against licensees and advisers. Storm Financial had been ticked off as compliant by ASIC in 2007 – they were self licensed?*" Some other examples include, "*NOT ME – I HAVE NEVER BEEN LINKED TO ANY OF THOSE ISSUES*" and "*Not me!*" The obvious unclear wording, misunderstanding by respondents or multiple comprehensions or interpretations and perhaps perceived tone of question may have ultimately invalidated the measure as an indicator of the latent factor Legitimacy [b_3]. These deletions did not jeopardise the integrity of the theory or data but improved it. It solved the statistical problems of explaining the factors (Osborne & Costello 2005) so the main research question and investigative questions were better answered. Furthermore, deleting these measures ensured a more parsimonious model for CFA (Kline 2010; Byrne 2013).

A fourth problematic variable evident in the *a priori* model was Cognitive [a_{14}]. It displayed a higher estimate when loading onto b_4 than the *a priori* model. Despite this anomaly, it was decided to retain this variable in factor b_3, because no theoretical substantive reason to move it or remove it could be justified. In addition, no replacement variable was available to substitute it. Furthermore, its loading was greater than .30 and hence interpretable and persuasive enough.

The scree plot after E/CFA indicating three factors after the kink [Graph 5.10] confirmed the respecification as summarised in the pattern matrix after E/CFA shown in Table 5.4. Thus, as illustrated in Table 18 in Appendix 5.18, three hypotheses and survey questions, and hence variables, were discarded. Hence, only three factors out of the original pre-conceived four factor-model and 18 out of the original 21 measures remained for further analysis. Uni-dimensionality was achieved in the CFA model, because all measuring items have acceptable factor loadings for the respective latent construct and all factor loadings were positive. Therefore, using EFA within the CFA MLE framework resulted in the appropriate

Table 5.4 Pattern matrix[a] after E/CFA.

	Factor		
	1	*2*	*3*
Dual			.532
Simult			.611
BestRev			.508
ColAss	.711		
AlignAct	.921		
ColAct	.821		
FiducAct	.958		
CompAct	.580		
Regulative	.767		
Consequential	.932		
Procedural	.850		
Personal	.483		
Cognitive	.358	.378	
Trust		.866	
Independence		.767	
Professions		.759	
IPFPSB		.811	
EliminateCol		.689	

Note: Coefficients were suppressed above an absolute value of .35 during SPSS EFA estimation.
Extraction Method: Maximum Likelihood.
Rotation Method: Promax with Kaiser Normalisation.
a Rotation converged in five iterations.

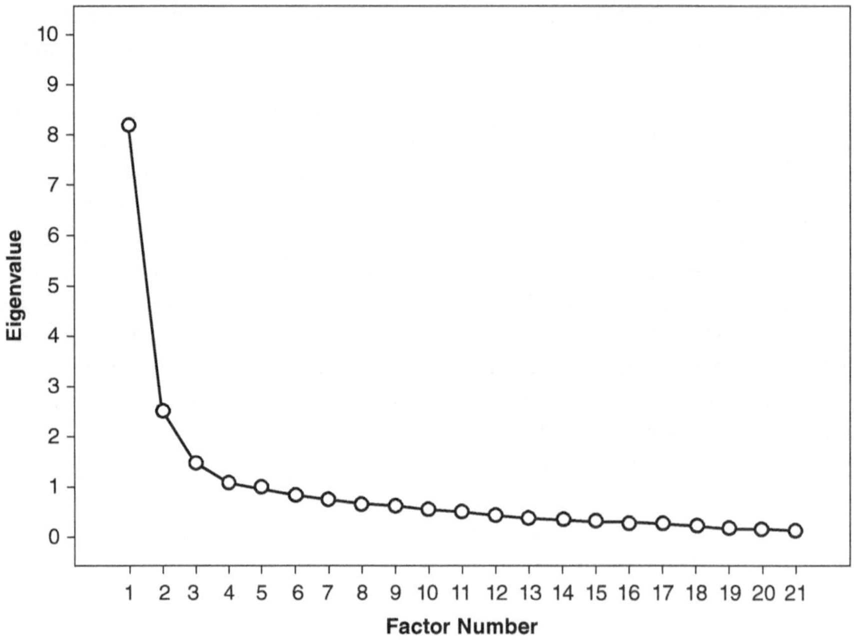

Graph 5.10 Scree plot after E/CFA indicating three factors after the kink.

number of factors and correct measures for each latent construct (Brown 2006) illustrated in Figure 5.4. Significant cross-loadings were fixed when evaluating the initial model against the pattern matrix. Subsequently, poorly selected indicators and error covariance were fixed to zero to see if they would further produce a refined model for CFA after MLE.

Confirmatory factor analysis maximum likelihood estimation results

After E/CFA was conducted, CFA using the EFA modified model in Figure 5.4 proceeded.

During MLE, there were no incidences of non-convergence, Heywood cases, improper solutions (Byrne 2013), any 'missing constraint' errors or indications the estimation was unable to reach its iteration limit (Gaskin 2016e). The standardised estimates indicated the latent variable and indicators, where the mean was equal to zero and the SD was equal to one, were all positive.

Although the EFA model fit had improved after E/CFA, it was not meeting the thresholds expected to achieve good fit. For instance, in column 2 of Table 5.5, the CMIN *p*-value is less than .05; an indication the model is different from the population's true covariance structure (Ke-Hai 2005; Bentler 2006; Hayduk *et al.* 2006; Barrett 2007). Given CMIN has been criticised for

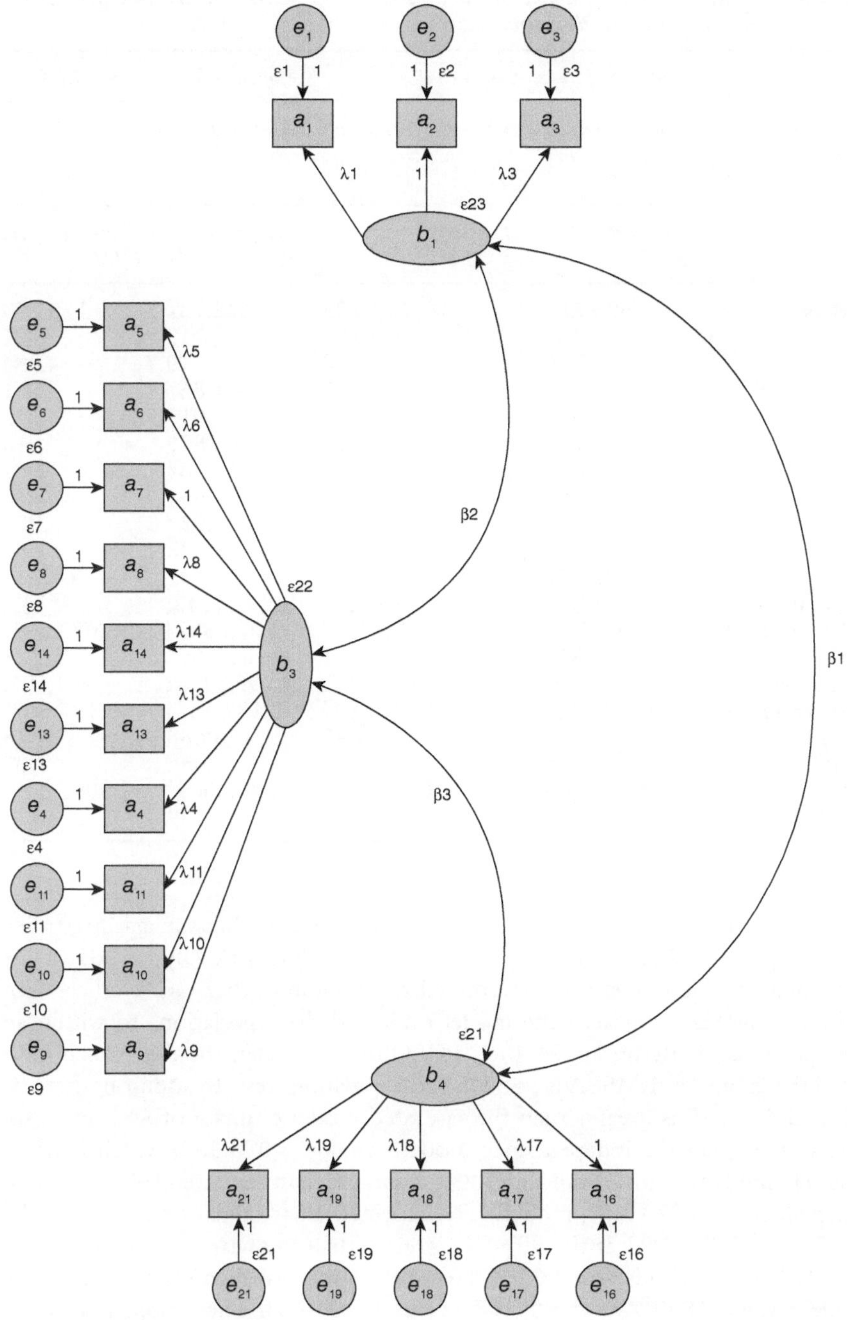

Figure 5.4 CFA measurement model prior to respecification using modification indices.

Table 5.5 Goodness of fit statistics of the bootstrapped MLE *a priori* model, after E/CFA and after CFA respecification.

	Column 1	*Column 2*	*Column 3*	*Column 4*
Measure	*a priori model before E/CFA and CFA*	*After E/CFA before respecification using MIs*	*After CFA respecified using MIs*	
	Bootstrap ex CLF	*Bootstrap ex CLF*	*Bootstrap ex CLF*	*Bootstrap cum CLF*
CMIN	536.537	374.725	222.131	128.339
DF	183	132	119	101
P	0	0	0	.034
CMIN/DF	2.932	2.839	1.867	1.271
GFI	.831	.859	.915	.95
AGFI	.787	.817	.878	.915
CFI	.884	.916	.964	.991
TLI	.866	.902	.954	.986
NFI	.835	.877	.927	.958
PCFI	.77	.79	.75	.654
AIC	632.537	452.725	326.131	268.339
[Saturated; *Independent*]	[462; 3,287.878]	[342.725; 3,073.337]	[342; 3,073.337]	[342; 3,073.337]
BIC	803.818	591.891	511.685	518.123
[Saturated; *Independent*]	[1286.288; 3,362.813]	[952.187; 3,137.567]	[952.187; 3,137.567]	[952.187; 3,137.567]
SRMR	.793	.0692	.0688	.0318
RMSEA	.086	.084	.058	.032
[90% CI]	[.078; .095]	[.074; .094]	[.046; .069]	[.009; .048]
PCLOSE	0	0	.139	.971

generally being unreliable for large *n*s greater than 250 (Matsunaga 2010) like this study of $n = 262$, on recommendations in the literature (Byrne 2013), the plausibility of the model was determined by including other GOF indices. For example, RMSEA indicated the model explained the correlations to within an average error of (Byrne 2013) .084. PCLOSE is less than the .05, which indicated the failure of 'RMSEA is good in the population' test. In addition, the AIC value of 452.725 is greater than the saturated model estimate of 342. Even so, it is smaller than the independence model of value 3,073.337, which is desirable. Desirable is the BIC value 591.891 is smaller than saturated [952.187] and independence [3,073.337] models. The expected cross-validation index [ECVI] is 1.735 [1.528; 1.971 at the 90% CI], greater than the saturated model's value of 1.310 at 90% CI [1.310; 1.310]. However, it was less than the independence model's value of 11.775 at 90% CI [11.103; 12.475]. The absolute fit index critical N [CN] is 103 [$p < .05$] and ten [$p < .01$], which is below the threshold sample size for accepting the model is correct (Schreiber *et al.* 2006). Therefore, together with the Hoelter at alpha .05 of 112 and at .01 of 121 results, it was concluded the model inadequately represents the sample data. Furthermore, the Bollen-Stine bootstrap $p = .005$ for testing the null hypothesis of a correct model confirmed the model is misspecified. So the model is a misfit and misrepresents a reasonable approximation to the population, which means it requires modifications (Byrne 2013).

On the grounds of inadequate fit, before making inferences and testing the hypotheses, CFA specification searches were performed using MI with a cut-off threshold greater than 4.0 (Brown 2006), because it provided recommendations to correct discrepancies or differences between the proposed and estimated model (Hermida 2015, p. 6).

A degree of overlap in item content (Byrne 2013) may arguably have been perceived by some respondents. Thus, starting with the covariances among measurement errors fixed to zero for the reason they were initially assumed unique to each indicator, it was evident several MI estimated at more than four was present. Consequently, after limiting modifications to 13 of the larger modifications greater than four, GOF was achieved within the thresholds specified in Table 5.5 columns 3 and 4. The modifications were justified on empirical and conceptual grounds (Maccallum & Necowitz 1992) to minimise what Hermida (2015) referred to as data-driven specifications searches leading to further model misspecification and overfitting. They claimed this avoids chance associations in the sample data by including unnecessary estimates. Therefore, adding the covariance between the errors to the model in Figure 5.4, to produce Figure 5.5 made sense and were reasonable (Harrington 2009) for reasons shown in Table 19 in Appendix 5.19. They were found to be all significant at $p < .05$ level.

Given the fit statistics indicated, the data fit the model adequately after respecification [columns 3 and 4 in Table 5.5] using MI, the standardised residual covariance estimates were only scrutinised, not used to produce better-fit statistics. It appeared the model did not account for the relationship between Cognitive [a_{14}] and Trust [a_{16}] [SRC = 4.069] and a_{18} [Professions] [4.415], because their SRCs were greater than the SRC critical value of 3.84 for one degree of freedom at the alpha level of .05 (Brown 2006). The data-driven EFA indicated a_{14} [Cognitive] would better load on [b_4] individual licensing, where individual licensing would facilitate a shared understanding of the difference between s923A *independent* advice and conflicted advice could explain this problem. Nevertheless, moving this variable could not be justified, nor was deleting it an option, because it is key to the theoretical basis for a_{14} [Cognitive] legitimacy. While this predictor was of value to the theoretical construct (Byrne 2010), no other measure-to-measure cognitive legitimacy was found. Unlike the original a_{12} [Structural], it could not be replaced with another measurement value, because none was available. As only two out of 171 SRCs showed values larger than four in the matrix, which amounted to only 1.17% of the covariance matrix, it was unnecessary to change the model, unless further problems were found down the track (Matsunaga 2010). Fortunately, no additional problems were identified for these variables further down the track and thus, were retained. Furthermore, additional deletions were not an option, because the variables left in the model added significant

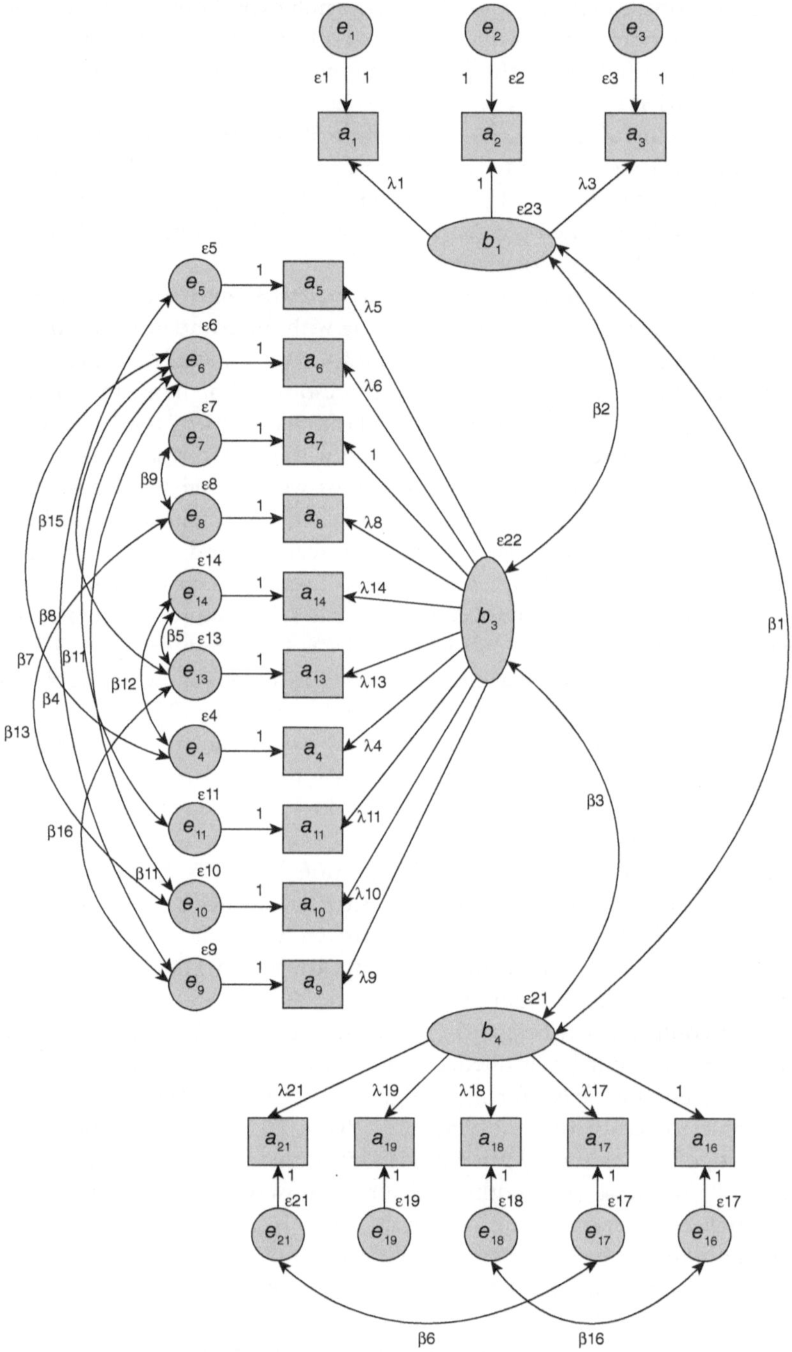

Figure 5.5 Respecified CFA unconstrained measurement model.

value to the theoretical construct (Byrne 2010) and were all significant at the $p < .05$ alpha level. Deleting any more variables would threaten the integrity of the data to solve the statistical problems of explaining the factors (Clark & Watson 1995; Osborne & Costello 2005). After model respecification to produce the model in Figure 5.5, the minimum sample required for MLE increased to 200 cases with effect size of .3, power of .8 and probability level .05. This was established by recalculating the minimum sample size using the online calculator developed by Soper (2016). This number was still below the *n* of 262, which indicated the sample size for this study was sufficient.

Cross-validation results

Thus, with tentative support for the notion, the evolving model was properly specified (Myung, Tang & Pitt 2009); the next step in the progression was cross-validation using another sample drawn from the population. The multiple group gender [male and female] formed the new sample from the same population specified and estimated in the same model, with freely estimated measurement parameters compared with measurement estimates constrained (Anderson & Gerbing 1988). Table 5.6 provides the results of the constrained models nested within less constrained models (Harrington 2009). Bootstrapping was used to generate the estimates, because χ^2 is sensitive to linearity, additivity, multicollinearity and normality (Joreskog 1978).

Table 5.6 indicates the χ^2 difference value is N.S.; therefore, the unconstrained model fits the data better than the constrained model. Consequently, the computed χ^2 statistic was less than the critical value in the χ^2 table value for a .05 probability level.[4] Thus, the null hypothesis verifying cross-validation is lacking could not be rejected. Consequently, the model in Figure 5.5 has real significance. With

Table 5.6 Model specification cross-validation of multigroup [male/female].

Model	*Unconstrained*	*Constrained*
χ^2	404.903	424.564
df	238	253
p	0	0
χ^2-square diff		19.661
df diff		15
χ^2-square diff p	Insignificant	.185
critical χ^2 -square $p < .05$ ♣		24.996
critical χ^2 -square $p < .01$ ♣		30.578
critical χ^2 -square $p < .001$ ♣		37.697
CFI	.943	.942
CFI diff		.001

Note: n = 216

♣ Values of the chi-squared distribution sourced from www.medcalc.org/manual/chi-square-table.php

the data cross-validated, it can be generalised (Myung & Pitt 2003), because it is not from capitalisation of chance (Hermida 2015). Then, the model provides a good predictor of future observations (Myung, Tang & Pitt 2009).

Invariance results

Table 5.7 summarising the invariance tests, in conjunction with Table 5.8 the invariance test GOF results, proves the model displayed configural [Model 1], metric [Model 2], latent factor mean difference test for scalar invariance [Model 3] and equality of uniqueness [residual variance] associated with observed variables [Model 4]. Simply, a parameter was invariant across the gender groups and the factor loadings were equal across the male and female groups resulting in metric invariance. For structural invariance, the equivalence of factor means [Model 5], equivalence of factor covariance [Model 6] and variance [Model 7] as recommended by various writers (Brown 2006, pp. 269–270; Schmitt & Kuljanin 2008) were tested. From Table 5.8 empirically MLE generated reasonable GOF for the unconstrained [Model 1] CFA solutions for male and female [χ^2 404.903; df 238; p .000; CMIN/df 1.701; GFI .862; AGFI .802; CFI .943; TLI .927; PCFI .734; RMSEA .052; 90% CI .043, .061; PCLOSE .335]. In this solution, the freely estimated unstandardised factor loadings were all statistically significant p <.001 [males] and p <.05 [females], apart from a_1, a_2 and a_3 loading on b_1. The standardised regression weights were all greater than this study's threshold of .35, except for a_1, a_2 and a_3. Recall from Chapter 4, χ^2 is influenced by sample size and hence model fit. Thus, different sample sizes will affect interpretability of the results. For instance, the female sample size is a small n = 44 and so will affect the results. Nonetheless, for male respondents n = 216, all the unstandardised regression weights were statistically significant at the p < .001 level with standardised regression weights all being greater than this research's threshold of .35. Therefore, overall invariance was proven, whereby the factor structure and loadings are equivalent across groups ensuring the variables measure the different underlying latent constructs for different groups within the sample and are thus generalisable across population (Vandenberg & Lance 2000). Configural [baseline] invariance has been proven based on the results of the χ^2 difference test for configural invariance [the p-value for the chi-square difference test for the configural model is N.S. at the p < .05 level]. Although it was unnecessary to go ahead with the metric invariance test (Schmitt & Kuljanin 2008), additional tests of invariance were performed out of curiosity with results in Table 5.7. The purpose was to see how restricting the model further affected the results, as well as in case reviewers and examiners wanted these tests performed.

According to the χ^2 difference test, the model has metric invariance, because the p-value for the chi-square difference test is N.S. at the p < .05 level [Table 5.7]. The χ^2 difference of 19.661 with 21 df is less than the critical χ^2 of 32,671 and it is N.S. with a p-value of .456 [Table 5.7]. This invariance is confirmed by the

Table 5.7 Model specification invariance tests of multigroup [male and female].

Invariance model	χ^2	*df*	χ^2 *diff*	*df diff*	*Critical* χ^2			χ^2 *Invariance*		*CFI invariance*		
					p <.05♣	*p <.01*♣	*p <.001*♣	*Significance p-value*		*CFI*	*CFI diff*	
Configural [Model 1]	404.903	238								.943		
Metric [Model 2]	424.564	253	19.661	15	28.869	34.805	42.312	N.S. p = .185	*	.942	.001	#
Structural covariance [Model 3]	425.945	259	21.042	21	32.671	38.932	46.797	N.S. p = .456	*	.943	0	#
Measurement Residual [Model 4]	467.982	290	63.079	52	69.832	78.616	89.272	N.S. p = .140	*	.94	.003	#
Configural of the latent mean [Model 5]	404.9	238								.943		
Structural equity of factor means [Model 6]	440.509	271	35.606	33	50.998	58.619	67.985	N.S. p = .347	*	.943	0	#
Structural equity of factor covariance [Model 7]	442.348	277	37.445	39	54.572	62.428	72.055	N.S. p = .541	*	.944	−.001	#
Structural variance [Model 8]	486.791	308	81.888	70	90.531	100.42	112.317	N.S. p = .157	*	.939	.004	#

* χ^2 invariant where p > .05 threshold
# CFI invariant where CFI difference < .01 threshold
♣ Values of the chi-squared distribution sourced from www.medcalc.org/manual/chi-square-table.php
N.S. Not significant

Table 5.8 Goodness of fit for invariance test for gender.

Measure	*Free estimate*	*Constrained estimate*					
	Models 1 and 5	*Model 2*	*Model 3*	*Model 4*	*Model 6*	*Model 7*	*Model 8*
CMIN	404.903	424.564	425.945	467.982	441.512	442.348	486.791
DF	238	253	259	290	274	277	308
P	0	0	0	0	0	0	0
CMIN/ DF	1.701	1.661	1.645	1.614	1.611	1.597	1.58
GFI	.862	.858	.856	.843			
AGFI	.802	.809	.81	.815			
CFI	.943	.942	.943	.94	.943	.944	.939
TLI	.927	.931	.933	.936	.936	.938	.94
NFI	.875	.869	.869	.856	.864	.864	.85
PCFI	.734	.788	.798	.89	.844	.854	.945
RMSEA	.052	.051	.05	.049	.049	.048	.047
90% CI	.043; .061	.043; .060	.041; .058	.041; .057	.04; .057	.04; .056	.039; .055
PCLOSE	.335	.394	.491	.59	.594	.638	.696

difference in CFI, because the value of .001 for Model 2 [Table 5.7] was less than .01 threshold (Cheung & Rensvold 2002). The factor loadings were considered equal across gender groups and shows the two groups have the same metrics. Thus, factor structure and loadings are equivalent across groups, which means the composite variables measure the same underlying latent constructs for different groups within the sample and are therefore generalisable across the population of interest (Vandenberg & Lance 2000).

From Table 5.7 empirically the data do display structural covariance invariance, because the χ^2 difference for gender of 21.042 with df of 21 is less than the critical χ^2 of 32.671 [Model 3] and therefore non-significant for the male/female group. Thus, covariance is equal across gender groups, meaning the two groups exhibited similar covariance. This invariance is further confirmed by the difference in CFI, because .000 was less than .01 threshold (Cheung & Rensvold 2002). Model 4 [Table 5.7] passes the strict invariance or equality of residual invariance test, because the χ^2 difference is non-significant [$p = .140$] and its difference of 63.079 with df of 52 is less than the critical χ^2 of 69.832. The residuals were equal across gender groups, meaning the two groups presented similar residuals. This result is further confirmed by the difference in CFI, because .003 was less than .01 threshold (Cheung & Rensvold 2002).

Recall, structural invariance is divided into three tests of equality, namely equivalence of factor variances, tests of equality of factor covariance and latent means. Structural invariance test the population heterogeneity (Brown 2006). To assess population heterogeneity, the invariance of the measurement and structural part of the MGCFA across two gender groups was tested. Differences between measurement errors, factor loadings and latent means among gender groups was expected, given measurement invariance was proven. Thus, by equivalence of factor means [Model 6] the difference in χ^2 observed across gender groups is N.S. [$p = .347$] [Table 5.7], because once again χ^2 difference of 35.606 with df 36 is less than the critical χ^2 of 50.998. This estimate point towards residual invariance, namely all items are related by their unique traits in the same way across groups. Furthermore, the results in Table 5.7 is confirmed by the CFI difference test. In addition, for equivalence of factor covariance [Model 7], the difference in χ^2 observed across gender groups is N.S. [$p = .541$], because χ^2 difference of 37.445 with df of 39 is less than the critical χ^2 of 54.572. Finally, the equivalence of factor variance [Model 8] across gender groups is proven with the difference in χ^2 observed as N.S. [$p = .157$], because χ^2 difference of 81.888 [df 70] is less than the critical χ^2 value of 90.531. The results from the respective fit indices for each model indicated a reasonably adequate fit, illustrated in Table 5.8, in all invariance test cases. As shown in Table 5.8, the differences between fit indices were negligible when the unconstrained models [Models 1 and 5] were compared with the constrained models [Models 2, 3, 4, 6, 7 and 8]. This measure provides support for the equivalency of factor loadings and the invariance of factor variance-covariance (Hewett, Money, & Sharma 2006), validating the two groups of gender may be analysed as one sample (Locander *et al.* 2015). Thus, it was unnecessary to explore and respecify the model, but to continue with model verification starting with validity and reliably tests.

Validity and reliability results

Convergent validity is evident in the EFA pattern matrix in Table 5.4, because the estimates of a given indicator loaded onto an underlying latent variable are above threshold of .35 [$n > 250$] and large and significant. Recall values above .30 (Harrington 2009) are interpretable. Additionally, the AVE is greater than .5 (Harrington 2009) for all the factors according to my calculations and recorded in Table 5.9. This outcome means the indicators have large degrees of true score common variance (Hermida 2015). For instance, AVE for the latent variables were estimated for the following: Dual [.548]; Legitimacy [.772]; and Individual licensing [.771]. Further evidence of convergent validity is the statistically highly significant $p = .001$ and $p < .001$ [*ex* CLF] [Table 20a in Appendix 5.20], and $p = .007$ and $p < .05$ [*cum* CLF] [Table 20b in Appendix 5.20], reflected in CFA MLE estimates in Amos.

Table 5.9 Reliability and validity.

Factor	*Cronbach's alpha*	*c.r.*	*AVE*	*MSV*	*ASV*
Dual	.563	.622	.548	.233	.186
Legitimacy	.937	.885	.772	.121	.177
Individual licensing	.880	.794	.771	.138	.129

Table 5.10 EFA factor correlation matrix with square root of the AVE on the diagonal.

	Dual	*Legitimacy*	*Individual*
Dual	.740		
Legitimacy	.483	.879	
Alternative licensing	.371	.348	.878

To assess discriminant validity, EFA and CFA tests were considered. The first EFA method was to examine the factor correlation matrix (Gaskin 2016b). Overall discriminant validity was established, because the EFA generated factor correlation matrix, in Table 5.10, whereby the correlation estimates in Table 21 in Appendix 5.21, indicated the correlations between factors were less than .85 (Harrington 2009). Thus, the indicators of the theoretical distinct constructs are not highly intercorrelated (Harrington 2009). Therefore, shared variance between factors is absent, which proved discriminant validity (Gaskin 2016b).

A second method was applied, namely examining the pattern matrix [Table 5.4] to establish any cross-loadings. With the exceptions of variable Cognitive [a_{14}], no shared variance where most variables loaded significantly onto one factor occurred (Gaskin 2016b). However, variable Cognitive [a_{14}] shows 'cross-loadings' by loading onto b_3 and b_4 factors. Furthermore, the Cognitive [a_{14}] loadings between these two factors differed by less than .02, which is of some concern for discriminant validity at indicator level, because it is less than the threshold of .20. A third method applied was to examine the AVE and ASV generated using CFA results in Table 5.9. If the AVE is greater than ASV, then the model displays discriminant validity (de Almeida *et al.* 2014).

Finally, Harrington (2009) proposed another method useful during CFA to establish discriminant validity, namely the CFA MLE correlations do not exceed .85 (see Table 21 in Appendix 5.21 Correlations of indicator variables. Hence, from Table 21 in Appendix 5.21, the indicators of the theoretical distinct constructs are not highly intercorrelated (Harrington 2009). Note, although CFA does assess convergent and discriminant validity (Curran, West & Finch 1996), Farrell and Rudd (2009) claimed EFA is the better technique to assess discriminant validity. Overall, on the basis of EFA analysis, discriminant validity was proven. Before the results of the respecified model were trusted, three methods of reliability tests were performed. Cronbach's alpha (Field 2014) was the first test and CR the second. A third test for reliability included congeneric, tau equivalent and parallel equivalent (Kline 2010) χ^2-square difference test (Yuan & Bentler 2004). Evident from the CR values in Table 5.11, they are not far off the Cronbach's alpha values. Field (2014) recommended when dealing with psychological constructs values, Cronbach's alpha of .8 is appropriate especially during the early stages of research. Thus, for purposes of this book, values as low as .5 were considered sufficient, and values greater than .7 was expected. Consequently, except for Dual latent variable, CR and Cronbach's alpha of the other two latent variables were greater than .8. Even though the Dual latent factor estimate was above .5, it was considered an acceptable alpha value for pioneering research according to Field (2014).

Table 5.11 Reliability and validity of multigroup gender.

Estimate	*Congeneric [Baseline]*	*Tau-equivalent*	*Parallel*
chi-squared	404.903	441.868	467.982
df	238	272	290
p	0	0	0
chi-square diff		36.965	63.079
df diff		34	52
critical chi-square $p < .05$*		48.602	69.832
critical chi-square $p < .01$*		56.061	78.616
critical chi-square $p < .001$*		65.247	89.272
Significance		N.S. $p > .05$	N.S. $p > .05$
RMSEA	.052	.049	.049
RMSEA low	.043	.041	.041
RMSEA high	.061	.057	.057
PCLOSE	.335	.553	.59
SRMR	.0727	.0735	.0732
CFI	.943	.942	.94
PCFI	.734	.838	.89

*Values of the critical chi-squared distribution sourced from www.medcalc.org/manual/chi-square-table.php and N.S. Not significant

Congeneric tests are unrestricted [Figure 5.5, Respecified CFA measurement model], unlike parallel and tau-equivalent (Curran, West & Finch 1996) when testing for scale reliability. Tau-equivalent tests have equal true score loadings [$\lambda_1 = \lambda_2$, *etc.*], but possibly different error variances [$\varepsilon_1 \neq \varepsilon_1$, *etc.*] [Figure 5.6, Tau-equivalent model to test reliability.] (Brown & Moore 2016). More restrictive is parallel [Figure 5.7, Parallel-equivalent model to test for reliability] where observed measures have equal factor loadings [$\lambda_1 = \lambda_2$, *etc.*] and equal error variances [$\varepsilon_1 = \varepsilon_1$, *etc.*] and measure the latent construct with the same level of precision, namely equivalent error variances (Brown & Moore 2016).

Applying the χ^2-square difference test to evaluate the number the nested model comparisons for tau and parallel equivalents (Yuan & Bentler 2004) from Table 5.11, the model displays convergent and discriminant validity. The congeneric model fit is better than the other tau- and parallel-constrained models. In addition, scale reliability was found, because this likelihood ratio test indicates at 34 df, chi-square difference of 36.965 is less than the critical 48.602 in Table 5.11. The chi-square and df value increase was N.S. by constraining the parameters. Thus, the reliability of the measures used does not compromise the statistical conclusions drawn after this and forthcoming chapters.

Common methods bias results

To test for a common method bias, a few different tests, recommended by Gaskin (2013), were implemented, namely the Harman test (Nebojsa 2014; Choi, Ullah & Kwak 2015), CLF test (Podsakoff *et al.* 2003; Podsakoff, MacKenzie & Podsakoff 2012) and CLF marker test (Podsakoff, MacKenzie & Podsakoff

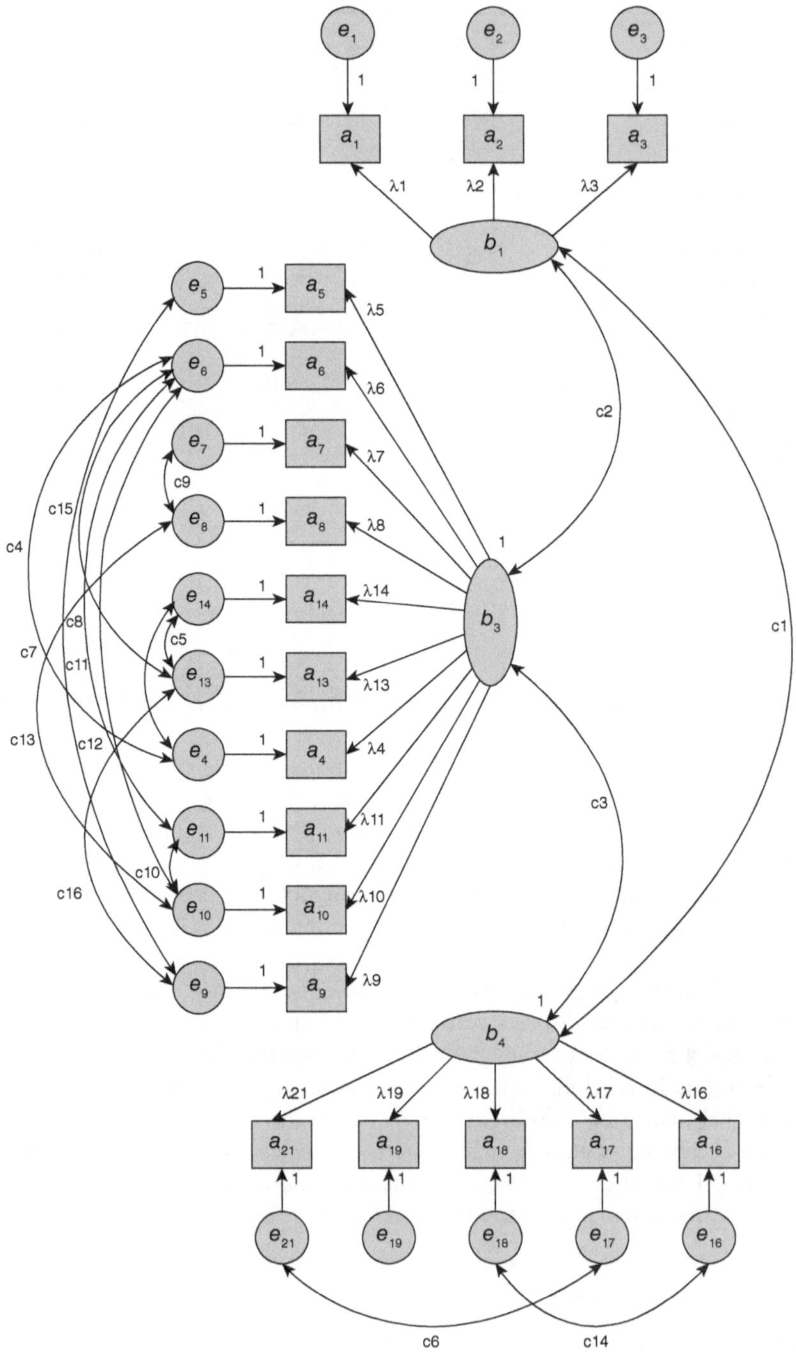

Figure 5.6 Tau-equivalent model to test reliability.

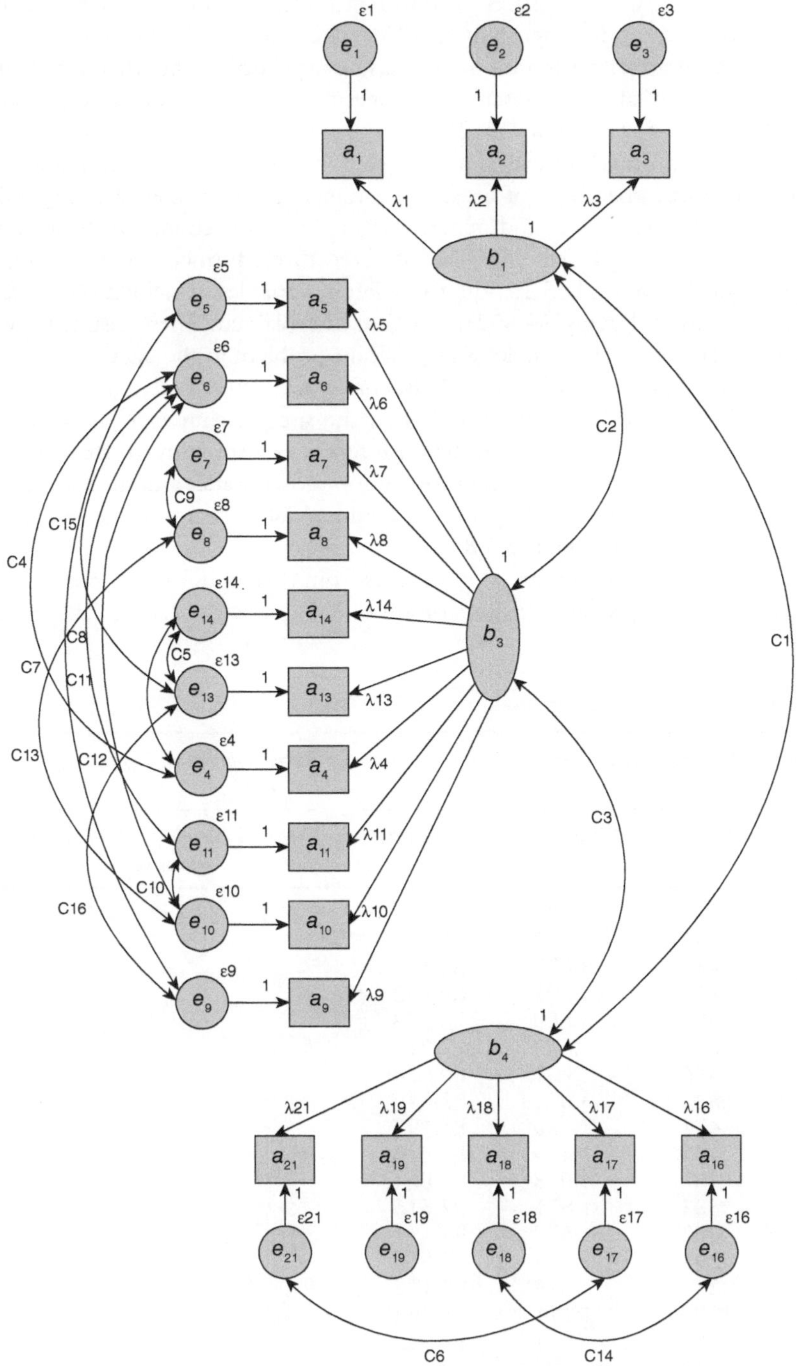

Figure 5.7 Parallel-equivalent model to test for reliability.

2012; Williams & O'Boyle 2015). From the results, in Table 5.12, empirically a single factor accounts for approximately 43% of the variance in the model by how much of the variance/covariance matrix can be explained, rather than how much of the variance in latent or observed endogenous variables is explained (Podsakoff, MacKenzie & Podsakoff 2012).

Thus, common method bias is a non-issue, because a single factor does not account for more than 43% of most the variance in the model. No single factor emerged in the results, and general factor did not account for most of the variance. An unrotated factor analysis extracted three distinct factors accounted for 65.148%. From Table 5.12, the three latent variables explained 65.148% of the total variation, leaving 34.852% variation unexplained. These results showed common method bias was unlikely a significant problem in the data.

Next, the CLF method [CLF] (Podsakoff *et al.* 2003; Podsakoff, MacKenzie & Podsakoff 2012) was applied. When the specific source of the common method bias cannot be identified, the CLF serves as a solution. In this method, the researchers utilised a CLF to capture the common variance among all observed variables in the model, by adding a single common latent factor to the respecified CFA model indicated in Figure 5.8.

When the standardised regression weights from this model are compared with the standardised regression weights of a model without the CLF [Table 5.13],

Table 5.12 Total variance explained.

Factor	*Initial eigenvalues*			*Extraction sums of squared loadings*		
	Total	*% of variance*	*Cumulative %*	*Total*	*% of variance*	*Cumulative %*
1	7.828	43.488	43.488	7.126	39.587	39.587
2	2.445	13.583	57.071			
3	1.454	8.077	65.148			
4	.827	4.595	69.743			
5	.684	3.800	73.543			
6	.661	3.673	77.216			
7	.596	3.31	80.526			
8	.544	3.021	83.546			
9	.477	2.650	86.197			
10	.437	2.429	88.626			
11	.367	2.038	90.664			
12	.333	1.851	92.515			
13	.302	1.677	94.191			
14	.295	1.639	95.830			
15	.238	1.323	97.153			
16	.200	1.111	98.264			
17	.169	.941	99.205			
18	.143	.795	100			

Source: *Extraction Method: Maximum Likelihood.*

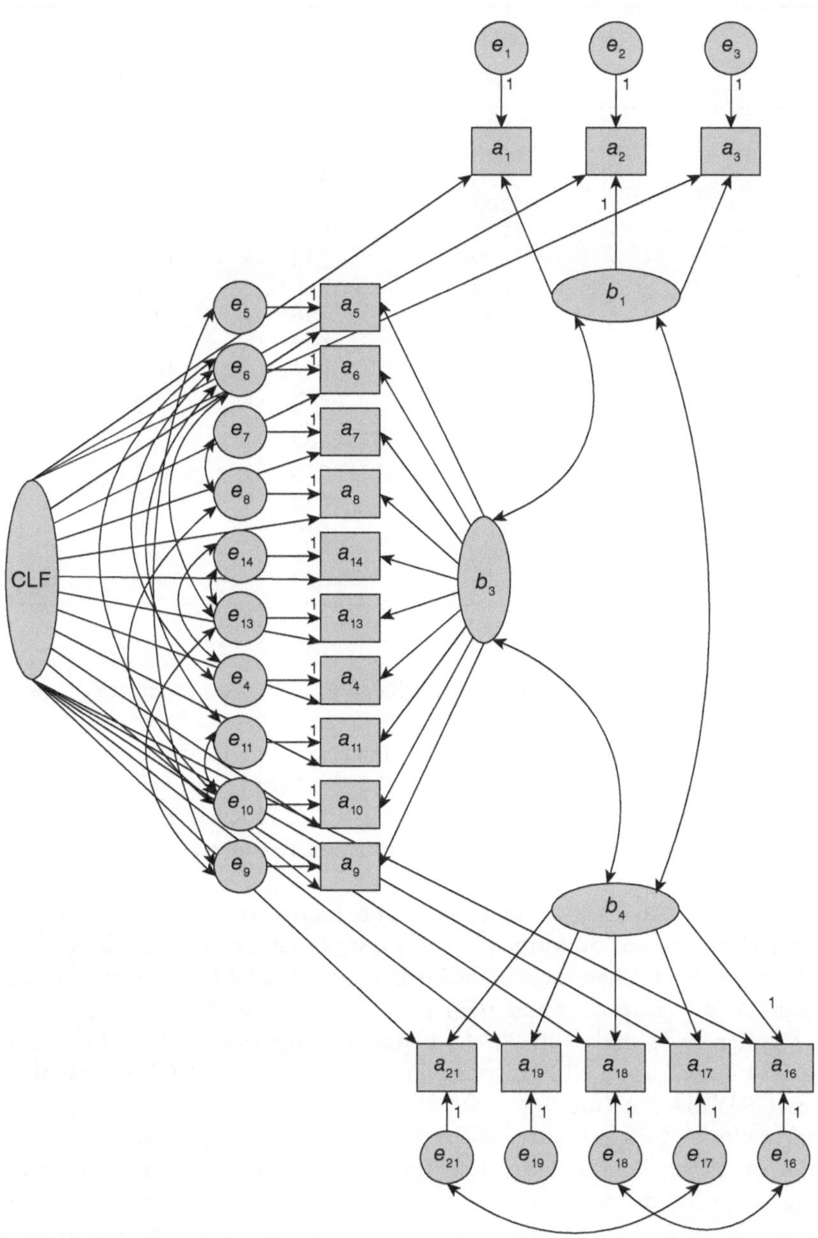

Figure 5.8 Common latent factor model.

Table 5.13 Comparison of standardised regression weights: [Group number 1 – Default model].

			Estimate		
			cum CLF	*ex CLF*	*Absolute difference*
a_1	<---	b_1	.604	.585	.019
a_2	<---	b_1	.689	.686	.003
a_3	<---	b_1	.375	.372	.003
a_{10}	<---	b_3	.794	.875	.081
a_{11}	<---	b_3	.781	.831	.050
a_{13}	<---	b_3	.679	.623	.056
a_{14}	<---	b_3	.682	.560	.122
a_4	<---	b_3	.740	.748	.008
a_5	<---	b_3	.810	.884	.074
a_6	<---	b_3	.773	.831	.058
a_7	<---	b_3	.821	.909	.088
a_8	<---	b_3	.679	.700	.021
a_9	<---	b_3	.727	.793	.066
a_{16}	<---	b_4	.745	.858	.113
a_{17}	<---	b_4	.662	.742	.080
a_{18}	<---	b_4	.711	.816	.105
a_{19}	<---	b_4	.695	.801	.106
a_{21}	<---	b_4	.536	.629	.093

undoubtedly differences between the model *cum* CLF and model *ex* CLF were less than .2.

Thus, on the basis of this test, it was unnecessary to retain the CLF when estimating the results (Williams & O'Boyle 2015), because the relationships are unaffected by common method (Groza, Locander & Howlett 2016). However, this test is not automatically considered the most reliable test, and thus additional tests were performed.

Subsequently, the CLF marker technique [zero constraint method/CFA marker technique] was performed. In this test, a marker variable [the CLF] is added [Figure 5.9]. Then each factor loading onto the CLF are initially unconstrained [as in Figure 5.5] and then constrained [as in Figure 5.9] (Podsakoff, MacKenzie & Podsakoff 2012), before a comparison of the estimates in Table 5.14 between the CLF unconstrained [Figure 5.5] and CLF constrained [Figure 5.9] models occurs.

The results of this re-estimation are provided in the right-most column of Table 5.14. Note, in this new model, zero constraints were imposed on the loadings from the methods factor to its indicators to obtain convergence. This procedure is consistent with the approach used by other researchers employing this approach (Podsakoff, MacKenzie & Podsakoff 2012). As can be seen from Table 5.14, the chi-square difference test came out as significant for difference in chi-squared 93.792 and difference in df 18, which indicated significant shared variance. Although one cannot be sure, the common methods variance may be

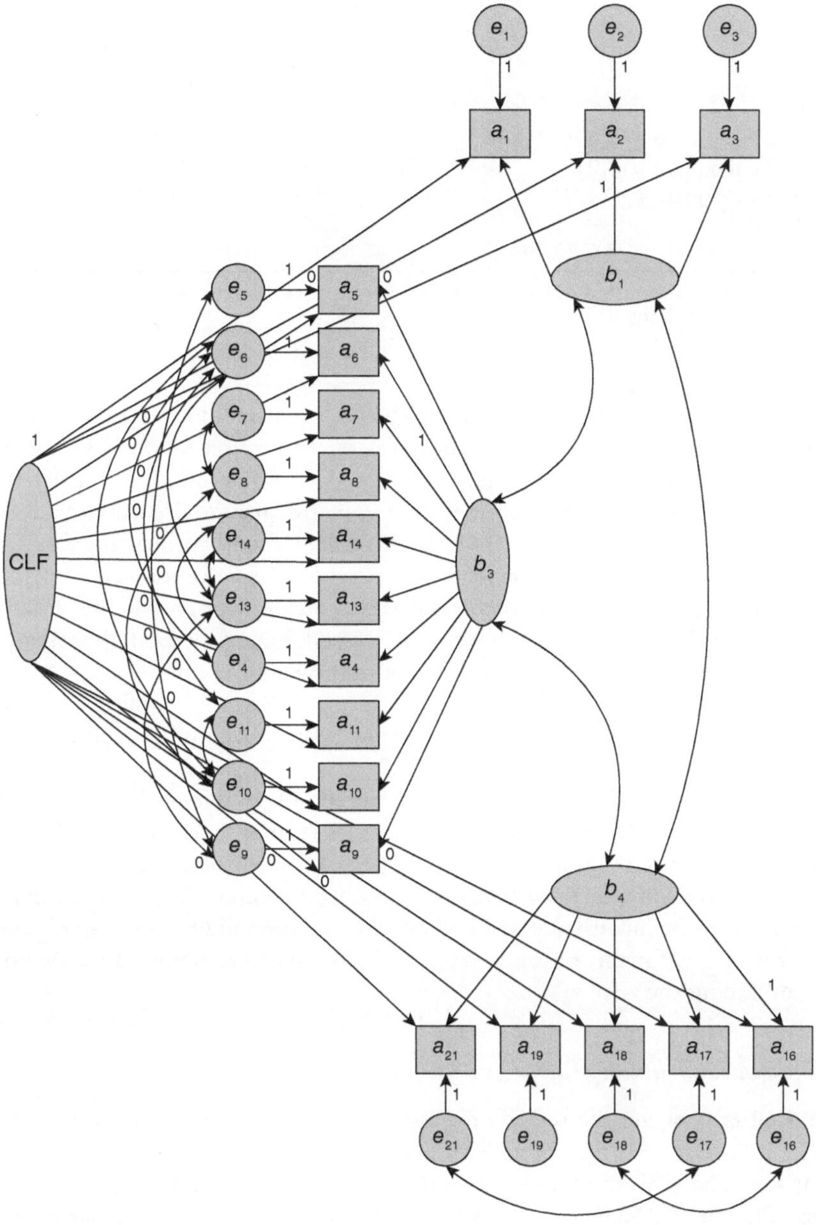

Figure 5.9 Common latent factor marker with zero constraint method.

Table 5.14 Common methods bias tests: CLF marker technique/zero constraint method/CFA marker technique.

Model	*CLF unconstrained*	*CLF constrained to zero*
χ^2	128.339	222.131
df	101	119
χ^2 difference		93.792
df difference		18
Critical chi-square $p < .05$*		28.869
Critical chi-square $p < .01$*		34.805
Critical chi-square $p < .001$*		42.312
Significance		S. $p < .001$
Common method bias if $p < .05$		Yes

* Values of the chi-squared distribution sourced from www.medcalc.org/manual/chi-square-table.php S. Significant

because a single questionnaire, rather than a multi-method approach (Brown 2003). Furthermore, common method bias might be a reflection of some advisers faking their responses (Biderman *et al. 2011)* on the grounds of the defensive responses of some of the respondents on the matter around licensing of advisers, based on the comments such as "*Again the RMIT should know better than to ask such a question.*" "*Duh! That's big business for you. They're not charities.*"

Interestingly, the common method bias was greatest for professions, followed by trust and IPFPSB. Thus, with the presence of common method, the researcher opted for retaining the CLF, namely the unmeasured common latent method factor during MLE (Podsakoff *et al.* 2003), because it controlled all systematic sources of bias during hypotheses testing of relationships between constructs (Podsakoff, MacKenzie & Podsakoff 2012).

Furthermore, on the grounds of a non-significant *p*-value of .310 for the CLF variance in Table 22 in Appendix 5.22, it was surmised common method bias should not threaten the validity of this enquiry's conclusions. Moreover, findings by Meade, Watson and Kroustalis (2007) showed common method bias may be in many cases be inconsequential and not impede the validity of the study's conclusions. Thus, for this research project, the results were reported by including and excluding the CLF.

Finalised confirmatory factor analysis model

Thus, after applying the remedy for common method bias, the most important GOF indices, namely the χ^2 test, RMSEA, GFI, AGFI, SRMR and PCLOSE, were analysed. The χ^2 was not larger than three times its df. The model has relatively good fit. The SRMR and RMSEA [Table 5.9, Goodness of fit for invariance test for gender] were within the specified limits of acceptability, satisfying the GOF criteria specified by numerous authorities. The GFI and AGFI are above the .90 threshold and are close to unity and close to perfect fit. Although overall GOF

[Table 5.9, Goodness of fit for invariance test for gender] validates reasonable approximate fit for this complex congeneric model with many indices, some relationships, particularly a_3 [BestRev] displayed the lowest loadings [Table 5.15]. Despite this low loading, further evidence suggests the sample matrix is produced reasonably well, overall, because all the estimates are significant at $p < .001$, apart from a_1 [Dual] with a significance value $p = .001$ *ex* CLF and $p = .007$ *cum* CLF.

From standardised regression weights estimates in Table 5.15, and the unstandardised factor loading estimates in Tables 20a and 20b in Appendix 5.20, it is clear the model's scale is reflective, rather than formative, because no proof of negative factor loadings [regression weights] was evident. Thus, from this Amos MLE solution the direction of the estimates was in accordance with the prediction of the theory. Namely, the indicators all have positive relationships with the latent constructs (Gaskin 2016b). Therefore, it was unnecessary to discard (Blunch 2008) any relationships during this phase of the CFA analysis. For example, predictors a_1, a_2 and a_3 are positively related to the construct Dual [b_1]. Their direction of causality was from construct to predictor. In Table 5.15 no evidence of any standardised regression weights below .35 was found. This the investigator considered acceptable thresholds for sufficient or significant factor loadings based on *ns* of 250 (Gaskin 2016b). The lowest bootstrapped *cum* CLF standardised regression weight was .375 for indicator BestRev [a_3]. The loadings meeting the excellent threshold of above .71 were a_4, a_5, a_6, a_7, a_9, a_{10}, a_{10}, a_{11}, a_{16} and a_{18}. The very good loadings above .60 included a_{13}, a_{14}, a_{17}, a_{19}, a_2, a_8 and a_1. In addition, only one variable a_{21} scored fair for being above .45, but not quite good [above .55]. On the basis of the literature's rules of thumb, no poor loadings below .32 (Tabachnick & Fidell 2007; Harrington 2009) were evident. However, these rules of thumb ignore *n*. For this study's *n* of 262, a loading of more than .35, based on an *n* of 250, is considered acceptable. Refer to Table 22 in Appendix 5.22, to obtain estimates of the variance in the unstandardised solution of all the indicators accounted for by the latent factors. The parameters in the CFA model include factor variance in the unstandardised solution. It includes error covariance [correlated errors of related indicators]. In these cases, these estimates measured influences other than the shared influence of the latent factor. Correlated errors could result from method effects, such as common measurement method of self-report or similar wording of items when testing for common methods bias. Overall, the variances are all highly significant, except for the CLF.

When measuring the precision or statistical accuracy, in other words the SE, in the estimates of the parameters, the overall SEs were considered reasonable as they are not too close to zero or too large. None of these parameters appeared statistically N.S. However, dual-agency indicators' SE magnitudes were inconsistent with the other variables' SE magnitudes. Thus, some concern for the SEs of the bootstrapped indicator estimates a_1 and a_2 forming part of factor Dual-agency b_1 was identified. The SE for a_1 and a_2 were particularly high compared with the other estimates in the model. The high SE has led to upper limits greater than one for the 95% CI. For instance, from Table 5.15, the 95% CI of the indicator a_1 factor loading [.585] verifies 95% certainty the true population value of

Table 5.15 Standardised regression weights: [Group number 1 – Default model].

Parameter	*Bootstrapped ex CLF*											*Bootstrapped cum CLF*[5]	
	Estimate	*p*	*SE*	*SE-SE*	*Mean*	*Bias*	*SE-Bias*	*95% CI*					
								Lower	*Upper*	*Range*	*p*	*Estimate*	*p*
Dual a_1 [b_1]	.585	.001	.215	.011	.616	.031	.015	.232	1.132	.900	.01	.604	.007
BestRev a_3 [b_1]	.372	***	.109	.005	.338	–.034	.008	.103	.590	.487	.01	.375	***
Regulative a_9 [b_3]	.793	***	.029	.001	.791	–.001	.002	.734	.850	.116	.01	.727	***
Consequential a_{10} [b_3]	.875	***	.026	.001	.872	–.003	.002	.817	.916	.099	.01	.794	***
Procedural a_{11} [b_3]	.831	***	.031	.002	.829	–.001	.002	.766	.884	.118	.01	.781	***
Personal a_{13} [b_3]	.623	***	.039	.002	.626	.003	.003	.535	.698	.163	.01	.679	***
Cognitive a_{14} [b_3]	.560	***	.047	.002	.567	.007	.003	.469	.657	.188	.01	.682	***
Independence a_{17} [b_4]	.742	***	.047	.002	.75	.008	.003	.653	.831	.178	.01	.662	***
Professions a_{18} [b_4]	.816	***	.042	.002	.816	.000	.003	.736	.895	.159	.01	.711	***
IPFPSB a_{19} [b_4]	.801	***	.039	.002	.804	.003	.003	.719	.872	.153	.01	.695	***
Simult a_2 [b_1]	.686	marker	.280	.014	.714	.028	.020	.313	1.264	.951	.01	.689	marker
Structural a_4 [b_3]	.748	***	.035	.002	.749	.001	.003	.674	.805	.131	.01	.740	***
AlignAct a_5 [b_3]	.884	***	.020	.001	.883	–.001	.001	.835	.923	.088	.01	.810	***
CoIAct a_6 [b_3]	.831	***	.029	.001	.833	.002	.002	.772	.885	.113	.01	.773	***
FiducAct a_7 [b_3]	.909	marker	.016	.001	.908	–.001	.001	.871	.937	.066	.01	.821	marker
CompAct a_8 [b_3]	.700	***	.039	.002	.699	–.001	.003	.620	.772	.152	.01	.679	***
EliminateCoI a_{21} [b_4]	.629	***	.051	.003	.636	.007	.004	.542	.738	.196	.01	.536	***
Trust a_{16} [b_4]	.858	marker	.035	.002	.857	–.001	.003	.780	.920	.140	.01	.745	marker

parameter is between .232 and 1.132 [*cum* bootstrap, *ex* CLF]. The 95% CI for particularly a_2 [Simult], a_1 [Dual] is quite wide for the bootstrapped data, followed to a lesser extent by a_3 [BestRev], which all load on the same factor Dual-agency. This result confirms the variable dual-agency shows some problematic results needing further investigation. Thus, caution is advised when considering these variables estimates, because the statistical significance tests of path coefficients may result in Type I errors with a risk of rejecting the models in error, if the chi-square is large (Menard 2002).

The chi-square estimates for this model was not considered large. This minimises the possibility of Type I errors. As far as the Dual-agency factor [b_1] is concerned, no error covariance was specified for its indicators during CFA MLE respecification using MI. Thus, all the covariation among its indicators shared the influence of the latent variables. In other words, the measurement error was considered random (Brown 2006). Yet, expectedly after considering the MI, 13 error covariance indicators covary. Respondents' comments confirmed these indicators were related somehow. Some of their covariation is from sources other than the shared influence of the latent factor (Menard 2002; Brown 2006). In addition, interesting, eight indicator error covariance for legitimacy and alternative licensing factors produced negative values [Table 23a and 23b in Appendix 5.23]. This means these estimates were out of range after modification. Generally, the presence of an error covariance indicates two indicators share systematic variance, which is unexplained by their common factor (Brown 2006). A negative covariance between error variables may indicate the relationship between two indicators is overestimated by the factor.[6] Evidently, the empirical covariance is smaller than the model-implied covariance. A reason for this outcome is the possible presence of two correlated factors instead of one. Recall, two correlated factors, namely Objectives of the Act factor b_2 with Legitimacy factor b_3 were merged. Yet E/CFA discounts this reason. Another reason found in the literature (Brown 2006) explained a method effect occurs when a positive effect on the first indicator and an undesirable effect on the second indicator is found. On the basis of the qualitative results, this latter reason is likely.

This study's measurement model involved a multiple-item questionnaire similarly worded, and given the controversial nature of the topic, hence emotional responses of some respondents, differentially prone to social desirability. A measurement issue deeper down, like skewness or kurtosis problems, or too much missing data, or a nominal variable are some other reasons (Gaskin 2016a). These were considered unlikely, because skewness and kurtosis were not a problem, missing data were minimal and there were no nominal variables. Literature-recommended remedies were applied to address the negative covariance estimates, including moving the latent variable path constraint of one to another path. They failed to fix the problem.

Another approach applied was to rectify these improper negative indicator covariance (Anderson & Gerbing 1988) by respecifying the model by fixing improper estimates to zero and performing a chi-square difference test [Table 24 in Appendix 5.24]. According to this chi-square test, fixing parameters to zero significantly worsened the GOF and χ^2 value. Then the investigator applied Anderson and Gerbing's (1988) proposed approach to preserve the confirmatory factor model, namely to fix these improper estimates to an arbitrarily small positive number, such as .005 [Table 24, Appendix 5.24]. This remedy worsened the model fit (Joreskog 1978). As the drop in chi-square was large compared with the difference in df, it indicated the negative covariance represents a real improvement and the drop in chi-square means the improvement in fit is not obtained by chance or sampling error and so these negative covariance parameters have real significance or meaning in this model (Joreskog 1978). Thus, this difficult negative error covariance was retained in the model. The relationship between these indicators was further confirmed from the comments made by survey respondents, notwithstanding it significantly helped with model specification and/or model fitting. Therefore, key to model specification were the positive and negative covariance between them.

When the reliability of the responses was measured, Graph 5.11, *Cum* CLF, square multiple correlations (r^2) in percent and Table 25 in Appendix 5.25 provide the squared multiple correlations of the data. Focusing on the *cum* CLF r^2 estimates in Graph 5.12, plainly only 14% and 31% of the variance of a_3 [BestRev] and a_{21} [EliminateCoI] are accounted for by the latent factor Dual and latent factor Individual licensing, respectively. This outcome means 86% and 69%, estimates of e_3 and e_{21}, respectively, are accounted for by unique variance or other factors.

Consequently, the estimated reliability of a_3 is only 14%, which is very low and puts a question mark on the reliability of the responses from the survey participants. Furthermore, a_8 [CompAct], a_2 [Simult], a_3 [Personal] and a_1 [Dual] have square multiple correlation estimates below 50%. An interesting statistic in Graph 5.11 and Table 25 in Appendix 5.25 is the CI of Simult [a_3], which is quite large and inconsistent with the other indicators in the model's r^2 95% CIs. Thus, indicators EliminateCoI, CompAct, Personal and particularly adviser's dual-agency role factor with low reliability values for Dual, Simult and BestRev, seemed problematic topics for the survey respondents. An analysis of the respondents' comments explained why the reliability for these five indicators were possibly so low. When some advisers considered the survey statement measuring a_1 [Dual]: Advisers authorised through third-party licensees face a dual-agency relationship, namely an adviser–licensee relationship and an adviser–client relationship, it seems they failed to see themselves as agents of licensees, but agents of clients only. "*My understanding of dual agency is where the agent represents the interests of both the buyer and the seller. As an adviser, we represent the interests of the client (buyer) but the interests of the licensee are not as a 'seller.' The licensee authorises/licenses advisers, they don't 'sell' advice which is what the client is 'buying.'*" "*Almost all advisers will tell you that their responsibility is to their clients. The fact that the law says there must be a relationship between licensee and adviser in the eyes of most advisers I know is purely because it has to be. I consider myself bound to my client before bound to the Licensee.*" Others viewed licensees merely as providing support services or authorising them to work and/or in some cases

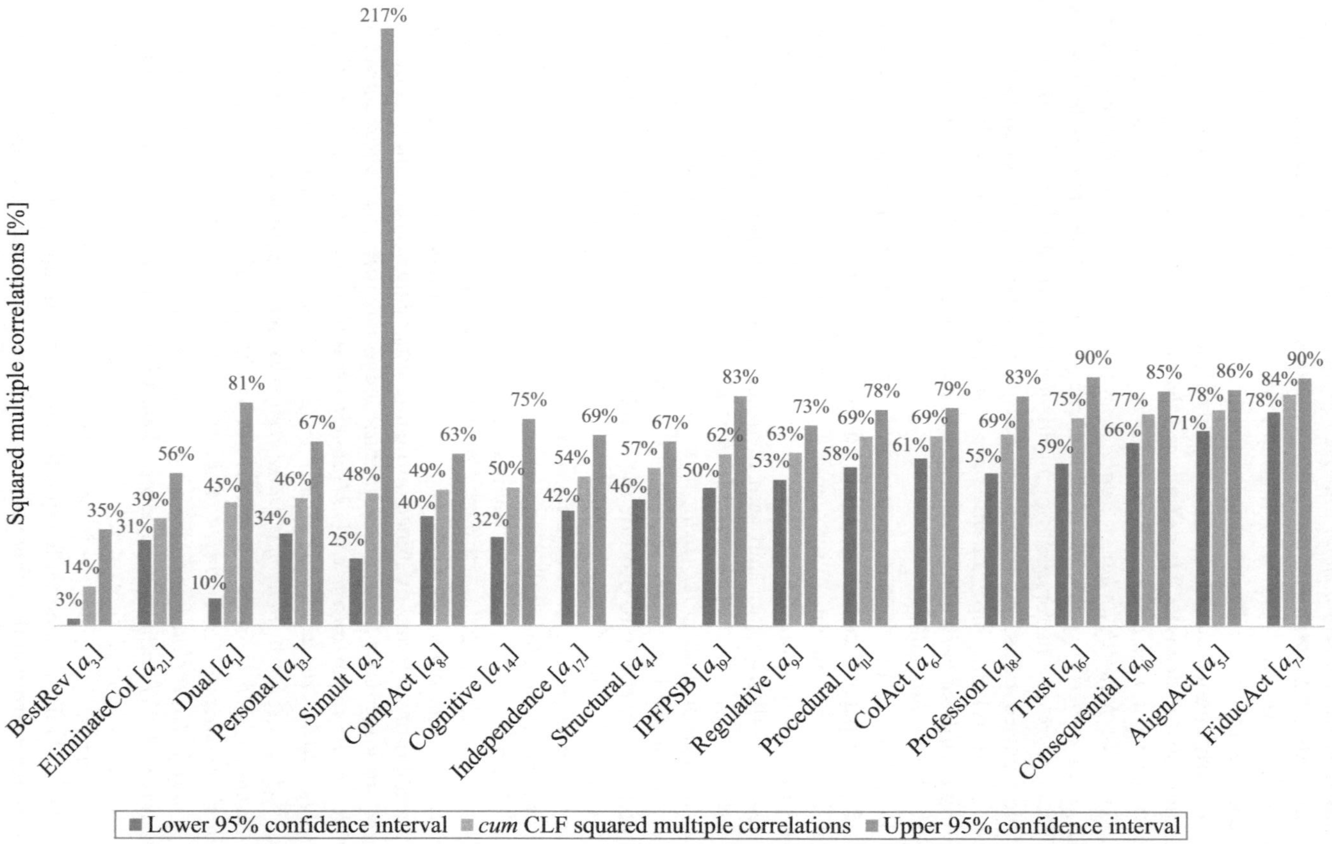

Graph 5.11 *Cum* CLF, square multiple correlations (r^2) in percent.

they feel licensees did not control them: "*Factually correct but I see the licensee as a servant/tool rather than a commander/controller.*" "*Not true. Licensees provide the framework for the adviser to service their clients on a day to day basis. The interest of the client always come first.*" Although not everyone agreed, because there were comments where advisers claimed they act as agents to distribute product of particularly aligned licensees or were limited and controlled by their licensees, depending on the licensee: "*It depends on who you are licensed with. An adviser who is licensee of a bank or a specific dealer group that does not have a wide authorised product list definitely do have a dual agency relationship and tend to be limited on the product offerings available to their clients. They also tend to be restricted in relation to processes and systems.*" Some did not seem to think any relationship with the licensee exists. While another added, they neglected to consider the licensee–client relationship: "*Licensees are required to ensure that the client's best interest is considered by its authorised representatives. Therefore Licensees also have a Licensee-client relationship.*"

When reflecting on the survey statement of a_2 [Simult]: Licensing advisers through third-party licensees' results in advisers serving the interests of their clients and licensees, simultaneously, seemingly advisers were very much focussed on prioritising their relationship with the clients. With only a few giving any thought with regard to their relationship with their licensees: "*Clients interest come first and foremost – and that is absolute. If there is a benefit to the licensee's interests and its not detrimental to the client, then I am happy to also benefit the licensee.*" Many did not see themselves serving the interests simultaneously; because the best interest duty is seen to override the interests of licensees. Whereas others did see themselves serving "*2 masters in this equation but this doesn't mean a licensee gets 'served' over the client. It depends so much on the licensee involved as to what their 'interests' are.*" When talking about interests, some respondents ignored the licensees' interests as if they are unimportant, non-existent or irrelevant: "*Not really; I don't give the licensee a second thought. I am not required to recommend their product or meet any quotas or targets.*" Whereas others seem to indicate the relevance, importance and existence of the interests being served simultaneously: "*Again, an undeniable fact, but the question makes no distinction to the relative % of service to and importance of each. My experience is that advisers serve their clients as close to 100% as the law allows, and their Licensee whatever % that leaves on the table.*" "*If licensee is a member of a dealer group that is an organisation listed on the stock exchange, then the there is a greater probability that the adviser will be working in the interests of the licensee and hence shareholder . . . Privately run dealer groups may be less inclined to do the above and cover costs only. Hence serve clients interests more.*" "*The adviser must service client's interests./The adviser only needs to serve the licensee's compliance interests.*" "*Whilst advisers need to be mindful of their licensee's interests, the client's needs must take priority, even where this may not 'suit' the licensee.*" Thus, an open-ended question in the main survey about the benefits licensees derive from authorising individual advisers was asked. A constant theme found for this question was the view the relationship between adviser–licensee is the licensee not only authorises advisers but also serves advisers: "*We are clients of the licensee and so they have to service me although I have to abide by their rules as they are responsible for the advice that I give. However, I can choose to change licensees or make sure I utilise one that provides sufficient breadth to provide the types of advice and use the products that I deem to be suitable.*" "*Many licensees have no interests other than compliance and reporting. It is important to separate out these two issues rather than assuming all licensees are the same.*" No clear consensus was present whether the adviser and licensee are assumed a unit acting on behalf of the client, or two separate units acting *independent*ly of each other: "*The interests of the Licensee should be to ensure the interests of the clients come first. Authorised Representatives activities are an extension of the Licensee's activities.*"

Advisers produced inconsistent responses to comments pertaining to a_3 [BestRev] measured by the statement: While serving the best interest of their clients, advisers generate revenue for their licensees. For instance, not all licensees were in business "*to make money*" or "*make money*" from FUM of product distribution on the basis of a few comments: "*Thankfully my dealergroup doesn't operate like this. They have a flat fee and there is absolutely no pressure to 'grow your business' to make more revenue for the dealer. Having done research back before I joined this group I can see from many others this is not the case.*" Licensee revenues were viewed as a means for advisers to pay their licensees for services rendered to support them in their roles or businesses: "*Revenue is required in order to cover expenses. Particularly given the high cost of ongoing education and compliance.*" ". . . *only in as much as we pay a fee for the licensee to provide us with a service, being research, technical, compliance etc. As a small business owner I contract with a lot of people to provide me with services: Telstra; Landlord; Mechanic etc.*" "*We certainly pay our licensee for services provided, however most dealer groups do not generate a profit, they simply break even.*" Whereas other licensees seem to use their advisers to distribute product for them: "*Yes, but overall most licences do not make a substantial profit, it is more to complement other services and other benefits of having distribution.*" "*Most licensees have preferred product lines that generate income for the licensee, and in many cases the adviser through share allotments in the licensee based on product volumes.*" "*Where licensees charge a % this may be true. My licensee charges a flat fee. So the licensee income is not tied to income generated by the adviser. However this is a relatively new system and mainly applies to new clients. Grandfathering provisions and the Approved Product List can create issues with serving the best interest of the client.*" Thus, the level of licensee control over their advisers, variety of business models, licensee–adviser agreements and remuneration arrangements were some of the other factors advisers thought about when reflecting on their response: "*Only if I select their products which I am not compelled to do.*" "*My practice is basically fixed fee with my AFSL. My AFSL doesn't make any more or less money from me irrespective of the source of my fees. That's why I am with them. If I worked for an Industry Fund or bank then I am in trouble. The answer would be maybe 75%.*" "*Yes this is true, depending on what the adviser makes money from. We generate money for the dealership, however the dealership gets volume rebates if we use their products. See where this is going?*" Licensee revenues was a touchy subject, because some advisers felt compelled to defend or rationalise licensees' revenues: "*Licensees are in the business of making money, but this has to be done transparently with the client, so that they understand the services they're paying for.*" "*I see no problem with that. All other professionals also generate revenue for themselves and/or an umbrella entity, and that has to be so that they are recompensed for their services.*" "*The Licensee is a business. They are not the enemy. They are there to provide a service, to assist us in our business, to be there if things go wrong. They provide our APL, the rules and the sandpit we need to play in. They are also the buffer between us and ASIC. Thank goodness they are there for us.*" Thus, from the foregoing, the issue of licensee revenues is a difficult issue for advisers.

The low squared multiple correlation for a_8 [CompAct] measured the question of whether licensing advisers through aligned licensees [e.g. ANZ, Westpac, NAB, CBA and AMP] limits advisers from competing on a level playing field within the industry indicating problems with reliability. From the comments, the advisers had different experiences or views concerning the issue of competition within the financial planning industry. Their lack of clarity on the topic of competition is reflected in their answers, which was influenced by whether they considered himself or herself aligned, non-aligned or s923A *independent*. For example, advisers seem to perceive competition as sales versus advice: "*The real distinction is advice vs. selling 'products'. Aligned advisers are driven/encouraged to sell products as a solution to clients' needs. Advice may result in no action at all e.g. aligned adviser encourages a client to mortgage the family home and invest in the stock market or managed funds. Best advice may be to do nothing.*" Some looked at the question from the perspective of product offered versus quality/suitability of advice: "*This assumes that advisers are competing in terms of their product offering not quality or suitability of advice. Surely it is the quality of advice that is important not the make or model of the product (if a product is offered)?*" On the other hand, others answered the question on competition from a marketing perspective: "*They have a huge brand advantage.*" Whereas one respondent looked at competition from the perspective of size or number of advisers or concentration of advisers within the industry: "*Bank advisers consist of 70% of the industry advisers. The IFA, we are 10–15% approx. Remainder is industry funds. It is not level. The IFA advice model has consistently ranked superior but the average consumer does not know this, or if they do, don't have the budget, where banks subsidise their advice delivery from vertical integration.*" Another adviser considered the size of the licensees: "*Alignment may seriously increase the competitive position of aligned advisers the strength of branding, systems & infrastructure, marketing resources and existing clientele. Nobody cares about level playing field. As an independent I have a serious disadvantage by comparison. Sometimes I wish I wasn't so conscientious.*" While another considered economies of scale: "*Only partly true. some platforms pass on some of their economies of scale to end clients and this is an area where our business, for example, cannot readily compete. On the other hand our fee model tends to result in lower overall costs because of the fact we do not take income from the platform.*" Whereas another looked at the capability of licensees to subside costs. "*Yes, the field is tilted in their favour as the licensee can afford to defray the costs or running the licensee onto other parts of their business, hence it is much easier for them to invest sufficiently into the very difficult compliance regime. Their large size also is a big advantage.*" Another ignored the intent of the question and offered an alternative explanation for their view, particularly approaching the question from a compliance point of view: "*Agree but for different reasons than intended by the question: The high licensee compliance standard places me at a competitive disadvantage against practitioner not subjected to such stringent standards. (And I DO understand the question and the intention of it!).*" Consequently, these different angles of answering the question may explain the low r^2 value.

The low squared multiple correlations for the survey question of whether contributions to the debate with the government surrounding the licensing of advisers by specific individual leaders of aligned licensees [e.g. ANZ, Westpac, NAB, CBA and AMP] are aimed to protect their product distribution channels, measuring a_{13} [Personal] may be explained by the following comments. The answers to Personal [a_{13}] moral legitimacy clearly do not explain the latent factor legitimacy completely, because other factors are at play, such as: (1) licensees "*hoping to protect their turf. But they are also trying to reduce the increase in administrative burden placed on financial advisers – raising the cost of advice to clients*"; (2) "*Contributions to the debate are around educating government and other interested parties in the profession and options for continual improvement. I disagree more to protect the advisers who look after the clients. With recent legislation changes some advisers have passed on the costs increased by the changes.*"

Respondents' comments explained the low squared multiple correlation for a_{14} [Cognitive] variable. Just considering the difference between independence and conflicted "*is too simplistic. There are other factors.*" For instance, one adviser claimed, "*Independent advice also has bias to some extent, while there may be a wider investment choice/selection available the planner is inherently biased towards funds/products they have already used and have a relationship with.*" "*The reason for confusion includes the rules that govern the use of certain banned words (independent, unbiased, etc.). However I also believe confusion would reduce if there was clarity in relation to the legal provider of the advice (i.e. the licensee).*" For another adviser, "*There is no 'independent advice.'*" Whereas another adviser disagrees, "*There is no conflict. Again, what would you suggest – if I was licensed with CBA, and then sold an AMP product, and an AMP adviser sold a CBA product – both products are still owned by someone. Would you prefer I set up my own managed fund for my clients to invest in? Where is the safety in that?*" "*I agree that the public has difficulty but not because of the existence of third party Licensees. I think the distinction should be about quality of advice. Product bias is a minor, secondary consideration. It is not the source of all evil. Bad advice can be delivered by any adviser; independent, self-licensed; aligned or in the employ of a bank.*" The emotional response in this example explains the lower r^2: "*The industry can't even work out what independent is. We have advisers who can receive an Independent Financial Adviser Award (IFA Magazine) yet who operate businesses as conflicted as a Bank's. The AFSL then leverages that publicity to appear as something they are not – appalling!! Is it any wonder the public has no trust.*" "*Really dont think most Australians would know the difference as it is not usually openly disclosed to them.*" For another, they "*hadn't thought of it that way before./Quite possibly./Need to make it easier to handle compliance of own AFSL?*"

Many respondents answered the survey in terms what should be the case, rather than answering the question by what is the case, which may explain the low squared multiple correlations and regression weights for these variables. In other words, the model may fit the data, but does not reproduce some indicator relationships well. It does not produce uniformly interpretable estimates, because the matter is more complex than was at first conceptualised. Even so, the model was not respecified to improve the parsimony and interpretability of the CFA model, because on the basis of the evidence from the comments made by the respondents, advisers are unclear about their role and identity. This lack of a clearly defined identity and role is evident in the financial planning literature, which is an important finding. As far as the estimates for the seven indicators with lower than 50% r^2 values are concerned perceptibly, advisers' identity, role and performance is still evolving and/or in an evolutionary, if not in a revolutionary phase.

Therefore, on the basis of the overall results, the model is properly specified and plausible (Kline 2010). It is similar to the population's true covariance structure (Kline 2010). Furthermore, all the fit indices for *ex* and *cum* CLF led to the same conclusion for the hypotheses.

Conclusion

To sum up the extended main study, the raw data were screened utilising Microsoft Excel and IBM SPSS software. After analysing the demographics, a data-driven EFA technique was applied within a CFA framework. The assumptions were tested using a data-driven EFA approach within a CFA method (Brown & Moore 2016) using MLE. EFA was important to implement, because as noted earlier, this study pioneered a new theoretical framework combining several different theories for the first time defining, modelling and measuring legitimacy. Beginning with the *a priori* model, the first initial misspecification source was too many factors. Consequently, the four indicators of the Objective of the Act factor were collapsed into one factor per the pattern matrix during EFA analysis by merging them into the legitimacy factor [b_3]. Unacceptable low loadings during initial E/CFA led to three indicators being deleted. Then one of the measures was replaced after it was validated appropriate per the pattern matrix during EFA analysis combined with interpreting the substantive theory. Thus, E/CFA provided the model a more realistic solution in line with the theory. Once the correct number of indicators and factors were identified, the analyses proceeded with CFA bootstrapped MLE specification searches using MI by adopting current practice in SEM. Sequentially, the model was modified 13 times until adequate fit was achieved. This respecification resulted in a more parsimonious model for CFA. Notably, SEM experts (Kline 2010; Byrne 2013) claimed simpler models are preferred. Then, using chi-square difference test between the multigroup containing males [n = 218] and females [n = 44], the data were cross-validated successfully. This positive result meant the data were generalisable and not because of capitalising on chance. The results passed all the invariance tests using the same male/female multigroup CFA MLE χ^2 difference test approach (Schmitt & Kuljanin 2008). Convergent together with discriminant validity was established using common statistical techniques. Scale reliability was proven using tau equivalent tests and the more restrictive parallel tests. High power and *p*-values confirmed little evidence of any Type II errors among the indicators. Type I errors based on the standard error values were not of concern. However, common method bias was observed when the well-known Harman test was applied. This test was further validated with more reliable tests, such as the CLF and CLF marker tests using χ^2 differences. Although the mean values may be distorted, common method bias was inconsequential and observed not to threaten the validity of this research's conclusions. With or without the remedy for common method bias [namely adding a CLF], all the estimates led to the same conclusions for the hypotheses. So the bootstrapped MLE results with [*cum*] and without [*ex*] CLF starting with the fit statistics were reported. To conclude, the respecified hypothesised model seemed a good fit for the data collected. For example, CFI showed the over-identification condition was met when comparing the estimated model with an ***independent*** and null model. BIC indicated the estimates are generalisable. The root mean-square error of approximation indicated the population matrix model was the same as the estimated or sample model's matrix. PCLOSE value verified the estimated model [sample] is a good fit to the population. Thus, given the GOF thresholds have been identified, remedied and met, the interpretation of the model's estimates together with testing the hypotheses proceeds confidently in the next chapter.

APPENDICES FOR CHAPTER 5

Appendix 5.1

Table 1 Frequency use of 'Other' option on the ruler-option scale.

Variable	*N*	*I don't understand the question*		*I don't know*		*Not applicable*	
		Frequency	*Percent*	*Frequency*	*Percent*	*Frequency*	*Percent*
a_1	3	1	.4	1	.4	1	.4
a_2	3	1	.4			2	.8
a_3	3	1	.4	1	.4	1	.4
a_4	2					2	.8
a_5	5			4	1.5	1	.4
a_6	5	1	.4	4	1.5		
a_7	6			5	1.9	1	.4
a_8	8	2	.8	5	1.9	1	.4
a_9	8	1	.4	6	2.3	1	.4
a_{10}	3	1	.4	2	.8		
a_{11}	8			8	3.1		
a_{12}	8	2	.8	5	1.9	1	.4
a_{13}	6	1	.4	5	1.9		
a_{14}	2	1	.4	1	.4		
a_{15}	5			4	1.5	1	.4
a_{16}	3			2	.8	1	.4
a_{17}	3	1	.4	2	.8		
a_{18}	3			2	.8	1	.4
a_{19}	6	1	.4	4	1.5	1	.4
a_{20}	6	1	.4	5	1.9		
a_{21}	2			1	.4	1	.4
Total	**98**	**15**		**67**		**16**	

Appendix 5.2

Table 2 Missing patterns [cases with missing values] for Section A of the questionnaire.

Case	*Missing no.*	*%*	*Missing and extreme value patterns*#									
			a_{12}	a_{21}	a_{14}	a_{15}	a_{16}	a_{17}	a_{3}	a_{8}	a_{2}	a_{4}
171	1	4.8			S							
165	2	9.5									S	S
261	3	14.3							S	S	S	
108	2	9.5	S	S								
198	3	14.3				S	S	S				

No.: Number of missing cases %: percentage of missing cases

 # Cases and variables are sorted on missing patterns.

Appendix 5.3

Table 3 Observations farthest from the centroid [Mahalanobis distance] [Group number 1].

Observation number	*Mahalanobis d-squared*	*p1*	*p2*	*Difference in Mardi d*
89	54.485	0	.004	2.546
90	51.939	0	0	1.067
65	50.872	0	0	.776
222	50.096	0	0	.456
86	49.640	0	0	1.385
109	48.255	0	0	.945
164	47.310	0	0	1.887
112	45.423	0	0	.179
64	45.244	0	0	.425
230	44.819	0	0	.176
136	44.643	0	0	.839
174	43.804	.001	0	1.717
99	42.087	.001	0	.892
123	41.195	.001	0	1.627
197	39.568	.002	0	.081
232	39.487	.002	0	2.516
69	36.971	.005	0	.555
134	36.416	.006	0	.015
43	36.401	.006	0	1.571
202	34.830	.010	0	.061
94	34.769	.010	0	.561
71	34.208	.012	0	.008
203	34.200	.012	0	.739

(*Continued*)

Table 3 (Continued)

Observation number	*Mahalanobis d-squared*	*p1*	*p2*	*Difference in Mardi d*
173	33.461	.015	0	.090
117	33.371	.015	0	.503
150	32.868	.017	0	.066
88	32.802	.018	0	.649
93	32.153	.021	0	.452
13	31.701	.024	0	.019
95	31.682	.024	0	.028
25	31.654	.024	0	.115
58	31.539	.025	0	.469
215	31.070	.028	0	.008
160	31.062	.028	0	.260
177	30.802	.030	0	.002
237	30.800	.030	0	.073
40	30.727	.031	0	.092
132	30.635	.032	0	1.049
84	29.586	.042	0	.696
85	28.890	.050	0	.072
246	28.818	.051	0	.265
92	28.553	.054	0	.107
252	28.446	.056	0	.154
61	28.292	.058	0	.537
209	27.755	.066	0	.246
1	27.509	.070	0	.090
242	27.419	.071	0	.149
157	27.270	.074	0	.051
156	27.219	.075	0	.296
184	26.923	.080	0	.243
12	26.680	.085	0	.032
182	26.648	.086	0	.016
20	26.632	.086	0	.401
139	26.231	.095	0	.013
133	26.218	.095	0	.077
253	26.141	.097	0	.123
155	26.018	.099	0	.213
191	25.805	.104	0	.785
126	25.020	.124	0	.053
50	24.967	.126	0	.499
97	24.468	.140	0	.220
127	24.248	.147	0	.182
52	24.066	.153	0	.092
185	23.974	.156	0	.143
198	23.831	.161	0	.051
54	23.780	.162	0	.030

Observation number	*Mahalanobis d-squared*	*p1*	*p2*	*Difference in Mardi d*
18	23.750	.163	0	.188
189	23.562	.170	0	.400
3	23.162	.184	.001	.122
120	23.040	.189	.001	.026
79	23.014	.190	.001	.293
217	22.721	.202	.003	.116
131	22.605	.206	.003	.451
81	22.154	.225	.018	.237
227	21.917	.236	.034	.350
213	21.567	.252	.089	.040
32	21.527	.254	.079	.088
152	21.439	.258	.082	.024
66	21.415	.259	.068	.069
74	21.346	.262	.067	.081
82	21.265	.266	.068	.094
103	21.171	.271	.073	.048
34	21.123	.273	.067	.026
119	21.097	.275	.056	.170
38	20.927	.283	.08	.132
208	20.795	.290	.098	.040
180	20.755	.292	.088	.066
178	20.689	.295	.087	.011
72	20.678	.296	.07	.021
259	20.657	.297	.059	.057
241	20.600	.300	.056	.005
214	20.595	.300	.044	.237
233	20.358	.313	.082	.001
194	20.357	.313	.065	.119
6	20.238	.32	.078	.017
19	20.221	.32	.065	.141
192	20.080	.328	.085	.149
104	19.931	.337	.113	.138
257	19.793	.345	.143	.037
76	19.756	.347	.131	.037

Appendix 5.4

Table 4a Outlier Dual [a_1] comments.

Case	*Score*	*Comment by respondent*
29	2	*This question is not entirely reflective of a relationship between FA and Licensee. A Licensee who is not aligned directly or indirectly with a product manufacturer, is unlikely to interfere with the client–adviser relationship. There is a very important distinction between belonging to an aligned and non-aligned licensee.*
44	10	*The real agency is with the client. The relationship with the third-party licensee is one of a service provided.*
158	11	*I do not see any conflict. In offering an adviser–client relationship, the adviser is still undertaking a commercially rewarding enterprise, as does any other professional, including medical practitioners.*
166	9	*Our greatest relationship is to our clients and as long as the approved list is wide it should not be a problem.*
194	0	*My understanding of dual agency is where the agent represents the interests of both the buyer and the seller. As an adviser we represent the interests of the client [buyer] but the interests of the licensee are not as a 'seller.' The licensee authorises/licenses advisers, they don't 'sell' advice which is what the client is 'buying.'*
197	0	*Adviser relationship is empirical to the client.*
227	0	*This would depend entirely on the type of licensee./In the proper world, the client–adviser relationship is paramount, the licensee would expect and respect that./The licensee should be merely facilitating the service the adviser provides to client, not influence it.*

Table 4b Outlier BestRev [a_3] comments.

Case	*Score*	*Comment by respondent*
25	1	*Only to pay for services provided . . . Audits, Research. Technical etc./ Licensees do not normally provide product, however, the licensee can be owned by a product provider.*
182	0	*My practice is basically fixed fee with my AFSL. My AFSL doesn't make any more or less money from me irrespective of the source of my fees. That's why I am with them. If I worked for an Industry Fund or bank, then I am in trouble. The answer would be maybe 75%.*
215	0	*Licensees should charge a fee which is independent of what an adviser does for a client.*
242	0	*Advice quality suffers.*
253	0	*This respondent declined to make any comments.*

Table 4c Outlier Personal [a_{13}] comments.

Case	*Score*	*Comment by respondent*
147	5	*I disagree more to protect the advisers who look after the clients. With recent legislation changes, some advisers have passed on the costs increased by the changes.*
179	0	*I am comfortable that AMPs intentions and involvement at a government level is genuinely intentioned to actually tell these bureaucrats how things actually work in reality, not via some cookie-cutter approach where one set of guidelines will provide the panacea to everybody's financial planning issues.*
194	0	*As far as I know, leaders of aligned licensees don't debate on this. The professional bodies FPA and AFA do this as bodies that represent adviser interests. Advisers don't recommend products unless they are competitive. The product providers protect their distribution channels by making their products competitive in the first place.*

Appendix 5.5

Table 5 Test for homogeneity of variance.

	N	*Range*	*Std. deviation*	*Range/std. deviation*
Dual [a_1]	262	100	30.942	3.232
Simult [a_2]	262	100	35.417	2.824
BestRev [a_3]	262	100	28.602	3.496
CoIAss [a_4]	262	100	33.091	3.022
AlignAct [a_5]	262	100	38.252	2.614
CoIAct [a_6]	262	100	37.456	2.670
FiducAct [a_7]	262	100	37.031	2.700
CompAct [a_8]	262	100	37.314	2.680
Regulative [a_9]	262	100	37.780	2.647
Consequential [a_{10}]	262	100	36.670	2.727
Procedural [a_{11}]	262	100	38.140	2.622
Structural [a_{12}]	262	100	38.034	2.629
Personal [a_{13}]	262	100	29.044	3.443
Cognitive [a_{14}]	262	100	36.719	2.723
Defend [a_{15}]	262	100	34.066	2.935
Trust [a_{16}]	262	100	37.670	2.655
Independence [a_{17}]	262	100	36.096	2.770
Professions [a_{18}]	262	100	36.328	2.753
IPFPSB [a_{19}]	262	100	35.573	2.811
Takeover [a_{20}]	262	100	30.384	3.291
EliminateCoI [a_{21}]	262	100	35.082	2.850
Valid *N* (listwise)	**262**			

Appendix 5.6

Table 6 Collinearity statistics.

Relationships	*Tolerance*	*VIF* *>3< 4*	*Relationships*	*Tolerance*	*VIF* *>4< 5*	*Relationships*	*Tolerance*	*VIF* *>5< 10*
Dual*CoIAct	.278	3.593	Dual*AlignAct	.232	4.312	Dual*FiducAct	.198	5.038
Dual*Procedural	.28	3.572	Dual*Consequential	.244	4.098	Simult*FiducAct	.197	5.066
Simult*CoIAct	.278	3.598	Simult*AlignAct	.233	4.291	BestRev*FiducAct	.192	5.201
Simult*Procedural	.281	3.558	Simult*Consequential	.244	4.092	CoIAss*FiducAct	.193	5.191
BestRev*CoIAct	.278	3.599	BestRev*AlignAct	.232	4.314	CompAct*FiducAct	.195	5.128
BestRev*Procedural	.283	3.54	BestRev*Consequential	.244	4.098	Procedural*FiducAct	.193	5.186
CoIAss*CoIAct	.331	3.026	CoIAss*AlignAct	.232	4.314	Structural*FiducAct	.194	5.162
CoIAss*Procedural	.282	3.54	CoIAss*Consequential	.246	4.062	Personal*FiducAct	.198	5.05
AlignAct*Consequential	.26	3.839	AlignAct*FiducAct	.212	4.706	Cognitive*FiducAct	.194	5.158
AlignAct*CoIAct	.294	3.403	CoIAct*FiducAct	.207	4.842	Defend*FiducAct	.195	5.12
AlignAct*Procedural	.287	3.487	CoIAct*Consequential	.244	4.093	Trust*FiducAct	.192	5.195
CoIAct*Procedural	.282	3.54	CoIAct*AlignAct	.245	4.075	Independence*FiducAct	.192	5.206
FiducAct*Consequential	.258	3.87	CompAct*Consequential	.244	4.098	Professions*FiducAct	.192	5.206
FiducAct*Procedural	.281	3.558	CompAct*AlignAct	.237	4.225	IPFPSB*FiducAct	.192	5.199
FiducAct*AlignAct	.256	3.905	Regulative*Consequential	.248	4.025	Takeover*FiducAct	.192	5.201
FiducAct*CoIAct	.298	3.355	Regulative*AlignAct	.237	4.218	EliminateCoI*FiducAct	.192	5.2
CompAct*Procedural	.28	3.566	Regulative*FiducAct	.208	4.816			
CompAct*CoIAct	.287	3.485	Consequential*AlignAct	.247	4.046			
Regulative*Procedural	.304	3.288	Consequential*FiducAct	.203	4.916			
Regulative*CoIAct	.278	3.591	Procedural*AlignAct	.237	4.218			
Consequential*Procedural	.313	3.194	Structural*AlignAct	.233	4.299			
Consequential*CoIAct	.278	3.603	Structural*Consequential	.245	4.082			
Procedural*Consequential	.273	3.665	Personal*Consequential	.244	4.092			

Procedural*ColAct	.28	3.576	Personal*AlignAct	.232	4.319
Structural*ColAct	.278	3.602	Cognitive*AlignAct	.232	4.309
Structural*Procedural	.282	3.552	Cognitive*Consequential	.244	4.099
Personal*ColAct	.279	3.583	Defend*AlignAct	.232	4.316
Personal*Procedural	.282	3.541	Defend*Consequential	.246	4.06
Cognitive*ColAct	.28	3.567	Trust*AlignAct	.232	4.31
Cognitive*Procedural	.282	3.552	Trust*Consequential	.245	4.088
Defend*ColAct	.279	3.587	Independence*AlignAct	.233	4.284
Defend*Procedural	.282	3.551	Independence*Consequential	.244	4.099
Trust*ColAct	.277	3.606	Professions*AlignAct	.232	4.316
Trust*Procedural	.28	3.572	Professions*Consequential	.244	4.096
Independence*ColAct	.279	3.591	IPFPSB*AlignAct	.233	4.293
Independence*Procedural	.282	3.542	IPFPSB*Consequential	.244	4.096
Professions*ColAct	.277	3.607	Takeover*AlignAct	.235	4.26
Professions*Procedural	.281	3.563	Takeover*Consequential	.246	4.065
IPFPSB*ColAct	.277	3.604	EliminateCoI*AlignAct	.237	4.225
IPFPSB*Procedural	.28	3.57	EliminateCoI*Consequential	.245	4.088
Takeover*ColAct	.277	3.606			
Takeover*Procedural	.292	3.426			
EliminateCoI*ColAct	.278	3.593			
EliminateCoI*Procedural	.282	3.544			

Appendix 5.7

Table 7 Gender split of survey respondents.

		Frequency	*Percent*
Valid	Male	216	82.4
	Female	44	16.8
	Total	260	99.2
Missing	System	2	.8
Total		**262**	**100**

Appendix 5.8

Table 8 Frequency of age of survey participants.

		Frequency	*Percent*
Valid	Gen Y/Millennial [1981–2001]	14	5.3
	Gen X [1965–1980]	98	37.4
	Baby Boomers [1946–1964]	146	55.8
	Traditionalists [Born prior to 1946]	3	1.1
	Total	261	99.6
Missing	System	1	.4
Total		**262**	**100**

Appendix 5.9

Table 9 Frequency of location of survey respondents.

State	*Frequency*	*Percent*	*Valid percent*	*Cumulative percent*
New South Wales [NSW]	78	29.8	29.8	29.8
Queensland [QLD]	55	21.0	21.0	50.8
Tasmania [TAS]	7	2.6	2.6	53.3
Western Australia [WA]	30	11.5	11.5	64.9
South Australia [SA]	32	12.2	12.2	77.1
Victoria [VIC]	53	20.2	20.2	97.3
Australian Capital Territory [ACT]	5	1.9	1.9	99.2
Northern Territory [NT]	2	.8	.8	100
Total	**262**	**100**	**100**	

Appendix 5.10

Table 10 Frequency of the number of years of AR status of survey respondents.

Years	*Frequency*	*Percent*	*Valid percent*	*Cumulative percent*
1	3	1.1	1.2	1.6
2	7	2.7	2.7	5.5
3	3	1.1	1.2	5.0
4	2	0.8	.8	5.8
5	6	2.3	2.3	8.1
6	5	1.9	1.9	10.1
7	4	1.5	1.6	11.6
8	5	1.9	1.9	13.6
9	9	3.4	3.5	17.1
10	19	7.3	7.4	24.4
11	6	2.3	2.3	26.7
12	7	2.7	2.7	29.5
13	8	3.1	3.1	32.6
14	10	3.8	3.9	36.4
15	13	5.0	5.0	41.5
16	15	5.7	5.8	47.3
17	6	2.3	2.3	49.6
18	12	4.6	4.7	54.3
19	5	1.9	1.9	56.2
20	19	7.3	7.4	63.6
21	7	2.7	2.7	66.3
22	9	3.4	3.5	69.8
23	13	5.0	5.0	74.8
24	6	2.3	2.3	77.1
25	9	3.4	3.5	80.6
26	9	3.4	3.5	84.1
27	5	1.9	1.9	86.0
28	5	1.9	1.9	88.0
29	5	1.9	1.9	89.9
30	12	4.6	4.7	94.6
31	1	.3	.4	95.0
32	6	2.3	2.3	97.3
33	2	.8	.8	98.1
35	2	.8	.8	98.8
38	2	.8	.8	99.6
40	1	.3	.4	100
Missing	4	1.5		
Total	**262**	**100**	**100**	

Appendix 5.11

Table 11 Frequency of the highest and financial planning AQF qualifications achieved.

	N	*Percent*	*N*	*Percent*
Certificate I: Some high school, no diploma	3	1.1		
Certificate II: High school graduate, diploma or the equivalent	5	1.9		
Certificate III: Some college credit, no degree	1	.4		
Certificate IV: Trade/technical/vocational training	1	.4	2	.8
Diploma	33	12.6	87	33.2
Advanced Diploma	52	19.8	93	35.5
Bachelor Degree	65	24.8	14	5.3
Bachelor Honours degree, Graduate Certificate, Graduate Diploma	43	16.4	33	12.6
Masters Degree	59	22.5	23	8.8
None of the above			6	2.3
Missing			4	1.5
Total	**262**	**100**	**262**	**100**

Appendix 5.12

Table 12 Frequency of professional association membership.

	Frequency	*Valid percent*	*Missing*	*Valid percent*
Financial Planning Association [FPA]	186	71.0	76	29.0
Self-Managed Super Fund Association [SMSF]	45	17.2	217	82.8
Association of Financial Advisers [AFA]	41	15.6	221	84.4
Not a member of any association	23	8.8	239	91.2
Chartered Accountants Australia and New Zealand [CA ANZ]	21	8.0	241	92.0
Certified Practising Accountants [CPA]	19	7.3	243	92.7
Financial Services Institute of Australasia [FINSIA]	18	6.9	244	93.1
The Tax Institute [TTI]	7	2.7	255	97.3
Asian Institute of Chartered Bankers [AICB]	6	2.3	256	97.7
Independent Financial Advisers Association of Australia [IFAAA]	5	1.9	257	98.1
Mortgage & Finance Association of Australia [MFAA]	3	1.1	259	98.9
Stockbrokers Association Australia [SAA]	2	.8	260	99.2

	Frequency	*Valid percent*	*Missing*	*Valid percent*
Boutique Financial Planner Principals' Group [BFP]	2	.8	260	99.2
Australian and New Zealand Institute of Insurance and Finance [ANZIIF]	2	.8	260	99.2
Association of Superannuation Funds of Australia [ASFA]	1	.4	261	99.6
Responsible Investment Association Australasia [RIAA]	1	.4	261	99.6
Association of *Independent*ly Owned Financial Professionals [AIOFP]	1	.4	261	99.6
Finance Brokers Association of Australia Limited [FBAA]	1	.4	261	99.6
Institute of Certified Management Accountants [ICMA]	1	.4	261	99.6
International Academy of Collaborative Professionals [IACP]	1	.4	261	99.6

Appendix 5.13

Table 13 Frequency of professional qualifications of survey respondents.

	Valid		*Missing*	
	Frequency	*Percent*	*Frequency*	*Percent*
Certified Financial Planner [CFP]	141	53.8	121	46.2
No professional qualifications	67	25.6	195	74.4
Self-Managed Super Specialist [SSA]	40	15.3	222	84.7
Certified Practising Accountant [CPA]	22	8.4	240	91.6
Chartered Accountant [CA]	21	8.0	241	92.0
Other professional qualifications	11	4.2	251	95.8
Fellow Chartered Financial Practitioner [FChFP]	9	3.4	253	96.6
Life Risk Specialist [LRS]	9	3.4	253	96.6
Accredited Estate Planning Strategist [AEPS]	5	1.9	257	98.1
Chartered Life Practitioner [ChLP]	3	1.1	259	98.9
Certified Financial Analyst [CFA]	1	.4	261	99.6
Stockbrokers and Financial Advisers Association of Australia Professional Diploma in Stockbroking™	1	.4	261	99.6
Certified Management Accountant [CMA]	1	.4	261	99.6

Appendix 5.14

Table 14 Frequency of authorised representative status of survey participants.

	Frequency	*Percent*	*Valid percent*	*Cumulative percent*
Employee AR	63	24	24	24
Self-employed AR	199	76	76	100
Total	**262**	**100**	**100**	

Appendix 5.15

Table 15 Frequency of licensee status of survey respondents.

	Frequency	*Valid percent*	*Cumulative percent*
Aligned licensee	125	47.7	47.7
Non-aligned licensee	97	37.0	84.7
s923A *independent* licensee	39	14.9	99.6
Other licensee	1	.4	100
Total	**262**	**100**	

Appendix 5.16

Table 16 Initial pattern matrix[a] during E/CFA analysis.

Parameter	*Factor*			
	1	*2*	*3*	*4*
Dual [a_1]		.250	.558	
Simult [a_2]			.647	
BestRev [a_3]			.461	
ColAss [a_4]	.544			.284
AlignAct [a_5]	.850			
ColAct [a_6]	.450			.703
FiducAct [a_7]	.897			
CompAct [a_8]	.525			
Regulative [a_9]	.786			
Consequential [a_{10}]	.987			
Procedural [a_{11}]	.934			
Structural [a_{12}]		.217		
Personal [a_{13}]	.501	.260		
Cognitive [a_{14}]	.312	.397		
Defend [a_{15}]	.248	.293		
Trust [a_{16}]		.874		
Independence [a_{17}]		.775		
Professions [a_{18}]		.769		
IPFPSB [a_{19}]		.818		
Takeover [a_{20}]		.214		
EliminateCoI [a_{21}]		.699		

Extraction method: Maximum likelihood.
Rotation method: Promax with Kaiser normalisation.
a Rotation converged in five iterations.

Appendix 5.17

Table 17 Initial structure matrix during E/CFA.

Parameter	*Factor*			
	1	*2*	*3*	*4*
Dual [a_1]		.366	.586	
Simult [a_2]	.343		.665	
BestRev [a_3]			.419	
CoIAss [a_4]	.754	.454	.35	.605
AlignAct [a_5]	.870	.406	.262	.530
CoIAct [a_6]	.800	.400	.312	.928
FiducAct [a_7]	.900	.395	.301	.530
CompAct [a_8]	.660	.393	.397	.422
Regulative [a_9]	.780	.374	.332	.388
Consequential [a_{10}]	.890	.381	.254	.401
Procedural [a_{11}]	.854	.412	.269	.356
Structural [a_{12}]		.264	.210	
Personal [a_{13}]	.614	.500	.289	.286
Cognitive [a_{14}]	.571	.598	.354	.361
Defend [a_{15}]	.386	.423	.261	
Trust [a_{16}]	.376	.824		.214
Independence [a_{17}]	.394	.788	.314	.209
Professions [a_{18}]	.374	.763	.243	.218
IPFPSB [a_{19}]	.362	.783		.231
Takeover [a_{20}]	.236	.298	.233	
EliminateCoI [a_{21}]	.302	.687	.267	.216

Extraction Method: Maximum Likelihood.
Rotation Method: Promax with Kaiser Normalisation.

Appendix 5.18

Table 18 Hypotheses and/or related survey question discarded during E/CFA.

Variable	*Empirical test*	*Respecification*	*Reason*
H1(d): Financial advisers significantly agree licensing advisers through aligned licensees leads to conflict of interest from *association*.			
a_4 [b_1]	Licensing advisers through aligned licensees (e.g. ANZ, Westpac, NAB, CBA and AMP) results in conflict of interest from association.	Hypothesis deleted	On the basis of substantive theoretical reasons and reviewing the original theory, extending and applying the theory, the data responses for this statement were moved to measure H3(d): Financial advisers significantly agree the current 'authorised representative' licensing model does *not* have structural normative legitimacy.
H3(d): Financial advisers significantly agree the current 'authorised representative' licensing model does *not* have structural normative legitimacy.			
a_{12} [b_3]	Licensing professionally qualified advisers through third-party licensees means that when these advisers leave their licensee, unless they sign up with another licensee, they lose their ability to work as a professional financial adviser.	a_{12} replaced by a_4	Data not interpretable, because factor loadings for a_{12} were below .30. Therefore, removed from analysis.
H3(g) Financial advisers significantly agree that a financial adviser of product-aligned licensees must defend their relationship/association/affiliation with their licensee to clients.			
a_{15} [b_3]	Since the media has exposed the financial planning scandals, financial advisers have had to defend their relationship/association/affiliation with their licensee to clients.	Hypothesis deleted	Data not interpretable, because factor loadings were below .30. Therefore, removed from analysis.
H4(e): Financial advisers significantly agree the lack of independence from conflicted licensees exposes the financial planning industry to a 'takeover' by the accounting profession as the accountants redefine or reposition financial planning within their self-regulatory model.			
a_{20} [b_4]	Strategic *independent* advice is being taken over by the accounting profession, as accountants redefine and re-position financial planning within their self-regulatory model.	Hypothesis deleted	Data not interpretable, because factor loadings were below .30. Therefore, removed from analysis.

Appendix 5.19

Table 19 Argument for the reasonableness of including 13 covariances in the model.

Parameter	*Reason*
ColAct e_6 <>Structural e_4	If there is structural legitimacy whereby licensing advisers through aligned licensees [e.g. ANZ, Westpac, NAB, CBA and AMP] does not result in conflicts of interest from association, then the objective of the Act to minimise conflicts of interest is achieved. Therefore, these two measures are related.
Personal e_{13} <>Cognitive e_{14}	If contributions to the debate with government surrounding the licensing of advisers by specific individual leaders of aligned licensees [e.g. ANZ, Westpac, NAB, CBA and AMP] are not primarily aimed to protect their product distribution channels, then this should have some influence on the identity, role and performance of authorised representatives. Therefore, these measures are related.
Independence e_{17} <>EliminateCoI e_{21}	Where there is no conflict of interest from association, there is independence, *vice versa*. Therefore, these measures are related.
AlignAct e_5 <>Regulative e_9	If licensing advisers through aligned licensees [e.g. ANZ, Westpac, NAB, CBA and AMP] leads to unintentional compliance breaches by their advisers, such as providing product-biased advice because of their affiliation to product issuers, then the objective of the Act to align the interests of the adviser to the client is breached. Therefore, these measures are related.
ColAct e_6 <>Procedural e_{11}	If licensing advisers through aligned licensees [e.g. ANZ, Westpac, NAB, CBA and AMP] results in sales policies, procedures, and practices is designed by licensees to give the appearance [window dressing] of complying with the regulatory requirements, then the objective of the Act to eliminate or reduce conflicts of interest is breached. Therefore, these measures are related.
FiducAct e_7 <>CompAct e_8	If the objective of the Act of the best interest duty obligations to clients is achieved, then this should assist in achieving the objective of the Act to encourage competition within the financial planning/services industry. Therefore, these measures are related.
Consequential e_{10} <>Procedural e_{11}	There is a relationship between the commercial interests of licensees [any business in general] and their sales policies, procedures and practices.
ColAct e_6 <>Consequential e_{10}	If the commercial interests of aligned licensees [e.g. ANZ, Westpac, NAB, CBA and AMP] do not compromise their advisers' best interest duty obligations, then it can be argued the objective of the Act of eliminating or minimising conflicts of interest has been achieved. Therefore, these measures are related.

(*Continued*)

Table 19 (Continued)

Parameter	*Reason*
Cognitive e_{14} <>Structural e_4	If the Australian public can clearly distinguish between advisers who provide *independent* advice [as defined by the Act] and product-conflicted advisers, then licensing advisers through aligned licensees [e.g. ANZ, Westpac, NAB, CBA and AMP] should not result in conflict of interest from association. Therefore, these measures are related.
CompAct e_8 <>Consequential e_{10}	If the commercial interests of aligned licensees [e.g. ANZ, Westpac, NAB, CBA and AMP] do not compromise their advisers' best interest duty obligations, then it can be argued the objective of the Act of encouraging competition within the financial services industry is achieved. Therefore, these measures are related.
Trust e_{16} <>Professions e_{18}	Professions such as the accounting, legal and medical are considered trusted professions. Therefore, these measures are related.
CoIAct e_6 <>Personal e_{13}	The objective of the Act to encourage authorised representatives to eliminate or reduce conflicts of interest would influence the role of leaders to lobby government to retain [or not] their product distribution channels. Therefore, these measures are related.
Regulative e_9 <> Personal e_{13}	Unintentional compliance breaches by advisers because of their affiliation to product issuers may be the result of specific individual leaders of aligned licensees [e.g. ANZ, Westpac, NAB, CBA and AMP] primarily lobbying government to protect their product distribution channels. Therefore, these measures are related.

Appendix 5.20

Table 20a Unstandardised regression weights *ex* common latent factor: [Group number 1 – Default model].

Parameter	*ex and cum Bootstrap*[1]		*ex Bootstrap*[1]		*cum Bootstrap*								
	Estimate	*p-value*	*SE*	*c.r.*	*95% CI*								
					SE	*SE-SE*	*Mean*	*Bias*	*SE-Bias*	*Lower*	*Upper*	*Range*	*p-value*
Dual [a_1]	.746	.001	.229	3.256	.683	.034	.94	.194	.048	.175	3.166	2.991	.01
BestRev [a_3]	.438	***	.123	3.555	.186	.009	.43	–.008	.013	.063	.831	.768	.01
Regulative [a_9]	.891	***	.051	17.456	.038	.002	.89	–.001	.003	.807	.966	.159	.01
Consequential [a_{10}]	.953	***	.044	21.607	.039	.002	.952	–.002	.003	.87	1.021	.151	.01
Procedural [a_{11}]	.941	***	.049	19.091	.04	.002	.942	0	.003	.856	1.016	.16	.01
Personal [a_{13}]	.538	***	.046	11.698	.048	.002	.546	.007	.003	.448	.645	.197	.01
Cognitive [a_{14}]	.611	***	.06	10.186	.058	.003	.623	.012	.004	.521	.749	.228	.01
Independence [a_{17}]	.829	***	.065	12.752	.063	.003	.842	.014	.004	.71	.969	.259	.01
Professions [a_{18}]	.917	***	.07	13.098	.063	.003	.92	.003	.004	.818	1.037	.219	.01
IPFPSB [a_{19}]	.882	***	.063	13.961	.065	.003	.888	.006	.005	.74	1.019	.279	.01
Simult [a_2]	1				0	0	1	0	0	1	1	0	. . .
Structural [a_4]	.735	***	.047	15.771	.047	.002	.738	.003	.003	.647	.83	.183	.01
AlignAct [a_5]	1.004	***	.045	22.309	.035	.002	1.006	.002	.002	.938	1.076	.138	.01
ColAct [a_6]	.925	***	.048	19.169	.045	.002	.93	.005	.003	.839	1.017	.178	.01
FiducAct [a_7]	1				0	0	1	0	0	1	1	0	. . .
CompAct [a_8]	.775	***	.06	12.815	.056	.003	.775	0	.004	.668	.88	.212	.01
EliminateCoI [a_{21}]	.682	***	.066	10.374	.068	.003	.695	.012	.005	.545	.833	.288	.01
Trust [a_{16}]	1				0	0	1	0	0	1	1	0	. . .

[1]*including Bollen-Stine bootstrap*

Table 20b Unstandardised regression weights *cum* common latent factor: [Group number 1 – Default model].

Parameter	*ex and cum Bootstrap*[1]		*ex Bootstrap*[1]		*cum Bootstrap*			
	Estimate	*p-value*	*SE*	*c.r.*	*95% CI*			
					Lower	*Upper*	*Range*	*p-value*
Dual [a_1]	.766	.007	.286	2.676	.051	1.574	1.523	.039
BestRev [a_3]	.439	***	.121	3.642	.054	.889	.835	.01
Regulative [a_9]	.903	***	.059	15.207	.747	.987	.24	.01
Consequential [a_{10}]	.957	***	.049	19.416	.829	1.097	.268	.01
Procedural [a_{11}]	.98	***	.071	13.844	.781	1.077	.296	.01
Personal [a_{13}]	.649	***	.125	5.193	.338	.866	.528	.01
Cognitive [a_{14}]	.824	***	.216	3.817	.22	1.228	1.008	.01
Independence [a_{17}]	.852	***	.077	11.035	.087	1.302	1.215	.027
Professions [a_{18}]	.92	***	.082	11.211	.357	1.269	.912	.01
IPFPSB [a_{19}]	.881	***	.073	12.075	.341	1.679	1.338	.01
Simult [a_2]	1				1	1	0	
Structural [a_4]	.805	***	.089	9.073	.545	1.021	.476	.01
AlignAct [a_5]	1.019	***	.053	19.14	.915	1.141	.226	.01
CoIAct [a_6]	.952	***	.063	15.101	.805	1.101	.296	.01
FiducAct [a_7]	1				1	1	0	
CompAct [a_8]	.833	***	.091	9.162	.59	1.015	.425	.01
EliminateCoI [a_{21}]	.67	***	.078	8.625	.082	1.019	.937	.037
Trust [a_{16}]	1				1	1	0	

[1]*including Bollen-Stine bootstrap*

Appendix 5.21

Table 21 Correlations of indicator variables: [Group number 1 – Default model].

Parameter			*cum Bootstrap & ex CLF*									*cum Bootstrap & cum CLF*	
			Estimate	*SE*	*SE-SE*	*Mean*	*Bias*	*SE-Bias*	*95% CI*			*Estimate*	*p-value*
									Lower	*Upper*	*p-value*		
e_6	<>	e_4	.343	.078	.004	.339	–.004	.006	.164	.499	.01	.35	***
e_{13}	<>	e_{14}	.275	.061	.003	.276	.001	.004	.152	.399	.01	.119	.316
e_{17}	<>	e_{21}	.338	.083	.004	.331	–.007	.006	.172	.491	.01	.35	***
e_5	<>	e_9	–.294	.07	.004	–.287	.007	.005	–.426	–.151	.01	–.294	***
e_6	<>	e_{11}	–.222	.105	.005	–.239	–.016	.007	–.444	–.039	.033	–.211	.001
e_7	<>	e_8	–.261	.087	.004	–.267	–.006	.006	–.448	–.107	.01	–.265	***
e_{10}	<>	e_{11}	.184	.103	.005	.18	–.004	.007	–.02	.394	.071	.199	.012
e_6	<>	e_{10}	–.213	.087	.004	–.214	–.001	.006	–.386	–.051	.013	–.202	.003
e_{14}	<>	e_4	.154	.062	.003	.15	–.004	.004	.034	.279	.018	.075	.276
e_8	<>	e_{10}	–.181	.087	.004	–.176	.005	.006	–.358	–.004	.047	–.173	.018
e_{16}	<>	e_{18}	–.373	.207	.01	–.378	–.005	.015	–.884	–.065	.013	–.492	***
e_6	<>	e_{13}	–.169	.071	.004	–.171	–.002	.005	–.33	–.034	.01	–.133	.04
e_9	<>	e_{13}	–.148	.054	.003	–.15	–.002	.004	–.271	–.06	.011	–.131	.056

Appendix 5.22

Table 22 Variances bootstrapped *ex* and *cum* CLF: [Group number 1 – Default model].

	Bootstrapped ex CLF							*Bootstrapped cum CLF*						
	Estimate	*SE*	*c.r.*	*P*	*Lower*	*Upper*	*P*	*Estimate*	*SE*	*c.r.*	*P*	*Lower*	*Upper*	*P*
b_1	587.673	193.722	3.034	.002	124.469	1909.519	.01	593.552	202.065	2.937	.003	−309.289	2639.257	.14
b_3	1128.062	118.886	9.489	***	948.423	1293.762	.01	920.795	315.515	2.918	.004	348.358	1266.734	.01
b_4	1040.192	130.995	7.941	***	825.423	1268.077	.01	784.721	266.638	2.943	.003	-1769.751	1094.179	.331
e_1	627.000	114.994	5.452	***	−283.944	896.793	.116	526.230	117.738	4.469	***	172.600	842.038	.015
e_2	661.896	179.660	3.684	***	-722.675	1123.446	.199	648.138	171.316	3.783	***	-1424.758	941.175	.203
e_3	702.158	68.389	10.267	***	518.060	864.655	.01	698.405	67.186	10.395	***	489.767	854.846	.01
e_5	319.743	33.488	9.548	***	222.435	427.546	.01	316.230	33.878	9.334	***	212.767	421.132	.01
e_6	432.923	43.871	9.868	***	299.874	561.788	.01	435.759	43.647	9.984	***	287.569	561.680	.01
e_7	238.029	26.491	8.985	***	172.207	321.971	.01	220.033	26.897	8.181	***	140.478	303.601	.01
e_8	706.449	65.820	10.733	***	544.577	859.943	.01	702.116	65.316	10.750	***	531.287	814.238	.01
e_9	529.790	50.945	10.399	***	393.928	652.832	.01	529.011	50.977	10.378	***	378.158	653.750	.01
e_{10}	312.399	33.739	9.259	***	214.727	429.892	.01	309.897	33.947	9.129	***	202.484	437.386	.01
e_{11}	449.588	44.790	10.038	***	313.789	603.058	.01	453.562	44.866	10.109	***	308.859	605.073	.01
e_{13}	515.544	46.822	11.011	***	399.181	630.719	.01	452.324	53.817	8.405	***	275.171	598.510	.01
e_{14}	921.024	81.833	11.255	***	734.703	1095.086	.01	669.111	107.249	6.239	***	297.773	912.250	.01
e_{16}	373.386	63.122	5.915	***	218.672	548.864	.01	347.496	61.404	5.659	***	140.157	564.890	.039
e_{17}	583.908	60.611	9.634	***	404.636	744.806	.01	595.592	60.511	9.843	***	381.495	736.097	.011
e_{18}	440.116	63.350	6.947	***	244.966	616.633	.01	401.777	61.129	6.573	***	223.918	579.930	.01
e_{19}	450.885	51.006	8.840	***	290.567	626.904	.01	474.902	50.501	9.404	***	179.529	628.223	.02
e_{21}	741.617	70.500	10.519	***	556.669	892.213	.01	748.486	70.755	10.579	***	540.359	894.448	.01
e_4	478.564	43.888	10.904	***	371.255	585.924	.01	464.577	43.289	10.732	***	349.473	574.844	.01
CLF								79.046	77.799	1.016	.31	7.512	381.920	.01

Appendix 5.23

Table 23a Factor and indicator covariance: [Group number 1 – Default model].

Parameter			*Bootstrapped ex CLF*											
			Estimate	*SE*	*c.r.*	*P*	*SE*	*SE-SE*	*Mean*	*Bias*	*SE-Bias*	*95% CI*		
												Lower	*Upper*	*P*
b_1	<>	b_4	230.357	68.838	3.346	***	79.734	3.987	197.015	–33.342	5.638	22.468	351.541	.035
b_1	<>	b_3	315.377	94.774	3.328	***	127.179	6.359	289.678	–25.699	8.993	38.387	516.798	.01
b_3	<>	b_4	487.600	80.375	6.067	***	77.426	3.871	493.280	5.680	5.475	357.843	657.646	.01
e_6	<>	e_4	156.129	33.458	4.666	***	41.008	2.050	151.925	–4.205	2.900	63.577	241.192	.01
e_{13}	<>	e_{14}	189.176	45.327	4.174	***	47.005	2.350	188.940	–.236	3.324	95.350	275.796	.01
e_{17}	<>	e_{21}	222.379	50.432	4.409	***	69.007	3.450	215.215	–7.164	4.880	91.695	355.171	.01
e_5	<>	e_9	–120.940	29.964	–4.036	***	31.671	1.584	–117.120	3.821	2.239	–181.110	–57.103	.01
e_6	<>	e_{11}	–98.067	28.838	–3.401	***	43.352	2.168	-101.62	–3.550	3.065	–196.180	–14.875	0.033
e_7	<>	e_8	–107.150	30.110	–3.559	***	35.184	1.759	–107.900	–.750	2.488	–176.610	–45.774	.01
e_{10}	<>	e_{11}	69.008	29.486	2.340	.019	43.870	2.193	69.793	.784	3.102	–5.492	164.776	.071
e_6	<>	e_{10}	–78.244	25.548	–3.063	.002	32.089	1.604	–77.263	.981	2.269	–140.440	–17.239	.013
e_{14}	<>	e_4	101.913	37.805	2.696	.007	39.309	1.965	97.165	–4.747	2.780	22.369	182.874	.018
e_8	<>	e_{10}	-84.935	33.283	–2.552	.011	38.776	1.939	–80.785	4.149	2.742	–157.760	–2.137	.047
e_{16}	<>	e_{18}	–151.120	47.476	–3.183	.001	63.370	3.169	–143.130	7.987	4.481	–278.570	–33.429	.013
e_6	<>	e_{13}	–80.065	29.442	–2.719	.007	33.897	1.695	–79.552	.512	2.397	–153.400	–14.897	.01
e_9	<>	e_{13}	–77.235	34.607	–2.232	.026	27.969	1.398	–77.541	–.306	1.978	–138.470	–27.410	.011

Table 23b Factor and indicator covariance: [Group number 1 – Default model].

Parameter			*Bootstrapped cum CLF*						
			Estimate	*SE*	*c.r.*	*P*	*95% CI*		
							Lower	*Upper*	*P*
b_1	<>	b_4	182.050	103.529	1.758	.079	–309.800	285.035	.856
b_1	<>	b_3	338.064	107.862	3.134	.002	–199.040	480.896	.178
b_3	<>	b_4	667.935	113.358	5.892	***	–198.260	810.914	.261
e_6	<>	e_4	157.537	33.393	4.718	***	74.618	223.590	.01
e_{13}	<>	e_{14}	65.264	65.081	1.003	.316	–135.420	213.704	.431
e_{17}	<>	e_{21}	233.544	50.810	4.596	***	90.648	336.901	.017
e_5	<>	e_9	–120.140	29.852	–4.025	***	–180.650	–48.485	.01
e_6	<>	e_{11}	–93.911	28.802	–3.261	.001	–187.140	–13.326	.031
e_7	<>	e_8	–104.040	31.025	–3.353	***	–170.510	–28.201	.01
e_{10}	<>	e_{11}	74.699	29.707	2.514	.012	–3.999	178.976	.058
e_6	<>	e_{10}	–74.233	25.307	–2.933	.003	–140.110	–17.668	.01
e_{14}	<>	e_4	41.827	38.404	1.089	.276	-60.281	147.282	.29
e_8	<>	e_{10}	–80.769	34.024	–2.374	.018	–156.450	1.992	.055
e_{16}	<>	e_{18}	–183.810	45.725	–4.020	***	–279.700	–39.051	.018
e_6	<>	e_{13}	–58.997	28.711	–2.055	.04	–127.800	–1.043	.048
e_9	<>	e_{13}	–64.255	33.588	–1.913	.056	–133.050	–2.013	.045

Appendix 5.24

Table 24 Error covariance constraint chi-square difference test [Bootstrapped *ex* and *cum* CLF].

ex CLF										
Model	*chi-square*	*df*	*p*	*chi-square diff*	*df diff*	$p < .05$*	$p < .01$*	$p < .001$*	*CFI*	*CFI diff*
Unconstrained	222.131	119	0	Significant		critical chi-square threshold			.964	
Zero error covariance constraint	290.565	127	0	68.434	8	15.507	20.09	26.124	.943	.021
Small positive value of.005 error covariance constraint	290.57	127	0	68.439	8	15.507	20.09	26.124	.943	.021

cum CLF										
Model	*chi-square*	*df*	*p*	*chi-square diff*	*df diff*	$p < .05$*	$p < .01$*	$p < .001$*	*CFI*	*CFI diff*
Unconstrained	128.339	101	.034	Significant		critical chi-square threshold			.991	
Zero error covariance constraint	188.8	109	0	60.461	8	15.507	20.09	26.124	.972	.019
Small positive value of.005 error covariance constraint	188.8	109	0	60.461	8	15.507	20.09	26.124	.972	.019

* *Values of the Critical chi-squared distribution sourced from www.medcalc.org/manual/chi-square-table.pp*

Appendix 5.25

Table 25 Squared multiple correlations: [Group number 1 – Default model].

Parameter		*Bootstrapped ex CLF*										*Bootstrapped cum CLF*				
		Estimate	*SE*	*SE-SE*	*Mean*	*Bias*	*SE-Bias*	*95% CI*				*Estimate*	*95% CI*			
								Lower	*Upper*	*P*	*Range*		*Lower*	*Upper*	*P*	*Range*
Structural	a_4	.560	.052	.003	.562	.002	.004	.454	.648	.01	.194	.574	.458	.669	.01	.211
EliminateCoI	a_{21}	.395	.065	.003	.407	.012	.005	.294	.545	.01	.251	.390	.311	.555	.01	.244
IPFPSB	a_{19}	.642	.062	.003	.648	.006	.004	.516	.760	.01	.244	.623	.501	.834	.01	.333
Profession	a_{18}	.665	.069	.003	.668	.003	.005	.542	.801	.01	.259	.694	.554	.833	.01	.279
Independence	a_{17}	.550	.069	.003	.564	.014	.005	.426	.691	.01	.265	.541	.417	.693	.01	.276
Trust	a_{16}	.736	.060	.003	.735	0	.004	.609	.847	.01	.238	.754	.588	.902	.01	.314
Cognitive	a_{14}	.314	.054	.003	.324	.010	.004	.220	.431	.01	.211	.502	.322	.752	.01	.430
Personal	a_{13}	.388	.049	.002	.393	.005	.003	.286	.487	.01	.201	.463	.335	.669	.01	.334
Procedural	a_{11}	.690	.051	.003	.688	−.001	.004	.586	.782	.01	.196	.687	.576	.784	.01	.208
Consequential	a_{10}	.766	.045	.002	.762	−.005	.003	.668	.838	.01	.170	.768	.663	.851	.01	.188
Regulative	a_9	.628	.046	.002	.627	−.002	.003	.538	.722	.01	.184	.628	.530	.728	.01	.198
CompAct	a_8	.490	.055	.003	.490	0	.004	.384	.596	.01	.212	.494	.398	.625	.01	.227
FiducAct	a_7	.826	.029	.001	.824	−.002	.002	.759	.878	.01	.119	.839	.775	.898	.01	.123
CoIAct	a_6	.691	.048	.002	.695	.004	.003	.596	.783	.01	.187	.688	.607	.791	.01	.184
AlignAct	a_5	.781	.035	.002	.779	−.001	.002	.697	.852	.01	.155	.783	.707	.856	.01	.149
BestRev	a_3	.138	.078	.004	.126	−.012	.005	.011	.348	.01	.337	.143	.025	.350	.01	.325
Simult	a_2	.470	.773	.039	.588	.118	.055	.098	1.598	.01	1.500	.481	.245	2.173	.01	1.928
Dual	a_1	.343	.294	.015	.425	.082	.021	.054	1.282	.01	1.228	.448	.099	.812	.02	.713

Notes

1 p1 is the probability of any observation exceeding the squared Mahalanobis distance of that observation. Problematic is when the Mahalanobis distance is high or shows a larger difference compared with any of the other variables in the same table. Small numbers of p1 less than 0.05 are generally expected.
2 p2 shows the probability that the largest squared distance of any observation would exceed the Mahalanobis distance computed. However, small numbers of less than 0.01 in the p2 column, on the other hand, indicate observations far from the centroid under the hypothesis of normality (Arbuckle 1997).
3 Recall in Chapter 4 we mentioned using an online SEM sampling calculator (Soper 2016) to calculate a minimum sample size of 137 cases with anticipated effect size .3, statistical power .8 and probability level .05 as sufficient to perform MLE analysis given the *a priori* model in Figure 4.4.
4 All critical χ^2 values were sourced online from MedCalc Software (2016). A modified copy of their table of the critical chi-square values is available in Table 20 in Appendix 5.20.]
5 We were unable to generate standardised regression weight's 95% confidence intervals in Amos using bootstrap *cum* CLF.
6 Negative covariance in CFA? – ResearchGate. Available from: <www.researchgate.net/post/negative_covariance_in_CFA> [accessed 26 November 2016].

6 Analysis of the AFSL-AR licensing regime

Introduction

Once the thresholds of the most important GOF indices were met, the next step was to identify, explain and/or remedy any bias in the data, run the final bootstrapped MLE *ex* and *cum* CLF and proceed with interpreting the results. Thus, this chapter homes in on the major quantitative results.

Overall results of AFSL-AR licensing

In the CFA models, depicted in Figure 6.1, all the estimated bootstrapped standardised regression weights in the respecified model are highly significant, except factor b_1 [adviser dual-agency role]. Critical ratios of all the unstandardised factor loadings far exceeded the threshold values of 1.96 [alpha .05] or 1.65 [alpha .01] or 2.58 [alpha .001], displayed in Tables 6.1 to 6.5. The correlation coefficients were highly significant, except between b_1 [dual-agency] and b_4 [individual licensing] *cum* CLF model [Figure 6.1]. However, this exception was interpreted with caution, because its N.S. $p = .079$ value was good news. Advisers cannot be dual agents while concurrently being licensed via a single ***independent*** professional financial planning standards board. Overall, the results indicated, all the theories in this model were useful in evaluating the licensee–adviser licensing model's legitimacy. Although not ideal, the negative covariance for factor b_3 [legitimacy] indicated overestimations of the relationships between its indicators. These relationships were retained, because they were central to the model.

Visibly the mean values indicated the extent of the level of agreement was close to undecided [a neutral value of 50%] for (1) Regulative illegitimacy [a_9] with a mean level of agreement of 48%, (2) CompAct [a_8] with mean of 51% and (3) EliminateCoI [a_{21}] with mean of 52% [Table 26 in Appendix 6.1 and Graph 6.1]. Whereas the highest mean level of agreement of 78% for BestRev [a_3] and Personal illegitimacy [a_{13}] indicated advisers strongly agree they earn revenues for licensee, while serving their best interest duty, while their leaders of aligned licensees focus to protect product distribution. Four variables scored a mean level above 70%, namely Dual [a_1], BestRev [a_3], Structural illegitimacy [a_4] and Personal illegitimacy [a_{13}]. The mean level of agreement above 50%, but below 60%, included FiducAct [a_7],

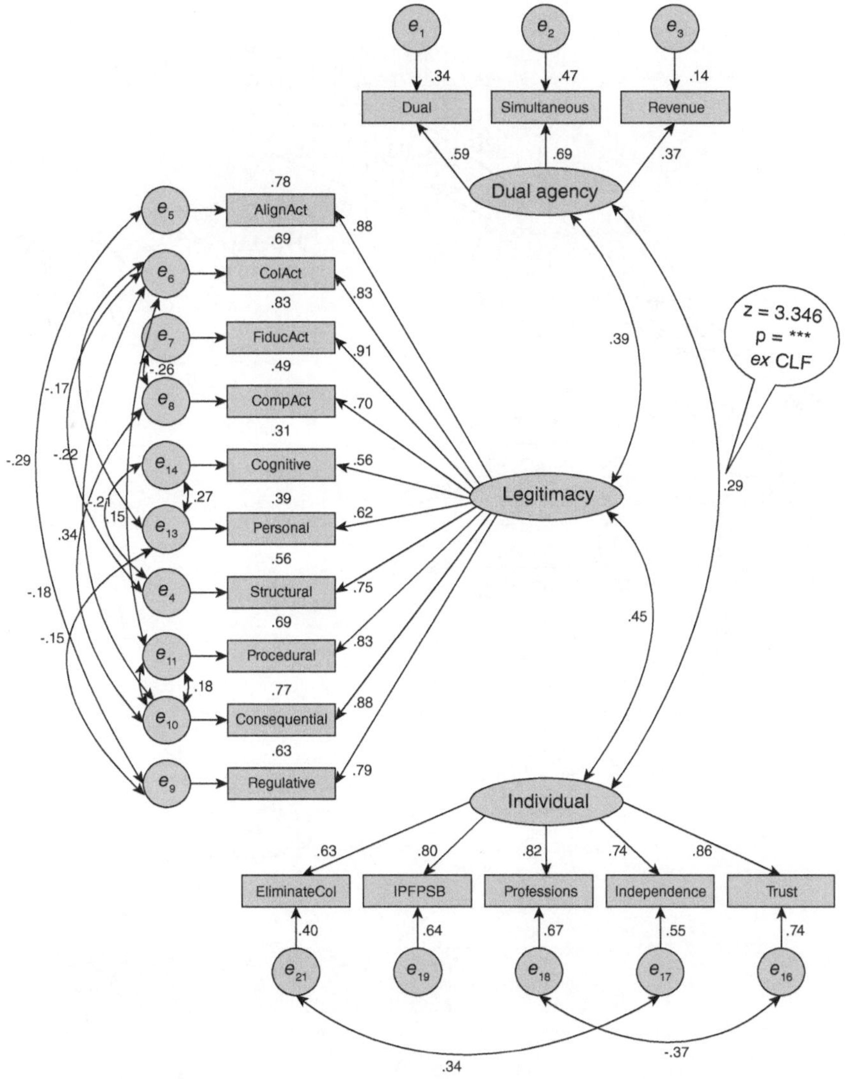

Figure 6.1 Confirmatory factor analysis model standardised regression weights after bootstrapped MLE *ex* and *cum* CLF.

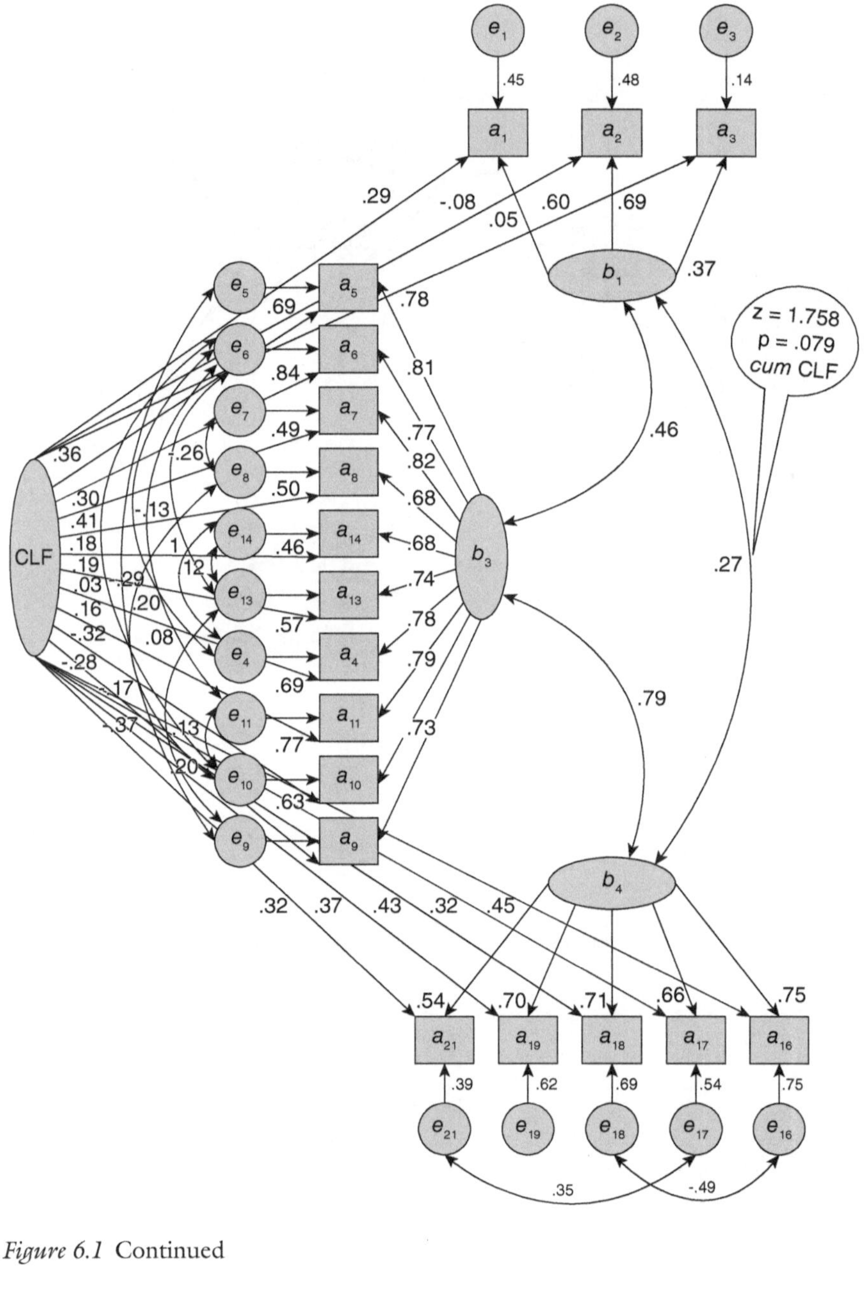

Figure 6.1 Continued

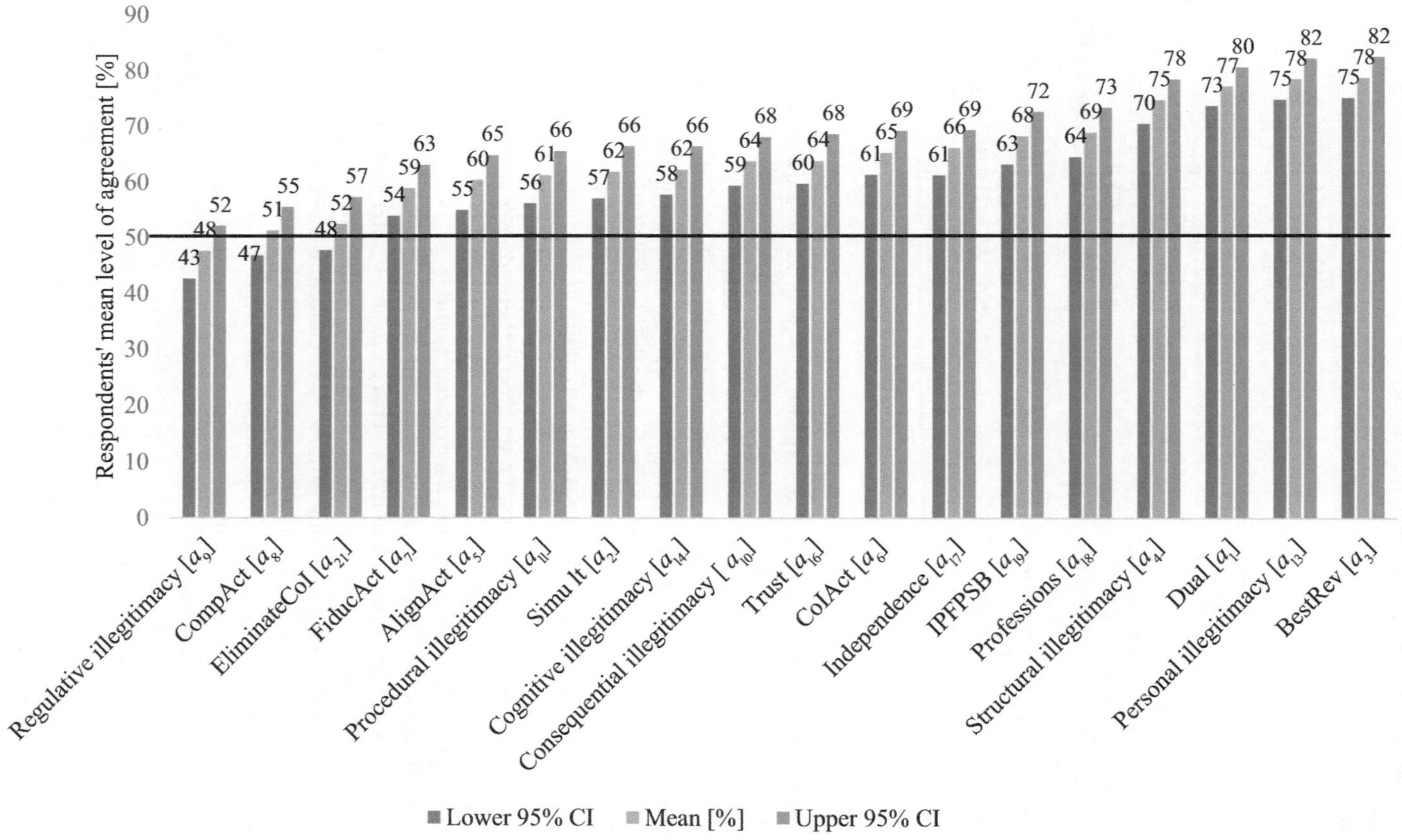

Graph 6.1 Respondents' mean level of agreement with 95% confidence interval.

Table 6.1 Structural part of the theoretical model.

Outcome	*Parameter*	*Evidence* β*; SE [95% CI] c.r. p-value [ex CLF]* β*; c.r. p-value [cum CLF]*
Dual-agency role and the legitimacy of the current licensing model are significantly correlated.	b_1<> b_3	.387 .102 [.112, .503] 3.326 p = *** [*ex* CLF] .257; 3.134 p = .002 [*cum* CLF]
Illegitimacy of the current licensing model and the individual licensing model is significantly correlated.	b_3<> b_4	.45 .061 [.335, .571] 6.067 p = *** [*ex* CLF] .786; 5.892 p = *** [*cum* CLF]
No significant correlation between dual-agency role and individual licensing	b_1<> b_4	.295 .128 [.016, .504] 3.346 p = *** [*ex* CLF] .267; 1.758 p = .079 [*cum* CLF]

Correlation (β) Standard error (SE) Confidence interval [CI] Critical ratio (c.r.)

CompAct [a_8] and EliminateCoI [a_{21}]. Apart from EliminateCoI [a_{21}], Simult [a_2], AlignAct [a_5], CoIAct [a_6], Consequential [a_4], Procedural [a_{21}], Cultural-cognitive [a_{14}], while the rest of the indicators for the factor individual licensing [b_4] had mean values between 60% and 70%. From Graph 6.1 the mean scores of the indicators for individual licensing factor [b_4] were consistent. Overall, the bootstrap 95% CIs were narrow in range and had CI p-values of .01 for all the estimates. For instance, the smallest value for the 95% CI 6.962 for indicator Dual [a_1]. Whilst the largest range value amounted to 9.821 for indicator AlignAct [a_5].

Furthermore, the structural part as conceptualised in Chapter 4, depicted on the left in Figure 6.2, ended up looking like the structural path on the right with its bootstrapped maximum likelihood estimates. Recall the indicators of factor b_2 was merged into b_3, thus the beta [β] estimates between b_1 and b_2, b_2 and b_3, as well as b_2 and b_4 were lost. Thus, leaving β's between b_1 and b_4, b_1 and b_3, as well as b_3 and b_4 in the respecified CFA model of Figure 6.1 in this chapter. From Table 6.1 above, there is no significant relationship between b_1 and b_4 after adding the CLF. The dual-agency role [b_1] and individual licensing [b_4] relationship was insignificant at the $p < .05$ level scoring a p-value of .079 as evidenced in Table 6.1. Thus, this relationship was discarded in the final structural part of the model.

Empirically, all the investigative questions and hypotheses were supported. Consequently, overall advisers support the notion-licensing advisers via multiple third-party licensees creates a dual-agency role. They claimed licensing advisers via third parties is inconsistent with four of the objectives of the Act. Linked to the objectives, advisers confirmed current licensing lacks legitimacy based on Suchman's theoretical legitimacy framework. This illegitimacy of AFSL-AR licensing strengthens arguments for individual licensing through a single *independent* professional body, like other professions, which advisers support. In sequence of the

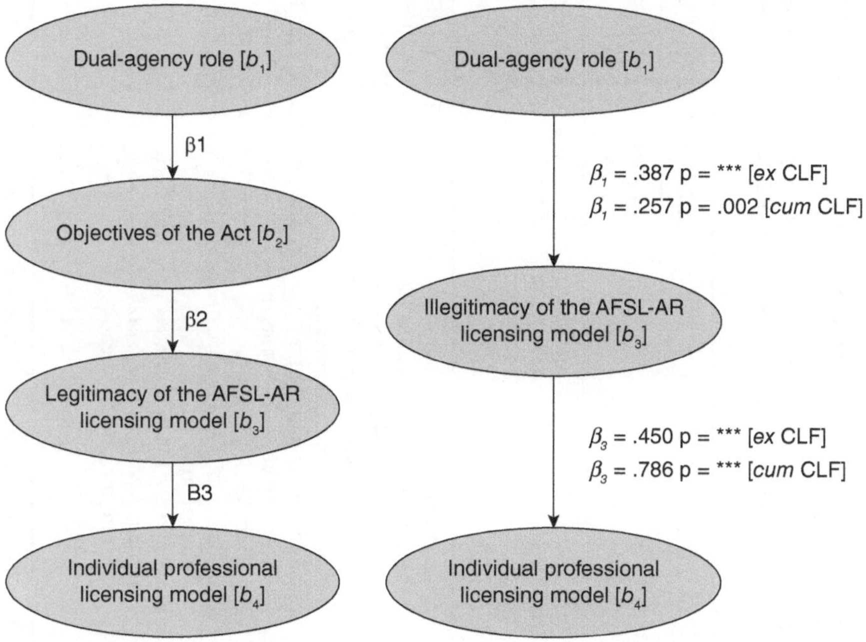

Figure 6.2 Structural part of the model *a priori* model on the left and the finalised model on the right with their correlation estimates.

model discussed in the literature review, a more detailed account of these overall findings is presented.

Dual-agency role uncertainty

Summarised in Table 6.2 mean [Table 26 in Appendix 6.1] agreement levels distributed from 62% to 78% confirmed prevailing licensing created a dual-agency role between licensee–adviser (Smith & Walter 2001; Gor 2005) and adviser–client (Corones & Galloway 2013). Additionally, results confirmed Kingston and Weng's (2014) claim, serving both principals simultaneously leads to conflicts of interest. Furthermore, the moderate standardised regression weights [Table 5.16] substantiate mixed perceptions, which meant uncertainty is evident among respondents when reflecting on the licensee–adviser–client agency role. This mixed response reflected in the commentary informants offered. However, when evaluating these results in conjunction with the results of unavoidable conflict of interest from association [Table 6.3] and structural illegitimacy [Table 6.4], it was clear advisers do perceive licensing advisers via third-party licensees leads to a conflict of interest from association. The moderate SE for predictor dual-agency role differed from the SE magnitudes of the indicators for factors b_3 and b_4 in the

Table 6.2 Summary of findings for adviser dual-agency role [b_1].

Q1: To what extent do financial advisers agree licensing via third-party licensees creates a dual-agency role, whereby they serve the commercial interests of licensees and the best interests of clients simultaneously, leading to conflict of interest from association?

H1: Financial advisers on the ASIC Adviser Register significantly agree licensing via third-party licensees creates a dual-agency role, whereby they serve the commercial interests of licensees and the best interests of clients simultaneously, as specified in the Act, which leads to conflict of interest from association.

PAR	*LITERATURE REVIEW*	*SUB-HYPOTHESES SUPPORTED*	*EMPIRICAL TEST*	*EMPIRICAL EVIDENCE* *λ SE [95% CI] c.r. p-value (ex CLF)* *λ c.r. p-value (cum CLF)* *M [95% CI] MSE c.r. p-value*
a_1	Licensee-adviser (Gor 2005; Smith & Walter 2001) and adviser–client relationship (Corones & Galloway 2013).	H1 (a): Financial advisers significantly agree advisers authorised via third-party licensees face a dual-agency role, namely an adviser–licensee relationship and an adviser–client relationship.	Advisers authorised through third-party licensees face a dual-agency relationship, namely an adviser–licensee relationship and an adviser–client relationship.	.585 .215 [.232, 1.132] 3.256 p = .001 .604; 2.676 p = .007 77 [73, 80] 1.912 40.266 p = ***
a_2	Advisers serve the interests of licensees & clients, simultaneously (Kingston & Weng 2014).	H1 (b): Financial advisers significantly agree licensing advisers through third-party licensees results in advisers serving the interests of their clients and licensees, simultaneously.	Licensing advisers through third-party licensees results in advisers serving the interests of their clients and licensees, simultaneously.	.686 .280 [.313, 1.264] marker p = *** .689 marker p = *** 62 [57, 66] 2.188 28.234 p = ***
a_3	Dual role creates conflicts of interest (Kingston & Weng 2014).	H1 (c): Financial advisers significantly agree while serving the best interests of their clients, advisers also generate revenue for their licensees.	While serving the best interest of their clients, advisers also generate revenue for their licensees.	.372 .109 [.103, .59] 3.555 p = *** .375; 3.642 p = *** 78 [75, 82] 1.767 44.416 p = ***

Parameter (Par) Question (Q) Hypothesis (H) Standardised regression weight (λ) *Standard error* (*SE*) *Critical ratio* (*c.r.*) *Mean* (*M*) *Mean standard error* (*MSE*)

Table 6.3 Summary of findings for objectives of the Act [b_2].

Q2: To what extent do financial advisers perceive the current 'authorised representative' licensing model achieves four objectives of the Act?
H2: Financial advisers on the ASIC Adviser Register significantly agree the current 'authorised representative' licensing model does not achieve the four identified objectives of the Act.

PAR	*LITERATURE REVIEW*	*SUB-HYPOTHESIS SUPPORTED*	*EMPIRICAL TEST*	*EMPIRICAL EVIDENCE* *λ SE [95% CI] c.r. p-value (ex CLF)* *λ c.r. p-value (cum CLF)* *M [95% CI] MSE c.r. p-value*
a_5	Encourage aligning advisers' interests with their clients' best interest (Goedecke 2001).	H2 (a): Financial advisers significantly agree the current 'authorised representative' licensing model, as specified in the Act, makes it difficult for advisers to align their interests with the best interests of the client.	Licensing advisers through aligned licensees sometimes makes it difficult for these advisers to align their interests with the best interests of their clients.	.884 .020 [.835, .923] 22.309 p = *** .810, 19.14 p = *** 60 [55, 65] 2.363 25.528 p = ***
a_6	Manage, control or avoid conflicts of interest (Tuch 2005; Pearson 2006a; Schwarcz 2009; Valentine 2008, 2013).	H2 (b): Financial advisers significantly agree the current 'authorised representative' licensing model, as specified in the Act, results in conflict of interest from association because they are affiliated to product issuers.	Advisers authorised through aligned licensees face unavoidable conflict of interest from association by being affiliated to product issuers.	.831 .029 [.766, .884] 19.169 p = *** .773, 15.101.169 p = *** 65 [61, 69] 2.315 28.137 p = ***

(*Continued*)

Table 6.3 (Continued)

Q2: To what extent do financial advisers perceive the current 'authorised representative' licensing model achieves four objectives of the Act?
H2: Financial advisers on the ASIC Adviser Register significantly agree the current 'authorised representative' licensing model does not achieve the four identified objectives of the Act.

PAR	*LITERATURE REVIEW*	*SUB-HYPOTHESIS SUPPORTED*	*EMPIRICAL TEST*	*EMPIRICAL EVIDENCE* *λ SE [95% CI] c.r. p-value (ex CLF)* *λ c.r. p-value (cum CLF)* *M [95% CI] MSE c.r. p-value*
a_7	Ensure compliance of the statutory fiduciary duty (Banister *et al.* 2013; Bateman & Kingston 2014).	H2 (c): Financial advisers significantly agree the current 'authorised representative' licensing model, as specified in the Act may lead to unintentional breaches of advisers' statutory fiduciary duty obligations.	Licensing advisers through aligned licensees puts their advisers at greater risk of unintentionally breaching their best interest duty obligations to clients.	.909 .016 [.871, .937] marker p = *** .821, marker p = *** 59 [54, 63] 2.288 25.717 p = ***
a_8	Promote competitive behaviour between financial service providers (Steen, McGrath and Wong 2016).	H2 (d): Financial advisers significantly agree that the current 'authorised representative' licensing model limits fair competition within the financial planning sector.	Licensing advisers through aligned licensees limits advisers from competing on a level playing field within the industry.	.700 .039 [.62, .772] 12.815 p = *** .679, 9.162 p = *** 51 [47, 55] 2.303 22.267 p = ***

Parameter (Par) Question (Q) Hypothesis (H) Standardised regression weight (λ) *Standard error* (*SE*) *Critical ratio* (*c.r.*) *Mean* (*M*) *Mean standard error* (*MSE*)

Table 6.4 Summary of findings for Suchman's legitimacy criteria [b_3].

Q3: To what extent do financial advisers agree the current AFSL-AR licensing model is legitimate based on the criteria of Suchman's theoretical legitimacy framework?

H3: Financial advisers registered on the ASIC Adviser Register significantly agree the current AFSL-AR licensing model is illegitimate based on the criteria of Suchman's (1995) theoretical legitimacy framework.

PAR	*LITERATURE REVIEW*	*SUB-HYPOTHESIS*	*EMPIRICAL TEST*	*EMPIRICAL EVIDENCE*
				λ SE [95% CI] c.r. p-value (ex CLF)
				λ c.r. p-value (cum CLF)
				M [95% CI] MSE c.r. p-value
a_9	Perception of compliance with laws operating within some socially acceptable system (Suchman 1995).	H3 (a): Financial advisers significantly agree the current licensee–adviser licensing model does not have regulative legitimacy.	Licensing advisers via aligned licensees can lead to unintentional compliance breaches by their advisers, because of their affiliation to product issuers (Bitektine 2011; Chelli *et al.* 2014).	.793 .029 [.734, .850] 17.456 p = *** .727, 15.207 p = *** 48 [43, 52] 2.337 20.365 p = ***
a_{10}	Acceptable specified ethics of socially value outputs/ outcomes (Suchman 1995).	H3 (b): Financial advisers significantly agree the current licensee–adviser licensing model does not have consequential normative legitimacy.	Licensing advisers via aligned licensees leads to the commercial interests of these aligned licensees compromising their advisers' best interest duty obligations (Smith 2009, p. 62; Pain 2013; Moran 2014; Maclean & Behnam 2010).	.875 .026 [.817, .916] 21.607 p = *** .794, 19.416 p = *** 63 [59, 58] 2.264 28.111 p = ***

(*Continued*)

Table 6.4 (Continued)

Q3: To what extent do financial advisers agree the current AFSL-AR licensing model is legitimate based on the criteria of Suchman's theoretical legitimacy framework?

H3: Financial advisers registered on the ASIC Adviser Register significantly agree the current AFSL-AR licensing model is illegitimate based on the criteria of Suchman's (1995) theoretical legitimacy framework.

PAR	*LITERATURE REVIEW*	*SUB-HYPOTHESIS*	*EMPIRICAL TEST*	*EMPIRICAL EVIDENCE* *λ SE [95% CI] c.r. p-value (ex CLF)* *λ c.r. p-value (cum CLF)* *M [95% CI] MSE c.r. p-value*
a_{11}	Perception of socially acceptable practices, standards & procedures (Suchman 1995).	H3 (c): Financial advisers significantly agree the current licensee–adviser licensing model does not have procedural normative legitimacy.	Licensing advisers via aligned licensees sometimes results in sales policies, procedures and practices designed by licensees to give the appearance [window dressing] of complying with the regulatory requirements (Valentine & Hollingworth 2015; Valentine 2013; Newnham 2012; Sampson 2010; West 2009).	.831 .031 [.766, .884] 19.901 $p =$ *** .781, 13.844 $p =$ *** 61 [56, 66] 2.356 25.956 $p =$ ***
a_4	Adopting acceptable formal structures acceptable to society (Suchman 1995).	H3 (d): Financial advisers significantly agree the current licensee–adviser licensing model does not have structural normative legitimacy.	Licensing advisers via aligned licensees results in conflict of interest from association (Steen, McGrath and Wong 2016; Valentine 2013; Smith 2009, p. 317; Parliamentary Joint Committee on Corporations & Financial Services 2009a, 2009b).	.748 .035 [.674, .805] 15.771 $p =$ *** .740, 9.073 $p =$ *** 75 [70, 78] 2.041 36.477 $p =$ ***

(*Continued*)

Table 6.4 (Continued)

Q3: To what extent do financial advisers agree the current AFSL-AR licensing model is legitimate based on the criteria of Suchman's theoretical legitimacy framework?
H3: Financial advisers registered on the ASIC Adviser Register significantly agree the current AFSL-AR licensing model is illegitimate based on the criteria of Suchman's (1995) theoretical legitimacy framework.

PAR	*LITERATURE REVIEW*	*SUB-HYPOTHESIS*	*EMPIRICAL TEST*	*EMPIRICAL EVIDENCE*
				λ SE [95% CI] c.r. p-value (ex CLF)
				λ c.r. p-value (cum CLF)
				M [95% CI] MSE c.r. p-value
a_{13}	Perception of acceptable leader's role to exert personal influence to dismantle/create existing/new entities (Suchman 1995; Goretzki *et al.* 2013; Carnegie & O'Connell 2012).	H3 (e): Financial advisers significantly agree the current licensee–adviser licensing model does not have personal normative legitimacy.	Contributions by specific individual leaders of aligned licensees to the debate with the government surrounding the licensing of advisers are aimed to protect their product distribution channels (Bird &Gilligan 2015a, 2015b; Sampson 2010).	.623 .039 [.535, .698] 11.698 *p* = *** .679, 5.193 *p* = *** 78 [75, 82] 1.797 43.594 *p* = ***
a_{14}	Perception of a shared understanding of actors' identity, role and performance to perpetuate an institutional order based on cognition or awareness (Santana 2012; Kury 2007; Meyer 2007; Suchman 1995; Zimmerman & Zeitz 2002, p. 420; Scott 2014).	H3 (f): Financial advisers significantly agree the current licensee–adviser licensing model does not have cultural-cognitive legitimacy.	Licensing advisers via third-party licensees is one of the reasons why the Australian public cannot clearly distinguish between advisers who provide *independent* advice (as defined by s923A of the Commonwealth Corporations Act 2001) and those who provide advice may be conflicted by product bias (Morris 2013).	.560 .047 [.469, .657] 10.186 *p* = *** .682, 3.817 *p* = *** 62 [58, 66] 2.268 27.401 *p* = ***

Parameter (Par) Question (Q) Hypothesis (H) Standardised regression weight (λ) Standard error (SE) Critical ratio (c.r.) Mean (M) Mean standard error (MSE) model. On the basis of the comments by survey respondents, their view of their role compared with what the theory implied, and the law intended, differed significantly. This is explained further by evaluating each indicator.

Licensee-adviser and adviser–client relationship issues

With high *cum* CLF, mean level of agreement of 77% [73%, 80%], moderate *cum* CLF regression weight of .604 in Table 6.2 tells us a licensee–adviser and adviser–client agency relationships exists. However, their dual-agency role is definitively different in the minds of advisers in practice compared to perhaps what the legislation intended, and financial planning literature describes.

Empirically advisers considered the legal adviser–licensee relationship as unimportant or "*purely legal, compliance related,*" because for "*almost all advisers . . . their responsibility is to their clients.*" The empirical results revealed agency theory, models and propositions produced in textbooks of personal financial planning in Australia (e.g. Beal & McKeown 2009; Banister *et al.* 2013) were mainly incorporated into the client–adviser relationship: "*The real agency is with the client. The relationship with the third-party licensee is one of a service provided,*" because "*the client relationship is distinct from and trumps the Licensee relationship in all cases.*"

Seemingly, the "*Best Interest Duty overrides the dual agency relationship, as the adviser is left in no doubt about the fact his fiduciary duties are to the adviser–client relationship.*" However, this matter is complicated, because the evidence suggests, "*It depends on who you are licensed with. An adviser who is licensee of a bank or a specific dealer group that does not have a wide authorised product list do have a dual agency relationship and tend to be limited on the product offerings . . . if the licensee is unaligned then the dual agency is not relevant. If the licensee is aligned with a product provider, then there is a stronger relationship with the product provider.*"

Apparently, advisers are "*bound by the licensee rules and regulations,*" whereas licensees are merely seen "*as a servant/tool,*" "*supplying compliance, audit and PD training,*" "*relevant legislation; education*" and "*assesses the products available in the market.*" These last points of view were more evident among non-aligned and s923A *independent* advisers. Evident in the commentary are licensee–client relationships affecting the adviser–client and the licensee–adviser relationship.

Advisers serve licensees and clients simultaneously

Although advisers seem to agree, they are "*TRYING to serve the interests of both parties, in practice it is often one or the other.*" Thus, with a mean of 12% above the neutral agreement level of 50%, together with a moderately high *cum* CLF effect size of .689, licensing advisers through third-party licensees results in advisers serving the interests of their clients and licensees, simultaneously (Kingston & Weng 2014, p. 294). "*One eye is forward towards our clients' (best interests) and one eye in the rear-view mirror, as we get audited and queried on both sides. The AFSL restricts for example the products we can recommend,*" according to one commentator.

Yet when the investigator considered the squared multiple correlation value of.481 [.245, 2.173], which indicated how much this indicator is explained by the factor dual-agency role detectably 52% is unexplained by the dual-agency role. Some other issues at play as per the comments of survey respondents, for instance: "*Irrespective of my Licensee and their alignment to a parent company, I have always served the interest of my client first and foremost. The interest of my licensee does not even come in to it.*" A sentiment expressed by several advisers. "*We are clients of the licensee and so they have to service me although I have to abide by their rules as they are responsible for the advice that I give.*" Following the "*rules*" of the licensees was a term used by several informants. "*Serving the interests of clients is the only consideration for advisers. Licensees provide tools and services to advisers to assist them to best serve the interests of their clients.*"

Once again, advisers point to the best interest duty having changed the relationship between licensee–adviser from advisers as agent acting on behalf of licensees to advisers being serviced by licensees. From Table 27, not all advisers agree there is or should be a difference in advice provided by aligned, non-aligned and *independent* advisers. On the basis of the responses, surprisingly only 49% agreed there was a difference. Combine some of the adviser comments here with the results from asking to survey respondents: 'What are the benefits to institutional licensees appointing, authorising and supervising authorised representatives?' Control product distribution, in Table 28 in Appendix 6.3, seems a key agenda issue for licensees. Although advisers "*should always serve their clients. However licensees have their own agenda depending who they are aligned to.*"

Predominant sentiments indicated simultaneously serving licensees' and clients' interests is evident "*where the third party licensee is also a product provider and/or has financial relationships with product providers to promote to the authorised representative. Where the licensee is itself independent and operates in the interests of clients then the relationship is much different.*" Thus, serving both parties simultaneously "*depends on whether the licensee is independent or not.*" Furthermore, "*it is possible to have a conflicted/product aligned AFSL and still give good advice from a limited solution set, provided, the products meet a certain quality or performance standard. However, my experience is that there remains an expectation from employer/AFSLs for an internal product bias.*" Serving the interests of the licensee "*depends on the extend of the control exerted by the Licensee.*" Threats made to advisers by licensees of "*Do what the AFSL says or lose your job.*" While others argued, the quality of advice is adversely influenced by remuneration conflicts: "*The power of the licensee completely overwhelms the best interests of the client. With live computerised reviews the licensee is now more closely monitoring to ensure advise is provided in the nest commercial interests of the licensee.*" Furthermore, remuneration models are key, because "*this would not be the case should the FA be with a non-aligned licensee and pays a fixed flat fee to the licensee. In other words, no commissions or percentage based fee income.*" Listed public companies versus private companies is another matter to consider with regard to serving licensees' interest "*if licensee is a member of a dealer group that is an organisation listed on the stock exchange, then the there is a greater probability that the adviser will be working in the interests of the licensee and hence shareholders. Privately run dealer groups may be less inclined to do the above and cover costs only. Hence serve clients interests more*", " *BUT within guidelines*," of licensees. Notwithstanding, "*Where licencees are product providers there is an inherent conflict of interest . . . played out in the Approved Product List which limits products that may be appropriate. Advice is also limited to the level of risk a licencee is prepared to accept.*" For some, serving the interests of the licensee and client simultaneously, "*sometimes confuses*" and makes for "*a bad model*," because it "*reduces the quality of advice.*" The types of licensee interests articulated by some advisers were "*compliance interests*," "*reporting*" and "*commercial interests of the licensee*" or "*to make money.*" This is further confirmed from the detailed description of the comments in Appendix 6.3 and further summarised in Table 28 in Appendix 6.3, when considering the benefits AFS licensees derive by licensing advisers.

Tension between licensees' revenues and clients' best interest

Despite scoring jointly with personal illegitimacy [a_{13}], the overall highest mean level of agreement of 78% [75%, 82%], the regression weights of .375 and the squared multiple correlation, measuring the reliability of the responses, of .143 [.025, .35] were the lowest compared with all the other indicators in the CFA model. Further investigation of the qualitative data revealed earning revenues for the licensees, while serving clients' best interests was a difficult conundrum for the advisers. In their commentary, licensee revenues was something they chose not to think about or want to think about. On the basis of the emotional responses of some, it is clear this topic was confronting and difficult for several advisers to reflect upon.

The most interesting quantitative combined with the qualitative results was the low squared multiple correlation values for hypothesis H1 (c) [.138 *ex* CLF and.143 *cum* CLF in Table 25 in Appendix 5.25] reflecting the discomfort to openly address this issue of licensee revenues. Yet the .9999 observed statistical power confirmed its statistical significance, especially as "*commercial interests of the licensee*" and "*to make money*" ranked in the top three benefits advisers felt licensees received by authorising them as recorded in Table 28 [Appendix 6.3].

Combining the findings of this question with informants' comments explained the reasons for this low reliability in conjunction with its moderate effect size. Advisers' explanation points to oblivion, ignorance, conflict, emotionality, myopia, lack of interest, notwithstanding even discomfort when they were asked about licensees' benefits. For some advisers, "*The revenue of the licensee is never a consideration.*" Whereas for others, "*Licencees are in the business of making money.*" However, "*this must be done transparently with the client, so that they understand the services they're paying for.*" Not everyone agrees "*it is a compulsory part of the process that advisers generate revenue for licensees as licensees can be the only party that legally collects revenue and therefore they are empowered to deduct their fees with or without adviser permission.*" "*Without the Planner the Dealer group gets no revenue*," because how and whether advisers generate revenue for licensees "*depends on the licencee model, flat fee or percentage of revenue*," "*on the product sold, or any dealer split of fees charged for advice*," "*product and platform fees from the companies*" and/or whether the "*dealership gets volume rebates if we use thier products*," notwithstanding "*how they charge advisers to use their services.*" If a licensee charges a flat fee, then "*the licensee income is not tied to income generated by the adviser.*" "*Some dealer groups aim to cover costs only.*" "*My licencee takes less than 2% of the income I generate.*" Thus, "*overall most licences do not make a substantial profit, it is more to complement other services and other benefits of having distribution.*" For example, they "*make money out of providing the services like compliance, research, software, that they get cheaper than an individual planner can get it.*" "*The majority of licencees though do expect their advisers to generate revenue through*" "*preferred product lines.*" "*And that's the conflict.*" Despite compliance requirements, the revenues earned by their licensees is non-transparent "*marginal revenue for any product placement (information to which I am not privy) depends on what we actually do.*"

Infringements of the objectives of the Act

With overall moderate *cum* CLF mean levels of agreement, strong squared multiple correlations [reliability] and standardised regression weights, current licensing is perceived as failing to achieve the four objectives of the Act. Evident from the results of the indicators for the factor objectives of the Act b_2 [Table 6.3] were high reliability, because the squared multiple correlations were high [Table 25 in Appendix 5.25]. Licensing advisers via third-party licensees makes aligning adviser–client's interests, eliminating conflict of interest from association, nonviolations of the statutory best interest duty, and fair competition, challenging. On the basis of scoring the overall highest squared multiple correlation values [.826 *ex* CLF and .839 *cum* CLF] [Table 25 in Appendix 5.25] and overall the highest regression weight [.909 *ex* CLF and .821 *cum* CLF] [Table 6.3], a key finding was advisers claimed unintentional [including "*intentional*"] best interest duty contraventions were the key variable delegitimising licensee–adviser licensing. The second highest overall estimate was the misalignment of adviser–client interests evident under the present licensing regime.

Unintentional breaches of the best interest duty

Advisers agree at a 59% [54%, 63%] mean level of agreement, a strong regression weight of .821 in Table 6.3 and the highest overall reliability score [r^2] of 83.90% [77.50%, 89.80%] [Table 25 in Appendix 5.25], licensing advisers through aligned licensees puts their advisers at greater risk of unintentionally [and in some instances "*intentionally*"] breaching their best interest duty obligations. Although "*Best Interest Duty should override these conflicts. Great in theory, but not always implemented in practice.*"

Although licensees manage conflicts of interest, qualitative data indicated otherwise, because "*aligned dealer groups spend most of their money working out ways to legally argue that their advisers are not at risk, or that they are satisfying best interest. Their SoAs are littered with statements to this effect and are fairly standard to all their clients, regardless of how different the circumstances.*" Even though the "*Licensee has rigorous standards and an uncompromising audit regime,*" compliance "*is all about protecting the licensee and adds no value to the client. It also adds cost and complexity, so the adviser and client lose out.*"

Allegedly, "*aligned licensees have a business model that deliberately breaches the best interest duty obligations. It is not the advisers that breach the obligations it is the licensee.*" If "*an organisation has a poor culture, then this could occur.*" With regard to culture, "*pressure from BDMs may influence new advisers.*" Especially, aligned licensees "*pressure the Planners to sell products.*" This is a problem. "*When there is pressure to use a particular product there is a much higher risk of breaching best interest duty.*" "*The major banks have the greatest influence as their advisers are also employees and if they do not achieve targets their job is in jeopardy.*" Advisers face ethical dilemmas, based on "*examples where aligned advisers by direct employment have had their employment directly and repeatedly threatened if they did not put the employer's interest first and only.*" Seemingly, advisers are powerless in some instances to prevent infringements of the best interest duty when licensed via third parties.

An unlimited APL may not necessarily be the answer, because "*the practicality of relatively small 'non aligned' businesses being capable of representing the full universe of investment options . . . can be misleading as well. Finite resources often demand that independent advisers narrow their focus to 'favourites'!*" Evident when advisers are faced with one-off approval applications, "*it just makes their business inefficient by having to apply for one-off approval.*" Whereas others deny affiliation to product issuers results in unintentional best interest duty: "*There is clarity around what is required to meet the best interest duty and if a licensee has structured their business in a way that the adviser is unable to meet this standard advisers will exit and that licensee's business will fail.*" This issue of best interest duty is a thorny matter, because "*this depends more on the processes they have to follow in making their recommendations – rather than the affiliation. For example, it depends more on the wording in the Statement of Advice and whether they have the freedom to alter the words and therefore the intent. To some degree they are limited by the products they can offer.*"

If this issue of serving the best interest of their clients is considered in combination with the qualitative results from the question asking advisers if they ever prepare SOAs without product recommendations, then it is clear most of the respondents [77%] rarely make product recommendations in every SOA. Sometimes they provide only strategic advice. More details about this issue can be found in Appendix 6.4. A solution proposed "*to act in the client's best interests is via an Independent (as defined by the Act) AFSL.*" "*The product makers should be separate from the product sellers.*"

Misalignment of adviser–client interests

Advisers agree at a mean level of 60% [55%, 65%] agreement, with strong r^2 of .783 [.707, .856] and effect size in the regression weight .810 [Table 6.3], licensing advisers through aligned licensees "*sometimes*," if not "*in most cases*" made it difficult to align adviser–client interests. With the second highest r^2 and regression weight overall, it was clear that transgression of this objective is the second highest reason delegitimising licensing advisers via third parties.

Apparently, "*it is more the licensee that has the conflict rather than the planner. The licensee has no relationship with the client and only with the planner so the relationship is driven by money.*" Although it seems the "*ethics of the adviser will determine this.*" To the contrary, misalignment results in "*even for the most ethical advisers trying to fit a client into one of the aligned products.*" Whereas another did not think it was that simple: "*There are many levels to this. They all have aligned AFSLs that place ARs somewhere from almost independent to tightly limited. Best Interests applies to everyone equally. The only difference is the Approved Product List and level of authorisation.*"

The success of aligning adviser–client interests "*depends on their model of business.*" For instance, "*major banks and not so much AMP*" were cited as the main culprits of causing this misalignment. Misalignment of interests depended "*on the licensee. AMP has a very open APSL and has had for many years, whereas I don't think a bank aligned planner would write non bank alined products. Very common for an AMP planner to be advising on industry/external funds from the AMP group.*" Thus, advisers confirmed declarations by Goedecke (2001), Australian "*major banks*" are the main culprits. "*Having worked for NAB, I would say in general that it is extremely difficult for these advisers to align their interests with the best interests of the client.*" "*The Bank aligned practices would be 100%. I was offered MLC/NAB and the terms are pretty bad.*" "*Bank advisers would certainly have incentives to recommend their own products.*" "*The banks talk about putting clients first, but all procedures are designed to put themselves first.*" "*Especially when you have sat in a room and heard a distribution manager plead with advisers to support the upstream owner's product to ensure the continuation of the dealer group without any reference to best interest.*"

Furthermore, there "*is a difference between an employee adviser and a licensee adviser.*" "*It depends because if they are in house, then they have to be employees. However, if they own their own practices, even though they are licensed through AMP, they try to provide best advice to their clients – usually these FPs are fee for service.*" Despite the legislation dealing with conflicts of interest from remuneration between licensee and adviser, seemingly remuneration models continue to influence advisers based on the claim, it is "*all about how the advisers are remunerated/incentivized.*" Specifically, the licensee–adviser relationship is "*driven by money,*" by a "*'Share of wallet' and 'sales' culture proven to be a conflict,*" which arises from ownership structures.

"*The pressures within aligned licensees to use the 'in-house' product is very high, and bonuses are often predicated upon certain percentages of 'in-house' products being utilised.*" However, uncertainty concerning this matter of sales pressure is prevalent. Some claims advisers "*do not know what other licencees do, but my licensee places no pressure or suggestions to use aligned products. From what I have read I believe this may be an issue with some.*" In other instances, instead of remuneration incentives, "*advisers are KPI to write the aligned product.*" "*Whilst some aligned licensees have removed sales/income targets for their FAs, the FA is still captured under a 'performance review' which determines their employment.*" "*The pressure is always there to get the sale as this is how the Bank makes its money. (This is from experience – not heresay). The banks like it when their employees have personal debt and are hungry to 'write the business.' Making a no action recommendation to the client does not pay, and in fact costs money if you have to write an SOA.*"

Advisers are controlled by "*restricted choice (ie 'cookie cutter model') means advice may not be in the client's best interests.*" "*Limited APL prevents choice for the client.*" Consequently, "*it is impossible to satisfy the client's best interest where product providers require advisers to use their approved product lists on which only their own products sit.*" Yet APLs do not limit every adviser. Licensees "*Apogee, RI advice, Charter etc (true aligned licensees) have wide Approved Product Lists, limiting the conflict. The adviser can pay more in licensee fees to have the licensee research more products for them, but most advisers choose not to. If you work for a bank, or AMP directly, the APL is smaller and limited and you can't increase it.*" Furthermore, "*there is an APSL that we follow but we've had successful approvals for products outside of this list.*"

Not everyone is able to apply for or is granted one-off approvals, because an adviser claimed, "*There are times I would like to use a strategy or give product advice that my Licensee and PI insurer will not allow me to do*". This latter issue is confirmed if analysed in conjunction with the results from the open-ended survey question: 'Have you ever applied for one-off approvals for financial products or investments not on you licensees' APL? Why or why not?' Note, 79% [Appendix 6.5] of the survey respondents said they have done so, when dealing with government-backed super funds, industry super funds, LICs, new exchange-traded funds, ethically responsible funds or life insurance bonds for aged care clients or when it was in the clients' best interest. Reasons why one-off approvals were unnecessary included the APL was sufficient to meet the clients' needs, as well as the APL was sufficiently broad, extensive and/open especially among the self-licensed managing their own APLs. Some advisers experienced one-off approvals to be "*difficult, time consuming and not always productive*" and they were "*not interested in the PI hassle.*"

Unavoidable conflict of interest from association

The evidence indicated a decent mean level of agreement of 65% [61%, 69%] with high regression weight of .773 [Table 6.3] and a high reliability r^2 of .688 [.607, .791], in Table 25 in Appendix 5.25, licensing advisers through product-biased licensees does lead to unavoidable conflict of interest from association.

Licensees' control over advisers, with a culture geared towards product distribution, is a problem. Instead of obvious product sales-targeted KPIs, some licensees have moved to performance reviews or "*cultural pressure from the parent company, in many instances*" as a method to influence advisers' recommendations to specific product solutions, which for salaried "*employee*" advisers, is forcing them into ethical dilemmas they may not be able to control. These "*employee*" advisers face inducement to mis-sell, because it is "*difficult to retain their job or obtain bonuses*" for non-performance of increasing volumes of "*writing product not strategy/optimal product for the client.*"

Once again, advisers point the finger at "*the limitation of product (APL).*" Thus, "*the application of APLs and the level of control from overseers*" and "*one-off approval for products not on APSL,*" linked to PI creates a problem. "*There will always be conflicts as it is not possible to have every product available in the market on an approved product list due to PI insurance reasons as well as other compliance reasons.*" Thus, "*the licensees choose to impose the conflicts by not having open approved product lists.*"

Again, advisers confirming the difficulty of achieving this objective of the Act seem more evident amongst those who "*work for a product manufacturer,*" especially if they are "*employee*" advisers or own financial planning practices with "*BOLR*" terms. Yet advisers who disagreed felt "*all conflicts of interest are 'avoidable' – sometimes an extra administrative step is required to justify it is within the client's best interest.*" "*Conflicts can often be managed. Depends largely on the integrity of the Adviser*" was a response by the dissenters with regard to this topic. Ultimately, it seems "*it is up to the adviser to avoid conflicts of interest and ensure clients best interests are paramount. That has become easier in recent years but not with all licensees.*" The solution to these unavoidable conflicts offered by advisers included "*Less of an issue with a very open/Broad APL*" and "*One-off approval for products not on APSL help meet Best Interest.*" "*This conflict is unavoidable unless it is very clearly and publicly stated that the advisers only have one master – the client. This has not happened in Australia but has happened at least once in the UK (until that bank was taken over by RBS).*"

Concerning was the comment in some cases, licensees set a "*minimum requirements for certain % of business to be placed through the product manufacturer.*" Evident was the same theme, namely it is "*all about how the adviser is remunerated, how the licensee is remunerated.*" "*Employee*" advisers were particularly incentivised, influenced or coerced to promote the licensees' products. Interestingly, despite legally banning conflicts of interest from remuneration, advisers still claimed, "*remuneration model is far more likely an indication of a conflict of interest from association. It is not a 'moral' choice on the part of the adviser. If AFSLs wanted to demonstrate Best Interests they would remove all conflicted remuneration models. They never will.*" Allegedly, "*Best Interest Duty should override these conflicts. Great in theory, but not always implemented in practice.*" A surprising comment was, "*These conflicts can be avoided but if all advisers avoid them, the dealer groups will fold.*"

Anti-competitive behaviour between financial services providers

Concerning the question asking whether authorising advisers through aligned licensees limits advisers from competing on a level playing field within the industry, generally, advisers seem close to undecided with a mean level of agreement at

51% [47%, 55%] with a moderate regression weight of .679 as shown in Table 6.3. Its reliability r^2 is .494 [.398, .625] [Table 25 in Appendix 5.25].

While licensing's failure on the first three objectives is clear, less clear is its failure about competition. One explanation for this close to neutral level of agreement is the view, "*Its the Licensees that are competing not the advisers.*" An adviser claimed, "*The question assumes the licensee dictates terms.*" The context advisers answered the question varied, which could explain this lack of clarity in the responses: "*This assumes that advisers are competing in terms of their product offering not quality or suitability of advice. Surely it is the quality of advice that is important not the make or model of the product (if a product is offered)?*"; "*There is more to financial advice than recommending a product. Product is only a solution or tool, the strategy is the important thing and the adviser must have the knowledge and understanding required of strategies in order to compete on a level playing field within the industry.*"; and "*My experience suggests that getting numbers through the door is more important. Competition in this space appears minimal when it comes to the client relationship selling.*"

Despite the lack of clarity on the issue of competition, others were clearer by the context: "*Uneven playing field exists between commercial advisers and those that work for Industry Superannuation funds as Industry planners do not have the same level of disclosure on fees and the industry funds mask their fee structure by applying no advice fees then charge huge SOA fees and consultation fees.*" In addition, "*Alignment may seriously increase the competitive position of aligned advisers due to the strength of branding, systems & infrastructure, marketing resources and existing clientele . . . an independent . . . have a serious disadvantage by comparison.*" Thus, "*marketing budgets and support from aligned dealer groups are substantial . . . these institutions providing outstanding support services, including advertising and referrals.*" Once again, support services provided by the larger aligned licensees afford greater "*access to training, conferences, fund managers, resources, research materials etc.*" "*When you are not aligned the cost of PI is huge.*" Additionally, "*aligned adviser has generally the power of third line forcing. Eg to get your loan you have to have insurance and you need to see our financial adviser before the loan can proceed.*"

Although it was conceded, a disadvantage of being licensed via a large licensee is the "*high licensee compliance standard places*", the adviser is "*at a competitive disadvantage against practitioner not subjected to such stringent standards.*" Particularly, "*banks rely on the use of their products to generate more revenue from their networks.*"

Then the "*banks subsidise their advice delivery from vertical integration.*" The "*large size*" means, "*the licensee can afford to defray the costs or running the licensee onto other parts of their business, hence it is much easier for them to invest sufficiently into the very difficult compliance regime.*" "*The ability of aligned licensees to subsidise their advice channels from product margin can actually make the independent licensees uncompetitive.*"

In addition, "*aligned advisers will sell this to clients as an advantage saying that they are backed by some of the largest institutions in the country. Unfortunately what they don't tell the clients that they are also backed by some of the largest legal teams in the country protecting the Licensee and not the client.*" Therefore, "*advisers licensed through aligned licensees actually have a competitive advantage due to price that independents cannot compete against.*" This contrasts with "*the non aligned advisers who aren't on a level playing field.*" Consequently, "*many clients and potential clients think they are safe with the perceived security.*"

Once again, the data revealed remuneration models are an issue contributing to anti-competitive behaviour. Some respondents proposed solutions: "*Best practice for client outcome would, in my view, be an open APL with highly experienced advisers who can truly tailor an insurance portfolio. For advisers? Aligned advisers get trusting customers directed to them as 'targets,' independent advisers have to find their own.*"

AFSL-AR licensing fails Suchman's legitimacy tests

Further assessment of the existing licensing's legitimacy was grounded on Suchman's (1995) complete legitimacy theoretical framework. On the grounds of overall moderate to strong mean scores, regression weight values and squared multiple correlations, from the adviser's perspective, current licensing using criteria from Suchman's model combined with the objectives of the Act, is illegitimate. Overall, advisers felt licensing via third parties failed the tests of achieving the objectives of the Act and failed the tests for regulative, consequential moral, procedural moral, structural moral, personal moral and cultural-cognitive legitimacy.

The significant high regression weights [Table 6.4], prove current licensing is illegitimate from a regulative point of view, because unintentional compliance infringements are problematic. Additionally, consequential moral illegitimacy is evident, because licensees' commercial interests do compromise advisers' best interest duty as anticipated in several financial planning studies (Smith 2009, p. 62; Maclean & Behnam 2010; Finke & Langdon 2012; Pain 2013; Moran 2014). Combining the results of hypothesis H3(b) with H1(c), empirically advisers acknowledge licensee revenues as a problem, but find contemplation of the matter difficult. The strong results [Table 6.4] attest licensees' sales procedures, standards and practices are designed to reinforce product distribution, while giving the appearance of satisfying regulatory compliance requirements. Thus, confirming the inferences during the literature review (West 2009; Sampson 2010; Newnham 2012; Valentine 2013; Valentine & Hollingworth 2015), AFSL-AR licensing lacks procedural moral legitimacy. Valentine's (2013) claim, conflict of interest from association is present, was validated by the results in Table 6.4. Thus, this confirmed multiple third party licensing is structurally debase and illegitimate. The findings [Table 6.4] found existing licensing is deficient in personal moral legitimacy too. Additionally, individual leaders of aligned licensees do aim, as claimed by several authors (Sampson 2010; Bird & Gilligan 2015a) during the secondary study, to protect their distribution channels. Advisers agree with mixed feelings, the Australian public cannot clearly distinguish between advisers defined as s923A *independent*. This outcome of cultural-cognitive illegitimacy is in line with Roy Morgan's survey findings (Morris 2013; Vickovich 2013; Boutique Financial Planners 2014).

From the foregoing discussion, none of the legitimacy tests were met. Hence, the licensee–adviser licensing structure is convincingly illegitimate. Next, each legitimacy criterion is unpacked in more detail, using the qualitative data, to understand the quantitative findings of the illegitimacy of current licensee–adviser licensing.

Regulative illegitimacy

Although strong evidence suggested licensing is shown to fail the regulative legitimacy test based on the effect size of .727, based on the mean level of agreement, noticeably advisers were on average unsure [close to undecided at a 47% mean level of agreement] whether the legally socially constructed licensing via third parties caused advisers to unintentionally breach regulatory compliance when dealing with clients.

Surprising was the mixed response was close to 50%, which is the neutral or undecided mean agreement level score. The emotional comments of survey informants explained this mixed response. For some it was "*impossible not to breach*" unintentionally. Although the focus of this research was on unintentional violations, seemingly "*those breaches you read about from bank-aligned advisers are NOT unintented!!!!!!*" Even though compliance contraventions by aligned advisers were "*often intentionally as well!*", apparent "*it depends upon the adviser and the culture of his superiors. Sales pressure can be extreme in some of those larger institutions.*" Not everyone agreed it was a problem for only the aligned advisers, because one adviser stated, "*all advisers from all Licensees have this problem.*"

Purportedly, "*the pressure to earn income . . . causes the unintentional compliance breach and not the product.*" A "*pressure the licensee brings to bear on the adviser to generate income for the licensee which may lead to shortcuts which breach compliance.*" Among several reasons blamed were "*the business models of the aligned licensees*" and "*their remuneration models encourage intentional compliance breaches.*"

Respondents offered many examples of such pressure leading to the contraventions, for instance, "*those who have to meet sales target can misunderstand directions they receive (or they did not misunderstand and did exactly what they were told).*" Troubling was, "*some aligned advisers thrive in this environment and are condoned for their actions despite many clients paying for inappropriate advice. eg an aligned adviser switching super to licensee's product and to get unnecessary insurance that costs more than the client's annual contributions.*" "*Especially where product sales volumes are rewarded in various ways.*"

Additionally, the "*legislative demands are what causes accidental breaches. They are draconian.*" Aligned employee "*in-house Advisers*" were cited to be at higher risk than self-employed aligned advisers or *independents* of unintentional infringements.

The APL was provided as a reason for the unintentional compliance contraventions: "*If it is not on your APL you can't write it and I have seen numerous time clients in expensive products written by an aligned adviser where a more cost effective option with a different provider would do the same – how does this relate to best interest?*" Additionally, "*breaches will be at the licensee level (e.g. via limited APLs, etc.) and not likely to come from the adviser who spends most of his or her day on compliance.*"

Furthermore, compliance infringements were not limited to product only, but other compliance demands such as "*didn't file note a conversation in time, or they accidentally provided verbal 'hold' advice not realising it was advice and therefore didn't provide an advice document.*" Contrary views explained, "*A compliance breach is the Adviser's responsibility. It is up to the Adviser to ensure that the advice is compliant.*" Besides, "*large licensees have very strict and comprehensive compliance checks.*" Moreso than "*independents.*" "*Compliance managers make sure that advisers will not be uncompliant.*" Seemingly, there is the perception that "*under the big licensees there are less compliance breaches, due to strict compliance audits.*" Consequently, "*breaches from the adviser are actually less likely because of the strict controls imposed upon them.*"

Consequential illegitimacy

Additionally, consequential moral illegitimacy was evident, because advisers with the third highest reliability [squared multiple correlation, namely .766 and .768, *ex* CLF and *cum* CLF, respectively] [Table 25, Appendix 5.25], and the third overall highest standardised regression weights [.875 and .794, *ex* CLF and *cum* CLF, respectively] [Table 6.4] strongly confirmed the theory. Licensees' commercial interests do compromise advisers' best interest duty (Smith 2009, p. 62; Maclean & Behnam 2010; Finke & Langdon 2012; Pain 2013; Moran 2014). The mean level of agreement was moderate scoring 64% [59%, 68%] by advisers; current licensing does not display consequential moral legitimacy.

Advisers clearly see tension between the commercial interests of aligned licensees and their advisers' best interest duty obligations. Combining the results of hypothesis H3(b) with H1(c), empirically advisers acknowledge licensee revenues as a problem, but find contemplation on the matter difficult. For instance, some argue "*fee for service eliminates this former problem,*" which once again implies remuneration models plays a role. Although Adviser RR claimed there is no tension by penning: "*Not anymore. Client's best interests are key. Perhaps the big banks provide sales pressure.*" It seems tension is "*more likely if the adviser is a direct employee representative of a financial product provider/bank.*" In line with shareholder wealth maximisation theory, "*instos are there to serve shareholders . . . they want returns and money.*" "*The profits of the company are put ahead of the client's best interests as the licensee makes up only part of the company's profit. The Funds Management business makes far more money than the Advice business but both are only part of the companies profits and the large financial institutions concentrate on shareholder profit.*" They claimed, "*Commercial interests control the content of the APL.*" Furthermore, licensee commercial interests compromising best interests "*can potentially happen if performance and KPI is linked to funds under advice and remuneration, number of new clients.*" For instance, "*The bank financial advisors (those who operate from branches or branded offices) . . . are sales people meeting KPIs.*" However, "*not all aligned licensees push their commercial interests on to their advisers.*" Furthermore, this commercial-best interest tension "*depends on the type of Practice.*" Seemingly, "*the institution is to blame not the planner. Our system blames the Planner.*" Although, it is argued, this "*is a problem from licensees end not advisers*" contentiously, "*a strong willed, well credentialed adviser can still resolve these issues when they arise.*" From the evidence, some advisers feel "*it comes down to ethics.*" Another argued, "*As a professional . . . ethics training plus a higher moral ethical overlay . . . means the licensee cannot control me against my client.*"

When considering the results in conjunction with the qualitative data, reported in Appendix 6.3, about benefits licensees gain from authorising advisers, profit is in the top three benefits, after the benefit of controlling product distribution.

Procedural illegitimacy

The evidence shows, with a strong regression weight of .781 [Table 6.4] and moderately strong squared multiple correlation of .687 [.576, .784] [Table 25 in Appendix 5.25], current licensing lacks procedural legitimacy. At a mean of 61% [56%, 66%] level of agreement among advisers, licensing advisers through aligned licensees sometimes results in sales policies, procedures and practices designed by licensees to give "*on paper appearance of compliance.*"

"*Verbally, or in practice, advisers encouraged to act in ways which do not comply.*" For example, "*Recent cases of some aligned licensees have shown that the companies concerned have not been driven by the ethos that is embedded in the regulatory requirements.*" Experienced by an adviser, it was "*often in the best interest of area managers to push advisers to use in-house products and override the best interest duty.*" Advisers are expected to jump "*hurdles . . . daily to make the best choices combined with the culture and the 'education' would make it incredibly difficult. But this is magnified by the 'unethical' advisers being feted and the ethical ones seen as 'non-performing' because they do the extra paperwork, rather than just sell.*" Commentary suggests there is "*a growing list of advisers receiving poor audit results for process (not advice) reasons.*" The "*newer advisers will not be able to tell these processes from a structured 'advice' process.*" While "*experienced advisers may simply choose to use a successful and 'compliant' sales process to generate themselves more revenue. ie. 'if it comes from the Licensee, it must be fine with compliance and my auditor.'*" Respondents would explain from the perspective of their experience: "*I have worked in management with AFSLs. I have seen aligned AFSLs dress-up as independents (Financial Wisdom – owned by CBA and Colonial) but set an internal sales budget of $1billion in platform recruitment to CFS FirstChoice. Same at MLC with specific targets for product placement from its more 'independent' AFSLs.*"

Seemingly the practices "*are hidden. I have recently taken on a client who is a friend, sold duplicated insurance by the CBA with no advice. How they get away with this is quite frankly disgusting, and we find it hard to compete against this fraudulent efficiency.*" Using the legislation to window dress product distribution is an alarming finding: "*Compliance is all about window dressing. The licensee makes it so strict so as to protect themselves against the charge of pushing product.*" "*Compliance is all about lip service and covering your arse. The client never ever reads the provided documentations. FSG, SOA, PDS are all about protecting the licensee and the adviser. 'But we disclosed everything.' [Subtext; not my fault you are stupid enough to require advice and can't or won't read.*"

Despite licensees providing "*'open' APL but really internally the approach is to use the aligned product.*" Then some situations where "*some licensees focus on compliance but overlook instances where advisers only use in-house products.*"

However, the minority counter-arguments seem to offer hope based on the comment: "*Many of the aligned licensors believe that they are seeking to act in client interest. However they also have a duty to their stakeholders . . . there is a genuine objective to provide the client with a good outcome, within a profit model.*" Allegedly, these practices do not go unnoticed and should not be of any concern according to some respondents, because "*licensees are well aware of the scrutiny of ASIC and Adele Ferguson, so no window dressing is applied.*" Notwithstanding the scrutiny by "*ASIC to ensure regulatory compliance.*"

Structural illegitimacy

Furthermore, this research proves strong support at a mean level of 75% agreement and regression weight of .740 [Table 6.4] and judicious squared multiple correlations of .574 [.458, .669] [Table 25 in Appendix 5.25] current licensing does not display structural moral legitimacy.

The frequency of comments was the highest in this part of the survey responses. Conflict of interest from association by licensing advisers via third-party licensees "*is what is causing most of the problems in the Financial Planning industry.*" "*This is the cancer that has led to the current situation of advisers being attacked from all political corners.*" It is a "*major confliction.*" "*This is the crux of the problem with financial planning.*"

Questionable, according to one adviser, is, "*How can best interest possibly be served with these conflicts?*" Apparently, "*the advisers fight very hard against the conflicts and aim to serve their clients first, but the licensees are able to use compliance as a tool to put themselves ahead of the client. The advisers are then scared of their licensee burning them and are forced to choose between the client and the licensee.*" This implies licensees have power to control adviser behaviour, rather than advisers having the power to self-control their own behaviour. From experience, an adviser wrote, "*Having come from this system originally we were pressured to sell the product. If your advice didn't match the product that you had available they made life very difficult.*" However, he was not the only one sharing this experience: "*Worked for a major bank for 9 years. This is DEFINITELY a conflict of interest. Aligned advisers are under pressure and inducement to use aligned products and services.*" Thus, "*under a sales culture . . . the pressure on managers to perform is very high.*" "*Where an individual adviser has specific KPI triggers to use products owned by their licensee there is a huge conflict between what is best for the client and what is best for the adviser/licensee to reach bonuses/profit etc.*" Thus, "*aligned advisers put their licensee before the clients best interest./They are conflicted by their ownership and their own products.*" One adviser observed, affiliation or ownership is "*only a conflict if you use the aligned licensee's product.*" Another adviser acknowledged, "*Most Licensees will encourage their advisers to use their products, however under our best interest duty we can only use our licensees' products if they are suitable for our clients.*" However, they are in the minority. Some advisers "*chose to leave the dealership . . . because of its bias towards its own platform.*" It is claimed licensing advisers via licensees ensures the "*client is not aware of these associations. If they go to a Holden dealership they only expect to buy a new Holden. Clients do not understand they are walking into a dealership when they walk into an aligned business – they do not know that the adviser has a limited suite of platform to choose from (not investments) there is a difference.*"

The few holding contrary views, by disagreeing conflict of interest from association is the problem, pointed at other possible reasons. For instance, it "*is more about disclosure than affiliation. If the affiliation is disclosed the conflict is minimal. Unfortunately, that disclosure is usually hidden deep in small print.*" In addition, "*The Licensee does own a product issuer license and has aligned platforms. However Advisers can use other products and platforms if on the APSL or also can seek one-off approval to use off-APSL products and platforms.*" Yet it was found mentioned earlier, one-offapprovals were rarely readily granted.

Interestingly, although "*licensing through aligned licensees does create conflicts of interest . . . it would be a mistake to believe that a non-aligned licensee doesn't have a conflict, it simply has different conflicts.*" Therefore, "*conflicts apply across all industries and regardless of whether a planner is aligned or not.*"

Once again, it seems "*employee reps conflicted*" and self-employed "*auth reps limited conflict*" when it comes to conflict of interest from association. Likewise, "*Wherever there is vertical integration there are inherent conflicts of interest. I have seen a number of studies that shows that advice from vertically integrated advisers is extremely heavily biased towards the parent company.*" However, not everyone agrees: "*The inherent bias comes from within the Approved Products list construction, but even this can be widened with a reasonable alternative and a good reason. In truth, conflicts of interest by association are more about perception than reality.*" For advisers to practise their craft, they "*need a licence, that licence is with a bank. This does not influence our decisions on our client outcomes!*" Ultimately, for another adviser it is "*up to the adviser to accept these 'inducements' or not. Some of us paid the higher fees to be licensed so that we were NOT influenced.*" Overall, most agree, "*adviser must address this conflict with integrity of a professional, but until this connection is removed there will always be the appearance of conflict of interest.*" Unexpectedly, "*an aligned licensee will mostly recommend the product from the licensee due to BOLR agreement.*" Even if it is "*up to the adviser to accept these 'inducements' or not,*" the overall quantitative results indicate structural illegitimacy.

A solution offered for the structurally corrupt licensing system is for licensee–adviser licensing advisers to be "*dismantled immediately for the sake of the clients and the profession.*"

Personal illegitimacy

Seemingly, current licensing does not display personal moral legitimacy given by the level of agreement of advisers sitting at 78% with a standardised regression weight effect size of .679 [Table 6.4] and squared multiple correlation of .463 [.335, .669] [Table 25, in Appendix 5.25] when advisers were asked whether contributions by specific individual leaders of aligned licensees to the debate with the government surrounding the licensing of advisers have a "*a vested interest*" to protect their product distribution channels.

"*Leaders of aligned licensees will not only protect their distribution channels when discussing the topic with the govt, they will also band together to control the information going to the government. ie FSC.*" Combine these results with the findings on consequential illegitimacy, and it is clear licensees' "*first obligation is to shareholders or employer,*" because they "*care about one thing, that is their bottom line. Client outcomes is a long way down the list.*" A problem again is "*the continuum of Financial Advice Business models.*" Thus, "*leaders will do what suits their particular business at the time. They are there to make a profit. If they could sell their product direct to the public and cut out the adviser, they would do it in a heartbeat. Life Insurance Framework is a good indication of that.*" The insurance debate was mentioned several times by respondents: "*Look at the new insurance proposals designed to reduce adviser commissions etc but not increase benefits to consumers via better definitions*" and the "*so called 'Churn Debate' in relation to insurance is a case in point.*"

Furthermore, combine the results with structural illegitimacy, albeit "*they don't have the integrity to admit this. All these institutions also OWN INSURANCE companies who have significant 'Direct' distribution – group – through industry funds and elsewhere, and on-line). These are also being protected in public debate. There is no proper research on outcomes for consumers.*" Although the leaders are claimed to "*try but their model does not reside on good, long term, client outcomes.*"

However, some advisers did not see a problem with licensees leaders lobbying "*to protect their revenue*" with a "*focus on retention of FUM*" as evidenced by "*their Annual Reports and see where they are making the massive profits.*" "*Of course, wouldn't any company want to preserve its sales arm?*" An additional argument proposed was "*business interests have every right to protect their ongoing survival and deserve to fail in business, fail their associates and fail to protect the interests of their clients if they did not do so.*" Thus, some advisers attempted to justify leaders protecting product distribution: "*What do you expect? We live in a capitalist country where competition within the market and access to the market rules. The institutions have been at it for 100s of years in some cases. Delivering benefits to policy holders and superannuants; paying wages to staff and all the supporting infrastructure. Of course they have a vested interest.*" Although "*it is natural for any business to protect its business model. It is up to Govt to decide if the business model is illegal or detrimental to society.*" Yet commentary indicates lobbying by aligned licensees "*is true, but can't the same be said about the leaders of non aligned groups??? Weaven and Whitely spring readily to mind.*" "*Every new regulation has ended up benefitting the big players and transferred wallet share away from advisers directly to the product providers.*"

Thus, Australian policymakers, in the eyes of some advisers, seem somewhat responsible for listening to the lobby groups, and Federal and State politics seems to play a significant part in some of the woes the industry faces. For instance, "*The Wallis enquiry could have fixed most of the industry problems by banning product manufacturers from owning advice businesses (and banning all commissions) . . . big instos' influence on politicians prevented this. Influence comes from industry funds as well of course.*" In addition, "*Government really has not considered what happened in the UK and the FSC has pushed their own agenda and this is what is being listened to – even the professional associations have caved in to pressure from the FSC.*"

Culture-cognitive illegitimacy

For this test, the *cum* CLF level of agreement was 62% with a moderate standardised regression weight effect size of .682 [Table 6.4] and r^2 .502 [.322, .752] [Table 25 in Appendix 5.25]. Consequently, advisers indicated licensing does not display cultural-cognitive legitimacy, whereby clients can clearly distinguish between s923A *independent* advisers and product-conflicted advisers. Respondents indicated "*the public has difficulty but not because of the existence of third party Licensees.*" To them, it "*is too simplistic. There are other factors,*" which is confirmed by the r^2 of .502 [.322, .752].

Among the other factors suggested by respondents are "*quality of advice. Bad advice can be delivered by any adviser; independent, self-licensed; aligned or in the employ of a bank.*" "*Clients value good, solid, professional planning that meets their goals and aspirations no matter how licensed.*" Moreover, "*It's the individual advisers ethics, best interest etc. no amount of legislation will combat a crook or someone who is unethical.*" Additionally, "*They just want what is clearly good and easy to understand advice from an Adviser with understanding and empathy.*" "*What we do not know is the level of literacy and comprehension individuals have.*"

Whereas for another, "*the reason for confusion includes the rules that govern the use of certain banned words (independent, unbiased, etc.).*" Allegedly, the "*industry can't even work out what independent is. We have advisers who can receive an Independent Financial Adviser Award (IFA Magazine) yet who operate businesses as conflicted as a Bank's. The AFSL then leverages that publicity to appear as something they are not – appalling!! Is it any wonder the public has no trust.*" The term "*independent*" remains a controversial matter among some advisers based on the comment "*we should be able to use the word independent, unlike the banks who manufacture and sell their own product. The word independent should be legislated for those satisfying a criteria.*" Confusion among advisers is apparent around the term "*independent,*" because it is alleged "*non aligned advisers are independent but don't meet the definition.*" Furthermore, it seems "*having your own AFSL does not mean that you don't have an arrangement with a product provider.*" "*It's in the private financial planning firms both 3rd party aligned and with their own AFSL where independence is foggy.*" An interesting comment was: "*There is no definition of the advice provided in s923A, it is concerned with the use of certain words. It relates to remuneration models not the type of advice provided.*" "*As a non-aligned adviser of an independently-owned Dealership, the difference is clear. Best interests of the client come first. Decisions about product are made towards the end of the process. Aligned advisers are (arguably) looking to sell a product to the client. In my experience the product was aligned to the dealer group/bank with sales targets to meet.*" Thus, the foregoing suggests that in differentiating the services they offer in practice, some advisers base it on ownership, product and/or remuneration practices.

Apparently, there is the perception the "*confusion would reduce if there was clarity in relation to the legal provider of the advice (i.e. the licensee).*" Specifically, the misperception has "*to do with labelling. People might expect MLC product from a MLC adviser, but Godfrey Pembroke is a different matter. A lot of this would be cleared up if product providers did not have advice businesses.*" Apparently, "*the aligned licensees hide behind multiple business names – no transparency exists.*" Seemingly, "*most Australians would not know the difference as it is not usually openly disclosed to them.*" Allegedly, the problem is not as apparent "*if a client walks into one of the big 5,*" because "*then they would expect to get a big 5 product.*" Furthermore, "*it's the old contracts/books that are sold where the majority of the 'independence' damage is done i.e. protectionist actions by the instos.*"

Arguably, this issue of identifying the nature of the licensee "*is covered by disclosure to each client.*" Thus, to help clients distinguish s923A *independent* advice from conflicted, "*the public are given a Financial Services Guide at the first meeting which shows who the Dealer Group is aligned to or not. So the public can distinguish the differences.*" Yet, to the contrary, "*even though FSGs are provided, consumers don't really understand any conflicts that may arise depending on licensing.*" "*Disclosure has become so complicated that most of the public do not understand what they are reading.*" Thus, disclosures are rarely done effectively. Notwithstanding that "*most Australians would not know the difference as it is not usually openly disclosed to them.*" "*Most people who seek advice have no idea that there could be a possibility of a conflict.*"

Disturbing is the adviser view that "*the public are not really interested in the issue.*" There is the perception that "*clients don't care whether their adviser is licensed through a 3rd party or independently. I have never had a client walk away because of who my Licensee is.*" The reason for this outcome in the qualitative data is "*the Australian public have a relationship with the adviser not the licencee. The trust is with the adviser.*" Surprisingly, advisers claimed, "*Most clients don't even ask about independence*" and "*Clients don't care about independence.*" They "*trust that the best advice will be given.*" Several respondents proposed a solution. For instance, "*There should not be product providers who also have advice arms to their businesses.*"

Support for individual licensing via a single body

From the results, current licensing is convincingly illegitimate. Accordingly, this illegitimacy strengthens arguments to replace the existing licensing model with individual licensing. Advisers reveal with moderate to high regression weights, mean levels of agreement and r^2, their support for such a model [Table 6.5]. Advisers strongly agree the most important factor to influence whether a person seeks financial advice, namely clients' trust (Balasubramnian, Brisker & Gradisher 2014), would improve with individual licensing. They acknowledged it would provide them with much needed independence from product-conflicted licensees. Furthermore, they are in favour of modelling adviser licensing on other professions. Interestingly, the preference is individual licensing via a "*single body.*" However, most of them expressed some reservations and concerns about the practical implementation of disconnecting them from licensees. Specifically, they were unsure what an individual licence would entail. Additionally, they feared the costs involved as well as wanting to know where the "*subsidised*" support services "*research, compliance, marketing and training support*" were going to come from, which "*from aligned dealer groups are substantial.*"

Public trust and confidence will improve

When asked whether client trust and confidence would improve under a single licensing regime, advisers agreed at a *cum* CLF of 64% [60%, 68%] mean level of agreement [Table 6.5], a high regression weight estimate of .745 and reliability of r^2 = .754 [.588, .902] [Table 25 in Appendix 5.25].

Qualitative data disclose that at "*100% the dealer group model is broken. It has not achieved what it was meant to do, give a higher quality of advice to the public.*" "*Apart from applying for your own license,*" individual licensing "*is the only way to remain truly client focussed,*" "*if the regulating body did a good job of monitoring and enforcing.*" Besides, "*advisers would then also be more PERSONALLY accountable.*" Thus, let "*individuals actions/service etc. be the distinguishing factor.*" "*This would go a long way to 'level the playing field' and break down the current underlying distribution based model.*"

In line with the views of O'Brien and Gilligan (2014), "*there is no longer a place for large institutions to be able to offer licencing services and to also be product manufacturers. The Law should requre they chose to do one but not both.*" Another "*really like[s] this idea, but . . . cant see it happening,*" nor "*how this would work in practice.*" Although "*consumers would have more confidence, this may be based on a perception only.*" A sentiment expressed in the survey was "*the existing vested interests and huge investment in infrastructure by the biggest players would stop this in its tracks.*" Besides, according to some, single licensing was not considered a viable solution to "*exclude bad advisers from the system*" or prevent those "*who deliberately set out*

Table 6.5 Summary of findings for individual licensing [b_4].

Q4: To what extent do financial advisers agree the current licensee–adviser licensing model of individual financial advisers should be replaced with an *independent* individual licensing system, like other professions?
H4: Financial advisers on the ASIC Adviser Register significantly agree the current 'authorised representative' licensing model of individual financial advisers should be replaced with individual licensing.

PAR	*LITERATURE REVIEW*	*SUB-HYPOTHESIS*	*EMPIRICAL TEST*	*EMPIRICAL EVIDENCE* *λ SE [95% CI] c.r. p-value (ex CLF)* *λ c.r. p-value (cum CLF)* *M [95% CI] MSE c.r. p-value*
a_{16}	Lack of trust & confidence (Hely 2012; ASIC 2013a; Morgan & Levine 2015) prevents the public from seeking advice (Balasubramnian *et al.* 2014).	H4 (a): Financial advisers significantly agree clients' trust and confidence in financial advisers would be restored if the licensing of individual financial advisers was via a single individual licence with professional standards of education, appointment, registration, regulation, discipline and cessation.	Clients would have more confidence and trust in financial advisers if advisers were licensed under a single individual licence with professional standards of education, appointment, registration, regulation, discipline and cessation.	.858 .035 [.780, .920] marker p = *** .745, marker p = *** 64 [60, 68] 2.327 27.386 p = ***

(*Continued*)

Table 6.5 (Continued)

Q4: To what extent do financial advisers agree the current licensee–adviser licensing model of individual financial advisers should be replaced with an *independent* individual licensing system, like other professions?
H4: Financial advisers on the ASIC Adviser Register significantly agree the current 'authorised representative' licensing model of individual financial advisers should be replaced with individual licensing.

PAR	*LITERATURE REVIEW*	*SUB-HYPOTHESIS*	*EMPIRICAL TEST*	*EMPIRICAL EVIDENCE* *λ SE [95% CI] c.r. p-value (ex CLF)* *λ c.r. p-value (cum CLF)* *M [95% CI] MSE c.r. p-value*
a_{17}	Institutional commercial licensee favoured over individual professional adviser (Sanders & Roberts 2015, p. 18) leads to problems (O'Brien & Gilligan 2014; Sampson 2010). Individual licensing to disconnect advisers from product issuers may lead to a culture shift (Steen, McGrath and Wong 2016; O'Brien & Gilligan 2014; Parliamentary Joint Committee on Corporations & Financial Services. 2009a, 2009b) to independence (North 2015; ASIC 2017a; Smith, Clarke & Rogers 2017).	H4 (b): Financial advisers significantly agree a single individual licence will promote independence from those licensees who may be conflicted by product bias.	A single individual licence for individual advisers will promote independence from those licensees who may be conflicted by product bias.	.742 .047 [.653, .831] 12.752 $p =$ *** .662, 11.035 $p =$ *** 65 [61, 69] 2.230 29.147 $p =$ ***

a_{18}	Financial advisers have been likened to other professionals (Ap 2011; Bruce 2012; Knutsen & Cameron 2012; Burke *et al.* 2015). Professional regulation evident in law/medicine is critical to the proper functioning of financial services industry (Omarova 2010).	H4 (c): Financial advisers significantly agree the licensing of individual Australian financial advisers should be modelled on those of other professions, such as accounting, legal and medical.	It is 'appropriate' to license advisers with an individual licence in line with other professions, such as the accounting, legal and medical professions.	.816 .042 [.736, .895] 13.098 p = *** .711, 11.211 p = *** 69 [64, 73] 2.244 30.618 p = ***
a_{19}	Individual license (Hoyle 2017; Sanders & Roberts 2015; Parliamentary Joint Committee on Corporations and Financial Services. 2009a, 2009b, 2014; Tuch 2005) via single monopoly body = most effective way to regulate the future financial planning profession (Kingsford Smith 2014).	H4 (d): Financial advisers significantly agree they would prefer an individual licence regulated through a single *independent* registration, competency, education, conduct, standards and disciplinary board.	You would prefer an individual licence regulated through a single *independent* registration, competency, education, conduct, standards and disciplinary board.	.801 .039 [.719, .872] 13.961 p = *** .695, 12.075 p = *** 68 [63, 72] 2.198 30.969 p = ***
a_{21}	Conflict of interest from co-habitation leads to institutional- professional conflicts and ethical dilemmas (Smith,2009) Therefore, disconnecting advisers from control by product distributors by a cultural shift (Steen, McGrath and Wong 2016; O'Brien & Gilligan 2014). Thus, it should eliminate this conflict.	H4 (e): Financial advisers significantly agree Individual licensing of advisers through a single *independent* professional standards board will eliminate conflict of interest from association.	Individual licensing of advisers through a single *independent* professional standards board will eliminate conflict of interest from association.	.629 .051 [.542, .739] 10.374 p = *** .536, 8.625 p = *** 52 [48, 57] 2.167 24.188 p = ***

Parameter (Par) Question (Q) Hypothesis (H) Standardised regression weight (λ) *Standard error* (*SE*) *Critical ratio* (*c.r.*) *Mean* (*M*) *Mean standard error* (*MSE*) *to deceive*" for the simple reason that "*any industry that . . . makes a lot of money quickly, someone will ALWAYS try to push the envelope. Also different ARs will have different attitudes.*" While a former "*senior government bureaucrat*" respondent perceived individual licensing via a single body to build trust and confidence would flop "*if it ended up being run by bureaucrats.*" Because "*from experience . . . most have no understanding of the commercial world or private sector. That's why so many government contracts both state & federal end up in tears.*" He was not the only adviser fearing individual licensing would "*increase the size of bureaucracy.*"

A single body "*would produce a licensee with too much power . . . Better to have many licensees for competition and none that issue product.*" Furthermore, they did not want a professional association involved, because "*so much would depend on the structure, administration and interests of the single licensee. The FPA, for eg, has multiple conflicts of interest.*" Other counter-arguments to this new form of licensing suggested, "*confidence and trust in financial advisers is not built on a licensing arrangement but on the integrity of the individual financial adviser's ethics and integrity.*" Therefore, there was the argument suggesting, "*what needs to be pushed is the high level of consumer protection there is under the current rules.*" The naysayers were not the only ones with hesitations. Those in favour of individual licensing reluctantly admitted, "*big organisation provides more confidence to a person than a small local business.*" Furthermore, "*most Clients actually don't know or care,*" because "*they don't even realise that I'm licensed/Authorised in many cases.*" Trust is with the individual adviser the client deals with, even though "*clients approach and trust a firm or company in the initial approach.*" Concerns expressed by advisers around a single licensing body continued to grow. On the evidence participants did not want a professional association involved, because the "*FPA, for eg, has multiple conflicts of interest. eg. the FPA delivers the 'CFP' designation which it claims is he 'pinnacle' of adviser qualifications. However, it is also the only institution licensed to provide the training.*"

For a few, to encourage trust and confidence in advisers is "*simple . . . remove all remuneration from product, whether that's insurance, platform, investment. Income for the Adviser can only be sourced through Fee for Service, no volume bonus schemes etc.*" Interestingly, not everyone was "*sure what you mean by 'single individual license,'*" because they asked "*Do you mean financial planning as a profession? With all the professional barriers to entry? Then yes,*" "*just like Accountants and Solicitors.*" "*Accounting provides a good model.*" "*Doctors are not licensed by hospitals or clients.*" Thus, "*the model of doctors, lawyers and accountants*" "*is a real possibility, given the Professional Development education we are required to complete to sustain our AR title presently.*" "*Financial advisers need to be like other professionals and charge a fee for service. Then clients will totally trust them. The majority of clients are aware that commissions distort advice given.*"

Independence from conflicted licensee control

A 66% [61%, 69%] level of agreement with a standardised regression weight of .662 *cum* CLF [Table 6.5] and r^2 .541 [.417, .693] [Table 25 in Appendix 5.25] supported a single individual licence for individual advisers to promote independence from conflicted licensees.

Advisers who agree felt, "*it would also mean that advisors aren't effectively bonded to an employer,*" because the "*problem is not the adviser – it is the model which allows a Licensee to own manufacture AND distribution. The banks & union super funds routinely abuse and exploit this.*" Yet others believed independence is a myth, because irrespective of the licensing model, "*you cannot have good advice without product recommendations.*" Thus, "*product bias is going to be there for some advisers aligned or not,*" especially for advisers who "*work for a bank or an industry fund.*"

A consistent theme was, "*an employee of a product provider still succumbing to bonuses etc to sell their products.*" Therefore, there "*will still be the potential to be conflicted if product providers are able to reward advisers for product volumes.*" Some advisers are convinced, "*providers will always try to provide incentives for advisors to recommend their products.*" Alternatively, the "*conflicted licencee will always try to bring pressure to get the sales and revenue either by coercion or demand.*" However, expressed in the viewpoint is "*it's not about licensing, it's about the ethics, standards and morals and education of the adviser.*"

Adding to the foregoing misgivings are some problems with the practical application of individual licensing to promote independence according to advisers. For instance, "*who guarantees that the research and monitoring of the products will be maintained?*" and "*who would provide the APL or would any promoter have access to advisers?*" Additionally, "*who will rigorously set out, apply, monitor, administer, and enforce the standards required for those who do not do the right thing; and make sure they have IP insurance; and deal appropriately with client complaints etc. Put ASIC in charge? A professional body?*" "*In practice the amount of red tape and regulation means that most advisors may still need a 3rd party licensee to provide support so conflicts may still occur.*" Thus, uncertainty as to "*how the compliance frame work would operate*" exists. Evident was the fear, individual licensing will "*place a much greater burden on individual advisers and/or practices to review and select appropriated investments.*"

Another major concern expressed was "*the cost will be high.*" Specifically, "*the costs of PI Insurance and administration of running a self-licensed practice would cause the costs of providing a service on a $Flat fee basis too expensive. This would marginalise the majority of the public who couldn't afford to pay the fees.*"

However, despite the misgivings, advisers acknowledged like doctors, advisers could have "*multi layered licence to determine specialist from generalists.*" Desirable by many respondents is "*a Single individual licensee will need to be independent of the regulator, institutions and Govt.*"

Adviser licensing like other accredited professions

Advisers indicated a moderately high mean level of agreement of 69% [64%, 73%] with a high standardised regression weight of .711 [Table 6.5] and r^2 of .694 [.554, .833] reliability [Table 25 in Appendix 5.25] it is 'appropriate' to license advisers with an individual licence in line with other professions, such as the accounting, legal and medical professions.

"*Trouble is the legislation is all wrapped up around product advice, whereas the other professions have legislation around professional standards rather than product. The law does not seem to envisage the provision of financial advice without use of a product.*" Financial advisers "*want to be considered a profession and yet . . . are corralled and controlled like sales cattle. How many accountants, solicitors and medical professionals do you see being 'franchised' by banks?*" "*It would clarify the issues and advisers would be answerable to their clients and the regulator.*"

Yet respondents' support for separation from licensees is conditional on several aspects, such as it is affordable, ensures ongoing *independent* compliance audits, is self-regulatory and excludes AFS licensees, professional associations and government-owned institutions, while remaining focussed on rigorous professional standards in line with other true professions. Specifically, advisers want to be "*able to afford the cost incurred as a result of compliance, insurance and ongoing education. All of which help to ensure that the client is receiving good advice that is in their best interest.*" Important is "*affordable professional indemnity insurance with a low level of policy excess.*" A concern for individual advisers is they "*don't have easily obtainable funds available to them to meet claims, should they arise.*" Again, it was expressed, "*as long as they are independently audited to maintain standards, it would be ideal.*"

Additionally, advisers want to be judged "*by . . . peers and reported for misconduct by peers as currently happens in the legal and accounting professions.*" They want the licensing body to be "*run by a NON-Government Body like the Law Society, ICA; Board of Surgeons,*" without interference by "*by banks and instos which is currently the case. There is too much fat in subscriptions to these groups and sponsorship by instos which then pollutes policy and ultimately credibility.*" Individual licensing "*needs . . . a vigorous framework . . . which doesn't currently exist. Allow the advisers to be a part of developing that framework.*"

Once again, concern was uttered about the practical workings of "*monitoring and supervision of individually licensed advisers*" and "*whether that system would support advisers enough.*"

Advisers who strongly disagreed with new licensing suggested, "*not on your nelly. I pay almost $30,000 per year for the privilege of providing advice to my clients. That is the cost of my license. for that, my licensee provides all research, compliance, reporting. I provide advice on Super, Insurance, estate planning, budgeting, investing, lending, health and wellbeing. There is so much more than 'product.'*" The same misgivings as earlier included the "*compliance burden of this scenario.*" "*Cost to end client would be much greater,*" is yet again a concern.

The self-licensed failed to see the need for individual licensing, because they were "*already under those regulations*" as in their view "*that option exists today – individuals can obtain an AFSL.*"

Independent ***professional financial planning standards board***

The support was moderately strong for an individual licence regulated through a single *independent* registration, competency, education, conduct, standards and disciplinary board. Extent of adviser agreement was measured to score a mean level of 68% [63%, 72%] with moderately high standardised regression effect size of .695 [Table 6.5] and moderate r^2 of .623 [.501, .834] [Table 25 in Appendix 5.25].

From these survey results, advisers are coming around to being licensed via a "*'single' body.*" An informant felt "*it would put all advisers on the same page and distinguish the aligned ones.*" However, once again, the self-licensed with their "*own AFSL,*" suggested it was unnecessary to pursue any new *independent* licensing, because they were "*already in that space*" where they "*operate as an independent (as defined by the Act).*"

A couple of respondents recognised this "*has all been tried before.*" Particularly, the "*FPA has tried to move down this track but has been largely ignored.*" The reason it has been neglected is it is perceived as a "*little hard as after 15 years we're heavily invested into the current position with commercial property and such.*" However, advisers desire such a model, because it "*takes the conflict of industry bodies away who currently 'own' the designations (eg. CFP and FPA).*"

Although it was reported costs were a major concern, to the contrary, others perceived the "*costs could be drastically reduced due to numbers,*" and hence "*help reduce costs to an Adviser's practice.*" Once again, advisers who were in favour of individual licensing did so conditionally. They expect "*the services delivered by current licensee are available at reasonable cost*" by the new body, because they "*are already under extreme pricing pressure and compliance complexity.*" According to one respondent, if the costs were not kept "*feasible,*" then "*the product providers will somehow find a way to 'reward' advisers who use their product and pay their fee.*" Survey participants confirmed, "*licensees subsidise the cost of services to affiliated advisers.*" Furthermore, the question was raised, "*will the administration burden on advisers [be] reduced under an individual license?*" "*Economies of scale is important,*" because "*too much compliance work*" makes a single license unworkable according to some informants.

The expectations of respondents included the licensing body should have "*the resources required to monitor and manage,*" "*was run efficiently and fairly*" with "*no ties union or government influences*" nor "*indirectly controlled by the institutions in the form of 'corporate sponsorship'*" with "*vested interest.*" They want to see a new body "*decreases red tape . . . and makes doing business easier.*" Worrying for one respondent was "*no board has shown any ability to appear independent – they usually have some vested interest.*" What troubled advisers was the potential loss of "*the backing of a large financial institution who owns the AFS license and appoints authorised representatives and monitors and supervises them.*"

The forfeiture of subsidised support services licensees provides, such as "*business planning and development support,*" "*Professional Indemnity Ins, Adviser software, practice management support training/technical support etc,*" was seen as cannot be provided by a single board. However, another made counter claims "*back office and other support services can be delivered by other parties in competition with each other,*" whereby "*advisers can pay a registration fee to a single board and pay for services independently of their licence.*" This latter claim was supported with evidence, such as the likes of "*CPA Australia and ICA can survive independently and compete.*"

Some respondents added finer details of what they would like to see the board provide. "*Degree from a recognised university, post degree course administered by professional body, registration by government body.*" It should offer "*a single set of standards for example, asset allocation, standard terminology for clients to understand (and agreed benchmarks with narrow deviation) and very strict compliance and disciplinary standards for those who choose to not comply.*" An added problem highlighted was uncertainty as to "*how this would remove the bias towards in-house products as advisers would still have to work with APL and sales targets.*" Additionally, there should be "*appropriate distinctions for exactly what advice that 'professional' is licensed to provide. Eg Insurance specialists (no other services offered) are designated differently to investment specialist – and variation thereof (no insurance), different to those who offer a bit of both.*"

Stamp out conflict of interest from association

Generally, it seems advisers were unsure whether individual licensing of advisers through a single *independent* professional standards board will completely eliminate conflict of interest from association based on a mean level of agreement score of 52% [48%, 57%] with a moderate effect size of .536 [Table 6.5] and moderately low squared multiple correlations of .39 [.311, .555] [Table 25 in Appendix 5.25].

Although it might "*not eradicate conflicts,*" "*it will resolve possibly the biggest issue standing in the way of clients' best interest being satisfied (all of the time).*" The excuse is "*advisers can't know all the products in the market so well as to satisfy their know your product obligation for all of them, so a close alignment with a product provider is inevitable.*" Many respondents appeared to sit "*midway with this one.*" The difficulty appears, although they "*agree with a Professional Standards Board,*" they did not "*see how this will stop Conflicts of Interest.*" By eliminating conflicts interest would provide advisers with control to enforce better ethical culture within licensees. "*If financial planners hold a licence and can choose their association and change at will, more pressure on the institutions to comply with legislation and look after clients rather than push profits.*" To overcome this problem of control by licensees is to ensure "*the ability for advisers to get paid by the products are removed as well.*"

However, others argue, product bias will remain a problem despite the licensing regime, because there is a "*personal bias*" together with "*other sources of product bias such as business efficiency,*" as well as "*poor sales practices, or simply inexperienced advice or business processes lacking in structure.*" "*As long as advisers are involved in recommending product and implementing product solutions beyond SMSF set up, product providers will continue to try and influence advisers.*" At risk of the greatest influence by licensees are the employee advisers who "*still need to work through a company – at least initially to gain experience. These companies will have their preferences for products and platforms and will influence the services the advisers offer.*" It has been reported earlier, "*BDMs*" of licensees allegedly will continue to use "*sales incentives like commissions, marketing allowances, white labeled products etc.*"

It is contended "'*white label' products with the product manufacturers*" remain a problem and "*may compromise the independence depending on how it is incorporated into the business.*" "*Commercial reality will simply generate new conflicts*"is thus a reason put forward why a single body will fail. Mentioned again by advisers, the "*problem is conflicted remuneration rather than that created by association alone.*" For some, the conflicted association was an issue of ethics: "*Advisers are either conflicted or not. Licencing is not the issue. Ethics of advisers is the issue.*"

Despite these misgivings, advisers recognise a solution is to "*De-link product and advice*" and thus "*separate the product owner from the Adviser,*" because, while "*the two are connected, you have conflict.*"

Conclusion

The quantitative results clearly show current AFSL-AR licensing is illegitimate. This research answered the four investigative questions. First, advisers perceived a dual-agency role between Licensee-Adviser-Client. They agreed with financial planning literature claiming advisers serve the interests of the licensees and clients simultaneously leading to a conflict of interest. A conflict of interest they confirmed was indeed from association to third-party often commercially driven product-oriented conflicted licensees. Second, advisers empirically confirmed licensing advisers through third parties is inconsistent with four objectives of the Act. Third, the observed research confirmed in the eyes of advisers, current AR-AFSL licensing fails the legitimacy criteria of Suchman's legitimacy framework applied to financial planning theory. Finally, advisers cautiously indicated their favour of an alternative licensing option disconnecting them from third parties like other professions, such as accounting, medical and legal. They were in favour of considering a single *independent* professional financial planning standards board to regulate not only the education of individual advisers, but also their registration, competency, conduct, standards and disciplinary issues, as an option to eliminate conflict of interest from association.

However, observed in the commentary by advisers, licensing advisers is a difficult issue with many other variables at play, leading to more complexity and perhaps even confusion. Interestingly, best interest duty has changed the perception of whom advisers are working on behalf of, even though the legislation does not reflect this. Advisers find it challenging to attend the licensees' and clients' interests simultaneously. Furthermore, the diverse benefits licensees gain from authorising advisers is not as transparent as one would expect and seems a difficult matter for advisers to reflect on and discuss.

Misalignment of adviser–client interests includes a licensee–adviser and/or a licensee–client interest misalignment. Licensing advisers via a third party is problematic within the context of licensees' business models, remuneration models and culture. In addition, it seems the following may negatively affect the adviser–client relationship achieving the four objectives of the Act: (1) AR employee or self-employment status with the licensee, (2) licensee influence over advisers, (3) application of licensee APLs and (4) adviser KPIs or performance indicators implemented by licensees.

Statutory fiduciary duty is the most significant variable driving the illegitimacy of current licensee–adviser representative licensing. The second most important source of illegitimacy is the objective of the Act, aligning adviser–client interests. Interestingly, the tension between licensees' commercial interests and advisers' fiduciary duty is the third key factor delegitimising current AFSL-AR licensing. This means these variables, together with advisers' view clients would have more trust in advisers licensed via a single licensing model, were significant determinants driving the illegitimacy of current AFSL-AR licensing.

Consequently, survey respondents, albeit with some misgiving and reservations, support the argument to change current licensee–adviser licensing to individual professional adviser licensing via a monopoly professional *independent* regulatory body.

APPENDICES FOR CHAPTER 6

Appendix 6.1

Means or Intercepts: [Group number 1 - Default model]

Table 26 Means or Intercepts: [Group number 1 - Default model] Bootstrapped *ex* and *cum* CLF

Parameter	*Survey statement*	*Estimate*	*SE*	*c.r.*	*P*
Dual [a_1]	Advisers are dual agents	76.973	1.912	40.266	***
Simult [a_2]	Simultaneously serving licensee and client	61.779	2.188	28.234	***
BestRev [a_3]	Generating revenue for licensees	78.485	1.767	44.416	***
Structural [a_4]	Conflict of interest from association	74.519	2.043	36.477	***
AlignAct [a_5]	Aligning adviser–client interests is difficult	60.328	2.363	25.528	***
ColAct [a_6]	Unavoidable conflicts of interest present	65.137	2.313	28.159	***
FiducAct [a_7]	Greater risk of breaching best interest duty	58.836	2.288	25.717	***
CompAct [a_8]	Advisers limited from competing fairly	51.279	2.305	22.247	***
Regulative [a_9]	Risk of unintentional act compliance breaches	47.584	2.335	20.375	***
Consequential [a_{10}]	Licensee commercial interests compromising adviser best interest duty	63.630	2.263	28.112	***
Procedural [a_{11}]	Sales window dressed to comply with the Act	61.160	2.356	25.956	***
Personal [a_{13}]	Aligned leaders of licensees aim to protect their product distribution channels when lobbying	78.282	1.796	43.594	***
Cognitive [a_{14}]	Public cannot clearly distinguish s923A *independent* from conflicted advisers	62.172	2.269	27.401	***
Trust [a_{16}]	Individual licensing will improve public trust and confidence in advisers	63.733	2.327	27.386	***
Independence [a_{17}]	Individual licensing will promote independence from product-biased licensee	65.000	2.23	29.147	***
Professions [a_{18}]	Individual licence should be in line with other professions, such as medical	68.718	2.244	30.618	***
IPFPSB [a_{19}]	Advisers prefer individual licence through a single *independent* body	68.061	2.198	30.969	***
EliminateCoI [a_{21}]	Individual licensing will eliminate conflict of interest from association	52.424	2.167	24.188	***

Appendix 6.2

Difference in aligned, non-aligned and s923A independent advice

What is the difference in advice provided by aligned advisers, non-aligned advisers and *independent* advisers as defined by the Commonwealth Corporations Act 2001?

Table 27 Difference in aligned, non-aligned and s923A *independent* advice.

Respondents claims	*Frequency*	*Percent of n = 262*
There is a difference	128	48.85
There is no difference	40	15.27
There should not be a difference	32	12.21
Missing responses	24	9.16
Not much or very little	12	4.58
Don't know	11	4.20
Not committing an answer	10	3.82
It depends	5	1.91

On the grounds of the number of missing responses (24), don't know responses (11) and uncommitted responses, including "it depends" (ten) numbering 50 (19%) in total, it is apparent advisers found this question difficult to answer or did not want to answer it or chose not to answer the question. As already alluded to, by combining these findings with the findings of cultural-cognitive illegitimacy, it is clear advisers struggle with clearly defining their identity, role and performance. Evidence showed advisers differentiated between non-aligned and s923A independence. How advisers differentiated between aligned and *independent* licensees was based on APLs, remuneration models, presence of KPIs, product and the nature of the adviser–licensee relationship. As already alluded to, by combining these findings with the findings of cultural-cognitive illegitimacy, it is clear advisers struggle with clearly defining their identity, role and performance.

Appendix 6.3

Licensees benefits of appointing, regulating and supervising advisers

Table 28 shows the results of the question: What are the benefits to institutional licensees appointing, authorising and supervising 'authorised representatives'? Advisers' diverse and sometimes unclear responses indicated it is necessary to explore this question further. For example, although the question asked advisers about what benefits licensees derive, six participants explained the benefit ASIC derives, namely "*easier for regulators to monitor/supervise/regulate*" or "*Cheaper for ASIC.*" It was as if they tried to avoid answering the question by deflecting the

Table 28 Licensees' benefits of appointing, regulating and supervising advisers.

Respondents claims	*Frequency*	*Percent of 262*
Control product distribution	49	18.70
Financial benefits	47	17.94
Control the compliance obligations of advisers	29	11.07
Economies of scale benefits	24	9.16
Lower cost benefits	23	8.78
Adviser benefits mentioned ignoring licensee benefits	18	6.87
No benefits to licensees	16	6.11
Missing responses	15	5.73
Benefit when clients' best interests are met	12	4.58
Benefit from authorised representatives recruiting clients for licensees	12	4.58
Increased legal protection benefits for licensees by authorising advisers	12	4.58
Control back office management of administration, advice process, procedures and outcomes	12	4.58
Control management of the APLs	8	3.05
ASIC benefits	7	2.67
Do not know how licensees benefit	7	2.29
Sharing of compliance risk between licensee and adviser benefits	5	1.91
Increased public "brand" awareness benefits	5	1.91
Reduced competition benefits	4	1.53
Unspecified control benefits	4	1.53

issue towards ASIC. Empirically proven, product distribution is the main reason licensees appoint and regulated authorised representatives. Overall, it appeared 102 out of 262 (39%) advisers used the term "*control*" by product distribution; the compliance obligations of advisers; back office management of administration; advice process, procedures and outcomes; and management of the APLs.

Appendix 6.4

Statement of advice without product recommendations

To determine whether advice is SOA are only product related, the question asked: Have you ever prepared a SOA [Statement of Advice] without any product recommendations? [Why or why not?] Table 29 recorded results of the responses.

Table 29 Frequency of statement of advice without product recommendations

SOA with no financial product recommendations? [Yes/No]	*Frequency*	*Percent*
Yes	204	77.9
No	58	22.1
Total	262	100

Appendix 6.5

One-off approvals

Table 30 records the results of the question: Have you ever applied for one-off approvals financial products or investments not on your licensees' APL? Why or why not? As was the case with non-product SOAs, most respondents have applied for one-off product approvals. The reasons provided by the 21% who have not applied for one-off approvals were diverse. The 12 of the 55 [22%] claimed the APL was sufficient to meet the clients' needs, followed by nine out of 55 [16%] who claimed the APL they were using was broad, extensive and open. Thirteen percent of this group were self-licensed and managed their own APLs, whereas one participant claimed, "***I don't have an approved product list.***"

Table 30 Frequency of one-off approvals

One-off approval applications? [Yes/No]	*Frequency*	*Percent*
Yes	206	78.6
No	55	21.0
Missing response	1	.4
Total	262	100

7 Conclusion

Introduction

Although this research started with unconfirmed statements around the illegitimacy of current AFSL-AR licensing, there is now scientific evidence substantiating many of these troubled negative views. Thus, with a framework to define, model and measure this legitimacy, a more balanced view on what is clearly a controversial matter is now available. Therefore, this chapter makes concluding remarks about the illegitimacy of licensing individual advisers via multiple third-party licensees. To do so, a summary of the main findings is presented, while highlighting its importance. This is followed by recommendations for future work. A brief discussion on the policy implications, practical application and contributions, together with some of the assumptions and limitations, ends the book.

Summary of findings and significance

Judged by financial advisers, the current licensing model lacks legitimacy.

Adviser dual-agency role ambiguity

Advisers concur that under current licensing, they serve two masters as **dual** agents **simultaneously**. Advisers admit that serving the interests of licensees and clients simultaneously is confusing. Notwithstanding, the lack of structural independence adversely affects the quality of advice. They confirmed licensing advisers via third party commercially driven licensees leads to a **conflict of interest** from association. Mainly, because licensees are earning various permutations of technical, and hence questionable, types of revenue, while advisers serve their clients' best interests at the same time. Licensees, advisers claimed, have the power, notwithstanding the authority, to control the quality of advice, the flow of funds via APLs and the sources of revenue. The power of the conflicted licensee to use technology to monitor advisers' performance in terms of meeting the licensees' commercial interests and expectations was claimed to overwhelm the best interests of the client. This remuneration focus is reinforced by the fact licensees are the only party legally permitted to collect revenues from clients. Informants alleged licensees are empowered to deduct their fees. There was uncertainty among advisers exactly how much they were earning for the licensee as a revenue centre.

On the available evidence, the best interest duty obligation has changed the perceived view and practice of the licensee–adviser–client relationship. An interesting finding was advisers refute licensees are the principal in the licensee–adviser relationship any longer. Instead of working on behalf of licensees, advisers claimed licensees served the purpose of merely legally authorising them, while providing them with subsidised support services, such as compliance, legal, software, PI, professional and business development, back office support as well as APLs. In other words, advisers advocated they perceived themselves as clients of licensees, while their priority is to act in the best interests of clients above all.

In accordance with the emerging financial planning theory on the adviser–client relationship, in practice, advisers take their relationship with their clients seriously. While at the same time, mirrored in financial planning textbooks and tertiary education courses, they are disregarding their relationship with their licensees. In practice, advisers see the adviser–licensee relationship as merely an unimportant legal arrangement of compliance, which they must live with and accept. A disconnect between how the advisers defined their and their licensees' role in practice and how the Act defines these roles exists. Thus, s916A and s916B of the Act, where advisers are legislated to act on behalf of licensees, is either out of sync with practice or *vice versa*.

The results also revealed a neglected licensee–client relationship. The licensee–client relationship is not a specific conceptual focus in financial planning scholarly literature. This confirmed that not only is agency theory narrowly presented in many Australian financial planning literatures, but also the legislation does not represent the dynamics of the relationships between licensee–adviser–client, which is subsequently mirrored in practice. This is arguably a source of additional problems leading to conflicts of interest. Just like ASIC clarified the interpretation of s923A of the Act regarding terminology "non-aligned," "non-institutionally-owned" and "*independent*ly owned," the legal definitions of the licensee–adviser–client relationship should be reviewed for clarification within the context of financial planning theory, legislation and practice.

Contraventions of the objectives of the Commonwealth Corporations Act 2001

At the macro-level, institutional [social] illegitimacy is present in the licensing model. In support of the dual-agency role findings, it is empirically clear current licensing sanctions contraventions of the best interest duty, misalignment of adviser–client interests, conflict of interest from association and anti-competitive practices.

Best interest duty obligations is the top reason for delegitimising current AFSL-AR licensing. Importantly, of the four legislative objectives, the verdict is advisers take intentional and unintentional contraventions of the statutory fiduciary duty the most seriously. By implication, the objective of the Act to promote the best interest duty is an important issue. Uncontentious on the prevailing evidence, licensing advisers via third parties creates business models that place them at greater risk of unintentionally [and in some instances intentionally] breaching their best interest duty obligations.

Although it is well-recorded in the literature review best interest duty should override conflicts in theory, the evidence confirms, it is impractical to implement in practice. Specifically, in the presence of conflict of interest from association, complying with the best interest duty is tricky according to the data collected. Licensees and their advisers are unsuccessful in achieving this objectives of the Act, because the results reveal the presence of a poor product sales culture within aligned licensees. Additionally, licensees' compliance, business development, area and/or distribution managers 'encourage' them to sell the licensees' in-house financial products. Advisers explained licensees' control over them made them powerless from avoiding contraventions of the best interest duty. Although the advisers acknowledged some aligned licensees have removed sales or income targets for their authorised representatives, their in-house product sales performance is still captured under a 'performance review' which determines their employment. Therefore, instead of obvious product sales-targeted KPIs, some licensees have moved to performance reviews using cultural pressure as a method to influence advisers' recommendations to specific product solutions. Furthermore, licensees have the power to manipulate their employees with threats of dismissal or forfeiture of remuneration [specifically, bonuses and support services] if they fail to follow procedures designed to serve the licensees' interests. Advisers claimed salaried employee advisers are forced into ethical dilemmas they are unable to control. It seems if licensees dictate the terms or have influence over the adviser, then the adviser finds it harder to effectively manage, control and/or avoid conflicts of interest, in comparison to situations where the advisers dictate the terms of their licensee–adviser relationship. Accordingly, the influence of best interest duty on the illegitimacy of current licensing in the debate around it should not be underestimated. In effect, it is argued here, the best interest duty legislation has made this model of licensing individual advisers redundant.

Moreover, linked to the foregoing, empirically the second highest contributing factor delegitimising current adviser licensing is **misalignment of adviser–client interests**. The qualitative data highlight it was even difficult for the most ethical bank advisers facing limited APLs to align their interests with the best interests of the client. Advisers agree, it is difficult to manage conflicts if financial products on APLs are linked to professional indemnity insurance to reduce the licensees' risk. Although secondary evidence suggests PI's purpose is to reduce the licensees' risk, no mention is made of the potential risks clients of financial advisers face by the practice of linking PI to APLs. Thus, the practice of linking PI to products on the APLs is questionable. Clear from the qualitative results, not every adviser was permitted to apply for or even be granted one-off approvals. Some licensees disallow one-off approvals. Where licensees permit one-off approvals, they make the application process a time consuming, unproductive and fruitless endeavour for the adviser to discourage them from applying. Advisers confirmed the difficulty of achieving alignment of interests is particularly evident among employees and/ or BOLR[1] product-aligned advisers, who are incentivised, influenced or coerced by their licensees.

The greatest contributing factor to encourage **conflicts of interest from association** was the ever-present subject of conflicted *licensee* remuneration models, note not *adviser* remuneration models, was continually raised by respondents. The qualitative data suggested, apparently it is all in the way licensees frame the remuneration within the context of disclosures to comply with the legislation. Seemingly, respondents accuse some licensees of using terminology for various types of fees to mask the true nature of the remuneration. Advisers reported in the empirical study that the disclosures have not been as transparent as they were intended to be in the legislation. Although this conflict can be managed at licensee and adviser level, effective management of this conflict ultimately relies on the integrity of the adviser and the culture of the licensee.

When considering the objective of encouraging competition, the non-aligned *independent* advisers reported instances, such as vertical integration benefits, of what they considered as **anti-competitive behaviour**. Common among the aligned advisers was the practice of third line forcing, which occurs when a loan application is approved only if the client also obtains insurance from the same provider. By implication, product-aligned licensees improve their product distribution in this way. Furthermore, advisers alleged banks subsidise their advice delivery from vertical integration in practice by defraying the costs, *inter alia*, and support services of running the licence onto other parts of the business.

Therefore, the current licensing model is not doing the job it was meant to do, namely protect the public as the objectives of the Act defines. Mentioned earlier, these potential statutory compliance infringements can encourage class action, while leading to damaged reputations of legislators, regulators, licensees and advisers. Notwithstanding significant financial losses to the public.

Illegitimacy of licensee–adviser licensing

If the contraventions of the objectives of the Act are considered in conjunction with the legitimacy tests using the criteria of Suchman's (1995) theoretical framework, then it is clear, licensing advisers via multiple third-parties leads to strategic [organisational] illegitimacy of AFSL-AR licensing. In order of rank, current adviser licensing lacks consequential moral, procedural moral, regulative, structural moral, personal moral and culture-cognitive legitimacy.

Of all criteria used to assess legitimacy, **consequential moral illegitimacy** was recognised as the third most influential reason why licensing lacks legitimacy. Thus, in accordance with this criteria applied to financial planning theory, without a doubt licensees' commercial interests compromise best interest duty. Advisers were apathetic when reflecting on the matter of licensees' revenues, even though it is clearly a significant problem causing difficulties for current licensee–adviser licensing. Even though the clients' best interest duty should legally trump shareholders' interests in practice, the findings in this research suggest otherwise. The research reconfirms the conclusions by Smith (2009), namely when behaving ethically is perceived as unprofitable by licensees, then the question of what licensees influence their advisers to do, as opposed to what they should actually do to comply, are two different things. Discovered in the qualitative data, the aligned licensees were aware they put their company profits, from expressly funds under management, ahead of the clients' best interest, if they believe they can get away with it.

In terms of **procedural moral illegitimacy**, licensees window-dress sales policies, procedures and practices to appear to comply with the Act. Specifically, the qualitative results revealed commercial interests is a focus for licensees, even though it meant 'unethical' advisers were feted, and ethical ones ostracised as underperforming.

Concerning **regulative illegitimacy**, the evidence revealed that in practice there were not only unintentional compliance transgressions, but also occurrence of intentional breaches. Compliance violations are perceived by advisers as limited not only to aligned advisers. In addition, business and remuneration models, encouraging product sales volumes, were among several issues blamed for the compliance contraventions. Findings revealed, the level of the product 'sales' culture licensee leaders encouraged within their institutions determined the extent of compliance breaches. Advisers felt frustrated by their licensees' lack of any desire to implement consistent ethical behaviour and adviser conduct standards across their financial advisory groups. Furthermore, there were clear differences in opinion among respondents as to whether the licensees' compliance managers and the strict controls licensees imposed, prevented compliance violations or not. Also unclear among respondents was the issue as to who [advisers, or the licensees or both] was ultimately accountable and in what proportions after a compliance breach.

The underlying structural issue of ownership of advice by product issuers is the crux of the problems in the financial advisory sector. From the available data, advisers believe this is a contributing factor to why they are being attacked from all political corners. Thus, adviser licensing displays **structural moral** illegitimacy.

Seasoned survey respondents indicated, Federal and State politics seems to play a significant part in some of the woes the industry faces at present. Individual leaders of aligned licensees, according to advisers, aim to protect their product distribution channels when lobbying government during FOFA reform consultations. Thus, current adviser licensing fails to meet the criteria for **personal moral legitimacy**. In support of the findings in the Royal Commission, it is questionable whether private commercially oriented institutions can be trusted to regulate their advisers' activities in the public interest.

Despite ASIC's attempt to use the legislative process, the public cannot clearly distinguish between s923A *independent* from product-conflicted advisers. Advisers genuinely mistakenly, yet also intentionally, misunderstand and/or misinterpret the requirements of the legislation from a structural, operational and ethical perspective. Articulated by respondents, it appears they differentiate the services they offer in practice, purely on the basis of ownership, product and/or remuneration practices. In some instances, advisers are defining the terms of s923A in their own way, where some present themselves as *independent*, while having some invisible arrangements with third-party product-aligned institutions. While advisers are connected to licensees, they themselves are unclear of who they are [identity] and what they do [role] to achieve the four objectives of the Act [performance]. Thus, licensing advisers via third parties results in **cultural-cognitive** illegitimacy.

Individual professional licensing like other professions

In the company of minority critics, it is certain, the findings strengthen arguments for individual licensing through a single *independent* professional body, modelled on other professionals. The verdict is individual licensing will improve **trust and confidence** in advisers.

Empirically verified and validated here, most respondent advisers seek **independence** from licensees, because it would remove advisers from being bonded to an employer and/or licensee. However, advisers acknowledge the problem included, licensees manufacturing and distributing product were able to own advice businesses. To advisers, the problem is less the adviser, and more the licensing system of being authorised by third party conflicted licensees who control adviser behaviour in ways that is not always in the best interest of clients.

From the results, advisers agree they should be licensed in a similar way to other **professions**, such as the accounting, legal and medical professions. Being judged and reported for misconduct by your peers, as is the case in the legal and accounting professions, is an attractive proposition for most advisers responding to the survey. In the discussion so far, advisers confirm their individual capacity is being overridden by licensees and is an obstacle to financial planning becoming a true profession. Advisers claim licensees, particularly banks, have too much control over their advisers, especially employee ARs, who are keen to consider non-APL product recommendations, while tying the hands of their employees with processes and procedures. Advisers want the freedom to set their own standards of registration, education, practice, ethical conduct and discipline like other professions.

The primary qualitative data also indicated this support for entering an era of self-regulation is conditional. They demand it is well resourced to enforce compliance, ensure efficiency and fairness, while having no ties to union, government and professional associations, including the government-recognised FPA. Advisers were quite clear that it must exclude control by AFSL licensees, existing professional associations and the government. They claim professional associations, like the FPA, are indirectly controlled by the AFSL institutions in the form of 'corporate sponsorship' with vested commercial interest. The concern for increased costs of licensing was among the greatest concerns in most of the commentary in the survey.

Not everyone was pleased with the idea of individual licensing, especially among those with their own AFSL, who felt they were already operating in this space, because they run an AFSL purely, so they can operate as an ***independent*** [as defined by the Act]. The lack of support by self-licensed ***independent*** advisers of individual licensing via a single body was unsurprising, because many have already invested quite a bit of time and money to apply for their own licence, notwithstanding the costs incurred to ensure ongoing compliance.

Thus, the data collected highlight advisers' uncertainty pertaining to what an individual licence would entail. Furthermore, the lack of the finer implementation details, which is yet unresolved, is possibly leading to these respondents' uncertainty.

However, merely concentrating on conflicts from remuneration, professional standards, education and ethical standards to improve financial adviser conduct, is misguided. Following from the foregoing statement, FASEA could evolve or be superseded by a new *Independent* Financial Planning Professional Regulatory Body to take on this challenging task of transforming advisers into recognised and accredited professionals. Notably, support by a sample of advisers for IPFPSB comes with reservations and concerns. Specifically, advisers fear losing what they claim are well-funded subsidised support services licensees offer. For example, the loss of licensees' subsidised software, training, research, compliance, business, legal plus back office support is a major concern for many. Advisers are apprehensive about the impact on licensing costs and economies of scale should government make a move to individual licensing. Additional unresolved issues around licensing comprise practicality, PI, APLs, 'white' and 'private' label products, plus vertical integration.

Despite these reservations, advisers agree removing the licensee–adviser legislated relationship should **reduce conflict of interest from association**. They claim it will resolve possibly the biggest issue standing in the way of clients' best interest being satisfied [all the time]. Although, it seems conflicted remuneration has been removed, licensees are using 'other' forms of incentives to control advisers, such as concealed soft dollar incentives, including the subsidised support services and BOLR agreements. What is thought-provoking is that apparently AFS licensees will always find ways to incentivise advisers to distribute their products no matter what licensing regime is in operation.

However, the concerns raised should not demotivate policymakers from pursuing further reforms to license advisers as recognised accredited professionals. The way licensing is structured presently works against legislators' efforts to raise financial planning standards through the legislative process and regulatory reform to enforce industry compliance of the Act. Besides, existing licensing threatens independence, a key characteristic of a profession. Conflicted association between licensees and their advisers arises from their 'co-existence.' Yet, it is well documented in this book, elimination of conflicts is vital to a true professional.

Key policy implications and practical application

Within the context of the Ripoll, Murray and Hayne Inquiries, as well as senate, parliamentary, media and public debates, this study attempted to answer some important policy questions, albeit from a macro-perspective. Proven illegitimacy encourages policymakers, together with all financial planning stakeholders, to draw on the experience of other true professions, and hence work together towards disconnecting advisers from conflicted institutions.

From the conversation, the illegitimacy of the examined current licensing implies it should be superseded or revised. To promote a healthy functioning financial services industry where advisers are recognised as true professionals under the same legislative requirements as other accredited professionals requires structural change to licensing individual advisers. Besides, the undesirable consequences of AFSL-AR licensing are detrimental to all the stakeholders within Financial Services. Although this recommendation is tempered with a word of caution, namely this model's legitimacy must also be tested.

If the benefit of improved public trust and confidence, is weighed against the costs of independence, conflict of interest from association, unintentional contraventions of the statutory fiduciary duty, misalignment of adviser–client interests and the matter licensee commercial interests comprise ARs' best interest duty, then for the sake of public interest change is inevitable. Especially given the public backlash to the scandals appeared to have outweighed the benefits they may feel they would receive from obtaining financial advice. Notwithstanding the disparaging effect on the reputations of the government, regulators, licensees and advisers.

Recognised here, implementing change is accompanied by practical, political, social and business opportunities and threats for all stakeholders' interests. Each actor in the financial services sector will have different objectives in a future individual licensing regime. For the Australian Federal Government, it is to protect the Australian public from financial harm. For ASIC, it is to ensure successful and cost effective law enforcement on Corporations sufficient to build confidence, trust and transparency in the Australian Financial System. For the FASEA or any other adviser regulatory body, it is ensuring advisers comply with professional, educational and ethical standards to promote professionalism further. For professional associations, it is to continue supporting their licensee and adviser members of the emerging profession and the public interest, while helping advisers further their careers. For AFSLs, it is providing financial products and services to the Australian public cost effectively within a sustainable ethical profit model acceptable to society. For advisers, it is to make quality recommendations to clients ethically while serving their best interests without the encumbrances imposed by licensees. For the public, it is receiving professional unbiased financial advice they can trust, cost effectively. Finally, for the media, it is to continue delivering everyone with information around events, issues and characters in the Financial Services industry requiring attention. Thus, professional individual licensing is critical to ensure the interests of all stakeholders are served. Thus, it requires all stakeholders to contribute to developing a feasible individual licensing model that will encourage the public to seek financial advice.

If financial planning becomes a recognised accredited true profession, enjoyed by other true professions, then a likely benefit is it will incentivise university graduate talent to enter the financial advisory sector. It is well known that recognised accredited professions have status. Thus, younger advisers entering this emerging profession should go a long way to reduce any fears of shortages in *independent* advisers.

Recommendations for future research

While a great deal more is now known about licensing advisers via third parties in comparison to professional individual licensing, this investigation serves to merely lay initial groundwork for further future research. The broad scope of the research has left many areas unexplored, while raising more questions and problems requiring in-depth detailed investigation.

Having collected data from only one group of stakeholders, the advisers, valuable insights would further contribute to a balanced view by collecting data from policymakers, ASIC, FASEA, PSA, professional associations, licensees and clients with regard to their perceptions of the legitimacy of current licensee–adviser licensing.

Additional research should delve deeper into the agency roles between adviser–client, and the much-neglected licensee–adviser and licensee–client relationships, because the agency role is not as simple or clearly defined as seemingly proposed in financial planning literature. The results of the study advocate the financial planning theory concerning the principal agent relationship is not aligned with the legislation, nor is the legislation aligned with financial planning theory. What needs clarification is the inconsistent perceptions of legislative, theoretical and actual practices regarding advisers' agency role. The licensee–adviser relationship, advisers felt, is merely a legislated definition, which differs from the practical application of this definition in practice. Added to this latter point, it is uncertain whether the viewpoint that advisers no longer act on behalf of licensees comes from themselves or through conditioning, training or marketing from their licensees, or the financial planning literature, which needs further investigation.

Moreover, since the best interest duty was implemented, advisers no longer understand their agency identity and role by agency theory and as prescribed in law. The apparent disconnect between how the advisers defined their and their licensees' role in practice and how the Act defines these roles needs further assessment in future enquiry.

Within the financial advisory sector, other relationships include advisers and *independent* facilitating agencies. These principals assist advisers to implement financial plans for their clients. Facilitating agencies are specialists – such as rating agencies, lawyers, accountants, fund managers, research suppliers, paraplanners, investment banks or institutions. Given the foregoing explanation submits financial planning involves a wide range of relationships, this highlights the need for these associations to be reported in the financial planning literature.

Lacking in financial planning theory are the agency relationships between the decision-making management team [agents] and the shareholders [principals] of financial services institutions [AFSL holders]. However, a void in the literature on how these relationships interact with the licensee–adviser–client relationship is prevalent. Thus, this void should be addressed.

In addition, more detailed future investigation should consider the politics, conflicts and power play between licensees and advisers; advisers and their clients; and licensees and their clients. In addition, employee representatives compared with self-employed authorised representatives face the greatest challenge when it came to conflict of interest from association, because their licensee uses key performance indicators, sales targets and threats of job loss or loss of remuneration to control them. Therefore, an important area of research is to ascertain to what extent employee advisers can deal with these control mechanisms and still operate ethically. With new legislation on whistleblowing yet to be tested, a gap on the issues of power and influence within financial planning literature exists. Especially, the gap relating to the licensee–adviser relationship requires further enquiry. Consequently, the extent to which licensees influence [control] their advisers, and *vice versa*, should be assessed.

What is overlooked in the theory and confirmed in this empirical study is the continued lack of clarity or misinterpretation by some financial advisory sector participants in practice of the terms "aligned," "non-aligned" and "s923A *independent*." The backlash from advisers as reported in the media after ASIC provided guidance as to how to interpret s923A and the use of these terms has demonstrated further work is necessary to distinguish *independent* from conflicted advisers.

Researchers should examine topics concerning adviser concerns and unresolved issues raised regarding a new licensing regime. For example, the practical applicaton of individual licensing caused unease among many in favour of individual licensing. Specifically, more light should be shed on the actual social and opportunity costs of changing to professional individual licensing systems, the impact on ongoing compliance costs and perceived loss of subsidised support services, notwithstanding the impact on established business models within the advisory sector. For example, the exact cost breakdown of providing subsidised support services per adviser in conjunction with a breakdown of the size of the subsidy licensees offered should be empirically verified and validated.

For some stakeholders, redundancy and changes to business models is surmised an inevitable outcome if financial planning is to become a true profession via an individual licensing. Further research can be conducted to determine the level of disruption to the various Financial Services stakeholders to come up with solutions to mitigate these.

The lack of consensus on some of the other concerns and unresolved issues raised during this research, such as disclosures, APLs, BOLR agreements and economies of scale of current licensing versus professional individual licensing demands further investigation.

Additionally, inquiries into the extent to which licensees may be contributing to the illegitimacy at a micro level would add a richer understanding of the problems confronting current licensing.

Notwithstanding, examining the benefits and costs AFSL licensees derived from appointing, supervising and overseeing advisers, in more depth, will make for fascinating findings.

If recommending evolving or superseding FASEA to set and enforce professional education and ethics standards, while licensing advisers individually, then future work should involve empirical verification of its legitimacy to ensure it is and continues to be fit for purpose.

The illegitimacy findings and support for individual licensing affects the current and future role, including the performance of advisers, and other financial services stakeholders. Thus, a worthwhile piece of research would be an examination of their current role and performance, as well as their expected future role and performance of these stakeholders if individual licensing develops. This research could potentially provide valuable insights into how best to implement change given the practical implementation concerns of a new licensing regime.

Financial planning academic scholars have overlooked risks associated with a specific licensing regime. Therefore, additional inquiry into the key risks stakeholders faced will further illuminate the strengths and weaknesses of each licensing model considered.

Furthermore, information technology advances and online information technology solutions could be of value during the implementation of disconnecting advisers from licensees and the ongoing management of individual licensing via their professional body. This is another avenue of research important to the future of adviser licensing.

Outside the scope of this study, numerous respondents blamed industry super fund licensees to have a conflict of interest from association. This is interesting, given industry superannuation funds allegedly serve to benefit their members, including ploughing any profit the fund earns back to their members. Therefore, the extent to which industry super fund advisers face a conflict of interest from association and whether it is a problem, could address these unconfirmed claims.

Future researchers are encouraged to use, adapt or modify the conceptualised framework of this research to study other complex business-related problems within other disciplines. Additionally, this includes replicating this research to confirm the findings; converting it into a longitudinal study to see how perceptions of survey participants change over time; or even applying the model within the context of other nations' jurisdictions, such as the US and the UK.

Although various researchers (see Suchman 1995; Zimmerman & Zeitz 2002) offered a selection of legitimation strategies for responding to a legitimacy crisis (Tilling 2004b; Chelli, Durocher & Richard 2014), these strategies were excluded from this study to be addressed in future research.

To present a more detailed account of this topic, perhaps future research could use other types of research paradigms and methodologies, which are yet to be applied, tried or tested, and reported in Australian financial planning literature. In this way, to fill other gaps in the study of the licensing of individual advisers or to further enhance the conceptualised model developed, and hence the survey questionnaire. Thereby, this should enrich the theory of this infant, emerging, financial planning academic discipline further, especially given this is a preliminary inquiry, viewed from a macro- or strategic level, rather than at micro-level of detail.

Given the qualitative evidence played a minor role, as well as how sensitive, if not emotional, about the topic informants were during this investigation, there is room for more extensive qualitative research incorporating all stakeholders' views on the numerous issues raised here superficially.

The recommendations provided in the foregoing are a few preliminary reflections of the void in the theory and empirical research. From the discussion, it is clear the surface of the underlying issues around licensing individual advisers has barely been touched. Further room to research this complex phenomenon with research teams comprising financial advisory services stakeholders from various disciplines and academic and private sector institutions to advance financial planning theory and practice is evident.

Contributions

With current licensing clearly verified by the internal actors as illegitimate, this proof in turn has led to significant contributions to the financial planning discipline.

Theoretical contributions

Financial planning theory building is in its infancy, with this work addressing an issue where no prior theory or research evidence was available. By relying on the experience of the researcher, literature review of multiple disciplines and innovative thinking to develop the framework for this study, the work may be considered ground-breaking. It is ground-breaking in the sense it builds new financial planning theory by developing a model on the back of several theories sourced from other disciplines, specifically law, accounting, medicine and management.

The critical theoretical analysis, extension and application of agency theory, legislation, legitimacy theory by Suchman (1995, p. 574) and expected standards of accredited true professionals are important theoretical contributions to empirically evaluate and verify the legitimacy of current licensing of individual advisers. The framework provided an opportunity to develop a standard instrument for future empirical analysis using dimensions such as regulative, consequential, structural, procedural, personal and cultural-cognitive as criteria to capture the perceptions of ARs regarding the desirability, propriety or appropriateness of current AR licensing.

This enquiry also considered an alternative solution, namely individual licensing. Providing a preliminary theoretical foundation to not only assess the problem of the legitimacy of any licensing where the source of its legitimacy is dependent on public trust and confidence, independence, conflicts of interest and a licensing body, but also address possible solutions. The application of several theories to the main research problem advances financial planning theory, while providing a scholarly platform for future empirical research to address complex problems in other social science disciplines.

Entering unchartered areas within a financial planning context added to the established financial planning body of knowledge with theory to guide future policy on suitable financial planning policies, procedures and practices. This project provides extensive scope to pursue additional valuable research in the field of financial planning, specifically matters relating to professionalising advisers.

Empirical contributions

The empirical contributions are twofold. First, this research has advanced application of research methodology for the social science financial planning discipline. Second, it has contributed to bringing together theory, application of research methodology and practice in a novel way. These two contributions will be discussed next.

Research design application

A fresh approach to financial planning research involved starting with simplifying the complex problem by formulating a series of linked questions to develop the hypotheses. Then these questions and hypotheses were conceptualised into an *a priori* measurement construct. After deciding on the sampling technique, the legitimacy was evaluated from a specific research paradigm and methods approach leading to SEM technique application unseen in financial planning research before. Thus, notable contributions of this enquiry to the financial planning discipline are (1) the novel integration of several theories to formulate linked investigative research questions and hypotheses, (2) application of post-positivist research paradigm and mixed methodology involving parallel convergent research design and (3) combining SEM [quantitative] with constant comparative [qualitative] techniques to generate the findings. In other words, for the first time in financial planning research, the definition, modelling and quantification of a complex problem was reflected in a different research design compared with other studies. In the process, a new body of knowledge with regard to application of quantitative research methodology and methods for financial planning to solve difficult, yet politically, legally and socially important problems, was produced.

New to the Australian academic financial planning discipline is the manner in which the researcher collected data, developed and evaluated their measures and analysed them. By new contributions to the collection of data, this project moved financial planning away from convenience sampling to stratified probability random sampling. Furthermore, the traditional data collection approach commonly used in financial planning research and SEM surveys have been Likert scales. However, on the basis of compelling evidence provided by Yusoff and Mohd Janor (2012), the Likert scales were replaced with a new continuous RO scale customised for purposes of this study.

Financial services industry practice

A major contribution to practice is replacing the myths and hearsay with substantiated evidence on the difficult topic of licensing. It serves as the beginning of a more balanced empirically verified and validated view on the matter, rather than in the past, a discussion based on harmful unconfirmed proclamations. Although the study did not cover every aspect of licensing because of its complexity, it does provide a solid foundation to pursue additional topics surrounding the matter. This research and Royal Commission stimulated debate on this political subject from a more scholarly perspective. Examining licensing scientifically aims to remove emotion out of the debate. A specific contribution of this enquiry was to offer a scholarly 'voice' to advisers about issues affecting them, namely their dual-agency role, conflict of interest from association, the objectives of the Act, AFSL-AR licensing, public trust and confidence, independence and professional individual licensing. The media interest highlights the value to researchers to take on more challenging topics. Most important, this research serves to help navigate areas of argument around licensing with a framework politicians, academics and practitioners can use as a guide to ask additional questions around some of the difficult political and practical financial planning topics needing answers. Thus, providing policymakers evidence to make better decisions on contentious issues such as licensing individual advisers as true professionals.

Assumptions and limitations

Despite designing the study at each stage to produce valid results to report and describe the extent of the legitimacy of current licensing, several limitations became evident during theory development and the empirical phase, which influenced the project on several fronts.

Assumptions

This research is grounded on the assumption, if advisers are to become an accredited recognised profession, then they should be structurally licensed in a similar manner to other professions. This means advisers must comply with the same standards and be subject to the same rules as other accredited professions.

Although examples of professions referred to were limited to law, accounting and medicine, it does not preclude the other numerous accredited professions and professional bodies.

This study assumed the sample and the population distributions have the same shape and meaning. The enquiry's findings are conditional on the assumption the bootstrap sampling distribution sourced from the sample is representative of the population, despite the multivariate non-normal data.

Theoretical and empirical limitations

A limitation of this research is applying the Act, agency theory, with legitimacy theory to financial planning theory for the first time, which may have resulted in the exclusion of many other relevant theories and variables. However, including all relevant variables or theories would have made the scope of this already complex and difficult study too large to simplify into one study.

Although most indicators in the model displayed acceptable reliability, three variables and their hypotheses were abandoned during the E/CFA analysis process. This ensured the model makes theoretical sense, was parsimonious and fit the data adequately for reliable interpretation.

The theoretical construct evaluated legitimacy from a macro-level or strategic level, rather than from a narrowly focussed micro-level of evaluation. Hence, the legitimacy criteria are not all inclusive, which Zimmerman and Zeitz (2002) advised is typical in research. Legitimacy criteria could be applied only at a superficial level given the complexity of conflict of interest. Thus, more in-depth analysis of the topic is required. Nonetheless, this project was merely a starting point to explore further the problems and solutions around conflict of interest from association.

Without enough peer-reviewed financial planning literature supported by sound definitions, principles, models, norms and decision rubrics (Paulo 2003), it was difficult to find and present a balanced view. Therefore, this research was limited to the negative unsupported arguments in the media and the limited financial planning scholarly secondary sources.

Not all agency relationships within the context of licensing of individual advisers were included to narrow the scope of the study. Although these agencies are outside the scope of the study, it is acknowledged they may have indirect influences on the licensee–adviser–client relationship and hence AFSL-AR licensing.

Although industry superannuation funds, such Australian Super, HESTA, Cbus *etc.*, may be important, they were excluded from this study, because trade unions and industry bodies with a not-for-profit motive originally started them, where any profits are returned to their members. The project was scoped to include profit-motivated institutions who serve shareholders' interests only.

Conclusion

Financial Services continues to be scrutinised for the ongoing contraventions of legislation implemented to protect the public. Specifically, serious violations of the Act by AFS licensees and their advisers remains in the spotlight. In this damaging environment, the legitimacy of current AFSL-AR licensing is questioned. Until this enquiry, no academic has attempted to evaluate the legitimacy of existing licensee–adviser licensing, because seemingly the conceptual construct was difficult to define and quantify. Therefore, the rectification of this difficulty involved critically integrating financial planning theory with several other theories forming a normative foundation to examine the legitimacy [or what was found to be the illegitimacy] of prevailing licensing.

Utilising this model, results revealed advisers do presume licensing advisers via product aligned, commercially oriented institutions, which creates a dual-agency role between licensee–adviser–client. This produces conflict of interest from association. Since the implementation of advisers' best interest duty, conflict of interest from association can no longer be tolerated. Results revealed licensing advisers via multiple third parties is inconsistent with four objectives of the Act. Specifically, the top three issues delegitimising licensing, in order of rank, are (1) contraventions of the legislated best interest duty to clients, (2) misalignment of the interests of adviser–client and (3) the commercial interests of AFS licensees compromises the best interest duty to clients. Clearly, on the available evidence presented, the current licensing does not result, in order of rank, in consequential moral, procedural moral, regulative, structural moral, personal moral and culture-cognitive legitimacy. Accordingly, arguments for individual licensing via a single body was strengthened by the adviser support for such a solution observed in the findings.

It is recommended FASEA or some other regulatory body should be tasked with more than just professional standards, education and ethics. FASEA or a single disciplinary body should evolve or be superseded to appoint, register, regulate, discipline and cease individual advisers to practice their craft like true accredited professionals operating within a recognised profession. Yet, before launching into any new regime, it is imperative further research must be conducted to address the perceived challenges detected in this study around implementing individual licensing. Additionally, illegitimacy puts the identity, role and performance of all stakeholders on notice. Therefore, this study holds implications for all Australian stakeholders within the advisory sector, not to downplay the importance of the findings for the international financial advisory sector.

Although the conclusions can be challenged, they are compelling and timely. Notwithstanding, important for the advice sector for several obvious reasons. Extending several theories for the first time, provides (1) a more balanced view on a controversial topic, (2) the foundation to advance financial planning research by closing a void, (3) policymakers domestically and internationally with credible evidence to make evidence-based policy decisions around licensing advisers and (4) a scholarly platform to raise additional questions for future empirical research. Therefore, with a shared sense of purpose, on the basis of the findings, all stakeholders need to work together collaboratively to overcome their differences. With the resolve not only to restore trust and confidence in advisers, while boosting growth in the numbers of *independent* advisers by encouraging graduates to pursue a professional career in financial planning, but also to find more fitting solutions to protect the public. Thus, this research and its international implications potentially puts Australia at the international forefront of licensing advisers professionally, like other professions.

Note

1 Recall from Chapter 3 some aligned institutions restrict adviser ownership of the clients introduced to the licensee by, for example, offering buyer of last resort (BOLR) terms (*Independent* Financial Adviser News 2016c). These agreements require self-employed advisers to leave the clients with the licensee when they

transfer to another licensee. The abandoned licensee purchases the clients they 'own' indirectly, from the adviser leaving, on the basis of some formula or multiple of revenue specified in the BOLR agreement. Unless, of course the leaving adviser sells these clients to an authorised representative who is already authorised or approved by the abandoned licensee. BOLR is also being used to purchase clients within networks to pass onto the younger up-and-coming 'authorised representatives' of the product-aligned licensee when advisers retire (Pokrajac 2013).

Bibliography

Abernethy, M.A. & Wai Fong, C. 1996, 'A field study of control system "Redesign": The impact of institutional processes on strategic choice', *Contemporary Accounting Research*, vol. 13, no. 2, pp. 569–606.

Accounting Professional & Ethical Standards Board Limited. 2011, *APES 110 Code of Ethics for Professional Accountants*, 28 January 2012, Accounting Professional and Ethical Standards Board, viewed December 2011, <www.apesb.org.au/uploads/revised-apes-110-dec-2010/apes-110-code-of-ethics-for-professional-accountants-december-2010-final.pdf>.

Accounting Professional & Ethical Standards Board Limited. 2012, *Proposed Standard: APES 230 Financial Planning Services*, Accounting Professional & Ethical Standards Board Limited, viewed 31 May 2016, <www.cpaaustralia.com.au/~/media/corporate/allfiles/document/professional-resources/financial-planning/submission-apes-230-cpa-icaa.pdf?la=en>.

Accounting Professional & Ethical Standards Board Limited. 2013, *APES 230 Financial planning services*, 1, Accounting Professional & Ethical Standards Board Limited, viewed April 2013, <http://apesb.org.au/download.php?codeP=221>.

Adams, M.A. 2002, 'Financial sector reform and professional advice', *Commercial Law Quarterly*, vol. 16, no. 3, pp. 20–26.

Adamson, C. 2012, 'Regulating in a new era of professionalism: What does the FSA want to see from the industry?', paper presented to Financial Services Authority (FSA) to the Marketforce and the Institute of Economic Affair's (IEA) 15th Annual Conference, 14 June, viewed 15 February 2016, <www.fsa.gov.uk/library/communication/speeches/2012/0614-ca.shtml>.

Aguinis, H. & Edwards, J.R. 2014, 'Methodological wishes for the next decade and how to make wishes come true', *Journal of Management Studies*, vol. 51, no. 1, pp. 143–174.

Aguinis, H., Gottfredson, R.K. & Joo, H. 2013, 'Best-practice recommendations for defining, identifying, and handling outliers', *Organizational Research Methods*, vol. 16, no. 2, pp. 270–301.

Akbulut, Y. 2015, 'Predictors of inconsistent responding in web surveys', *Internet Research*, vol. 25, no. 1, pp. 131–147.

Akhtar, J. 2011, 'Determinants of service quality and their relationship with behavioural outcomes: Empirical study of the private commercial banks in Bangladesh', *International Journal of Business & Management*, vol. 6, no. 11, pp. 146–156.

Al-Debei, M.M., Akroush, M.N. & Ashouri, M.I. 2015, 'Consumer attitudes towards online shopping', *Internet Research*, vol. 25, no. 5, pp. 707–733.

Al-Dossary, S. 2008, A study of the factors affecting student retention at King Saud University, Saudi Arabia: Structural equation modelling and qualitative methods, thesis, University of Stirling, edsble database, <http://ezproxy.cqu.edu.au/login?url=http://search.ebscohost.com/login.aspx?direct=true&db=edsble&AN=ethos.015923966&site=eds-live&scope=site>.

Al Qeisi, K. & Al Zagheer, H. 2015, 'Determinants of knowledge sharing behaviour among personnel in banking industry', *International Journal of Business and Management*, vol. 10, no. 4, pp. 49–59.

Al-Shirawi, A., El-Hajjar, S. & Charles, D. 2014, 'An empirical study to develop a structural equation model showing the impact level of market orientation among the financial services providers in a resource-based economy', *International Journal of Innovation and Knowledge Management in Middle East & North Africa*, vol. 3, no. 3/4, pp. 227–258.

Alexander, S. 2011, 'Surviving and thriving on change regulatory reform: The future of financial advice', *Journal of the Australian & New Zealand Institute of Insurance & Finance*, vol. 34, no. 4, pp. 12–14.

Aliyu Ahmad, A., Muhammad Umar, B., Rozilah, K. & David, M. 2014, 'Positivist and non-positivist paradigm in social science research: Conflicting paradigms or perfect partners?', *Journal of Management and Sustainability*, vol. 4, no. 3.

Anderson, J.C. & Gerbing, D.W. 1988, 'Structural equation modeling in practice: A review and recommended two-step approach', *Psychological Bulletin*, vol. 103, no. 3, pp. 411–423.

Andon, P., Free, C. & Sivabalan, P. 2014, 'The legitimacy of new assurance providers: Making the cap fit', *Accounting, Organizations and Society*, vol. 39, no. 2, pp. 79–96.

Angel, J. & McCabe, D. 2013, 'Ethical standards for stockbrokers: Fiduciary or suitability?', *Journal of Business Ethics*, vol. 115, no. 1, pp. 183–193.

Anonymous. 2011, 'Regulation: RDR around the world', *Anonymous*, p. 38.

Ap, M. 2011, 'The future of financial advice reforms: Restoring public trust and confidence in financial advisers – an unfinished puzzle', *Canberra Law Review*, vol. 10, no. 3, p. 188.

Aras, G. & Crowther, D. 2011, *Governance and social responsibility: International perspectives/Güler Aras and David Crowther*, Palgrave Macmillan, Houndmills, Basingstoke; New York, 2012, cat00311a database, <http://ezproxy.cqu.edu.au/login?url=http://search.ebscohost.com/logsin.aspx?direct=true&db=cat00311a&AN=cqu.900811&site=eds-live&scope=site>.

Arbuckle, J. L. (1997). *AMOS user's guide version 3.6*, SmallWaters Corporation, Chicago, Illinois as per AU note 4.

Arbuckle, J.L. 2014, *IBM SPSS Amos™ 23 user's guide*, IBM Corporation, viewed 29 August 2015, <ftp://public.dhe.ibm.com/software/analytics/spss/documentation/amos/23.0/en/Manuals/IBM_SPSS_Amos_User_Guide.pdf>.

Arghode, V. 2012, 'Qualitative and quantitative research: Paradigmatic differences', *Global Education Journal*, vol. 2012, no. 4, pp. 155–163.

Argyrous, G. 2011, *Statistics for research: With a guide to SPSS*, 3rd edn, Sage, Los Angeles, cat00311a database, <http://ezproxy.cqu.edu.au/login?url=http://search.ebscohost.com/login.aspx?direct=true&db=cat00311a&AN=cqu.885706&site=eds-live&scope=site>.

Ariely, D., Amir, O. & Lobel, O. 2008, 'Predictably irrational: The hidden rocks that shape our decisions', *Columbia Law Review*, vol. 108, pp. 2098–2099.

Arman, J. & Shackman, J. 2012, 'The impact of financial planning designations on financial planner income', *The Service Industries Journal*, vol. 32, no. 7–8, pp. 1393–1409.

Arnold, A.J. & McCartney, S. 2008, 'The transition to financial capitalism and its implications for financial reporting: Evidence from the English canal companies', *Accounting, Auditing & Accountability Journal*, vol. 21, no. 8, pp. 1185–1209.

Arteta, S. 2016, 'How to become a lawyer in Australia?', The Law Dictionary, viewed 13 March 2016, <http://thelawdictionary.org/article/how-do-you-become-a-lawyer-in-australia/>.

Arthurs, J.D. & Busenitz, L.W. 2003, 'The boundaries and limitations of agency theory and stewardship theory in the venture capitalist/entrepreneur relationship', *Entrepreneurship: Theory and Practice*, vol. 28, no. 2.

Aschkenasy, J. 2009, 'Seeking independence: Is now the time to move to an *independent* business model?', *Journal of Financial Planning*, pp. 6–7.

Atkin, B., Toberman, A., Wintersgill, D. & Wood, A. 2013, *RDR adviser population and professionalism research – 2012 survey*, viewed 25 August 2017, <www.fca.org.uk/publication/research/rdr-survey-2012-rs-consulting.pdf>.

Australian Bankers' Association Inc. 2014, *Submission to the financial systems inquiry _first submission*, viewed 5 July 2016, <http://fsi.gov.au/files/2014/04/ABA_1.pdf>.

Australian Banking & Finance. 1999, 'The changing shape of the Australian financial system', *Australian Banking and Finance*, vol. 8, no. 12, pp. 12–20.

Australian Bar Association. 2016, 'Australian Bar Association', viewed 13 March 2016, <www.austbar.asn.au/>.

Australian Government. 2016, 'ASIC – Australian financial services authorised representative dataset', viewed 2 April 2016, <www.data.gov.au/dataset/asic-afs-authorised-representative>.

Australian Government Corporations and Markets Advisory Committee. 2012, *Managed Investment Schemes*, viewed 18 July 2016, <www.camac.gov.au/camac/camac.nsf/byheadline/pdffinal+reports+2012/$file/mis_report_july2012.pdf>.

Australian Government The Treasury. 2014, *Details-stage regulation impact statement. Future of Financial Advice Amendments*, viewed 8 March 2015, <https://ris.govspace.gov.au/files/2014/03/03Final_details_stage_RIS1.pdf>.

Australian Government The Treasury. 2016, *Turnbull Government bolsters ASIC to protect Australian consumers*, Australian Government The Treasury, viewed 20 April 2016, <http://sjm.ministers.treasury.gov.au/media-release/042-2016/>.

Australian Government Treasury. 2009, *Inquiry into financial products and services in Australia*, Senate Printing Unit, Parliament House, Canberra.

Australian Medical Association (AMA). 2009, 'Good medical practice: A code conduct for doctors in Australia', *Australian Medical Council*, viewed 28 November 2012, <www.health.nt.gov.au/library/scripts/objectifyMedia.aspx?file=pdf/39/02.pdf>.

Australian Securities and Investments Commission. 2003, 'Survey on the quality of financial planning advice', *ASIC*, viewed 1 August 2013, <http://download.asic.gov.au/media/1310341/Advice_Report.pdf>.

Australian Securities and Investments Commission. 2004, *Report 30: Disclosure of soft dollar benefits*, viewed 27 September 2017, <http://download.asic.gov.au/media/2243023/rep30-published-june-2004.pdf>.

Australian Securities and Investments Commission. 2006, *Report 69: Shadow shopping survey on superannuation advice*, viewed 1 August 2013, <http://download.asic.gov.au/media/1347026/shadow_shop_report_2006.pdf>.

Australian Securities and Investments Commission (ASIC). 2007, *Regulatory Guide 104 Licensing: Meeting the general obligations*, viewed 1 August 2013, <https://download.asic.gov.au/media/3278615/rg104-published-1-july-2015.pdf>.

Australian Securities and Investments Commission. 2009, *Regulatory Guide 200: Advice to super fund members*, viewed 1 Augsut 2013, <https://asic.gov.au/regulatory-resources/find-a-document/regulatory-guides/rg-200-advice-to-super-fund-members/>.

Australian Securities and Investments Commission. 2010a, 'Access to financial advice in Australia', viewed 3 June 2014, <www.asic.gov.au/asic/pdflib.nsf/LookupByFilNane/rep223.pdf/$file/rep224.pdf>.

Australian Securities and Investments Commission. 2010b, *Access to financial advice in Australia*, viewed 8 March 2016, <http://download.asic.gov.au/media/1845586/rep407-published-17-september-2014.pdf>.

Australian Securities and Investments Commission. 2011, *Report 251: Review of financial advice industry practice report*, ASaI Commission, Canberra, viewed 6 July 2016, <http://download.asic.gov.au/media/1343702/rep251-published-13-September-2011.pdf>.

Australian Securities and Investments Commission. 2012a, *Regulation Impact Statement: Future of Financial Advice: Best interests duty and related obligations*, viewed 7 May 2014, <http://download.asic.gov.au/media/2125918/rg175-ris.pdf>.

Regulatory Guide 244: Giving information, general advice and scaled advice. 2012b.

Australian Securities and Investments Commission. 2012c, *Report 279: Shadow shopping study of retirement advice*, <www.asic.gov.au/asic/pdflib.nsf/LookupByFileName/rep279-published-27-March-2012.pdf/$file/rep279-published-27-March-2012.pdf>.

Australian Securities and Investments Commission. 2013a, *Regulation impact statement: Future of financial advice: Best interests duty and related obligations*, viewed 19 March 2014, <www.asic.gov.au/asic/pdflib.nsf/LookupByFileName/RIS%20-%20FOFA%20-%20Best%20Interests%20Duty%20and%20Related%20Obligations.pdf/$file/RIS%20-%20FOFA%20-%20Best%20Interests%20Duty%20and%20Related%20Obligations.pdf>.

Regulatory Guide 246: Conflicted remuneration. 2013b.

Australian Securities and Investments Commission. 2013c, *Review of financial advice industry practice: Phase 2, Report*, viewed 6 July 2016, <https://dv8nx270cl59a.cloudfront.net/media/1344368/rep362-published-31-July-2013.pdf>.

Australian Securities and Investments Commission. 2013d, *Senate inquiry into the performance of the Australian securities and investments commission*, viewed 10 February 2015, <www.abc.net.au/4corners/documents/2014/BANKING/ASIC_Submission_Senate_Inquiry.pdf>.

Australian Securities and Investments Commission. 2014a, 'About FSR', viewed 30 May 2014, <www.asic.gov.au/asic/asic.nsf/byheadline/About+FSR>.

Australian Securities and Investments Commission. 2014b, 'Accountants and financial advice', viewed 27 May 2014, <www.asic.gov.au/asic/ASIC.NSF/byHeadline/Removal%20of%20accountants%20exemption>.

Australian Securities and Investments Commission. 2014c, 'FOFA- background and implementation', viewed 27 May 2014, <www.asic.gov.au/asic/ASIC.NSF/byHeadline/FOFA%20-%20Background%20and%20implementation>.

Australian Securities and Investments Commission. 2014d, 'FOFA – ASIC guidance', viewed 27 May 2014, <www.asic.gov.au/asic/ASIC.NSF/byHeadline/FOFA%20%20-%20Consultation%20and%20guidance>.

Australian Securities and Investments Commission. 2014e, 'Future of financial advice', viewed 19 March 2014, <www.asic.gov.au/asic/ASIC.NSF/byHeadline/Future%20of%20financial%20advice>.

Australian Securities and Investments Commission. 2014f, *Report 407: Review of the financial advice industry's implementation of the FOFA reforms*, viewed 8 March 2016, <http://download.asic.gov.au/media/1845586/rep407-published-17-september-2014.pdf>.

Australian Securities and Investments Commission. 2016a, *16–004MR ASIC bans former ANZ bank adviser for ten years*, Australia Securities and Investments Commission, Canberra, 14 January 2016, <http://asic.gov.au/about-asic/media-centre/find-a-media-release/2016-releases/16-004mr-asic-bans-former-anz-bank-adviser-for-ten-years/>.

Australian Securities and Investments Commission. 2016b, *16–343MR Findex Group Limited and Financial Index Australia Pty Ltd pay $21,600 in penalties*, Australian Securities and Investments Commission, 10 October 2016, <www.asic.gov.au/about-asic/media-centre/find-a-media-release/2016-releases/16-343mr-findex-group-limited-and-financial-index-australia-pty-ltd-pay-21–600-in-penalties/>.

Australian Securities and Investments Commission. 2016c, *16–460MR ASIC takes action against Westpac entities in relation to the 'best interests duty' and superannuation customers*, Australian Securities and Investments Commission, 22 December 2016, <http://asic.gov.au/about-asic/media-centre/find-a-media-release/2016-releases/16-460mr-asic-takes-action-against-westpac-entities-in-relation-to-the-best-interests-duty-and-superannuation-customers/>.

Australian Securities and Investments Commission. 2016d, 'ASIC licensing kit', viewed 19 August 2016, <http://asic.gov.au/for-finance-professionals/afs-licensees/applying-for-and-managing-an-afs-licence/afs-licensing-kit/>.

Australian Securities and Investments Commission. 2016e, *ASIC targets financial services licensees using the term "independent"*, Australian Securities and Investments Commission, Wednesday, 2 March 2016, <http://asic.gov.au/about-asic/media-centre/find-a-media-release/2016-releases/16-056mr-asic-targets-financial-services-licensees-using-the-term-*independent*/>.

Australian Securities and Investments Commission. 2016f, 'Financial Adviser Register', viewed 4 March 2016, <http://asic.gov.au/for-finance-professionals/afs-licensees/financial-advisers-register/>.

Australian Securities and Investments Commission. 2016g, 'FOFA – background and implementation', Australian Securities and Investments Commission, viewed 8 March 2016, <http://asic.gov.au/regulatory-resources/financial-services/future-of-financial-advice-reforms/fofa-background-and-implementation/>.

Regulatory guide 181. Licensing: Managing conflicts of interest. Chapter 7 – financial services and markets. 2016h.

Australian Securities and Investments Commission. 2016i, *Report 474: Culture, conduct and conflicts of interest in vertically integrated businesses in the funds-management industry*, viewed 21 March 2016, <http://download.asic.gov.au/media/3583028/rep474-published-21-march-2016.pdf>.

Australian Securities and Investments Commission. 2016j, *Report 478: Overview of licensing and professional registration applications: July to December 2015*, pp. 1–55, viewed 3 June 2016, <http://download.asic.gov.au/media/3875857/rep478-published-31-may-2016.pdf>.

Australian Securities and Investments Commission. 2016k, *RG 105 Licensing: Organisational competence*, viewed 12 December 2017, <www.asic.gov.au/regulatory-resources/find-a-document/regulatory-guides/rg-105-licensing-organisational-competence/>.

Australian Securities and Investments Commission. 2017a, *17–206MR ASIC clarifies its position on the use of 'independently owned' under s923A*, 27 June 2017, viewed 27 June, <http://asic.gov.au/about-asic/media-centre/find-a-media-release/2017-releases/17-206mr-asic-clarifies-its-position-on-the-use-of-*independent*ly-owned-under-s923a/>.

Australian Securities and Investments Commission. 2017b, *17–206MR ASIC clarifies its position on the use of 'independently owned' under s923A*, 27 June 2017, <www.asic.gov.au/about-asic/media-centre/find-a-media-release/2017-releases/17-206mr-asic-clarifies-its-position-on-the-use-of-*independent*ly-owned-under-s923a/>.

Australian Securities and Investments Commission. 2017c, *17–229MR NAB makes corrective disclosure to customers about relationships within its wealth management business*, 7 July, <http://asic.gov.au/about-asic/media-centre/find-a-media-release/2017-releases/17-229mr-nab-makes-corrective-disclosure-to-customers-about-relationships-within-its-wealth-management-business/>.

Australian Securities and Investments Commission. 2017d, *Regulatory guide 175 licensing: Financial product advisers-Conduct and disclosure*, viewed 22 September 2017, <http://download.asic.gov.au/media/4191992/rg175-published-22-march-2017.pdf>.

Australian Securities and Investments Commission. 2017e, *Report 515: Financial advice: Review of how large institutions oversee their advisers*, viewed 29 March 2017, <http://download.asic.gov.au/media/4186280/rep515-published-17-march-2017.pdf>.

Awasthi, P. & Sangle, P. 2013, 'The importance of value and context for mobile CRM services in banking', *Business Process Management Journal*, vol. 19, no. 6, pp. 864–891.

Bacon, L.D. 1997, 'Using Amos for structural equation modelling in market research', viewed 21 July 2017, < https://www.researchgate.net/publication/237658357_Using_Amos_for_Structural_Equation_Modeling_in_Market_Research>.

Bagozzi, R.P. 2007, 'On the meaning of formative measurement and how it differs from reflective measurement: Comment on Howell, Breivik, and Wilcox (2007)', *Psychological Methods*, vol. 12, no. 2, pp. 229–237.

Bailey, K. 2000, 'Financial planning costs in spotlight', *Herald Sun*, 11 November 2000, p. 91, viewed 20 March 2014, n5h database, <http://ezproxy.cqu.edu.au/login?url=http://search.ebscohost.com/login.aspx?direct=true&db=n5h&AN=200011110911860798&site=ehost-live>.

Baily, M.N., Klein, A. & Schardin, J. 2017, 'The impact of the Dodd-Frank Act on financial stability and economic growth', *RSF: The Russell Sage Foundation Journal of the Social Sciences*, vol. 3, no. 1, pp. 20–47.

Bakir, C. 2003, 'Who needs a review of the financial system in Australia? The case of the Wallis inquiry', *Australian Journal of Political Science*, vol. 38, no. 3, pp. 511–534.

Balasubramnian, B., Brisker, E. & Gradisher, S. 2014, 'Financial adviser background checks', *Financial Services Review*, vol. 23, no. 4, pp. 305–324.

Bamber, M.E. & Iyer, V.M. 2002, 'Big 5 auditors' professional and organizational identification: Consistency or conflict?', *Auditing: A Journal of Practice & Theory*, vol. 21, no. 2, p. 21.

Banister, P.M. 2016, *Australian financial planning handbook 2016–17*, Thomson Reuters, Pyrmont, NSW.

Banister, P.M., Campbell, J., Davies, B.K., Day, J.K., Fenton, N., Fitton, G.D., Flack, G.R., Graham, S.D., Hayes, T.P., Jones, S.C., Kiddell, R.J.A., Pepper, T. & Prestney, S.J. 2013, *Australian Financial Planning Handbook 2012–2013*, Thomson Reuters Australia, Sydney.

Baran, M. & Jones, J. 2016, *Mixed methods research for improved scientific study*, Information Science Reference, an imprint of IGI Global, Hershey, PA.

Baris, J. & Cohn, H. 2012, 'How broker-dealer standards will change', *International Financial Law Review*, vol. 31, no. 5, p. 63.

Barrett, P. 2007, 'Structural equation modelling: Adjudging model fit', *Personality and Individual Differences*, vol. 42, no. 5, pp. 815–824.

Bateman, H. & Kingston, G. 2012, 'The future of financial advice and mySuper', *JASSA: The Finsia Journal of Applied Finance*, vol. 3, pp. 49–53.

Bateman, H. & Kingston, G. 2014, 'Regulating financial advice: Lessons from the United States, the United Kingdom and Canada', *JASSA: The Finsia Journal of Applied Finance*, vol. 4, pp. 7–13.

Batten, R. & Pearson, G. 2013, 'Financial advice in Australia: Principles to proscription managing to banning', *St. John's Law Review*, vol. 87, no. 2/3, pp. 511–559.

Baum, J.A.C. & Oliver, C. 1991, 'Institutional linkages and organizational mortality', *Administrative Science Quarterly*, vol. 36, no. 2, p. 187.

Beal, D. & McKeown, K. 2009, *Personal finance*, 4th edn, John Wiley & Sons Australia, Camberwell, Victoria.

Beal, D.J. & Dawson, J.F. 2007, 'On the use of Likert-type scales in multilevel data: Influence on aggregate variables', *Organizational Research Methods*, vol. 10, no. 4, p. 20.

Beaman, L. 2010a, 'AIOFP's status questioned', *Money Management*, vol. 24, no. 6.

Beaman, L. 2010b, 'Calls for a unified industry body', *Money Management*, vol. 24, no. 8, pp. 1–3.

Beaman, L. 2010c, '*Independent* advisers go it alone', *Money Management*, viewed 3 November, p. 8, heh database, <http://ezproxy.cqu.edu.au/login?url=http://search.ebscohost.com/login.aspx?direct=true&db=heh&AN=48921002&site=eds-live&scope=site>.

Bearden, F.C. 2002, 'Conflicts of interest in financial planning practice', *Journal of Financial Planning*, vol. 15, no. 2, p. 86.

Bearden, F.C. 2006, 'Curbing conflict', *Financial Planning*, vol. 36, no. 11, pp. 111–112.

Bell, H.F. 1975, 'The securities market – national control or self-regulation?', *Economic Record*, vol. 51, no. 135, p. 372.

Bender, R. 2011, 'Paying for advice: The role of the remuneration consultant in U.K. listed companies', *Vanderbilt Law Review*, vol. 64, no. 2, pp. 361–396.

Bendixen, M. & Yurova, Y. 2011, 'How respondents use verbal and numeric rating scales: A case for rescaling', *International Journal of Market Research*, vol. 54, no. 2.

Bennett, J. 2000, 'Financial planning down under', *Journal of Financial Planning*, vol. 13, no. 7, pp. 114–123.

Bentler, P.M. 2006, 'On tests and indices for evaluating structural models', *Personality and Individual Differences*, vol. 42, no. 2007, pp. 825–829.

Bergen, M., Dutta, S. & Walker Jr, O.C. 1992, 'Agency relationships in marketing: A review of the implications and applications of agency and related', *Journal of Marketing*, vol. 56, no. 3, pp. 1–24.

Bewley, M.D., Dwyen, B., Frueh, R.A., Gruben, J.B., Knight, B., Mettelman, M.C. & Mungenas, M. 2008, 'The CEO challenges of growth: Recruitment, regulation and consolidation in the Indy B-D world. (cover story)', *Journal of Financial Planning*, vol. 21, pp. 8–17.

Bhargava, N. 2009, 'Broker-dealers and investment advisers: The Administration's plans for the future of regulation', *Administrative Law Review*, vol. 61, no. 4, pp. 907–918.

Bhati, S. 2009, 'Competition and consumer regulation for Australian banks', *ICFAI Journal of International Business Law*, vol. 8, no. 3, pp. 53–67.

Bhattacharya, U., Hackethal, A., Kaesler, S., Loos, B. & Meyer, S. 2012, 'Is unbiased financial advice to retail investors sufficient? Answers from a large field study', *The Review of Financial Studies*, vol. 25, no. 4, pp. 975–1032.

Biderman, M.D., Nguyen, N.T., Cunningham, C.J.L. & Ghorbani, N. 2011, 'The ubiquity of common method variance: The case of the Big Five', *Journal of Research in Personality*, vol. 45, no. 5, pp. 417–429.

Bird, H. & Gilligan, G. 2015a, 'Financial services misconduct and the Corporations Act 2001 – paper 2', in Centre for International Finance and Regulation Research Working Paper Series, viewed 7 October 2016, <http://poseidon01.ssrn.com/delivery.php?ID= 394013103113029031121027103122069109050063050068079069007112000009071020107023127009034102098026110059062006088123092002002064045007060077040002019098080114117113070000035046002087003015030000081006084090098123084075028005014070027125031066026021071100&EXT=pdf>.

Bird, H. & Gilligan, G. 2015b, *Research working paper series: Financial services misconduct and the Corporations Act 2001 – paper 2*, viewed 16 August 2018, <https://papers.ssrn.com/sol3/papers.cfm?abstract_id=2656882>.

Bird, H., Gilligan, G., Godwin, A., Hegdges, J. & Ramsay, I. 2016, *Research working paper series: An empirical analysis of enforceable undertakings by the Australian Securities and Investments Commission between 1 July 1998 and 31 December 2015*, viewed 16 August 2018, <https://papers.ssrn.com/sol3/papers.cfm?abstract_id=2766134>.

Bird, H., Gilligan, G. & Ramsay, I. 2016, 'The who, why and what of enforceable undertakings accepted by the Australian Securities and Investments Commission', *Company and Securities Law Journal*, vol. 34, no. 7, pp. 491–517.

Bird, J. 2011, 'Regulating the regulators: Accountability of Australian regulators', *Melbourne University Law Review*, vol. 35, no. 3.

Bitektine, A. 2011, 'Towards a theory of social judgements of organisations: The case of legitimacy, reputation and status', *Academy of Management Review*, vol. 36, no. 1, pp. 151–179.

Black, B. 2005, 'Brokers and advisers – what's in a name?', *Fordham Journal of Corporate & Financial Law*, vol. 11, no. 1, pp. 31–56.

Black, J. 1996, 'Constitutionalising self-regulation', *The Modern Law Review*, vol. 59, no. 1, p. 32.

Black, J. 2012, 'Paradoxes and failures: "New Governance" techniques and the financial crisis', *Modern Law Review*, vol. 75, no. 6, pp. 1037–1063.

Black, K., Asafu-Adjaye, J., Khan, N., Perera, N., Edwards, P. & Harris, M. 2010, *Australasian business statistics.*, 2nd edn, Milton, QLD, John Wiley & Sons, cat00311a database, <http://ezproxy.cqu.edu.au/login?url=http://search.ebscohost.com/login.aspx?direct=true&db=cat00311a&AN=cqu.777611&site=eds-live&scope=site>.

Blunch, N.J. 2008, *Introduction to structural equation modelling using SPSS and AMOS*, Sage, Los Angeles; London.

Bollen, K. & Lennox, R. 1991, 'Conventional wisdom on measurement: A structural equation perspective', *Psychological Bulletin*, vol. 110, no. 2, pp. 305–314.

Bollen, K.A. & Bauldry, S. 2011, 'Three Cs in measurement models: Causal indicators, composite indicators, and covariates', *Psychological Methods*, vol. 16, no. 3, pp. 265–284.

Bollen, K.A. & Noble, M.D. 2011, 'Structural equation models and the quantification of behavior', *Proceedings of the National Academy of Sciences of the United States of America*, vol., pp. 15639–15646.

Bolton, P., Freixas, X. & Shapiro, J. 2007, 'Conflicts of interest, information provision, and competition in the financial services industry', *Journal of Financial Economics*, vol. 85, pp. 297–330.

Boone, N.M. 2000, 'My plumber is a financial planner?', *Journal of Financial Planning*, vol. 13, no. 1, pp. 30–33.

Bora, B. & Lewis, M.K. 1997, 'The Australian financial system: Evolution, regulation, and globalization', *Law and Policy in International Business*, vol. 28, no. 3, pp. 787–811.

Borsboom, D., Mellenbergh, G.J. & Van Heerden, J. 2003, 'The theoretical status of latent variables', *Psychological Review*, vol. 110, no. 2, pp. 203–219.

Boutique Financial Planners. 2014, *Submission to the financial system inquiry*, viewed 3 July 2016, <http://fsi.gov.au/files/2014/08/Boutique_Financial_Planners.pdf>.

Bowen, C., Hon. 2010, *The future of financial advice information pack*, p. 14, viewed 27 May 2014, <http://ministers.treasury.gov.au/Ministers/ceba/Content/pressreleases/2010/attachments/036/Future_of_Financial_Advice_Information_Pack.pdf>.

Boyle, L. 2015, 'An Australian August corpus: Why there is only one common law in Australia', *Bond Law Review*, vol. 27, no. 1, pp. 27–56.

Boynton, J. & Mathieson, M. 2009, 'Radical proposals', *International Financial Law Review*, vol. 28, no. 9, p. 15.

Brammall, D. 2012, 'How to find conflict-free financial advice', The *Independent* Financial Advisers Association of Australia, viewed 24 April 2014, <http://ifaaa.com.au/ifaaa.pdf>.

Brannan, M.J. 2017, 'Power, corruption and lies: Mis-selling and the production of culture in financial services', *Human Relations*, vol. 70, no. 6, pp. 641–667.

Breakey, H. 2017, 'Building ethics regimes: Capabilities, obstacles and supports for professional ethical decision-making', *University of New South Wales Law Journal*, vol. 40, no. 1, pp. 322–352.

Breakey, H. & Sampford, C. 2017, 'Employed professionals & ethical responsibilities in public service and private enterprise: Dilemma, priority and synthesis', *University of New South Wales Law Journal*, vol. 40, no. 1, pp. 262–301.

Brean, D.J.S., Kryzanowski, L. & Roberts, G.S. 2011, 'Canada and the United States: Different roots, different routes to financial sector regulation', *Business History*, vol. 53, no. 2, pp. 249–269.

Brito, C. & Pearl, J. 2002, 'A new identification condition for recursive models with correlated errors', *Structural Equation Modeling: A Multidisciplinary Journal*, vol. 9, no. 4, pp. 459–474.

Brittain, N. 2013, 'So you want to be a planner?', *Professional Adviser*, vol. n/a, p. 21.

Brown, B. 2007, 'Super dupers: Beware of dealers posing as financial advisers', *The Australian*, 16 March, viewed 9 May 2014, <www.strategyfirst.com.au/downloads/media/Australian_Newspaper.pdf>.

Brown, R. 2011, *APESB standard hits the mark*, Sydney.

Brown, R.M.C. 2008, 'Reinventing financial planning', *The Australian Journal of Financial Planning*, vol. 3, no. 1, pp. 17–27.

Brown, T.A. 2003, 'Confirmatory factor analysis of the Penn State Worry Questionnaire: Multiple factors or method effects?', *Behaviour Research and Therapy*, vol. 41, no. 12, pp. 1411–1426.

Brown, T.A. 2006, *Confirmatory factor analysis for applied research*, Guilford Press, New York.

Brown, T.A. & Moore, M.T. 2016, 'Confirmatory factor analysis', *Researchgate*, viewed 28 November 2016, <www.researchgate.net/profile/Michael_Moore8/publication/251573889_Hoyle_CFA_Chapter_-_Final/links/0deec51f14d2070566000000.pdf>.

Bruce, K. 2012, Conceptions of the professionalism of financial planners, PhD thesis, Central Queensland University.

Bruhn, A. & Miller, M. 2014, 'Lessons about best interests duty', *Australasian Accounting Business & Finance Journal*, vol. 8, no. 4, pp. 23–43.

Bulling, J. 2003, 'Financial services reform: The journey so far', *Keeping Good Companies*, vol. 55, no. 11, pp. 669–673.

Burke, J. & Hung, A.A. 2015, *Financial advice markets: A cross-country comparison*, Santa Monica, CA, viewed 7 March 2015, <www.rand.org/content/dam/rand/pubs/research_reports/RR1200/RR1269/RAND_RR1269.pdf>.

Burke, J., Hung, A.A., Clift, J., Garber, S. & Yoong, J.K. 2015, *Impacts of conflicts of interest in the financial services industry*, RAND Labor & Population, <www.rand.org/pubs/working_papers/WR1076.html>.

Byrne, B.M. 2010, *Multivariate applications series. Structural equation modeling with AMOS: Basic concepts, applications, and programming*, 2nd edn, Routledge, New York, NY.

Byrne, B.M. 2013, *Structural Equation Modeling with AMOS*, 2nd edn, Routledge, Moorebank, NSW.

Byrne, B.M., Shavelson, R.J. & Muthen, B. 1989, 'Testing for the equivalence of factor covariance and mean structures: The issue of partial measurement in variance', *Psychological Bulletin*, vol. 105, no. 2, pp. 456–466.

Caginalp, G. & Desantis, M. 2011, 'A paradigm for quantitative behavioral finance', *American behavioral scientist*, vol. 55, no. 8, pp. 1014–1034.

Calcagno, R. & Monticone, C. 2015, 'Financial literacy and the demand for financial advice', *Journal of Banking and Finance*, vol. 50, pp. 363–380.

Campbell, D.T. & Fiske, D.W. 1959, 'Convergent and discriminant validation by the multitrait- multimethod matrix', *Psychological Bulletin*, vol. 56, no. 2, pp. 81–105.

Campbell, J. 2014, 'Legal studies research paper no.14/26: Fiduciary relationships in a commercial context', paper presented to Corporate Law Conference of the Sydney Law School and the Supreme Court of NSW August 2012, Sydney, March, viewed 29 September 2017, <file:///C:/Users/Angelique%20McInnes/Downloads/SSRN-id2404202.pdf>.

Campo, R. 2014, *What is the future of financial advice?*, 19 March, viewed 19 March 2014, <www.industrysuperaustralia.com/what-is-the-future-of-financial-advice>.

Carlin, B.I. & Gervais, S. 2012, 'Legal protection in retail financial markets', *Review of Corporate Finance Studies*, vol. 1, no. 1, pp. 68–108.

Carnegie, G.D. & O'Connell, B.T. 2012, 'Understanding the responses of professional accounting bodies to crises. The case of the Australian profession in the 1960s', *Accounting, Auditing & Accountability Journal*, vol. 25, no. 5, p. 835.

Carnegie, G.D., Edwards, J.R. & West, B.P. 2003, 'Understanding the dynamics of the Australian accounting profession: A prosopographical study of the founding members of the Incorporated Institute of Accountants, Victoria, 1886 to 1908', *Accounting, Auditing & Accountability Journal*, vol. 16, no. 5, p. 790.

Carosa, C. 2012, 'What is a fiduciary (and why should we care)?', *Benefits Selling*, vol. 10, no. 2, p. 50.

Carr, L.T. 1994, 'The strengths and weaknesses of quantitative and qualitative research: What method for nursing?', *Journal of Advanced Nursing*, vol. 20, no. 4, pp. 716–721.

Carroll, P. & McGregor-Lowndes, M. 2001, 'A standard for regulatory compliance? Industry self-regulation, the courts and AS3806–1998', *Australian Journal of Public Administration*, vol. 60, no. 4, p. 80.

Carruthers, B.G. 1995, 'Accounting, ambiguity, and the new institutionalism*', *Accounting, Organizations & Society*, vol. 20, no. 4, pp. 313–328.

Certified Practising Accountants. 2014, *Submission: Financial systems inquiry*, viewed 31 May 2016, <www.cpaaustralia.com.au/~/media/corporate/allfiles/document/professional-resources/financial-planning/financial-system-inquiry-submission.pdf?la=en>.

Certified Practising Accountant. 2016, 'How to become a CPA?', viewed 13 March 2016, <www.cpaaustralia.com.au/>.

Certified Practising Accountants Australia. 2016, *Part 2 – how to select a licence holder key considerations*, viewed 17 July 2016, <www.cpaaustralia.com.au/~/media/corporate/allfiles/document/professional-resources/financial-planning/things-to-consider-when-you-are-choosing-a-licence-holder.pdf>.

Chalmers, K. & Godfrey, J.M. 2004, 'Reputation costs: The impetus for voluntary derivative financial instrument reporting', *Accounting, Organizations and Society*, vol. 29, no. 2, pp. 95–125.

Chan, L. & Bishop, B. 2013, 'A moral basis for recycling: Extending the theory of planned behaviour', *Journal of Environmental Psychology*, vol. 36, pp. 96–102.

Chaplin, D. 2015, 'Why financial planning needs more women', *Financial Review*, 25 February, viewed 22 March 2017, <www.afr.com/brand/asset/why-financial-planning-needs-more-women-20150223-13m784#ixzz4c0yGhaP6 >.

Chaston, I. 2013, '*Independent* financial advisors: Open innovation and business performance', *The Service Industries Journal*, vol. 33, no. 6, pp. 636–651.

Chater, N., Huck, S. & Inderst, R. 2010, *Consumer decision-making in retail investment services: A behavioral economics perspective: Final report*, viewed 30 September 2017, <http://ec.europa.eu/consumers/financial_services/reference_

studies_documents/docs/consumer_decision-making_in_retail_investment_services_-_final_report_en.pdf>.

Cheetham, G. & Chivers, G. 2005, *Professions, competence and informal learning*, Edward Elgar Publishing Inc, Northampton, MA.

Chelli, M., Durocher, S. & Richard, J. 2014, 'France's new economic regulations: Insights from institutional legitimacy theory', *Accounting, Auditing & Accountability Journal*, vol. 27, no. 2, pp. 283–316.

Chen, F., Bollen, K., Paxton, P., Curran, P. & Kirby, J. 2001, 'Improper solutions in structural equation models: Causes, consequences, and strategies', *Sociological Methods and Research*, vol. 29, no. 4, pp. 468–508.

Chen, J.C. & Roberts, R.W. 2010, 'Toward a more coherent understanding of the organization-society relationship: A theoretical consideration for social and environmental accounting research', *Journal of Business Ethics*, vol. 97, no. 4, pp. 651–665.

Chen, W.-L. 2009, 'What is "financial product advice"? Zhang v Minox securities', *Proctor*, vol. 29, no. 9, pp. 47–48.

Chene, D., Gold, J. & Gramlich, J. 2010, 'The scope and practice of comprehensive financial planning: Survey results, current standards, and engagement letter recommendations', *Journal of Financial Service Professionals*, vol. 64, no. 1, pp. 47–59.

Cheung, G.W. & Rensvold, R.B. 2002, 'Evaluating goodness-of- fit indexes for testing measurement invariance', *Structural Equation Modeling: A Multidisciplinary Journal*, vol. 9, no. 2, pp. 233–255.

Cheung, G.W. & Rensvold, R.B. 2009, 'Evaluating goodness-of-fit indexes for testing measurement invariance', *Structural Equation Modeling: A Multidisciplinary Journal*, vol. 9, no. 2, pp. 233–255.

Chiandotto, B. & Masserini, L. 2011, 'A two-level structural equation model for evaluating the external effectiveness of PhD', *Journal of Applied Quantitative Methods*, vol. 6, no. 4, pp. 72–87.

Chin, W.W. 1998, 'Issues and opinion on structural equation modeling', *MIS Quarterly*, vol. 22, p. 1.

Chiu, Y. 2014, Exploratory studies for Gaussian process structural equation models, thesis, University College London.

Choi, S., Ullah, S. & Kwak, W. 2015, 'Ethical leadership and followers' attitudes toward corporate social responsibility: The role of perceived ethical work climate', *Social Behavior and Personality*, vol. 43, no. 3, pp. 353–365.

Chou, C.P., Bentler, P.M. & Satorra, A. 1991, 'Scaled test statistics and robust standard errors for non-normal data in covariance structure analysis: A Monte Carlo study', *The British Journal of Mathematical and Statistical Psychology*, vol. 44, no. 2, pp. 347–357.

Christie, R. 2015, *ABA defends vertical integration*, FINSIA, 20 January 2015.

Chua, F. & Rahman, A. 2011, 'Institutional pressures and ethical reckoning by business corporations', *Journal of Business Ethics*, vol. 98, no. 2, pp. 307–329.

Clare, A., Thomas, S., Walgama, O. & Makris, C. 2013, *The impact of the RDR on the UK's market for financial advice: Challenge and opportunity*, CB School, City University London and BNY Mellon, viewed 11 March 2017, <www.cassknowledge.com/sites/default/files/article-attachments/bny-mellon-rdr-cass-knowledge.pdf>.

Clark, L.A. & Watson, D. 1995, 'Constructing validity: Basic issues in objective scale development', *Psychological Assessment*, vol. 7, no. 3, pp. 309–319.

Clark, V.L. & Creswell, J.W. 2008, *The mixed methods reader*, Sage, Thousand Oaks, CA.

Classen, S, Lopez, E.D.S., Awadzi, K.D. & Garcan, C.W. 2007, 'Population-based health promotion perspective for older driver safety: Conceptual framework to intervention plan', *Clinical Interventions in Aging*, vol. 4, no. 4, pp. 677–693.

Clayton Utz Financial Services Reform Group. 2002, 'Insurance agents: Coping with the transition to the financial services reform', *Australian and New Zealand Institute of Insurance and Finance*, vol. 25, no. 5, pp. 31–34.

Clegg, S. 2010, 'The state, power, and agency: Missing in action in institutional theory?', *Journal of Management Inquiry*, vol. 19, no. 1, pp. 4–13.

Coghill, T. 2013, 'The great independence conundrum . . . part 9, v7', *Professional Adviser*, vol., p. 17.

Cohen, J. 1988, *Statistical power analysis for the behavioral sciences*, 2nd edn, Lawrence Erlbaum Associates, Hillsdale, NJ.

Cole, B.M. & Salimath, M.S. 2013, 'Diversity identity management: An organizational perspective', *Journal of Business Ethics*, vol. 116, no. 1, pp. 151–161.

Cole, D.A., Ciesla, J.A. & Steiger, J.H. 2007a, 'The insidious effects of failing to include design-driven correlated residuals in latent- variable covariance structure analysis', *Psychological Methods*, vol. 12, no. 4, pp. 381–398.

Cole, D.A., Ciesla, J.A. & Steiger, J.H. 2007b, 'The insidious effects of failing to include design-driven correlated residuals in latent-variable covariance structure analysis', *Psychological Methods*, vol. 12, no. 4, pp. 381–398.

Collier, B. 2003, 'The financial planning shadow shopping project – results and moving forwards', paper presented to Australian Investors' Association Annual Conference, 12 June, viewed 1 August 2013, <www.asic.gov.au/asic/pdflib.nsf/LookupByFileName/AIAspeech_120603.pdf/$file/AIAspeech_120603.pdf – 198k – [pdf] – 12 Jun 2013>.

Coltman, T., Devinney, T.M., Midgley, D.F. & Venaik, S. 2008, 'Formative versus reflective measurement models: Two applications of formative measurement', *Journal of Business Research*, vol. 61, no. 12, pp. 1250–1262.

Colwell, S.R. 2016, *The composite reliability calculator*, <www.thestatisticalmind.com/composite-reliability/>.

Commonwealth of Australia. 2014a, *Financial system inquiry final report*, viewed 14 March 2016, <http://fsi.gov.au/files/2014/12/FSI_Final_Report_Consolidated20141210.pdf>.

Commonwealth of Australia. 2014b, *Financial system inquiry: Final report*, viewed 30 December 2014, <http://fsi.gov.au/publications/final-report/>.

Commonwealth of Australia. 2014c, *Parliamentary debates. The Senate matters of public importance future of financial advice speech by Senator Peter Whish-Wilson (Hansard)*, Canberra, viewed 11 July 2016, <http://parlinfo.aph.gov.au/parlInfo/genpdf/chamber/hansards/7f9c768e-cf09-4d07-a8ab-7c7e2f355ade/0089/hansard_frag.pdf;fileType=application%2Fpdf>.

Commonwealth of Australia. 2014d, *Parliamentary debates. The Senate matters of urgency future of financial advice speech by Senator Catryna Bilyk (Hansard)*, Canberra, viewed 11 July 2016, <http://parlinfo.aph.gov.au/parlInfo/genpdf/chamber/hansards/83688ae6-f170-4f32-a8f6-d8a971c587c8/0106/hansard_frag.pdf;fileType=application%2Fpdf>.

Commonwealth of Australia. 2014e, *Parliamentary debates. The Senate matters of urgency: Future of financial advice speech by Senator John Williams (Hansard)*, Canberra, viewed 11 July 2014, <http://parlinfo.aph.gov.au/parlInfo/genpdf/cham

ber/hansards/83688ae6-f170-4f32-a8f6-d8a971c587c8/0107/hansard_frag.pdf;fileType=application%2Fpdf>.

Commonwealth of Australia. 2015, *Parliamentary debates. The Senate motions financial services speech by Senator Peter Whish-Wilson*, Canberra, viewed 11 July 2016, <http://parlinfo.aph.gov.au/parlInfo/genpdf/chamber/hansards/4eed2018-4d3f-44d9-9722-b4eb019d1634/0136/hansard_frag.pdf;fileType=application%2Fpdf>.

Commonwealth of Australia. 2016a, *Parliamentary debates. The Senate committees corporations and financial services report speech by Senator Deb O'Neill (Hansard)*, Canberra, viewed 11 July 2016, <http://parlinfo.aph.gov.au/parlInfo/genpdf/chamber/hansards/c59815f1-0832-42c3-b73b-d3ee21b57955/0257/hansard_frag.pdf;fileType=application%2Fpdf>.

Commonwealth of Australia. 2016b, *Parliamentary debates. The Senate motions financial services speech by Senator Peter Whish-Wilson (Hansard)*, viewed 11 July 2016, <http://parlinfo.aph.gov.au/parlInfo/genpdf/chamber/hansards/548f7e7e-68e6-4e9c-8f40-5e4a56df0b06/0182/hansard_frag.pdf;fileType=application%2Fpdf>.

Commonwealth of Australia. 2016c, *Parliamentary debates. The Senate questions without notice: Take note of answers Financial services, Australian securities and investments commission speech by Senator Deb O'Neill (Hansard)*, viewed 13 July 2016, <http://parlinfo.aph.gov.au/parlInfo/genpdf/chamber/hansards/2c377a45-ab6f-4df0-b658-a87819aec92e/0066/hansard_frag.pdf;fileType=application%2Fpdf>.

Commonwealth of Australia. 2016d, *Parliamentary debates: The Senate questions without notice financial services question by Senator Peter Whish-Wilson (Hansard)*, viewed 11 July 2016, <http://parlinfo.aph.gov.au/parlInfo/genpdf/chamber/hansards/1ea904ea-ae93-4f0c-bb20-3d8c33e83f81/0112/hansard_frag.pdf;fileType=application%2Fpdf>.

Commonwealth of Australia. 2018, *Interim report: Royal commission into misconduct in the banking, superannuation and financial services industry*, viewed 1 October 2018, <https://financialservices.royalcommission.gov.au/Documents/interim-report/interim-report-volume-1.pdf>.

Commonwealth of Australia. 2019, 'Royal commission into misconduct in the banking, superannuation and financial services industry', viewed 4 February 2019, <https://financialservices.royalcommission.gov.au/Pages/default.aspx>.

Complinet – Thomson Reuters – Governance Risk & Compliance. 2010, 'Retail distribution review: The supervision and enforcement of professional standards – a new era?', *Law and Financial Markets Review*, vol. 4, no. 6, pp. 616–618.

Considnine, M. & Ali Afzal, K. 2011, *Legitimacy*, The SAGE Handbook of Governance, Sage, London.

Cooper, D.J. & Robson, K. 2006, 'Accounting, professions and regulation: Locating the sites of professionalization', *Accounting, Organizations and Society*, vol. 31, no. 4–5, pp. 15–444.

Cooper, D.R. & Schindler, P.S. 2003, *Business research methods*, 8 edn, McGraw-Hill, New York.

Cooper, D.R. & Schindler, P.S. 2014, *Business research methods*, 12th edn, McGraw-Hill, New York.

Cooper, J. 2006, 'The integration of financial regulatory authorities-The Australian experience', paper presented to Comissao de Valores Mobiliarios (Securities and exchange commission of Brazil) 30th Anniversary Conference 'Assessing the Present, Conceiving the Future', Rio de Janeiro, Brazil, 4–5 September, viewed

23 October 2013, <www.asic.gov.au/asic/pdflib.nsf/LookupByFileName/integration-financial-regulatory-authorities.pdf/$file/integration-financial-regulatory-authorities.pdf>.

Coorey, P & Eyers, J. 2015, 'Senator Sam Dastyari to grill bank chiefs on financial planning scandals', *Financial Review*, 14 April, viewed 12 July 2016, <www.afr.com/news/politics/senator-sam-dastyari-to-grill-bank-chiefs-on-financial-planning-scandals-20150414–1mkwme#ixzz4E957Fm4H >.

Corbett, A. 1999, 'Self-regulation, CLERP and financial markets: A missed opportunity for innovative regulatory reform', *University of New South Wales Law Journal*, vol. 22, no. 2, pp. 506–534.

Corones, S. & Galloway, T. 2013, 'The effectiveness of the best interests duty – enhancing consumer protection?', *Australian Business Law Review*, vol. 41, no. 1, p. 5.

Corones, S. & Irving, K. 2016, 'Raising levels of awareness of rights and obligations in the provision of financial product advice to retail clients', *Company and Securities Law Journal*, vol. 32, no. 3, pp. 192–213.

Cotter, T. & Von Nessen, P. 2001, 'The general insurance industry in 2001: Prudential regulation and consumer disclosure', *Proctor*, vol. 21, no. 9, pp. 10–11.

Creswell, J.W. 2003, *Research design: Qualitative, quantitative, and mixed method approaches*, 2nd edn, Sage, Thousand Oaks, CA.

Creswell, J.W. & Plano Clark, V.L. 2011, *Designing and conducting mixed methods research*, 2nd edn, Sage, Thousand Oaks, CA.

Cull, M. 2009, 'The rise of financial planning industry', *Australasian Accounting Business & Finance Journal*, vol. 3, pp. 26–37.

Curran, P.J., West, S.G. & Finch, J.F. 1996, 'The robustness of test statistics to non-normality and specification error in confirmatory factor analysis', *Psychological Methods*, vol. 1, no. 1, pp. 16–29.

Davis, J. 2002, 'Don't get caught in the act are you ready for the new financial services rules?', *Journal of Banking and Financial Services*, vol. 116, no. 2, p. 2.

Davis, K. 1995, 'Bank deregulation, supervision, and agency problems', *Australian Economic Review*, vol. 111, p. 43.

Dawson, G.S., Watson, R.T. & Boudreau, M.-C. 2010, 'Information asymmetry in information systems consulting: Toward a theory of relationship constraints', *Journal of Management Information Systems*, vol. 27, no. 3, pp. 143–178.

de Almeida, SnOs, Dholakia, U.M., Hernandez, J.M.C. & Mazzon, J.A. 2014, 'The mixed effects of participant diversity and expressive freedom in online peer-to-peer problem solving communities', *Journal of Interactive Marketing*, vol. 28, no. 3, pp. 196–209.

de Queiroz, M.A.L., de Vasconcelos, F.C. & Goldszmidt, R.G.B. 2007, 'Economic rents and legitimacy: Incorporating elements of organizational analysis institutional theory to the field of business strategy', *Brazilian Administration Review*, vol. 4, no. 1, pp. 51–65.

Deephouse, D.L. 1996, 'Does isomorphism legitimate?', *Academy of Management Journal*, vol. 39, no. 4, pp. 1024–1039.

Degeling, S. & Hudson, J. 2014, 'Fiduciary obligations, financial advisers and FOFA', *Company and Securities Law Journal*, vol. 32, no. 8, pp. 527–539.

Deloitte. 2019, *A new era Actions from the Hayne Royal Commission for each sector*, viewed 10 February 2019, <https://www2.deloitte.com/content/dam/Deloitte/au/Documents/financial-services/deloitte-au-fs-new-era-actions-royal-commission-130219.pdf>.

Deloitte 2016, *Plotting a new course. Brexit -the financial advisory perspective*, viewed 11 March 2017, <https://www2.deloitte.com/uk/en/pages/international-markets/articles/brexit-financial-advisory-perspective.html>.

Deloitte & Financial Services Council. 2014, *A comparison of financial advice regulations – personal advice for retail clients-Financial Services Council's submission to a Senate inquiry on the Corporations Amendment (Streamlining of Future of Financial Advice) Bill 2014*, Deloitte, viewed 3 July 2017, <file:///C:/Users/Angelique%20McInnes/Downloads/27_suppl%20(1).pdf>.

Demina, P. 2014, 'Broker-dealers and investment advisers: A behavioural-economics analysis of competing suggestions for reform', *Michigan Law Review*, vol. 113, no. 3, pp. 429–459.

Den-Toll, K. 2001, 'Australia paints unified picture for financial services', *International Financial Law Review*, vol. 20, no. 2, pp. 37–41.

Diamantopoulos, A. & Siguaw, JA 2006, 'Formative versus reflective indicators in organizational measure development: A comparison and empirical illustration', *British Journal of Management*, vol. 17, no. 4, pp. 263–282.

Díez-Martín, F., Prado-Roman, C. & Blanco-González, A. 2013, 'Beyond legitimacy: Legitimacy types and organizational success', *Management Decision*, vol. 51, no. 10, pp. 1954–1969.

Doh, J.P., Howton, S.D., Howton, S.W. & Siegel, D.S. 2010, 'Does the market respond to an endorsement of social responsibility? The role of institutions, information, and legitimacy', *Journal of Management*, vol. 36, no. 6, pp. 1461–1485.

Dolan, P., Elliott, A., Metcalfe, R. & Vlaev, I. 2012, 'Influencing financial behavior: From changing minds to changing contexts', *Journal of Behavioral Finance*, vol. 13, no. 2, pp. 126–142.

Dolnicar, S. 2013, 'Asking good survey questions', *Journal of Travel Research*, vol. 52, no. 5, pp. 551–574.

Dolnicar, S., Grün, B. & Leisch, F. 2011, 'Quick, simple and reliable: Forced binary survey questions', *International Journal of Market Research*, vol. 53, no. 2, pp. 231–252.

Durocher, S., Fortin, A. & Côté, L. 2007, 'Users' participation in the accounting standard-setting process: A theory-building study', *Accounting, Organizations and Society*, vol. 32, no. 1–2, pp. 29–59.

Edwards, J.R. & Bagozzi, R.P. 2000, 'On the nature and direction of relationships between constructs and measures', *Psychological Methods*, vol. 5, no. 2, pp. 155–174.

Edwards, V. & Valentine, T. 1998, 'From Napier to Wallis: Six decades of financial inquiries', *Economic Record*, vol. 74, no. 226, p. 1.

Egan, L. 2008, '*Independent* advice clients more satisfied', *Money Management*, p. 24, bth database, <http://ezproxy.cqu.edu.au/login?url=http://search.ebscohost.com/login.aspx?direct=true&db=bth&AN=33434909&site=eds-live&scope=site>.

Egan, M., Matvos, G. & Seru, A. 2016, *The market for financial adviser misconduct*, 1 March 2016, <http://dx.doi.org/10.2139/ssrn.2739170>.

Eisenhardt, K.M. 1989, 'Agency theory: An assessment and review', *The Academy of Management Review*, vol. 14, no. 1, pp. 57–74.

Elliott, D. 2006, 'The road to independence', *IntheBlack*, vol. 76, no. 9, p. 30, viewed 27 July 2016, <http://search.proquest.com.ezproxy.lib.rmit.edu.au/docview/211300600?OpenUrlRefId=info:xri/sid:primo&accountid=13552>.

Ellis, G. 2010, 'Grimson backs finance reform', *Illawarra Mercury*, vol. 20, viewed 20 March 2014, <http://ezproxy.cqu.edu.au/login?url=http://search.ebscohost.com/login.aspx?direct=true&db=n5h&AN=SYD-5UAD9H83C501 14L2D6QW&site=ehost-live>.

Ellis, J.M. 2006, *Bringing legitimacy back in: An analysis of institutionalized myth*, 27 March, blog, <http://polisciprof.blogspot.com.au/2006/03/essay-on-legitimacy-in-social-science.html>.

English, B. 2008, '"Climate for ethics" and occupational-organisational commitment conflict', *Journal of Management Development*, vol. 27, no. 9, pp. 963–975.

Everingham, R. 2014, *Better investment outcomes: It's time to co-regulate the financial product advice chain*, Lonsec Research Pty Ltd, viewed 17 July 2016, <www.beyond.lonsec.com.au/files/bio-pdf>.

Evetts, J. 2011, 'A new professionalism? Challenges and opportunities.(Reconnecting professional occupations and professional organizations)', *Current Sociology*, vol. 59, no. 4, pp. 406–422.

Evetts, J. 2014, 'Chapter 2 The Concept of professionalism: Professional work, professional practice and learning', in Sea Billett (ed.), *International handbook of Research in professional and practice-based learning*, Springer International Handbook of Education, Dordrecht, pp. 29–58.

Facciolo, F.J. 2011, 'The revolution in investment adviser regulation', *The Investment Lawyer*, vol. 18, no. 10, p. 11.

Facciolo, F.J. 2013, 'Revolution in the regulation of financial advice: The U.S., the U.K. and Australia: Introduction', *St. John's Law Review*, vol. 87, no. 2/3, pp. 297–311.

Faherty, A. 2010, 'BFPPG hits back at independence of advice "perception"', *Money Management*, vol. 24, no. 12, p. 10.

Fain, J.A. 2010, 'Should we publish pilot/feasibility studies?', *The Diabetes Educator*, vol. 36, no. 4, p. 521.

Farrell, A.M. & Rudd, J.M. 2009, 'Factor analysis and discriminant validity: A brief review of some practical issues', paper presented to Australian and New Zealand Marketing Academy (ANZMAC)Conference 2009 Crown Promenade, Melbourne, Australia, 30 November–2 December 2009, viewed 8 November 2016, <www.duplication.net.au/ANZMAC09/papers/ANZMAC2009-389.pdf>.

Feldon, D.F. & Kafai, Y.B. 2008, 'Mixed methods for mixed reality: Understanding users avatar activities in virtual worlds', *Educational Technology Research and Development*, vol. 56, pp. 575–593.

Felsenthal, S.M. & Guttenberg, G. 2009, 'Proxy voting and the disclosure of conflicts of interest: A recent enforcement action under the US Investment Advisers Act', *Journal of Securities Law, Regulation & Compliance*, vol. 2, no. 3, pp. 232–235.

Ferguson, A. 2015, 'Senate inquiry: Pain must prompt change in financial planning', *The Sydney Morning Herald, Business Day*, 22 April, viewed 1 June 2016, <www.smh.com.au/business/comment-and-analysis/senate-inquiry-pain-must-prompt-change-in-financial-planning-20150421-1mq16q.html>.

Ferguson, A. 2016, 'Adele Ferguson on the cost of whistleblowing and need for a bank royal commission', *The Sydney Morning Herald Business Day*, 6 May, viewed 1 June 2016, <www.smh.com.au/business/workplace-relations/adele-ferguson-on-the-cost-of-whistleblowing-and-need-for-a-bank-royal-commission-20160505-gomxc4.html#ixzz4AIZdpkFV >.

Ferguson, A., Masters, D. & Christodoulou, M. 2014, 'Sales-driven culture within Commonwealth Bank's financial planning division examined', *ABC Four*

Corners, 5 May, viewed 10 August 2017, <www.abc.net.au/news/2014-05-05/four-corners-examines-the-cba-financial-planning-division/5429170>.

Fernandez-Aviles, G. & Davila, L. 2012, 'A business figure in crisis time: *Independent* financial adviser', *The International Business & Economics Research Journal*, vol. 11, no. 13, p. 1499.

Ferran, E. 2012, 'Regulatory lessons from the payment protection insurance mis-selling scandal in the UK', *European Business Organization Law Review*, vol. 13, no. 2, pp. 247–270.

Ferrier, S. 2015, 'Commonwealth bank compensation scheme for victims of financial planning scandal "a joke", Senate inquiry hears', *ABC News*, 28 October, viewed 10 August 2017, <www.abc.net.au/news/2015-10-28/cba-denying-compensation-to-victims-of-financial-planning/6892624>.

fi360 FiduciaryPath. 2015, *Seeking trustworthy advice for individual investors. Financial intermediaries indicate strong support for fiduciary standard. Findings of the 2015 fi360 Fiduciary Standard Survey*, <www.fi360.com/uploads/media/2015fiduciarysurvey.pdf>.

Field, A. 2014, *Discovering Statistics using IBM SPSS statistics*, 4th edn, Sage, London.

Financial Conduct Authority. 2013a, *Policy statement PS13/1 – payments to platform service providers and cash rebates from providers to consumers*, viewed 7 March 2016, <www.fca.org.uk/static/documents/policy-statements/ps13-1.pdf>.

Financial Conduct Authority. 2013b, *Supervising retail investment advice: How firms are implementing the RDR*, viewed 8 March 2016, <www.fca.org.uk/static/documents/thematic-reviews/tr13-05.pdf>.

Financial Conduct Authority. 2014a, *Post-implementation review of the retail distribution review*, Financial Conduct Authority (FCA), 16 December, <www.fca.org.uk/news/post-implementation-review-of-the-rdr>.

Financial Conduct Authority. 2014b, *Post-implementation review of the retail distribution review – phase 1*, viewed 5 February 2016, <www.fca.org.uk/static/documents/post-implementation-review-rdr-phase-1.pdf>.

Financial Conduct Authority. 2014c, *Retail distribution review: Post implementation review – Europe economics*, Financial Conduct Authority, viewed 8 February 2016, <www.fca.org.uk/your-fca/documents/research/rdr-post-implementation-review-europe-economics>.

Financial Conduct Authority. 2014d, *Retail investment advice: Adviser charging and services*, viewed 8 March 2016, <www.fca.org.uk/static/documents/thematic-reviews/tr14-21.pdf>.

Financial Conduct Authority. 2014e, *Supervising retail investment advice: Delivering independent advice*, viewed 8 March 2015, <www.fca.org.uk/static/documents/thematic-reviews/tr14-05.pdf>.

Financial Conduct Authority. 2014f, *Supervising retail investment firms: Being clear about adviser charges and services*, viewed 8 March 2016, <www.fca.org.uk/static/documents/thematic-reviews/tr14-06.pdf>.

Financial Conduct Authority. 2015, 'Appointed representatives and principals: Responsibilities', viewed 10 December 2015, <www.the-fca.org.uk/appointed-representatives-and-principals?field_fcasf_sector=unset&field_fcasf_page_category=unset>.

Financial Conduct Authority. 2016a, *Financial advice market review: Final report*, viewed 4 October 2016, <www.fca.org.uk/publication/corporate/famr-final-report.pdf>.

Financial Conduct Authority. 2016b, 'Financial conduct authority handbook', viewed 25 August 2017, <www.fca.org.uk/about/handbook>.

Financial Conduct Authority. 2016c, '*Independent* and restricted advice', *Financial Conduct Authority* (FCA), viewed 5 February 2016, <www.the-fca.org.uk/*independent*-and-restricted-advice?field_fcasf_sector=236&field_fcasf_page_category=unset>.

Financial Conduct Authority. 2017a, *Conduct of business sourcebook*, viewed 25 August 2017, <www.handbook.fca.org.uk/handbook/COBS.pdf>.

Financial Conduct Authority. 2017b, *FAMR financial market review baseline report*, viewed 12 December 2017, <www.fca.org.uk/publications/research/financial-advice-market-review-famr-baseline-report>.

Financial Planning Association. 2014b, *Submission exposure draft – FoFA amendments*, viewed 4 December 2016, <http://futureofadvice.treasury.gov.au/content/consultation/fofa_amendments/submissions/Financial_Planning_Association_of_Australia.pdf>.

Financial Planning Coalition. 2014a, *Consumers are confused and harmed: The case for regulation of financial planners*, viewed 11 February 2016, <http://financialplanningcoalition.com/wp-content/uploads/2014/06/Financial-Planning-Coalition-Regulatory-Standards-White-Paper-Final.pdf>.

Financial Rights Legal Centre, Choice & Consumer Action Law Centre. 2016, *Submission 161: Scrutiny of financial advice inquiry: Additional terms of reference on the life insurance industry*, viewed 30 May 2016, <www.aph.gov.au/Parliamentary_Business/Committees/Senate/Economics/Scrutiny_of_Financial_Advice>.

Financial Service Council & UBS Asset Management. 2016, *State of the industry*, FSCFaUA Management, viewed 29 February 2016, <www.fsc.org.au/downloads/uploaded/2016_0225_FSC%20UBS%20State%20of%20the%20Industry%20Report%20(FINAL)_1238.pdf>.

Financial Services Authority, F. 2010, *Delivering the RDR: Professionalism, including its applicability to pure protection advice, with feedback to CP09/18 and CP09/31*, pp. 1–98, viewed 22 March 2016, <www.fsa.gov.uk/pubs/cp/cp10_14.pdf>.

Financial Services Authority, F. 2012a, 'FSA factsheet for all firms: Applying for authorisation', viewed 8 February 2016, <www.fca.org.uk/static/fca/documents/fsa-applying-authorisation.pdf>.

Financial Services Authority, F. 2012b, *Retail distribution review: Independent and restricted advice*, FSA – FG12/15, viewed 10 December 2015, <www.bing.com/search?q=Finalised+Guidance%3A+Retail+Distribution+Review%3A+*Independent*+and+Restricted+Advice.&PC=U316&FORM=CHROMN>.

Australian Government, 2001, *Federal Register of Legislation, Financial Services Reform Act.* 2001, viewed 3 April 2017, < https://www.legislation.gov.au/Details/C2004A00891>.

Finke, M., Huston, S. & Waller, W. 2009a, 'Do contracts influence comprehensive financial advice?', *Financial Services Review*, vol. 18, no. 2, p. 177.

Finke, M, Huston, S. & Waller, W. 2009b, 'Do contracts influence comprehensive financial advice?', *Financial Services Review*, vol. 18, no. 2, p. 17.

Finke, M. & Langdon, T.P. 2012, 'The impact of the broker-dealer fiduciary standard on financial advice', *Journal of Financial Planning*, vol. 25, no. 7, pp. 28–37.

Fisher, D.G., Swanson, D.L. & Schmidt, J.J. 2007, 'Accounting education lags CPE ethics requirements: Implications for the profession and a call to action', *Accounting Education*, vol. 16, no. 4, pp. 345–363.

Fitzpatrick, J. 2011, 'A message from the CEO', *Journal of the Australian & New Zealand Institute of Insurance & Finance*, vol. 34, no. 4, pp. 4–5.

Fornell, C. & Larcker, D. 1981, 'Evaluating structural equation models with unobservable variables and measurement error', *JMR, Journal of Marketing Research (pre-1986)*, vol. 18, no. 000001, p. 39.

Fouliadi, R.T. 1998, Covariance structure analysis techniques under conditions of multivariate normality and nonnormality – modified and bootstrap based test statistics, paper presented at the annual meeting of the American Educational Research Association, San Diego, 14 April 1997, ER Information, <http://files.eric.ed.gov/fulltext/ED420717.pdf>.

Fox, B. 2014, 'Non-aligned licensees drive innovation', *Professional Planner*, August, p. 36, viewed 28 July 2016, <http://search.informit.com.au/documentSummary;dn=828114957768387;res=IELBUS>.

Francis, S. 2006, *Planning's dirty little secrets*, 9 August, <www.acleardirection.com.au/planning_s_dirty_little_secrets___eureka_report_article>.

Frumento, A.J. & Korenman, S. 2013, 'Professionalism and investment advisers', *Journal of Investment Compliance*, vol. 14, no. 1, pp. 32–41.

Garner, R. 2005, *The joy of stats*, 1st edn, Broadview Press, Canada.

Gaskin, J. 2011, *Multivariate outliers, Gaskination's statistics*, 1, Youtube, viewed 25 October 2016, <www.youtube.com/watch?v=0vtgynhkH60>.

Gaskin, J. 2012, *SEM series (2016) 6. Multivariate assumptions, Gaskination's StatWiki.*, YouTube, 22 April 2016, <www.youtube.com/watch?v=J2EkjIeK-PE&feature=youtu.be>.

Gaskin, J. 2013, *SEM series part 5b: Validating the measurement model, Gaskination's statistics.*, viewed YouTube, 28 October 2016, <www.youtube.com/watch?v=hqV9RUSwwdA>.

Gaskin, J. 2015, *#2.6 Determining homoscedasticity*, YouTube, <www.youtube.com/watch?v=3jgq1T9AJLY>.

Gaskin, J. 2016a, 'Confirmatory factor analysis, Gaskination's statistics.', viewed 26 October 2016, <http://statwiki.kolobkreations.com/index.php?title=Confirmatory_Factor_Analysis>.

Gaskin, J. 2016b, 'Exploratory factor analysis, Gaskination's statistics.', viewed 28 October 2016, <http://statwiki.kolobkreations.com/index.php?title=Exploratory_Factor_Analysis#Rotation_types>.

Gaskin, J. 2016c, 'Linearity, Gaskination's statistics.', viewed 26 October 2016, <http://statwiki.kolobkreations.com/index.php?title=Data_screening>.

Gaskin, J. 2016d, 'Multicollinearity, Gaskination's statistics.', viewed 26 October 2016, <http://statwiki.kolobkreations.com/index.php?title=Data_screening>.

Gaskin, J. 2016e, 'Validitymaster, stats tools package.', viewed 28 October 2016, <http://statwiki.kolobkreations.com>.

Gilligan, G., Ali, P., Godwin, A., Hedges, J. & Ramsay, I. 2015a, *Research working paper series: An analysis of penalties under ASIC administered legislation: Scoping the issues – paper 1*, viewed 16 August 2018, <https://papers.ssrn.com/sol3/papers.cfm?abstract_id=2649724>.

Gilligan, G., Godwin, A., Hedges, J. & Ramsay, I. 2017, 'Penalties regimes to counter corporate misconduct in Australia – views of governance professionals', *Law and Financial Markets Review*, vol. 11, no. 1, pp. 4–12.

Gilligan, G., Hedges, J., Ali, P., Bird, H., Godwin, A. & Ramsay, I. 2015b, 'Regulating by numbers: The trend towards increasing empiricism in enforcement reporting by financial regulators', *Law and Financial Markets Review*, vol. 9, no. 4, pp. 260–282.

Gillis, J.G. 1986, 'The self-regulation movement', *Financial Analysts Journal*, vol. 42, no. 3, pp. 16–18.

Gioia, D.A. & Pitre, E. 1990, 'Multiparadigm perspectives on theory building', *The Academy of Management Review*, vol. 15, no. 4, pp. 584–602.

Glaser, B.G. 1965, 'The constant comparative method of qualitative analysis', *Social Problems*, vol. 12, no. 4, pp. 436–445.

Global Accounting Alliance, Chartered Accountants Worldwide & charteredaccountantsanz.com. 2016, *Financial advice and regulations: Guidance for the accounting profession*, viewed 16 August 2016, <www.charteredaccountantsanz.com>.

Goedecke, M. 2001, 'Wealth management: Can the banks beat the accountants at their own game? The banks possess the huge customer bases and the resources to tackle the wealth management market. But as Mark Goedecke reports, they could be doing better', *Journal of Banking and Financial Services*, vol. 115, no. 6, p. 4.

Golant, B.D. & Sillince, J.A.A. 2007, 'The constitution of organizational legitimacy: A narrative perspective', *Organization Studies (01708406)*, vol. 28, no. 8, pp. 1149–1167.

Gor, L. 2005, 'The financial services licensee's derivative liability for the conduct of its representatives', *Law Society Journal: The Official Journal of the Law Society of New South Wales*, vol. 43, no. 7, p. 59.

Goretzki, L., Strauss, E. & Weber, J. 2013, 'An institutional perspective on the changes in management accountants' professional role', *Management Accounting Research*, vol. 24, pp. 41–63.

Gough, O. 2005, '*Independent* financial advisers – why they remain the strongest distribution route for pensions', *Service Industries Journal*, vol. 25, no. 5, pp. 709–720.

Grace, J.B. 2008, 'Structural equation modeling for observational studies', *Journal of Wildlife Management*, vol. 72, no. 1, pp. 14–22.

Graham, S. 2017, 'ASIC's Report 515 puts licensees' auditors under scrutiny', *Professional Planner*, viewed 2 May 2017, <www.professionalplanner.com.au/featured-posts/2017/05/02/asics-report-515-puts-licensees-auditors-under-scrutiny-55681/?utm_medium=email&utm_campaign=PP0007&utm_content=PP0007+CID_db16efb45a1002e41a8d3c87e55839b3&utm_source=Campaign%20Monitor&utm_term=Report%20515%20puts%20licensees%20auditors%20under%20scrutiny>.

Gray, L. & Ireland, J. 2011, 'Future of financial advice reforms', *Law Society Journal: The Official journal of the Law Society of New South Wales*, vol. 49, no. 11, p. 66.

Greenleaf, G. 2017, 'Technology and the professions: Utopian and dystopian futures', *University of New South Wales Law Journal*, vol. 40, no. 1, pp. 302–321.

Greenwood, R., Suddaby, R. & Hinings, C.R. 2002, 'Theorizing change: The role of professional associations in the transformation of institutional fields', *Academy of Management Journal*, vol. 45, no. 1, pp. 58–80.

Griffiths, M. 2007, 'Consumer debt in Australia: Why banks will not turn their backs on profit', *International Journal of Consumer Studies*, vol. 31, no. 3, pp. 230–236.

Groza, M.D., Locander, D.A. & Howlett, C.H. 2016, 'Linking thinking styles to sales performance: The importance of creativity and subjective knowledge', *Journal of Business Research*, vol. 69, no. 10, pp. 4185–4193.

Gualini, E. 2004, 'Integration, diversity, plurality: Territorial governance and the reconstruction of legitimacy in a European 'Postnational' State', *Geopolitics*, vol. 9, no. 3, pp. 542–563.

Hackethal, A., Haliassos, M. & Jappelli, T. 2012, 'Financial advisors: A case of babysitters?', *Journal of Banking & Finance*, vol. 36, no. 2, pp. 509–524.

Haigh, M. 2006, 'Managed investments, managed disclosures: Financial services reform in practice', *Accounting, Auditing & Accountability Journal*, vol. 19, no. 2, p. 186.

Hair, J.F., Black, W.C., Babin, B.J., Anderson, R.E. & Tatham, R.L. 2010, *Multivariate data analysis*, 6th edn, Pearson Prentice Hall, Upper Saddle River, NJ, cat00311a database.

Hair, J.F., Jr., Ringle, C.M. & Sarstedt, M. 2013, 'Partial least squares structural equation modeling: Rigorous applications, better results and higher acceptance', *Long Range Planning: International Journal of Strategic Management*, vol. 46, no. 1–2, pp. 1–12.

Halsey, F. & Halsey, M. 2014, 'Replacement of the "accountants' exemption" – the limited licence regime', *Taxation in Australia*, vol. 48, no. 7, p. 378.

Hancock, G.R. & Nevitt, J. 1999, 'Bootstrapping and the identification of exogenous latent variables within structural equation models', *Structural Equation Modeling*, vol. 6, no. 4, pp. 394–399.

Hanratty, P. 1997, *The Wallis report on the Australian financial system: Summary and critique*, 16 1996–97, Department of the Parliamentary Library, viewed 17 July 2017, <http://parlinfo.aph.gov.au/parlInfo/download/library/prspub/D2G30/upload_binary/D2G30.pdf;fileType=application/pdf#search=%221990s%20 1997%20publications%22>.

Hansen, S. 2008, 'So, whose client is it anyway?: Regulation S-P impacts that answer', *Journal of Financial Planning*, pp. 20–21.

Harding, D. 2001, 'Australia gets closer to financial services reform', *International Financial Law Review*, vol. 20, no. 8, pp. 57–63.

Hargovan, A. 2011, 'Director's breach of fiduciary and statutory duties – the decision in Hydrocool', *Keeping Good Companies (14447614)*, vol. 63, no. 7, pp. 414–417.

Harrington, D. 2009, *Confirmatory factor analysis*, Oxford University Press, Oxford; New York.

Hartnett, N. 2009, *Introduction to individual financial planning*, 5th edn, Pearson, Frenchs Forest, NSW.

Hartnett, N. 2010, 'Trust and the financial planning relationship', *JASSA: The Finsia Journal of Applied Finance*, vol. 1, pp. 41–46.

Harvey, B. & Schaefer, A. 2001, 'Managing relationships with environmental stakeholders: A study of U.K. water and electricity utilities', *Journal of Business Ethics*, vol. 30, no. 3, pp. 243–260.

Harvey, K. 2002, 'Financial sector reforms: Financial sector reforms catch lawyers and accountants napping', *Taxation in Australia*, vol. 37, no. 2, pp. 89–94.

Harvey, V. 2011, 'Why we are proud to be restricted', *Professional Adviser*, pp. 32–33.

Hayduk, L., Cummings, G., Boadu, K., Pazderka-Robinson, H. & Boulianne, S. 2006, 'Testing! testing! one, two, three – testing the theory in structural equation models!', *Personality and Individual Differences*, vol. 42, no. 2007, pp. 841–850.

Heath, J. 2009, 'The uses and abuses of agency theory', *Business Ethics Quarterly*, vol. 19, no. 4, pp. 497–528.

Hely, S. 2012, 'Pressure on planners', *Money (Australia Edition)*, vol. 144, p. 12.

Henderson, A. & Conifer, D. 2016, 'Commonwealth Bank boss Ian Narev says no-one sacked over CommInsure scandals', *ABC News*, 5 October, viewed 10 August 2017, <www.abc.net.au/news/2016-10-04/commonwealth-bank-boss-says-no-staff-axed-comminsure-scandals/7901884>.

Herda, D.N. 2013, 'Structural equation modeling in the accounting literature: Observations and suggestions', *Journal of Theoretical Accounting Research*, vol. 8, no. 2, pp. 103–138.

Hermida, R. 2015, 'The problem of allowing correlated errors in structural equation modeling: Concerns and considerations', *Computational Methods in Social Sciences*, vol. 3, no. 1, pp. 5–17.

Herremans, I., Herschovis, M. & Bertels, S. 2009, 'Leaders and laggards: The influence of competing logics on corporate environmental action', *Journal of Business Ethics*, vol. 89, no. 3, pp. 449–472.

Hewett, K., Money, R. & Sharma, S. 2006, 'National culture and industrial buyer-seller relationships in the United States and Latin America', *Official Publication of the Academy of Marketing Science*, vol. 34, no. 3, pp. 386–402.

Hewison, J. 2014, *The line in the sand has been drawn*, 17 April, Morningstar Media, viewed 17 April 2014, <www.ifa.com.au/blogs/13136-the-line-in-the-sand>.

Hii, S.-K. & Su-King, H. 2009, 'Tougher regulation is likely for AFS licensees and new applicants', *InFinance*, vol. 123, no. 5, p. 52.

Hiller, K., Mahlendorf, M.D. & Weber, J. 2014, 'Management accountants' occupational prestige within the company: A social identity theory perspective', *European Accounting Review*, vol. 23, no. 4, pp. 671–691.

Himstreet, J. 2012, 'Regulation and supervision of financial planning under the securities laws', *The Investment Lawyer*, vol. 19, no. 4, pp. 3–15.

Hofacker, C. 2007, 'Chapter 5: Ordinary least squares', openaccesstexts.org, <www.openaccesstexts.org/pdf/Quant_Chapter_05_ols.pdf>.

Holley Nethercoate Commercial & Financial Services Lawyers. 2014a, *Financial advice and regulations: Guidance for the accounting profession*, viewed 27 May 2014, <https://www.cpaaustralia.com.au/~/media/corporate/allfiles/document/professional-resources/financial-planning/financial-advice-and-regulations-for-accounting.pdf?la=en>.

Holley Nethercoate Commercial & Financial Services Lawyers. 2014b, *Information guide: Accountants' exemption reform and the limited licensing framework*, viewed 27 May 2014, <https://www.cpaaustralia.com.au/~/media/corporate/allfiles/document/professional-resources/financial-planning/information-guide.pdf?la=en>.

Horsley, M. & Thomas, D. 2003, 'Professional regulation and professional autonomy: Benchmarks from across the professions – the New South Wales experience.', *Change: Transformations in Education*, vol. 6, no. 1, pp. 34–47.

Howell, R.D., Breivik, E. & Wilcox, J.B. 2007, 'Reconsidering formative measurement', *Psychological Methods*, vol. 12, no. 2, pp. 205–218.

Hox, J.J. & Bechger, T.M. 1998, 'An introduction to structural equation modeling', *Family Science Review*, vol. 11, pp. 354–373.

Hoyle, S. 2016, 'Independence play – even planners unclear on "*independent*" meaning', *Professional Planner*, 8 December, viewed 20 April 2017, <www.professionalplanner.com.au/featured-posts/2016/12/08/independence-play-even-planners-unclear-on-*independent*-meaning-52876/>.

Hoyle, S. 2017a, 'Individual licensing: A bold step towards becoming a profession', *Professional Planner*, 11 May, viewed 22 May 2017, <www.professionalplanner.com.au/featured-posts/2017/05/11/individual-licensing-a-bold-step-towards-becoming-a-profession-55914/>.

Hoyle, S. 2017b, 'Industry leaders: The move to independence is critical', *Professional Planner*, 12 July, viewed 12 July 2017, <www.professionalplanner.com.au/featured-posts/2017/07/12/industry-leaders-the-move-to-independence-critical-57271/>.

Hoyle, S. 2017c, 'Licensees' futures are built on support for advisers', *Professional Planner*, 26 May, viewed 26 May 2017, <www.professionalplanner.com.au/featured-posts/2017/05/26/licensees-future-is-built-on-support-for-advisers-56200/?utm_medium=email&utm_campaign=PP0026&utm_content=PP0026+CID_6f758e88a6dd748a494b9f8846b35701&utm_source=Campaign%20Monitor&utm_term=Exactly%20how%20the%20nature%20of%20licensing%20for%20financial%20planners%20will%20change%20is%20still%20unsettled%20but%20one%20thing%20does%20seem%20certain%20%20licensees%20will%20have%20to%20adapt%20to%20a%20new%20role>.

Hoyle, S. 2017d, 'Professional codes only as strong as enforcement powers', *Professional Planner*, 13 June, viewed 14 June 2017, <www.professionalplanner.com.au/featured-posts/2017/06/13/professional-codes-only-as-strong-as-enforcement-powers-56611/?utm_medium=email&utm_campaign=PP0037&utm_content=PP0037+CID_eaa2f8c38c4ffcf2961d3b2af37c3841&utm_source=Campaign%20Monitor&utm_term=Professional%20codes%20only%20as%20strong%20as%20enforcement>.

Hoyle, S. 2017e, 'Reflection: Individual licensing starting to resonate', *Professional Planner*, 21 July, viewed 21 July 2017, <www.professionalplanner.com.au/featured-posts/2017/07/21/reflection-individual-licensing-starting-to-resonate-57437/?utm_medium=email&utm_campaign=PP0065&utm_content=PP0065+CID_8297fdcc69c6d2a3bc24571a103be9fb&utm_source=Campaign%20Monitor&utm_term=Professional%20Planners%20suggestion%20that%20financial%20planning%20would%20be%20better%20served%20if%20planners%20were%20accredited%20as%20individuals%20is%20starting%20to%20catch%20on>.

Hoyle, S. 2017f, 'Reflection: The disturbing question of licensing's legitimacy', *Professional Planner*, 17 November, viewed 23 November 2017, <www.professionalplanner.com.au/featured-posts/2017/11/17/reflection-a-disturbing-question-of-legitimacy-59937/?utm_medium=email&utm_campaign=PP00173&utm_content=PP00173+CID_7fa2da0d65927c0c14a359c8d72888e6&utm_source=Campaign%20Monitor>.

Hu, L.T. & Bentler, P.M. 1999, 'Cutoff criteria for fit indexes in covariance structure analysis: Conventional criteria versus new alternatives', *Structural Equation Modeling*, vol. 6, no. 1, pp. 1–55.

Hu, L.-T., Bentler, P.M. & Kano, Y. 1992, 'Can test statistics in covariance structure analysis be trusted?', *Psychological Bulletin*, vol. 112, no. 2, pp. 351–362.

Hutson, J. & Vonnessen, P. 2003, 'The FSRA transition: Preparing for the end', *Proctor*, vol. 23, no. 4, pp. 21–22.

ICFP. 1999, 'Ten years ago at the institute', *Journal of Financial Planning*, vol. 12, no. 9, p. 21.

Independent Financial Adviser News. 2014a, 'ASIC takes action against CBA dealer groups', 16 May, viewed 21 May 2014, <www.ifa.com.au/news/13222-asic-takes-action-against-cba-dealer-groups?utm_source=IFA&utm_campaign=IFA_Newsflash16_05_2014&utm_medium=email>.

Independent Financial Adviser News. 2014b, 'Murray mulls *independent*-aligned divide', *Independent Financial Adviser News*, 15 July, viewed 16 July 2014, <www.ifa.com.au/news/13439-murray-mulls-*independent*-aligned-divide>.

Independent Financial Adviser News. 2016a, 'Advice firm penalised for '*independent*' claims', 10 October, viewed 16 November 2016, <www.ifa.com.au/news/16907-advice-firm-penalised-for-*independent*-claims>.

Independent Financial Adviser News. 2016b, 'Financial planners rated low for ethics and honesty', 12 May, viewed 7 June 2016, <www.ifa.com.au/news/16162-financial-planners-rated-low-for-ethics-and-honesty>.

Independent Financial Adviser News. 2016c, 'Instos to soon get left behind, aligned advisers warned', 22 August, viewed 25 August 2016, <www.ifa.com.au/news/16692-instos-to-soon-get-left-behind-aligned-advisers-warned?utm_source=IFA&utm_campaign=22_08_16&utm_medium=email&utm_content=2>.

Inderst, R. 2009, 'Retail finance: Thoughts on reshaping regulation and consumer protection after the financial crisis', *European Business Organization Law Review*, vol. 10, no. 3, pp. 455–464.

Inderst, R. & Ottaviani, M. 2009, 'Misselling through agents', *American Economic Review*, vol. 99, no. 3, pp. 883–908.

Inderst, R. & Ottaviani, M. 2012a, 'Competition through commissions and kickbacks', *American Economic Review*, vol. 102, no. 2, pp. 780–809.

Inderst, R. & Ottaviani, M. 2012b, 'Financial advice', *Journal of Economic Literature*, vol. 50, no. 2, pp. 494–512.

Inderst, R. & Ottaviani, M. 2012c, 'How (not) to pay for advice: A framework for consumer financial protection', *Journal of Financial Economics*, vol. 105, no. 2, pp. 393–411.

Inderst, R. & Ottaviani, M. 2012d, 'How (not) to pay for advice: A framework for consumer financial protection', *Journal of Financial Economics*, vol. 105, pp. 393–411.

Inderst, R. & Ottaviani, M. 2012e, 'Regulating financial advice', *European Business Organization Law Review*, vol. 13, no. 2, pp. 237–246.

Industry Super Australia. 2014, *Submission 31 to the Senate economics legislation committee: Corporations amendment (streamlining of future of financial advice) bill 2014 Submission 31*, viewed 27 July 2016, <file:///C:/Users/Angelique%20 McInnes/Downloads/31.pdf>.

Industry Super Network. 2011, *90% sales, 10% advice. A snapshot of the financial planning industry*, IS Network, viewed 6 July 2016, <www.industrysuperaustralia.com/assets/Reports/A-snapshot-of-the-financial-planning-industry-110930-1010 version.pdf>.

Institute of Chartered Accountants of Australia. 2012, 'How to become a Chartered Accountant', viewed 23 November 2016, <www.charteredaccountants.com.au/Chartered-Accountants/Become-a-Chartered-Accountant-in-Australia>.

International Financial Law Review. 2009, 'Radical proposals in Australia', vol. n/a.

Ireland, J. & Gray, L. 2011, 'Future of financial advice reforms', *Law Society of NSW Journal*, vol. 49, no. 11, pp. 66–70.

Jackling, B. & Sullivan, C. 2007, 'Financial planners in Australia: An evaluation of gaps in technical and behavioral skills', *Financial Services Review*, vol. 16, no. 3, pp. 211–228.

Jackson, D.L., Gillaspy, J.A., Jr. & Purc-Stephenson, R. 2009, 'Reporting practices in confirmatory factor analysis: An overview and some recommendations', *Psychological Methods*, vol. 14, no. 1, pp. 6–23.

Jackson, D.L., Voth, J. & Frey, M. 2013, 'A note on sample size and solution propriety for confirmatory factor analytic models', *Structural Equation Modeling: A Multidisciplinary Journal*, vol. 20, no. 1, pp. 86–97.

Jacobson, D. 2016, *When is a financial services licensee "independent"?*, 28 July, Bright Legal Services Pty Ltd, <www.brightlaw.com.au/corporations-act/when-is-a-financial-services-licensee-*independent*/>.

Jamieson, S. 2004, 'Likert scales: How to (ab) use them', *Medical Education*, vol. 38, no. 12, pp. 1217–1218.

Janghorban, R., Roudsari, R.L. & Taghipour, A. 2014, 'Pilot study in qualitative research: The roles and values', *Journal of Hayat*, vol. 19, no. 4, pp. 1–5.

Jean Lee, S. 1992, 'Quantitative versus qualitative research methods – two approaches to organisation studies', *Asia Pacific Journal of Management*, vol. 9, no. 1, pp. 87–94.

Johnsen, B.D. 2010, 'Myths about mutual fund fees: Economic insights on Jones v. Harris', *The Journal of Corporation Law*, vol. 35, no. 3, p. 561.

Johnson, J. & Holub, M.J. 2003, 'Questioning organizational legitimacy: The case of U.S. expatriates', *Journal of Business Ethics*, vol. 47, no. 3, pp. 269–293.

Johnston, P. 2014, 'The AIOFP is dismayed and frustrated with market stakeholders continually blaming advisers for the industry's deficiencies regardless of mitigating circumstances', *Independent Financial Adviser News*, 7 July, viewed 16 July 2014, <www.ifa.com.au/blogs/13402-an-open-letter-to-the-fpa>.

Johnston, P. & Walker, B. 2017, *White paper: Amending s923A for the post FOFA advice era*, Association of *Independent*ly Owned Financial Professionals, Smart Compliance Pty Ltd, 24 August, <www.ifa.com.au/tmp/s923Awhite paper.pdf>.

Jones, E. 2009, 'The crisis and the Australian financial sector', *Journal of Australian Political Economy*, vol. 64, pp. 91–116.

Jones, R.M. & Welsh, M. 2012, 'Toward a public enforcement model for directors' duty of oversight', *Vanderbilt Journal of Transnational Law*, vol. 45, no. 2, pp. 343–403.

Jones, S. 2012, *Australian superannuation handbook*, Thomson Reuters (Professional) Australian Limited, Sydney.

Joreskog, K. 1978, 'Structural analysis of covariance and correlation matrices', *Psychometrika*, vol. 43, no. 4, pp. 443–477.

Journal of Financial Planning. 2009, 'Planners on par with brokers among mass affluent', vol. 22, no. 12, p. 10.

Julian, D. 2009, 'FED: Financial advisers shouldn't receive commissions: Report', *AAP Australian National News Wire*, viewed 20 March 2014, <http://ezproxy.cqu.edu.au/login?url=http://search.ebscohost.com/login.aspx?direct=true&db=n5h&AN=74C3307746292&site=ehost-live>.

Kaissar, N. 2016, *You deserve a better financial adviser*, Bloomberg, blog, 9 March 2016, 1:14 AM EAST, <www.bloomberg.com/gadfly/articles/2016-03-08/calling-for-better-financial-advisers>.

Kakkuri-Knuuttila, M.-L., Lukka, K. & Kuorikoski, J. 2008, 'Straddling between paradigms: A naturalistic philosophical case study on interpretive research in management accounting', *Accounting, Organizations and Society*, vol. 33, no. 2, pp. 267–291.

Kang, B. & Jindal, R.P. 2015, 'Opportunism in buyer – seller relationships: Some unexplored antecedents', *Journal of Business Research*, vol. 68, no. 3, pp. 735–742.

Kay, J. 2012, *The Kay review of UK equity markets and long-term decision making: Final report*, viewed 29 September 2017, <www.gov.uk/government/uploads/system/uploads/attachment_data/file/253454/bis-12-917-kay-review-of-equity-markets-final-report.pdf>.

Ke-Hai, Y. 2005, 'Fit indices versus test statistics', *Multivariate Behavioral Research*, vol. 40, no. 1, pp. 115–148.

Kell, P. 2012, 'The future of advice post FOFA: A speech by Peter Kell, Commissioner, Australian Securities and Investments Commission', paper presented to Association of Financial Advisers/Financial Services Council Leadership Forum, Sydney, 1 May, viewed 23 June 2015, <www.asic.gov.au/about-asic/media-centre/speeches/future-of-advice-post-fofa/>.

Kell, P. 2013, 'Are you ready for FoFA?', *InFinance: The Magazine for Finsia Members*, vol. 127, no. 1, pp. 25–27.

Kelleher, D.M., Hall, S.W. & Medina, F. 2016, 'The Dodd-Frank Act is working and will protect the American people if it is not killed before fully implemented', *North Carolina Banking Institute Journal*, vol. 20, no. 1, pp. 127–144.

Kendell, S. 2017, 'BOLRs drive poor client outcomes', *Financial Observer*, 4 October, viewed 4 October 2017, <www.financialobserver.com.au/articles/bolrs-drive-poor-client-outcomes>.

Kennedy, C. 2012, 'Financial advisers questioning practice ownership', *Money Management*, 23 August, p. 32, viewed 7 June 2016, <http://connection.ebscohost.com/c/articles/79837856/advisers-questioning-practice-ownership>.

Kennedy, L., McCoy, P. & Bernstein, E. 2012, 'The consumer financial protection bureau: Financial regulation for the 21st century', *Cornell Law Review*, vol. 97, no. 5, p. 1.

Kim, B., Pratt, T. & Wallace, D. 2014, 'Adverse neighborhood conditions and sanction risk perceptions: Using SEM to examine direct and indirect effects', *Journal of Quantitative Criminology*, vol. 30, no. 3, pp. 505–526.

Kingsford Smith, D. 2009, 'Regulating investment risk: Individuals and the global financial crisis', *University of New South Wales Law Journal*, vol. 32, no. 2, pp. 514–546.

Kingsford Smith, D. 2011, 'A harder nut to crack? Responsive regulation in the financial services sector', *University of British Columbia Law Review*, vol. 44, no. 3, pp. 695–742.

Kingsford Smith, D. 2012, 'Governing the corporation : The role of "soft regulation"', *University of New South Wales Law Journal*, vol. 35, no. 1, pp. 378–403.

Kingsford Smith, D. 2014, 'Submission to the financial system inquiry: An inquiry into the performance of the Australian Financial System', viewed 21 July 2017, <http://fsi.gov.au/files/2014/04/Kingsford_Smith.pdf>.

Kingston, G. & Weng, H. 2011, *Agency theory and financial planning practice*, Macquarie University, viewed 21 July 2017, <http://scholar.google.com.au/scholar_url?url=https://www.mq.edu.au/__data/assets/pdf_file/0006/74490/Agency12June2013.pdf&hl=en&sa=X&scisig=AAGBfm1sXV9-VJHe6t6aH1UTKKj4NljKmQ&nossl=1&oi=scholarr>.

Kingston, G. & Weng, H. 2014, 'Agency theory and financial planning practice', *Australian Economic Review*, vol. 47, no. 3, pp. 290–303.

Kirby, J.B. & Bollen, K.A. 2009, 'Using instrumental variable tests to evaluate model specification in latent variable structural equation models', *Sociological Methodology*, vol. 39, pp. 327–355.

Kline, R.B. 2010, *Principles and practice of structural equation modeling*, 3rd edn, Guilford Publications, New York, <http://RMIT.eblib.com.au/patron/FullRecord.aspx?p=570362>.

Knie-Andersen, M. 2002, 'Banks: Advisers or sellers of mortgage loans?', *Journal of Financial Services Marketing*, vol. 7, no. 1, p. 15.

Knutsen, J. & Cameron, R. 2012, 'The financial coaching advice model: An exploration into how it satisfies expectations of quality advice', *Australasian Accounting Business & Finance Journal*, vol. 6, no. 4, pp. 31–45.

Kofman, P. & Murawski, C. 2015, 'Policy forum: The Murray financial system inquiry: Does Australia need a new banking model?', *Australian Economic Review*, vol. 48, no. 2, pp. 200–202.

Koh, B. 2016, *Submission 162: Scrutiny of financial advice*, viewed 30 May 2015, <www.aph.gov.au/Parliamentary_Business/Committees/Senate/Economics/Scrutiny_of_Financial_Advice>.

Kohler, A. 2017, 'New standards and ethics authority will make the banks' day', *The Australian*, 10 April, viewed 5 May 2017, <www.theaustralian.com.au/business/opinion/alan-kohler/new-standards-and-ethics-authority-will-make-the-banks-day/news-story/3c097367a09eb4740bd733a688fb81b2>.

Kolb, S.M. 2012, 'Grounded theory and the constant comparative method: Valid research strategies for educators', vol. 3, no. 1, pp. 275–286.

Kostova, T. & Zaheer, S. 1999, 'Organizational legitimacy under conditions of complexity: The case of the multinational enterprise', *Academy of Management. The Academy of Management Review*, vol. 24, no. 1, pp. 64–81.

Krauss, S.E. 2005, 'Research paradigms and meaning making: A primer', *The Qualitative Report*, vol. 10, no. 4, pp. 758–770.

Kury, K.W. 2007, 'Decoupled earnings: An institutional perspective of the consequences of maximizing shareholder value', *Accounting Forum*, vol. 31, no. 4, pp. 370–383.

Kuzucu, Y. 2016, 'Do anger control and social problem-solving mediate relationships between difficulties in emotion regulation and aggression in adolescents?', *Kuram ve Uygulamada Egitim Bilimleri*, vol. 16, no. 3, pp. 849–866.

Kwon, J.W. 2013, 'The significance of regulatory orientation, political stability and culture on consumption and price adequacy in insurance markets', *The Journal of Risk Finance*, vol. 14, no. 4, pp. 320–343.

Laby, A.B. 2010, 'Reforming the regulation of broker-dealers and investment advisers', *Business Lawyer*, vol. 65, no. 2, pp. 395–440.

Lambert, B. 2013, 'A licence to lose', *Money Management*, 18 July 2013, p. 12, bth database, <http://ezproxy.cqu.edu.au/login?url=http://search.ebscohost.com/login.aspx?direct=true&db=bth&AN=89498473&site=eds-live&scope=site>.

Laughlin, R. 2004, 'Putting the record straight: A critique of "Methodology choices and the construction of facts: Some implications from the sociology of knowledge"', *Critical Perspectives on Accounting*, vol. 15, no. 2004, pp. 261–277.

Law Council of Australia (LCA). 2011, 'Australian solicitors' Conduct Rules', viewed 15 June 2014, <www.lawcouncil.asn.au/lawcouncil/images/LCA-PDF/a-z-docs/AustralianSolicitorsConductRules.pdf>.

Lazaro, C. 2013, 'The future of financial advice: Eliminating the false distinction between brokers and investment advisers', *St. John's Law Review*, vol. 87, no. 2 3, pp. 381–414.

Lee, H.W. 2011, 'An application of latent variable structural equation modeling for experimental research in educational technology', *Turkish Online Journal of Educational Technology – TOJET*, vol. 10, no. 1, pp. 15–23.

Lee, S.A. 2007, 'Be careful what you wish for large-firm financial planning in the wake of court ruling', *Journal of Financial Planning*, vol. 20, no. 10, pp. 28–35.

Leon, A.C., Davis, L.L. & Kraemer, H.C. 2011, 'The role and interpretation of pilot studies in clinical research', *Journal of Psychiatric Research*, vol. 45, no. 5, pp. 626–629.

Leslie, C.R. 2008, 'Cartels, agency costs, and finding virtue in faithless agents', *William and Mary Law Review*, vol. 49, no. 5, p. 79.

Lester, R. 2016, *Best interests part 1 – the aligned vs non-aligned debate* 23 February, Praxis Pty Ltd, <www.adviserratings.com.au/news/2016/february/best-interests-part-1-the-aligned-vs-non-aligned-debate/>.

Levy, B. 2010, 'Dealer groups fall out over contract', *Money Management*, 25 February 2010.

Lewis, G. 2013, 'Australia's regulatory panopticon', *AQ – Australian Quarterly*, vol. 84, no. 4, pp. 26–31.

Lichterman, P. 2015, 'Interpretive reflexivity in ethnography', *Ethnography*, vol., p. 1466138115592418.

Lindorff, M. & Peck, J. 2010, 'Exploring Australian financial leaders' views of corporate social responsibility', *Journal of Management and Organization*, vol. 16, no. 1, pp. 48–65.

Locander, D., Weinberg, F., Mulki, J. & Locander, W. 2015, 'Salesperson lone wolf tendencies: The roles of social comparison and mentoring in a mediated model of performance', *Journal of Marketing Theory and Practice*, vol. 23, no. 4, pp. 351–369.

Loewenstein, G., Cain, D.M. & Sah, S. 2011, 'The limits of transparency: Pitfalls and potential of disclosing conflicts of interest', *American Economic Review*, vol. 101, no. 2, pp. 423–428.

Lounsbury, M. 2007, 'A tale of two cities: Competing logics and practice variation in the professionalizing of mutual funds', *Academy of Management Journal*, vol. 50, no. 2, pp. 289–307.

Low, B. 2010, 'An institutional and network perspective of organisational legitimacy: Empirical evidence from China's telecommunications market', *Asian Academy of Management Journal*, vol. 15, no. 2, pp. 117–134.

Lowe, A. 2004, 'Methodology choices and the construction of facts: Some implications from the sociology of scientific knowledge', *Critical Perspectives on Accounting*, vol. 15, no. 2, pp. 207–231.

Lubke, G.H. & Muthen, B. 2005, 'Investigating population heterogeneity with factor mixture models', *Psychological Methods*, vol. 10, no. 1, pp. 21–39.

Lynch, S.M. 2003, *Missing data (Soc 504)*, <www.coursehero.com/file/25930493/missingdatapdf/>.

Lynch, S.M. 2006, *Introduction to applied Bayesian statistics and estimation for social scientists*, Springer, Berlin, viewed 5 April 2016, <http://citeseerx.ist.psu.edu/viewdoc/download?doi=10.1.1.177.857&rep=rep1&type=pdf>.

Maccallum, R. & Necowitz, L. 1992, 'Model modifications in covariance structure analysis: The problem of capitalization on chance', *Psychological Bulletin*, vol. 111, pp. 490–504.

Maccallum, R. 1986, 'Specification searches in covariance structure modeling', *Psychological Bulletin*, vol. 100, no. 1, pp. 107–120.

MacCallum, R.C. & Austin, J.T. 2000, *Applications of structural equation modeling in psychological research*, *Annual Review of Psychology*, vol. 51, pp. 201–226.

MacCallum, R.C. & Hong, S. 1997, 'Power analysis in covariance structure modeling using GFI and AGFI', *Multivariate Behavioral Research*, vol. 32, no. 2, pp. 193–210.

Macey, J. 2002a, 'Options for future regulation of financial planners, part II', *Journal of Financial Planning*, vol. 15, no. 7, pp. 90–97.

Macey, J.R. 2002b, 'Options for future regulation of financial planners, part I', *Journal of Financial Planning*, vol. 15, no. 6, pp. 92–99.

Mackenzie, N. & Knipe, S. 2006, 'Research dilemmas: Paradigms, methods and methodology', *Issues in Educational Research*, vol. 16, no. 2, pp. 193–205.

Maclean, T.L. & Behnam, M. 2010, 'The dangers of decoupling: The relationship between compliance programs, legitimacy perceptions, and institutionalized misconduct', *Academy of Management Journal*, vol. 59, no. 8, pp. 1499–1520.

Malhotra, N.K. & Dash, S. 2011, *Marketing research an applied orientation*, Pearson Publishing, London.

Markland, D. 2007, 'The golden rule is that there are no golden rules: A commentary on Paul Barrett's recommendations for reporting model fit in structural equation modelling', *Personality and Individual Differences*, vol. 42, no. 5, pp. 851–858.

Marsh, H.W., Hau, K.-T. & Wen, Z. 2004, 'In search of golden rules: Comment on hypothesis-testing approaches to setting cutoff values for fit indexes and dangers in overgeneralizing Hu and Bentler's (1999) findings', *Structural Equation Modeling: A Multidisciplinary Journal*, vol. 11, no. 3, pp. 320–341.

Marsh, H.W., Kit-Tai, H. & Zhonglin, W. 2004, 'In search of golden rules: Comment on hypothesis-testing approaches to setting cutoff values for fit indexes and dangers in overgeneralizing Hu and Bentler's (1999) findings', *Structural Equation Modeling*, vol. 11, no. 3, pp. 320–341.

Maslowsky, J., Jager, J. & Hemken, D. 2015, 'Estimating and interpreting latent variable interactions: A tutorial for applying the latent moderated structural equations method', *International Journal of Behavioral Development*, vol. 39, no. 1, pp. 87–96.

Matsunaga, M. 2010, 'How to factor-analyze your data right: Do's, don'ts, and how-to's', *Cómo analizar factorialmente tus datos: qué significa, qué no significa, y cómo hacerlo.*, vol. 3, no. 1, pp. 97–110.

May, J. 2014, 'Bank love for aligned licensees in question', *Financial Observer*, 17 September, viewed 28 July 2016, <www.financialobserver.com.au/articles/bank-love-for-aligned-licensees-in-question>.

Maykut, P. & Morehouse, R. 1994, *Beginning qualitative research A philosophic and practical Guide*, The Falmer Press, viewed 11 July 2017, <file:///C:/Users/Angelique%20McInnes/Downloads/Beginning_Qualitative_Research__A_Philosophical_and_Practical_Guide.pdf>.

Mazzola, D.G. 2013, 'A universal fiduciary standard: Does it eliminate confusion or protect investors?', *The CPA Journal*, vol. 83, no. 9, p. 10+.

McCoach, D.B., Black, A.C. & O'Connell, A.A. 2007, 'Errors of inference in structural equation modeling', *Psychology in the Schools*, vol. 44, no. 5, pp. 461–470.

McDermott, T. 2016, 'Independence, confidence and fairness', *Bloomberg*, 4 February, viewed 5 February 2016, <www.fca.org.uk/news/independence-confidence-fairness#>.

McDonald, R.P. 2011, 'Measuring latent quantities', *Psychometrika*, vol. 76, no. 4, pp. 511–536.

McFadyen, A.K, Maclaren, W.M. & Webster, V.S. 2007, 'The interdisciplinary education perception scale (IEPS): An alternative remodelled sub-scale structure and its reliability', *Journal of Interprofessional Care*, vol. 21, no. 4, pp. 433–443.

McInnes, A., Ahmed, A.D. & Delpachitra, S. 2014, 'An overview of the legitimacy of the current licensing of financial advisers', paper presented to The 3rd Annual Personal Finance and Investment Symposium, Flinders University, Victoria Square Campus, 182 Victoria Square, Adelaide, South Australia, 11th November 2014, <http://pfisymposium.wordpress.com>.

McKeown, W., Kerry, M. & Olynyk, M. 2014, *Financial planning*, 2nd edn, John Wiley & Sons Australia, Ltd, Milton, QLD.

McMeel, G. 2013, 'International issues in the regulation of financial advice: A United Kingdom perspective – the retail distribution review and the ban on commission payments to financial intermediaries.', *St. John's Law Review*, vol. 87, no. 2 3, pp. 595–627.

McNally, R.C. & Griffin, A. 2005, 'An exploratory study of the effect of relationship marketing institutionalization and professional and organizational commitment in business-to-business exchanges', *Journal of Business-to-Business Marketing*, vol. 12, no. 4, pp. 1–39.

Meade, A.W., Watson, A.M. & Kroustalis, C.M. 2007, 'Assessing common methods bias in organizational research', paper presented to 22nd Annual Meeting of the Society for Industrial and Organizational Psychology, New York, viewed 10 March 2017, <http://www4.ncsu.edu/~awmeade/Links/Papers/Methods_Bias(SIOP07).pdf>.

MedCalc Software. 2016, 'Values of the Chi-squared distribution', viewed 12 December 2016, <www.medcalc.org/manual/chi-square-table.php>.

Medical Board of Australia. 2012, 'Registration webpage', viewed 31 October 2012, <www.medicalboard.gov.au/Registration.aspx>.

Menard, S. 2002, *Applied logistic regression analysis*, 2nd edn, Sage, Thousand Oaks, CA.

Mennen, J. 2014, 'Financial advice disputes – recent developments', *Precedent*, vol. 121, p. 36.

Mennen, J. 2016, 'Life insurance reform legislation a missed opportunity?', *Precedent (Sydney, N.S.W.)*, vol. 134, pp. 14–19.

Mertens, D.M. 2005, *Research and evaluation in education and psychology: Integrating diversity with quantitative, qualitative, and mixed methods*, 2nd edn, Sage, Thousand Oaks, CA.

Meyer, J.W. 2007, *Chapter 34 Reflections on institutional theories of organizations*, Sage, <http://scripts.mit.edu/~cwheat/ess/papers/Meyer_6.pdf>.

Milne, N. 2007, 'Is regulation going too far? The financial services regime and its burden on directors and managers', *Commercial Law Quarterly*, vol. 21, no. 2, pp. 33–39.

Mitchell, J. 2014, 'Legislate between IFAs and salespeople: QC', *Independent Financial Adviser News*, 28 March, viewed 27 June 2016, <www.ifa.com.au/news/13063-legislate-between-ifas-and-salesmen-says-qc>.

Moisand, D. 2008a, 'The financial planning act of 2008', *Journal of Financial Planning*, vol. 21, no. 10, pp. 78–90.

Moisand, D. 2008b, 'A rant on RAND', *Journal of Financial Planning*, vol. 21, no. 1, p. 26.

Money Management. 2012, 'BFPPG lauds FPA's FOFA outcome', *Money Management*, vol. 26, no. 14, pp. 8–8, viewed 5 June 2014, heh database, <http://

ezproxy.cqu.edu.au/login?url=http://search.ebscohost.com/login.aspx?direct=true&db=heh&AN=74970370&site=eds-live&scope=site>.

Money Management. 2014, 'ASIC acknowledges conflicts in vertical integration', *Money Management*, vol. 28, no. 30, p. 5, viewed 23 April 2015, bth database, <http://ezproxy.cqu.edu.au/login?url=http://search.ebscohost.com/login.aspx?direct=true&db=bth&AN=98914518&site=eds-live&scope=site>.

Moran, P. 2014, *A submission to the parliamentary joint committee on corporations and financial services. Inquiry into proposals to lift the professional, ethical and education standards in the financial services industry*, <www.aph.gov.au/DocumentStore.ashx?id=36a169a1-3ef0-4601-81e6-302aab4b706b&subId=299183>.

Morgan, G. & Levine, M. 2015, *Roy Morgan image of professions survey 2015 – nurses still easily most highly regarded – followed by Doctors, Pharmacists & School Teachers*, viewed 8 December 2015, <www.roymorgan.com/findings/6188-roy-morgan-image-of-professions-2015-201504280343>.

Morgan, J.K. & Hanrahan, P. 2017, 'Professional indemnity insurance: Protecting clients and regulating professionals', *University of New South Wales Law Journal*, vol. 40, no. 1, pp. 353–384.

Morgan Stanley. 2018, *Global banks & diversified financials: Banking at the speed of light*, 29, January, viewed 24 April 2018, < https://www.morganstanley.com/ideas/global-banking-equities>.

Morris, J. 2014, *Submission 421: The performance of the Australian securities and investments commission*, viewed 14 July 2016, <www.aph.gov.au/DocumentStore.ashx?id=750d427e-37ca-4f47-82e6 . . . subId. . . >.

Morris, N. 2013, *On the money: New report examines Australia's changing attitudes to wealth, debt, superannuation and plans for their financial future*, Roy Morgan Research, 28 November 2013, <www.roymorgan.com/findings/5323-superannuation-and-wealth-management-report-launched-november-2013-201311280143>.

Moutsopoulos, J. 2005, 'Finance industry has duty to manage conflicts', *International Financial Law Review*, vol. 24, no. 2, pp. 41–43.

Mulaik, S.A. 1998, 'Parsimony and model evaluation', *The Journal of Experimental Education*, vol. 66, no. 3, pp. 266–273.

Mulaik, S.A. & Millsap, R.E. 2000, 'Doing the four-step right', *Structural Equation Modeling: A Multidisciplinary Journal*, vol. 7, no. 1, pp. 36–73.

Munro, C. 2011, 'Badged platforms not a FOFA panacea', *Money Management*, p. 8, bth database, <http://ezproxy.cqu.edu.au/login?url=http://search.ebscohost.com/login.aspx?direct=true&db=bth&AN=61208005&site=eds-live&scope=site>.

Murphy, B. & Watts, T. 2009, 'Financial planning in Australia: Industry or profession', paper presented to 14th FINSIA MCFS Banking and Finance Conference, Melbourne Centre for Financial Studies, Melbourne, Australia.

Mutton, A. 2001, 'Financial services reform bill 2001 set for big impact', *Australian Property Journal*, vol. 36, no. 7, pp. 1441–4929.

Myung, J. & Pitt, M.A. 2003, 'Model comparison methods', in L Brand & ML Johnson (eds), *Methods in enzymology, numerical computer methods, part D*, n.d., viewed 9 March 2017, <http://faculty.psy.ohio-state.edu/myung/personal/enzymology.pdf>.

Myung, J., Tang, Y. & Pitt, M.A. 2009, 'Evaluation and comparison of computational models', *Methods Enzymol*, vol. 454, pp. 287–304.

Nebojsa, D.S. 2014, 'The use and misuse of structural equation modeling in management research: A review and critique', *Journal of Advances in Management Research*, vol. 11, no. 1, pp. 47–81.

Nehme, M. 2010, Enforceable undertakings: An improved form of settlement, Doctor of Philosophy thesis, University of Western Australia.

Nevitt, J. & Hancock, G.R. 1998, Relative performance of rescaling and resampling approaches to model Chi-square and parameter standard error estimation in structural equation modeling, paper presented at the annual meeting of the American Educational Research Association, San Diego, 14 April 1997, viewed 28 February 2017, <http://www-01.ibm.com/support/docview.wss?uid=swg21476184>.

Nevitt, J. & Hancock, G.R. 2001, 'Performance of bootstrapping approaches to model test statistics and parameter standard error estimation in structural equation modeling', *Structural Equation Modeling*, vol. 8, no. 3, pp. 353–377.

Newnham, M. 2012, 'Financial body flexes its muscle', *The Age*, 24 February, p. 7, viewed 20 March 2014, <http://ezproxy.cqu.edu.au/login?url=http://search.ebscohost.com/login.aspx?direct=true&db=n5h&AN=SYD-63PH0YSLWMCSAPE3JKP&site=ehost-live>.

Newnham, M. 2017, 'Education standards may send old advisers back to school', *Professional Planner*, 3 May 2017, viewed 3 May 2017, <www.professionalplanner.com.au/featured-posts/2017/05/03/education-standards-may-send-old-advisers-back-to-school-55712/>.

Niemierko, A. & Goitein, M. 1990, 'Random sampling for evaluating treatment plans', *Medical Physics*, vol. 17, no. 5, pp. 753–762.

NMG Consulting. 2014, *Impact of the retail distribution review on consumer interaction with the retail investments market – a quantitative research report*, FC Authority, viewed 8 February 2016, <www.fca.org.uk/your-fca/documents/research/impact-rdr-on-consumer-interaction-with-the-retail-investments-market>.

North, G. 2015, 'The future of financial advice reforms: Will they achieve their long term objectives?', *Competition & Consumer Law Journal*, vol. 22, no. 3, pp. 197–217.

Nyberg, A.J., Fulmer, I.S., Gerhart, B. & Carpenter, M.A. 2010, 'Agency theory revisited: CEO return and shareholder interest alignment', *Academy of Management Journal*, vol. 53, no. 5, pp. 1029–1049.

O'Brien, J. & Gilligan, G. 2014, *Submission to the parliamentary joint committee on corporations and financial services inquiry into proposals to lift the professional, ethical and education standards in the financial services industry*, viewed 6 August 2016, <file:///C:/Users/Angelique%20McInnes/Downloads/Sub_008.pdf>.

O'Brien, R. 2007, 'A caution regarding rules of thumb for variance inflation factors', *International Journal of Methodology*, vol. 41, no. 5, pp. 673–690.

O'Dwyer, K. 2017, 'Financial adviser standards and ethics authority appointments', Australian Government, The Treasury, viewed 10 April 2017, <http://kmo.ministers.treasury.gov.au/media-release/033-2017/>.

O'Neill, P. 2006, *Was there an EM?: Explanatory memoranda and explanatory statements in the commonwealth parliament**, Parliament of Australia, viewed 12 December 2017, <www.aph.gov.au/About_Parliament/Parliamentary_Departments/Parliamentary_Library/Browse_by_Topic/law/explanmem/wasthereanEM>.

Ojo, M. 2011, 'Co-operative and competitive enforced self regulation', *Journal of Financial Regulation and Compliance*, vol. 19, no. 2, pp. 139–155.

Omarova, S.T. 2010, 'Rethinking the future of self-regulation in the financial industry', *Brooklyn Journal of International Law*, vol. 35, no. 3, pp. 665–706.

On Wall Street. 2003, 'Planners, funds cool to proposed self-regulatory organization', vol. 13, no. 3, p. 32.

Onwuegbuzie, A.J., Johnson, R.B. & Collins, K.M. 2009, 'Call for mixed analysis: A philosophical framework for combining qualitative and quantitative approaches', *International Journal of Multiple Research Approaches*, vol. 3, no. 2, pp. 114–139.

Osborne, J.W. & Costello, A.B. 2005, 'Best practices in exploratory factor analysis: Four recommendations for getting the most from your analysis', *Pan-Pacific Management Review*, vol. 12, no. 2, pp. 131–146.

Overland, J. 2007, 'Back to the future? The impact of financial services reform on insider trading in Australia', *Macquarie Journal of Business Law*, vol. 4, pp. 179–196.

Overton, R.H. 2008, 'Theories of the financial planning profession', *Journal of Personal Finance*, vol. 7, no. 1, p. 40.

Owen, L. 2003, 'Wealth management: Surviving the tough times: AXA Asia Pacific chief executive Les Owen explains why he retains faith in the wealth management industry – but also warns that too many providers are chasing too few customers. (Wealth Management).(Industry Overview)', *Journal of Banking and Financial Services*, vol. 117, no. 3, p. 4.

Pain, J. 2013, *Parliamentary commission on banking standards*, 24 June, <www.publications.parliament.uk/pa/jt201314/jtselect/jtpcbs/27/27ix_we_j20.htm>.

Palazzo, G. & Rethel, L. 2008, 'Conflicts of interest in financial intermediation', *Journal of Business Ethics*, vol. 81, no. 1, pp. 193–207.

Parker, C. 1999, 'Compliance professionalism and regulatory community: The Australian trade practices regime', *Journal of Law & Society*, vol. 26, no. 2, p. 215.

Parker, C. 2004, 'Law firms incorporated: How incorporation could and should make firms more ethically responsible', *University of Queensland Law Journal*, vol. 23, no. 2, pp. 347–380.

Parliament of Australia. 2001, *Financial Services Reform Bill 2001*. Bills Digest No. 26 2001-02, < https://www.aph.gov.au/Parliamentary_Business/Bills_Legislation/bd/bd0102/02bd026>.

Parliamentary Joint Committee on Corporations and Financial Services. 2009a, *Inquiry into financial products and services in Australia*, Commonwealth of Australia, Canberra.

Parliamentary Joint Committee on Corporations and Financial Services. 2009b, *Inquiry into financial products and services in Australia*, Senate Printing Unit, Parliament House, Canberra.

Parliamentary Joint Committee on Corporations and Financial Services. 2014, *Inquiry into proposals to lift the professional, ethical and education standards in the financial services industry*, Commonwealth of Australia, Canberra.

Parliamentary Joint Committee on Corporations and Financial Services. 2015, *Lifting the professional, ethical and education standards in the financial services industry: Consultation on recommendations of the Parliamentary joint committee on corporations and financial services' inquiry into proposals to lift the professional, ethical and education standards in the financial services industry*, Canberra, viewed 12 March 2016, <www.treasury.gov.au/ConsultationsandReviews/Consultations/2015/Lifting-the-standards-in-the-financial-services-industry>.

Paulo, S. 2003, 'Epistemology, research methodology and rule 702 of the federal rules of evidence versus eva ', *Journal of Business Ethics*, vol. 44, no. 4, pp. 327–341.

Pearson, G. 2006a, 'The place of codes of conduct in regulating financial services', *Griffith Law Review*, vol. 15, no. 2.

Pearson, G. 2006b, 'Risk and the consumer in Australian financial services reform', *Sydney Law Review*, vol. 28, no. 1, pp. 99–137.

Pearson, G. 2008, 'Reconceiving regulation: Financial literacy', *Macquarie Law Journal*, vol. 8, pp. 45–58.

Pellegrino, C. & Lodhia, S. 2012, 'Climate change accounting and the Australian mining industry: Exploring links between corporate disclosure and the generation of legitimacy', *Journal of Cleaner Production*, vol. 36, no. 2012, pp. 68–82.

Peretz, P. & Schroedel, J.R. 2009, 'Financial regulation in the United States: Lessons from history', *Public Administration Review*, vol. 69, no. 4, pp. 603–612.

Perkins, M. & Monahan, R. 2011, *Estate planning: A practical guide for estate and financial service professionals*, 3rd edn, LexisNexis Butterworths, Australia.

Perri, J. 2014, *Life is about balance – a lesson for industry and government*. Connect Financial Services Brokers, <www.connectfsb.com.au/wp-content/uploads/2012/08/Connect-FSB-Media-Release-February-2014.pdf>.

Pitt, M.A. & Myung, J. 2002, 'When a good fit can be bad', *Trends in Cognitive Sciences*, vol. 6, no. 10, pp. 421–425.

Pittayachawan, S. 2013. *Structural equation modeling (SEM) workshop*. RMIT University, Australia, 20 January, viewed 20 February 2017, < https://www.academia.edu/2448000/Structural_equation_modeling_SEM_workshop>.

Podsakoff, P.M., MacKenzie, S.B. & Podsakoff, N.P. 2012, *Sources of method bias in social science research and recommendations on how to control it*, 0066–4308.

Podsakoff, P.M., Podsakoff, N.P., MacKenzie, S.B. & Lee, J.-Y. 2003, 'Common method biases in behavioural research: A critical review of the literature and recommended remedies', *Journal of Applied Behavioral Science*, vol. 88, no. 5, pp. 879–903.

Pokrajac, M. 2013, 'AIOFP compliance review', *Money Management*, vol. 27, no. 45, p. 5.

Pokrajac, M. 2014, 'Vertically integrated advice vs self-licensing and non-aligned advice', *Money Management*, 31 March, viewed 19 May 2014, <www.moneymanagement.com.au/analysis/financial-planning/2014/vertically-financial-advice-licensing-non-aligned>.

Powell, III, R.J. 2008, 'How do planners regard regulation?', *Journal of Financial Planning*, vol. 21, no. 12, pp. 10–11.

Power, T. 2015, 'How many advisers operate in Australia?', *SuperGuide*, 17 November, viewed 19 August 2016, <www.superguide.com.au/comparing-super-funds/how-many-financial-advisers-operate-in-australia>.

Power, B. 2016a, 'Do hard yards on professionalism, or it's all just "theory and fluff"', *Professional Planner*, 6 October 2016, viewed 6 October 2016, <www.professionalplanner.com.au/magazine/2016/10/06/do-hard-yards-on-professionalism-or-its-all-just-theory-and-fluff-49850/?utm_medium=Email&utm_source=ExactTarget&utm_campaign=PPO927>.

Power, T. 2016b, 'Financial advice: Only 78 *independent* financial advisers in Australia', *SuperGuide*, 25 July, viewed 2 August 2016, <www.superguide.com.au/the-soapbox/truly-*independent*-financial-advisers-in-australia>.

Power, T. 2017, 'Only 85 *independent* financial advisers in Australia', *SuperGuide*, p. 14 August, viewed 17 August 2017, <www.superguide.com.au/the-soapbox/truly-*independent*-financial-advisers-in-australia>.

Professional Planner. 2017a, 'The Australian financial planning market – full licensee listing', viewed 12 May 2017, <www.professionalplanner.com.au/licensees/2017/05/09/the-australian-financial-planning-market-full-licensee-listing-55649/>.

Professional Planner. 2017b, 'To boldly go where every other profession has gone before', *Professional Planner*, vol. 97, pp. 6–12.

Professional Standards Councils. 2014, 'White paper: Professionalisation of financial services', viewed 13 July 2016, <www.psc.gov.au/sites/default/files/NEW-PSC%20Whitepaper_final.pdf>.

Professional Standards Councils. 2015, *Submission to the parliamentary joint committee on corporations and financial services' inquiry in professional standards of financial advisers*, viewed 22 August 2016, <www.psc.gov.au/news-and-publications/latest-news/PJC-on-Corporations-and-Financial-Service>.

Raar, J. 2008, 'A basic user utility preference to reduce uncertainty: A dissent to reporting and asset measurement', *Critical Perspectives on Accounting*, vol. 19, no. 5, pp. 785–804.

Rantall, M. 2014, 'FoFA regulatory freeze welcomed by advice profession', *AdviserVoice*, viewed 26 March 2014, <www.adviservoice.com.au/2014/03/fofa-regulatory-freeze-welcomed-advice-profession/>.

Rao, H. 2004, 'Institutional activism in the early American automobile industry', *Journal of Business Venturing*, vol. 19, no. 3, pp. 359–384.

Rao, H., Morrill, C. & Zald, M.N. 2000, 'Power plays: How social movements and collective action create new organizational forms', *Research in Organizational Behavior*, vol. 22, no. 2000, pp. 237–281.

Raykov, T. 1997, 'Estimation of composite reliability for congeneric measures', *Applied Psychological Measurement*, vol. 21, no. 2, pp. 173–184.

Raykov, T. 2004, 'Behavioral scale reliability and measurement invariance evaluation using latent variable modeling', *Behavior Therapy*, vol. 35, no. 2, pp. 299–331.

Reddacliff, T. 2017, 'A professional sector needs a professional structure', *Professional Planner*, 16 May, viewed 19 May 2017, <www.professionalplanner.com.au/featured-posts/2017/05/16/a-professional-sector-needs-a-professional-structure-56026/?utm_medium=email&utm_campaign=PP0021&utm_content=PP0021+CID_b62d6bddc0fb6213b3a6f73b28eb149d&utm_source=Campaign%20Monitor&utm_term=A%20professional%20sector%20needs%20a%20professional%20structure>.

Rees, R. 1985, 'The theory of principal and agent: Part 2', *Bulletin of Economic Research*, vol. 37, no. 2, p. 75.

Reese, R. 2011, 'Planning to share advice & client bases: The Future of Financial Advice (FoFA) reforms underway are likely to have a profound effect on the way accountants and financial planners interact', *Australian Banking & Finance*, vol. 3, no. 9, p. 19.

Reichman, C. 2013, 'Safe and sound: Has RDR de-risked advice?', *Professional Adviser*, vol. n/a, pp. 5–7.

Reise, S.P., Widaman, K.F. & Pugh, R.H. 1993, 'Confirmatory factor analysis and item response theory: Two approaches for exploring measurement invariance', *Psychological Bulletin*, vol. 114, no. 3, pp. 552–566.

Riaz, S., Buchanan, S. & Bapuji, H. 2011, 'Institutional work amidst the financial crisis: Emerging positions of elite actors', *Organisation*, vol. 18, no. 2, pp. 187–214.

Rigdon, E.E. 1994, 'Calculating degrees of freedom for a structural equation model', *Structural Equation Modeling: A Multidisciplinary Journal*, vol. 1, no. 3, pp. 274–278.

Rigdon, E.E., Preacher, K.J., Lee, N., Howell, R.D., Franke, G.R. & Borsboom, D. 2011, 'Avoiding measurement dogma: A response to Rossiter', *European Journal of Marketing*, vol. 45, no. 11–12, pp. 1589–1600.

Ring, P.J. 2015, 'Analysing the reform of the retail financial advice sector in the United Kingdom from an agencement and performativity perspective', *Competition & Change*, vol. 19, no. 5, pp. 390–405.

Roberts, P. 2012, 'The missing pieces', *Money Management*, vol. 26, no. 4, pp. 18–19.

Rocha, R.S. & Granerud, L. 2011, 'The search for legitimacy and organizational change: The agency of subordinated actors', *Scandinavian Journal of Management*, vol. 27, pp. 261–272.

Rogers, J., Smith, D.K. & Chellew, J. 2017, 'The large professional service firm: A new force in the regulative bargain', *University of New South Wales Law Journal*, vol. 40, no. 1, pp. 218–261.

Rogers, T. 2004, 'Managing in the interprofessional environment: A theory of action perspective', *Journal of Interprofessional Care*, vol. 18, no. 3, pp. 239–249.

Rossiter, J.R. 2002, 'The C-OAR-SE procedure for scale development in marketing', *International Journal of Research in Marketing*, vol. 19, no. 4, pp. 305–335.

Rossiter, J.R. 2008, 'Content validity of measures of abstract constructs in management and organizational research', *British Journal of Management*, vol. 19, no. 4, pp. 380–388.

Rovine, M.J. & Molenaar, P.C.M. 2001, 'A structural equations modeling approach to the general linear mixed model', in L.M. Collins & A.G. Sayer (eds), *New methods for the analysis of change, decade of behavior*, American Psychological Association, Washington, DC, pp. 67–98, psyh database, <http://ezproxy.cqu.edu.au/login?url=http://search.ebscohost.com/login.aspx?direct=true&db=psyh&AN=2001-01077-003&site=eds-live&scope=site>.

Rubin, G.D. 2015, 'Advisers and the fiduciary duty debate', *Business and Society Review*, vol. 120, no. 4, pp. 519–548.

Salka, A. 2015, 'Lessons from the United Kingdom', *LIMRA's MarketFacts Quarterly*, vol. 3, pp. 87–88.

Sampson, A. 2009, 'ASIC's radical adviser rethink', *The Sydney Morning Herald*, vol. 6, viewed 20 March 2014, <http://ezproxy.cqu.edu.au/login?url=http://search.ebscohost.com/login.aspx?direct=true&db=n5h&AN=SYD-5QMVZM8362CVFKM7A5R&site=ehost-live>.

Sampson, A. 2010, 'Tangled web of asset-based fees', *The Sydney Morning Herald*, 7 July, viewed 20 March 2014, n5h database, <http://ezproxy.cqu.edu.au/login?url=http://search.ebscohost.com/login.aspx?direct=true&db=n5h&AN=SYD-5V68AWFZMSO1MIU2X1AY&site=ehost-live>.

Sanders, D. 2014, 'Reinventing regulation', *Law and Financial Markets Review*, vol., pp. 98–102.

Sanders, D. & Roberts, A. 2015, 'White paper: Professionalisation of financial services', viewed 13 July 2016, <www.psc.gov.au/sites/default/files/NEW-PSC%20Whitepaper_final.pdf>.

Sandlant, R. 2011, 'Consumer financial protection: Future directions', *JASSA: The Finsia Journal of Applied Finance*, vol. 4, pp. 42–47.

Santacruz, L. 2016a, 'ASIC to consider protecting term "*independent*ly-owned"', *Independent Financial Adviser News*, 25 October 2016, viewed 16 November 2016, <www.ifa.com.au/news/16966-asic-to-consider-protecting-term-*independent*ly-owned>.

Santacruz, L. 2016b, 'ASIC to consider whether asset-based fees are conflicted', *Independent Financial Adviser News*, 18 November, viewed 18 November 2016, <www.ifa.com.au/news/17082-asic-to-consider-whether-asset-based-fees-are-conflicted>.

Santacruz, L. 2016c, 'Findex responds to ASIC "*independent*" penalty', *Independent Financial Adviser News*, 11 October, viewed 12 October 2016, <www.ifa.com.au/news/16911-findex-responds-to-asic-*independent*-penalty?utm_source=IFA&utm_campaign=11_10_16&utm_medium=email&utm_content=1>.

Santana, A. 2012, 'Three elements of stakeholder legitimacy', *Journal of Business Ethics*, vol. 105, no. 2, pp. 257–265.

Santhebennur, M. 2014, 'License to practice: Pros and cons of AFSL ownership', *Money Management*, 7 August, viewed 17 July 2016, <www.moneymanagement.com.au/news/financial-planning/license-practice-pros-and-cons-afsl-ownership>.

Schapiro, M. 2009, 'Talking point: SRO for planners?', *Journal of Financial Planning*, vol. 22, no. 8, p. 18.

Schmitt, N. & Kuljanin, G. 2008, 'Measurement invariance: Review of practice and implications', *Human Resource Management Review*, vol. 18, pp. 210–222.

Schmitt, T.A. 2011, 'Current methodological considerations in exploratory and confirmatory factor analysis', *Journal of Psychoeducational Assessment*, vol. 29, no. 4, pp. 304–321.

Schreiber, J., Nora, A., Stage, F., Barlow, E. & King, J. 2006, 'Reporting structural equation modeling and confirmatory factor analysis results: A review', *The Journal of Educational Research*, vol. 99, no. 6, pp. 323–338.

Schuchardt, J., Bagwell, D.C., Bailey, W.C., DeVaney, S.A., Grable, J.E., Leech, I.E., Lown, J.M., Sharpe, D.L. & Xiao, J.J. 2007, 'Personal finance: An interdisciplinary profession', *Journal of Financial Counseling & Planning*, vol. 18, pp. 61–69.

Schulaka, C. 2009, 'Ready, set, select', *Journal of Financial Planning*, vol., p. 3.

Schumacker, R.E. & Lomax, R.G. 2010, *A beginner's guide to structural equation modeling*, 3rd edn, Routledge, New York and London.

Schwarcz, D. 2014, 'Transparently opaque: Understanding the lack of transparency in insurance consumer protection', *UCLA Law Review*, vol. 61, pp. 394–2068.

Schwarcz, S.L. 2009, 'Regulating complexity in financial markets', *Washington University Law Review*, vol. 87, no. 2, p. 211.

Scott, W.R. 2013, *Institutions and organizations: Ideas, interests, and identities*, 4th edn, Sage, Thousand Oaks, CA.

Scott, W.R. 2014, *Institutions and organizations: Ideas, interests and identities*, 4th edn, Sage, Thousand Oaks, CA.

Sekaran, U. 2000, *Research methods in business. A skill-building approach*, 3rd edn, John Wiley & Sons, New York.

Senate Economics References Committee. 2014, *Issues paper: Corporate whistleblowing in Australia: Ending corporate Australia's cultures of silence*, viewed 30 May 2016, <www.aph.gov.au/Parliamentary_Business/Committees/Senate/Economics/Scrutiny_of_Financial_Advice>.

Serpell, A.J. 2008, 'The future of financial services regulatory reform in Australia: Conduct and disclosure obligations', *Macquarie Journal of Business Law*, vol. 5, pp. 329–352.

Serpell, A.J. 2012, 'The future of financial advice reforms', *Company and Securities Law Journal*, vol. 30, no. 4, pp. 240–252.

Shah, R. & Goldstein, S.M. 2006, 'Use of structural equation modeling in operations management research: Looking back and forward', *Journal of Operations Management*, vol. 24, no. 2, pp. 148–169.

Sheehan, P. 2016, *Why FAR is not far enough*, 6 June, Morningstar Media, blog, 6 June 2016, <www.ifa.com.au/blogs/16284-why-far-is-not-far-enough?utm_source=IFA&utm_campaign=07_06_16&utm_medium=email>.

Shook, C.L., Ketchen, D.J., Hult, G.T.M. & Kacmar, K.M. 2004, 'An assessment of the use of structural equation modeling in strategic management research', *Strategic Management Journal*, vol. 25, no. 4, pp. 397–404.

Siddiqui, M.H. & Sharma, T.G. 2010, 'Analyzing customer satisfaction with service quality in life insurance services', *Journal of Targeting, Measurement and Analysis for Marketing*, vol. 18, p. 221.

Simes, R., Harper, I. & Green, H. 2008, 'Implementing best practice regulation in a dynamic marketplace: Consultation and accountability', *Economic Papers*, vol. 27, no. Special edition, pp. 24–40.

Sinodinos, A. 2013a, 'Address to the association of ***independent***ly owned financial professionals (AIOFP) National Conference, Hobart, Tasmania', paper presented to Association of ***Independent***ly Owned Financial Professionals (AIOFP) National Conference, Hobart, Tasmania, 17 November, viewed 27 May 2014, <bhttp://axs.ministers.treasury.gov.au/speech/002-2013/>.

Sinodinos, A. 2013b, *Delivering affordable and accessible financial advice*, viewed 20 December, <http://axs.ministers.treasury.gov.au/media-release/011-2013/>.

Sinodinos, A. 2013c, 'Plenary address to the association of financial advisers, National Conference, Gold Coast', paper presented to Association of Financial Advisers' National Conference, 13 October, viewed 27 May 2014, <http://axs.ministers.treasury.gov.au/speech/001-2013/>.

Sinodinos, A., 2013d, *Address to the Association of Independently Owned Financial Professionals (AIOFP) National Conference.* Hobart, Tasmania, 7 November, viewed 27 May 2014, < http://axs.ministers.treasury.gov.au/speech/002-2013/>.

Sinodinos, A. 2014, 'Keynote address to the 2014 Insurance Council of Australia regulatory update seminar', paper presented to 2014 Insurance Council of Australia Regulatory Update Seminar, 28 February, viewed 27 May 2014, <http://axs.ministers.treasury.gov.au/speech/008-2014/>.

Sitkoff, R.H. 2014, 'The fiduciary obligations of financial advisers under the law of agency', *Journal of Financial Planning*, vol. 27, no. 2, pp. 42–49.

Slattery, A. 2014, 'A new licensing model would protect consumers' best interests', *Professional Planner*, vol. 65, pp. 38–40.

Slattery, D.J. & Nellis, J.G. 2005, 'Product development in UK retail banking. Developing a market-oriented approach in a rapidly changing regulatory environment', *International Journal of Bank Marketing*, vol. 23, no. 1, pp. 90–106.

Smith, D.K., Clarke, T. & Rogers, J. 2017, 'Banking and the limits of professionalism', *University of New South Wales Law Journal*, vol. 40, no. 1, pp. 411–455.

Smith, J. 2009, Professionalism and ethics in financial planning, PhD thesis, Victoria University, Melbourne, Australia.

Smith, J., Armstrong, N. & Francis, R. 2009, 'Professionalism and ethics in financial planning', *Journal of Business Systems, Governance and Ethics*, vol. 2, no. 1, pp. 1–10.

Smith, R.C. & Walter, I. 2001, 'Rating agencies: Is there an agency issue?', viewed 8 July 2014, <http://papers.ssrn.com/sol3/papers.cfm?abstract_id=1294460>.

The Social Research Centre. 2011, *Adult financial literacy in Australia: Full report of the results from the 2011 ANZ survey*, viewed 30 September 2019, <www.financialliteracy.gov.au/media/465153/2011-adult-financial-literacy-full.pdf.pdf>.

The Social Research Centre. 2015, *ANZ survey of adult financial literacy in Australia: Full report of the results from the 2014 ANZ survey*, viewed 30 September 2017, <www.anz.com/resources/3/1/31cbc1fd-9491-4a22-91dc-4c803e4c34ab/adult-financial-literacy-survey-full-results.pdf>.

Soin, K. & Huber, C. 2013, 'The sedimentation of an institution: Changing governance in U.K. financial services', *Journal of Management Inquiry*, vol. 22, no. 3, pp. 260–280.

Sonpar, K., Pazzaglia, F. & Kornijenko, J. 2010, 'The paradox and constraints of legitimacy', *Journal of Business Ethics*, vol. 95, no. 1, pp. 1–21.

Soper, D.S. 2016, *A-priori sample size calculator for structural equation models [software]*, <www.danielsoper.com/statcalc>.

Spits, J. 2013, 'FPA calls for self-regulation through association membership', *RiskInfo*, 9 July 2013, viewed 8 May 2017, <http://riskinfo.com.au/news/2013/07/09/fpa-calls-for-self-regulation-through-association-membership/>.

Spits, J. 2014a, *Aligned versus non-aligned advice*, 4 February, Peter Sobels, 26 June 2016, <http://riskinfo.com.au/news/2014/02/04/aligned-versus-non-aligned-advice/>.

Spits, J. 2014b, *Consumers taking back seat to self interest*, 4 February 2014, Peter Sobel, <http://riskinfo.com.au/news/2014/02/04/consumers-taking-back-seat-to-self-interest/>.

Spits, J. 2015, 'Non-aligned advisers emerge from fog of numbers', *Money Management*, 1 August, viewed 29 July 2016, <www.moneymanagement.com.au/features/top-100/non-aligned-advisers-emerge-fog-numbers>.

Sposito, V.A., Hand, M.L. & Skarpness, B. 1983, 'On the efficiency of using the sample kurtosis in selecting optimal l p estimators', *Communications in Statistics – simulation and Computation*, vol. 12, no. 3, pp. 265–272.

Staff Reporter. 2011, 'Class action filed against Commonwealth Financial Planning', *Independent Financial Adviser News*, 9 February 2011, viewed 14 May 2014, <www.investordaily.com.au/31975-class-action-filed-against-commonwealth-financial-planning>.

Starke, A. 2013a, 'Authorised reps loaded with liability?', *Professional Planner*, 11 June, viewed 12 February 2015, <www.professionalplanner.com.au/featured-posts/2013/06/11/authorised-reps-loaded-with-liability-21310/>.

Starke, A. 2013b, 'A case of vertical integration: The future of financial advice (FoFA) legislation has already out-lasted the government that first championed the sweeping reforms but will its legacy ultimately be one of honourable intent tarnished by unintended consequences?', *Asia-Pacific Banking & Finance (AB+F)*, vol. 5, no. 9, p. 3.

Steen, A., McGrath, D. & Wong, A. 2016, 'Market failure, regulation and education of financial advisors', *Australasian Accounting Business & Finance Journal*, vol. 10, no. 1, pp. 3–17.

Steinmetz, H., Schmidt, P., Tina-Booh, A., Wieczorek, S. & Schwartz, S. 2009, 'Testing measurement invariance using multigroup CFA: Differences between educational groups in human values measurement', *International Journal of Methodology*, vol. 43, no. 4, pp. 599–616.

Stevens, J.P. 1984, 'Outliers and influential data points in regression analysis', *Psychological Bulletin*, vol. 95, no. 2, pp. 334–344.

Stewart, T. 2013, 'Approved product lists under scrutiny', *Money Management*, 18 January, viewed 7 June 2016, <http://search.proquest.com.ezproxy.lib.rmit.edu.au/docview/1270851348?accountid=13552&rfr_id=info%3Axri%2Fsid%3Aprimo>.

Stolz, R.F. 2009a, 'Richard Salmen on regulation, the financial crisis, and planners as leaders', *Journal of Financial Planning*, vol. 22, no. 1, pp. 14–18.

Stolz, R.F. 2009b, 'SEC Chairman Mary L. Schapiro on SEC effectiveness and the regulation of financial planners', *Journal of Financial Planning*, vol. 22, no. 8, pp. 16–18,20.

Streiner, D.L. 2006, 'Building a better model: An introduction to structural equation modelling', *The Canadian Journal of Psychiatry-Research Methods in Psychiatry*, vol. 51, no. 5.

Structural equation modeling (SEM) workshop powerpoint slides. 2013, RMIT University, Australia, 20 January.

Suchman, M.C. 1995, 'Legitimacy: Strategic and institutional approaches', *Academy of Management Journal*, vol. 20, no. 3, pp. 571–610.

Suciu, T. 2011, 'Financial innovation and moral hazard', *Bulletin of the Transilvania University of Brasov. Series V: Economic Sciences*, vol. 4, no. 1, pp. 177–182.

Suddaby, R. & Greenwood, R. 2005, 'Rhetorical strategies of legitimacy', *Administrative Science Quarterly*, vol. 50, no. 1, pp. 35–67.

Swift, L. & Piff, S. 2010, *Quantitative methods for business, management & finance*, 3rd edn, Palgrave MacMillan, Basingstoke, cat00311a database, <http://ezproxy.cqu.edu.au/login?url=http://search.ebscohost.com/login.aspx?direct=true&db=cat00311a&AN=cqu.885705&site=eds-live&scope=site>.

Tabachnick, B.G. & Fidell, L.S. 2007, *Using multivariate statistics*, 5th edn, Pearson/Allyn & Bacon, Boston, cat00311a database, <http://ezproxy.cqu.edu.au/login?url=http://search.ebscohost.com/login.aspx?direct=true&db=cat00311a&AN=cqu.607306&site=eds-live&scope=site>.

Taneja, S., Taneja, P. & Gupta, R. 2011, 'Researches in corporate social responsibility: A review of shifting focus, paradigms, and methodologies', *Journal of Business Ethics*, vol. 101, no. 3, pp. 343–364.

Taylor, M. 2011, 'FOFA failing on most counts – AFA', *Money Management*, vol. 25, no. 37, p. 8.

Taylor, M. 2012, 'FOFA alone won't stop another Trio', *Money Management*, 24 May, p. 19, viewed 25 July 2017, <http://ezproxy.cqu.edu.au/login?url=http://search.ebscohost.com/login.aspx?direct=true&db=bth&AN=76360926&site=ehost-live>.

Taylor, M. 2014, 'FSR a chance to move beyond FOFA', *Money Management*, 30 January, p. 1, viewed 28 August 2016, heh database, <http://ezproxy.cqu.edu.au/login?url=http://search.ebscohost.com/login.aspx?direct=true&db=heh&AN=94506759&site=eds-live&scope=site>.

Taylor, S. & Juchau, R. 2017, *Financial planning in Australia-advice and wealth management*, 7th edn, LexisNexis Butterworths Chatsworth, Australia.

Taylor, S., Juchau, R. & Houterman, B. 2013, *Financial planning in Australia*, 5th edn, LexisNexis, Butterworths, Chatsworth, Australia.

Teale, J. 2008, *Insurance and risk management*, John Wiley & Sons Australia Limited, Milton.

Teo, T. 2010, 'Using structural equation modelling (SEM) in educational technology research: Issues and guidelines', *British Journal of Educational Technology*, vol. 41, no. 6, pp. E117–E119.

Thompson, D. 2001, 'FPA white paper to look at future regulation of planners', *Journal of Financial Planning*, vol. 14, no. 10, pp. 34–36.

Thorpe, R. 2012, 'Retail advisers' RDR checklist', *Financial Adviser*, vol., p. n/a.

Thynne, I. 2011, 'Symposium introduction: The global financial crisis, governance and institutional dynamics', *Public Organization Review*, vol. 11, no. 1, pp. 1–12.

Tilling, M.V. 2004a, *Refinements to legitimacy theory in social and environmental accounting*, Flinders University, South Australia, 1441–3906, <www.flinders.edu.au/sabs/business-files/research/papers/2004/04-6.pdf>.

Tilling, M.V. 2004b, 'Some thoughts on legitimacy theory in social and environmental accounting', *Social and Environmental Accountability Journal*, vol. 24, no. 2, pp. 3–7.

Tittsworth, D.G. 2013, 'H.R. 4624: The pitfalls of a self-regulatory organization for investment advisers and why user fees would better accomplish the goal of investment adviser accountability. (Revolution in the Regulation of Financial Advice: The U.S., the U.K. and Australia)', *St. John's Law Review*, vol. 87, no. 2–3, pp. 477–510.

Tom, L. 1995, 'The professionalization of accountancy: A history of protecting the public interest in a self-interested way', *Accounting, Auditing & Accountability Journal*, vol. 8, no. 4, pp. 48–69.

Tomarken, A.J. & Waller, N.G. 2005, Structural equation modeling: Strengths, limitations, and misconceptions, *Annual Review Clinical Psychology*, vol. 1, pp. 31–65.

Tomlinson, D. 2001, 'Aussie financial law delayed', *Business Insurance*, vol. 35, p. 16.

Tran, M. 2017, 'ASIC simplifies IFA terms', *Financial Observer*, 28 June, viewed 28 June 2017, <www.financialobserver.com.au/articles/asic-simplifies-ifa-terms>.

Treasury, H.M. 2015, *Financial advice market review (FAMR): Call for input*, 005136, Financial Conduct Authority (FCA), viewed 5 February 2016, <www.fca.org.uk/your-fca/documents/famr-cfi>.

Trone, D.B. 2009, 'Standing on principle', *Financial Planning*, vol. 39, no. 12, pp. 75–76.

Trowbridge, J. 2015, *Review of retail life insurance advice: Final report*, 26 March 2015, <https://1-afa.cdn.aspedia.net/sites/default/files/uploaded-content/field_f_content_file/trowbridge_final_report.pdf>.

Trudeau, M. 2012, 'Forget *independent* versus restricted: Sanlam's RDR plans', *Financial Times Business*, viewed 29 July 2016.

Tuch, A. 2005, 'Investment banks as fiduciaries: Implication for conflicts of interest', *Melbourne University Law Review*, vol. 29, no. 2, pp. 478–517.

Tucker, S. 2009, 'Taking the next step: Consumers' growing demands for trust and transparency following the GFC', *InFinance: The Magazine for Finsia Members*, vol. 123, no. 4, pp. 10–14.

Tuffin, J. 2009, 'Responsible lending laws: Essential development or overreaction?', *Queensland University of Technology Law & Justice Journal*, vol. 9, no. 2, pp. 280–310.

Tyson-Chan, D. 2006, 'Bloch pushes for FPA co-regulation alongside ASIC', *Money Management*, vol. 20, no. 31, p. 1.

U.S. Securities and Exchange Commission. 2011, *Study on investment advisers and broker-dealers*, viewed 28 August 2016, <www.sec.gov/news/studies/2011/913studyfinal.pdf>.

Ullman, J.B. 2006, 'Structural equation modeling: Reviewing the basics and moving forward', *Journal of Personality Assessment*, vol. 87, no. 1, pp. 35–50.

Ullman, J.B. & Bentler, P.M. 2012, 'Structural equation modeling', in I. Wiener (ed.), *Handbook of psychology*, 2nd edn, John Wiley & Sons, online, <http://dx.doi.org/10.1002/9781118133880.hop202023>.

United Kingdom House of Commons Treasury Committee. 2011, *Retail distribution review: Written evidence*, viewed 25 August 2017, <www.parliament.uk/documents/commons-committees/treasury/rdrwrittenevvolumetwo.pdf>.

United States Department of Labour. 2017, *Definition of the term "Fiduciary"; Conflict of interest rule – retirement investment advice; best interest contract exemption (prohibited transaction exemption 2016–01); class exemption for principal transactions in certain assets between investment advice fiduciaries and employee benefit plans and IRAs prohibited transaction exemption 2016–02); prohibited transaction exemptions 75–1, 77–4, 80–83, 83–1, 84–24 and 86–128*, vol. 82, pp. 16902–16908, United States Department of Labour, viewed 6 July 2017, <www.gpo.gov/fdsys/pkg/FR-2017-04-07/pdf/2017-06914.pdf>.

United States Department of The Treasury. 2009, *Financial regulatory reform: A new foundation*, viewed 15 December 2015, <www.treasury.gov/initiatives/Documents/FinalReport_web.pdf>.

United States Securities and Exchange Commission. 2017, *A plain English handbook – SEC*, viewed 25 August 2017, <www.sec.gov/pdf/handbook.pdf>.

Valentine, S. & Hollingworth, D. 2015, 'Communication of organizational strategy and coordinated decision making as catalysts for enhanced perceptions of corporate ethical values in a financial services company', *Employee Responsibilities and Rights Journal*, vol. 27, no. 3, pp. 213–229.

Valentine, T. 2008, 'The regulations of investments', *Economic Papers*, vol. 27, no. 3, pp. 272–285.

Valentine, T. 2013, 'The problems with investment advice', *JASSA: The Finsia Journal of Applied Finance*, vol. 4, pp. 42–46.

Van der Stede, W.A., Young, S.M. & Chen, C.X. 2005, 'Assessing the quality of evidence in empirical management accounting research: The case of survey studies', *Accounting, Organizations and Society*, vol. 30, no. 7, pp. 655–684.

van Teijlingen, E.R. & Hundley, V. 2002, *The importance of pilot studies*, 40, Royal College of Nursing, Great Britain, 27 April 2014, <sru@soc.surrey.ac.uk.>.

Vandenberg, R.J. & Lance, C.E. 2000, 'A review and synthesis of the measurement invariance literature: Suggestions, practices, and recommendations for organizational research', *Organizational Research Methods*, vol. 3, no. 1, p. 4.

Varriale, G. 2012, 'Open access: US investment advisers react to self-regulator proposal', *International Financial Law Review*, vol. 31, no. 4, p. 37.

Venable, J. 2013, 'A framework for comparing IS research paradigms: How is design science related to other research paradigms?', paper presented to 24th Australasian Conference on Information Systems 2013, Melbourne, 4–6 December 2013.

Vessenes, K. 1997, 'Avoiding lawsuits based on a conflicts of interest', *Journal of Financial Planning*, vol. 10, no. 6, pp. 22–24.

Vickovich, A. 2013, 'Clients in dark on insto ownership', *Independent Financial Adviser News*, 2 August, viewed 17 July 2016, <www.ifa.com.au/news/12172-clients-in-dark-on-insto-ownership>.

Vickovich, A. 2014a, 'General advice loophole requires 'IFA' redefinition', *Independent Financial Adviser News*, 16 May, viewed 21 May 2014, <www.ifa.com.au/news/13216-general-advice-loophole-requires-ifa-rethink?utm_source=IFA&utm_campaign=IFA_Bulletin16_05_2014&utm_medium=email>.

Vickovich, A. 2014b, '*Independent* advice AFSL proposed', *Independent Financial Adviser News*, 14 April, viewed 3 May 2014, <www.ifa.com.au/news/13111-spaa-takes-up-mantle-of-*independent*-advice>.

Vickovich, A. 2014c, 'Individual licensing solves ASIC "invisibility"', *Independent Financial Adviser News*, 30 October, viewed 5 February 2015, <www.ifa.com.au/news/13849-individual-licensing-solves-asic-invisibility>.

Vickovich, A. 2014d, 'Licensees to step up self-regulation', *Independent Financial Adviser News*, 2 July, viewed 2 July 2014, <www.ifa.com.au/news/13389-licensees-to-step-up-self-regulation?utm_source=IFA&utm_campaign=IFA_Bulletin02_07_2014&utm_medium=email>.

Vickovich, A. 2015, 'IFAAA president launches dealer group', *Independent Financial Adviser News*, 17 February, viewed 24 February 2015, <www.ifa.com.au/news/14218-ifaaa-president-launches-dealer-group?utm_source=IFA&utm_campaign=IFA_Bulletin17_02_2015&utm_medium=email>.

Vickovich, A. 2017a, 'IFAs still suffer under 'institutional control'', *Independent Financial Adviser News*, 3 April, viewed 5 April 2017, <www.ifa.com.au/news/17638-ifas-still-suffer-under-institutional-control?utm_source=IFA&utm_campaign=03_04_17&utm_medium=email&utm_content=1>.

Vickovich, A. 2017b, 'Lobbying commences for s923A repeal', *Independent Financial Adviser News*, 28 June, viewed 28 Jun 2017.

Vickovich, A. 2017c, 's923A reform white paper launched', *Independent Financial Adviser News*, 24 August, viewed 24 August 2017, <www.ifa.com.au/tmp/s923Awhitepaper.pdf>.

Vickovich, A. & Garber, S. 2014, 'Senator questions authorised rep model', *Independent Financial Adviser News*, 29 October, viewed 5 February 2015, <www.ifa.com.au/news/13844-senator-questions-authorised-rep-model#comment-8192>.

Vickovich, A. & Micallef, R. 2013, 'Flying solo: A post-FOFA guide to obtaining an AFSL ', *Independent Financial Adviser News*, 3 May, viewed 3 May 2014, <www.ifa.com.au/features/cover-stories/12483-flying-solo-a-post-fofa-guide-to-obtaining-an-afsl>.

Vickovich, A. & Stewart, T. 2014, 'ASIC cuts raise licensing fees alarm', *Independent Financial Adviser News*, 14 May, viewed 15 May 2014, <www.ifa.com.au/news/13201-asic-cuts-raise-licensing-fees-alarm?utm_source=IFA&utm_campaign=IFA_Bulletin14_05_2014&utm_medium=email>.

Waddell, M. 2017, 'Regulators approve 18-month delay, postponing Obama's "fiduciary rule"', *The National Law Journal*, viewed 30 August 2017, < http://www.nationallawjournal.com/id=1202796756320/Regulators-Approve-18Month-Delay-Postponing-Obamas-Fiduciary-Rule?slreturn=20170730035200#>.

Walker, B. 2006, 'No strings attached', *Money Management*, vol. 20, no. 42, pp. 16–17, viewed 13 July 2016, <http://ezproxy.cqu.edu.au/login?url=http://search.ebscohost.com/login.aspx?direct=true&db=bth&AN=23191611&site=eds-live&scope=site>.

Walker, G.A. 2012, 'U.K. regulatory revision-a new blueprint for reform', *The International Lawyer*, vol. 46, no. 3, pp. 787–828.

Walton, S. 2012, 'Back to the future: The debate over the future of financial advice reforms has some surprising similarities to the debate that accompanied the introduction of secret commissions laws over a century ago.', *Law Institute Journal*, vol. 86, no. 9, p. 6.

Wang, J. & Wang, X. 2012, *Structural equation modeling applications using mplus, structural equation modeling -applications using mplus*, John Wiley & Sons, Hoboken.

Wasserman, N. 2006, 'Stewards, agents, and the founder discount: Executive compensation in new ventures', *Academy of Management Journal*, vol. 49, no. 5, pp. 960–976.

Waterson, L. & Vickovich, A. 2017, 'Experts weigh in on s923A breach penalties', *Independent Financial Adviser News*, 13 July, viewed 14 July 2017, <www.ifa.com.au/news/18108-experts-weigh-in-on-s923a-breach-penalties?utm_source=IFA&utm_campaign=13_07_17&utm_medium=email&utm_content=1>.

Watts, T. & Murphy, B. 2009, 'Assessing professionalism: The case of financial planning', *JASSA: The Finsia Journal of Applied Finance*, vol. 2, pp. 40–45.

Webb, D.A., Sweet, D. & Pretty, I.A. 2002, 'The emotional and psychological impact of mass casualty incidents on forensics odontologists', *Journal of Forensic Science*, vol. 47, no. 3, pp. 539–541.

Wei, S., Hengwen, L., Yichao, P. & Hengqing, T. 2010, 'Evaluation of social risk using structural equation model', *I-Business*, vol. 2, no. 2, pp. 188–192.

Wenzel, M. & Jobling, P. 2006, 'Legitimacy of regulatory authorities as a function of inclusive identification and power over ingroups and outgroups', *European Journal of Social Psychology*, vol. 36, no. 2, pp. 239–258.

West, M. 2009, 'Ripoll does little to stop another Storm', *The Sydney Morning Herald*, 25 November, viewed 20 March 2014, <http://ezproxy.cqu.edu.au/login?url=http://search.ebscohost.com/login.aspx?direct=true&db=n5h&AN=SYD-5RZNG5LWXDW4HH0CFT&site=ehost-live>.

Westland, C.J. 2010, 'Lower bounds on sample size in structural equation modeling', *Electronic Commerce Research and Applications*, vol. 9, pp. 476–487.

Wilkins, G. 2015, 'Victims of Commonwealth Bank financial planning scandal and consumer group Choice question scheme's independence and reach', *The Sydney Morning Herald*, 26 January, viewed 10 August 2017, <www.smh.com.au/business/banking-and-finance/victims-of-commonwealth-bank-financial-planning-scandal-and-consumer-group-choice-question-schemes-independence-and-reach-20150120-12uncb.html>.

Williams, L.J. & O'Boyle, E.H. 2015, 'Ideal, nonideal, and no-marker variables: The confirmatory factor analysis (CFA) marker technique works when it matters', *Journal of Applied Psychology*, vol. 100, no. 5, pp. 1579–1602.

Willmott, H. 1993, 'Breaking the paradigm mentality', *Organization Studies*, vol. 14, no. 5, pp. 681–719.

Wimmel, A. 2009, 'Theorizing the democratic legitimacy of European governance: A labyrinth with no exit?', *Journal of European Integration*, vol. 31, no. 2, pp. 181–199.

Wiseman, A. & Anderson, E. 2013, 'Introduction to Part 3: Conceptual and methodological developments', *International Perspectives on Education and Society*, vol. 20, pp. 85–90.

Worthington, A.C. 2006, 'Predicting financial literacy in Australia', *Financial Services Review*, vol. 15, no. 1, pp. 59–79.

Yanamandram, V. & White, L. 2010, 'An empirical analysis of the retention of dissatisfied business services customers using structural equation modelling', *Australasian Marketing Journal*, vol. 18, no. 4, p. 222.

Yeung, K. 2009, 'Presentational management and the pursuit of regulatory legitimacy: A comparative study of competition and consumer agencies in the United Kingdom and Australia', *Public Administration*, vol. 87, no. 2, pp. 274–294.

Young, S. & Thyil, V. 2014, 'Corporate social responsibility and corporate governance: Role of context in international settings', *Journal of Business Ethics*, vol. 122, no. 1, pp. 1–24.

Yuan, K.-H. & Bentler, P.M. 2004, 'On chi-square difference and z tests in mean and covariance structure analysis when the base model is misspecified', *Educational and Psychological Measurement*, vol. 64, no. 5, pp. 737–757.

Yun, M. 2012, 'The next phase in supporting women at work: Balancing fiduciary duties and corporate legitimacy', *Wisconsin Journal of Law, Gender & Society*, vol. 27, p. 65.

Yusoff, R. & Mohd Janor, R. 2012, 'A proposed metric scale for expressing opinion', paper presented to International Conference on Statistics in Science, Business and Engineering (ICSSBE 2012), Langkawi, Kedah, Malaysia, 10–12 September 2012, viewed 15 September 2015, <www.researchgate.net/profile/Rohana_Yusoff/publication/261389634_A_proposed_metric_scale_for_expressing_opinion/links/551ca2b20cf2fe6cbf792f35.pdf>.

Yusoff, R. & Mohd Janor, R. 2014, 'Generation of an interval metric scale to measure attitude', *SAGE Open*, vol. 4, no. 1.

Zabel, J. 2010, 'Easing the transition to independence', *Journal of Financial Planning*, vol. July/August, p. 11.

Zammit, P. 2004, 'Conflict: Part of life, part of business', *Money Management*, vol. 18, no. 31, pp. 20–20, bth database, <http://ezproxy.cqu.edu.au/login?url=http://search.ebscohost.com/login.aspx?direct=true&db=bth&AN=14358948&site=eds-live&scope=site>.

Zimmerman, M.A. & Zeitz, G.J. 2002, 'Beyond survival: Achieving new venture growth by building legitimacy', *Academy of Management Review*, vol. 27, no. 3, pp. 414–431.

Index